LIVE BY THE SWORD

THE SECRET WAR AGAINST CASTRO AND THE DEATH OF JFK

GUS RUSSO

bancroft
press

Baltimore   1998

Computer modeling pages 478–479
from the video, *Secrets of a Homicide,*
courtesy Dale Myers Animation.
(www.jfkfiles.com)

Published by Bancroft Press
P.O. Box 65360, Baltimore, MD 21209
(800)637-7377 *(for general inquiries)* and
(888) 40-READS *(for book orders)*
www.bancroftpress.com

Library of Congress Catalog Card Number 98-072307
ISBN 1-890862-01-0

Printed in the United States of America
First Edition
1 3 5 7 9 F10 8 6 4 2
Distributed to the trade by National Book Network, Lanham, MD.

CONTENTS

Photographic section near book's middle.

INTRODUCTION

On November 22, 1963, the day President John F. Kennedy was assassinated, I was a 13-year-old freshman attending Mount St. Joseph's High School, a Catholic school in Baltimore, Maryland. I remember exactly where I was when I heard the first whispered rumor—in the hallway on my way to a sixth period biology class. I recollect just as distinctly what I heard: "Some Cuban guy working for Castro shot the President!" It wasn't long before I heard a new explanation for the president's murder: "It was a Russian agent working for Khrushchev!" None of us knew which was the more shocking or potentially dangerous rumor.

In the blur of that first horrible day came yet another news report, this one stating that the President had been shot by a former Marine hiding in a book warehouse and using a German Mauser-type rifle. Hours later, the Dallas police took such a man into custody five miles away, in a Dallas movie theater. Two days later, by the end of that paralyzingly sad weekend, the story of JFK's assassination had turned 180 degrees: Now, according to most of the reports, the President had been shot in the back of the head by a Castro sympathizer using an Italian rifle.

I couldn't help but be intrigued.

After the suspect, Lee Harvey Oswald, was gunned down on the way from one Dallas jail to another, President Lyndon Johnson put together an august body, headed by Supreme Court Chief Justice Earl Warren, to find out definitively (or so it was thought) who had killed the president and why. Ten months later, without any equivocation, it concluded that Oswald, an American and a former Marine, had acted alone with no clear motive, and certainly without evidence of any involvement by Cuba, the Soviet Union, or any other foreign nation.

My own initial skepticism over the 1964 Warren Commission findings was fueled by the naivete (perhaps it was the arrogance) of a seasoned teenager who had read all the James Bond novels. I knew about spies, and fake defectors, and sharpshooters, and patsies. The government couldn't fool me! My suspicions were heightened by the obvious government secrecy over the investigation, especially the sealing of the Warren Commission records for 75 years. Thus, I, like many of my age group, became an amateur investigator pursuing the ultimate truth—what exactly happened on November 22, 1963.

In 1966, with the publication of Mark Lane's book *Rush to Judgment,* I became convinced that the government itself was covering up the true nature and cause of the JFK assassination. Others, encouraged by the popularity of Lane's book, accused the federal government of conspiring to murder JFK. Years later, I would come to realize Lane's tome for what it was: a lawyer's masterful brief for his "client," the deceased Lee Oswald. Reading it as a teenager, I had no inkling of the ease with which a competent attorney could find discrepancies in any murder investigation, let alone one in which 25,000 interviews were conducted. In truth, Lane went far beyond the pale, taking evidence and testimony so far out of context that their original import (if any) was unrecognizable. His treatment of Jack Ruby's testimony was a virtual masterpiece of lawyerly obfuscation. But it took a while for me to come to this realization.

In 1968, I gravitated to the anti-war candidacy of Robert Kennedy, spending many an after-school evening as a volunteer in his presidential campaign headquarters. It was there that a senior RFK aide told me obliquely of Bobby's secret investigations into his brother's death. In June of 1968, I was to attend a picnic, for campaign volunteers, at RFK's Hickory Hill home, where I hoped to ask the Senator about his interest in President Kennedy's death. Instead of a picnic, however, there was a funeral. The tragic assassination of Robert Kennedy in June of 1968 only strengthened the sense of paranoia many of us were feeling. My interest in JFK's murder intensified. I was hooked.

In my early "investigations," which began soon after Bobby's death, I called witnesses on the phone and heard their stories first-hand. I tracked down some hard-to-find players (and got them to talk). I began assisting on research projects that others were doing for books, magazine articles, and television specials.

With the bootleg release of the Zapruder film in 1975, conspiracy fever reached its high mark. The home movie seemed to show JFK reacting to a shot from the front, while Oswald's "sniper's nest" (as termed by the Warren Commission) had been behind the presidential motorcade. Like many others, I was convinced that the Zapruder film proved Kennedy was shot from the front. I also was persuaded that Oswald wasn't a talented enough shooter to pull off the shooting alone. On both counts, I was wrong.

This entire period—from 1963 through 1975—was marked by a continual barrage of ideologically-driven books on the Kennedy assassination. Ideologues are dangerous enough, but the books and authors of this time inspired a clique of followers, all with a pathological hatred of the U.S. government. These "conspirati" would make any leap of logic necessary in order to say that Lee Oswald had been an unwitting pawn of the evil government conspirators. And anyone believing otherwise was branded as a CIA agent (more than one prominent critic has labeled me as such), or a gullible lackey. The atmosphere of intellectual anarchy frightened off almost every serious historian. If they looked at the Kennedy murder, they concluded, they too would be branded as "kooks."

When the House Select Committee on Assassinations (HSCA) began gearing up in 1978, I spoke often with its staff members, directing them to areas I believed important. It was their meticulous photographic, forensic, and ballistic work that convinced me that Oswald alone shot President Kennedy. From that point on, only one question remained for me to answer: Was Oswald a hired gun?

Over the next dozen years, I suggested to numerous broadcast entities that they should reinvestigate the Kennedy assassination in a long-form TV documentary. PBS showed some interest, and a research grant I was given produced some interesting interviews. But none of the media wanted to pursue the matter further.

Temporarily abandoning the idea of a documentary, I resuscitated an old fictional screenplay I had written as a roman á clef on the Kennedy killing. However, in the Hollywood of 1990, the number of directors interested in making political statements could be counted on one finger. His name was Oliver Stone.

The brilliantly talented Stone seemingly showed interest in my screenplay. By sheer coincidence, and unbeknownst to me, the powerful filmmaker had recently decided to write and direct a film on JFK's murder. I was invited to meet with Stone in Dallas. To my shock, Stone informed me, apparently without consulting anyone who had studied the case for decades, that he would base his film on the most flawed and controversial character ever connected with it, the District Attorney of New Orleans, Jim Garrison. Stone said he rejected my screenplay, among other reasons, because it was a work of fiction. In the drink-filled haze of the Stoneleigh Hotel bar, I tried to tell him that Garrison's story was fictional, too. At the same time, Stone also plunked down $80,000 for the rights to an obviously concocted story peddled by some local "entrepreneurs." Their tale purported to prove that a Dallas cop, moonlighting as an international assassin, really had shot Kennedy.

I headed back east to pitch PBS' Frontline on my documentary idea. I hooked up with Emmy Award-winning reporter W. Scott Malone, who joined with me in drafting a proposal for Frontline. Months later, I came back to Dallas. Stone had graciously granted me total access to his movie set, where he sought to recreate the shooting. Walking with Stone one day, I heard him tell a tag-along press member about the sinister sealing of the Warren Commission records for seventy-five years. I was stunned. Although that had been President Johnson's original intention, public pressure had actually forced the release of most of the Commission's records within three years of the 1963 murder.

I managed to pull Stone aside, and informed him that the records we investigators really coveted were the HSCA's sealed files, numbering hundreds of thousands of pages, as well as those of other federal agencies, whose holdings could be in the millions of pages. He asked me to write down this information, which I did. I also suggested that Stone use the outcry his film was sure to generate to demand that these records be released. I proposed two things: first, that the last thing the movie audience should see was a statement informing them of the hidden records; and second, that pre-addressed postcards be handed out

at theaters, given to patrons wishing to lobby Congress for a law bringing all
these documents to the public's purview. I envisioned millions of postcards
flooding Congressional offices.

Next, I made a trip back east to confer with former HSCA investigator Kevin
Walsh. Since his days with the HSCA, Walsh, now a private detective, had
become a one-man lobby. For ten years, he had mounted a behind-the-scenes
campaign to encourage legislation freeing the HSCA's material. Kevin gave me a
letter he had been trying to get to Stone that essentially corroborated what I had
been trying to tell the Oscar-winning director. Upon returning to Dallas, I hand-
delivered the letter to Stone. By now, he was convinced.

The closing credit phrase was inserted, and while Warner Brothers printed
up some postcards, the film's distributor eventually backed out of this strategy.
Instead of giving up, a few volunteers and I decided to stand outside theaters to
hand out the few hundred postcards we managed to obtain.

As I had hoped, Stone's film, while completely misleading, created a hurri-
cane of controversy, and made the Congress see the political benefits of freeing
the records. A number of us began working feverishly with the relevant politicians to draft legislation. Among those who deserve acknowledgement are Kevin
Walsh, Jim Lesar, Eric Hamburg, and Mark Zaid. Oliver Stone himself should
also be recognized for his travels to Capitol Hill. They encouraged the legislation's passage. As it turned out, public support for the bill was virtually unanimous; many on the outside of the policy-making loop were convinced that total
disclosure would indicate the government's role in JFK's assassination, while the
politicians they implicated were convinced the released material would vindicate them. The legislation (the so-called JFK Act) passed easily in 1992.

In 1994, the JFK Review Board (mandated by the new law) was seated, and
within a year, the documents began flowing. The board ceases to exist on
September 30, 1998, and by then, it is estimated that over three million pages
will have been released.

Meanwhile, in 1991, I began a professional association with PBS' Frontline
program, researching the life of Lee Harvey Oswald. The 1993 production,
"Who Was Lee Harvey Oswald?" was a massive undertaking, with executive pro-
ducers David Fanning and Michael Sullivan showing great courage to get it
made and aired. With a huge research budget, we divided into four teams. All of
us were given great latitude. I was allowed to follow up on every lead (conspiratorial and otherwise) I had always wanted to test. We went everywhere Oswald
went, from Minsk, Russia to Atsugi, Japan. I crisscrossed the U.S. for eighteen
months. It was a dream assignment, and the first (and likely, the last) undertaking of its kind.

The research generated literally thousands of interviews, most of which,
because of the program's time constraints, were never aired. The "Oswald" portion of this book greatly benefited from those previously unseen interviews,
which Mike Sullivan graciously allowed me to draw upon.

My combined work over the years with PBS and other media interests allowed me to interview thousands of individuals who claimed to know something about the case—from Sergio Arcacha, who ran the Cuban Revolutionary Council in New Orleans, to Master Sergeant James A. Zahm, head of training at the Marine Quantico unit—and everyone in between. Many were helpful, but some seemed only too aware that one of the easiest ways to turn a profit or attain celebrity status was to feed off the public's natural paranoia regarding THE GOVERNMENT.

During many of my years of research, I was convinced that all the truths surrounding the Kennedy assassination would never be known—that a complete story could never be told. After the House Committee's work of 1979, I was more convinced than ever of Oswald's complicity. But there were huge gaps in the case that left me with the pervasive feeling that all was not being told. My inquiries were purely personal; I never intended to write a book on this case. In fact, I never thought anyone could write a good book on this subject because all the secrets were well beyond the grasp of anyone without subpoena power. To my complete surprise, and when I least expected it, two key events forced me to change my mind.

It was while in New Orleans for Frontline that I had my first inkling of the "ultimate truth," the one explanation that resolved everything for me: Oswald's apparent lack of a motive; the Kennedy family's reluctance to say anything about Jack's death; Robert Kennedy's unrelenting grief; the secrecy surrounding the two key cities in Oswald's life (New Orleans and Mexico City).

More important by far was the release of the JFK documents required by the JFK Act. Measured in man-hours, I spent practically a full year combing the files. They enabled me to see that the big question wasn't WHO done it, but WHY.

Aided by the decision of RFK intimates to tell me their stories, and the Review Board's release of over three million pages of previously classified documents, I am able, for the first time, to speak the unspeakable. My research has convinced me that John and Robert Kennedy's secret war against Cuba backfired on them—that it precipitated both President Kennedy's assassination and its coverup.

On April 19, 1994, I was back at my alma mater, giving a lecture about my interest in the Kennedy assassination. I stood perhaps 50 feet from the place where, 31 years earlier, I had first heard of JFK's death. Here at Mount St. Joseph's High School I now learned that the president's widow, Jackie Kennedy, had died. The eerie synchronicity of being in virtually the same spot for both events was almost beyond description. For years, I had continued to hero worship the Kennedys. Jack and Jackie had been my idols—they seemed part of my Italian Catholic family. Now I knew for sure that "Camelot" was indeed over, though for years, I had intellectually recognized the Kennedy-Camelot comparison for what it was: myth.

In the ensuing years, not only have Jack and Jackie been turned into caricatures, but so have Oswald, Jack Ruby (the man who killed Oswald), the FBI, and the CIA, to name a few. There certainly are one-dimensional individuals in this world—people who are either pure good or pure evil. Those "types," I have learned, had nothing to do with JFK's murder.

I learned that the Bobby Kennedy I so admired in 1968 had been a polar opposite as his brother's Attorney General: dangerously inexperienced, and, worst of all, reckless. In the time it took for a hyper-velocity rifle bullet to traverse 100 yards, Bobby was converted to an introspective man of peace. He and other members of the Kennedy clan went on to give much to the country. Their contributions to the impoverished, the handicapped, and the racially excluded have been legendary and heroic. After the 1968 assassination of Martin Luther King, Jr., when Bobby pleaded to enraged blacks "Make gentle the life of this world," he truly meant it, and many listened.

But a different Bobby Kennedy, five years earlier, had berated government officers 20 years his senior for their slow pace in eliminating Cuban dictator Fidel Castro.

More than most, Bobby himself appreciated the importance of his personal transformation following the assassination. Toward the end of his life, he mused, "I have wondered at times if we did not pay a very great price for being more energetic than wise about a lot of things, especially Cuba."

He was right.

Gus Russo
Baltimore, MD
August 1998

CAST OF CHARACTERS

(In chronological order by section)

Members of the U.S. Intelligence Community

Allen Welsh Dulles . . . . CIA Director during the Cold War
Warren Commissioner

Richard Bissell. . . . . CIA Director of Covert Operations

Jake Esterline . . . . CIA Coordinator of Bay of Pigs

Lyman Kirkpatrick . . . . CIA Inspector General

John McCone . . . . CIA Director after Allen Dulles

E. Howard Hunt . . . . CIA CubaProject Officer;
Watergate burglar

Joseph Caldwell ("J.C.") King . . . . CIA Western Hemisphere Chief

Robert Maheu . . . . CIA freelancer; Former FBI Agent

Charlie Ford . . . . CIA Case Officer(Mafia-CIA liaison)

Richard Helms. . . . . CIA Deputy Director of Plans
CIA Director (after Dulles)

William King Harvey . . . . CIA Officer in charge of ZR/RIFLE
Coordinator of Task Force W

Sam Halpern . . . . CIA Executive Assistant to William Harvey
the Cuba Project; and, later, Desmond FitzGerald

Theodore Shackley. . . . . CIA Station Chief, JM/WAVE (Miami)

Desmond FitzGerald . . . . CIA Special Affairs Staff, Cuba

Lt. Commander John Gordon III (USN) . . . . Naval Intelligence Officer
Office of Field Intelligence
Guantanamo Bay

Win Scott. . . . . CIA Station Chief, Mexico City

David Atlee Phillips . . . . CIA Director of Covert Operation
Cuban Affairs, Mexico City

James Angleton . . . . CIA Counterintelligence Chief

American Politicians

John Fitzgerald Kennedy (JFK). . . . . President (1961-1963)

Robert Francis Kennedy (RFK) . . . . Attorney General (1961-1964)

Lyndon Baines Johnson (LBJ). . . . . Vice-President (1961-1963)
President (1963-1969)

Joseph Kennedy Sr. . . . . Father of John F. Kennedy and Robert F. Kennedy

Dwight D. Eisenhower . . . . President (1953-1961)

Richard Nixon . . . . Eisenhower's Vice-President; Later President

John Connally . . . . Governor of Texas

Bobby Baker . . . . Friend of Lyndon Johnson

Anti-Castro Cubans and other Anti-Castro Activists

Sergio Arcacha Smith (Arcacha) . . . . . . Cuban Revolutionary Council Delegate
New Orleans

David Ferrie . . . . Anti-Castro activist for Arcacha;Freelancer for Banister

Fulgencio Batista . . . . President of Cuba before Fidel Castro took power

Manuel Artime . . . . Military Leader of Brigade 2506
Second Naval Guerrilla organizer
Founder of the Movement for Revolutionary Recovery

Rolando Cubela Secades (Cubela) . . . . AM/LASH
(Proposed assassin of Fidel Castro)

Gerry Hemming . . . . American mercenary
Anti-Castro activist

Layton Martens. . . . . Volunteer with Cuban Revolutionary Council
New Orleans

Guy Banister. . . . . Detective, New Orleans
Former FBI Special Agent in Charge, Chicago

Enrique "Harry" Ruiz-Williams . . . . Former member of Brigade 2506
Friend of Robert F. Kennedy

Roberto San Román (Roberto). . . . . Commander of Brigade 2506
Friend of Robert F. Kennedy

Pepe San Román (Pepe). . . . . Commander of Brigade 2506
Friend of Robert F. Kennedy

Pro-Castro Individuals (and Their Loved Ones)

Fidel Castro . . . . Cuban President

Lee Harvey Oswald . . . . Murderer of John F. Kennedy

Raul Castro . . . . Brother of Fidel Castro, and second-in-line for presidency

Che Guevara . . . . Second-in-command to Fidel Castro

Marina Oswald . . . . Wife of Oswald

Marguerite Oswald . . . . Mother of Oswald

Organized Crime Figures, Gamblers, and Associates

Meyer Lansky . . . . Organized crime leader
dispensed casino franchises in Batista's Cuba

Norman Rothman . . . . Associate of Meyer Lansky
Cuban casino manager

Santos Trafficante, Jr . . . . Mafia leader, Tampa, FL
controlled Cuban casinos in Batista's Cuba

Johnny Rosselli . . . . Las Vegas Mafia: "Mr. Smooth"
worked with CIA on assassination plots
especially Phase One

Sam Giancana . . . . Chicago Mafia Don

Michael (Mike) McLaney . . . . Shareholder in Hotel Nacional
Friend of Joseph Kennedy, Sr.

William McLaney . . . . Brother of Mike McLaney (in New Orleans)

Carlos Marcello . . . . New Orleans Mafia Don

Soviet Leaders and Diplomats

Nikita Khrushchev . . . . Premier

Valery Kostikov. . . . . KGB agent;Consular Official
Russian Consulate, Mexico City

American Planners and Officials

Robert McNamara . . . . Secretary of Defense

Admiral Arleigh Burke . . . . Chief of Naval Operations

General Maxwell Taylor . . . . Chairman of the Joint Chiefs of Staff

Brigadier General Edward Lansdale . . . . White House Coordinator of
Operation MONGOOSE

Dean Rusk . . . . Secretary of State

Admiral Robert Dennison. . . . . Commander in Chief of the Atlantic Fleet
(CINCLANT)

General Alexander Haig . . . . Cuban Coordinating Committee
Deputy to Joseph Califano
Military assistant to Cyrus Vance

Cyrus Vance . . . . Secretary of the Army; Cuban Coordinating Committee

Joseph Califano. . . . . Director of the Cuban Coordinating Committee

Nicholas Katzenbach . . . . . Deputy Attorney General under Robert F. Kennedy
Attorney General after RFK

Presidential Aides

Arthur Schlesinger, Jr. . . . . Special Assistant to President John F. Kennedy

McGeorge Bundy. . . . . National Security Advisor to John F. Kennedy

Walt Rostow . . . . Advisor to John F. Kennedy and Lyndon Johnson

FBI Officials

J. Edgar Hoover . . . . Director of the FBI

Jim Hosty. . . . . FBI Agent in Dallas; Case Officer for Oswald

Warren DeBrueys . . . . FBI Special Agent in Charge, New Orleans

Investigators and Others

G. Robert Blakey . . . . Chief Counsel for the House Select Committee
on Assassinations (after Richard Sprague)

Sylvia Duran . . . . Secretary to the Consul, Cuban Consulate, Mexico City

J.D. Tippit . . . . Police Officer, Dallas

Jim Garrison . . . . District Attorney, New Orleans

Earl Warren. . . . . Chief Justice of the U.S. Supreme Court
Chairman of the Warren Commission

Gerald R. Ford. . . . . Warren Commissioner; Later President

Clay Shaw. . . . . Private citizen, New Orleans

Nelson Rockefeller. . . . . Gerald Ford's Vice-President
Director of the Rockefeller Commission

Frank Church. . . . . . . Senator, Idaho (D); Chairman of the Church Committee

Richard Sprague. . . . . Chief Counsel of the House Select
Committee on Assassinations (HSCA)

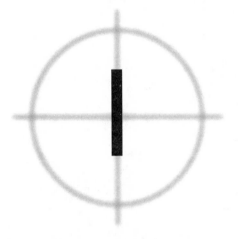

KENNEDY

CHAPTER ONE

THE STORY BEGINS

The Backstory: Cuba in the 1950's and the Emergence of Fidel Castro

"Cuba seems to have the same effect on American administrations as the full moon used to have on werewolves."
—Wayne Smith, Former U.S. State Department Officer in Havana

At the center of it all was Cuba—a small tropical island a mere 90 miles off the U.S. coast. Its recent, tumultuous, and largely secret past is the hidden key which unlocks the mysteries of the century's most important mystery. Only by coming to grips with Cuba can any of us truly understand that catastrophic day in Dallas, when President John F. Kennedy was assassinated, and when the trust between a nation and its citizens began to crumble. Nor, in an intelligent way, can U.S. foreign policy be crafted and executed without knowing what motivated U.S. leaders to wage an undeclared war against the tiny, and seemingly insignificant, country of Cuba.

In the United States of the 1950's and early 1960's, Cuba was a ticking time bomb. During a lengthy period of Cold War hostility, the antagonism between Cuba and the United States became so well-established that in 1963, when John Kennedy was killed, many Americans felt that the U.S.-Cuban disputes had been going on forever. Actually, the conflict was quite young. But by making it their Alpha and Omega, the brothers Kennedy escalated the tensions beyond all reason, and thus guaranteed their own downfall. For while the U.S. government preached its own brand of jingoism, it was matched by the feverish activities of those who believed Cuba's leader, Fidel Castro, to be a virtual Messiah. The polarities that created such volatile obsessions are rooted in Cuba's unique history.

For years, Cuba had been an American vassal. The U.S. had forced itself into the Cuban constitution with the inclusion of the notorious "Platt Amendment," which allowed for U.S. intervention whenever it felt the urge. Until Castro's 1959 revolution, Cuba was ruled by a series of dictators who redefined the terms graft and corruption. The most corrupt of these was President Fulgencio Batista, who controlled the country until the Castro takeover. And, as pointed out by historian Michael Beschloss, Batista had ingratiated himself nicely with his neighbors to the north:

> During World War II, he enlisted Cuba behind the Allies, protecting the American naval base at Guantanamo and selling Cuba's 1941 sugar crop to the United States at bargain prices. By the 1950's Americans owned 40 percent of the Cuban sugar industry, 80 percent of Cuban utilities, and 90 percent of Cuban mining.[1]

Under Batista, Cuba's economic involvement with the U.S. exploded. By the 1950's, 75 percent of Cuba's imports were from the United States, which benefited from the fact that its commodities enjoyed a unique exemption from Cuban import duties. By 1958, American investments on the island were approaching the 1 billion dollar mark. The signs of American business and culture were inescapable in Cuba. The Chase Manhattan Bank, Procter and Gamble, Colgate, Texaco, Goodyear, Remington, Borden, Sears, Ford, U.S. Rubber, Standard Oil, Coke, Pepsi—all had substantial holdings on the island.

The Kennedys themselves were among those to benefit from this tropical nest-egg. According to some reports, Joseph Kennedy Sr. had owned stock in a profitable Coca-Cola franchise on the island with Irish tenor and Coke spokesman Morton Downey, Sr.[2] In addition, Robert Kennedy's father-in-law, George Skakel, had financial holdings in Cuba, represented there by Cuban attorney Dr. Carlos Johns.[3] Skakel's company, Great Lakes Carbon, had made the family wealthy. Great Lakes' worldwide holdings included some in Batista-era Cuba, where the firm supplied filters used in the sugar industry. Skakel maintained close friendships with CIA officers, often supplying them with intelligence data he received from the island, some of which would later be used to plan the Bay of Pigs invasion. When the Castro enterprise began, his daughter, Ethel, was known to fear its revolutionary tendencies, and pray for its defeat.[4]

Castro also profited from the excesses of the Batista era and its relationship with the United States. His father had made money from the American-owned United Fruit Company, which had a presence on the island. The young Fidel even tried to cash in on the U.S.-Cuban relationship in professional baseball. In the 1940's, legendary American baseball scout Joe Cambria twice turned down Fidel Castro, then a young, athletic baseball player. "Uncle Joe scouted Castro and told him he didn't have a major league arm," said Washington Senators' owner Clark Griffith, who employed Cambria to milk Latin America for its raw baseball talent.

Fellow scout Ruben Amaro jokes, "[Cambria] could have changed history if he remembered that some pitchers just mature late."[5] And Castro's pitching did mature. By the late 1940's, he became known for his wicked curve ball. One Pittsburgh Pirates scout recalled, "He could set 'em up with the curve, blow 'em down with the heater." By 1949, Castro was indeed offered a contract with the New York Giants and a $5,000 signing bonus. But by then Castro's law studies and political interests had taken root. "We couldn't believe he turned us down," remembered a Giants scout. "Nobody from Latin America had [ever] said 'no' before."[6]

Other beneficiaries of the Batista regime included prominent representatives of organized crime. Havana had become a kind of offshore Las Vegas, and Mafia enterprises were obscenely profitable. Raw opium from South America (and possibly from Asia) was processed on the island. Cuban children suffered from disease and malnutrition, but the casinos reaped huge profits ($100 million profit from gambling alone, according to the best estimates).[7] These were supplemented by earnings from abortion services and prostitution. The island was a great draw for American tourists.

The corrupt Batista even hired U.S. mob boss Meyer Lansky to (in the dictator's words) "clean up" the casinos. Lansky, at the time a fugitive from the IRS, was happy to accept the offer. Soon, crime figures from Las Vegas, Miami, Cleveland, and elsewhere were moving in on Havana, where Lansky doled out the casino franchises.

Batista's corruption was recently summarized by historian Thomas G. Paterson:

Probably 20 to 25% of government expenditures represented graft and payoffs. Batista's personal wealth stood somewhere between $60 and $300 million. In 1959 revolutionary government officials opened his safe deposit boxes and found $20 million…When Batista and his close corruptionists fled the country as 1958 turned into 1959, they took with them—nobody knows how much for sure—some 350 million pesos of the national treasury (one peso equaled one dollar).[8]

But the bubble was soon to burst, for Batista's greed began to foster strong revolutionary movements which threatened to topple the dictator. When Castro started his movement in the early 1950's, many key players in Cuba, weary from extortion by the Batista regime, were willing to assist. For a time, according to Cuban soldier Ramon Conte, Castro enlisted the CIA's help and himself became a CIA informant.[9] CIA agent Ross Crozier, who was assigned to work with Fidel in the mountains as he prepared his final push against the Batista regime, recently corroborated this: "[CIA Western Hemisphere Chief] J.C. King had come down to talk to Fidel in 1959."[10] Castro so wanted the Americans' support, according to Crozier, that he readily supplied Crozier with details of his own troop movements. "Fidel gave us much intelligence. I went on the Manzanillo raid with him." Crozier still possesses a letter of introduction, written on his behalf by Fidel, in which the Cuban leader instructed his associates to give "Mr. Ross" all the cooperation he needed, including access to Raul Castro, his brother.

In December 1958, President Dwight D. Eisenhower sent a representative to Havana to persuade Batista to resign. However, on January 1, 1959, before Batista could respond, Castro marched victoriously into the streets of Havana, declaring, "For the first time, the Republic will really be entirely free." He later declared, "The Platt Amendment is finished."

One of Castro's first acts as Cuba's leader was to close the largely American-owned casinos (together with many of the country clubs), which the emerging dictator turned into schools and hospitals. "When the barbudos ('bearded ones') from the hills marched into Havana the day after New Year's of 1959," a historian of the period recently wrote, "the first thing the happy street throngs did was to smash parking meters and slot machines in the casinos, the most immediate symbols of the American presence in their lives."[11] Fidel next nationalized all international businesses on the island. Huge enterprises like Coca-Cola and United Fruit, not to mention their owners, suffered greatly.[12]

Batista's departure and Castro's takeover began a huge influx of disenchanted and fearful Cubans to the nearby coasts of the United States, particularly Miami and New Orleans. No wonder. On his island nation, Castro was orchestrating a political purge, dominated by trials and executions of "war criminals." The year following his takeover of Cuba, he presided over the machine-gun executions of thousands of handcuffed opponents, who were then bulldozed into mass graves. Thousands more were left to rot, naked, in solitary cells on the Isle of Pines. The year 1961 was officially declared "The Year of the Firing Squad" by Castro lieutenant Captain Antonio Jimenez.[13]

To emphasize their tenure in America as temporary, Cubans fleeing to the safety of the U.S. called themselves "exiles," rather than refugees.

In the early months of the revolution, Castro hoped for American support for his endeavor. "I am going to the United States to gather men and money," Castro had told his people. "I'll come back to see you and we shall plan what we have to do for our military training."[14] But the nationalization of American-owned property, combined with Fidel's firing squad purges, had so outraged U.S. citizens and officials that, in April 1959, when Fidel flew to Washington to seek aid for his fledgling regime, President Eisenhower refused to see him. Not only did the United States refuse any assistance to Cuba, but Eisenhower virtually planted the kiss of death on the revolution by banning all Cuban sugar imports to the America Castro was surely disappointed. The United States had been silent during the excesses of the Batista regime. But now, it seemed, Eisenhower was doing his best to drive Cuba into the Soviet sphere.

What followed was an all too-familiar stroke of opportunism by the Soviets. In October 1959, the Soviets sent an envoy to Cuba—Alexander Alexyev. When word of the U.S. sugar ban reached Soviet Premier Khrushchev, he immediately dispatched a cable to Alexyev to forward to Castro. "When I handed this to Fidel, it said that 'we, the Soviet Union, were ready to buy all the sugar, those 700,000 tons rejected by the Americans. And not only that year's assignment, but also all the next year's.' That was really an event! I was at the rally. There were one million people there. I could see for myself the joy of the Cuban people. They were throwing their berets in the air. They were dancing."[15]

In the U.S., debate raged as to whether Castro's dealings with the Soviet Union represented merely financial opportunism or a political alliance. Castro himself supported the view that his alignment was transient and pragmatic. As if to drive home the point of his non-allied independence, he said, "I hate Soviet imperialism as much as Yankee imperialism! I'm not breaking my neck fighting one dictatorship to fall into the hands of another."[16] However, as historian Bernard Weisberger has written:

> For Washington's security planners, the controversy was wastefully abstract. The brutal fact to deal with was that before 1959, Cuba had been within the American sphere of interest…and now it was literally an enemy island in the very waters that lapped at the U.S. Gulf. An unthinkable Soviet foothold, ten minutes from Miami by jet plane.[17]

In Castro, the U.S. seemed to have quite a potential adversary. Maurice Halperin wrote of the country's charismatic head, "Like all political leaders…he has been a disciple of Machiavelli, capable of inconsistency, opportunism, and deceit but not for their own sake, and always weighing anticipated profits against costs in any political operation." More forebodingly, Halperin quoted Castro as often saying, "We [Cuban revolutionaries] are not afraid of danger. As a matter of fact, we thrive on it. And besides, everyone has to die sooner or later."[18]

The Eisenhower-Nixon Covert Model

In the American public, a vast tide of fear and hatred towards Cuba was rising up. Yet, Dwight D. Eisenhower did not immediately react militarily towards Cuba's new government. As a Cold War president, he had developed innovative strategies towards burgeoning Communist governments, and his administration would rely on these strategies to take care of Castro.

Having seen the horrors unleashed by world war, Eisenhower believed that another such confrontation, now likely nuclear, had to be avoided by any means necessary. That meant stamping out Communist regimes early, before they could gain global allies.

"Ike" further worried about the built-in dangers of the expanding military-industrial complex, which he believed might trigger a world war if given the slightest provocation. Thus, he turned to the Central Intelligence Agency as his personal counter-insurgency weapon, giving that agency a charge unintended by its founder (President Harry S Truman). The pie was sweetened by the fact that CIA covert operations were much cheaper than anything the U.S. military could undertake. What transpired under Ike's direction led Blanche Cook, author of The Declassified Eisenhower, to label him "America's most covert President." Implicit in Eisenhower's demand for counter-insurgency was the need for detailed planning: any undertaking was to commence not one moment before every possible contingency had been addressed. In addition, Ike demanded total deniability for the President, and he got what he wanted: after counter-insurgent escapades, the CIA burned the entire paper trail of its communications with the President.

In 1953, the first year of his presidency, Eisenhower, already caught up in Communist "domino theory" fears, instructed CIA director Allen Dulles to implement Operation Ajax: the overthrow of Iran's leader, Mohammed Mossadegh. The fervent nationalist Mossadegh had had the audacity to nationalize U.S. oil businesses and legalize the Communist party's right to participate in elections. In response, the CIA adopted a British coup plan in the making for over a decade. When the CIA's Kim Roosevelt successfully deposed Mossadegh, Eisenhower was so ecstatic that he secreted him into the White House and bestowed on him the National Security Medal.

The following year, when Guatemala's Jacabo Arbenz nationalized the U.S. multinational United Fruit Company, Ike had Dulles initiate an operation coded PBSUCCESS. On this occasion, Ike told Dulles, "I want you all to be damn good and sure you succeed. When you commit the flag, you commit to win."[19] The coup planning, known only to Ike and the Dulles brothers (Allen of the CIA, and John Foster, Secretary of State), proceeded for over a year before Eisenhower gave the go-ahead. When this coup also proved successful, the White House-CIA covert partnership became entrenched.

After the Guatemalan coup, Ike commissioned an internal report on covert activity. In March 1954, his National Security Council passed Resolution 5412/2, which was intended to give definition and direction to the CIA's covert action capability. The directive resulted in the formation of the "5412 Committee" (later renamed "the 40 Committee," then the "303 Committee," and finally, "The Special Group"). This committee set the standard for the U.S. policy planners:

> *Create and exploit troublesome problems for International Communisim...and facilitate covert and guerrilla operations...U.S. Government responsibility for [covert operations] must not be evident...and if uncovered the United States can plausibly disclaim any responsibility for them. Specifically, such operations shall include sabotage, anti-sabotage, demolition, subversion against hostile states...*

The following September, Ike endorsed "The Doolittle Report," which intoned: "There are no rules in such a game—norms of human conduct do not apply. We must try to subvert, sabotage, and destroy our enemies by more clever and more effective methods."[20]

It was against this backdrop that Vice-President Richard Nixon, a legendary anti-Communist, convinced President Eisenhower that something had to be done about Cuba. Nixon thus became one of the first in the Eisenhower administration to urge Castro's overthrow. This came as no surprise, given Nixon's role as White House Chair of the "5412 Committee." It was Nixon's gung-ho spirit that initiated not only the idea of invading Cuba, but, quite possibly, the use of political assassination as well.

After meeting Fidel Castro in Washington in the spring of 1960, Nixon became, in his own words, "the strongest and most persistent advocate for setting up and supporting" covert action to end Fidel Castro's regime.[21] Nixon's resolve was reinforced by the opinions of his close friend, William Pawley. Pawley, a World War II hero, became a highly successful capitalist in the Havana of the Batista regime. Ousted after the revolution, Pawley developed a pathological hatred of Castro, and went on to work with both Nixon and the CIA to help launch sabotage raids against the island.

Nixon, as he would later write in 1962, concluded that the U.S. should move "vigorously to eradicate this cancer on our hemisphere and to prevent further Soviet penetration."[22] According to CIA Cuba Project officer (and later Watergate burglar) E. Howard Hunt, Nixon at this time was the "[Cuba] project's action officer within the White House." The U. S. Ambassador to Cuba Philip Bonsal called Nixon "the father of the operation."[23] "Nixon was a hard-liner," says Eisenhower's National Security Advisor, Colonel Philip Corso. "He wanted to get rid of him [Castro]. He wanted him hit hard...when he was Vice-President. He was a rough customer."[24]

As his first step, Nixon drafted a secret four-page memo to Eisenhower, CIA Director Allen Dulles, and Secretary of State Christian Herter (who succeeded John Foster Dulles following his death). "Castro is either incredibly naive about Communism, or is under Communist discipline," Nixon wrote. All those who received the memo, as well as Nixon himself, were well aware that Castro was not naive. Eisenhower agreed with Nixon's conclusions, and made him the point man for the new operation, thereby initiating a policy that led to many years of invasion and assassination plots against the Castro regime.

Nixon's next step was to appoint General Robert E. Cushman, Jr. as his executive assistant for national security affairs. Cushman's purpose was to coordinate communication between Nixon and the CIA's team: Allen Dulles, Richard Bissell (Director of Covert Operations), and Jake Esterline (who was soon given the role of planning a Cuban invasion).

Cushman has gone on record as saying that Nixon was the one in the White House applying the pressure, via him, to the CIA.[25] The President, a sober military realist, had misgivings about predictions of success from over-enthusiastic bureaucrats. He had been there before, and demanded slow and deliberate planning before he would give the go-ahead. Ike told his Defense Liaison Andrew Goodpaster that the invasion planning was merely a "Contingency plan," and he put little faith in it. Goodpaster warned that the momentum in the Cuban exile community might become unstoppable, to which Ike replied, "That won't happen as long as I'm here." Goodpaster then told Ike that he wouldn't be in office when the plan came to fruition in early 1961. Ike then said (prophetically), "Well, that's going to be a problem for my successor."[26]

Nixon, however, proceeded full-speed ahead. Years later, mired in the war in Southeast Asia, Nixon wrote of Eisenhower's painstakingly-slow planning pace, "The liberals are waiting to see Nixon let Cambodia go down the drain the way Eisenhower let Cuba go down the drain."[27]

From 1959 on, Cuba's Fidel Castro became the chief focus of assassination plots hatched by the United States government. Another target of these attempts was Patrice Lumumba of the Congo. In Congressional hearings two decades later, CIA officials, driven by their relished role of secret-keepers, refused to name the originator of the plots, but insisted that the assassination plans were originally approved by someone at a high political level in the Eisenhower administration. That person appears not to have been President Eisenhower. Richard Nixon may have been the original instigator of these plots.

Recent interviews strongly suggest that Nixon, along with his Military Aide, General Robert Cushman, secretly undertook an anti-Castro operation that operated outside of Presidential and Security Council controls. He enlisted trusted power brokers in Washington and exiles in Miami to hatch not only of a Cuban peso counterfeiting scheme, but also to assemble an assassination squad. The goal was to invade Cuba while Castro was being executed—all prior to the November 1960 election—thus aiding Nixon's presidential bid.

Although Nixon pressed for action before the all-important November presidential election, it was not to happen then. The exile forces proved too difficult to coalesce in such a brief time. The plan would reach fruition sometime in the spring of 1961, and become known as the Bay of Pigs operation.

Cuba and Politics

President Kennedy's inauguration in January 1961 came on the heels of a campaign pitting one Cold War sabre-rattler against the other. Though he proved the louder and the more adept, Kennedy's personal history with Cuba gave little indication of the strategy that Kennedy, the campaigner, would later adopt.

Kennedy first visited the Havana casinos in December 1957 during a period of marital troubles. According to the widow of mobster/casino owner Meyer Lansky, young senator Kennedy asked Lansky if he could set him up with women. Kennedy traveled to the island with his friend, Senator George Smathers, Democrat of Florida, who has said, "Kennedy liked Cuba. He liked the style. He liked the people...Once they started looking after you, which they naturally would a senator, why it was just elegant." It proved so enjoyable that the two pals returned to Cuba again in 1958. Regarding politics, Smathers recalls, "I don't think I ever heard Kennedy express any feeling about Batista or Castro either way."[28]

By the time of his presidential campaign in 1960, John Kennedy knew innately that the political necessities of demonization and hyperbole could create international monsters where none existed. But before succumbing to the rhetoric of the campaign trail, Kennedy authored *"The Strategy of Peace,"* in which he wrote sympathetically of Castro's mission. In that piece, Kennedy compared Castro to the "George Washington of South America," Simon Bolivar, whose leadership freed much of South America from Spanish colonialism.[29] As he later remarked to a friend, "I don't know why we didn't embrace Castro when he was in this country in 1959, pleading for help...Instead of that, we made an enemy of him, and then we get upset because the Russians are giving them money, doing for them what we wouldn't do."[30] Shortly before his death in 1963, in an interview with Jean Daniel of the *Paris Express*, President Kennedy elaborated:

> *I believe there is no country in the world, including the African regions, includ-*
> *ing any and all the countries under colonial domination, where economic col-*
> *onization, humiliation, and exploitation were worse than in Cuba, in part*
> *because of my country's policies during the Batista regime. I believe that we*
> *created, built, and manufactured the Cuban movement, without realizing it.*[31]

However, in the 1960 presidential campaign, both major party candidates, Nixon and Kennedy, recognized the votes to be gained by being tough on Castro.[32] This shared anti-Castroism would prove to be Kennedy's fatal mistake. In his zeal to win the presidency, John Kennedy chose to vilify Castro. He saw it as a convenient way to polarize the electorate. Kennedy's soon-to-be Secretary of State, Dean Rusk, was startled by the intensity of Kennedy's new anti-Castro feelings and thought that Kennedy "had it in for Castro." Historian Bernard Weisberger concluded, "Future positions were frozen. Kennedy became rooted in absolute hostility to Castro."[33]

In late October 1960, with the election near and its outcome very much in doubt, Kennedy told advisor and speechwriter Richard Goodwin to prepare a "real blast" for Nixon.[34] From written questions the public submitted to the candidate at his major evening stops, Goodwin had noticed that Americans feared Cuba and Castro more than the USSR and its leader, Nikita Khrushchev. In fact, Castro had come to personify the conflict between communism and Americanism. He was public enemy number one. The idea of a communist outpost 90 miles from Florida disturbed Kennedy's listeners more than any other foreign policy issue.[35] "It was almost as if the communists had taken over southern Florida," Goodwin remembered later.[36]

Tapping into this large reservoir of fear and anger seemed a good way to juice up the campaign, and it was consistent with his past conduct. During his terms in the House and Senate, Kennedy had been a stalwart Cold Warrior. Nothing in his background gave Kennedy's speechwriters pause before attacking Nixon for "losing" Cuba, much as the Republicans had attacked the Democrats on the equally ridiculous charge of "losing" China to communism in the late 1940s.

Thus did Cuba become a "major" campaign issue in 1960, as Goodwin, who was partly responsible for making it so, would put it:[37]

> *In dozens of speeches we assailed Nixon and the Republicans for losing Cuba*
> *to our communist adversaries. ("Ike didn't lose it," Kennedy scribbled in the*
> *margin of one of his speeches, "he gave it away.") We censured the feeble*
> *Republican response to this new danger; proposed further sanctions, a step-up*
> *of propaganda, action to "quarantine" the Cuban revolution, increased support*
> *for those Cubans, in exile and elsewhere, who opposed the Castro regime.*[38]

Goodwin composed the "real blast for Nixon" one evening late in October. It attacked the Republicans for weakly opposing the perceived menace of communist Cuba. But this one went further than its predecessors by decrying the Eisenhower administration's feeble support of anti-Castro forces, both in exile in the U.S. and underground in Cuba, offering "eventual hope of overthrowing Castro." Those "fighters for freedom" deserved greater support, Goodwin wrote.

The speech, which was released to the press before the candidate approved it, provoked criticism for its "rash" call for government aid in overthrowing Castro: a clear violation of international law in general and the Inter-American treaty in particular. Nixon professed outrage at Kennedy's recklessness in advocating American-sponsored revolution or invasion. Either, he said, would greatly harm American interests by demonstrating Washington's willingness to baldly breach its international responsibilities and commitments. Unknown to the public, this was a striking display of Nixon's deviousness. The vice-president had been largely responsible for the training of a force of Cuban exile guerrillas—training that President Eisenhower approved in March 1960.

Kennedy's campaign strategy, according to Nixon, was no less devious than his own. He believed that Kennedy had been briefed by CIA chief Allen Dulles about plans for the Bay of Pigs invasion (Dulles later denied the charge). Therefore, according to Nixon, Kennedy was aware that the Eisenhower administration was going after Fidel, and knew that Nixon was incapable of responding to Kennedy's charges because of the project's secrecy. Nixon would later write in his memoirs:

> In order to protect the secrecy of the planning and safety of thousands of men and women involved in the operation, I had no choice but to take a completely opposite stand...the most uncomfortable and ironic duty I have had to perform in any political campaign.

Recent disclosures indicate that Nixon was correct that JFK had inside information about the planned invasion of Cuba. Not only was Kennedy said to have secretly met with the leader of the invasion brigade (Manuel Artime) in July of 1960, as will be seen later to be the case, but it is now known that Kennedy had still another source for the sensitive intelligence.

John Patterson, then Democratic governor of Alabama, had been told of the Cuban operation in October of 1960 by his friend George R. "Reid" Doster, a National Guard instructor assigned to train the invaders. Patterson, a Kennedy campaigner, immediately flew to New York and briefed Kennedy—before the final TV debate with Nixon. (Patterson said precisely this in his oral history for the Kennedy Library, only to find it censored by library officials.)[39]

While the campaigning continued, the Bay of Pigs invaders were hard at work trying to coalesce a 1,500 man force in training camps in Guatemala. The invaders were assigned consecutive badge numbers, which, oddly, started with the number 2,500. According to one Brigade member, "We were trying to appear larger than we were." When Brigade member 2506 (Carlos Santana) fell to his death during training, CIA coordinator Barney Hidalgo suggested, "We should name the force after him, as a memorial."[40] Thus was born the force known forever after as "Brigade 2506."

Prescriptions for Disaster

John F. Kennedy came to the White House with promises to toughen Eisenhower's supposedly weak commitment to getting rid of Castro—and "when you become an advocate of a point of view," as Goodwin would put it in retrospect, "you tend to believe it. I think everybody got to feel that way about Castro. And Kennedy's desire to prove himself in foreign policy by getting Cuba back was important."

But as the newly-elected president took the reins of power, the invasion plans, already beset with problems, suffered from the expected inadequacies of a young, inexperienced Chief Executive, and the predictable degree of chaos any changing-of-the guard brings with it. The key problem, however, may have been Kennedy's own inattention to the whole Cuban issue after it served his electioneering purpose. Kennedy aide Harris Wofford later wrote:

> *Kennedy paid Cuba little heed in February [1961]. His trouble spot that month was Laos, where the Communist-led Pathet Lao continued to do well. There was, therefore, a vacuum of inattention in which the landing scheme moved into its final phase, and in that silence all parties to the operation acted out a perfect scenario of how to march, with all good will and intelligence, straight into a disaster.[41]*

Kennedy, however, was acutely concerned with the potential for negative political fallout, and demanded that a new plan, providing him deniability, be prepared in only four days. Calling the proposed plan "too noisy," he wanted it substituted for a "less spectacular" one that would remove all administration fingerprints.

One such plan involved a newly-formed exile umbrella organization called the Cuban Revolutionary Council (CRC). The CRC was a wing of the Frente Revolutionario Democratico (FRD), formed in May 1960 by prominent Cuban expatriates such as Dr. Manuel Artime and Dr. Aureliano Sanchez Arango. After its organization in Mexico, the FRD created the CRC to be its official liaison to Washington. The Kennedy White House noted: "The United States regards the Revolutionary Council as the central point of contact in its dealings with the Cuban exile and underground activity." The memo added that the CRC would be allocated one million dollars per year, and "retain contact with the White House."[42] This plan also heralded both Washington's and the Kennedys' liaisons with Cubans in New Orleans, where the CRC maintained a key outpost.[43]

Exile leader and former Castro supporter Nino Diaz was assigned by his CIA controllers to lead a mission so sensitive that certain aspects were withheld from Diaz himself. Diaz was sent to New Orleans to command a rust-bucket fishing boat called the Santa Ana, which had been leased by the CIA for $7,000 a month. "They gave me this beat-up old ship. Nothing worked on it," recalls Diaz.[44] Although he was told his mission was to "create a front in the Oriente province [of Cuba]," Diaz is now convinced "this was a lie." He and his men were told to dress in Cuban Army uniforms and fly the flag of Costa Rica.

The Santa Ana mission was prepared in New Orleans, with the assistance of the Cuban Revolutionary Council's delegate Sergio Arcacha Smith. That effort, Arcacha says, was coordinated directly by Bobby Kennedy. It's now known that Diaz's mission was personally approved by the President.[45] The provocation gambit was originally proposed to the President by his friend Senator George Smathers of Florida in the weeks prior to the attack.[46]

Historically, Diaz' mission has been portrayed as a diversionary tactic, drawing Castro's firepower away from the Bay of Pigs landing site towards the Santa Ana, which would arrive at Oriente. However, the mission was cancelled at the last moment when Diaz, by U.S. accounts, got "cold feet."[47]

Recent testimony suggests that the ploy may have had a more sinister agenda. A CIA agent testified in 1978 that Diaz' exiles, dressed like Castro's troops, were to appear as a "tripwire"—a fake attack against the U.S. naval forces at Guantanamo that would justify the Bay of Pigs invasion.[48]

"We were lied to," says Diaz. "We weren't even told about the landing at the Bay of Pigs until we were near our landing site. The CIA knew Castro's troops were waiting for us—we were to be sacrificed."[49]

The Invasion Plan

In its initial formulation, the invasion actually made some sense: a daylight beach landing at Trinidad, at the foot of the Escambray Mountains. Because of the cover provided by U.S. air strikes, the exiles would, at the very least, enter Cuba, escape to the mountains, and encourage the locals to initiate guerrilla warfare, that, over time, might overthrow the Castro government.

For three decades, the Marine in charge of planning the invasion has remained silent about the Bay of Pigs operation. Recently, however, Colonel Jack Hawkins described the initial thinking:

The Trinidad Plan was actually a good plan. The force could have been inserted into the mountains very easily where they could have remained for a very long time. We had agents in Trinidad who reported that the people there were very pro-guerrilla and anti-Castro. Fundamental to it all was—we were going to destroy Castro's Air Force by using 40 sorties of B-26's. We met every week for briefings at the White House. I was appalled at what I was hearing. Bissell was briefing the President, not [Joint Chiefs Chairman] Lemnitzer or the other military present. They were all afraid of [Defense Secretary] McNamara. One month before the invasion, [Secretary of State] Rusk, with Kennedy's agreement, vetoed the Trinidad landing as "too noisy." Bissell and McNamara stood silent. Bissell gave us four days to arrive at a new plan. Rusk demanded a landing near an airstrip. The only place that fit that requirement was the Bay of Pigs. We had almost no sleep for the four days. When I gave Bissell the plan, I said, "We can land there, but we can't hold it long. It's just not suitable." The final plan provided for 40 [air] sorties.[50]

Now, after eight months of planning, and with only weeks to go, the invasion evolved into a night-time amphibious assault landing at a swamp known as the Bay of Pigs. There were only two problems with this approach: first, there was no escape route from the Bay to the Escambray Mountains; and second, the exiles had no training in this newly-revised tactic. In February 1961, the official report of the Joint Chiefs of Staff on the invasion planning gave a strong clue as to how the events would transpire. "The amphibious element of the [invasion] force," wrote Chairman Lemnitzer to Defense Secretary Robert McNamara, "has received no amphibious training and is not now scheduled to receive any prior to the operation...Against moderate, determined resistance, this plan will fail to provide adequate logistic support."[51]

McNamara, however, remained silent about this memo in subsequent cabinet planning meetings. His failure to convey "the damning analysis in Lemnitzer's report," wrote Bissell, "is part of the pattern of incomplete interaction that continued throughout the period leading up to the actual invasion."[52] But, as will be seen, Bissell also withheld vital information—and from the President himself.

The plan further suffered from the tight internal security placed on the operation. Knowledge of it was so tightly held that experts who should have been consulted were left completely out of the loop. Because he was unable to ask, Bissell never learned that his early reports of dissent in Castro's regime were dreadfully overestimated. By February 1961, Castro had excoriated his political enemies, and enjoyed widespread popularity, but Bissell, Dulles, and others were out of touch.

Furthermore, the internecine rivalry between the various Miami-based exile leaders should have been enough alone to scare off the U.S. planners. As Bissell himself later came to admit:

The leaders of the Cuban exile community, centered in Miami, were in competition with one another for U.S. funds, supplies, and support....It was disheartening to hear [radio] broadcasts by exile program managers who seemed more concerned with serving the political ambitions of Cubans in Miami than with the situation of those trapped on the island.[53]

Kennedy Administration officials would never develop much respect for the Cuban exiles, whose apparent selfishness caused considerable infighting. Desmond FitzGerald, the CIA official later tabbed by the Kennedys to bring about Castro's downfall, wrote his daughter Frances, "I have dealt with a fairly rich assortment of exiles in the past, but none can compare with the Cuban group for genuine stupidity and militant childishness. At times I feel sorry for Castro—a sculptor in silly putty."[54]

To make matters worse, the media, most notably the *New York Times* and the *New Republic*, leaked word that Cubans were training for an imminent invasion. When he read Tad Szulc's New York Times article, "Anti-Castro Units Trained to Fight at Florida Bases," JFK fumed, "Castro doesn't need agents over here. All he has to do is read our papers."

In fact, Castro agents had already infiltrated every aspect of the Bay of Pigs operation. Former CIA executive assistant Lyman Kirkpatrick, Jr. wrote that, "the leaks about the operation from its very inception were horrendous."[55] Philip Bonsal, former U.S. Ambassador to Cuba, recalled, "The nature of the activities and the number of people involved made concealment impossible. I assume that Castro's intelligence service knew of the project within weeks, perhaps days, of the operation."[56]

Raphael "Chi Chi" Quintero, a Brigade leader at the camps, was one of the first to arrive at the training base. "We definitely had spies at the [Bay of Pigs] training camps [in Nicaragua]," he recently affirmed. One of the few who was there before Quintero was later found to be a Castro spy. "This man actually helped construct the camps," says Quintero. "One month after the Bay of Pigs invasion, I secretly infiltrated to Cuba and saw this same man working in Castro's security force."[57]

Captain Albert "Buck" Persons was one of the American pilots who flew in the invasion, as well as helping with the training in Nicaragua and Guatemala. He recalls:

It would have been very easy for Castro to have infiltrated our camps. We had AWOLs all the time. He knew there was an invasion coming, and he had very good intelligence. Still, I believe we could have established a beachhead, if we had stayed with the original plan and landed at Trinidad. It was a city of 20,000 people who were known to be friendly with the Castro resistance in the nearby Escambray Mountains. But Kennedy changed the landing site because he wanted to disguise our participation in the invasion. It was insanity. Everyone would know in ten seconds that the U.S. was involved, no matter where we landed.[58]

Lyman Kirkpatrick, the CIA's Inspector General, wrote:

[Castro] obviously knew about the [U.S.-sponsored] training camp in Guatemala. He was certain that some sort of major blow against his regime was in the making...As a result, Castro directed his security forces to round up all known or suspected members of the opposition. Nearly 100,000 were arrested and taken to detention camps all over the island. This was the first catastrophic blow to the Bay of Pigs operation, because here was the hard core of those who might have rallied to the support of the beachhead.[59]

In 1961, Kirkpatrick conducted an internal CIA review of the operation, the only copy of which was withheld from public scrutiny for thirty-seven years. When finally released in 1998, the report stated one of its conclusions: "Such massive preparations could only be laid to the U.S....Plausible denial was a pathetic illusion."

Rafael Nuñez, then serving as Castro's Diplomatic Attaché in Costa Rica, recently recalled how in early 1961 he picked up one of Raul Castro's counter-intelligence chiefs, General Fabian Escalante, at the Costa Rican airport. "He told me that his main objective was to gather intelligence on the exile training camps," Nuñez recalls. "He told me they were in training to invade Cuba near the Zapata Peninsula. When the Bay of Pigs occurred, Castro was waiting for them."[60]

Castro's supporters were not at all amused by what they were learning. In late March 1961, barely nine weeks into the Kennedy presidency (and two weeks before the Bay of Pigs invasion); the first of an unending series of anti-Kennedy threats emanating from Havana was apparently made. At the time, the President's wife, Jackie, and three-year-old daughter, Caroline, were spending the Easter holiday at the Kennedy estate in Palm Beach, Florida. Secret Service surveillance teams were closely monitoring a group of four Cubans living in Miami known to have close ties to pro-Castro activists in Havana. One of the Cubans was heard to remark, "We ought to abduct Caroline Kennedy to force the United States to stop interfering with Cuba's Castro government."

The Secret Service, taking the threat very seriously, expected the group to attack the family while at St. Edward's Catholic Church on Easter Sunday. To keep close tabs on the threatening Castroites, the agency used the intelligence network of the recently-formed anti-Castro group known as the Cuban Revolutionary Council (CRC). The subjects were watched around the clock, and the threat never materialized.[61]

This assistance, combined with the CRC's support for the Diaz mission, her-alded the beginning of a long relationship between the Kennedy White House and CRC members. According to a Congressional investigation, the CRC had been formed to coordinate anti-Castro activities with the U.S. government. The report further conceded, "The new organization had direct access to President Kennedy and top White House aides." The CRC went on to maintain a strong presence in New Orleans, where, in two years, the President's future assassin would arrive.

On April 9, 1961, eight days before the invasion, Castro appeared on Havana TV warning, "the extremely vigilant and highly-prepared Cuban people would repel any invasion attempt by the counter-revolutionaries now massing in Florida and Guatemala who are sponsored and financed by the United States."[62]

Col. Hawkins concluded the obvious:

This thing was going to be an utter disaster. During the preceding months, Castro had a massive military buildup, drafting 200,000 militia. He had fifty tanks. So I went to see Jake [Esterline, the CIA coordinator]. Jake agreed with my assessment and said, "We have got to go to Bissell and get him to stop this thing." The next day, Sunday, we went to him. He refused to call it off, and we both threatened to resign. To keep us on, Bissell promised to persuade the President to increase the airpower.[63]

Thirty-four years later, Hawkins and Esterline would learn that this promise was a lie told to prevent their resignations. In 1995, when Bissell's presidential briefing memos were released, it was learned that Bissell, before his confrontation with Hawkins and Esterline, had agreed with Kennedy to cut the air support.

Not only were American coordinators wanting out of the invasion, but key Cuban leaders, such as FRD founder Aureliano Sanchez Arango, sensed imminent disaster, and would have nothing to do with it.

But if JFK had any qualms about proceeding, he quickly dismissed them when he met with CIA Director Allen Dulles. The young president revered Dulles. Dulles would later painfully confess, "I confronted an inexperienced President Kennedy directly with the argument, 'Do you want to be perceived as less anti-communist than the great Eisenhower?'"[64] Dulles assumed that Kennedy would give adequate air support. When told the night of the invasion that Kennedy had reduced the air attacks, he said, "The President must be confused."[65]

Before approving the invasion, Kennedy briefed Senator William Fulbright, Chairman of the Senate Foreign Affairs Committee. Fulbright urged him to leave Castro alone because he and his regime were a "thorn in the flesh" but not a "dagger in the heart."[66] Fulbright considered the invasion illegal and immoral, as well as badly planned. Behind the invasion, he said, was fundamentally the same "hypocrisy and cynicism for which the United States is constantly denouncing the Soviet Union."[67] But as historian Bernard Weisberger said, Kennedy's position by this time was "frozen."

Kennedy told aide Ted Sorenson, "I know everybody is grabbing their nuts on this," but he wasn't going to be "chicken."[68] Yet Kennedy's macho stand was fatally weakened by his overriding concern for deniability. He insisted that the invasion should in no way be traced to his White House. But with the plan now revised to land the exiles in the suicidal, enclosed swamp, the CIA's Dick Bissell concluded, "the long-touted guerilla option was as much a myth as plausible deniability."[69]

At the last moment, Robert Kennedy was warned not to proceed with the operation by Constantine "Gus" Kangles, a Chicago-based attorney in the unique position of being a Democratic pol friendly with the brothers Kennedy, as well as being a longtime friend of the brothers Castro. He thus became an invaluable source of Cuban intelligence for the Kennedys. "I told Bobby [that] Castro knew everything—he was waiting for them. Not only did Castro know, but he enjoyed huge popularity. As far as an uprising, I told Bobby, 'It ain't gonna happen.' But Bobby didn't care. He wanted him [Castro] out."[70]

Unknown to Kangles, Bobby may have had a secret basis for confidence in green-lighting the operation. In a recent interview, Kennedy's great friend

Senator George Smathers recalled walking with the President on the White House South Lawn just prior to the invasion. At one point, Kennedy disclosed to Smathers what was about to happen at the Bay of Pigs. According to Smathers, Kennedy told him, "There is a plot to murder Castro. Castro is to be dead at the time the thousand Cuban exiles trained by the CIA hit the beaches."[71]

Kennedy admitted as much to CIA officer Hans Tofte. One month before the invasion, Tofte was briefing the President on guerrilla activity in Colombia. Tofte was also aware of the upcoming invasion, and boldly suggested to the President that Castro should be killed as a prequel, to give the operation any chance of success. Kennedy responded, "That is already in hand. You don't have to concern yourself about that."[72]

What happened next, regardless of who should shoulder the blame, would set off a chain of sinister events that would culminate in Dallas in 1963 and guarantee that any investigation of the death of President John F. Kennedy would be woefully, and intentionally, incomplete.

The Bay of Pigs Invasion

The attempted invasion of Cuba at the Bay of Pigs on April 17, 1961 quickly won a high place among America's worst debacles in foreign affairs. The troops who made the landing, 100 miles southeast of Havana, were Cuban exiles formed into Brigade 2506. Quickly apparent was the conclusion that the White House and CIA would not repeat their 1953 success in replacing the elected government of Iran with Shah Mohammed Reza Pahlevi, and in overthrowing Guatemala's leftist government of Jacabo Arbenz the following year.

Within hours of the botched landing through hull-gutting coral (of which intelligence had failed to warn), the attempts to hide America's massive participation, not to say conception and direction at every stage, were coming apart. Within days, they appeared farcical to most of the world. The predictions of success—two chances out of three, as Bobby Kennedy was assured when first briefed about the venture—now seemed equally absurd. Bobby had also been promised that another kind of success would be achieved even if Castro were not immediately overthrown. The invaders, operating as guerrillas from the mountains, would harass Castro, much as Castro had harassed and eventually disposed of his predecessor, Fulgencio Batista. Then again, these predictions were based on the Trinidad landing scenario.

When the invasion took an instant turn towards disaster, and the Brigade members turned into cannon fodder, the planners approached the president for more sea and air reinforcement. Over the next few days, the CIA repeatedly begged Kennedy for it. Instead, he cut the first wave of air attacks by 80 percent. "We found out about it only hours before the invasion," Hawkins recently recalled. The reduction was the exact opposite of what was promised when Esterline and Hawkins had their showdown with Bissell weeks earlier. (When his

White House launched a coup against Guatemala, Eisenhower, in sharp contrast to Kennedy, had been the driving force behind providing air support.)

The CIA's Jake Esterline was "ashen-faced" as he broke the news to Hawkins. Hawkins said, "Goddamnit, this is criminal negligence!"[73] Esterline added, "This is the goddamnest thing I have ever heard of." Years later, in separate interviews, key planners assessed the disaster. Hawkins remembered these "devastating orders" coming from the White House: "Military failure was now virtually assured."[74] When the second wave of air strikes was canceled, the exiles, who had been promised air support, were left to fend for themselves in the cold, dark swamp. Kennedy's own Chairman of the Joint Chiefs of Staff, General Lyman Lemnitzer, would later comment, "Pulling the rug like that was unbelievable....absolutely reprehensible, almost criminal."[75]

"I called Bissell and Rusk right away," remembers Hawkins. "Kennedy had conveniently left town, of course. Rusk called Kennedy, and without explaining why we needed the air cover, he advised that Kennedy's plan should proceed without changes. Kennedy agreed. Bissell didn't take the phone."[76]

In the invasion, Captain Eduardo Ferrer led the exile air force—he had trained with them in Guatemala. He pulls no punches about where the blame should be placed: "The failure was Kennedy's fault," he says. "Kennedy was immature, a little bit chicken. Today, ninety percent of the Cubans are Republicans because of Kennedy, that motherfucker."[77]

"Bissell and Kennedy thought they had some kind of magic bullet for the Bay of Pigs—assassination," says Jake Esterline. "Of course, they weren't going to support air strikes. The Kennedys were so egotistical to think they could pull this off. They thought one of these assassination things was going to work."[78] When none of them did, and air support was canceled, disaster was guaranteed.

"We were sending those Cubans to their deaths," concludes Hawkins:

> "Everybody knew that's what they were doing. Kennedy knew that's what he was doing. Don't think he didn't. Fifteen hundred men's lives were not as important as his political purposes. It was one of the most disgraceful things I ever had to be a part of. I've regretted it all my life."

In a last-ditch attempt to salvage the operation, Chief of Naval Operations Arleigh Burke begged the President for permission to use a U.S. aircraft carrier to annihilate Castro's air force, and bring amphibious landing craft to evacuate the troops from the swamp. The president refused.[79] Kennedy later attempted a different spin, telling aide Dave Powers, "They were sure I'd give in to them and send the go-ahead order to [the aircraft carrier] The Essex. They couldn't believe that a new president like me wouldn't panic and try to save his own face. Well, they had me figured all wrong."[80]

Of course, saving face was precisely what the president was attempting to do. When the first American ashore, Grayston Lynch, found out about the cancelled air strikes, he said it was like "finding out that Superman is a fairy."[81]

Rushing armor and infantry to the Bay of Pigs, Castro's defenders caught the invaders in the swamp. Ninety of the 1,300-odd men of Brigade 2506 were killed. Most of the others were captured, to Castro's intensely self-satisfied glee, and the invaders were utterly crushed. The last message the U.S. received from Brigade Commander José "Pepe" San Román read, dismissively, "How can you people do this to us?" Almost two years later, JFK confided to San Román that the real reason he withdrew the air support was that after the initial (April 15) air strike, he was secretly warned by the Soviets that they would attack West Berlin if he continued. Kennedy thus had to choose, in his own mind, between the lives of the 1,300 invaders and a possible nuclear conflagration.[82] (There is no independent corroboration that the Soviets actually issued this threat.)

Rubbing salt into the Kennedys' wounds, the Cuban premier took to the microphone ridiculing capitalism in general and the United States in particular, and his listeners cheered in delight. He strutted about the battlefield, showing foreign correspondents, with immense satisfaction, how his forces had humiliated the invaders and their Yankee sponsors.[83] Soon he was delivering arm-waving, chest-thumping speeches about why the imperialists had lost: they counted on geography and weapons, whereas socialists counted on hearts and minds. Castro had a huge sign erected at the invasion site that read: "Welcome to the Site of the First Defeat of Imperialism in the Western Hemisphere."

Perhaps the most ludicrous aspect of the Bay of Pigs venture was the political judgment on which the military strategy had been based—the analytical underpinning of the entire operation. Even before the landing, skeptics wondered how a single brigade of 1,300 exiles—never mind how well-trained and led they were—could defeat a home army of 200,000 men, operating on their own soil, with proportionate knowledge of the terrain and a good supply of war materials. The unabashed answer was that the Cuban people would rise to join the exiles in overthrowing Castro, whose rule they had come to detest. "How did I ever let it happen?" Kennedy asked later. "I know better than to listen to experts. They always have their own agenda. All my life I've known it, and yet I still barreled ahead."[84]

For Kennedy, the fiasco assumed consuming proportions. Dozens of commentators debated the degree of his responsibility. Was it diminished because he had inherited the invasion plan from President Eisenhower, whose military competence Kennedy naturally refrained from questioning? That was the administration's claim, stated most impatiently by Bobby Kennedy: "It was Eisenhower's plan. Eisenhower's people all said it would succeed."[85] Or, to the contrary, did the president's longstanding drive to demonstrate how tough he could be—an old inclination of the Kennedy family—make him even more guilty? The question is, of course, unanswerable, but the attitudes of the Kennedy family as manifested in Jack and Bobby are relevant, for they would bear on the full course of the tragedy that lay ahead.

Furthermore, while President Eisenhower had indeed approved the training of the Cuban exiles for a possible invasion, he never did more than that. He never ordered the invasion that actually took place—and if he had, it is fair to assume that, with his usual caution and military expertise, he would have insisted on changes in the deeply flawed CIA plans. Richard Goodwin, a member of the high councils of the Kennedy administration, was among those who later concluded that Eisenhower would not have approved the invasion at all. "On the basis of Eisenhower's general record [i.e., of nonintervention], we have to give him the benefit of the doubt and assume he would not have invaded."[86]

In either case, the defeat was officially Kennedy's responsibility, and the first major defeat of his life. Manolo Reboso, a member of Brigade 2506 who escaped from the beach head and went on to work with Bobby Kennedy on future Cuban projects, agreed with domestic observers: "The passion of the Kennedys over Cuba was because they had never lost anything in their lives."[87] The daughter of one of the five CIA pilots who lost their lives in the invasion (officially denied for 17 years) put it more bluntly: "Life was a series of touch football games. The Kennedys wanted to win 'the football game' in Cuba."[88] In their mind, Castro had only won the first round.

In future years, many of the principal players, except the Kennedys and their sycophants, came to agree on the causes of the Bay of Pigs failure. Two of the most incisive statements came from former CIA Directors. Allen Dulles said, "One never succeeds unless there is a determination to succeed, a willingness to risk some unpleasant political repercussions, and a willingness to provide the basic military necessities. At the decisive moment of the Bay of Pigs operation, all three of these were lacking."[89] John McCone, Dulles' successor, explained, "The 'stand down' of the air cover...was the fatal error that caused the failure of the Bay of Pigs operation[90]...The responsibility rests squarely on the shoulders of President Kennedy."[91]

The Aftermath

The Bay of Pigs represented not merely a stunning military loss for Kennedy. It was also a personal humiliation. To Richard Nixon, whom he had so recently defeated for the presidency, the president described the debacle several days later as "the worst experience of my life."[92] The Castro-hating Nixon, during this same April 20 phone conversation, advised the confused young President, "I would find a proper legal cover and go [back] in. There are several legal justifications that could be used, like protection of American citizens living in Cuba and defending our base in Guantanamo."[93]

On the first night of the invasion itself, Robert Kennedy anticipated the disaster, saying that "the shit has hit the fan. The thing has turned sour in a way you wouldn't believe!" By all accounts, the President was stunned and devastated. Kenny O'Donnell, a long-time aide from Boston, remembered him as more distraught—"as close to crying"—as he had ever seen him.[94] Bobby Kennedy took it just as badly. "They can't do this to you," he said privately to Jack after other advisors had retired that evening, and Jack paced the White House grounds alone for nearly an hour. "Those black-bearded communists can't do this to you."[95]

On April 19, just two days after the disaster, RFK let it be known that he wanted revenge. He dictated a letter to his brother: "Our long-range policy objectives in Cuba are tied to survival far more than what is happening in Laos or in the Congo or any other place in the world...The time has come for a show-down, for in a year or two years the situation will be vastly worse." And in a phrase that would most likely haunt him, Bobby added, "If we don't want Russia to set up missile bases in Cuba, we had better decide now what we are willing to do to stop it."[96] What they ultimately did is now believed by many to have instigated the very occurrence they tried to prevent. On June 1, 1961, RFK issued a memo that declared, "The Cuba matter is being allowed to slide...mostly because nobody really has an answer to Castro."[97]

Robert Kennedy saw that his brother was "more upset at this time [the Bay of Pigs] than he was at any other"—so upset that it produced a physical reaction in the President who was always fully composed in public; who took great pains to conceal stress from even his closest advisors.[98] In private, he kept shaking his head and rubbing his hands over his eyes.[99] The President told advisor Clark Clifford that a "second Bay of Pigs" would destroy his presidency. "It was the only thing on his mind, and we just had to let him talk himself out," remembered friend Charles Spalding. His depression reached such depths that he told his friend LeMoyne Billings, "Lyndon [Johnson] can have it [the presidency] in 1964," saying that the presidency was the "most unpleasant job in the world."[100]

One of the job's more unpleasant aspects was foisting all the blame on someone else's shoulders in order to protect the president's own reputation. A week before the invasion, Presidential Special Assistant Arthur Schlesinger Jr. had foreshadowed this possible necessity in a long memo he composed for the new president. "The character and repute of President Kennedy constitute one of our greatest natural resources," wrote Schlesinger, who had originally opposed the Cuban venture but later sought to ensure its successful execution. "Nothing should be done to jeopardize this invaluable asset."[101] Another memo, which was entitled "Protection of The President," went on to suggest a course of action that now seems to have been followed: "When lies must be told, they should be told by subordinate officials." In the event of failure, Schlesinger recommended placing the blame on the CIA, painting them as "errant idealists and soldiers-of-fortune working on their own."[102] (In Dulles' papers is a non-published memo on the Bay of Pigs, in which he wrote of the Schlesinger tactic, "I deplore the way this is being done...If what is written goes entirely unanswered and without critical examination, it will go down as the history of the event. It is not the true story."[103])

After a suitable period of time, the CIA's Allen Dulles and Richard Bissell were asked to resign, which they did by the end of 1961. Dulles had dutifully offered his resignation to the President when it became obvious that the invasion had failed. Kennedy initially refused the tender,[104] but it soon became apparent that he needed scapegoats. Kennedy told Allen Dulles that he and Bissell, men he had personally liked and admired, would have to leave their posts after things quieted down. "Under a parliamentary system of government, it is I who would be leaving office. But under our system, it is you who must go."[105] E. Howard Hunt *concluded,* "Both Bissell and Mr. Dulles were slated to go, scapegoats to expiate administration guilt."[106]

The *New York Times* later ran a front page story, which documented how Kennedy, in the wake of the failed invasion, had railed at the CIA. He would, he threatened, "splinter the CIA in a thousand pieces and scatter it to the winds."[107] In fact, Kennedy's actions were exactly the opposite. Over the following weeks and months, Dulles and the President spoke often, and Dulles would later say of Kennedy, "There was never one harsh or unkind word said to me by him at any time thereafter."[108]

At a White House meeting, when Vice-President Lyndon Johnson attempted to point the finger of blame for the invasion's failure at the CIA, Kennedy admonished him. "Lyndon, you've got to remember [that] we're all in this, and that when I accepted responsibility for this operation, I took the entire responsibility on myself. We should have no sort of passing the buck, or backbiting, however justified."[109]

JFK went out of his way to defend Dulles in this trying time. Shortly after the Bay of Pigs invasion, one of the Kennedys' Palm Beach neighbors, Charles Wrightsman, with whom Dulles had often stayed, told the president that when he (Wrightsman) next came to Washington, he would not see Dulles. Kennedy then invited Wrightsman for a drink at the White House. Unbeknownst to Wrightsman, Kennedy also invited Allen Dulles. Dulles' biographer recounts what happened next: "When Allen walked in—Wrightsman was already settled down—Kennedy stood up and, in case the rich man from Florida did not get the message, the beleaguered president put his arm around Allen's shoulders to lead him to a comfortable chair."[110] Kennedy summed up his opinion of Dulles at a luncheon held just days after the botched invasion. Speaking privately with *New York Times* publisher Arthur Hays Sulzberger, Kennedy said, "It's not that Dulles is not a man of great ability. He is. Dulles is a legendary figure, and it's hard to operate with legendary figures."[111]

There were solid political reasons for Kennedy to take this "colossal mistake" so seriously. The new administration wanted dearly to protect an image of a reborn America striving for a new order based on justice and ethical principles. Kennedy had entered the White House proclaiming that "the torch had passed to a new generation of Americans," and promising a new kind of leadership for the free world. He would lead it in new, saner, and more humane directions, away from anything smacking of rigidity or behavior that could prompt memories or mistaken images of America as an imperialist power. And much of the free world responded enthusiastically to those promises. From the first, Kennedy was relatively more popular in many countries of Europe and Latin America than at home.

Days before the invasion, when rumors about it were rampant in Washington, Kennedy made an unequivocal public announcement that "there will not be, under any circumstances, any intervention in Cuba by the United States armed forces."[112] After the debacle, despite administration efforts to portray the operation as the work of Cuban exiles without American support, few in the world took this patent fiction seriously. During the pre-invasion week, James Reston of the *New York Times* thought that Allen Dulles was "lying like hell" when he denied CIA involvement. After the Cuban Foreign Minister reported air strikes on the island—and identified the planes as American—the United Nations scheduled an emergency session, during which Adlai Stevenson, the American Ambassador to the UN, promised that his government would do anything possible to insure that "no American participate in any action against Cuba." Stevenson had not been informed that Americans were participating for all they were worth. When he learned the truth, the Ambassador considered his previous statement "the most humiliating experience" of his public life.

If it was humiliating for Stevenson, it was an even greater personal disgrace for Robert Kennedy. Earlier, he had stifled administration dissension about, and even outright opposition to, the invasion. Now Bobby worried that the Bay of Pigs harmed his brother's "standing as President and the standing of the United States in public opinion throughout the world."[113] He worried that, abroad, "The United States couldn't be trusted," for either honesty or competence.

Until the invasion's failure, Bobby Kennedy's role in the administration had been somewhat limited. He was to fulfill his function as Attorney General, and to advise the president on a wide range of issues whenever the president solicited his opinion. The April failure prompted the president to retrench; to reach back to the kid brother he most trusted among his advisors; to elevate Bobby to the President's right hand. Now Bobby would also advise on foreign affairs—and not only advise, but also implement action in some of the most sensitive matters.

He was appointed to the Cuba Study Group, which included retired General Maxwell Taylor; Admiral Arleigh Burke, the Chief of Naval Operations; and Allen Dulles, the CIA Director. The committee met in a Pentagon basement, where Bobby took notes with an intense desire for action—in this case, to find out what went wrong in order to get it right the next time.[114] During the next six weeks, the Cuba Study Group would interrogate 50 witnesses about the failure at the Bay of Pigs, and come to the conclusion the White House wanted to hear: that the chief cause had been the new administration's reluctance to oppose plans proposed by President Eisenhower, America's "greatest military man." In support of that highly questionable judgment, Bobby asserted that not to have gone ahead with the project "would have showed that [President Kennedy] had no courage."[115] However, the Study Group also concluded that the proximate cause of the failure was the direct result of the inability to destroy Castro's air force.[116]

No matter how much Americans disliked Fidel Castro, the apparently greater Administration need was to demonstrate Kennedy's courage by invading a sovereign nation. (The President himself manifested the same concern to Ted

Sorenson days before the invasion. The longtime aide and chief speechwriter concluded that Kennedy would not listen to the plan's critics at that stage because he was not going to be cowardly.)[117]

Even more revealing was Bobby's behavior at a meeting, less than a week after the debacle, of Kennedy's Cuban advisors. Undersecretary of State Chester Bowles advised that, practically speaking, nothing could be done about Castro, as he was now firmly entrenched. Other aides such as Richard Goodwin agreed. However, when Bowles finished his presentation, Goodwin would write, "Bobby exploded" at the notion that nothing could be done to shake Castro from power. "That's the most meaningless, worthless thing I've ever heard," Bobby screamed. "You people are so anxious to protect your own asses that you're afraid to do anything…We'd be better off if you just quit and left foreign policy to someone else."[118]

That was not the language of Cabinet room discussions. Goodwin and the others blinked at the "harsh polemic…the embarrassing tirade." The rest of the group sat silently, "stunned by the ferocity of his [Robert Kennedy's] assault." Bowles himself called the atmosphere "almost savage…The President and the U.S. government had been humiliated and something must be done."[119] Bowles also described the President at this time as being in "a dangerous mood."

Bowles was one of the earliest to sense what was happening. He pleaded with the President to not let the situation "deteriorate into a head-to-head personal contest between the President of the United States and Fidel Castro." The seasoned, experienced Bowles, realizing that the Kennedys were newcomers to foreign policy matters, feared that they were easy targets for "military-CIA-paramilitary type answers."[120]

Bowles himself had less reason than others to be stunned by Bobby's Cabinet room exchange. He had earlier felt Bobby's fury—a fury that others described as without bounds. The episode occurred when Bobby concluded, wrongly, that Bowles was the source of a leak to the press about opposition to the invasion. Bobby was convinced that the purpose of the leak was not to save the country from a huge mistake, but to embarrass his brother. Encountering Bowles in a corridor, he lashed out at him with scathing remarks, emphasizing them with pokes to the chest with his finger. Bowles later denied that physical contact occurred, but the denial may well have been diplomatic. "His teeth hurt from that finger in his chest," a Bowles friend later remembered.[121]

Bobby's rage at Bowles persisted. A few months later—in the summer of 1961—he would call Bowles a "gutless bastard" for obstructing a plan to land troops on the Dominican Republic in order to install a friendly regime there.[122] Bowles wrote that Bobby was "slamming into anyone who suggested we go slowly." But the thrust of Bobby's anger at the Undersecretary came from Bowles' opposition to the Bay of Pigs adventure—opposition greatly justified, it turned out—and for what he felt was insufficient anti-Castro militancy. Unlike Jack, Bobby frequently and unrestrainedly spit out his animosity. He had "a tremendous capacity for love and hate," as William Hundley, chief of the

Organized Crime division in Kennedy's Justice Department, put it. "You would-n't want to get on his wrong side."[123] And Castro was as far on his wrong side as possible.

General Edward Lansdale, a counter-insurgency expert who later worked intimately with the Attorney General trying to destabilize Communist rule in Cuba, joined almost every observer in concluding that Bobby felt the April defeat even more strongly, and even more personally, than Jack. "He was pro-tective of his brother, and he felt his brother had been insulted at the Bay of Pigs. He felt the insult needed to be redressed rather quickly."[124] This is not to say that President Kennedy could not be vengeful, or that his friends never felt the "cruel whip" of his arrogance and self-absorption.[125] During Bobby's Cabinet room expression of fury, Richard Goodwin watched the seemingly calm, relaxed pres-ident tap the tip of a pencil against his teeth. Goodwin knew this as a sign that "some inner tension was being suppressed." He also knew "there was an inner hardness, often volatile anger beneath the outwardly amiable, thoughtful, care-fully controlled demeanor of John Kennedy." He became certain that Bobby's anger represented the silent President's own feelings, which he had privately communicated to his brother in advance.[126]

It is also not to say that Jack, in his own way, didn't want to settle the score with Castro as much as Bobby. A CIA Deputy Director of Intelligence felt that both brothers were "deeply ashamed after the Bay of Pigs, and they were quite obsessed with the problem of Cuba. They were a couple of Irishmen who felt they had muffed it...and being good fighting Irishmen, they vented their wrath in all ways that they could."[127]

According to documents held for 35 years, Che Guevara, Castro's second in command, met with Kennedy's Latin America advisor, Richard Goodwin, at a cocktail party four months later in Uruguay. At Guevara's insistence, Goodwin was brought to the 2 a.m. session, where he was offered a Cuban olive branch. Guevara's proposal was sweepingly attractive: Cuba was ready to foreswear any political alliance to the USSR, pay for confiscated U.S. property, and consider ending its support for communist insurgents in the area. All Castro wanted in return was a Kennedy pledge to cease hostile operations against his regime.[128] According to Goodwin (who, playing hardball politics as he had during the 1960 election, advised Kennedy against the idea), "Guevara's proposal was never pursued."[129]

Castro rankled Kennedy more than could be explained by any real threat to American interests. Of course, some threat was there, but it in no way justified the out-of-proportion U.S. response. Many analysts have pointed out that America shared responsibility for the mutual antagonism between Washington and Havana—by backing the corrupt dictator Batista for so long, by failing to see Castro in the tradition of Simon Bolivar, as an expression of a yearning desire for liberation, and by resorting to a boycott too soon after Castro's Marxist pro-fessions. Cuba had become for Kennedy what Khrushchev liked to call his "bone in the throat." Presidential historian Michael Beschloss put it this way, "What he [JFK] resented more were the costly political choices forced upon him by Castro's rise to power and his alliance with Moscow. He told friends that sooner or later, every politician acquired an albatross: 'I've got Cuba.'"[130]

The Kennedy Dynamic

In his autobiography, published just prior to his death in 1996, the CIA's Richard Bissell refers to fear of failure, an oft-described Kennedy family dynamic, and how it manifested itself in Jack and Bobby on the subject of Cuba:

> *The Kennedys wanted action and they wanted it fast. Robert Kennedy was willing to look anywhere for a solution... From their perspective, Castro had won the first round at the Bay of Pigs. He had defeated the Kennedy team; they were bitter and they could not tolerate his getting away with it. The President and his brother were ready to avenge their personal embarrassment by overthrowing their enemy at any cost. To understand the Kennedy administration's obsession with Cuba, it is important to understand the Kennedys, especially Robert.*[131]

Joe, the Kennedy patriarch, had used questionable and unscrupulous means in his drive to amass an immense fortune, and inculcated in his children a singular stress on the importance of winning. Joe was no ordinary father in his ambition for his children. Even after making himself extremely rich, he remained extraordinarily compelled to assert himself, partly through them. He raised his sons under an extremely rigorous set of values. As one biographer concluded, "Failure was not to be tolerated, passivity was a disgrace."

Kennedy family members agree on the key point of Joe's child-rearing philosophy. "The thing he always kept telling us," remarked Joe's daughter Eunice, "was that coming in second was just no good. The important thing was to win— don't come in second or third. That doesn't count—but win, win, win."[132]

By all accounts, Joe Kennedy's mandate as family patriarch achieved its fullest expression in Bobby. Most agree with the views of RFK biographers Lester and Irene David, who wrote, "He was just like the old man, Joseph Kennedy."[133] In describing her husband, Ethel Kennedy once said of Bobby:

> *"For him, the world is divided into black and white hats. The white hats are 'for us,' the black hats are 'against us.' Bobby can only distinguish good men and bad. Good things, in his eyes, are virility, courage, movement, and anger. He has no patience with the weak and the hesitant."*[134]

A number of RFK acquaintances have volunteered that Bobby's headstrong focus on results displayed a classic case of "short man complex." Physically, he had no reason for a Napoleonic complex — he stood over five feet, nine inches tall. But he was small in comparison to his siblings—which, of course, was the milieu in which he developed. "In a fiercely competitive family," Richard Goodwin noted, "[Bobby] had to battle more ferociously, recklessly, in order to hold his own." "Bobby grew up to be the runt," biographer William Shannon observed, "... in a family where all the other men were six feet or taller."[135] Bobby's mother Rose recalled a fear that he might grow up puny and girlish because he was the smallest and thinnest of the boys—but "we soon realized there was no fear of that." In fact, he went the opposite way, becoming a young man who had to distinguish himself daily to a family of "provers." Some thought Bobby tried the hardest and accomplished the least, intellectually as well as physically. But his overriding qualities derived precisely from the attempt.[136]

As Jack's presidential campaign manager, the younger Bobby channeled his own thrusting ambition into becoming the elder brother's servant, protector, henchman—and, when he felt it necessary—hatchet man. As an old friend of Jack, LeMoyne Billings, once observed, Bobby had "put his brother's career absolutely first; and [cared] nothing about his own career whatsoever."[137] As Attorney General, and de facto intelligence czar, Bobby Kennedy realized that part of his job was to deflect criticism of his brother. "The President," Bobby once said, "has to take so much responsibility that others should move forward to take the blame. People want someone higher to appeal to...It is better for ire and anger to be directed somewhere else."[138]

Bobby became the caustic, ornery executive officer who cracked down on his shipmates in order to run a tight ship for his beloved skipper—beloved, in Jack's case, because of his personal charm. The executive officer doesn't care that he is hated, because that comes with the job. A high CIA official once said that Bobby "always talked like he was the President, and he really was in a way."[139] Bobby was much more than Jack's right-hand man. He would also become the prime mover—inspirer and instigator—of some of the most secret (and dangerous) facets of the President's personal foreign policy.

"He's always been a lightning rod for Jack, trying to take the heat away from the presidency. It's not important what happens to him. What is important is what happens to Jack. I would say few men have ever loved a brother more." So spoke Bobby's successor, Ramsey Clark, Attorney General under Lyndon Johnson.[140] From the standpoint of presidential deniability, this seemed to play nicely when Bobby took charge of the Cuban initiatives.

On the difference between Jack and Bobby, Papa Joe once remarked, "Not that Jack isn't just as courageous, but Bobby feels more strongly for or against people than Jack does—just as I do."[141] Another remark by his father was more direct: "Everyone in my family forgives—except Bobby."[142] This trait was also a chip off Papa Joe, who once said of himself, "When I hate some son of a bitch, I hate him till I die."[143] Jack was incomparably better than Bobby at controlling his expressions of displeasure, reducing them to a dismissal or cold stare. Bobby tended to get hot quickly, releasing his fury indiscriminately

Jack, too, was competitive in his way, and could be quite aggressive. For example, newsman Walter Cronkite years later recalled how he felt JFK's wrath during the 1960 campaign. Cronkite had asked Kennedy about the impact of his Catholicism on the election. Cronkite later learned that a furious JFK contacted

CBS president Frank Stanton and bellowed, "When I become president, I get to name the members of the FCC, which controls your license [to operate]."[144]

But Bobby's competitiveness had a rawness to it, and Jack's did not. This difference reflected itself in their domestic life styles. While the White House glowed with grace, elegance, and culture, Hickory Hill, Bobby's estate in nearby McLean, Virginia, was a place where he challenged his guests to physical encounters. No one ever broke a bone visiting Jack, "but chipped fingers, wrist fractures, loosened teeth, torn muscles and ligaments, and even broken legs were not uncommon at Hickory Hill," as one RFK biographer put it.[145]

Evelyn Lincoln, the President's personal secretary, made a skillful stab at summing up the brothers' dissimilarities. "The difference between Bobby and Jack," Lincoln offered, "was this: Jack was evolutionary, Bobby was revolutionary."[146] Her observation was quite perceptive. A photographer covering Bobby once suggested to him that he was really a revolutionary. After some thought, Bobby acknowledged that the photographer, in a large sense, was right.[147] He was a revolutionary in the way he attacked whatever issues were on his agenda at the moment. While Jack, the cool skeptic, was keenly aware of the value of good appearances, Bobby, the firebrand, often appeared disheveled, just like a good revolutionary should. While Jack liked ideas, Bobby preferred action. Kennedy aide Harris Wofford observed during his brother's administration, "[Bobby] was always saying, 'Don't sit there thinking, do something!'"[148]

These differences between the brothers were not absolute. But in terms of how they expressed their antipathy to "that guy with the beard," as Bobby often called Castro, they were very important. They helped explain why the younger brother was "a man driven by demons" in the secret war with Cuba. "Bobby was emotional as he could be," Ray Cline, Deputy Director of Intelligence for the CIA, would remember. "He was always bugging the Agency about the Cubans."[149]

The personal differences also explained why the White House's chief occupant could have been pictured as a man of peace—which he was in many critical ways not concerning Cuba—while his brother, his trusted right hand, was deep in Florida's Everglades, on secret visits to personally supervise quasi-legal acts of war against Fidel Castro and the sovereign nation of Cuba. This was the Bobby who, with his heavy preference for action over contemplation, was "fascinated by all that covert stuff, counter-insurgence, and all the garbage that went with it," as Undersecretary of State George Ball once put it.[150] This was also the brother whom no one had to like because he wasn't running for anything, or furthering his own ego, but merely serving Jack. And it was the brother so widely known as ruthless by those who worked with and under him.

With his intellectual curiosity, and his knowledge of history and other leaders' mistakes, John Kennedy grew remarkably as a statesman during his 34 months as president. He took courageous steps toward peace with many adversaries. But Cuba remained the exception. As his father opined, "Cuba gave this administration a chance to be great." Tragically, it was an opportunity not seized.

The Kennedy Connections

John F. Kennedy inherited more than a family characteristic for stubbornness. He inherited his family's resources, its wealth, and connections as high as the CIA and as low as the Chicago underworld. Joseph Kennedy had built a network of trustworthy men, which JFK expanded while he occupied the highest office in the land. The men in this large network would protect him during his presidency (and after his death), but couldn't protect him from the repercussions of his brother's actions, taken either on his behalf or according to his orders. This network of powerful friends has been pointed to as evidence of an anti-Kennedy conspiracy. The truth is just the opposite.

Patriarch Joe Kennedy founded a Kennedy tradition when he entered the bootlegging business in the 1920's. His relationship with the Mafia would grow, culminating when he approached the underworld for its support in JFK's 1960 presidential campaign. Joe Kennedy's contacts in that area would also prove invaluable when Robert Kennedy was later looking for "unofficial" intelligence opportunities in Cuba. The Mafia had been almost entirely shut out by the Castro regime, and they very badly.wanted to return to Cuba. RFK was not opposed to using them to get what he and his brother were after.

The Kennedys had informal bonds with CIA members long before John F. Kennedy was inaugurated. Robert Kennedy's wife's family, the Skakels, maintained close relationships with CIA officers. In 1966, the closeness of the Skakels with the CIA was noted when George Skakel, Jr. (then running Great Lakes) and three friends chartered a plane for a hunting trip in Idaho. When the plane crashed, killing all aboard, it was reported that 15-year CIA veteran Lewis Werner was one of the victims. In charge of the St. Louis division of the CIA at the time, Werner often traveled to Cuba with Skakel to hunt wild boar.

In addition, a variety of New England liberals such as Allen Dulles, Des FitzGerald, Richard Bissell, Richard Helms were part of a social/intellectual clique that included Joseph P. Kennedy. CIA executive Bill Harvey referred to this group as "Fifth Avenue cowboys." As historian Burton Hersh points out, "Most of the leadership of the CIA was enlightened, preponderantly Democratic, with emerging senior managers like Tracy Barnes and Dickie Bissell quite dedicated social reformers."[151] Comparisons to the Kennedys are inescapable.

The Kennedy brothers had also preserved a long-lasting association with Allen Dulles, then CIA Director. Letters in both the Kennedy and Dulles collections reflect that John and Robert Kennedy maintained correspondence with both Dulles brothers from at least 1955. Traveling in the same social sphere, Allen Dulles and John Kennedy were "comfortable with one another and there was a lot of mutual respect," Richard Bissell said in an interview. In fact, Kennedy was known to regard Dulles as a legendary figure. Historian Herbert Parmet wrote, "Dulles often went to the Charles Wrightsman estate near Joe Kennedy's Palm Beach House. As far back as Jack's early days, they socialized down in Florida, much of the time swimming and playing golf."[152] Dulles himself said, "I knew Joe quite well from the days when he was head of the Securities and Exchange Commission."[153]

But Papa Joe Kennedy's relationship with Dulles extended far beyond that of neighbor and occasional golf buddy. On January 13, 1956, when Allen Dulles was CIA Director, Joseph Kennedy was appointed to President Eisenhower's Presidential Foreign Intelligence Advisory Board (PFIAB).[154] "PFIAB is a sort of holding ground for people who couldn't obtain, or didn't want, Congressional approval [to serve the U.S. government]," explains Colonel Alan D. Campen, who served under President Reagan as Director of Command and Control Policy in the office of the Secretary of Defense.[155] Historian Michael Beschloss adds, "After exerting himself to win appointment to Eisenhower's intelligence board, he [Joe Kennedy] improved his acquaintance with Dulles."[156]

Among other commonalities, Joe Kennedy and Allen Dulles were both outspoken isolationists at the start of World War II. Kennedy was often called pro-Nazi (by, among others, Lyndon Johnson) when he publicly insisted that the German-English "feud" had nothing to do with U.S. interests.[157] Likewise, Dulles, whose law firm, Sullivan and Cromwell, represented many German and U.S. investors, told businessmen who belonged to the German SS that he believed that many of their objectives were well-founded. At one point, Dulles remarked to a German SS member that he was "fed up with listening all the time to outdated politicians, émigrés, and prejudiced Jews."[158]

Dulles first met Jack Kennedy at the Kennedy Florida compound in 1955. They became fast friends. "Our contact was fairly continuous," Dulles later said. "When [JFK] was in Palm Beach, we always got together."[159] Jack came to revere both Dulles' intellect and accomplishments.

Robert Kennedy, too, was clearly impressed with Dulles. Regarding his performance at the time of the Bay of Pigs, Robert Kennedy later recalled, "Allen Dulles handled himself awfully well, with a great deal of dignity, and never attempted to shift the blame. The President was very fond of him, as I was."[160] He elaborated to historian Arthur Schlesinger, "He [JFK] liked him [Dulles]— thought he was a real gentleman, handled himself well. There were obviously so many mistakes made at the time of the Bay of Pigs that it wasn't appropriate that he should stay on. And he always took the blame. He was a real gentleman. JFK thought very highly of him."[161]

Dulles kept a variety of Kennedy secrets from the public. For example, when John Kennedy won the election in November 1960, the CIA under Dulles conducted a background investigation of Kennedy in anticipation of his first intelligence briefing as President-elect on November 18. Such investigations were designed to predict how the subject would respond when informed of the full range of CIA operations, and to show Dulles the most effective method of appeal. Prepared by CIA psychologists, the study included hot evidence from the FBI: the indiscretion of a youthful Jack Kennedy, at the height of World War II, with alleged Nazi spy Inga Arvad Fejos.[162] In 1942, while serving in the Office of Naval Intelligence in Washington, Jack Kennedy had established this potentially dangerous liaison. The FBI, which had wiretapped Arvad, initially compiled the file. Historian Thomas Reeves wrote:

> When Jack's relationship with the woman became known to Navy officials, the assistant director of the Office of Naval Intelligence wanted to cashier the young ensign from the Navy. A witness remembered the officer being "really frantic." Reminded of Joe Kennedy's prestige, however, the official eventually calmed down and consented merely to give Jack a speedy transfer to an ONI outpost in Charleston, South Carolina.[163]

(FBI sources state that it was Hoover's direct pressure that brought about the transfer.[164] The potential value of this kind of political dynamite was most assuredly never lost on the FBI Director. It was just the kind of file that kept Hoover's power inviolate for so long.[165])

Dulles' decision, or favor, to keep this matter secret was quite possibly rewarded later, when Kennedy, as president-elect, retained Dulles as CIA Director. It may also have played a part in Kennedy's initial refusal to accept Dulles' resignation after the Bay of Pigs fiasco.

The CIA after the Bay of Pigs

> "In the course of the past few months I have had occasion to again observe the extraordinary accomplishments of our intelligence community, and I have been singularly impressed with the overall professional excellence, selfless devotion to duty, resourcefulness and initiative manifested in the work of this group."
> — President Kennedy, in a letter of commendation to new CIA Director John McCone, January 9, 1963

After thinking it over, it was clear to John Kennedy that the blame for the Bay of Pigs was largely his and not the CIA's. And although Kennedy needed public scapegoats in his administration, he drew the line at a public indictment of the original Eisenhower-era planners of the invasion. Kennedy's Secretary of State, Dean Rusk, later testified, "President Kennedy was very angry when some people around him tried to share responsibility with President Eisenhower because President Kennedy knew that he and his senior advisors had a chance to look at that and made their own judgment on that, and he did not like the idea of having to share the buck."[166]

Although Kennedy's threat to "splinter the CIA into a thousand pieces and cast it to the winds" has long been used to support theories that the CIA had reason to hate JFK, just the opposite is true. Kennedy's "threat" was a knee-jerk reaction to the failed invasion. Years later, E. Howard Hunt, the CIA's liaison to the Cuban exiles, surmised, "For him [Kennedy] to have said that was probably a way of disguising from himself the fact that he himself was responsible for the fiasco, and I'm sure that's something that haunted him for the rest of his days."[167]

All of John Kennedy's other statements regarding the CIA were nothing short of glowing. On November 28, 1961 Kennedy went to Langley, Virginia to dedicate the CIA's new headquarters, which came to fruition under the outgoing Director, Allen Dulles. Addressing the large throng, Kennedy said:

I want, first of all, to express my appreciation to you all for the opportunity of this ceremony to tell you how grateful we are in the government and in the country for the services that the personnel of this Agency render to the country. It is not always easy. Your successes are unheralded—your failures are trumpeted. I sometimes have that same feeling myself. But I am sure you realize how important is your work, how essential it is—and, in the long sweep of history, how significant your efforts will be judged.

In addition to the dedication, Kennedy had planned a surprise for his loyal friend. Dulles' biographer, Peter Grose, described the event:

Allen greeted the presidential helicopter at the landing pad hidden among the trees of the campus. Interrupting the carefully scripted ceremony that followed, with more than six hundred CIA professionals in attendance, Kennedy turned to the dais behind him. "Would you step forward, Allen." On his lapel he pinned the National Security Medal. Short of knighthood or lordship, it was the highest honor of the United States government.[168]

Turning to address Dulles, Kennedy said, "I want to express my appreciation to you now, and I am confident that in the future you will continue to merit the appreciation of our country, as you have in the past." The next day, JFK dashed off a letter expressing his great admiration and affection for Dulles. In closing, Kennedy wrote, "You leave behind you, as witness to your great service, an outstanding staff of men and women trained to the nation's service in the field of intelligence." In what appears to be a genuinely heartfelt letter to his old friend Dulles, the President added, "I am sure you know you carry with you the admiration and affection of all of us who have served with you. I am glad to be counted among the seven Presidents in whose administrations you have worked, and I am also glad that we shall continue to have your help and counsel…Your integrity, energy, and understanding will be a lasting example to all."[169] Two years later, in the wake of JFK's assassination, Dulles' kinship with John Kennedy would play a role in Dulles' decision to withhold critical information from his fellow Warren Commission members.

On March 1, 1962, JFK would similarly honor Bissell with the same National Security medal. In ceremonies at the White House, Kennedy made it clear that he still held Bissell in high esteem. In part, Kennedy said:

During his more than twenty years of service with the United States government, he has invested a rich fund of scholarship and vision. He has brought about returns of direct and major benefit to our country. In an area demanding the creation and application of highly technical and sophisticated intelligence techniques, he has blended theory and practice in a manner unparalleled in the intelligence profession. Mr. Bissell's high purpose, unbounded energy, and unswerving devotion to duty are benchmarks in the intelligence service.[170]

The Kennedys and the CIA

After the Bay of Pigs, as both he and his brother Robert began to understand the intended role of the CIA, John Kennedy would oversee one of the greatest budget increases for the intelligence community in U.S. history. "You have to always bear in mind how the Agency was originally set up," instructs one high-ranking Agency official. The CIA, he reminds us, was instituted as the intelligence arm of the Executive branch—the President and official Washington have never been confused about that fact. First conceived by President Harry S Truman, the CIA was established and organized by the National Security Act of 1947 (Truman submitted it to Congress, which passed it on July 26, 1947).

The CIA's charter is unambiguous in stating that the Agency would function only in response to directives of the President and of the President's own intelligence apparatus, the National Security Council. Nowhere in the charter is there any inference that the CIA would be allowed to initiate policy. JFK, a close student of history, was undoubtedly aware of the Eisenhower-CIA partnership that had toppled regimes in both Iran and Guatemala. The Directors of the CIA, appointed by the President, take their loyalty to the President seriously, and often have performed tasks against their own better judgment at their bosses' behest.

In return for this loyalty, Kennedy often went out of his way to shield the CIA from unwelcome scrutiny. At a news conference in November 1963 (six weeks before his death), Kennedy responded to a question regarding the CIA. A newsperson had asked Kennedy if the CIA was conducting unauthorized activity in South Vietnam. Kennedy rose to its defense, saying:

> *I think that while the CIA may have made mistakes, as we all do, on different occasions, and has had many successes which may go unheralded, in my opinion in this case it is unfair to charge them as they have been charged. I think they have done a good job.*

Robert Kennedy also knew where the buck stopped. In 1967, when the CIA was criticized for giving illegal financial support to the National Student Association, Bobby refused to let the CIA take the rap. He went on record as saying that the CIA policies were approved at the highest levels of presidential administrations. "If the policy was wrong," Bobby said, "it was not the product of the CIA but of each administration."[171] When Kennedy family friend Jack Newfield tried to goad Bobby into criticizing the Agency, Bobby again rose to its defense, saying, "What you are not aware of is the role the CIA plays within the government. During the 1950's...many liberals found sanctuary in the CIA. So some of the best people in Washington, and around the country, began to collect there. One result of that was the CIA developed a very healthy view of Communism, especially compared to State and some other departments. So it is not so black and white as you think."[172]

The Kennedy brothers, Bobby more than Jack, soon became smitten with the clandestine world the CIA inhabited. Author and intelligence expert John Ranelagh most accurately summarized the relationship. According to one CIA man with whom Ranelagh spoke, "Robert Kennedy, in his shirtsleeves, delved into the inner workings of the agency. In the end, he did not shake it up as his brother had wanted, but fell in love with the CIA and the concept of clandestine operation." Ranelagh added:

> Jack Kennedy realized, as he told Clark Clifford—an influential and trusted Kennedy advisor and Democratic power broker—"I have to have the best possible intelligence," and soon reversed his decision to punish the CIA. Both brothers saw that alone of the agencies of government the CIA was willing to take action and had tried to do in Cuba what the President wanted. The Bay of Pigs failure meant that the agency would not resist tighter control. Rejection of the agency was not necessary: the windmill was now the Kennedys' to turn and direct. They were determined to make it work under their close direction.[173]

CHAPTER TWO

THE CUBA PROJECT

"Everyone at CIA was surprised at Kennedy's obsession with Fidel. There was no gung-ho [anti-Cuban] spirit among the officers at the JM/WAVE station in Miami. They thought it was a waste of time. We all knew he [Fidel] couldn't hurt us. Most of us at CIA initially liked Kennedy, but why go after this little guy? One thing is for sure: Kennedy wasn't doing it out of national security concerns. It was a personal thing. The Kennedy family felt personally burnt by the Bay of Pigs and sought revenge. Papa Joe taught his sons well: 'Don't get mad, get even.'"

—Sam Halpern, CIA executive assistant to William Harvey and the Cuba Project[1]

Bobby Takes Charge

During the 1960 presidential campaign, candidate John F. Kennedy mused aloud, "There are two people I'd like to get out: Jimmy Hoffa and Castro." [2] And towards Castro, there was a certain, special level of ridicule. "Why doesn't he take off those fatigues? Doesn't he know the war is over?" In the wake of his Bay of Pigs debacle, now-president Kennedy appointed his brother as de facto head of all intelligence operations, including those of the CIA. From the time he became President-elect, Kennedy had hinted at such a move. In November 1960, Kennedy asked CIA Director of Covert Operations Richard Bissell whether it would be "useful to have an individual executive to pull the whole Cuban situation together who would know precisely at all times what State, CIA, and the military were doing and who could answer questions directly?" Now JFK had determined that that man should be his most trusted advisor, and the best organization man he knew—his brother.[3]

John Kennedy had concluded what the real mistake had been in the Bay of Pigs operation. The Agency just didn't have any idea how far the Kennedy brothers wanted to go to "get rid" of Castro. They were soon to find out. The President told aide Kenny O'Donnell, "I should have had Bobby in on that from the start." Jack also said, "I made a mistake putting Bobby in the Justice Department. Bobby should be in CIA."[4] Kennedy advisor Arthur Schlesinger, Jr.

remembered the chain of events, saying, "After the Bay of Pigs, Robert Kennedy took a personal interest in the CIA and became an informal presidential watchdog over covert operations."[5] Bobby became "the untitled overseer of the intelligence apparatus in the Kennedy administration," as chroniclers of American intelligence activities later put it.[6] Soon Bobby Kennedy's iron grip on CIA covert activities was complete.

The first result of this reshuffling was Bobby Kennedy's appointment of the Taylor Commission to investigate what had gone wrong at the Bay of Pigs. It consisted of Allen Dulles, General Maxwell Taylor, and Admiral Arleigh Burke, and was overseen by Bobby Kennedy. Six weeks later, Bobby concluded:

> We have been struck with the general feeling that there can be no long term living with Castro as a neighbor. It is recommended that the Cuban situation be reappraised ... and new guidance be provided for political, military, economic, and propaganda action against Castro.[7]

Aware of the recent coup successes of the previous administration, and with the CIA's Allen Dulles still on board, the Kennedys were brimming with confidence. Bobby made it clear to his charges that Public Enemy Number One was Fidel Castro. One Kennedy intimate has written, "From inside accounts of the pressure Bobby was putting on the CIA to 'get Castro,' he seemed like a wild man who was out-CIA-ing the CIA."[8] The same source concluded that the "Attorney General was the driving force behind the clandestine effort to overthrow Castro." Dick Bissell said, "That pressure was exerted, all right. I felt that pressure, mainly from Bobby."[9] After a few weeks on the job, Bissell complained, "Bobby is a wild man on getting rid of Castro."[10] Richard Helms, CIA Deputy Director of Operations, also knew what Bissell was experiencing. "My God, these Kennedys keep the pressure on about Castro," Helms remarked.[11]

While the Taylor Commission was in session, the assassination plots against Castro, begun before the Bay of Pigs, continued. The CIA later admitted that the plots were never terminated, but were always considered a "going operation."[12] While Phase One of the Cuban Project was failing dismally, Phase Two (post Bay of Pigs) was already in the planning stages.

The second result of this reshuffling was a new operation, overseen by Robert Kennedy and unprecedented in the annals of the American intelligence community. As Bobby instructed his charges, "My idea is to stir things up on the island with espionage, sabotage, general disorder..."[13] He planned to topple what he considered the Castro "insurgent movement" with his own movement. His idea was not new. In military circles, it was known by its true name—counterinsurgency.

The Kennedys and Counterinsurgency

"Guerrillas must move among the people as fish swim in the sea."
    —John F. Kennedy, giving his "bastardized" version of Mao Tse
    Tung's famous maxim[14]

Since World War II, the U.S. military establishment had been concerned with the possibility that the Soviet Union would eclipse the West in its ability to conduct "special warfare." Also referred to as counterinsurgency, special warfare allowed a nation to respond to a foreign threat in a manner short of all-out war, and before the threat was fully realized. The Pentagon's Field Circular for low intensity conflict defines counterinsurgency this way: "The art and science of developing and using the political, economic, psychological, and military powers of a government, including police and internal security forces, to prevent or defeat insurgency."[15] According to a 1947 Army review entitled "A Study of Special and Subversive Operations," the specific counterinsurgent techniques to be employed included:

The control of movement of civilians, rendering civilian cooperation with our forces desirable, eliminating guerrilla sources of supply, the holding of hostages, reprisals against civilians [etc],...In general, means must be devised to remove any guerrilla logistic support, to alienate the civilian population from the guerrillas, to isolate the underground, and to prevent support for them by air, sea, or land.[16]

Many of these tactics were used against the Castro regime.

In 1947, U.S. military planners studied guerrilla movements in the Philippines, the Balkans, and the Soviet Union to formulate their policy. It became clear that effective counterinsurgency demanded a capability for sabotage, hit-and-run raids, control of the airwaves, arson, terror, and assassination.

These studies led to the formation of the Army's elite Special Forces unit. Although clearly concerned with the new dimension of statecraft, the military remained reluctant to elevate pre-emptive counterinsurgence to the strategy of first choice. With centuries of proven tactical warfare theory, the military planners felt more secure in devoting their continued energies to the tried and true methods of full-scale war. (This kind of thinking precipitated America's all-out involvement in Korea in the 1950s and Vietnam in the late 1960s.) Sensing what full-scale war would mean with either Cuba or Vietnam, President Kennedy knew there had to be another answer, and he believed he found it in counterinsurgency. The Special Forces had been a small, highly trained, and rarely used cadre. That would change almost immediately after Kennedy's inauguration.

On February 1, 1961, ten days after assuming office, President Kennedy met with his National Security Council (NSC) to formulate National Security Action Memorandum 2 (NSAM2). The document called for "an expanded guerrilla program," the addition of 3,000 men to the Army's 1,000-man Special Forces, funded by a budget increase of $19 million, and a re-allocation of $100 million within the Defense Department for "unconventional wars." Historian Michael McLintock observed:

> *The counterinsurgency era began with John F. Kennedy's call for a radical reappraisal of U.S. special warfare. His fascination with the Special Forces and the idea of American guerrillas meshed neatly with his Cold War view that the small wars of subversion and insurgency on the periphery of the "Free World" posed the greatest challenge to our national security. In particular, Kennedy emphasized counterinsurgency's use for political and economic reform.[17]*

McLintock points out that NSAM2 was just the beginning. In his March 28 message to Congress (just prior to the Bay of Pigs invasion), the President delivered what the historian referred to as Kennedy's "seminal statement" on counterinsurgency. On this occasion, Kennedy declared:

> *The free world's security can be endangered not only by a nuclear attack, but also by being nibbled away at the periphery...by forces of subversion, infiltration, intimidation, indirect or non-overt aggression, internal revolution, diplomatic blackmail, guerrilla warfare or a series of limited wars...*

> *Much of our effort to create guerrilla and anti-guerrilla capabilities has in the past been aimed at general war. We must be ready now to deal with any size of force, including small externally supported bands of men; and we must help train local forces to be equally effective.*

But it was clear that Kennedy wanted to go beyond merely training "local forces." America, the President went on to say, had an obligation to contribute "highly mobile forces trained in this type of warfare." On May 11, in the wake of the Bay of Pigs embarrassment, Kennedy issued National Security Action Memorandum 52. Its first and keystone clause stated that the U.S. objective (preventing a Communist takeover in South Vietnam) had caused the White House "to initiate, on an accelerated basis, a series of mutually supportive actions of a military, political, economic, psychological and covert character designed to achieve this objective." The practical result was that CIA Saigon station chief William Colby formed the highly secret Special Operations Group (SOG), which infiltrated saboteurs and agents into the sovereign nations of North Vietnam, Laos, and Cambodia.[18]

On May 25, Kennedy addressed a joint session of Congress and requested a one-half billion dollar increase in the Defense Department budget to further this new strategy. Elaborating to the Congress on the "type of warfare" he was talking about, Kennedy spoke of the enemy using "guerrillas striking at night, by assassins, acting alone." By employing "this type of warfare," Kennedy was letting the world know that the United States was preparing, in his words, to "respond in kind." The United States was about to enter not only the "counterinsurgency era," but also the assassination era. Stung by the Bay of Pigs one month earlier, Kennedy was informing the world (and especially Cuba) that America's gloves were off.[19]

Throughout the summer of 1961, the U.S. mounted a series of disorganized offensives against Cuba *(details to follow)* that went nowhere. It wasn't until then that a frustrated Bobby Kennedy suggested putting some shape to the amorphous policy.

In October 1961, two momentous events occurred. First, the CIA, ostensibly corroborating the allegations of exile leader Miro Cardona of a planned second invasion of Cuba, was instructed by President Kennedy to conduct a study which would be called "If Castro Were to Die." If Fidel were removed "by assassination" or other causes, what would be the effect on his regime? The CIA response: "If Castro were to die by other than natural causes, the U.S. would likely be charged with complicity." As will be seen, this conclusion would have no effect on the assassination plotting that was to follow.

Secondly, Kennedy asked the Joint Chiefs of Staff to prepare an invasion plan for Cuba. The top secret plans, months in the preparation, said the military could be mobilized within eight days of the go-ahead.[20] All that was needed now was a White House coordinator for the intensified Cuba Project. The man President Kennedy chose was Brigadier General Edward Lansdale.

Edward Geary Lansdale

"Robert Kennedy was the driving force behind a continued operation against Castro, and Edward Geary Lansdale was his official instrument."
—**Richard Bissell**[21]

The subject of two best-selling novels (Graham Greene's *The Quiet American*, and *The Ugly American*, by William Lederer and Eugene Burdick), Lansdale had become a mythic figure by the time John Kennedy assumed the presidency in 1961. As one of the few military men to champion the use of counterinsurgency, he was consistently considered an "outsider" by his Pentagon peers. Lansdale, however, had established a record of success that spoke for itself. Former CIA Director William Colby wrote of Lansdale:

Lansdale was a maverick, and big bureaucrats do not suffer mavericks kindly....When an order appeared wrong, he simply ignored it and went on doing what he thought was right (and frequently it was). His style made him few friends among the more traditional bureaucrats and, more seriously, kept him from appointment to the kind of leadership where he might have been able to make major changes in American foreign policy...But he left a legacy. He inspired many with his empathy for Asians, particularly with the simplest Asians in the rice paddy or in the street stall. He was a patriot for all that is best in America...[22]

Lansdale had a strong ally at CIA: director Allen Dulles became his patron, eventually intervening with the Air Force to have Lansdale promoted to

Brigadier General.[23] In 1951, Edward Lansdale was thus inducted into the CIA's Office of Policy Coordination, where he was assigned the task of assisting the Philippines' Minister of Defense, Raymond Magsaysay, in suppressing a rebellion by the Communist Huk guerrillas. Against great odds, Lansdale won over the peasant population with a program of road building, health center construction, and improved agricultural programs. In time, the Huks were defeated, with Lansdale and Magsaysay becoming popular heroes. (Lansdale incurred the wrath of fellow CIA officers by acquiring such a heroic public persona. Magsaysay went on to win the Philippine presidency by a landslide.)

Lansdale's next challenge was Vietnam. President Eisenhower had hoped that Lansdale would have similar success assisting South Vietnam's President Ngo Dinh Diem in repelling a similar Communist insurrection. Diem, however, was no Magsaysay. Lansdale's techniques of reform and tolerance were not appreciated by Diem, who was intolerant of any opposition.

This is not to say that Lansdale was a pacifist. True to his military calling, the General was not averse to the use of "bullets over butter," but advocated their use only against an armed and intransigent enemy, not against a wavering populace as an instrument of terror. When Eisenhower refused to pressure Diem into accepting reforms, Lansdale requested a transfer. He was promoted to the influential position of Deputy Director of the Pentagon's new Office of Special Operations. It was here that he wrote a 25-page study about the Vietnam situation entitled "Binh Hung: A Counter Guerrilla Case Study." The report, unlike typical upbeat military prognostications, painted a bleak, but realistic, picture of the situation in Asia. As if written by a military heretic, the study advised that the only way to defeat the Vietcong would be by enlisting the sincere loyalty and support of the peasants through agricultural and social reform. Lansdale wrote:

> The great lesson [of Malaya and the Philippines] was that there must be a heartfelt cause to which the legitimate government is pledged, a cause which makes a stronger appeal to the public than the Communist cause…When the right cause is identified and used correctly, the anti-Communist fight becomes a pro-people fight.[24]

President Kennedy read the report two days before his inauguration. Impressed by the report's candor, JFK instructed military advisor Walt Rostow, "Get to work on this."[25]

On January 28, 1961, the weekend following his inauguration, John Kennedy summoned Lansdale to a cabinet meeting. The president told Lansdale how impressed he was with the general's Vietnam study. After the meeting, Kennedy pulled Lansdale aside. "Did Dean [Rusk, the secretary of state] tell you that I'd like you to go over there [South Vietnam] as the new ambassador?" he asked. Although a stunned Lansdale had been lobbying for just such a post, he thought it better to act demure and to decline the offer, hoping the president would insist. He didn't. Lansdale later recalled, "I still couldn't catch on that he was being serious about it. I guess he was."[26]

Three months later, the Bay of Pigs left Kennedy deeply suspicious of optimistic predictions from both CIA and Defense. The President needed a pragmatist, and in Lansdale, who had strongly objected to the Bay of Pigs invasion, he knew he had one. Like the rest of the Kennedys' New York-Boston clique, Lansdale fit in nicely. "Ed was another Madison Avenue grey-suiter," is the way one Cuba Project officer remembers him. It was Lansdale's influence that led to the President's demands on Congress for increased funding for counterinsurgency. Kennedy began reading the works of other famous guerrilla leaders, including Mao Tse Tung and Che Guevara. So enthralled was he that Kennedy even began quoting their maxims in public.

Not long after, at Robert Kennedy's suggestion, the President offered Lansdale the Cuba Project. By 1962, the Kennedy administration had formed the Special Group Augmented (SGA), and made Bobby Kennedy the chairman. Bobby had teamed up with JFK aide Richard Goodwin in suggesting a "command operation" to deal with Cuba. The seminal document was a November 1, 1961 Goodwin memo to JFK proposing the new concept.

"The beauty of such an operation...is that we cannot lose," the youthful Goodwin naively guaranteed. "I believe that the Attorney General would be the most effective commander of such an operation," Goodwin continued. "The one danger here is that he might become too closely identified" with the project. Therefore, Goodwin advised, "His role should be told to only a few people at the top."[27]

Robert Kennedy made his first formal presentation of the proposal to the Special Group on November 22, 1961. On November 30, 1961, President Kennedy issued the following proclamation to the Special Group: "We will use our available assets to go ahead with the discussed project in order to help Cuba overthrow the communist regime. This program will be conducted under the general guidance of General Lansdale, acting as Chief of Operations." Lansdale, in fact, had proposed NSAM2 to Kennedy. This new, overarching program, conceived on a scale grander than anything before it, was bestowed the name "Operation Mongoose." [28]

Operation Mongoose

> "It is the age of arson, sabotage, kidnappings and murder for political purposes; it is the age of hit-and-run terrorist activities coordinated on a global scale."
> — **Robert Kennedy, to the first graduating class of the International Police Academy, February 1964**[29]

> "MONGOOSE: A carnivorous predator known for its lightning-fast reflexes. After killing its prey, it steals its eggs. Also known as 'The Perfect Killer.'"
> — **The Encyclopedia of the Animal World, Vol. 7.**

"In keeping with the Presidential memorandum of 30 November 1961, the United States will help the people of Cuba overthrow the Communist regime from within Cuba... The U.S. recognizes that final success will require decisive U.S. military intervention."

— This early guideline written by Lansdale became the mantra for a reckless new anti-Castro program spearheaded by the Kennedy White House[30]

While Lansdale formulated policy in the White House, the practical logistics, predictably, were to be carried out by the CIA, where the new Cuban "Task Force W" was headed by Bill Harvey. By this time, the White House had removed the Cuban component from where it traditionally resided, in the CIA's Western Hemisphere Division, run by J.C. King. This allowed Task Force W to come under the direct control of Bobby Kennedy and the Kennedy White House. However, JFK installed a direct "red phone" line to J.C. King's private study at home to seek his counsel when needed throughout his term. "That phone rang at all hours of the day and night," King's daughter Marguerita recently recalled.[31]

The first item for Bill Harvey and his staff was the choice of a code name, or crypto, for the new program of sabotage. The CIA's longtime crypto reference officer recommended the diagraph MO, which was the agency's code for Thailand—in hopes of briefly confusing the unauthorized who learned the code name. A list of words beginning with "MO" was submitted to Cuba Desk officer Sam Halpern, who chose Mongoose.[32] (The apt mongoose/cobra analogy was an unintended coincidence.)

Although CIA budgets are still classified, insiders all agree that Operation Mongoose received a bloated allocation, with estimates ranging from $50 million to $150 million per year (over $500 million in 1998 dollars.) Mongoose was headquartered in Miami and the CIA station there was given the code-named acronym JM/WAVE. It employed over 700 Americans and over three thousand Cubans, and was overseen by former Saigon Station Chief Theodore Shackley. Shackley, Bill Harvey's protegé in Berlin, had also served as the head of the Western Hemisphere Division of Clandestine Services.[33]

Mongoose's strategy of sabotage consisted of contaminating Cuban sugar exports, inciting guerrilla warfare, counterfeiting Cuban currency, conducting military raids against refineries and copper mines, disseminating anti-Castro propaganda, and carrying on espionage.

Although the CIA's charter forbids domestic intelligence operations, one would never know it by the Mongoose logistics. Ray Cline, the Deputy Director of Intelligence, remembers Mongoose as "a real anomaly. It was run as if it were in a foreign country, yet most of our agents were in the state of Florida. People just overlooked the fact that it was a domestic operation."[34] "We ran 2,123 missions out of the Florida CIA station," CIA agent Grayston Lynch remembered.[35]

Working the Cuba Desk at Langley in Virginia, Sam Halpern wasn't certain the project was legal, and sought advice from CIA General Counsel Lawrence Houston. Houston noted that Congress had provided the funds, and added, "If the President says it's okay, and the Attorney General says it's okay, then it's okay."[36]

The Cuba Project had as its sole purpose the removal from office of Castro, now known by his CIA cryptonym AM/THUG. The White House contingent met daily, often for six and seven hours at a stretch. Its scope and intensity astounded even seasoned staffers.

From Kennedy With Love

Just prior to the Bay of Pigs, the White House released a list of JFK's favorite books. Number nine was Ian Fleming's James Bond adventure *From Russia With Love*, a piece of fiction chock full of assassinations and womanizing. That Kennedy took such a hankering to Fleming's work received wide coverage in the press. As it turned out, Kennedy's passion for Fleming was shared by his friend and CIA director, Allen Dulles, who wrote that he was first recommended to the Fleming books in 1957 by Jackie Kennedy. "She gave me *From Russia With Love*," Dulles later recounted. From then on "President Kennedy and I often talked about James Bond."[37] What was not as well reported was that the previous spring Fleming had been Senator Kennedy's houseguest at his Georgetown home (another guest was CIA agent and close friend of Allen Dulles, John Bross).

According to Fleming biographer John Pearson, while coffee was being served, Kennedy asked Fleming what James Bond would do if his superior "M" asked him to get rid of Castro. Fleming replied that the U.S. was making too much fuss over the dictator, thereby inflating his importance in the eyes of his followers and the rest of the world. He then proceeded to regale the dinner guests with his proposals for "ridiculing" the Cuban leader. Claiming that there were only three things that mattered to Cubans—money, religion, and sex— Fleming suggested the following three-pronged approach:

- *The United States should send planes to scatter Cuban money over Havana, accompanying it with leaflets showing that it came with the compliments of the United States.*

- *. Using the Guantanamo base, the United States should conjure some religious manifestation in the sky (a cross of sorts), which would induce the Cubans to look constantly skyward.*

- *The United States should send planes over Cuba dropping pamphlets, "compliments of the Soviet Union," stating that the American A-Bomb tests had poisoned the atmosphere over the island; that radioactivity is held longest in beards; and that radioactivity makes men impotent. Consequently, the Cubans should shave off their beards, and, as the logic follows, without bearded Cubans, the revolution would collapse.*[38]

Ian Fleming died in 1964 and therefore did not live to read the report of the Church Committee in 1975, or the 1967 CIA "Inspector General's Report" released in 1993. He would have been proud. All of his proposals were acted on by the CIA at the urging of the Kennedy's Mongoose coordinator, General Edward Lansdale. As we will see, the CIA attempted to make Castro's beard fall out, considered staging a "religious event" off the coast using Guantanamo-based submarines, and was involved in a plot to flood Cuba with counterfeit currency. Allen Dulles wrote that after he was turned on to the Bond books by the Kennedys, he met and became great friends with Bond's creator, Ian Fleming. "I kept in constant touch with him," Dulles wrote after Fleming's death. "I was always interested in the novel and secret 'gadgetry' Fleming described from time to time...They did get one to thinking and exploring, and that was worthwhile because sometimes you came up with other ideas that did work."[39]

The most unsavory aspect of the administration's anti-Castro plotting, its use of the Mafia, also bore the Fleming stamp—but may in fact have been a case of Kennedy inspiring Fleming. It recalls what many consider Judy Campbell's most controversial allegation: while she was John Kennedy's lover, she passed Castro assassination plans from Kennedy to Chicago mob boss Sam Giancana. One year after Campbell says she performed this function, Fleming published *On Her Majesty's Secret Service* (1963), In that novel, James Bond falls in love with the daughter of an organized crime syndicate leader. Bond proceeds to use his lover as a go-between with her father, and together they attempt to kill the sinister leader of an international terrorist organization.

At one Mongoose meeting, the President indicated to Lansdale that the decorated warrior seemed to embody the essence of JFK's favorite fictional hero, James Bond. Lansdale disagreed and informed Kennedy that America's real James Bond was the man coordinating the Cuba Project at CIA, the man who had been in charge of ZR/RIFLE, William Harvey. Soon, President Kennedy would meet the legendary Harvey face-to-face. On that occasion, the President was said to remark, "So you're our James Bond."[40] Although initial meetings with Harvey went well, it soon became apparent that the Kennedys and the old pro from CIA were at strategic loggerheads.

Bill Harvey was assigned to coordinate Mongoose from the CIA headquarters in Langley. He was rightly perceived as a single-minded man who got things done. Along with Lansdale, his task was to make Mongoose a success within a single year. But Harvey and Lansdale disagreed on the strategy needed to incite a popular uprising in Cuba. Harvey hoped to use professional tradecraft, to create an infrastructure of agents, and to put it in place on the island. This took time, and the Kennedys let Lansdale know that they were in a rush. "To the White House, it was just pressing buttons," recalled Harvey's assistant Sam Halpern. "They didn't understand how long it took. Spies don't grow on trees."[41]

"We want boom and bang on the island," Lansdale countered.[42] Harvey's handwritten notes of an early meeting with Robert Kennedy underscore the determination involved: "Top priority in U.S. Gov't...All else is secondary

...Nothing to stand in way of getting this done."[43]

The differing strategies of the White House and Harvey were not the only problems confronting the Cuba Project. In fact, this difficulty was dwarfed by another obstacle: practically everyone remaining in Cuba supported Fidel, and gave no indication that they would rise up against him, even if incited. Harvey had managed to place some agents in Havana, and their reports were discouraging. No support networks existed on the island for the Kennedy-backed exiles, as the exiles had promised. A popular, CIA-sponsored uprising was a fantasy. But no one in the White House, it appeared, was reading the intelligence reports. Consequently, Mongoose proceeded full speed ahead.

Robert F. Kennedy—"Mr. Mongoose" [44]

"Bobby Kennedy could sack a town and enjoy it."
> —**General Maxwell Taylor, JFK's Chairman of the Joint Chiefs of Staff, after watching RFK berate the Special Group**[45]

"Bobby went bonkers on counterinsurgency. We [at CIA] were up to our bloody eyeballs in counterinsurgency. Those of us at the 'troop' level did not like what was going on. We objected."
> —**Sam Halpern, CIA Executive at the Cuba Desk**[46]

After the Bay of Pigs, Colonel Jack Hawkins wrote an "after-action" report. "It concluded," Hawkins later explained, "that Castro is too strong to be overthrown by para-military action, and that no further action should be taken. If Bobby Kennedy even read my report, he must have thought, 'Hawkins is a fool.'"[47] The Kennedy administration plowed ahead.

Key players in the Kennedy administration were well aware that Bobby Kennedy maintained a "hands-on" approach to all things Cuban, especially those matters involving his covert counterinsurgent footsoldiers. George Ball, for example, then-Undersecretary of State, recalled, "Bobby was always for that kind of thing. He was fascinated by all that covert stuff, counterinsurgency, and all the garbage that went with it."[48]

"Counterinsurgency," as epitomized by Operation Mongoose, had become the buzzword of the day, and Bobby reveled in it. Kennedy aide Harris Wofford noted that RFK's interest was far more than intellectual. "He would invite Green Berets for weekends at Hyannis Port and watch them demonstrate their prowess swinging from trees and climbing over barricades."[49] Thomas Parrott, a CIA officer assigned as Secretary to Bobby Kennedy's Special Group, recently complained, "Everybody in the Army—even lieutenants in the finance corps—had to have a course in counterintelligence. We in the CIA would refer to Lansdale as the FM—for Field Marshall."[50] As Bobby himself recalled, "Yes, I was involved in it all the time—Cuba. I was trying to do things, mostly trying to get them to come up with some ideas about things to be done."[51]

Bobby Kennedy even made frequent clandestine appearances at the CIA base in Florida. "In 1962 and 1963, RFK was running the anti-Castro operation in Florida by himself. I saw him down here myself many times. Everybody knew it. Everybody knew it!" said CIA contractor/exile organizer/Watergate burglar, Frank Sturgis.[52] As will be seen, Army Captain Bradley Ayers, on loan to JM/WAVE as an instructor, saw the Attorney General at the Florida base twice in 1963, when he was inspecting the Everglades training camps. He had come by private helicopter from the family compound in West Palm Beach.[53] While at the secret base, Bobby worked the phone incessantly, calling Harvey regularly to play cheerleader. Grayston Lynch remembers the RFK phone calls to the CIA's safe houses in Florida. "I'd come into the safe house in the morning," says Lynch, "and they would say, 'Bobby says this, and Bobby says that.'"[54]

CIA photo analyst Dino Brugioni recently recalled Bobby's regular presence at CIA headquarters in Langley. At the time, Brugioni's office was using U-2 photos to monitor the damage inflicted by the Mongoose troops. "Bobby used to stop by after going home for lunch [in nearby McLean], or on his way home from work late in the afternoon," says Brugioni. "He wanted to be kept up on how the sabotage was going. We provided a room for him where he could call the White House."

Brugioni remembered that Bobby was especially keen on blowing up the island's oil refineries.[55] "It was obvious he was the eyes and ears of his brother. He was like a prizefighter, pumped up for action." Brugioni later wrote, "Frequently, [Bobby] would chat with [CIA Director] Mr. McCone, but more often he would want to discuss the latest covert operations against Cuba with officers in the Directorate of Plans."[56] When Bobby couldn't make it to Langley, CIA officers brought surveillance photos over to his D.C. office.

CHAPTER THREE

MURDER AND MISSILES

Hashshasin—The "hashish-users." A fanatical Moslem sect that flourished
in Persia over a thousand years ago and who considered murder of their enemies a sacred duty; the origin of the modern word, assassin.

W hen the Kennedy administration took office in January 1961, it inherited
not just the Bay of Pigs operation, but the programs of assassination
directed against several foreign leaders, including Castro. Insiders wondered
how Kennedy's policy-making would affect the anti-Castro mayhem instituted
by Eisenhower and Nixon. Incredibly, due to the effects of the Bay of Pigs fiasco
on the vaunted Kennedy pride, the new administration upped the ante to dramatic, and tragic, heights. Whereas the previous administration had failed in all
its attempts to do away with Lumumba (Congo), Trujillo (Dominican Republic),
Diem (Vietnam) and Castro (Cuba), the Kennedys seemed determined to claim
the title of first American administration to successfully murder a foreign leader.
This was accomplished four months after Kennedy's inauguration, when Trujillo
was murdered. Two and a half years later, the Diem brothers were killed. But it
was Castro's head that was most coveted.[1]

Close friend Senator George Smathers encountered a distraught John
Kennedy soon after the Bay of Pigs. Recalling what he had told Smathers prior
to the invasion, Kennedy again brought up a sensitive secret. Smathers remembered Kennedy saying that he "had been given to believe by the CIA that Castro
would be dead before the attack went in. Someone was supposed to knock him
off."[2] Eight months later, just after his retirement, CIA Director Allen Dulles
admitted to a national television audience, "We were not looking for a spontaneous uprising, but for other developments."[3] The CIA's Bay of Pigs planner
Richard Bissell was less discreet in 1984, when he stated, "There was the thought
that Castro would be dead before the landing. Very few, however, knew of this
plan."[4]

Three decades later, details are beginning to emerge about what Dulles
termed "other developments."

The Pre-Invasion (Phase One) Castro Assassination Attempts

As has been stated, even before John F. Kennedy made it to the White House, there were plans for a Castro assassination. The pre-Kennedy phase of the operation began when the CIA's Western Hemisphere chief, J.C. King, wrote an internal memo suggesting the "elimination" of Fidel Castro. King's daughter Eloise recently recalled the period and her father's frame of mind. "He felt very strongly about this country. If he honestly felt it would help this country, I believe he would have done it." Eloise recalls that her father was caught up in the Cold War mindset of the times, much like the Kennedys.[5] Another daughter, Marguerita King, adds, "It also stems from the great friendships he developed with the Cuban exiles living in Miami."[6] Soon, a handwritten note appeared indicating that both CIA Director Allen Dulles and Richard Bissell, the director of Covert Operations, approved King's recommendations (including assassination).[7] (Dulles and King were very close friends. Dulles was even the godfather of one of King's daughters.) Bissell placed his subordinate, Sheffield Edwards, in charge. This pre-Bay of Pigs period came to be known as Phase One of the assassination plots. These efforts were clearly designed to provide the coup de grace for the upcoming Bay of Pigs invasion.

Edwards' plan was to utilize members of organized crime to eliminate Castro. It was a fact known to all that the U.S. mob had been reaping vast sums from the Cuban casinos it controlled under the previous regime, and the gangsters badly wanted to return to Havana. Edwards surmised that there should be an extensive Mafia network already in place on the island, and that they had murderers at their disposal, so the mob seemed an obvious choice. "I learned of the Mafia plots early on," says CIA planner for the Bay of Pigs, Jake Esterline. "I often wished I hadn't. I controlled the purse strings and had to sign off on it, in this case, without being told what the money was to be used for. I told J.C. King that I refused to O.K. it." The next day, Esterline was given a detailed briefing by [CIA Director] Allen Dulles. "I couldn't believe what I was hearing," says Esterline. "Dulles told me, 'It's alright. This is money approved by the President.'"[8]

The first CIA-mob liaisons have gone largely unreported. In the summer of 1960, Charles Siragusa, Washington-based deputy Director of the Bureau of Narcotics (and the bureau's liaison with the CIA), was approached by a CIA friend, who said, "We are forming an assassination squad...There's some foreign leaders we'd like dead." Siragusa knew that one such leader had to be Castro.[9] An unnamed middleman, it was later learned, was used to enlist a number of mobsters, including Santos Trafficante. It now appears that that mobster middleman—Norman Rothman—was the partner of Meyer Lansky, and had links to Richard Nixon.[10]

Before Castro's takeover, Rothman, together with mob partners Meyer Lansky and Gabriel and Sam Mannarino, owned the Batista-era Sans Souci Casino in Havana, where Rothman was known to share his profits ("the skim") with Batista and his family. After the revolution, Rothman, like many others, fled to Miami. Rothman, however, was one of the few with the moxie to return to Havana and attempt to enlist Castro's bodyguards in an assassination attempt against the new dictator. Rothman was apparently the "go-between" for the CIA, sources have revealed. "Rothman was in touch with several CIA agents," a former CIA officer recalls. "They had many meetings concerning assassination plots against Castro." According to this agent, Rothman tried to enlist fellow mobsters Santos Trafficante of Tampa, the Mannarinos of Pittsburgh, Sal Granello and Charles Tourine of New York, and Johnny Rosselli of Las Vegas.[11]

According to *Time* magazine, the CIA obtained mobsters' aid by promising that they would be allowed to recover the booty left behind if they would assist the Agency in recruiting "their old contacts on the island to set up a small network of spies." The CIA specifically wanted them "to pinpoint the roads that Castro might use," so that they would be in the best position possible to kill him.[12]

Unable to enlist the help of Castro's protectors, Rothman returned to Miami, where he bought a hotel with Batista's relatives. Soon, the bodyguard he had attempted to enlist, Frank Sturgis, turned against Castro and fled to Miami, where he hooked up with Rothman. From unknown sources, Rothman channeled money to Sturgis' new anti-Castro group, The International Anti-Communist Brigade.[13]

Sheffield Edwards next contacted former FBI man/Howard Hughes aide/CIA freelancer, Robert Maheu.[14] The CIA's James O'Connell was assigned as Maheu's case officer.

"I'm no saint," Maheu has said. "I am a religious man, and I knew that the CIA was talking about murder." O'Connell told Maheu, however, that the U.S. and Cuba were, in effect, at war, and drew Hitlerian analogies. "If Fidel, his brother Raul, and Che Guevara were assassinated, thousands of lives might be saved," O'Connell told the reluctant go-between. Wrestling with his decision at home the night Edwards contacted him, Maheu finally assented to the CIA's requests.[15]

Johnny Rosselli, whose name had been floated during the previous Rothman plot attempts, was the point man the CIA selected to implement the assassination plots. He was the Mafia's "Mr. Smooth," assigned to run operations in Los Angeles in the 1930's, and later in Las Vegas, where he oversaw the mob's takeover of the gambling industry. Maheu's role was to draw Mr. Smooth into the operation. Maheu had met Rosselli in the spring of 1959 in Las Vegas. Like many before him, Maheu was charmed by Rosselli, and later wrote that he considered him a friend.

"Me? You want me to get involved with Uncle Sam?" responded an astonished Rosselli on meeting with Maheu in L.A. "The Feds are tailing me wherever I go...Bob, are you sure you're talking to the right guy?" Maheu eventually succeeded in convincing Rosselli to come aboard for the project. Although some have speculated that Rosselli was attempting to leverage a deal in order to get the government off his back, Maheu remembers it differently. "The truth, as corny as it may sound, is that down deep he thought it was his patriotic duty," Maheu later wrote.[16]

After being recruited by Maheu, Rosselli introduced (the CIA's) O'Connell to Sam Giancana, boss of the Chicago mob, and Santos Trafficante, who had been the Mafioso in charge of the casinos in pre-Castro Havana. Like the White House, the mobsters wanted back into Cuba, and told O'Connell that they could find a Cuban to kill Castro.

The initial planning meeting was held in Miami Beach's Fontainebleau Hotel, where the assassins-to-be were offered $150,000 by the U.S. government to kill Fidel Castro. O'Connell told the mobsters he wanted Castro gunned down in a gangland-style killing, à la "The Untouchables." The Mafiosi rejected this as too dangerous and suggested something "nice and clean"—poison in the form of pills or something else that would disappear without a trace. Months later, the CIA's Technical Services Division perfected a botulism toxin, which Maheu passed, in the form of deadly capsules, to a Cuban at the same Fontainebleau Hotel.[17]

After the Kennedy administration had been installed, a news service reported that Castro was ill, and in fact, on his deathbed. The planners assumed that their poison pill had been involved. According to Joe Shimon, who attended some of the Fontainebleau sessions, Robert Maheu called him, saying, "Boy, we've got it made. Bobby's going to be very happy!" (Shimon would later say that the news accounts were planted by Castro, who knew in advance that the plotters were coming. "Castro wasn't even sick," Shimon said. "The people that took that stuff over there disappeared.")[18]

In fact, the Giancana gambit was a total disaster, but not for Castro. Although the U.S. government shelled out $150,000 to the "don's" organization, the contacts Giancana provided never delivered. (There is also a widespread belief that Giancana himself never intended on following through—his agreement with the feds was a scam to ease FBI harassment of him.[19])

Although it has been widely reported that the U.S. government engaged members of organized crime to assassinate Fidel Castro as a prelude to the Bay of Pigs invasion, it is not so well-known that Cuban exile murder teams were working in league with the CIA toward that same end.

"I volunteered to assassinate Fidel Castro, and the Americans took me up on it," says Felix Rodriguez, a Cuban exile and longtime CIA agent. According to Rodriguez, while the Kennedy administration was being installed in January 1961, his CIA superior provided him with a "beautiful German bolt-action rifle" and a backup support team. The team was transported to a "safe house" in the Florida Keys, where they trained. The team made three attempted infiltrations into Cuba, two of which were thwarted by Castro's patrol boats. The third attempt was scrubbed by the American advisors, who unbeknownst to Rodriguez' "Grey Team," had shifted their hopes to yet another Cuban hit squad.[20]

In 1975, Congress heard testimony from a CIA officer who admitted to being in charge of the pre-invasion assassination attempts. That officer, John Henry Stephens, a Covert Actions Operations officer on loan to the CIA from Special Forces, told investigators of two occasions where he led five-man assassination teams. After training in Guatemala, the teams were flown over the island and parachuted in. His team members were not Cubans, but "Poles, Germans, or Americans." His teams, he testified, were equipped with "assassination packages," consisting of a variety of weapons, including grenades and an "assassination gun."

Stephens, now deceased, told his family at the time of the inquiry that the committee was pressing for more details. According to his sister, Flora May Stephens, John told the family little of the operation. His training in Latin America was so secretive that the family didn't hear from him for three months and presumed him dead. Later, he confided that the CIA wanted complete deniability should he be captured. He went into the island under the name "John Simpson." At the time of the Congressional hearings, Stephens told his sister, "They're trying to make me talk. But if I talk, I die."[21] Stephens gave the investigators operational details, but no names. The Congressional summary of the Stephens interview states:

This gun was a 9 mm. weapon made in England, of which there were only "9 or 10 in the world." It consisted of two pieces of pipe, which when disconnected from each other, looked like simple pieces of pipe rather than a weapon. These pieces screwed together into a "clip," containing ammunition and a firing mechanism, and was inserted into one piece, creating a gun. According to Stephens, the gun, when fired, made only a slight "woosh" sound, and was otherwise silent.[22]

CIA cables released in 1994, not necessarily connected to Stephens' operation, shed more light on assassination operations going on at the time, which were overseen by a CIA Cuba group known as "Branch Four." In late March 1961, cables began arriving at CIA headquarters from a Cuban plotter, codenamed "NOTLOX." The messages were addressed to "JMBELL," and said, in part:

(March 23): I told Luis Bueno to ask your opinion regarding sabotage of electric company in order to leave Havana ten days without power. We can coordinate with attempt against Fidel. Suggest attempt against Fidel in accordance with general plan. Reply urgent, Monty

(Plan (4) 9 April): Fidel will talk at the Palace. Assassination attempt at said place followed by a general shutting off of main electric in Havana....Answer before 1 April. Agent 2637 (pictured page 55)

[NAMES DELETED] was advised below-listed names provided by Guat secret service with statement they [are] all Cubans except as noted who are on way or in Guat with mission assassination.

Brigade leader Raphael Quintero recently disclosed, "I was part of that NOT-LOX plot. There was going to be a big boxing match and we knew Castro was supposed to be present. We planned to have him hit with a bazooka." Quintero says that the CIA gave the final go-ahead to another exile group, but it was ill-equipped for the mission.[23] Other cables referred to an airdrop of "Springfield rifles with telescopic sights," presumably to have been used for the NOTLOX attempt.

After the Bay of Pigs failure in April, the assassination plotting continued. On May 3, 1961, JMBELL received a cable from a Cuban agent code-named TEK-LOK. The cable stated:

> We are contacting all groups (DOS) to organize one united front with a coordinator. You name him or we elect him. Tell us. Will try kill Fidel today. Andres OK but still hiding. His men gone to hill. Want to know what can be used. Luis Jorge (pictured page 56)

These attempts continued after the Bay of Pigs, according to other cables. Here is one example. On June 4, 1961, the CIA's Deputy Director of Plans (DDP) Richard Helms received the following:

> Functionary Italian Embassy by the name of Moratori says he works for one intelligence organization of yours, he says he is in contact with Martin Elena and others and that you have plans for invasion within 30 days after killing Fidel, advise if we can confide in Moratori.[24]

Despite the attempted secrecy, Castro's intelligence apparatus had, typically, penetrated the plots from the start, dooming them to disaster. In the first of Stephens' attempts, one member of the parachuted-in team actually succeeded in reaching his appointed hotel site on the island. Upon entering his room, he radioed Stephens in Guatemala. Stephens testified that this individual's radio transmission was interrupted by gunfire and no more was heard from him. On the second attempt, two men were captured or killed at the drop zone where they made their parachute landing in Cuba.

After the unsuccessful Bay of Pigs invasion, a number of laughably futile plans were concocted to bring about Castro's demise. Some of the earliest attempts on Castro were designed to destroy his character, if not his person. The plotters had hoped to at least erode Castro's public image, or as one Congressional investigator called it, "the magnetic charisma he seemed to exert for the Cuban people."[25] One idea was to be carried out during Castro's trips out of the country. When he left his boots outside his hotel door for polishing, the CIA would sprinkle thallium, a strong depilatory, into them. As a consequence, the CIA determined, Castro's beard would fall out, and his rule would be irreparably weakened without the symbol of his masculinity and power. The CIA abandoned the scheme when intelligence determined that Castro's trips abroad were infrequent and well guarded.

Subsequent attempts were, in the summary of the same Congressional investigator (Loch Johnson), "still more fantastic, requiring a suspension of disbelief

```
  843                    CLASSIFIED MESSAGE                          ROUTING
                                                              1              4
DATE :  29 Mar 61                                             2              5
                                                              3              6
TO   :  [        ]        RX Filing telec't code.
                          No Cm Record Value.  Destroy.
FROM :  [        ]        fil file and copy as indicated
                          Branch and y filed to indicated      MAR 29  2136Z  61
ACTION: [        ]        the thousand since chan.
                          Marked  [ ]        None required [ ]
                                                             OPERATIONAL IMMEDIATE
INFO :  DDP, COP, ADDP/A, WH 3, OC 6, [    ] 5/C

                              #2                               IN 0665

TO  [        ] WAVE           INFO                   CITE  [        ] 9956
    [        ]
    [        ]
```

FOLLOWING RECEIVED [   ] AT 292036Z:

NR2 CK110 QSP

OCHO SEIS X PLAN NUEVE X NUEVE ABRIL X FIDEL (RECD: HIDEL) HABLA EN PALACIO X
ATENTADO EN DICHO LUGAR SEGUIDO APAGAN (RECD: APAGJN) GENERAL EN HAVANA VELADURA
PRINCIPALES PLANTAS ELECTRICAS X TOMA DE PLAZA CIVICA CIA (RECD: 19A) CIA (RECD:
CCA) X CIA TELEFONOS CIA ATARES Y X Y MINFAR X MINFARX ACCION TODA LA ISLA COMBINAN
DESEMBARCO UDS POR SALADO X SALADO Y X Y SANTA (RECD: YANTA) MARIA MAR X NECESITAN
ENTREN ARMAS HABANA X TENEMOS SUFICIENTES (RECD: SZFICIENTES) HOMBRES Y X Y VALOR
(RECD: VCLOR) X ESTADO ANIMO DESESPERADO (RECD: DESESLERADO) IMPOSIBLE (RECD: IMPOS
AGUANTAR MAS X CADA (RECD: CAKA) DIA SITUACION (RECD: SITUACIOP) PEOR DETENCIONES
DIARIAS X PODEMOS VOLAR CIA ELECTRICIDAD CUALQUIER (RECD: VUALQUIER) MOMENTO X PIE
LO QUE NOS REPRESENTA DESPUES DE LA ACCION X RESPONDA ANTES (RECD: ANTEN) UNO ABRIL

                    END OF MESSAGE

<u>WH/4 Translation:</u>

86.. PLAN (FOR) 9 APRIL. FIDEL WILL TALK AT THE PALACE. ASSASSINATION ATTEMPT AT
SAID PLACE FOLLOWED BY A GENERAL SHUTTING OFF OF MAIN ELECTRIC PLANTS IN HAVANA
VELADURA. OCCUPY THE PUBLIC SQUARE, TELEPHONE COMPANY. ATARES (ARSENAL) AND
MINFAR (MINISTERIO DE FUERZAS ARMADES REVOLUCIONARIO -ARMED FORCES MINISTRY).
ACTION THROUGHOUT THE ENTIRE ISLAND COMBINED (WITH) YOUR DEBARKATION AT SALADO
AND SANTA MARIA (DEL) MAR. WE MEDLARS ENTER HAVANA. WE HAVE SUFFICIENT MEN
AND COURAGE. STATE OF MIND DESPERATE IMPOSSIBLE TO ENDURE THIS LONGER. EVERY DAY
SITUATION WORSE DAILY ARRESTS. WE CAN BLOW UP ANY ELECTRIC COMPANY AT ANY TIME.
CONSIDER WHAT THIS REPRESENTS FOR US AFTER THE ACTION. ANSWER BEFORE 1 APRIL. sgc:
AGENT 2637.

2	5
3	6

1 [ ]

2 [ ]

3 [ ]

4 COP, ADDP/A, WH, OC 6, [ ] S/C

RE Filing (check one):
No CS Record Value. Destroy. ☐
RI file this copy as indicated ☒
Branch copy filed as indicated ☐
RE Indexing (check one):
Marked ☐ None required ☒
Signature:

#5

MAY 3 2138Z 61

OPERATIONAL IMMEDIATE

IN 1283

[ ] WAVE CITE [ ] 5540.

[ ] [ ]

FOLLOWING RECEIVED FROM [ ] AT Ø32Ø11Z: NR 3 CK 46

35. WE ARE CONTACTING ALL GROUPS (DOS) TO ORGANIZE ONE UNITED FRONT WITH A COORDINATOR YOU NAME HIM OR WE ELECT HIM TELL US. WILL TRY KILL FIDEL TODAY. ANDRES OK BUT STILL HIDING. HIS MEN GONE TO HILL. WANT KNOW IN WHAT CAN BE USED. (AS RCVD)

[ ]

END OF MESSAGE

RI COPY

APPROVED FOR RELEASE 1993
CIA HISTORICAL REVIEW PROGRAM

1389 Use Previous Editions

RELEASED PER P.L. 102-526 (JFK ACT)
NARA BT DATE 9-20-95

few serious novelists would ask of their readers." One focused on Castro's cigars, which were to be impregnated with a chemical that would cause temporary disorientation. There was also a plan to spread the word on Cuba that the Second Coming of Christ was imminent, and that he would vanquish the anti-Christ Castro. A submarine would then surface near the island and send up starshells—supposedly a manifestation of the Second Coming, which would lead to Castro's overthrow. Walt Elder, Assistant to the CIA Director, sarcastically referred to this plan as "elimination by illumination."[26] "This is absolutely true," an intelligence officer felt it necessary to assure the Church Committee, which investigated these plots some 15 years later.

Plot followed plot—the latest more overwrought than the last: using the deadly botulism poison on his cigars to kill on contact; placing a bomb in an exotic seashell certain to attract Castro's attention when he went skin diving; exploding the bomb from a nearby submarine; or just having an intermediary present Castro with the gift of a skin diving suit contaminated with still another exotic poison.

The Story of Lt. Commander John Gordon III (USN)

It now appears that assassination plots employed not only Cuban exiles and mobsters, but also Naval Intelligence officers, gamblers, or anyone else who seemed to have access to Fidel Castro's person.

"The last words that were said to me when I left Washington were, 'Get Castro!' It was an ugly business." Quoting these instructions, a senior officer in the Office of Naval Intelligence (ONI) describes his marching orders as he prepared to leave for his command post at the Navy's Guantanamo (Cuba) Base in the wake of the Bay of Pigs defeat. "It was a shooting war going on down there," remembers the officer, who prefers to remain anonymous. "Castro shot thirty base employees one morning."[27] Like the pre-Bay of Pigs plots supervised by John Stephens, these post-Bay of Pigs attempts were also thwarted by Castro's superior intelligence operation. The ONI officer remembers, "Castro was picking up on these things as fast as they got started."

John Gordon, one ONI officer given the task of furthering the Kennedy administration's murder plots, would suffer for three decades as a result of his involvement in the futile schemes. By 1961, 40 year old career Naval Intelligence Officer John Gordon III had established himself as a man with a bright future in the military. Successful tours overseas and assignments with the brass in the Pentagon made it clear to all that he was on a fast track. He would gain his Ph.D. in maritime history from Harvard, and become the senior researcher for a renowned Harvard historian, Samuel Elliott Morison. Later, he would become an assistant professor of maritime history at Framingham State College, a prestigious New England institution of higher learning, and eventually the director of a college in South Carolina, where he remained until his death in 1987.[28]

But in 1961 something happened to John Gordon that caused permanent mental anguish, characterized by periods of isolation and hospital stays for nervous breakdowns. He never talked in detail about what happened that summer, but left enough small bits of information around for those who needed to know—his family, closest friends, and attorneys—that it is possible to piece the story together for the first time. Gordon left behind documents that he urged his family to keep in a safe place. The documents were coded, cut up into six parts, and sent to six different family members, with the key to the code left behind for his daughter to find at the author's urging. A surprising amount of his story would be corroborated by a future Congressional investigation (see Chapter Nineteen).

In the spring of 1961, in the wake of the Bay of Pigs disaster, Gordon became aware of a secret meeting at the Pentagon held to determine how to deal with the victorious Castro. Gordon would later tell his attorney, F. Lee Bailey, that those present included CIA Director Allen Dulles, Secretary of State Dean Rusk, Chief of Naval Operations Arleigh Burke, and Attorney General Robert Kennedy. The result of this meeting was to direct certain Naval Intelligence officers in Guantanamo, Cuba to oversee an assassination plot against Fidel and Raul Castro.

Burke, who had once received a medal from former Cuban leader Batista, was on record as favoring the assassination plots. At the National Security Council's Special Group meeting of March 9, 1961, Burke stated "that any plan for the removal of Cuban leaders should be a package deal, since many of the leaders around Castro were even worse than Castro."[29] (Two years later, when it was believed that Admiral Burke might oppose Kennedy in the upcoming 1964 presidential elections, his personal files on Cuba [including those possibly pertaining to Gordon] were stolen. Burke believed the culprit was a member of Kennedy's team.[30] Given how involved Burke was, there's reason to think he may have been right.)

In an interesting coincidence, when Bobby Kennedy's phone logs were (partially) released in 1994, a June 7, 1961 "while you were out" message—at the time Gordon was getting set up in Guantanamo—showed that Bobby Kennedy received a call from the CIA's Western Hemisphere Chief J.C. King, the originator of the Castro assassination plots in 1959.[31] King, as noted by Bobby's secretary, called to say he "has info about five Cubans that Mr. [Bobby] K asked him to find out about."

It was in this spring of 1961 that Gordon, accompanied by his wife and two children, relocated to "Gitmo." He became the acting officer in charge of Intelligence there. Gordon once showed his daughter Heather his military records, pointing out a two month gap in the summer of 1961 (while they were in Guantanamo). Gordon's sister Caroline recalls, "He told me he met with Bobby Kennedy in Guantanamo also. He didn't respect Bobby. All John told me was that something was supposed to happen that didn't."

John Gordon's assistant in the Field Intelligence Office was Jack Modesett.

Modesett introduced Gordon around the base to both the military and the local Cubans. Modesett denies vehemently that there was any talk then of an assassination. However, when pressed, he admits, "There was something regarding Raul [Castro] that I don't think I can talk about."[32] Gordon's close friend, historian, and college director Mack Daniels remembers, "John told me he was involved in some planning in Guantanamo. I always assumed he meant the Bay of Pigs. He never told me the details. He did once say something about the assassination of Castro, but I didn't pay much attention."[34]

According to his daughter Heather, John Gordon worked around the clock, pushing himself to the point of total exhaustion. John spoke fluent Spanish and was always having Cubans over to their home. "I remember dad going out at night in civilian clothes with a Cuban named 'Big Louie.'"[34] The Cubans told Gordon's wife about plots to kill Castro, and their suspicion that one of their associates named Gonzalez was a double agent, reporting back to the Cuban dictator. Gordon's daughter remembers November 22, 1963: "When President Kennedy was killed, and it was announced that a man with Cuban ties had been arrested and was seeking a lawyer well-known for defending communists, dad pointed to Oswald and said, 'He's a dead man.' To his dying day he felt that Oswald was hired by Cuba in retaliation." John Gordon would often tell his family, "That bastard Bobby got his brother shot."

In early 1964, in the wake of the Kennedy assassination, Gordon sent coded documents detailing sites, operational details, and a list of over 50 of his Gitmo contacts to six family members. His daughter retained "the key" document. The operation was code-named "OP # 922H 2 D4" later changed to "922H 1E." Some of the shooters brought in, included on the list, were Luis Balbuena, also known as "El Gordo" (most likely "Big Louie" from daughter Heather's memory) and Alonzo Gonzalez.[35]

According to court documents filed by Gordon's attorney, one of the shooters recruited in the plot was turned around by Castro, and instructed to return and inform the planners (RFK, et al) that "for the vicious plot, he [Fidel] would have President John F. Kennedy assassinated."[36] Heather Gordon remembers, "Dad found out that one of his Cuban double agents was a triple agent reporting back to Fidel. He had him arrested."[37]

In late 1961, after his Guantanamo stint, Gordon suffered a nervous breakdown and was sent to Bethesda Naval Hospital for mental evaluation. He was not allowed to see any member of his family for eight months. He told his family it was really a debriefing, and the extended stay an effort by the Kennedy administration to put the fear of God into him. After vowing to remain silent about the plots he had discovered at Guantanamo, Gordon won reassignment, serving out his career at posts in the Pentagon, Florida, New Orleans, and the Boston Naval Shipyards. During the latter part of this period, one incident stands out in Heather Gordon's memory. "I remember in 1968, when Bobby was killed, dad jumped for joy. It was like a millstone was removed from his neck. He knew Bobby and felt that if he was elected, we'd have a mobster president."

After retiring from the military in 1969, Gordon became bitter over what he perceived to be medical malpractice performed by military physicians on his wife. He wrote letters that may have contained veiled threats to reveal what he knew if his wife were not taken care of. The military threatened to lobotomize Gordon and keep him in Bellevue Hospital for life. His daughter Heather says: "They were afraid he'd write about Cuba. He was not the kind of guy you wanted mad at you, and he was a prolific writer." Gordon's sister-in-law says emphatically that Gordon told her he was going to write a book. Gordon, while stationed in New Orleans, told the details of the Cuba episode to fellow ONI officer Guy Johnson. Johnson, coincidentally Guy Banister's attorney, thought Gordon could use Cuba as leverage over the military. Johnson had good contacts in Washington, and noted attorney F. Lee Bailey eventually took Gordon's case. Bailey negotiated with the Pentagon. A deal was struck that accommodated Mrs. Gordon's needs with the agreement that her husband remain mum on Guantanamo, and the matter was dropped.[38]

John Gordon went on to become assistant professor of history at Framingham State College. In 1970, two CIA officers showed up at his house in Framingham and brought Gordon to Washington, D.C., where he testified in closed session before the Senate Judiciary Committee (among whose members was Ted Kennedy). Consequently, according to court documents, Judiciary Committee member Senator Ed Long of Missouri gained "knowledge of where a record of the (Guantanamo) meeting may be maintained." That proof has never surfaced, and Sen. Long's own papers are voluminous and unindexed.

In 1976, Gordon relocated to Georgetown, SC, where he was Director of University of South Carolina's Coastal Carolina College. He retired in 1986 and died of a heart attack on Sept 27, 1987, never being able to prove his own stories true.

For years, the seeds of doubt were rampant in the minds of the Gordon family. Was John Gordon exaggerating his experiences? How could they believe his stories? Eventually, vindication would appear for John Gordon and all those who stuck by him in the face of 33 years of government denials. With the passage of the JFK Act in 1992, sensitive government documents began being declassified, shedding light on much of the secret government operations of the Kennedy administration, including the Guantanamo affair. One investigation would conclude that the Guantanamo plotting likely had its origins in the stratagem that was micro-managed by Robert Kennedy—Operation Mongoose. *(For further details on John Gordon, see Chapter Nineteen.)*[39]

Camelot, /aka/ "Murder, Incorporated"

On January 25, 1961, just five days after the president's inauguration and three months before the Bay of Pigs, JFK's White House instructed CIA Director of Covert Operations Richard Bissell to create a permanent assassination capability. Bissell's assistant, Tracy Barnes, remarked, "JFK was tough. He knew the difference between who you have to kill and who you don't have to kill."[40]

Bissell would initially testify that the idea of a permanent assassination capability probably had come from one of JFK's top national security advisors, either McGeorge Bundy or Walt Rostow: "There is little doubt in my mind that Project RIFLE [the CIA's cryptonym for the assassination project] was discussed with Rostow, and possibly Bundy." One month after making this statement, Bissell would waffle, asserting his earlier testimony to be mistaken.[41] However, in later years, Bissell slowly began to retreat from the party line. In 1975, he testified to the Senate that when he and Allen Dulles briefed President-elect Kennedy in Palm Beach in the fall of 1960, he said it was his "opinion" that Dulles told Kennedy "obliquely of this auxiliary operation, the assassination attempt."

Thirty years after JFK's 1963 assassination, Bissell began to open up more. "Allen Dulles had reason to believe that JFK knew [about the assassination plots], and there is no doubt that it was fully known to the Attorney General [Robert Kennedy]," he told author Richard Reeves.[42] Finally, in 1994, in his last interview just prior to his death, Bissell removed any remaining doubt when he spoke with the daughter of a CIA pilot killed at the Bay of Pigs. She asked him directly about the assassination plots. Bissell replied, "There was never anything undertaken without presidential approval."[43]

Almost apologetically, Bissell conceded in this final interview, "I was probably taken in by Kennedy's charisma. He was such a complicated mix of accomplishment and mistakes that when he died, my children didn't know whether to laugh or cry."[44]

In complying with the White House directive and Bobby's pressure, Bissell initiated a project known as "Executive Action." Bissell tapped the CIA's version of James Bond, William Harvey, to plan the program. Harvey's notes quote Bissell as saying, "The White House twice asked me to create such a capability."[45] Immediately after Bissell and Harvey received their orders from the White House, Harvey contacted the CIA's wizard from the office of Science and Technology, Dr. Sidney Gottlieb. "I've been asked to form this group to assassinate people and I need to know what you can do for me," Harvey told Gottlieb.[46] The scientist proceeded to develop lethal poisons for use against foreign leaders, especially Fidel Castro. And Harvey entered one of the most controversial periods of his illustrious career.

William King Harvey Plays "M"

Bill Harvey called the assassination capability "the magic button," while the CIA's internal code name for the undertaking was ZR/RIFLE. It was intended to be the most secure operation at the CIA's headquarters in Langley, Virginia. The directives and guidelines in the Agency's action file were clear: "No projects on paper." The magic button would "require professional, proven, operationally competent, ruthless, stable CE [counter-espionage]-experienced ops [operations] officers."[47]

William King Harvey certainly fit the bill. He was a large, pear-shaped man who drank heavily, but who remained perfectly capable of performing his professional tasks.[48] Harvey had spent much of the 1950's in West Berlin, where he supervised one of the CIA's most publicized success stories, the Berlin Tunnel. The 600 yard-long tunnel from West to East Berlin was actually an elaborate system to tap Soviet military phone conversations. The setup functioned for almost a year before being discovered by the Soviets. (Since it is now known that the Soviets knew of the tunnel from its inception, the issue has been raised that perhaps all Harvey obtained was disinformation. However, in 1997, the CIA's Berlin Station Chief at the time, David Murphy, recalled that Harvey's tunnel reaped huge benefits for U.S. intelligence.)[49]

Prior to the tunnel, Harvey made a name for himself by discovering the KGB's legendary "mole," Kim Philby, who was successfully penetrating both the British and U.S. intelligence services for years. Brought back to the U.S., Harvey was appointed to head up ZR/RIFLE at first, and also, later, the newly-formed Task Force W—the Cuba Project. "Bill was brought in to mop up the mess after the Bay of Pigs," says a longtime CIA fellow officer and confidante.

Considered a diamond in the rough, Harvey was a perfect match for the "James Bond"-loving JFK. CIA historian Thomas Powers described Harvey's traits:

> *He once told an acquaintance that he had been to bed with a woman every day of his life since he was twelve. Colleagues remember him as the only CIA officer who carried a gun. He often left it in plain view on his desk. Sometimes he loaded the gun while he talked [to visitors]. Not just a gun, but a different gun every day, from the large collection he kept in a case at home.*[50]

"There was absolutely no doubt what the subject was," Harvey later said of his initial conversation with Bissell. "We were not talking about propaganda or a planted bank account, or a planted morals charge, or et cetera, et cetera, et cetera. We were talking about direct elimination, assassination."[51] When it came time to implement America's assassination capability, Harvey called upon an asset the CIA had used before in the Congo to attempt to assassinate Premier Patrice Lumumba. The CIA's hired assassin's name has only recently (1996) been revealed as Jose Mankel, operating under the cryptonym QJ/WIN.[52]

Mankel-QJ/WIN was a drug smuggler and mercenary from Cologne, Germany. He was described by a senior CIA official as a man without scruples, a man who would do anything—including assassination.[53] He was provided with plastic surgery and a wig before being sent into the Congo. Over a four year period from 1960 to 1964, when the CIA claims it terminated his contract, it paid him $18,000. The CIA also claims he never fulfilled the assignment.[54] Harvey later testified that QJ/WIN indeed became a candidate in the Cuba Project, but would never seriously apply himself. (His contract was eventually terminated in February of 1964.)[55]

All the while, Bobby Kennedy kept pushing the throttle. Former Director of Operations Richard Helms later testified: "The Attorney General was on the phone to me, he was on the phone to Mr. Harvey...he was on the phone even to people on Harvey's staff, as I recall it."[56] In these conversations, Bobby Kennedy made it clear that "the terrors of the earth" should be brought to bear against Castro.[57]

Jake Esterline, CIA Staff Officer in charge of the Cuba Project, recently recalled, "These things were known: that the Kennedys instigated the plots to assassinate Castro. Bill Harvey was working for Bobby Kennedy...Bobby was a terrier, he was a protector of his brother...The Kennedys were behind everything. I know this."[58] Kennedy's Defense Secretary Robert McNamara cut to the chase: "We were hysterical about Castro at the time of the Bay of Pigs and thereafter, and there was pressure from JFK and RFK to do something about Castro."[59]

Phase Two assassination attempts used both Mankel and Rosselli, and again failed miserably. Often, the assassins-to-be got cold feet, or their proficiency came up short. The Kennedys, however, were convinced that sooner or later, one of their attempts would hit the mark. They therefore considered plans for a re-invasion to be coordinated with Castro's death. On May 4, 1961, José Miró Cardona, President of the White House-backed Cuban Revolutionary Council, met with JFK and received, by Cardona's account, a formalized "pact which called for a new invasion."

While gambits with Rosselli and Mankel were being explored, the CIA initiated discussions with the man to be the focal point of the 1963 (Phase Three) assassination attempts, Rolando Cubela Secades, a high-ranking member of an anti-Batista movement which also became "disgusted" with Castro soon after the revolution. Initially contacted by the CIA in Mexico City in March 1961, Cubela, over the next two years, would engage the CIA in discussions that would center on his assassinating Castro with CIA assistance.[60] The CIA would then secure asylum for Cubela in the U.S. The CIA kept him on hold for two years, only to be activated as AM/LASH-1 in the fall of 1963.[61]

With the Harvey actions proceeding, Robert Kennedy was growing impatient. He called Bissell into his office in November 1961. A CIA official who was present would later tell Congress that "Bissell was chewed out in the Cabinet Room by both the President and the Attorney General for, as he put it, 'sitting on his ass and not doing anything to get rid of Castro and the Castro regime.'"[62]

All effort now was aimed at destroying Castro, not coming to terms with him. In August 1961, when Castro's second-in-command, Che Guevara, approached JFK aide Richard Goodwin in Uruguay, and offered to broker a peace with Castro and Kennedy, Goodwin reported that Cuba didn't expect an understanding with the U.S., but "they would like a *modus vivendi*." The Kennedy brothers essentially said, "Thanks, but no thanks."[63] Being Kennedys, they were playing to win.

As 1961 was drawing to a close, *New York Times* correspondent Tad Szulc attended an informal dinner with JFK and his aide Richard Goodwin. "What would you think if I ordered Castro assassinated?" Kennedy asked a stunned Szulc. The reporter replied that it was not only immoral, but useless, as others such as Raul Castro were waiting in the wings.

Kennedy then said he was under extreme pressure to do away with Castro, but that he strongly opposed the idea. "I'm glad you feel the same way," Kennedy said. The President then hinted at the source of the "extreme pressure" when he said to Szulc, "Look, I'd like you to talk to my brother."[64] Szulc later wrote of the episode:

> I cannot say to what extent [President Kennedy] knew that November about a scheme elaborated by Military Intelligence officers soon after the Bay of Pigs (and of which I was vaguely aware of at the time) to kill Castro and his brother Raul, the Deputy Premier and Defense Minister, using Cuban marksmen who were to be infiltrated into Cuba from the United States Naval Base at Guantanamo on the island's southeastern coast.[65]

Szulc's information appears to corroborate the conclusions of John Gordon, who believed the plots to be authorized by Bobby Kennedy. John Kennedy's confidante Senator George Smathers recently acknowledged, "Jack would be [saying] all the time, 'If somebody knocks this guy off, O.K., that'd be fine…But Kennedy had to say he could not be a party to that sort of thing with the damn Mafia." When asked if Bobby Kennedy knew of the assassination plots, Smathers responded, "Sure."[66]

The Kennedys' Unofficial Anti-Castro Campaign

Bobby and Jack Kennedy seemed to doubt from the start that their administrative charges would accomplish Castro's elimination. And they probably were right to be dubious. Grayston Lynch, a CIA officer assigned to Operation Mongoose, is representative of his peers when he says, "If the CIA had been left to its own devices, the Agency would have ended the Cuba Project much earlier. The CIA wasn't gung-ho about Cuba. It amounted to nothing but harassment, and at a terrific cost. We all understood that JFK wanted revenge for the Bay of Pigs."[67]

Indeed, it now is clear that the Kennedy brothers decided early to hedge their bets. They would develop their own contacts in the continuing effort to have Castro killed.

In February 1962, President Kennedy's Operation Mongoose adviser, Edward Lansdale, wrote a memo that resuscitated the Phase One strategy: using the Mafia to eliminate Castro. In one of his proposals to the president, Lansdale suggested "attacks on the cadre, including key leaders…Gangster elements might provide the best recruitment potential for actions against police-G2 [Cuban intelligence] officials." Lansdale, however, saw this action as only the capstone to an internal revolt—a revolt that would have to be on the verge of success before assassinations were attempted.[68]

This suggestion clearly carried weight with Bobby Kennedy, who put Lansdale's idea into action. Frustrated with ZR/RIFLE and Mongoose's snail-like pace, Bobby supplemented the CIA's efforts to kill Castro using a new entrée to

Papa Joe's sometime allies in organized crime. (There is a wealth of evidence now available that indicates Joe had no qualms about utilizing the mob's talents, whether it was for the delivery of bootleg-era booze or for ballots in his son's 1960 election.[69])

The CIA's Cuba Desk executive assistant Sam Halpern recently recalled the period:

> One officer in the Agency was permanently assigned by Bobby Kennedy to maintain liaison with organized criminals. Bobby hoped that some of them still maintained their underground contacts in Cuba, and that they could be utilized in the anti-Castro operations.[70]

Halpern says that the officer so-assigned spent so much time in mob havens such as Chicago, New York, and Las Vegas, that he [Halpern] used to jokingly address the guy (named Charlie) using an "Italian-sounding" name. In describing the activity to historian Max Holland, Halpern recalled, "It was Bobby and his secretary [Angie Novello] who called Charlie on what used to be called at the Agency a secure line, [to] give him a name, an address, and where he would meet with Mafia people." Halpern remembers the agent going to places like Chicago, Miami, and even Canada. "The time, the place was all arranged by Bobby Kennedy and his Mafia contacts." Like Bobby's other attempts at "clandestine" activity, this gambit was also viewed by intelligence professionals as reckless and highly insecure. "We thought it was stupid, silly, ineffective, and wasteful," Halpern recently stated. "But we were under orders, and we did it."[71]

The agent was in fact named Charles Ford. "We gave him the nickname 'Fiscalini,'" said Halpern, who added that Ford was also referred to as "Rocky." Both Ford's real name and nickname appear in RFK's phone logs.[72] "It was a tightly-held operation," says Halpern. "Only Bill [Harvey], Bobby, and I knew of Charlie's activity." He also appeared at RFK's office. At no other time in his professional career, said Halpern, did he hear of a CIA case officer showing up in the Attorney General's office to discuss an operation. "Absolutely never. It was unique."

The 1978 investigation by the House Select Committee on Assassinations (HSCA) offered a peek into Robert Kennedy's personal dealings with other Cuban-focused mobsters—names included.

According to deposition testimony he supplied the FBI, former Havana casino operator Norman Rothman participated in clandestine meetings, arranged by RFK, inside the White House, where Rothman's possible assistance in providing Cuban-based contacts was explored. Initially, Rothman had been in touch with the Justice Department in an effort to avoid a prison term for a gun-running conviction. At the time, he informed the FBI that he had "considerable knowledge concerning the Cuban underground." When the summary report passed RFK's desk, he wrote on it, "press rigorously all angles." Two days later (June 26, 1961), according to the FBI, Rothman was again interviewed "at the request of the Attorney General." He now indicated that "he was in a position to procure the liquidation of Fidel Castro." The offer was forwarded to Bobby Kennedy's Deputy Attorney General, Byron White (JFK's longtime friend and later a Kennedy appointee to the U.S. Supreme Court). Soon, Rothman was invited to the White House.

At a White House gathering, attended by both RFK aide John Seigenthaler and JFK's Congressional Liaison, Henry Hall Wilson, the subjects of Castro's assassination and leniency for Rothman were broached. Both Wilson and Rothman's attorney, Harry Riddle, were close friends of JFK buddy, Governor Terry Sanford of North Carolina. This suggests a possible mechanism for how Rothman came to the attention of the White House in the first place.

Thereafter, Rothman began receiving mysterious telegrams summoning him back to the White House for a series of meetings. Pleading poor memory, Rothman told later investigators that someone brought up the subject of assassination in a "casual way," but he forgot the exact wording.[73] Given Rothman's history and bravado, such a topic of conversation would not be surprising. Rothman had been linked to a pre-Kennedy assassination plot (on Castro) and to the formation of a mob spy network in Cuba. Recall also that Charles Siragusa, who admitted helping form an assassination squad, was known to have met with Bobby in his office, where the subject had also been Cuba. Siragusa later became a very close friend of Robert Kennedy. According to mutual friend Constantine Kangles, a Chicago-based attorney, who knew Fidel Castro, he and Siragusa were called into private meetings with Bobby in the Attorney General's office to discuss Cuba.

In Rothman's Congressional testimony, he provided some details about his trips to the White House and the Attorney General's office. Although Bobby didn't attend the meetings, his aides escorted Rothman:

> *[We went] to the Attorney General's office, and then from there to a big conference room...[Bobby's] wife or some member of his family was hanging pictures. They must have just moved into the office....They started off by saying...that they would be helpful to me [with the appeal]....They asked me if I would help them...or if I wished to become a part of some group in the government in establishing communications in Cuba—contacts. I told them that I was not interested in helping myself...I was not interested in discussing anything...They sent me another telegram after that. [Again he was brought to Bobby's office.] They wanted me to give them names and I refused to do it....One of them approached me and discussed what method [of assassination] I would suggest if it were me....I told them I was at no liberty to involve others with them... I do not think we got along in our discussion, and the matter more or less dropped, on my part.[74]*

Rothman's links to Bobby, however, weren't confined to meetings in Washington. Recently, another RFK/Rothman link surfaced.

When Bobby Kennedy visited southern Florida, one of his exile bodyguards was a young Cuban named Angelo (who later adopted the last name of

"Kennedy" as an homage to the brothers' concern for the exiles' plight.) Only recently has Angelo agreed to be interviewed. With much reluctance, Angelo divulged that on more than one occasion, he accompanied Bobby to the Star Island (Miami) home of a "fat cat from up north." Angelo conceded that "We knew there was something wrong with this guy—Mafia maybe." When pushed for the name, Angelo initially declined to answer. Eventually, he gave up the name "Normie Ross."[75] It took all of five minutes to learn from another Miami resident that "Normie Ross" was the name often used by Star Island resident Norman Rothman.[76]

In still another attempt to jumpstart the plots, the Kennedys again went around "official" controls, seeking out an old family friend with a similar grudge against the Cuban dictator.

Michael McLaney

"I liked old man Joe Kennedy," said renowned sports hustler/casino operator Mike McLaney. "We used to golf together two or three times a week at the Palm Beach Country Club."[77] McLaney also played golf with President John F. Kennedy. And he met Bobby "many times," though he was quick to add that, of the Kennedy clan, Bobby was "the only one I didn't like."

McLaney, in fact, had known Joe Kennedy so long that he no longer remembers exactly how they met, but was sure it had something to do with golf. McLaney's longtime right-hand man "Steve Reynolds" (pseudonym) remembers McLaney being introduced originally to Joe Kennedy at the Palm Beach Country Club by one of Joe's few Jewish friends, Carroll Rosenbloom, the controversial Baltimore Colts football owner. "Joe, Jack, and Bobby used to sit with Mike on the veranda, where they could have private conversations," recalls Reynolds.[78] (Mike McLaney and Joe Kennedy were part of a clique of golf-playing Irishmen in Florida.)

Reynolds added, "If you want to understand the Kennedys and Cuba, think about how Mike [McLaney] got involved with the casino. Then investigate Joe Kennedy's days in Hollywood." Reynolds refused to elaborate. The trail, however, leads to Meyer Lansky, Bugsy Siegel, and Johnny Rosselli, all of whom traveled in the same circles as Joe Kennedy when he was a Hollywood player. Joe Kennedy, among other things, had helped to form RKO Pictures.

McLaney told Congressional investigators in 1978 (withheld until 1997) how he had known Joe Kennedy since the early 1950's, and had visited the family's Palm Beach estate. "I had drinks at the home...I liked the President very much. I thought Bobby was a mess, but the President I thought was a very nice human being, a very warm and likeable human being."[79] The investigators felt it wasn't necessary to pursue the nature of McLaney's relationship with the Kennedys, though it was clear they weren't merely discussing their latest golf scores. McLaney even teased them with the admission that he presented his operational ideas to JFK's friend, George Smathers. Still, the Congressional investigators didn't take the bait. When asked what the topic of conversation had been, Reynolds, who accompanied Mike to the Kennedy estate, pointed towards Cuba.

In a rare interview, just prior to his death from Parkinson's Disease, McLaney for the first time related the details of a series of anti-Castro operations, undertaken with the blessing of the Kennedy patriarch and his sons. McLaney was a player in pre-Castro Cuba who had the firepower and the moxie to launch his own raids against the dictator. He was one of the big losers wanting back in, and the Kennedys needed all the help they could get. Tragically, the McLaney liaison would be the first of a number of unofficial operations whose scope would become known to, and inspire, Lee Harvey Oswald.

The story of Mike McLaney is the stuff of movies. A born athlete, he did a brief stint as a deputy sheriff in New Orleans before deciding to cash in on his real talents, golf and tennis. As a young tennis player, McLaney was the Louisiana state champion eight years running. He won the national amateur doubles tennis championship in 1962 with Gardner Mulloy, proudly displaying for the author the inscribed pewter plate to prove it. He numbered among his friends tennis great Bobby Riggs, and many players on the men's pro golf and tennis tours.

As to why McLaney did not turn pro during the 1950's and 1960's, his long-time caddy, Larry Murphey, makes the answer quite clear, "Do you know what the pros made winning tournaments in those days? We made that much [hustling amateurs] on the first hole."[80] Mike McLaney's decision to hustle golf proved a smart one. He made a fortune on the links: "I once took [NFL owner] Carroll Rosenbloom for a quarter million on one round," he remembers. He amassed enough capital to place him in contact with the kind of operators able to help him realize his dream of owning his own casino. With the permission of the legendary mob financial whiz Meyer Lansky (the mob's man in Cuba), McLaney purchased a huge share of the 450-room Hotel Nacional Casino in Havana. In doing so, he became partners with Baltimore Colts owner Carroll Rosenbloom. "He [Rosenbloom] was a killer at heart. Everybody who did business with him hated him," remembered McLaney in 1994.

The Nacional was a regular watering hole for members of the crime syndicates from Chicago and New York. The casino had been purchased by McLaney and Rosenbloom in September 1958, but by the spring of 1959, the new leader, "El Maximo Lider" Fidel Castro, had nationalized the Nacional—incredibly bad timing for Mike McLaney.[81] Lansky was banished from the island, and some operators, including McLaney, were imprisoned for a time. What made it even worse for McLaney was that he had sold his stock in Universal Controls (a conglomerate that included American Totalizator racetrack computers and Seven Arts Motion Picture Company) to finance his purchase of the casino. The arrangement had been that, should things go wrong, he could buy the stock back, but the stockholders, among them McLaney's former partner and hustling "mark" Carroll Rosenbloom, reneged. In short, McLaney may have been as upset about Cuba as the sons of his golfing buddy, Papa Joe Kennedy.

Along with his former Nacional lieutenant, Sam Benton, Mike McLaney constantly concocted schemes for launching attacks on Castro. Benton provided liaison with the Cuban exiles. "Benton knew Bobby Kennedy too," says anti-Castro activist Gerry Hemming. "Bobby sent him up and down the east coast in a sting operation involving a stolen securities fraud investigation being run by the Justice Department," says Hemming.[82] McLaney had explosives experts at the ready; he had private planes lined up, prepared to drop bombs on the Cuban oil refineries. One would think that Mike McLaney would get a call from his fellow Irishmen. In the year following the Bay of Pigs defeat, he did.

Steve Reynolds was a witness to meetings held with his boss Mike McLaney at Joe Kennedy's Palm Beach compound. "They were all there—Joe, Bobby, the President," says Reynolds. "It was when the Cuba thing really started to get going. Mike operated as a go-between for the White House and the Cuban exiles." Reynolds says the talk was of "getting rid" of Castro. It was made clear to McLaney that the Kennedys would be most appreciative if Castro was "taken out." As Reynolds recalls it, "We could have had him [Castro] killed in 10 minutes. But Mike was against it. He knew it would destroy the White House if it got out. Mike favored harassment." McLaney's feelings about assassination were to change, perhaps after continued prodding from Washington.

Eventually, McLaney's plans for bombing the Esso, Shell, and Texaco refineries in Cuba got back to the oil companies. Pressure was immediately exerted to stop him. The oil companies were hoping to recoup the refineries intact after Castro fell. Columnist Jack Anderson wrote that McLaney got an urgent phone call warning him to call the refinery raids off.[83] However, Gerry Hemming was told differently. "It was a face to face meeting in Miami Beach. And it was with Robert Kennedy. Three of my close associates were there. [Hemming's mercenary unit ran security for various anti-Castro groups.] It took place on the houseboat that was used in an old TV series in the Surfside area, near where McLaney lived. Bobby was thrusting his index finger into McLaney's chest telling him to stay away from the refineries."[84] Steve Reynolds, McLaney's aide, was present, and corroborated the confrontation with Bobby. "The houseboat was owned by Mike," says Reynolds, "and he had it docked at the Kingston Hotel in Vista Park, where the meeting took place. The boat was used in the TV show 'Surfside Six.' Bobby Kennedy was there all right. The gist of his remarks was that the refineries would be needed in the post-Castro period."[85]

Mike McLaney, before he died in 1994, consistently cut off all conversation when it turned to his possible involvement in the assassination plots against Castro. However, explosives expert Ed Arthur leaves little doubt about what happened. Arthur told former FBI man-turned author Bill Turner in 1974 that a McLaney lieutenant, Sam Benton, whom he had recently met, took him to McLaney's house in Miami Beach to discuss a "lucrative assignment" with a man who looked exactly like Mike McLaney, who lived in the house listed to him, and whom he would later positively identify as McLaney from a photo.

At the house, McLaney offered Arthur $90,000 to assassinate Fidel Castro. "We have access to an airplane and 500 pound bombs and other munitions. What about flying over the Presidential Palace and dropping bombs?" McLaney asked. As they drove off, Benton offered Arthur one other inducement: the assassination project "had the approval of certain well-connected people in Washington," he said. Arthur backed out of the assignment when he realized it would link him to the syndicate-owned clubs in Havana.

In the months prior to his death, McLaney claimed not to remember the Kennedys' request to kill Fidel Castro. However, Steve Reynolds, who is said by his associates to have a photographic memory, is adamant that the request was made. A clue to McLaney's apparent memory loss may reside in a statement he gave to former FBI agent Bill Turner in 1974. Turner wrote:

> McLaney did not see the wisdom of talking about other aspects of his campaign against Castro. "They have long memories up in Washington," the gambler said, "and they might not recognize that the statute of limitations has run out."[86]

McLaney, in his Congressional testimony of 1978, did hint at who had signed off on his operation. Whenever the FBI threatened his anti-Castro activities, his boys used this standard response:

> Oh, we got the money from a fellow by the name of "John" from the CIA and he said Bobby Kennedy gave it to him. So they would call back and they would ask Bobby Kennedy, or whoever was on the other end of the phone. Then everybody would faint and they would run out of the place. There was no charges for nothing because they did not want the publicity of Bobby Kennedy.[87]

Finally, in 1997, Steve Reynolds offered information that left no doubt as to who had approved the plots:

> After the ceremony at the Orange Bowl [in Miami, during December 1962], President Kennedy stopped by Mike's house while I was there. Kennedy was staying at the Fontainebleau, and Mike lived right across Indian Creek— within view of the hotel. Kennedy merely told his driver to take a left instead of a right. Mike and Jack went to sit on the back patio, where they were joined by an emissary of Sam Giancana's. They spoke for about twenty minutes.[88]

Asked if the emissary was Johnny Rosselli, Reynolds would merely say, "No comment."

Before McLaney had a falling-out with Rosenbloom, and strains were put on his relationship with the Kennedys,[89] the Kennedys, according to Reynolds, performed one favor for him. Planning another assault against Fidel in the summer of 1963, Mike McLaney stored some explosives at the summer cottage of his brother William on Lake Ponchartrain near New Orleans. When the FBI raided the cottage, some saw it as a Kennedy crackdown on rogue hoodlums—hoodlums later considered "suspects" in the Kennedy assassination. The FBI, however, took pains at the time to deny the raid, and when no one was ever charged or even arrested, locals became suspicious. Reynolds makes it clear why nothing happened, "The Kennedys took care of it. They were aware of that operation from the start."

As will be seen, the FBI's raid on the cottage was front page news in New Orleans. And there is strong evidence to indicate that a pro-Castro agitator named Lee Harvey Oswald read all about it.

Bobby's First Coverup

Meanwhile, the FBI's seemingly omniscient director, J. Edgar Hoover, had used his own channels to learn of the Sheffield Edwards/Johnny Rosselli Phase One plots against Castro. In 1961, Sam Giancana, the Chicago mafia boss, hired Robert Maheu to wiretap Giancana's girlfriend Phyllis McGuire, of the McGuire Sisters, whom he suspected of infidelity with the comedian Dan Rowan. Hoover had been trying to make a case against the Las Vegas mob—which coincidentally included Maheu and Rosselli. In April 1961, after Maheu was caught in the act of wiretapping, the FBI finally spoke with Maheu, who told them that he was working with the CIA on the anti-Castro plots, leaking this information beyond the Agency for the first time.

Hoover was furious that his investigation was complicated by this relationship between the CIA and the mob. He demanded an explanation from the CIA. On May 3, 1961, Sheffield Edwards admitted to Hoover that Maheu was right, and gave Hoover details of the operation. Bissell was said to be shocked that Edwards revealed so much to Hoover.[90] On May 21st, Hoover dashed off a memo to Bobby Kennedy detailing Edwards' report on the plots. Hoover evidently felt it necessary to protect himself by getting something on the record. Significantly, there is no record that RFK did anything about the plots after receiving the Hoover memo. The FBI's liaison to the CIA, Sam Pappich, would tell a future Congressional investigator that the Bureau kept Bobby Kennedy advised on what it knew of the CIA/mob operations. According to Pappich, Kennedy's reaction was not one of disapproval, but that he "was concerned that this operation would become known, and [he] didn't want it to get out."[91]

If Robert Kennedy wanted to stop the plotting, he had more than ample opportunity. He was in almost daily contact with CIA Director Allen Dulles. Between April 22 and May 30, 1961, Kennedy met with Dulles at least 21 times (on the record). At the time, they were overseeing the Taylor Board of Inquiry into the Bay of Pigs defeat. For his part, Hoover kept after the Las Vegas crowd, and in one year he gathered information from Nevada that could incriminate not only the mob, but the Kennedys as well.

In the winter of 1962, Hoover's continuing surveillance of Johnny Rosselli produced big dividends. In the process of monitoring Rosselli's acquaintances, the FBI came across Judith Campbell, also a friend of Sam Giancana. In a routine trace, shocked FBI agents learned that one recipient of her numerous calls was none other than President John Fitzgerald Kennedy. The President's philandering, of which Hoover was already aware, had finally caught up with him. As Vice President Lyndon Johnson remarked to a *Time* magazine reporter, "J. Edgar Hoover has Jack Kennedy by the balls."[92]

Hoover realized that if Campbell ever talked, she might also implicate the President directly in the Rosselli/CIA plots, as well as tie him to the underworld through not only Rosselli, but also Sam Giancana. This was just the kind of political dirt Hoover so coveted. On February 27th, Hoover sent a memo to the Attorney General, laying out the problem. Hoover backed this up by also sending a copy to JFK's close friend and aide, Kenny O'Donnell—virtually guaranteeing that the President would see it. On March 22, Hoover met with JFK, and according to Hoover aide Cartha DeLoach, told the President what he knew of the affair, pressing Kennedy to call it off. Years later, the Church Committee stated that the contact with JFK's "good friend" ended that night. In fact, according to both Campbell and White House phone records, the affair continued for at least eight more months.

The next day, Hoover sent a memo to the CIA, demanding an official explanation. On April 10th, Hoover heard from the CIA's Sheffield Edwards, who again asked Hoover not to prosecute Maheu.

Hoover's strategy was brilliant. He established a paper trail clearing himself of any involvement in the plots on Castro—whereas Bobby Kennedy's only record was the memo received from Hoover a year earlier informing him of the plots. His failure in the ensuing year to stop the plotting effectively incriminated him. The Attorney General had to move fast to establish a new record, praying that the old one would never surface. He set about devising a memo to protect himself from incrimination.

On May 7th, Bobby held a meeting with Sheffield Edwards, and the CIA's counsel, Lawrence Houston. At this meeting, on hearing of the plots, RFK feigned surprise and outrage. Houston would later say, "[RFK] was mad as hell...but what he objected to was our involvement with the Mafia. He was not angry about the assassination plot."[93] Houston and Edwards later drafted the all-important new memo for the Attorney General's files describing his outrage. The memo read, in part:

> *Mr. Kennedy stated that upon learning CIA had not cleared its action in hiring [Maheu, Rosselli] and Giancana with the Department of Justice he issued orders that CIA should never again take such steps without checking with the Department of Justice.*[94]

The new memo served two distinct functions. First, it gave the impression that Bobby Kennedy was "outraged" at the plots, and secondly, it implied that the plots were to be ended. Edwards next wrote an internal memo which noted that the Rosselli plots were now terminated. Nothing could be farther from the truth. William Harvey later testified that the Edwards memo "was not true, and

Edwards knew it was not true." Rosselli would later say that the plots were always "a going operation." Harvey then ventured a guess as to why the internal memo was created, saying, "If this ever came up in the future, the file would show that on such and such a date, he was advised so and so, and he was no longer chargeable with this." It was, he continued, "an attempt to insulate against what I would consider a very definite potential damage to the Agency and to the government."[95]

J. Edgar Hoover not only recognized RFK's display as a sham, but he let him know it, in so many words. On October 29, 1962, four months after Bobby's disingenuous show of outrage, the FBI Director sent RFK a memo detailing an interview of a mob informant who claimed to have strong ties in Cuba as well as with the Meyer Lansky mob. The informant had recently told the FBI that his connections could "buy practically any Cuban official...He believes some of these underworld figures still have channels inside Cuba through which the assassination of Castro can be successfully arranged."[96] Knowing that Kennedy's earlier protestations had no real meaning, Hoover passed this information on to RFK, possibly intending to incriminate him with it. There is no record of Bobby's reaction.

Lawrence Houston, the CIA's General Counsel who attended the May 1962 briefing of Robert Kennedy on the Mafia plots, told author Thomas Powers, "All I know is that Robert Kennedy knew about one of them [the assassination plots] in very great detail." Powers concluded:

> The record is clear, then, that Kennedy was thoroughly briefed about the details of an attempt to murder Castro during his brother's presidency. The record is clear that the attempts to kill Castro continued [with Phase Three]. And the record is clear that despite his knowledge of the earlier attempt, Robert Kennedy did not protest to the CIA, to its director John McCone, to Helms, or to anyone else in the Agency for that attempt.[97]

Assassination to the Forefront

> "There was a rumor around the Agency that the Kennedys wanted Castro out by the Congressional elections of 1962."
> —Bruce Cheever, CIA officer on the Cuba Project[98]

> "We need not preoccupy ourselves over the politics of President Kennedy because we know, according to prognostication, that he will die within the present year."
> —Morse Zabola, Communist Party cell leader, January 5, 1962[99]

On October 5, 1961, National Security Action Memorandum 100, "Contingency Planning for Cuba," was issued. Consisting of only twenty words, it stated: "In confirmation of oral instructions conveyed to Assistant Secretary of State [Robert Frobes] Woodward, a plan is desired for the indicated contingency." Earlier that same day, Thomas Parrott, a CIA officer serving as the SGA's secretary, intended to meet with Woodward to elucidate the meaning of "the contingency." Because Woodward was leaving the country, he advised Parrott to meet with his Deputy, Wymberley Coerr. In a memo discussing that October 5, 1961 meeting, Parrott wrote, "What was wanted was a plan against the contingency that Castro would in some way or other be removed from the Cuban scene."[100] Parrott added: "I mentioned to Mr. Woodward the President's interest in this matter, before General Taylor told me he preferred this not be done...[Woodward] understood this fully and volunteered that it could be presented as an exercise emanating from his own office." For future reference, Parrott suggested how the paper trail be worded: "I asked that this aspect be kept completely out of the picture." Woodward clearly understood the need for presidential deniability.

The same contingency would be mentioned again in an August 8, 1962 memo from Lansdale to the SGA. On page 7073 of that memo, a "contingency to assassinate Castro and his handful of top men" is noted. The "contingency" referred to in John F. Kennedy's National Security Action Memo 100 was clearly the assassination of Castro.

Throughout that fall, word passed throughout the White House that something big was afoot. An increasingly unhappy Vice-President was yelling about it all the way to Texas.

"That son of a bitch Bobby wants to kill the whole fuckin' world," Lyndon Johnson barked into the telephone. He was responding to a query by fellow Texan, Lonnie Hudkins. Prior to his career as a reporter for the *Houston Post*, Hudkins had been a sometime contract agent for the CIA. In this capacity, he occasionally "ran guns" to Central American anti-Communists, and became friends with such CIA luminaries as David Atlee Phillips, Win Scott, and others. Hudkins had often received interesting offers from these men, but the most recent was so bizarre that he sought confirmation from above.

"One of my CIA contacts asked me in 1962 to get involved in an operation that involved assassinations of both Cuba's Castro and Cheddi Jagan of Guyana," recalls Hudkins. "I frankly didn't think this kind of thing could possibly be sanctioned, First, I called [Senator] George Smathers. He told me to call Johnson, which I did."[101] Hudkins says Johnson knew all about it, telling Hudkins that the project indeed had White House authorization, "but it's unofficial." Recently, Air Force Colonel Howard Burris, Johnson's Military Aide, fellow Texan, and friend of over thirty years, affirmed that LBJ was aware of both Mongoose and the assassination plots. According to Burris, Johnson had back-channel sources at the CIA that kept him apprised of such matters. "Johnson found the whole policy distasteful," Burris said.[102]

Hudkins and his cohorts decided against joining up, not for Johnson's reasons, but for more pragmatic ones. "We figured we couldn't knock off Castro without forfeiting our own lives, " says Hudkins. "We said to hell with that—money doesn't do you any good if you're dead."[103]

Robert Kennedy had wanted to start 1962 on a high note. Calling a meeting of all Mongoose principals on January 19, 1962, the Attorney General read them the riot act, saying, " a solution to the Cuban problem [carries] top priority in the U.S. government. No time, money, effort, or manpower is to be spared." Only the day before, he continued, the President had indicated to him that "the final chapter had yet to be written—it's got to be done and will be done."[104]

Although he differed with Bill Harvey on strategy, and completely underestimated the Cuban people's loyalty to Fidel, Bobby faced his most formidable obstacles in his brother's own administration. The White House's own SGA (Special Group Augmented) constantly shied away from approving Bobby's sabotage proposals. None could legally go forward without its approval. SGA Executive Secretary Thomas Parrott recalled, "Bob Kennedy was very difficult to deal with. He was arrogant. He knew it all, he knew the answer to everything. He sat there, tie down, chewing gum, his feet up on the desk. His threats were transparent. It was, 'If you don't do it, I'll tell my big brother on you.'"[105]

Harvey's proposals were countered by time-consuming deliberations, and by demands for paperwork from the military members of the SGA. Harvey complained to Richard Helms, Deputy Director of Plans, about the SGA's head, General Maxwell Taylor, then Chairman of the Joint Chiefs of Staff: "Taylor never approves anything...Can't you do something about this?"[106] Taylor implies he denied the Kennedy/Harvey requests in response to Robert Kennedy's attitude: "I don't think it occurred to Bobby in those days that his temperament, his casual remarks that the president would not like this or that, his difficulty in establishing tolerable relations with government officials, or his delight in causing offense, was doing harm to his brother's administration."[107]

CIA executives like Richard Helms privately agreed with the SGA that Mongoose limit itself to intelligence gathering. While the SGA was responsible for deciding on specific items of sabotage, both Helms and Bobby Kennedy were aware that the Special Group had no control system for assassination activity.[108] On that score, the Kennedys had free rein. They were soon to exert it.

Although typically perceived as a strategy of last resort, the counterinsurgent use of assassination soon became the method of choice for the increasingly frustrated Kennedys. In August 1962, the SGA met to assess the lack of progress in Cuba. With Bobby Kennedy present, Robert McNamara delivered a staggering judgment, "The only way to get rid of Castro is to kill him...and I really mean it." To which Richard Bissell responded, "Oh, you mean Executive Action." According to aide Richard Goodwin, no one objected, although some were privately against the idea.[109]

"I was surprised and appalled to hear McNamara propose this," remembers Goodwin. "He [McNamara] said that Castro's assassination was the only productive way of dealing with Cuba."[110]

The increasing talk of assassination was tightly held, with only those in a "need-to-know" position informed. "We in Operation Mongoose were told nothing about assassination plans against Castro," remembered Grayston

Lynch, the first American to land on the beach at the Bay of Pigs. "In fact, that kind of talk was forbidden."[111] Lynch may have occupied an important position in the conduct of raids under Mongoose, but he was not in the loop, even ex officio.[112] He wasn't told what his bosses, Bill Harvey and General Edward Lansdale, the Mongoose military commander, knew, or what others assumed as fact.

It wasn't just the "grunts" who were out of the loop. CIA Director John McCone was not part of the assassination planning—but that, apparently, was by his own wish. McCone later wrote, "Through the years, the Cuban problem was discussed in terms such as 'dispose of Castro, 'remove Castro,' 'knock off Castro,' etc."[113] It was common knowledge with the upper echelons that McCone would never approve such activity. Bill Harvey later testified that the decision to keep McCone in the dark was made by Richard Helms.[114] McCone, having just converted to Catholicism, was known to have strong moral objections to murder. He told assistants that he feared ex-communication. According to Helms' personal assistant, George McManus, Helms knew that "if McCone had been asked to approve an assassination, he would have reacted violently immediately." Helms indeed knew for certain because McCone's assistant Walt Elder told him so. Elder would later testify: "I told Helms that Mr. McCone had expressed his feeling...that assassination could not be condoned and would not be approved...Mr. Helms responded, 'I understand.'"[115]

Bill Harvey testified as to what happened next: "There was a fairly detailed discussion between myself and Helms as to whether or not the Director should...be briefed...We agreed that it was not necessary or advisable."[116] However, Harvey made it clear that another VIP was aware of the plots. His name was Robert Kennedy. As Harvey would tell the FBI in 1968, "Robert Kennedy was knowledgeable of the operation which had been devised by the CIA with the collaboration of Rosselli and his cohorts...Kennedy is in an extremely vulnerable position if it were ever publicized that he condoned an operation which involved U.S. Government utilization of hoodlum elements."[117] Seven years later, testifying under oath before Congress, Harvey said, "I was completely convinced during this entire period that this operation had the full authority of every pertinent echelon of the CIA and had the full authority of the White House."[118]

In 1991, McCone's assistant, Elder, added a subtle but important addition to this story. While attending a CIA seminar commemorating the 30th anniversary of the Bay of Pigs, Elder remarked that McCone had not been inadvertently left out of the loop. He had taken himself out. Elder said that McCone, upon learning of the administration's intentions, instructed Helms to not tell him about the murder plots. He didn't want to know about them. Helms complied with his wishes.[119] (As with many others involved in the Cuba Project, McCone may have been a tad disingenuous. A Congressional investigator, later going through McCone's files, would find a memo authored by McCone in which he stated that the ultimate objective of U.S. policy toward Cuba should be "to encourage dissident elements in the military...to bring about the eventual liquidation of the Castro/communist entourage.")[120]

The Early Reinvasion Plans

Simultaneous with Mongoose and the assassination plotting, the Kennedys' pressure for "action" on Cuba caused the Joint Chiefs of Staff (JCS) to produce intensive operational plans. The JCS formulated an elaborate series of OPLANS to provide a pretext for an all-out U.S. invasion of the island, according to documents withheld from the public until 1997. The invasion was to be overseen by the Commander in Chief of the Atlantic Fleet (CINCLANT), Admiral Robert "Denny" Dennison. Favored ploys preceding the invasion included:

- Creating "incidents around Guantanamo...to give the genuine appearance of being done by hostile Cuban forces."

- Creating "the appearance of an [air] attack on Guantanamo...we could blow up a U.S. ship...[or] paint an F-86 to look like a Cuban MIG type aircraft [and] have it destroy a U.S. drone aircraft."

- Using the MIG mock-up to "shoot down a U.S. charter airline drone" that would appear to have been filled with U.S. college students.[121]

On April 10, 1962, the JCS wrote to the Secretary of Defense, "Joint Chiefs of Staff believe that the Cuban problem must be solved in the near future... Accordingly, we believe that military overthrow by the United States will be required to overthrow the present Communist regime." The project's secrecy is noted in the postscript: "This paper NOT be furnished to the Chairman, U.S. Delegation, United Nations Military Staff Committee." Nine days after this memo was sent, John Kennedy paid a secret visit to CINCLANT headquarters, where Admiral Dennison briefed him in depth on Polaris missile firing procedures.[122] The JCS sent a "memo to CINCLANT on February 22nd: "Plans supporting OPLAN 314-61 Be Completed as Expeditiously as Possible."

The OPLAN noted that, when the pretext for invasion had occurred, U.S. troops would be massed in nearby U.S. states, like Florida and Texas, ready to commence hostilities.

All this plotting should have given someone pause, and it did. On January 17, 1962, the Army coordinator for the Cuba Project sent a memo to Lansdale warning, "The Soviets could provide Castro with a number of ballistic missiles with nuclear warheads."[123] The alert was given short shrift and the planning escalated.

In fact, the warning was right on target—the American-backed sabotage and plotting was not going unnoticed, either by the Cubans, or by their powerful sponsor, the Soviet Union. As a result, the Kennedys' fanatical desire to avenge the Bay of Pigs defeat was about to take the world to the brink of thermonuclear war.[124] And, incredibly, it was JFK himself who let the cat out of the bag.

On January 31, 1962, the President met with Khrushchev's son-in-law,

Aleksei Adzhubei. The two were engaged in a wide-ranging conversation when the President brought up the topic of Cuba. "If I run for re-election and the Cuban question remains as it is—then Cuba will be the main problem of the campaign, [and] we will have to do something," Kennedy said to a startled Adzhubei. Digging himself a deeper hole, Kennedy added, "[After the Bay of Pigs,] I called Allen Dulles into my office and dressed him down. I told him: 'You should learn a lesson from the Russians. When they had difficulties in Hungary, they liquidated the conflict in three days.'"[125]

Adzhubei dashed off a secret communiqué to Khrushchev summarizing the conversation with Kennedy. One week later, on February 8, 1962, the Soviet Presidium approved a $133 million military assistance package for Cuba—a proposal that had been stalled for over four months. On February 21, the head of the Soviet KGB sent a memo to the Kremlin, warning, "Military specialists in the USA had revised an operational plan against Cuba, which according to this information, is supported by President Kennedy." In an indication of how competent Soviet intelligence was, the memo added that the assault would "be supported by military air assets based in Florida and Texas."[126]

"An attack on Cuba is being prepared," Soviet Premier Nikita Khrushchev said. "And the only way to save Cuba is to put missiles there." It was May 27, 1962 and Khrushchev was addressing a Soviet delegation on its way to Cuba to convince Castro of his need for Soviet nuclear weapons.[127] Khrushchev continued, "For the salvation of the Cuban revolution, there is no other path than one which could equalize the security of Cuba with the security of the United States. And this logically could be done only by our nuclear missiles, our long-range missiles. So try and explain it to Fidel."[128] With Castro's rapid concurrence, Soviet missiles, in what was called Operation Anadyr, began arriving in Cuba in mid-July 1962. A Soviet bonus, as Khrushchev later wrote, was that the U.S. now would have to reappraise a worldwide missile imbalance favoring the West—and its response could specifically affect the U.S. deployment of missiles on the Soviet border, in Turkey.

Serge Mikoyan, son of Khrushchev's Deputy Premier, Anastas Mikoyan, summed up the Soviet apprehension: "In the Spring of 1962, we in Moscow were absolutely convinced that a second Bay of Pigs was at hand—that a new military invasion of Cuba was at hand—but this time with all the American military might, not only with proxy troops."[129] The U.S. Secretary of Defense, Robert McNamara, recently stated, "If I had been a Cuban leader at that time, I might well have concluded that there was a great risk of a U.S. invasion. And I should say, as well, if I had been a Soviet leader at the time, I might have come to the same conclusion."[130]

At the end of the summer of 1962, it was clear that Mongoose was having no effect on Fidel Castro's regime. Bobby Kennedy was now frantically trying to be creative. At the August 21, 1962 SGA meeting, the CIA gave the group an update on the unsuccessful sabotage operations. With Bobby's frustration mounting, he reintroduced the idea of instigating a fake Cuban provocation.

The previous March, Bobby's Mongoose coordinator, Edward Lansdale, had asked the Joint Chiefs of Staff to prepare a report entitled "Justification for U.S. Intervention in Cuba." One of the JCS's recommendations was a scenario in which the U.S. would blow up one of its own battleships at Guantanamo and place the blame on Cuba.[131]

According to CIA Director John McCone's notes, Bobby now asked the SGA to consider "what other aggressive steps could be taken, questioning the feasibility of provoking an action against Guantanamo which would permit us to retaliate, or [of] involving a third country in some way."[132] This gambit recalled the Nino Diaz' Santa Ana mission prior to the Bay of Pigs invasion.[133] The idea went nowhere fast, though for Bobby, the provocation ploy was far from dead.

As Mongoose and the assassination plots proceeded into the fall of 1962, the Kennedy brothers apparently gave little heed to the possible reaction of the Soviet Union, and less still to that of Fidel Castro—this despite CIA intelligence reports showing thousands of Soviet military and technicians arriving on the island. Instead of slowing the anti-Castro fervor, these reports played into the hands of the most hawkish Kennedy plans for a full-scale re-invasion of Cuba. Despite earlier warnings that the Soviets might respond to the U.S.' anti-Cuban escalation, the Kennedy administration continued to push the envelope.

On October 6, 1962, thousands of troops were positioned, along with support equipment and planes, prepared to implement military OPLANS being considered by the President. In charge of the operation was Admiral Robert "Denny" Dennison, Commander in Chief of the North Atlantic Fleet (CINCLANT). The plans called for everything from small amphibious landings, to a full-scale invasion by over 18,000 U.S. troops. On October 10, the White House obtained permission from the British government to use the Bahamas as an invasion base camp. D-Day was to be October 20, 1962.[134]

In 1986, Admiral Dennison's account of the OPLANS was released under the Freedom of Information Act. The report leaves little doubt that the Kennedy administration was going to make its move against Cuba in October 1962. However, something even bigger intervened. It became known as the Cuban Missile Crisis.[135] Thus, on the morning of October 16, 1962, the Kennedys awoke to find out how the Soviets were responding to their Cuba policies. Although the administration had been receiving intelligence reports for many months, the CIA now supplied clear U-2 photos that told the President nuclear missiles were in Cuba.

When informed in "detail" of the crisis, the American public was led to believe that the heroic Kennedy brothers had stood at the brink, skillfully defusing the risk of nuclear annihilation in the entire northern hemisphere. The citizenry, however, was not informed of the Kennedys' anti-Castro plotting—the very reason tens of millions of lives were jeopardized in the first place.

And that risk was quite real. If the U.S. had decided to invade Cuba to remove Castro or Soviet missiles by force, the Soviets might have employed their *tactical* nuclear weapons (those with a 30-mile range) on the battlefield. The U.S.

knew that *those* weapons were operational.

The Demise of Operation Mongoose

> *"Mongoose was poorly conceived and wretchedly executed. It deserved greatly to fail. It was Robert Kennedy's most conspicuous folly."*
> —**Arthur M. Schlesinger, Jr.**[136]

The resolution of the Cuban Missile Crisis produced the U.S.' hollow agreement to cease its subversive activities against Cuba, including Operation Mongoose. In later years, Mongoose coordinator General Lansdale would tell General Sam Williams that the Cuba Project was "probably the most frustrating damn thing I've ever tackled." He added that he wished he had never become involved in the Cuba Project.[137] The crisis not only ended Mongoose, it also brought about the CIA's demotion of William Harvey. It was a huge irony: The Mafiosi with whom Harvey dealt were allowed to stay in the U.S. fold, while Harvey himself was sent packing.

It is a matter of some contention as to why Bill Harvey was reassigned so far from the Cold War battlefronts in which the CIA played so large a role. During Mongoose, Harvey had repeated run-ins with the Kennedys, especially Bobby, regarding operational strategy. A typical encounter was described by reporter David C. Martin:

> During one meeting, Kennedy rattled off a series of questions to Harvey, finishing with "and I've got ten minutes to hear the answer." When Harvey exceeded his time limit, Kennedy walked out. Harvey kept talking.[138]

Cuba Project officer Sam Halpern recalls another RFK rant directed at Harvey:

> I happened to be in Harvey's office one day when he got a telephone call from Bobby Kennedy. And he started to bawl Harvey out and point out that he, Kennedy, thought that when we did things secretly, how come it ended up in the press. And Harvey had to explain in words of one syllable that when you blow something up, it's going to make headlines somewhere. And it was the Kennedy brothers who were demanding the 'boom and bang' all over the island."[139]

Like Ted Shackley and other officers-in-charge of the Cuba Project, Harvey violently opposed Bobby Kennedy's personal relationships with the exiles. CIA analyst Dino Brugioni wrote, "Harvey argued unsuccessfully that someone of Bobby's stature and position should not be known to the covert operatives, much less be seen with them." Harvey once remarked to a fellow officer that "Bobby was carving a path in the operations so wide that a Mack truck could drive through."[140] Once, when Bobby was visiting the CIA station in Miami, he was, according to one witness, "barking orders at everyone like he knew what the hell was going on." Later, Kennedy tore a printout from a teletype machine which was connected to headquarters. As he started to walk out the door with a strip of sensitive, coded CIA paper, Harvey screamed, "Hey! Where are you going with that?" walked up to the Attorney General, and tore the paper from his hand. The confrontation most likely sealed Harvey's fate.[141]

Harvey was, officially, relieved of his command for breaching security during the missile crisis. The Kennedy line was that at the height of the crisis, with delicate negotiations going on between the Soviet Union and the U.S., Harvey took it upon himself to send two-man subs to Cuba to assist, should a possible shooting war break out. At least two teams landed on Cuban shores while the blockade was in effect. When the National Security Council was advised not only of the landing, but that the men were out of communication and could not be recalled, all hell allegedly broke loose.[142] Harvey's CIA associates recall it differently.

"The CIA doesn't have subs. Where do you think we got them?" is the rhetorical question posed by Harvey's assistant Sam Halpern. "Bill was working with the Joint Staff of the Joint Chiefs of Staff," he continued. According to Halpern and Cuba Desk Officer Jake Esterline, Harvey was booted for two reasons, the sub uproar and his poor relationship with Bobby Kennedy. Halpern says that at the height of the missile crisis, at an already tense cabinet meeting, Harvey had the effrontery to yell at the President: "If you hadn't screwed up in the first place [referring to the Bay of Pigs], we wouldn't be here now."[143]

Lest there be any doubt how the protective, thin-skinned Bobby reacted, one witness recalled the expected blast from "little brother." General Charles Johnson, an SGA member, remembers RFK turning to Harvey and starting on a "damned tirade—a shocking thing." Johnson said it all stemmed from a failure of a series of "operations by the CIA. Mr. McCone was there and did not say a word in defense of Harvey. The incident lasted quite a while, eight to ten minutes." When it was over, according to Johnson, Harvey said little in response. "I was surprised at the vehemence of this thing," Johnson remembered. "It couldn't have been a tirade for just a failure to make Mongoose succeed, I don't think. It seemed to be something beyond that—a failure beyond that."[144]

According to one high-ranking CIA officer, when Harvey returned to headquarters, he said that he and Bobby had taken turns calling each other liars and sons-of-bitches.

Jake Esterline states what many at the CIA felt: "Bill [Harvey] was seen by the Kennedys as failing in the Castro assassination attempts."[145] John Evans (pseudonym), who worked closely with Harvey on the Cuba Desk, told the author, "Bobby found Bill uncooperative, and Bill was constantly confronting Bobby with what he thought Kennedy was doing that was wrong."

What Bobby didn't know (and has not been revealed until now) was that the plots may well have been doomed from the start. And the reason, according to Evans, was that Bill Harvey himself was "sandbagging" them. Evans' information corroborates Harvey's own handwritten notes, which said that assassination is "the last resort beyond last resort and a confession of weakness." As

Harvey himself said to his operative/friend Johnny Rosselli regarding the plots, "There's not much likelihood of this going anyplace."[146] Evans, who insists on anonymity, worked closely with Harvey on the ZR/RIFLE and Rosselli assassination projects. In 1995, he said:

> *Bill gave the attempts only a half-hearted effort at first, but soon decided against going through with them for a variety of reasons. First, it went against his Hoosier upbringing [Harvey was from Indiana]. I remember Bill pacing the office saying, "Bobby's plan to kill Castro is the worst thing I've seen in my career. How on earth can I convince that idiot that this is so wrong?" Bill used to say that Bobby couldn't grasp the meaning of 'unattributable' operations ....[He felt that] the Kennedys thought of it as a game. Bill knew that this was no game. It was serious business. I know that Bill personally stopped the plots in their tracks. Any efforts that continued had nothing to do with Bill Harvey and everything to do with Bobby Kennedy.[147]*

Whatever his role, Harvey certainly had scored no points with the Attorney General. "Bobby was still smarting over the teletype incident in Florida. He never forgave Harvey for it," says one CIA officer. RFK went to Richard Helms, demanding that Harvey be shipped out. Helms gave Bill Harvey his choice of out-of-the-way assignments, with Harvey selecting the CIA station in Rome. Although Harvey was later made to look like a bumbling buffoon, his co-officers at Langley knew the truth. Allen Dulles would eventually bestow on Harvey the Distinguished Intelligence Service medal. The Cuba Task Force at CIA tried to cheer Harvey up by throwing a going-away party for him. Most there felt Harvey had been "shafted." His co-workers performed a satire of Shakespeare's *Julius Caesar*. In this version, however, it was Harvey who was stabbed in the back. "When Harvey's turn came," recalled one agent in attendance, "he picked up the cue. 'Brutus was Bobby,' he said."[148]

The folding of Mongoose and the resolution of the missile crisis has long fostered the perception that the efforts to assassinate Castro were put on hold. Harvey had been exiled to Rome, Bissell dismissed for his role in the Bay of Pigs, and Lansdale moved on to other ventures. But, in fact, the plotting was to continue, with only the strategies subject to change. It was these new strategies that ironically placed John F. Kennedy, not Fidel Castro, in mortal danger.

The Kennedys now called upon an old family friend, the head of the CIA's Far East Division, Desmond FitzGerald, to take over the CIA's newly-reconstituted Cuban Task Force, now named the Special Affairs Staff or SAS (Task Force W having been disbanded). FitzGerald and Allen Dulles had been old friends and neighbors in Manhattan, and Des was in fact coaxed into the Agency by Dulles. Dulles' biographer, Peter Grose, notes that FitzGerald "was ready to drop everything to accept Allen's call to Washington."[149] Like Allen Dulles, FitzGerald became an important ally of the Kennedys in the Cuba Project.

"The Kennedys and Des were old friends," recalls one CIA officer brought in by FitzGerald to assist in this phase of the assassination program.[150] They were so close that, though it was not true, many at CIA believed John Fitzgerald Kennedy and Des FitzGerald were related.[151]

The familiarity of their relationship was underscored by Bill Harvey, who later testified that FitzGerald addressed the younger Kennedy as "Bobby," not "Mr. Attorney General." This does not mean to indicate that FitzGerald was as close to Bobby as he was to JFK. Quite the contrary. FitzGerald's daughter Frances recently recalled that Des thought Bobby was a "young punk." Barbara Lawrence, FitzGerald's stepdaughter, recently stated, "[Des] was scared of Bobby's power. He felt threatened by him. He felt Bobby was there just because he was the President's brother. He thought he was an amateur."[152] The feeling was mutual. Years later, Bobby recalled, "Des FitzGerald came up with some ideas. At least we got some projects going. But then every time he got a project ready, nobody wants to have a go. Got scared of it."[153]

Soon after taking his new post, FitzGerald was asked by a colleague if he was having "any fun." FitzGerald responded, "All I know is that I have to hate Castro."[154]

Like Harvey, FitzGerald's tenure was met by skepticism by those under him in the operation. But FitzGerald knew something they didn't know. They were going to get Castro. "You don't know what you're talking about," he told one of the doubters.[155]

There is some evidence that the Kennedys had gone back to looking for "James Bond" type gadgets, even now that their "James Bond," Bill Harvey, had been taken off the project. "I started to get suspicious when I realized that every time Des came in with these weird ideas—exploding seashells, poisoned wet-suits, etc.—it was on a Monday following a weekend off, probably with the Kennedy brothers. I'm sure that's where the ideas originated," recalls FitzGerald's assistant Halpern.[156] When Halpern questioned the wisdom of the seashell ploy, FitzGerald shot back, "The President wants this."[157]

FitzGerald's bizarre assassination plans never came close to fruition, but an assassin with a more conventional approach, Rolando Cubela Secades (aka AM/LASH), would be activated by FitzGerald in the fall of 1963.

Unbeknownst to John Kennedy, Castro was not only warned in advance of these plots—official and otherwise—but all those that were to follow. The Church Committee of 1975 stated that it found at least eight CIA plots to assassinate Castro from 1960 to 1965. In 1975, Castro gave Senator George McGovern, who was then visiting Cuba, materials that described 24 incidents, stressing that the 24 were not all-inclusive. In most cases, the plot participants were thrown into Cuban prison, where they divulged the details of their CIA contacts.[158] In November 1993, Castro stated, somewhat ambiguously, that there had been 30 plots and 300 attempts, including those based on "a mask that produces a fungus" and a wide variety of other instruments distributed by the United States.[159] The figures differ, but the implications are clear: Castro knew a good deal about the plots, and would have been simple-minded not to take them very seriously. There is now evidence that Castro's knowledge of those attempts, and the Kennedys' desire to keep them secret, played a key role in the official whitewash of John Kennedy's death, if not in the murder itself.

Historian Thomas G. Paterson concluded that Kennedy's actions regarding Cuba "thus helped create major crises, including the October 1962 missile crisis. Kennedy inherited the Cuban problem—and made it worse."[160] Put another way, although John F. Kennedy is historically praised for peacefully resolving the 1962 Missile Crisis, it might be argued that through his continued antagonizing of Fidel Castro, he pushed the dictator into the Soviet's nuclear corner in the first place. Though the missiles were in place only from July through October of 1962, the evidence is compelling that the Kennedy administration tried to murder Castro from January 1961 until the president's last day in office on November 22, 1963. Castro knew about it. And both Robert Kennedy and Lyndon Johnson knew that Castro was so informed. After the 1963 Dallas assassination, that shared knowledge became the foundation upon which future policy would be fashioned. Although the survivors immediately grasped the possibility that Castro had caused Kennedy's death, it was understood that, for the good of all concerned, the matter should not be pursued.

Former Kennedy aide (later a senator) Harris Wofford observed, "As the President turned more and more to his brother, and together John and Robert Kennedy committed themselves to counter-insurgency, covert action, and increased military effort as a way to counteract the Cuban defeat...I wondered what whirlwind they would reap."[161]

That whirlwind, in fact, would include a decades-long coverup of the Kennedys' provocative foreign policies. It also included among its debris a young, emotionally vacant Castro admirer who sought a place in history. His name was Lee Harvey Oswald.

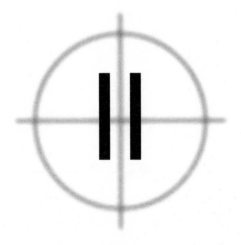

OSWALD

CHAPTER FOUR

THE CHILD IS
THE FATHER TO THE MAN

"Lee Harvey Oswald was born in October, 1939 in New Orleans, La. the son of a Insurance Salesmen whose early death left a far mean streak of independence brought on by neglect."
> —Lee Harvey Oswald about himself, from his manuscript "The Collective" (misspellings in original)

"Lee Harvey Oswald is...not...an easy man to explain."
> —G. Robert Blakey, former Chief Counsel for the House Select Committee on Assassinations[1]

Lee Harvey Oswald, the man who would kill John Kennedy and help produce, unknowingly, the most massive coverup in U.S. history, was nothing less than an enigma. George DeMohrenschildt, one of Oswald's only friends in the later years of his life, once characterized Lee Oswald as "the most honest man I knew." At other times, he severely disparaged Oswald as a "mixed-up...unstable...semi-educated hillbilly."

It was a dichotomy that well-characterizes the man. Others, too, have spoken highly of the infamous assassin. Nelson Delgado, a Marine corporal who once shared a cubicle in a Quonset hut with Oswald, was impressed by Oswald's intelligence and how he used it to cut officers down to size. Delgado, a Puerto Rican, also liked Oswald for treating him as an equal. In 1959, an airline stewardess met Oswald and was charmed by his intellectual curiosity and ability to admit areas where he had no knowledge or experience. To that woman, who had a long talk with the 20-year-old Marine, he seemed to be "totally guileless."[2] Another Marine, James Botelho, with whom Oswald roomed for six months, called him "the best roommate I ever had...an honest, scrupulously loyal gentleman." "You couldn't find a better friend," says James Botelho. "If you dropped a five-dollar bill, he would return it, even though he was always broke...[He was] the most patriotic American in history."[3]

Ed Butler, the host of a New Orleans radio show on which Oswald appeared in 1963, was impressed with Oswald's ability to think on his feet and to hold his own "against great odds" in a debate with much older, more skillful opponents. The self-educated Oswald, Butler remembers, tended to use words like "superfluous" without knowing the correct pronunciation. Still, he was "nobody's fool and certainly not the image that most Americans still have of a patsy. He was a formidable character [with] a lot more ability than most people give him credit for."[4]

Every observer agrees that Oswald genuinely loved his children—and other children too, with whom he sometimes played peacefully and generously.[5] Speaking of the time before his second daughter was born, Priscilla McMillan, author of *Marina and Lee*, called his first daughter June the "happiest and best" thing in his life. McMillan, Marina's biographer, would write, "June was the one person he lived for and whom he loved, and he played with her every night when he put her to bed. He also played with her during the day. When he was doing exercises to practice going to Cuba, she ran after him and laughed..."[6]

A neighbor, whose son played together with Lee and his daughter June, observed how pleased Lee was by his second baby. "I didn't feel he was pleased to have the children just as an extension of himself. He paid real attention to them."[7]

On the morning of the assassination, Lee left a note for Marina before going to work. It said that he had left some money on the bureau, and that she should be sure to buy shoes for the children.

All this suggests that the initial depiction of Oswald as a simple-minded murderer—a characterization that generally persists in America's mainstream press[8]—is itself simple-minded. But if Oswald's "positive" qualities impressed some, his negative ones struck a much larger number. The history of his young life provides fertile ground for developing those negative qualities. While it goes without saying that not every difficult childhood engenders a capacity to kill, it does provide a framework in which to understand the adult Oswald.

Who Was Lee Harvey Oswald?

"I dislike everybody."

—Lee Oswald at age 13 (1953), to his court-appointed psychiatrist[9]

Oswald was born in October 1939. His mother, Marguerite, was a pretty, popular girl from a poor but apparently stable New Orleans family. Like her son, she was a one-parent child. Her mother died when she was two years old.[10]

Lee's father, an insurance premium collector named Robert Lee Oswald, died suddenly two months before his birth. Marguerite was viewed by his horrified family as cold and selfish because she decided against having a funeral for him. A funeral, she told them, would take time away from her and the baby she was carrying. That baby would be named Lee Harvey Oswald. The father's family never spoke to Marguerite again.[11]

Instability followed. Lee's elder brother Robert recalls that family members thought of Lee as a "beautiful, adorable child." An aunt who helped raise him would agree. But Lee's childhood was a succession of wrenchings from one shaky home to another in New York, Louisiana, and Texas. The fragile youngster grew up in a relentless series of household moves, no less than thirteen of them before he was ten years old. Virtually everyone who knew Marguerite Oswald blames Lee's mental state on her dysfunctional parenting.

Marguerite had two other sons, Robert and John Pic, Lee's half-brother from an earlier marriage that ended in divorce. Those two other boys may have turned out with a healthier mental profile because, during their formative years, they benefited from having a father figure. Lee wasn't so fortunate. Often plunged into poverty, sometimes on the edge of panic, Marguerite transferred her family from one house or apartment to another, often "prison-like," as characterized by one of the brothers. As their living conditions spiraled downward, gloom took over, and rootless young Lee spent hours in lonely brooding. The uncertainty, as Gerald Posner recently wrote with admirable understatement, "prevented Lee from ever settling into a single neighborhood and school."

Another mother might have provided more stability, but Marguerite had little emotional reservoir from which to draw to cope with her family problems on her own—and too much disagreeableness to sustain another marriage. She gave her boys mixed signals, alternating between wild abandonment (leaving them with relatives or in orphanages), coddling-and-spoiling, and dominating them. Self-absorbed, and groping for security, she had the emotional development of a spoiled child. Jealous and resentful of people who had better luck and easier lives, the self-pitying woman quarreled with friends and neighbors, blaming others for her troubles and nursing a sense of abject persecution.

After the Kennedy assassination, John Pic ventured that Lee, if guilty, had received "a little extra push from his mother in the living conditions that she presented to him."[12] Lee's brothers would remember their mother as lacking maternal love, but possessing an inclination to try to control them: a woman with whom it was difficult to live. The "little extra push" she may have given him was a tendency to lie and dissemble. A Secret Service agent who was on the team that held her in protective custody just after the assassination learned that she would help herself get nursemaid jobs by dressing in a uniform with a small Red Cross—and bragging about her training. This made Robert Oswald, Lee's full brother, laugh, since this "nurse" never had a day of training in her life.

Robert Oswald has volunteered considerable information about his mother's tendency to fancy herself someone other than who she was. Marguerite, he would recall, "had the same type of imagination [as Lee]. She could become somebody from New York real easy when she's [actually] from Texas, putting on airs." According to Robert, his mother also bred another tendency in Lee. She nurtured in him a feeling of abiding grievance—a grudge at having been dealt a bad deal by the world, which withheld from her what she thought was properly due. Robert poignantly recalled to a Secret Serviceman that when Lee was a toddler, Marguerite would rock him in her lap in a rocking chair—and carp about the dishonesty of government. She was convinced the government was cheating her out of a veteran's pension for Lee's father. "If the government had paid me as they should have, we wouldn't have all these problems now," she would say.[13]

John Pic, Lee's half-brother, remembers how Lee was nonetheless special in his mother's eyes. While the two older brothers slept in a screened-in porch, Lee slept in his mother's bed. Pic says, "Lee slept with my mother until [he was] almost eleven years old."[14] Evelyn Strickman Siegel, the social worker who once was called on to analyze Lee, couldn't help but analyze Marguerite, writing, "I honestly don't think that she sees him as a person at all but simply an extension of herself." Her interview with Marguerite led her to conclude: "She was defensive, rigid, selfish and very much a snob."[15] Reviewers of Marguerite's biography (*A Mother in History* by Jean Stafford) drew conclusions like, "Mrs. Oswald is as grotesque a character as one can find,"[16] and "a woman sick with a spiritual and emotional malignancy."[17] They could have been describing the adult Lee Oswald.

If an even more twisted home life were needed to explain Oswald's convoluted development, it is found in an orphanage where Marguerite placed Lee when he was three years old. One writer recently called the atmosphere of the Bethlehem Children's Home "relaxed" and Lee's two-year stay there "uneventful." But Allen Campbell, who was in the institution at the same time, described its conditions as "deplorable...We were fed water and four-day-old bread for breakfast."[18]

Campbell also described the Bethlehem Home as "a house of horrors" that "severely affected not only me but also Lee and the other children who were there at the time." The chief horror arrived when the girl residents, upon turning 16, were sexually molested by the priest who headed the orphanage. Terrified of being killed, the girls asked some boys to watch, which they did from a hiding place in a crawl space. It was, Campbell says, "the only defense mechanism the girls had....We would watch to make sure that this individual didn't kill those girls after he raped them." Incredibly, four-and a-half-year-old Lee Oswald was among the group of boys who saw the atrocities first-hand. Witnessing the rapes "shattered" Lee. Campbell continues:

> He was up in the crawl space with two other people and it was demoralizing, it was depressing, it was scary. We cried at the end of it but it was something we had to do because of the girls. They were our friends and we were the only defense they had. I know it affected all of us tremendously. We would go into a state of depression for days and days after...It affected me, it affected Lee, it affected the other two boys. It's indescribable. You'd have to be there to know how bad it was.[19]

Ruth Paine, a woman who would later befriend Oswald's future wife, had an opportunity to observe Oswald during the months just prior to the assassination because he occasionally visited her at her home in suburban Dallas.[20] Though she lacked formal training in analysis, as well as the details of his childhood, she arrived at the conclusion that Lee's childhood had badly scarred him. She felt this way about Marina too, whom she knew better because they would live together for months at a time. (Lee's visits were shorter.) Interviewed in later years, Paine opined:

> *From what I know now, as somebody who's studied psychology since then, I really feel that both Lee and Marina were abused children. I think that Lee was very injured emotionally early on. He didn't really understand—or know or feel—love in a normal way…And Marina was very abused as a child. Some of the ways she reacted to him—her tolerance of the way he behaved and her thinking it was something she'd done wrong or that she wasn't good enough— was also the behavior of a grown-up who'd been abused as a child.[21]*

Oswald's thirteen childhood moves were in Louisiana and Texas, most of them in and around New Orleans, Dallas, and Fort Worth. The fourteenth was to New York City. In August 1952, Marguerite took herself and thirteen-year-old Lee from Fort Worth to Manhattan, depositing themselves with Lee's elder step-brother John Pic, who had joined the Coast Guard and was stationed in New York. The cramped little apartment quickly filled with tension. Soon after the Oswalds' arrival, Pic's wife of one year asked Lee to lower the volume of the television set. The teenager responded by threatening her with a knife. His mother rushed into the room and told him to put the knife away. He punched her in the face. The Pics asked them both to leave.[22] Marguerite moved again with her troubled boy, this time to a one-room apartment in a Bronx basement.

Lee's year and a half in New York was disastrous for his emotional development. Some evidence suggests that before that profoundly alienating experience, he had at least a hope of overcoming his severely disadvantaged childhood, despite the effects of the orphanage. Lee had attended the Ridglea West Elementary School for three years, longer than any other school in his life—before moving to New York. One of his Ridglea teachers would remember him as deeply introverted and friendless.[23] But at least one Fort Worth friend, Pat O'Connor, would remember Lee as a "normal kid [who] liked to do the normal-type things"—movies, ball-playing, swimming at swimming holes, spending the night at a friend's house. O'Connor described Lee and himself as "very good friends." He considered Lee to have "a good personality" and was of the opinion that "everybody liked him." "He was a regular kid. You'd have never known he didn't have the same aspirations as everyone else had." O'Connor also observed a "very smart young man…[who] seemed to stand out above the rest of us."

If Lee's aspirations did differ, it was because they were wider and higher. He loved to read. When a book-mobile visited the school, Lee was the first in line to use it and make his choice of books. O'Connor perceived Lee to be a leader, whom "everyone" enjoyed and looked up to. But he saw a noticeably different boy when Lee returned from New York[24]—as did others: now he was more with-drawn, more bruised, more arrogant.

No wonder. Even for a single-parented adolescent partially inured to the trauma of being plucked from one neighborhood and dropped into another one, the New York months were an emotional nightmare. A Bronx probation officer came to the conclusion, which tests appeared to confirm, that Lee had no deep-seated psychiatric problems, although he often had become angry and disruptive in school. He was having "an adjustment problem." In a recent inter-view, the officer stated, "Oswald didn't like school. He didn't like the boys there. He felt it was a waste of time. He wasn't doing well. He said he had more impor-tant things he could do."[25]

A social worker at a New York Youth House prepared a diagnostic report on Oswald. She remembers him as "a skinny kid dressed in blue jeans and a leather jacket. No kids in New York wore that in those days."[26] She too found no deep-seated mental problem:

He was not a mentally disturbed kid. As a matter of fact, his IQ was better than average. He was just emotionally frozen. He was a kid who had never developed a really trusting relationship with anybody...Our feeling was that unless he got therapy...he would have to be placed in a home, a school for juvenile delinquents. He needed therapy very badly.

Both the probation officer and social worker had involved themselves with young Oswald because of his chronic truancy in the New York junior high school. Absent 47 of 64 school days, he was failing most of his courses. Instead of going to school, where his southern accent and Texas clothes were targets for mockery, he stayed home and read, or prowled the city by subway and on foot.

The probation officer and social worker agreed that Lee's anti-social behav-ior grew from a sense of detachment that deprived him of the ability to express normal emotions. The social worker blamed the boy's mother. She saw little of her, but little was enough to convince her that the "very self-absorbed" Marguerite was a substantial part of Lee's problem. The "very smartly dressed, gray-haired woman" struck the social worker as "detached herself...not a warm person...She seemed to me to have very little emotional feeling for any of her kids"—and was "clearly annoyed" by the city's attempts to help Lee, which she took as interference in her life. The probation officer put it more directly. He felt Marguerite "may have been as disturbed as the boy," so pre-occupied with her-self that the officer doubted that "she really had an awareness as to the boy's own problems and fears."[27]

Still another professional assigned to Lee, psychiatrist Dr. Renatus Hartogs, made the conclusions unanimous, writing, "Lee has to be diagnosed as person-ality pattern disturbance with schizoid features and passive-aggressive tenden-cies....an emotionally quite disturbed youngster who suffers under the impact of really existing emotional isolation and deprivation, lack of affection, absence of family life, and rejection by a self-involved and conflicted mother....[He is] a seriously detached, withdrawn youngster..."[28]

Marguerite left the basement apartment every day around seven o'clock in the morning and returned at seven in the evening, leaving Lee to fend for himself during the entire day. Instead of receiving "very badly" needed therapy, "you got the feeling of a kid nobody gave a darn about. He was just floating along in the world with no emotional resources at all," says Lee's brother Robert, commenting on this period. "Mother was working all the time. Lee had no brothers around, no father figure around, no adult he was acquainted with that he could talk to and rely on. He was on his own," Robert says. "To me, mother and Lee did not belong in New York. They belonged in Fort Worth or New Orleans."

The court-appointed professionals added that both son and mother belonged on a psychiatrist's couch, but Mrs. Oswald wouldn't hear of it. Lee's older brother, Robert, rightly concludes, "If she had faced it, if she had seen to it that Lee received the help he needed, I don't think the world would ever have heard of Lee Harvey Oswald."[29]

Oswald also began to exhibit a tendency for violence when his very nasty temper erupted. Once, he chased his half-brother with a butcher knife, then hurled it at him. A Fort Worth neighbor, where the Oswald's would soon move, thought him not only quick to anger but also "a bad kid...vicious almost."[30] Baby-sitters hired by the mother would also refer to Lee as a bad child and quickly refuse another baby-sitting job.

In his wanderings, Oswald encountered something that would quickly channel him towards a radical turning. If fate is the cards one is dealt and destiny is how one plays them, this was a classic illustration of both: a chance happening that would have hardly affected a better nourished ego; an accident that assumed critical importance because it seemed to light a path from emotional emptiness toward explanation and fulfillment.

The Emergence of Oswald's "Politics"

"Oswald turned to politics because of a lack of happiness, of achievement, of knowing what to fill his life with. A man who knows he can do something but has nothing to do...it creates a terrible tension if he realizes this dilemma: this tremendous energy he has, this will power—and no achievement."

—Volkmar Schmidt, an acquaintance of Oswald in Fort Worth

"[Oswald's] interest in Communism may have grown out of the desire to be knowledgeable about something about which a lot of other people weren't knowledgeable."

—Dr. Dale Cameron, psychiatrist, testifying before the Warren Commission, June 23, 1964[31]

From his earliest years, Lee Harvey Oswald had been fond of dissembling. A compulsive liar, he lied about little things, even when it served no discernible purpose except, perhaps, to treat himself to the satisfaction of asserting his will and merit by fooling others. His elder brother Robert would conclude that Lee used intrigue as a way of escaping the drabness of his young life—which would have seemed all the more unfortunate to those who saw how "beautiful" and "adorable" the pristine child had been. In any case, Lee grew up wanting to "be something different, something unique,"32 as Robert Oswald would put it. He also developed a passion for secrets, mystery, and role-playing. As a boy, he loved a radio program called "Let's Pretend." While his brother and half-brother were off doing more physically active things, Lee immersed himself in what Robert would call his "fantasy life." "I think he just liked the atmosphere where you could do anything you wanted to, or could imagine you could do anything....He seemed to really get involved with it and hang on to it after the programs were over."33

In the late 1940's, when Lee was ten or eleven years old, television, in the form of a small black-and-white set, made its debut in the Oswald home. His favorite program was "I Led Three Lives," based on the exploits of an FBI informant who posed as a communist spy. Robert Oswald remembers Lee watching it intensely when he, Robert, left the home to join the Marine Corps in 1952. "My opinion of what he got out of 'I Led Three Lives' and other programs with a similar nature was the fact that he could put on a facade and pretend to be somebody he wasn't." Robert would later consider the meaning for Lee:

> It probably opened up a new world for him...[where] you could appear to be something, then appear to be somebody else...To me, that was a training ground...If you're playing "Cowboys and Indians," you stop being the cowboys and the Indians when you stop playing. But with Lee, with the "I Led Three Lives" type show, he was still being somebody even though the show was over, the game was over. He still played another role.

As an adult, his favorite show became "The Fugitive," a television series about a man always on the run because he was wrongly accused of murdering his wife. Also as an adult, he was fascinated with the "James Bond" spy novels, and when he would return from his Soviet stay, his reading would include *How to Be a Spy*. In the Marines, he studied the Russian language. When playing chess, he used red pieces to represent the Red Army. For those reasons, some fellow Marines would call him a Russian spy—which he liked.34

But now, in New York, he took his first steps in this new direction. A pamphlet was handed to him as he wandered through the city. It described the Rosenberg case, still very fresh in the memory of many Americans. Julius and Ethel Rosenberg were two American citizens executed in June 1953, for passing atomic secrets to Soviet agents.35 In this—the protest against what seemed a hideous injustice perpetrated by an ungenerous authority—Oswald found a cause. It was the far left wing, specifically, that organized and led the protests against the Rosenberg convictions. Oswald's brother Robert reasons that "the appeal to Lee of something like Marxism, communism, socialism would be something different, something unique."

But it was more. It was a way for Lee to ameliorate his sense of hurt with acceptance, praise, recognition, admiration. "I think Lee Harvey Oswald... was looking for acceptance in some way, shape or form, and never could achieve it in what he called a capitalist system," a fellow Marine would remember.[36] "Being himself, he's not going to have acceptance in what he calls a capitalist world, and so he has to turn to something else." Oswald himself said that he was like "a very religious man opening the Bible for the first time" when he made his first acquaintance with Marxist literature, soon after leaving New York. This was a new, much more promising kind of fantasy. It was fantasy mixed with what seemed to Lee the reality of the socialist world—which, by definition, was supposedly the opposite of the capitalist world. By attaching himself to that other, better world, Oswald could unify his wants with universal problems. He could imagine a much finer life and much more comfortable mental state than he could from watching his favorite television programs about pretense.

Rather than receive the help both she and her son desperately needed, Marguerite Oswald took Lee from New York and fled for New Orleans, where Lee attended a junior high school—his tenth school. By this point, he professed himself a communist. The appeal of Marxism varies considerably with each individual attracted to it. Lee would later explain he had been looking for "a key to my environment."[37] But if a single reason can explain his attachment to that alien belief—alien in the context of the overwhelming American fear and loathing of communism—it probably lay in his need to join a cause that would rescue him from his loneliness and hurt, and provide him what he sensed he had been deprived of in childhood. This profoundly lonely teenager craved recognition and appreciation; he needed to belong to something.

Among the American adherents of Marxism-Leninism, he was hardly alone in those needs. It's just that in the context of his personal problems, his attraction to the cause seems clearer than that of more intellectual believers. One of his young classmates, William Wulf, sensed Oswald had "a real identity problem" and "needed something to identify with"—which is why he "looked for something to belong to." In his case, that something was a communist cell "to participate with and push the communist ideal."[38]

Wulf's father had been an active social democrat in Hamburg, Germany following World War I, where he developed a strong dislike for communism. In the service of the Soviet Union's nationalist interests, it had perverted socialism, he thought. Overhearing Lee's praise of Soviet socialism, the father tried to explain its defects, but Lee would hear none of it. The teenager told the old man he didn't know what he was talking about, and was ordered to leave his house.

Young Wulf was struck by Oswald's radicalism, and Oswald's fascination with guns—which Wulf linked to "the whole idea of being an active communist if he could find some way to exhibit that activity."[39] At that time, in his New Orleans junior high school, Lee was indeed trying to acquire his own weapon—by stealing it. He made a careful plan to snatch a revolver from a store window.

He even produced a glasscutter, and persuaded another school friend to help him reconnoiter the premises. He dropped the plan only when the friend noticed the metal strip around the window that would trigger an alarm if the glass were broken.[40]

Meanwhile, 15-year-old Oswald remained an outsider, "living in his own world," as Edward Voebel, the co-conspirator in the plot to steal the revolver, noticed. Oswald also struck neighbors and acquaintances of his mother as difficult, arrogant, and sometimes unbearable. Voebel noticed his dislike for authority. He seemed "bitter" and believed life had given him a raw deal.[41]

Lee's commitment to what was generally practiced as communism endured from that point on. Some writers challenge this, but incorrectly. Like many who believed in Marxism-Leninism, Oswald, despite his reading from pamphlets and library books, understood little about the precepts of Lenin, let alone Marx. For instance, when he arrived in Moscow, the American Consul discovered, after some questions about fundamental Marxist tenets, that Oswald's knowledge was rudimentary. Oswald also possessed a large dose of naiveté in these matters. He would later discuss with fellow marine Nelson Delgado the books he was reading, including George Orwell's *Animal Farm*, and *1984*. Oswald spoke of them as if they were pro-communist tracts, completely missing the point of the anti-communist satires.[42]

But all that didn't matter because Oswald's commitment was far more emotional than intellectual. He became convinced that a better social system existed in which he would find a happier place—and be appreciated. His disillusionment with Soviet socialism would not change his basic vision of Marxism as a cure for his personal problems as well as for social injustice.

In July 1956, Lee was relocated, for the twenty-first time in his sixteen years, when his mother trundled him off to Fort Worth, Texas. Soon, he would drop out of still another school, and appear interested in only two pursuits: communism, and escape from his mother. In October of that year, Oswald wrote a letter to the Socialist Party of America, stating, "I am sixteen years of age and would like more information about your youth League...I am a Marxist and have been studying Socialist principles for well over fifteen months"[43] *(pictured on following page).*

Simultaneously, Oswald joined the Marines. His decision to enlist in October of 1956 can be understood as an escape from what we know of Oswald's desperately twisted home life. Virtually all the people who knew him as a child agree that his sole motive in signing up was to escape his dysfunctional situation. His enlistment had nothing to do with patriotism, and almost everything to do with his mother. The remarks of his brother and half-brother are typical. As noted by author Gerald Posner, Oswald's half-brother John Pic stated: "He did it for the same reason that I did it and Robert did it...to get from out and under the yoke of oppression from my mother." Even Robert admitted that Lee "had seen us escape from mother that way. To him, military life meant freedom."[44]

DEAR Sirs;
      I am sixteen years
of age and would like more
information about your
youth League, I would
like to know if there
is a branch in my area,
how to join, ect., I am
a marxist, and have been
studying socialist principles
for well over fifteen months
I am very interested in
your Y. P. S. L.

            Sincerely
Lee Oswald

        (ADDRESS OVER)

Oswald in the Marines: A Different Kind of Cuban Obsessive

Oswald's early Marine period, while stationed in various Pacific outposts, was noteworthy for only two reasons. His constant brushes with authority often resulted in disciplinary action against him, including a stint in the "brig." (Dan Powers, a fellow Marine, characterized Oswald in this way: "I think just as...in any part of society that we live in today, there's a certain amount of screwups in there—and he was one of the all-time screwups.")[45] Oswald also stood out in the Marines for his unabashed proselytizing of communism, especially the Cuban version.

Following basic training and his time in the Pacific, Oswald was assigned to the Marine Corps Air Station at El Toro, California. There, he was a member of a radar crew of less than a dozen officers and men, one of whom was Owen Dejanovich. Dejanovich remembers Oswald as being entranced with Cuba:

> He used to talk quite a bit about Fidel Castro being a great leader and how the United States wasn't treating him right. He talked about how Castro really needed Americans to go down there and help him, and how he wanted to go down and do that. He wanted to do anything he could to help Cuba. He went to the point of even dealing with one of the guys who lived in our barracks, Nelson Delgado, to have him teach him Spanish.[46]

Corporal Nelson Delgado of Brooklyn, characterized by his commander as "very dependable," did try to teach Oswald some Spanish. He and Oswald shared a Quonset hut cubicle and stood the same watches in a radar bubble— their job was aircraft surveillance. They had hours and hours to talk and they became good friends. They shared a mutual interest in Fidel Castro, who had won his first revolutionary battle at the beginning of 1957. Buoyed by his friend's sympathy for Fidel, Oswald confided that he desperately wanted to go to Cuba and help train Castro's army.[47]

Oswald's conversations and plans with Delgado deserve examination as evidence not only of his ardor for a revolutionary mission, but also of his ability to take at least some action in that direction. He kept talking about his desire to go to Cuba and fight for the noble cause there. Encouraging Delgado to join him, Oswald cited the example of a former American army sergeant named William Morgan, whom Castro personally commissioned a Major in his army after Morgan had arrived in Cuba and renounced his American citizenship. Morgan, as a Castro agent, lured anti-Castro rebels to Cuba and into various traps.[48]

This was certainly in keeping with Oswald's longstanding fascination with men who assumed double or triple identities and lived a life of seeming fantasy, lying and deceiving for a noble cause. There is every reason to believe that the thought of becoming a double agent for Castro—carrying out a mission of penetrating anti-Castro groups in order to serve Fidel—allured him, and would motivate some otherwise puzzling activities of his in New Orleans (where White House-sponsored anti-Castro activities had a base) during the summer before he shot President Kennedy.

Oswald went so far as to press Delgado for ideas about how to make contact with revolutionary Cuba. Delgado suggested writing the Cuban Embassy in Washington, and soon noticed that Oswald, who until then had received very little mail, began getting letters several times a week. Some of them, he discovered while looking in his friend's locker for a tie to borrow, bore the "unmistakable" seal of the Cuban Consulate.

The two men began taking the bus to Los Angeles, a trip of about 90 minutes. In the city, Oswald would visit the Cuban Consulate, he revealed in time. Delgado "started getting scared" when he saw that Oswald was "actually making plans."[49] By this time, Castro, whose revolution originally appeared to be liberal-democratic, had begun declaring adherence to Marxism. He was derided in the American press. Oswald argued that the American media was highly propagandistic and distorted Castro's position. It seems reasonable to question whether the 20-year-old Oswald, with his drive to make himself more important than he was, actually did make contact with the Cuban Consulate.

There is evidence that he did. An American mercenary, Gerry Hemming, remembered (together with others) seeing an American in civilian clothes at the home of the Cuban Consul, which Hemming was guarding. He gave his name as Oswald and said he was living in Santa Ana, where the El Toro base was located. He said he wanted to get on a flight to Cuba that would deliver arms hidden in the Consul's house—and join the revolution. Hemming was suspicious: how did the stranger know about the top-secret flight or its purpose? Suspecting a threat rather than an asset, Hemming brushed Oswald off, then followed him seconds later to try to copy down his license plate number. But Oswald disappeared before then. Hemming concluded that Oswald drove off or was picked up.[50] He could not have left on foot, Hemming reasoned, for he would have seen him somewhere on the long, straight street.

The young Marine's behavior with Nelson Delgado was also suspicious. Near the end of his service at the El Toro base, Delgado saw that Oswald had a stack of "spotter" photographs of a fighter plane—the kind used for aircraft identification in training classes—among his papers. Together with other possessions, Oswald put them in a duffel bag, which he asked Delgado to take to a bus station locker and bring him back the key—in return for which, Delgado remembers, Oswald gave him two dollars.[51] What was the purpose of that maneuver? Did Oswald plan to offer the photographs to representatives of Cuba to ingratiate himself with them? In New Orleans during the summer before the assassination, he would give a Marine handbook to ingratiate himself with anti-Castro Cubans so as to "penetrate" them. In any case, he was evolving a method of operation. And later, when Delgado asked Oswald whether he still planned to go to Cuba after his discharge, Oswald pretended not to hear him.[52]

Soon, Oswald began suiting up in a coat and tie during his off hours, telling Delgado he was visiting the Cuban Consulate (corroborated by Hemming's sighting). Delgado recalled what happened next, while on guard duty late one night with Oswald. "I got a call from the MP guard shack...that Oswald had a visitor at the front gate. This man had to be a civilian; otherwise, they would have let him in...I had to find somebody to relieve Oswald."

Delgado passed by the same front gate an hour later and witnessed Oswald in a heated discussion with a man attired in a topcoat—odd to Delgado, this being a hot night in California. Although Oswald never told Delgado who the man was, Delgado (for reasons he can't now recall) formed the impression that the rendezvous had something to do with "the Cuba business."[53]

When Oswald returned home after his discharge, he told an elder brother that he was thinking of going to Cuba—to acquire experience, he said, and write about it, "like Hemingway."[54] (Although wide reading allowed Oswald to express himself with imagination, his prose was tortured. Handicapped by slight dyslexia as well as by a weak formal education, he made constant errors in spelling, and his grammar was poor.) Oswald felt it unnecessary to divulge his true plans to his family. When he spoke about Cuba to his brother in September 1959, he made no mention of planning to leave for Russia, which he did several days later—a stunning move in those Cold War days for any American, let alone a young man from a disadvantaged background, just discharged from the Marines.[55] Nor did Oswald feel compelled to reveal his political thoughts or obsessions to his family. But his "Hemingway" reason for wanting to go to Cuba, as stated to Robert Oswald, may have derived from his ultimate motives: a search for acceptance and recognition, a need for fame and glory.

Some have pointed out the seeming contradiction in Oswald being both a communist and a Marine—or, to put it another way, reasonable minds doubted he ever truly believed in communism because anyone who did could not have joined the Corps, which was "always prepared" to fight communism. But at a deeper level, there was no contradiction at all, any more than there was a mystery about why Oswald so wanted change—a profound change from his present circumstances, whatever they were, so that he could find acceptance and peace: the proper home he never had.

Code Name: "Nalim"—Oswald In Moscow

"I think Oswald wanted to be exceptional, to be famous. It was the main goal of his life, and he was striving for it. But he could not achieve it in a usual way: to be a prominent businessman, or be a prominent musician or so forth. So he decided to find the only way for him to be very extraordinary—to do something which all ordinary people would never dare to do."
—Oswald's Russian tour guide, Rimma Shirakova, in 1993

By the summer of 1959, Oswald had become known to his fellow Marines as a "commie." And in his own mind, he believed he was. On August 17, 1959, he applied for a dependency discharge, saying he had to return to Fort Worth, Texas to care for his ill mother. His stated reason was a lie. After only three days in Texas, he went on to New Orleans, and on September 17th gained passage on the SS Marion Lykes on the first leg of his journey to the USSR. He would later write his brother, Robert, that he had planned to defect for a year.[56]

Arriving in Moscow on a six-day tourist visa obtained in Helsinki, the young American visitor was assigned an Intourist guide, Rimma Shirokova, for the usual routine of carefully routed sightseeing from limousines and totally untypical meals in the handful of expensive Intourist restaurants into which almost all Western tourists were herded. Rimma would become a genuine friend, who would maintain contact with young Oswald during his entire two-and-a-half year stay in Russia.

Rimma recalls, "He was a very modest, serious young boy. He was wearing military shoes, and didn't correspond at all to my views of an American tourist. I had him driven around town, although he showed no interest in seeing the sites. He wanted to change his life."[57] On his second day with the (sympathetic) Rimma, he announced his intention to remain in the Motherland of Socialism. "Oswald explained that he was a communist who did not approve of the American way of life...or the policy of the United States abroad, with its wars. He wanted to live in the Soviet Union, where people were very good to each other, 'like brothers and sisters.'"

Rimma recalls being shocked. Because Oswald could neither write nor speak Russian, she agreed to help him draft letters to the passport office and the Supreme Soviet in furtherance of his desire.[58] While awaiting the Soviet decision, Oswald was interviewed by Aline Mosby, an American journalist in Moscow. "He appeared totally disinterested in anything but himself," she later recalled. "He talked almost non-stop like the type of semi-educated person of little experience who clutches at what he regards as some sort of unique truth."[59]

Five days later, Oswald received the news that his citizenship request had been turned down. Rimma would remember the news' devastating effect—a "very tragic feeling"—on him. He "couldn't believe his ears. He said, 'No, it's impossible.'" Oswald then begged Rimma Shirokova to help him see the Soviet authorities. He revealed that he had served in the Marines and had something to tell them. When Rimma reported this, a middle-aged woman she assumed to be a KGB officer saw Oswald—in her presence. "He told her everything she asked about"—his parents, his life, his political views, his reasons for wanting to stay, his military service—"but did not produce a good impression on the lady. That was my opinion."

Inconsolable, Oswald wrote in his diary, "I am shocked! My dreams! I have waited two years to be accepted...my fondest dreams are shattered." He attempted suicide by slashing his wrists. Rimma remembers, "That same afternoon, we were to meet downstairs as usual. Some time passed and he didn't appear. Certainly I was nervous and wanted to know what had happened. So that's when I rushed upstairs and knocked on the door, but there was no answer."[60]

Accompanied by hotel security, who broke down the locked door, Rimma found Oswald in his underwear, lying unconscious in a bathtub filled with a mixture of blood and water. He was rushed to Botkin Hospital, where he was placed in the "psychosomatic" ward.

Dr. Lydia Mikhailina, the psychiatrist who treated him, describes Oswald's action in terms usually reserved for a petulant child. "It was my impression that this was a 'show suicide' attempt since he was refused political asylum, which he had been demanding."[61]

Oswald's KGB file shows that he was given the code name "Nalim," which is Russian for turbot, or river fish.[62] For thirty years after the Kennedy assassination, the KGB maintained that they never talked to (or "debriefed") Lee Harvey Oswald, or had any interest in recruiting him. However, in 1993, after the fall of communism, the former head of the KGB who handled the Oswald case, Vladimir Semichastny, finally came clean and admitted the obvious. Oswald, in fact, was contacted in Botkin Hospital. Semichastny recalls:

There were conversations, but what he had to say was hardly useful information. There was nothing new in it. It was the kind of information we had been talking about for a long time already and then Oswald tells us about it. It was of no interest to a high level organization like ours....The general impression was that he wasn't talking about anything that, as we say in Russia, "the sparrows on the trees aren't already singing about."[63]

Oswald offered the KGB secrets of America's new spy plane, the U-2. Stationed in Atsugi, Japan, he had been assigned to the radar "bubble" that tracked the new plane. But soon after Oswald's defection, the Soviets would shoot down a U-2 piloted by Francis Gary Powers. Of Oswald's proffer, Semichastny says, "Oswald knew very little. We knew a lot more than he was able to tell us. He didn't have any operational knowledge. He knew his own number at the U-2 base, but that was all...By the time we were fucking around with Oswald, he'd been here some months. Then the U-2 was shot down, we had Powers in jail, and he was a far better source than Oswald could have ever been."

The CIA agrees wholeheartedly about Oswald's lack of useful information. "That's the biggest pile of bull," laughs the CIA's chief U-2 photo analyst of the period, Dino Brugioni. "The Soviets already knew how to track the U-2's, so what the hell could he tell them? All he could give them was the fact that there were U-2's at Atsugi, and they already knew that. The actual photo targets were a tightly-held secret, and there is no way a radar operator had that information."[64]

Semichastny says Oswald was nonetheless considered for recruitment by both the KGB's intelligence and counter-intelligence divisions. We now know that the name of the man who had to make the final decision on whether to recruit Oswald was Vasili Petrov, the head of the Belarus KGB. According to his son, Petrov determined that Oswald "didn't have the intellectual capacity to be a professional agent." (After the Kennedy assassination, Petrov would tell his son, "Thank goodness I made the right decision.")[65]

Operatives tracking Oswald in the field were said to be offended that there were serious deliberations on the subject. KGB agent Nechiporenko recalls, "They wondered if the enemy considered us so stupid that they would send us this 'garbage.'"[66] Eduard Shirkovsky, the present Bylorussian KGB Chairman, read the Oswald file, then went so far as to admit that drugs may have been used on "Nalim," saying, "Well, maybe they did drop a few tablets in his glass, but just the kind to make him let down his guard and be a little more talkative."[67] Semichastny elaborates on just what the KGB wanted to know:

> If he [Oswald] were going to live here, could he be used against the Americans? Would he have the ability to be used against the Americans, and those Americans living here? And espionage was interested in whether he could work over there, and could he be of interest to Intelligence? They both studied him but unfortunately could not find any abilities at all, in either field.[68]

The Second Chief Directorate, responsible for counterintelligence, made his decision without any equivocation, saying, "Who the hell needs Oswald?"[69]

Semichastny asserts that Oswald wasn't working for American intelligence either. His "intellectual training and capabilities were such that it would not show the FBI and CIA in a good light if they used people like him."[70]

One of Oswald's best Russian friends, Pavel Golovachev, later said, "I would say that he wasn't a spy because when he bought a camera, he couldn't even put film in it. And it was a very basic camera, a Smena-2, which even a Soviet school-child could use, and he couldn't." Regarding his work in the Minsk Byelorussian Radio and Television Factory, Pavel also said that Oswald couldn't repair the simplest defect in a radio. "He locked up the condensers."[71] His childhood friend Allen Campbell remembers, "Lee was the biggest geek in the whole world. That the CIA or the KGB would hire him is ludicrous."[72]

After being released from the hospital seven days later, Oswald visited the American Embassy to request revocation of his American citizenship. He went in person, probably because he wanted to impress the Soviet authorities. With good logic, he reasoned they would hear his statements through bugging devices, and calculated they would be more inclined to permit him to stay. The consular official Oswald saw was Richard Snyder, who, by his own admission in 1993, served for a time in a clandestine branch of the CIA. Due to those connections, Snyder's assessment of the "very, very uptight" Oswald was telling. "Here's a dumb kid. Twenty years old and he hasn't got the faintest idea of what this country [the Soviet Union] is about…He said he was a Marxist and I told him he was going to be a lonely man in the Soviet Union because Marxism was already a faded religion there."[73]

According to Semichastny and other KGB officials, Oswald's suicide attempt was seen as "political blackmail" by a person they viewed as "very simple or primitive, not a very interesting person." Once it was determined that Oswald was not working for U.S. intelligence,[74] the sentiment was, "Let him stay! [We wanted] to avoid an international scandal over such a character," Semichastny explains. The KGB officer continues:

We decided to send him further away from Moscow since we were not convinced that this would be his last effort at blackmail. We were sure that he would try something again, and we didn't want to deal with that in Moscow, and so we decided to send him to Minsk.

Code Name: "Likhoy"—Oswald in Minsk

Oswald's transfer to the industrial city of Minsk, 450 miles to the southwest of Moscow, did not occur instantly, however. He spent two lonely months in the Metropole Hotel in Moscow waiting for his Stateless Persons ID and financial assistance to arrive.

On January 4th, 1960, two days after 42-year-old Senator John Kennedy announced he was a candidate for president, Oswald was given papers granting him temporary residency in the Soviet Union. During Kennedy's nine months of campaigning and first 17 months as President, the ex-Marine would be in Minsk, at first buoyed by the novelty of living Soviet life somewhat like a Soviet citizen—and by the perks and privileges that distinguished his life from the average—but then chafing with disillusionment and personal disappointment.

Lee Oswald, called "Alik," the nearest Russian equivalent to Lee, was eventually given work at the Byelorussian Radio and Television Factory, which employed between 5,000 and 10,000 workers. Combining his salary and his regular Red Cross stipend, Oswald was making as much as the factory's director. This relative affluence for the unskilled Oswald led some to suspect a special relationship between Oswald and the Soviet government. However, documents later released by the Soviets, and interviews with former KGB officers, make it clear that all defectors were initially given this sort of special treatment.[75] Oswald was also given, by Minsk standards, a very nice (if modestly furnished) apartment overlooking the Svisloch river.

Oswald was initially distressed to learn he would be working as a metal-worker in a factory. He had hoped to become an influential political spokesman. But as time progressed, and as he began to relish his celebrity (he was referred to by a co-worker as "the man from Mars"), Oswald seemed, for the first and perhaps only time in his life, to be genuinely happy. He seemed to actually be living the "American dream" instead of the revolutionary Marxist one. He dated often, had numerous girlfriends, and spent his spare time at the movies, opera, and going on picnics. The KGB file says that he showed no interest in politics— "he only wants to have a good time." His letters home to his brother Robert attested to his new-found tranquility.

Within a matter of months, however, his celebrity wore off, and so did his enthusiasm for life in Russia. "Some of his friends had begun to see him as much less a figure than they believed when they first met him, when they assumed that an American would be well educated and highly cultured," says his Russian friend Ernst Titovets.[76] Soon his co-workers and his KGB babysitters were aware of his deficiencies. "He really did not work hard, and some of his colleagues noticed that he was not a radio technician at all," says present KGB Chief Vacheslev Nikonov.[77] According to co-worker Leonid Botvenik, Oswald even complained about the food in the canteen. Botvenik recalls, "Honestly, he was not a good worker. He would bring all kinds of magazines to read at work, and he was always dissatisfied."[78]

Another co-worker, Leonid Tsagoikov, said, "Oswald was a lazybones who always put his feet up on his worktable"—a shocking breach of etiquette in the Soviet Union.[79] Other workers spoke of Alik's growing disillusionment at the job, citing his "sit down strikes, minor incidents in the cafeteria, and general indifference." KGB Chairman Vadim Bakatin added that Oswald was a "slacker at work."[80] The KGB file suggests that the factory wanted to fire Oswald, but was prevented from doing so because of his perceived instability.[81]

"He was a fellow who needed attention. He was a new fellow in Minsk, a new American, so they were all interested in him. And they lost interest in him eventually. So he became nothing again. So he got disgusted with it."
—**Oswald's friend George DeMohrenschildt, to the Warren Commission**

The KGB was in a tough spot. It was clear that Oswald knew next to nothing about Marxism, and his time in Minsk didn't enhance his knowledge or interest. Oswald's close friend Pavel Golavachev says, "He never talked politics. He avoided the subject." Ivan Lunyov, an official archivist for the Communist Party and the KGB, says, "Oswald was a radish: red on the outside and white on the inside." This was in fact the way he was referred to by the KGB at the time—"the radish."[82] Vacheslav Nikonov was the first post-communist KGB official to review the Oswald file. According to him, "He [Oswald] didn't attend any Marxist classes, he didn't read any Marxist literature, and he didn't even attend the labor union meetings. So the question was: what was he doing here?"[83]

There was some possibility, the KGB reasoned, that Oswald, now code-named "Likhoy" by the Minsk KGB office (a play on the name "Lee Harvey"), might be a "sleeper agent," programmed without his own knowledge. CIA officials, while claiming never have to have perfected the capability, nonetheless admit that the Soviets were worried that the U.S. possessed it and would someday attempt to deploy it.[84]

Consequently, the KGB assigned over a dozen full time agents to watch "Likhoy" Oswald. His apartment was bugged from above, below, and inside. His phone was tapped. Surveillance photos were taken constantly. His co-workers, including his best friends, were reporting back to the KGB. This would continue, at no small cost to the KGB, for Oswald's entire stay in Russia. Conversations were monitored until Lee left the apartment for good in 1962. Photos would be taken of him until he boarded the train bound for the border on his way out of the country.

Oswald's increasing discontent with his situation was put on temporary hold when he met Ella Germann, arguably the first true love of his life. She was a dark-haired, fair-skinned Jewish girl he had met at the factory. His diary reflects the fact that he fell for her the minute he saw her. Although they would date for over six months, the feeling of love was never mutual. Ella was interested in having an American friend, and someone with whom she could enjoy the symphony and opera, but nothing more. She remembers:

> *I saw him more out of habit than love. I didn't have a deep feeling for him. And then I felt that he fancied me. I didn't want to upset him. I had in mind that he was here alone, he had no relatives here or any close friends to turn to, to give him support when he needed it. And it went on like that until he pushed me into saying "yes" or "no."* [85]

After spending New Year's Eve 1961 with Ella and her family, Oswald proposed marriage. The subject of marriage had come up before, but only in passing. Ella recalls that she would ask Alik about his background, and she became aware of what others would refer to as Oswald's lifelong predilection for lying. "All the answers that he gave me were not satisfactory and this created an atmosphere of mistrust between us," Ella remembers. "Because of that, I wasn't able to agree to marry him." Oswald wrote in his diary, "She hesitates than [sic] refuses, my love is real but she has none for me...I am stunned she snickers at my awkwardness in turning to go (I am too stunned to think) I realize she was never serious with me...I am miserable [sic]."[86]

Soon after Ella's rejection, Oswald would write that he was reconsidering his desire to stay in the USSR. In retrospect, his proposal to Ella represented one of his several attempts to live a "normal" life with a stable woman. For the second time in his life, an important female figure had refused to rescue him from his inner demons.

One last woman would have the opportunity to "rescue" Oswald. However, she would be more psychologically akin to Lee and his mother than to the mature, stable Ella. Her name was Marina Prusakova.

Lee and Marina

> I may curse you later
> Your features;
> To love you is like a disaster
> To which there is no end
> There is no friend, no comrade
> Who could drag me out of this conflagration
> In the broad light of day.
> Despairing of salvation
> I dream in the daytime
> And live near you
> As near an earthquake.

—From a poem Marina Oswald kept in her notebook

On March 16, 1961, six weeks after being rebuffed by Ella, and consumed by depression over the rejection, Alik/Lee met Marina Prusakova. Marina had told two young men (without each other's knowledge) she would be their date to the Trade Union dance. Her biographer says that this was typical behavior for her—that she reveled in the attention and jealousy this situation induced. However, she left the dance with a third young man she had been introduced to that night as Alik. Of course, his real name was Lee Harvey Oswald. One month later, Lee proposed marriage and Marina accepted. Within another two weeks, the couple received official approval and were married on April 30, 1961. Lee was 21 years old (although he told Marina he was older), and Marina was 19.

The uncommon speed with which they were able to obtain the marriage license has held sinister implications for some writers. However, KGB Chief Semichastny says that the government's position was: "Let the poor devil marry. The [Minsk authorities] even thought that he might calm down and wouldn't jump up and down so much."

"Soon after we broke up, I learned that he had got married," Ella now says. "I thought on the whole that he did it that quickly to get [back] at me. I feel that kind of behavior is quite normal in people who are in love and are rejected."[87] Lee himself would write in his diary that he was still in love with Ella after marrying Marina—that he did it "to hurt Ella."[88] Both Lee and Marina would have many second thoughts about the wisdom of the marriage, often calling it a mistake.

That is not to say there was no attraction between Lee and Marina. In fact, it is universally agreed that Marina Prusakova was an uncommonly beautiful woman. The man who introduced them, Yuri Merezhinski, recalls:

She was the most attractive woman in the room. She was surrounded by lots of admirers. She didn't pay any attention to him, but he still wanted to get to know her better...He [Oswald] fell in love with her at first sight. He was under her spell. He had fallen for her in a big way because she was going with a lot of men and was having sex with them.[89]

The Lee/Marina mix was certain to be volatile. Marina, like Lee and his mother before him, was a one-parent child. Born illegitimate, she never knew the identity of her father. Her mother told her that her father had died in the war, and that she was the legally adopted daughter of her stepfather, Alexander Medvedev. Both were lies. When Marina was fifteen, her mother died. One year later, when she obtained her birth records, Marina learned that she was the illegitimate daughter of someone named Nikolai, and worse, her stepfather never legally adopted her. Her feeling of loneliness was overwhelming. It was only then that she learned that her legal last name was Prusakova, her mother's maiden name. To her great embarrassment, she had to change her last name back to Prusakova in order to obtain work permits. This only added to the scorn she now felt for her mother.

After Marina's mother's death, her "stepfather" felt unrestrained to express his true emotions about the young girl. "Don't come to me bringing a baby in your skirts," he warned her. "Go to Minsk. You're in my way. I don't want any prostitutes around me!"[90] With these words, the second husband of Marina's mother threw sixteen-year-old Marina out of their Leningrad house. He had spread the word to other relatives throughout Russia that Marina was a prostitute. In many cultures, a beautiful woman who likes to have carnal fun is often branded a prostitute, but such a characterization may have been unfounded in Marina's case.

However, what does become important is that Marina was widely regarded as an easy woman to bed, and more importantly, her friends say she wanted out of the USSR. One of the young men Marina dated, Oleg Tarusin, says that Marina was "desperate to leave the USSR."[91] This exact sentiment is reinforced by Vanda Kuznetsova, a roommate of Marina, who remembers Marina as anxious to marry a foreigner and leave the country.[92] Another of the roommates, Galia Printseva, says that the thing she remembers most about Marina was her desire to marry an American.[93] KGB officer Oleg Kalugin refers to Marina as a "light" woman (meaning low sexual morals) who was looking for a "good thing" in a western man.[94]

Feeling unloved and totally alone, Marina became apathetic and passive. She was mischievous in school, where she was known as "matchstick" because of her slim body and because "she would flare up in an explosion of words whenever anyone addressed her."[95] She was expelled from pharmacy school for academic failure and poor attendance. All of this curiously parallels the childhood of young Lee. Predictably, Marina became, according to her biographer, a rebel. Dirt poor, she survived by her wits and, by many accounts, her good looks. Marina said, "I simply lived off chance acquaintances."[96] She had an unending stream of boyfriends, mostly foreigners, to whom she felt more attracted than Soviet natives.

That the beautiful Marina wanted to leave Russia, and that she behaved like a totally liberated female, would certainly help explain their whirlwind courtship and marriage. It would also explain the many violent rows that their brief marriage would endure. Like Ella, Marina would catch Lee in lies about his background: saying he was older, claiming his mother was dead, etc. And Marina's influence was anything but calming. A Communist Party archivist who has seen the Oswald file says that Marina was a "complete slag" and that Lee tried to strangle her. Other officials agree, adding, however, that Marina held her own physically and would often beat up Lee. These rows were all overheard by the KGB. A KGB official who is privy to the surveillance tapes says, "She hurt him too. They had active [physical] fights."[97]

The marriage turned sour almost from the start, and both partners spoke of divorce, but tried to reconcile when they learned that Marina was pregnant. By this time, Lee had already initiated the arduous process of convincing authorities in both the U.S. and the USSR to allow him to repatriate to America. According to his diary entries, he told Marina in late June 1961 that he was eager to return to the United States.

In fact, as early as January 4, 1961, precisely a year after he had been issued his residence permit in Moscow, he was summoned to the passport office in Minsk and asked whether his request for Soviet citizenship remained valid. It didn't, he said. He asked only for an extension of his residence permit, confiding to his diary: "I am stating [sic] to reconsider my disire [sic] about staying. The work is drab. The money I get has nowhere to be spent. No nightclubs or bowling allys [sic] no places of recreation acept [sic] the trade union dances. I have had enough."

Less than a month after visiting the passport office, Lee wrote the American Embassy in Moscow, stating his desire to return to the United States. He wanted to be assured that any legal proceedings against him would be dropped. Richard Snyder, a U.S. Embassy official, was not surprised. On the basis of his experience with Oswald more than two years earlier, he felt absolutely certain he would hear from the young man again. "I heard from him a little sooner than I had expected," Snyder recalls. Actually, Oswald had written the Embassy even earlier, but the first letter, and many others, were apparently intercepted by the Soviet authorities. Current KGB Chief Vacheslav Nikonov describes the tone of the letters: "We really have the story of a man whose heart is breaking. Between the wife, the life in Minsk, which he didn't very much like, and his family, his brother...he was really homesick at this point."[98]

However, according to KGB surveillance, it was unclear if Marina would accompany her husband to the U.S. "You idiot!" she was heard to scream. " I'm not going anywhere with you...(sobbing) Out of my sight, you dog! You scoundrel!...Go to hell, you bastard! You can go to your America without me, and I hope you die on the way."[99] History shows that Marina had a change of heart, and on June 1, 1962, both Lee and Marina were finally able to leave for the United States.

While the couple waited for the paperwork to be processed, and it was determined that "Likhoy/Nalim" was not an American operative, one would expect the KGB authorities to lessen their surveillance of him. But considering Oswald's increasingly bizarre behavior, it can now be seen why that was impossible. In 1992, the KGB began granting western journalists limited access to their Oswald file. With this information, the position in which the KGB had been placed can be better understood. The KGB files also shed new light on Oswald's ability to obtain an exit visa when he was ready to return to the U.S. KGB Colonel Oleg Nechiporenko, who has reviewed the entire Oswald file, writes of a most unsettling episode:

Days before the new year [1962], operatives uncovered that Nalim had a new pastime. He had decided to build bombs. This was not a hypothetical hobby, since he had already built two iron casings, one box-shaped and the other cylindrical. Each contained two compartments; one filled with shot and the other with explosives. He had also prepared paper-tube fuses, 4-5 centimeters long and 2 millimeters in diameter. They were to be filled with gunpowder, with the fuse designed to last approximately two seconds. Nalim concealed his new toys from his wife and stored them at home. Nothing related to the con-

struction of the bombs was done at the factory, where it would have undoubt-
edly attracted attention.[100]

The file reflects the KGB's satisfaction when Oswald gave up the bomb project because he couldn't acquire the amount of gunpowder required. The operatives were, however, unsettled by Oswald's attachment to his rifle, which he prominently displayed on the wall of his apartment (this in a household rife with domestic abuse). The KGB held its collective breath when Oswald boarded a crowded streetcar with his rifle in plain sight—something that might have gone unnoticed in the deep south of the U.S., but was unheard of in Russia. The KGB operatives, expecting the worst, breathed a sigh of relief when Oswald ended up taking the rifle to a local shop and pawning it.[101]

Still more bizarre activity was emanating from the Oswald sphere. Oswald spent much time with his friend Ernst Titovets, helping him with his English. Lee would read from Shakespeare, or ad lib being interviewed into a tape recorder for Titovet's future phonetic studies. In one such interview, Oswald played the role of a mass murderer. The tape was broadcast for the first time in 1993 on PBS' Frontline. Excerpts from the interview are chilling in retrospect:

Titovets: Tell us about your last killing.

Oswald: Well, it was a young girl under a bridge. She came in carrying a loaf of bread and I just cut her throat from ear to ear.

Titovets: What for?

Oswald: Well, I just wanted the loaf of bread of course.

Titovets: What do you take to be your most famous, ah, in your life?

Oswald: Well, the time I killed, ah, eight men on the Bowery that were on the sidewalk there. They were just standing there loafing around. I didn't like their faces so I just shot them all with a machine gun. It [the murder] was very famous. All the newspapers carried the story.[102]

Considering all of Oswald's unsettling activity and the burden he placed on his KGB "babysitters," it comes as no surprise that the Soviets approved his exit visa. Former KGB Chief Semchastny recalls, "He was always changing his jobs [assignments within the factory] and behaving in a rather unsatisfactory way. So when he eventually asked to go back, I said, 'By all means let him—I mean, put no obstacles in his way'."[103]

The American response to Oswald's return request, like most everything else, has been viewed with skepticism. When the Americans not only granted Oswald's request, but also assisted him financially, suspicions were fueled that Oswald was a spy. However, this treatment was, in fact, unremarkable, as the House Select Committee on Assassinations (1977-1979) later learned. HSCA Chief Counsel G. Robert Blakey summed up U.S. practices during a 1993 interview:

One of the most troubling things for me, on the hypothesis that Oswald was connected to American intelligence, was the seeming ease with which he got out of the Soviet Union. The American government gave him a visa to get out, financed him, facilitated it all the way. I was deeply troubled by that because it seemed to me unusual. To test that hypothesis, we did a defector study. We analyzed 22 American defectors—found that what happened with Oswald wasn't unusual. Incredibly, that was the way the American government treated all its defectors.

On May 22, 1962 the Oswald family, which now included the couple's three-month old daughter June, spent their last night in Minsk at their friend Pavel Golovochev's apartment. Because the Oswalds were still under surveillance, the KGB tapes record Marina's last words to Lee as they walked out the door: "You fucking guy, you can't even carry a baby."

Oswald's behavior patterns were clearly consistent: once he became disillusioned with his current sanctuary, whether with his mother, the Marines, Russia, or his wife, he soon became what his early psychological profiles had predicted all along—manic, schizoid, and passive-aggressive. Owen Dejanovich, who knew Oswald from his Marine days, saw him as a loner, an outsider, a seeker of attention by "being on the edge of discipline," and flouting the Marine tradition of "all for one and one for all." In Russia, Oswald had been a poor workman at a radio factory. When he returned to the U.S., and again found work, he again became a disciplinary problem.

When Oswald returned to the U.S., he completed his break with his mother. After joining the Marines, he had had only minimal contact with her, and then not of his own volition. Now, he stopped seeing her entirely until she visited him in prison after the assassination. At that time, she was not even aware of the birth of Lee's second child and Lee reacted strongly when he found that his wife had brought his mother to visit him in jail. He said to Marina, "Why did you bring that fool with you? I don't want to talk to her."[104]

If Oswald served neither American nor Soviet intelligence in the Soviet Union, he did serve a powerful compulsion of his own: to be appreciated as an important person with great political and intellectual abilities and to make a mark on the world. And if the Soviet Union had failed to live up to his expectations, it only served to crystallize and focus his attention on his original idol: Fidel Castro.

CHAPTER FIVE

BACK IN THE USA

"I have lived under both systems, I have sought the answers and although it would be very easy to dupe myself into believing one system is better than the other, I know they are not. I despise the representatives of both systems, whether they be socialist or Christian democracies."
   —Lee Oswald on the ship bearing him back to America after his years in Russia (spelling mistakes corrected)

"Immediately after coming to the United States, Lee changed. I did not know him as such a man in Russia...He helped me as before, but he became a little more of a recluse...He was very irritable, sometimes for a trifle."
   —Marina Oswald

"Ever since he was born and I was old enough to remember, I always had the feeling that some great tragedy was going to strike Lee in some way or another ...I figured, well, when he defected and came back—that was his big tragedy. I found out it wasn't."
   —John Pic, Oswald's half-brother, to the Warren Commission

B y mid-June, 1962, Lee and Marina Oswald were back in Fort Worth, Texas, staying temporarily with Oswald's brother, Robert. Lee's time was taken up with job-hunting, getting his Russian memoirs typed, and subscribing to various publications of the Communist Party, U.S.A.

On July 17th, Oswald landed a job as a sheet metal helper at the Leslie Welding Company in Fort Worth. He would cease working by October, lying to Marina that he had been fired (he never even told his employers he was quitting—he just stopped showing up). At the time, the Oswalds were living in a shabby $60-per-month bungalow.

This period is relatively unremarkable, except that all the previously established patterns in Oswald's life continued: his fighting with Marina, his constant lying (for instance on job applications), and his interest in Marxism. Yet, despite the low-key nature of his life, Oswald became of interest to the U.S. government.

For it was 1962, the height of the Cold War, the year of the Cuban Missile Crisis, and a pro-Marxist defector like Oswald had the potential to be a "sleeper" Soviet agent. He was monitored.

The FBI and Oswald

At the time of Oswald's original defection to Russia, Fort Worth FBI agent John Fain conducted a routine investigation. Thus, it was considered appropriate that Fain reopen the file upon Oswald's return. The agency was equally interested in Marina, who, as a young and well-educated immigrant from the Soviet Union, fit the bureau's criteria for investigation. Agent Jim Hosty, who helped Fain review Marina's Immigration file, says that the FBI had information that the Soviets were planning to use moles— "we called them sleepers"—to infiltrate the U.S. in their guise as refugees. In fact, Hosty claims to have uncovered a few sleepers. Thus, Marina was considered a potential mole.[1]

On June 26th, Fain, assisted by FBI agent Tom Carter, interviewed Oswald at the FBI's Fort Worth headquarters. The agency was most interested in determining if Oswald had been recruited by Soviet Intelligence. The tense, two-hour interview was filled with Oswald displays of temper. As usual, Oswald's answers were replete with lies: he claimed never to have requested Soviet citizenship, or to have offered the Soviets radar information. The interview ended with Oswald's assurance that he would contact the FBI if the Soviets attempted to contact him. Fain summarized Oswald as "impatient and arrogant during most of the interview," and sufficiently evasive to warrant a follow-up.

Two months later, armed with confidential informants' reports that the Oswalds had nothing to do with the local communist party, Fain reinterviewed Oswald at Oswald's apartment. As a result of this subsequent interview, Fain recommended that the FBI close its file on Oswald. He had determined that Oswald posed no apparent danger. "You don't keep a case going if there's nothing to do, and there was nothing to do," says Jim Hosty. "He'd defected, become disillusioned, and came back, and Fain was under the impression that he'd seen the light and was going to behave himself."

Marina's file was kept open, but as one of forty such cases, it was not given a high priority. When Fain retired in 1963, Hosty took over his case investigations. "I think it was March 31st [1963] that I went to Forth Worth," Hosty recalls. "I found out they [the Oswalds] were gone, tracked them to Dallas, and found out that the landlady there had expelled them. She said they were fighting, so she evicted them." The landlady pointed to another rental house down the street, but when Hosty went there, he found they weren't home. The purpose of Hosty's visit to Dallas was simply to size the Oswalds up, to get a feel for them. The approach was friendly. Hosty says that the typical conversation would include letting them know that "we're here to help them out, blah, blah, blah. It's not an accusatory interview...the British call it 'vetting.'"

Had Hosty arrived a few hours later on his initial interview attempt (March

31), he would have stumbled upon an event that would have certainly heightened the Bureau's interest in Lee Harvey Oswald. (But this, and later attempts to interview Oswald at this address, failed. Soon, Lee Oswald would "skip town.")

Odd Photos and Fantasies: The Politics of Lee Harvey Oswald

In the late afternoon of March 31, 1963, Lee Oswald descended the back stairs of the cheap second-floor apartment on West Neely Street. The 23-year-old former Marine and recent returnee from Russia was of medium height, slender, and ordinarily solemn-looking except when a slight smile—often taken for a smirk—appeared on his face. His head seemed small for his body, prompting a man who would encounter him four months hence in New Orleans—an ardent political enemy who nevertheless came to appreciate Oswald's quick intelligence—to think that he had "the face of a parrot on the neck of a bull."[2] But anyone who happened to see him walking down the back stairs of the tired house that afternoon would not have looked first at his face. Oswald was carrying an old bolt-action rifle he had just bought by mail. It was the rifle from which all the shots would be fired in Dealey Plaza almost eight months later. It was the weapon that would kill John Kennedy.[3]

From the back stairs of 214 West Neely Street, Oswald entered the building's postage stamp-sized backyard. He was dressed entirely in black, with a revolver, also bought by mail, strapped in a holster on his hip. The smirk for which he would soon become known—and which would infuriate police officers and journalists after his capture on November 22nd—played about his lips. Marina, the wife he had married in the Soviet Union, was hanging up diapers for their baby daughter. When he came into view, she burst out laughing and asked what on earth he was doing in his costume. He told her to take a picture of him and handed her a camera. "Are you crazy? I've never taken a picture in my life." Lee Oswald persisted. The afternoon sun was sinking and he was concerned about the shadows that would appear in the photograph. Marina resisted. "I'm busy and I don't know how. Take it yourself…What a weird one you are! Who on earth needs a photograph like that?"[4] Already disturbed by Lee's recent acquisition of the guns, Marina later said she thought Lee had "gone crazy."[5]

But she soon did his bidding, snapping the shutter repeatedly, and taking the photograph that would become his representation throughout the world. Before they went back up to their modest apartment, she asked him why he wanted his picture taken with guns, of all stupid things. Oswald answered that he was going to send it to *The Militant*, to show he was "ready for anything."[6] *The Militant* was one of two newspapers with which he had posed, holding them in one hand while grasping his rifle with the other. The second newspaper was *The Worker*, published by the American Communist Party. Oswald may not have known that the two supposedly fraternal papers were in fact at ideological war with each other, partly over Soviet dominance of socialist movements and interpretations of Stalin's role in history. Pressed to choose between the two, he probably would have chosen *The Militant.* Under a heading of "News and Views from Dallas"—where the newspaper's readers were very thin on the ground—the March 11th issue with which he posed contained a letter from an "L. H." of Dallas praising it as "the most informative radical publication in America."[7]

Most importantly, by the fall of 1963, *The Militant* was reporting to its subscribers Castro's belief that the United States, in contrast to its publicized desire to reduce world tensions, was in fact "increasing its efforts to tighten the noose around Cuba." Oswald's other Communist group contact, The Fair Play for Cuba Committee (FPCC), had been reporting to its members since the fall of 1961 that the Kennedys were planning a reinvasion of Cuba, using troops being trained in Guatemala, Nicaragua, and El Salvador.[8] Oswald agreed with Castro's (and the FPCC's) analysis, telling a Dallas friend, Michael Paine, "You could tell what they [the Kennedys] wanted to do by reading between the lines, reading the thing and doing a little reading between the lines." In fact, both Oswald and Castro were correct, though few in the United States knew it in 1963.[9]

After Oswald's death, some would insist that the photo-taking incident never occurred—that the photos were fakes, designed to implicate the innocent "patsy." From interviews and the HSCA work described later,[10] we now know that the photos are genuine, and that Oswald took pride in them.

On his return to America, Oswald applied to work for Peter Gregory, a Russian translator. This move opened Lee and Marina to the White Russian communities of Fort Worth and Dallas, and would introduce the Oswalds to their few friends in Texas. Names like George DeMohrenschildt, Michael and Ruth Paine, and Volkmar Schmidt became part of Lee and Marina's small world. It was at dinner parties with this community that the Oswalds found both assistance and an arena for political discourse.

One of the people who managed to befriend Lee on his return from Russia to the States was Ruth Paine, a Russian language student. Her husband, from whom she would be amicably separated for most of the eight months from now until the assassination, was a research engineer at Bell Helicopter. Michael Paine remembered Oswald well. His father had been active in leftist politics, and, with that in mind, Paine expressed his dislike for Lee's treatment of Marina. "One of the goals of communism is to stop the exploitation of man by man, and here was this guy treating his wife like a vassal. I was quite offended by that." He also took note of Oswald's conviction that capitalism could not be reformed or improved, and thus "had to be destroyed."

But even before he had time to appraise Lee's politics or relationship with Marina, Paine was startled by something the strange young man showed him at their first meeting, just after they introduced themselves:

> *Almost the next thing he does is to pick up this eight-by-ten glossy photo of himself in black with a rifle and a couple of pamphlets [the two newspapers]...I didn't know what to make of it because it was very different from what I had expected to find. I had known communists, and they were mostly intellectually interesting people...I'd been told he was a communist and I kind*

of expected a social idealist and couldn't see the connection between [that and] this picture of a guy with his rifle there in black clothing. It was so different, I just didn't put the two together. But he was obviously proud of that picture and...the first thing we did then was to talk about his times in Russia. His greatest disagreement—bitterness—toward Russia seemed to be that they wouldn't let him own a rifle unless he was a member of a paramilitary organization there.[11]

Coincidentally, at the time he met the Paines, Oswald was working at the graphic arts shop Jaggers-Chiles-Stovall, where he had access to the necessary equipment for processing the photos. His co-worker Dovid (Dennis) Ofstein recalls, somewhat haltingly:

About a month or two after Lee came to work for us, he asked me what the company policy was about using the company equipment for making personal photographs, enlargements of personal pictures, family pictures, that sort of thing. I told him at the time that the company policy was pretty much that you don't do it, but that people did it anyway, and as long as it didn't get out of hand, the company usually didn't say very much about it.[12]

It is now clear that Oswald sent these photographs precisely where he told Marina he would.[13] *The Militant*, published by the Socialist Workers' Party, was one of the few American periodicals where one could read "alternative" (pro-Castro) news and opinion. Oswald's reason for subscribing to it meshed with the passion for revolutionary Cuba he would express to Volkmar Schmidt and others during the coming months. Almost certainly, he sent the paper a print of one of the backyard photos to ingratiate himself with the publisher while giving notice of himself as important and resolute—and potentially as a useful Party agent in Dallas. Michael Paine thought the print Oswald showed him "represented an icon of just the way he'd like to be seen, the world to think of him, the way he thought of himself."[14] The way he thought of himself was as a soldier of revolution whose perspicacity and deeds would win him recognition and praise, perhaps make him a commander someday.

In fact, the photograph had the opposite effect when it arrived at *The Militant's* offices in New York. Sylvia Weinstein, who handled the paper's subscriptions, opened the envelope and thought the man in black was "kookie." In her opinion, he had chosen a "stupid" way to declare his loyalty to the publication. (Weinstein was struck by the apparent ignorance of the man who held *The Militant* and *The Worker* together in his hand. Anyone holding both, together with a gun, she said, would have to be assumed to be "really dumb and totally naive.")

Farrell Dobbs, National Secretary of the Socialist Workers' Party, was appalled and frightened. After suffering a witch hunt and being imprisoned during the McCarthy years, Dobbs feared something much more serious than "some weirdo" acting out his fantasies. Specifically, he feared a provocateur, and instructed Weinstein to immediately bring to his office any similar material if more arrived.[15]

—◇—

*"He was extremely critical of President Kennedy, and he was just obsessed
with what America did to support this invasion at the Bay of Pigs, obsessed
with his anger towards Kennedy."*
**—Volkmar Schmidt, describing a conversation he had with
Oswald soon after his return from Russia**[16]

The rifle that would fire the bullets in Dealey Plaza was a hoary veteran of World
War II. It arrived at a post office box assigned to "A. J. Hidell," the name under
which Oswald had bought the rifle and a revolver.[17] Just days before placing his
order, the rifle's new owner—a low-paid worker with few employable skills, dim
prospects, but a powerful desire to become a political luminary—had a rare long
talk at a dinner party with another guest named Volkmar Schmidt, a discussion
which might explain Oswald's desire to purchase the weapons. A geologist by
profession, Schmidt did research for Mobil Oil. His intelligence and psychological insights were admired in his upper middle class circle of worldly Dallasites.

The German-born scientist had no way of knowing that Oswald and his
pregnant, Russian-born wife, who was also at the party with their 13-month-old
child, were descending toward a relationship of severe strain, sometimes
relieved by moments of groping for each other, but increasingly battered by
insult and abuse. But Schmidt did notice that Oswald seemed emotionally
detached from his "lovely" wife and baby daughter. More than that, he felt certain that Oswald was "in deep, deep spiritual and emotional trouble...a lost
soul." The older man sensed an almost palpable emptiness and despair in the
younger one, "a state of mind that Dostoyevsky described as a suicide." Schmidt
added:

> I realized that Lee Harvey Oswald was a deeply troubled man who was spiri-
> tually totally empty...He was totally obsessed with his own political
> agenda...[He] would have found anybody of importance to assassinate—to
> become history, to leave a mark in the history books, no matter what.[18]

Schmidt was most worried by Oswald's seeming determination to give
meaning to his life by achieving something political—for which he had no
means. Even if his basic motives were good, as Schmidt perceived them, the
youth had an abnormal gap between his yearning and his possibilities.
Remembering that similar traits had driven fellow Germans to join the Bader
Meinhoff gang, the thoughtful geologist considered him "exceedingly dangerous." Oswald's inner tensions might lead him to explode—not, Schmidt then
imagined, into political assassination but perhaps domestic violence or something at that level.

The two discussed the Soviet Union, from which Oswald had returned some
nine months before the dinner party. Oswald's comments were far more interesting and seemingly intellectual than his meager formal education would
seemingly allow, and were uttered in a thin, controlled voice, with the wisp of

a southern accent. Schmidt thought he discerned the reason for at least some of Oswald's desperation: the young man had put a great deal of effort into learning Russian and going to the Soviet Union, but failed to find what he was seeking there. "Now his hopes were dashed; now what?" Back in America with his wife and little child, he was poor, struggling, anxious to assert himself—but empty. "He could not find anything positive to fill that void in his life."

Sitting near a window, the new acquaintances talked throughout most of the party (at least two hours). The conversation turned to domestic politics, and Schmidt could hardly help noticing that his new acquaintance was "extremely critical" of President Kennedy, chiefly because of the American-backed invasion at Cuba's Bay of Pigs in April 1961, a mere three months after Kennedy entered the White House. Oswald disparaged Soviet socialism but felt very differently about Cuba's.

On his return from Russia nine months earlier, Oswald had envisioned himself a luminary. A Russian immigrant who briefly defended him would remember that "he wanted to stand out. He wanted everybody to know he was the defector."[19] After great disappointment that a swarm of reporters hadn't greeted him when he disembarked from his ship in New York, the would-be celebrity studiously composed a list of questions for himself, then answered them. Was he a communist? he asked himself in question 7A. "Yes, basically, although I hate the USSR and [its] socialist system, I still think Marxism can work under different circumstances."[20] To anyone who listened, he would say, in one form or another, that the Soviet system was as bad as the American one, and in some of the same fundamental ways. But he retained his belief—as someone with his powerful longings had to retain it—that something better surely existed on this earth than the social systems under which he had, until now, been so deeply disappointed, deprived, and hurt. His new hope was Cuba.

In fact, Oswald appeared to have shifted his faith in and aspiration for Soviet socialism to the newer, seemingly purer and happier Cuban variety. In this, he resembled many believers in Marxism-Leninism of the time. Accepting the idea that the bureaucratic, repressive Soviet regime had deeply corrupted socialism's ideals—a corruption Oswald knew from his 30-odd months of disillusioning personal witness in the country—a large percentage of the thin ranks of American "sympathizers" were now convinced that Fidel Castro's socialistic version, which they pictured as enlightened, progressive, and fun-loving, had come to carry the banner of mankind's hope for the better life promised by freedom from capitalism.

Oswald's attachment to Castro was more than blind faith and shattered hopes on the rebound from his Soviet experience. Since Fidel, as his admirers happily called him, had begun capturing headlines in 1958 with daring guerrilla activities in Cuba's vast Sierra Maestra mountains, the intellectual campesino embodied a great romantic appeal for people of even moderately leftist feelings. The dashing rebel went on to overthrow a corrupt dictatorship that had pandered to American business interests, including the interests of Mafia bosses. He spoke a language of clarity and understandable human feelings, as opposed to the stupefying mumbo-jumbo of ritualistic dishonesty from Moscow. He seemed a genuine idealist—a visionary whose promises of hospitals, schools, and self-fulfillment for the masses sounded thrillingly attainable in his long, passionate speeches. This was the revolutionary figure of the age, and young Oswald quickly responded to him.

Oswald had had Cuba on his mind for a long time. His 30-odd months of residence in the Soviet Union gave him substantial knowledge of ordinary Soviet life, even with privileges that put him far above the average in living conditions and pay. For him, this was more than ample opportunity to become disenchanted with Soviet socialism. And if, as now seems clear, Marxism as a vehicle for protest and longing was the political constant in his life since discovering it at the age of 15, it is understandable that he transferred his full passion—or obsession, or contorted desire—to the brave new world he envisioned being constructed under the humane new leadership in Havana. His affection for Castro would become so strong that he would want to name his new baby "Fidel," a decision from which he retreated only because Marina insisted there would be no Fidel in their family.[21]

Without knowing Oswald's entire background, the temperate Volkmar Schmidt understood, in February 1963, that Oswald "idolized Cuba"—and hated President Kennedy for attacking it:

> He also very much idealized the socialist government in Cuba, and he was just obsessed with what Americans did to support this invasion...He really felt very angry about the support which the Kennedy Administration gave to the Bay of Pigs...I noticed that he was really, really obsessed with this idea and with his animosity towards Kennedy, just obsessed with his anger towards Kennedy.[22]

In the decades of speculation after the assassination, much attention would be given to Oswald's reported affection for Jack Kennedy. It would be based chiefly on statements by his wife Marina. "I'll go to the grave believing that Lee adored John Kennedy," she would say 25 years later. "How do you think I learned to like John Kennedy?"[23] But Marina's testimony about her husband—who kept her ignorant of many of his stranger thoughts and activities—was often highly contradictory. Some have pointed to the fact that Oswald borrowed one book by the President, and one about him, from the Dallas public library.[24] But Oswald also borrowed James Bond books—and one about the assassination of Huey Long.

In any case, a person's heightened interest in a public figure is no guarantee that the public figure is free from personal danger. Sometimes the contrary is true. John Lennon and Jody Foster are only two among many who were hunted by men whom they fascinated. One psychological theory has it that some disturbed people, with delusions of self-importance and a detachment from reality, imagine they will become the hero they kill. At least in passing, Oswald entertained notions that he or his children would serve in the White House.[25]

There is also evidence that Oswald spoke well of President Kennedy to friends in the Soviet Union, describing him as progressive. But by that time, he was probably fed up with the "Motherland of Socialism." And when his closest Russian friend, Pavel Golovachev, asked him how he would be able to satisfy his new (Russian) wife's materialistic demands when he returned to his native land, Oswald said that Golovachev didn't understand the United States. "You could always make a lot of money by shooting the President," he was reported to have answered. If that was a joke, its impulse came from the mind that conceived it.[26]

The host of the dinner party where Oswald unburdened himself was George DeMohrenschildt, a well-traveled oil geologist. DeMohrenschildt was a good friend of Schmidt—and also of Oswald. In fact, he was the only known friend of Oswald who might be called somewhat close after Oswald's return from Russia. A suave businessman and world traveler, DeMohrenschildt would assert shortly before his death in 1977 that "they made a moron out of [Oswald], but he was really smart as hell—ahead of his time, really, a kind of hippie of those days. In fact, he was the most honest man I knew. And I will tell you this—I am sure he did not shoot the President."[27]

However, the same DeMohrenschildt had painted a very different picture to the Warren Commission a decade earlier. Testifying there about the possibility of Oswald serving an intelligence function, he called the assassinated assassin "mixed-up," an "unstable individual" and a "semi-educated hillbilly," and said he "never would believe that any government would be stupid enough to trust Lee with anything important." And despite his later claim to be certain of Oswald's innocence, DeMohrenschildt had also stated that on first hearing of the news about Dealey Plaza, he thought that his young friend was the killer.[28]

Like thousands of other businessmen who traveled extensively, DeMohrenschildt was interviewed by CIA officers upon his return—a common practice by an agency desperate for Cold War intelligence. DeMohrenschildt was also known to socialize after hours with some of the Agency's people. After the assassination, conspiracy-prone readers seized upon these points. Wasn't there more to the relationship of the "Prince and the Pauper," as one writer called them—a relationship between a prosperous businessman and a despairing, down-at-the-heels, Marxism-hectoring loner half his age? Even though they met accidentally, at an émigré party, didn't DeMohrenschildt maintain the relationship with Oswald on directions from the CIA, in an attempt to debrief the returning defector?

The CIA has long maintained that it never debriefed Oswald after his return from the Soviet Union. That assertion—originally made at a time when the CIA took great pains to debrief some 25,000 tourists a year after visits to countries that interested the Agency—has to prompt grave doubt. CIA interest in the Soviet Union was understandably second to none. It seemed almost incredible that the Agency would not try to glean information from a young man who had lived in Minsk, a city about which far less was known than about Moscow and Leningrad.[29] The CIA even took the trouble to interview some tourists who had

---

visited Minsk in 1961, and copied a photograph those tourists had taken because it showed an Intourist guide the Agency suspected was a KGB informer.[30]

An unidentified American—the only one known to be in Minsk at the time—was also in that photograph. Though it happened to be Lee Oswald, the CIA said it realized that only after the Kennedy assassination.[31]

Minsk was also known as the site of a Soviet espionage school. But even if Oswald had had no contact with that establishment—and official documents reveal that some American security personnel suspected that wasn't the case — he had lived among Soviet citizens for 30-odd months. In Minsk, he had worked in a huge radio factory that employed as many as 10,000 people. The CIA was extremely keen to know not only about radios and possible other items of manufacture by ostensibly civilian Soviet plants, but also about plant rules, procedures, and conditions in general; daily routines, workers' morale, everything. That kind of intelligence-gathering was supposedly the Agency's primary mission. Why did it pass up such a rare opportunity with Oswald?[32]

In fact, it did not pass it up at all, but George DeMohrenschildt clearly had nothing to do with it. Oswald almost certainly was debriefed by the CIA, as he was by the FBI, probably after he disembarked from the Maasdam, the ship on which he returned to America after his Russian stay.

One month after Oswald's return to the U.S., Thomas Casasin, the Deputy Chief of the CIA's "6 Research Section" (specializing in the debriefing of returning defectors from the Soviet Union), wrote a memo to Walter P. Haltigan, Chief of the Soviet Section of the Paris Station, suggesting that Oswald be interviewed by the Office of Operations. Casasin also worried that Oswald "looks odd" and "may [have] been sent out of the Soviet Union by the KGB." In later Congressional testimony, both Casasin and Haltigan stated that they had no idea if the debriefing ever occurred. [33]

However, in 1978, an unnamed CIA officer testified to Congress that he remembered seeing a CIA debriefing report in 1962. It was about a Marine "re-defector" who was returning with his family from the Soviet Union, and it gave many details about the organization of a radio plant in Minsk, USSR—where Oswald worked.[34]

In 1993, the author tracked down that anonymous witness. It turned out to be Donald Denesleya, who admitted that when he testified before Congresss, he had not revealed the name of the man who had conducted the Oswald debriefing. Persuaded to appear on Frontline, he finally revealed the name:

I received across my desk a debriefing report. It was a debriefing of a Marine redefector. He was returning with his family from the Soviet Union and was back in the United States. The report was approximately four to five pages in length. It gave a lot of details about the organization of the Minsk radio plant. It was signed off by a CIA officer by the name of Anderson.

In 1993, several other CIA officers remembered a Major Andy Anderson who conducted debriefings for the CIA's domestic contacts division, and two recalled the debriefing of Oswald. Still, only Denesleya would go public with the information. Then, in August of 1993, John Newman, the author of *JFK and Vietnam* (and then working under contract on the Frontline project), was examining boxes containing Oswald's newly released CIA files. Among thousands of pages, he found traces of a notation in Oswald's 201 file—a personal record of people who interested the Agency. The traces were reversed, obviously bled-through from a document that wasn't meant to be photocopied. Newman turned it over, held it up to the light, and deciphered handwriting that read, "Anderson OO on Oswald." Barely legible, the writing that preceded "Anderson" appeared to read "Andy." In CIA language, OO is the symbol for the Domestic Contacts Division.

Years earlier, Denesleya told Congressional investigators that they might search a CIA volume on the Minsk Radio Factory in the CIA's Industrial Registry Branch (a component of the Office of Central Reference.) The investigators located the volume but it failed to contain the Oswald debriefing.[35]

Denesleya said in 1993, "My feeling at this point is the report is buried somewhere. I don't know where it is, but I'm sure it is probably in the contacts division, somewhere, or in one of the other filing systems at the Agency."

Oswald and Walker

"We didn't know [that Oswald shot at Walker] until a week or two after Kennedy's death. I didn't have to hear that in order to believe he had shot at Kennedy. That fits with the kind of thing that may have been in his mind. I think he was trying to find things he could do to bring about the revolution or something—bring about change. I supposed [with Walker], he was trying smaller little missions."
    —Michael Paine, Dallas friend of Lee Oswald[36]

"Lee Harvey Oswald had, on his own, made the move to learn Russian, which is no small feat for a young, uneducated American Marine. And he had moved to Russia to see for himself what life in a socialist country was about. You must say that this young man had a lot of courage and a lot of determination."
    —Volkmar Schmidt, Dallas acquaintance of Lee Oswald[37]

At George DeMohrenschildt's dinner party, which the oil man had arranged partly to introduce the struggling Oswald to people who might help him in Dallas, Volkmar Schmidt became "very concerned" about Oswald's "personal anger" at President Kennedy. Schmidt tried to soften it. He said that the many good things the President was doing made him the best hope for the Western world and the world as a whole—and although the Bay of Pigs may indeed have been a mistake, he commended Kennedy for trying to cure the country's domestic ills. In an attempt to "lure Oswald out of the emotional trap" he'd built for himself with his anger, he brought up something he believed truly deserved criticism: American bigotry and racism. Seeking to re-direct Oswald's outrage to "a more reasonable object of criticism," he mentioned General Walker as a personification of the bigotry and racism that had to be fought.[38]

General Edwin Walker was the former commander of the 24th Army Division, stationed in West Germany. In that recently-held post, his zeal stood out even among the Army's most vigorously anti-Communist officers during a powerfully anti-Communist time.

"We must throw out the traitors," he declared during the first spring of Kennedy's presidency—and with more than a hint at Kennedy's alleged softness on communism. "And if that is not possible, we must organize armed resistance to defeat the designs of the usurpers and contribute to the return of constitutional government."[39] The President forced Walker to resign in November 1961, after the general, among other unlawful political activities, distributed John Birch Society literature to his troops. Returning to the States, Walker was one of the leaders in the famous University of Mississippi integration riots in October 1962. Protesting the admission of black student James Meredith, Walker was arrested for inciting a riot. Walker eventually settled in Dallas. As a journalist would describe the radically conservative city, it was "the most appropriate command post for anti-Communist speaking tours and other right-wing activities."[40]

In February 1963, Walker joined extremist evangelist Reverend Billy James Hargis in "Operation Midnight Ride," a five-week national tour to bolster popular spirits, resolve, and anger in the fight against Communism. The tour took them to the University of Mississippi in February 1963, where they railed against the Kennedy administration's control of the press on the segregation issue. Some of the students Walker addressed became agitated enough to shoot and kill two reporters. Although Volkmar Schmidt did not believe that Walker had directly exhorted them to do this, he mentioned the violence to Oswald as illustration of bigotry's path to bad acts and to make it clear that he and DeMohrenschildt considered the General's racist views "very obnoxious."

After the 1963 incident in Mississippi, General Walker was charged with inciting a riot and Dallas-based FBI agent James Hosty supervised the FBI investigation. Coincidentally, he was also in charge of the Agency's casual watch on Oswald, and would later play a minor role in Oswald's life before the assassination. Hosty also learned later that George DeMohrenschildt had described Walker to Oswald as a "menace," adding that if Hitler had been shot in the early 1930s, World War II might have been avoided.[41] Marina's recollection of her husband's view of Walker supports Hosty's speculation about DeMohrenschildt's inadvertent stimulus. Lee told his wife that "[Walker] was a very bad man, that he was a fascist…the leader of a fascist organization…He said if someone had killed Hitler in time, it would have saved many lives."[42]

On the evening of April 10, 1963, Oswald shot at Walker with the intention of killing him.[43] The General was at a desk on his ground-floor dining room, working on his income taxes. Taking up an excellent position in back of the house, Oswald fired into the brightly-lit room through a window less than a hundred feet away. Walker instantly fell to the floor, crawled to a gun of his own, and ran out of the house.[44]

For many years, some students of the Kennedy assassination would question whether it was actually Oswald who made the attempt on Walker. Others would doubt that Oswald shot the President, or that the fatal shots came from him rather than one or more accomplices. In support of this, they would cite the failure to kill Walker from such close range.[45] How, they ask, could Oswald have hit the moving target in Dealey Plaza from a perch in the Texas School Book Depository when he missed the stationary, much closer Walker from ground level? That was evidence, the skeptics submitted, that Oswald's abilities with his rifle were too feeble to have allowed him to perform the more difficult Kennedy killing. "All it proved," two respected experts concluded in 1992, "was that Oswald couldn't hit a sitting target, much less a moving one."[46]

More evidence of Oswald's ineptitude with guns seemed to support their claims. For instance, his shooting amused and appalled his Russian friends. After an outing where he could hit nothing at all, his fellow hunters gave him rabbits to save him embarrassment when going home to Marina. His carelessness with his weapon made one member of a hunting party unwilling to go out with him again. That was how he handled a shotgun, but his record with the standard Marine M1 rifle seemed even more telling. Many of those who doubt he shot or shot alone have stressed that he was a poor rifleman who had to repeat his Marine test in order to attain the lowest score that would permit him to handle the weapon.

Examined more closely, however, the evidence points to the contrary. He was familiar with guns, had liked and played with them from an early age, and was competent or more in their use.

As for Oswald's inability to hit Walker with his Italian-made rifle, that was also subject to misinterpretation. Oswald had trained with his Mannlicher-Carcano in preparation for the attempt at Walker and would intensify his training in the weeks prior to shooting President Kennedy. Missing the reviled right-wing leader was no indication of poor marksmanship. Just at the instant of firing, Walker leaned forward at his desk to pick up a piece of carbon paper for his tax form, and the bullet whizzed directly above him.[47] (Kennedy would be an easier, more predictable target, in that he made no unexpected moves in his car. And although the presidential limousine was moving at the time Oswald fired, the limousine driver, after the first two shots, slowed it almost to a stop. In this sense, at the moment of the most accurate head shot, Kennedy was almost stationary.)

A police officer who conducted the Walker investigation concluded that "had he not moved at that instant, [the bullet] would have gone in one ear and out the other."[48] At the same time, a slat of the wooden window frame deflected Oswald's bullet slightly upward, causing the bullet to pass through the General's hair instead of his head. *(For details of Oswald's true shooting abilities, and a more thorough discussion of the physical evidence in the Kennedy shooting, see Appendix A.)*

Later, Volkmar Schmidt would be distressed by the thought that he may have unconsciously inspired Oswald to hunt down Walker.[49] Schmidt was probably wrong. He did not plant the idea in the future assassin. At most, he gave Oswald a push in the direction he was already taking. For one thing, Michael Paine found him "familiar with Walker…quite familiar" two days later.[50] And he had ordered his rifle on March 12th, not, as Schmidt believed, shortly after their conversation at DeMohrenschildt's party. Oswald told Marina that, two days prior to ordering the rifle, he had taken surveillance photos of Walker's home.

The Dallas media carried extensive stories about the city's most visible representative of the far right and his participation in "Operation Midnight Ride." *The Dallas Morning News*, for example, ran a front-page article about Walker and the Operation on February 14th, and there is evidence that Oswald—who liked to read newspapers and listen to broadcast news—was disturbed by Walker and his activities even then. The likelihood is that he had Walker in mind when he ordered his weapons. He told Marina that he had planned to kill him for two months.[51] Much has been written about the role of chance in Kennedy's killing, about the President becoming an unlikely target of opportunity for Oswald when he would hear, at almost the last minute, of the motorcade in Dallas that would pass the Texas School Book Depository where he worked. Actually, his activities earlier in November cast doubt on the supposition that his decision to act against Kennedy came quite so late. And the Walker attempt reveals he was determined to kill as early as April. At least as far as Oswald's ability to murder is concerned, there is no doubt that it was in place more than five months before it focused on Kennedy.

In any case, the more relevant facts about the Walker shooting concern Oswald's intent—no less murderous for the failure to kill his target, or for others to know about it. When he assumed that evening that he had successfully rid the world of Walker, Oswald was proud. The following morning, when the media indirectly informed him he had failed, he was disgusted. With his rebelliousness and withdrawal, Oswald had displayed a predilection for careful planning and organization in the service of his major designs—and never more than now. Experts concluded that a mere ten shots or so from his Mannlicher-Carcano, given his Marine experience, would be enough for him to adjust for the drift of the scope and otherwise make himself at home with that rifle. Oswald almost certainly fired at least that number. When Marina saw him carrying the hidden rifle, he assured her that the place where he practiced—presumably an uninhabited area called the Trinity River Bottom, 35 feet below a levee a short bus ride from his apartment—would not be discovered. He practiced three days in early April before burying his rifle near Walker's house, in woods near railroad tracks: the place he had picked out and photographed a month earlier.[52] This was not a spur-of-the-moment operation. Even the perceptive Volkmar Schmidt would have been surprised by the degree to which Oswald was "totally obsessed with his own political agenda."

The killer-but-for-a-window-frame had also carefully reconnoitered the

Walker house. He photographed it from the back, including an alley that led to the driveway, drew maps of the area, and compiled a collection of notes.[53] After working up his detailed plan, he executed it flawlessly—which might suggest that he would not have undertaken his more difficult shooting in Dealey Plaza, where he would be incomparably more vulnerable, without similar planning, especially for his getaway.

In this case, the escape into the residential and evening quiet was clever. Oswald told Marina he had run from Walker's house for all he was worth, hopped a bus to go back to where he had buried the rifle, then taken another bus home. He burst out laughing at a radio report of a neighbor who claimed to have seen two cars when leaving the scene just after the shooting. "Americans are so spoiled, they think you always have to have a car," he said. "I got away on my own two feet."[54]

But Oswald would lie and conceal crucial information from Marina in the coming months. Perhaps he didn't take a bus at all. Case Coleman, a 14-year-old Walker neighbor, said he saw two cars leaving immediately after the shot. At the sound of "this loud bang," young Coleman ran out of his house and, from the seat of his sister's bicycle, peered over a six-foot fence around a neighboring church. "That's when I noticed the black Ford that had been backed in [an alley] driving off down the alley. And there was a '58 Chevy with a guy [who] threw something in the back seat and then jumped in the car and headed toward Turtle Creek."[55] Coleman is supported by the recollections of Walker himself, who later stated that after the shot, he heard a car door slam followed by a car driving off.

The most important aspect of the Walker attempt is that it establishes once and for all that Oswald's "politics" did not exclude the idea of assassination. There is also the possibility, albeit small, that the attempt demonstrated Oswald's ability to conspire with others. The evening was dark. Case Coleman could not identify Oswald in any of the photographs shown him by the FBI. The cars might have been driven off by men who had attended a small church function that evening—which Oswald might have used as cover. The two cars might not deserve mention at all, except for Case's vivid memory of their connection to the shot—and the circumstances surrounding most of the critical moments in Oswald's life, from the Walker episode to shortly before his arrest after the assassination. As Robert Blakey would conclude after exhaustive study, he was "a loner who was never alone." Was this an early instance of Oswald possibly acting in concert with others?

More specifically, Oswald, despite keeping himself distant from people who might want to befriend him—perhaps that was why he kept himself distant— would be seen again and again during the coming months with drivers, escorts, and mute companions, many of them Latin. It is now impossible to identify them, and it will probably remain impossible forever. But not to acknowledge their possible existence is to portray the "lone nut" very differently than he was. Owen Dejavovich was one of the fellow Marines at Oswald's base at El Toro to whom Oswald revealed his great desire to help Fidel Castro. He is one of many former acquaintances who caught a glimpse of Oswald's secret life. Dejanovich recently stated:

Yes, at one time I recalled Oswald being a loner. But since the assassination of John F. Kennedy, other things stood out in my mind. I recall one incident where Oswald was talking through the chain-link [base] fence to two very dig-nified Hispanic-looking males who had driven up in a big, black Cadillac. To an enlisted man in the Marine Corps, they looked like quite influential people, and to see them with Oswald made a great impact on me...Looking back, I'd guess that Oswald was talking to someone from the Cuban Embassy, or some-body who'd come over from the Cuban hierarchy, about what he could do for them. [56]

This was at the same time when Oswald and Nelson Delgado, who shared radar watches and a Quonset hut, were talking about joining Castro. Oswald had also told Delgado he was visiting the Cuban Consulate in Los Angeles around this time.

Given the state of Oswald's private life, the Walker attempt does not seem at all out of context. Lee had just lost his job at the graphic arts shop Jaggers-Chiles-Stovall. A combination of reasons has been cited: he couldn't do the work; he was constantly bickering with co-workers; he didn't exactly endear himself to the management by bringing to work militant Communist literature. Co-worker Dovid Ofstein remembers, "Lee seemed to be very hell-bent, if you will, on getting through his day, getting through his job, getting on to other things. It rubbed some people the wrong way." Ofstein also recalls Oswald's lack of ability:

Lee Oswald was let go from Jaggers-Chiles-Stovall for an inability to master the techniques and the technical skills necessary to produce a quality product. Lee seemed to be very interested in learning how to do photography, commer-cial photography. [But] his skills didn't seem to go along with his eagerness. He was hired initially, as we all were, on a six month trial basis. At the end of that period, it was evident that he was turning out probably as much bad work as he was turning out good work. [57]

The Oswalds' marriage was at a low point, and becoming more violent. Lee was beating Marina regularly, and with his fists. He would at times give her black eyes, and a bloody nose. Most horrifying of all, according to Marina, was the look of pleasure in his eyes when he administered the abuse. Some neighbors were complaining. "I think he's really hurt her this time," warned one com-plainant when speaking to Mahlon Tobias, the Oswalds' apartment manager. Another neighbor told Tobias, "I think that a man over there is going to kill that girl."[58] Marina would say that February 1963 was the worst month of their mar-riage: "I'm tired of his brutality. I can't take it anymore." Once, when Marina's dress wasn't fastened properly, Lee reprimanded her in front of her friend Alex

Kleinlerer. Kleinlerer remembers:

He [Oswald] called to her in a very angry and commanding tone of voice just like an officer commanding a soldier. His exact words were "Come here!" in Russian, and he uttered them the way you would call a dog with which you were displeased in order to inflict punishment...He slapped her hard in the face twice. Marina had the baby in her arms.[59]

Marina's friends began to refer to Lee as a "megalomaniac," "unbalanced," "a psychopath." George Bouhe said, "I am scared of this man. He is a lunatic."[60] After reading an April 21 article, "Nixon calls for decision to force Reds out of Cuba," Oswald packed a pistol and threatened to use it against Nixon. Marina dissuaded him from going after the former vice-president, fearing the worst. (As it turned out, Nixon wasn't in Texas that particular day, but Lyndon Johnson was.)

Oswald's secret life continued. On April 19, 1963, the Fair Play for Cuba Committee (FPCC), a small pro-Castro organization based in New York, mailed him a stack of pamphlets. That was in response to a letter from Oswald in which he reported having recently distributed some 15 earlier leaflets in forty minutes. "I was cursed as well as praised by some," he wrote.

Oswald loved to exaggerate his significance, but this was almost certainly not an imagined boast. At about this time, two Dallas policemen reported seeing an unidentified white man of medium build passing out pro-Castro literature on a Main Street corner. He wore a placard with "Viva Fidel" over his white shirt. Local citizens complained. The man fled when the policemen arrived.[61]

Also about this time, as Oswald became more of a political activist, he forced Marina to write to the Soviet Embassy in Washington to ask that she be allowed to return to the USSR. However, the Oswalds would decide not to go back to the Soviet Union. Circumstances would bring Lee Harvey Oswald to New Orleans, to Mexico City, and back to Dallas, without ever finding a permanent home. And it all started when Marina Oswald said to her husband, "I'd like to see the city where you grew up," suggesting that Lee move to New Orleans in the spring of 1963 to look for work. With this innocuous suggestion, Marina was inadvertently placing Lee near one of the strategic pipelines of Bobby Kennedy's "secret war."

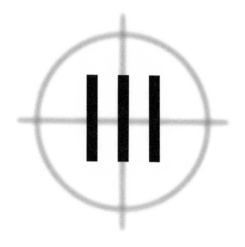

NEW ORLEANS

CHAPTER SIX

WASHINGTON, NEW ORLEANS, AND CUBA

"We call New Orleans a city of five hundred people because everybody seems to know each other."
—Stephen Tyler, Louisiana filmmaker[1]

"New Orleans is full of crazy people. I hate that place."
—Sergio Arcacha Smith, Cuban exile activist based in New Orleans in the early 1960s[2]

"Unethical behavior is a way of life in New Orleans."
—Layton Martens, a volunteer in 1961 with the Cuban exile movement[3]

When Lee Oswald moved to New Orleans in the spring of 1963, he inadvertently became enmeshed in a convoluted world of political intrigue that often led straight to John and Robert Kennedy. And this out-of-control world not only mirrored the world inside Lee Oswald's head, but later colored any study of the Kennedy assassination with a palette of conspiratorial possibilities. As Stephen Tyler says, "Everyone knew each other" in New Orleans. Everyone seemed to know a CIA agent, or a Naval Intelligence officer, or a Cuban exile training to reinvade the island.

In later years, this would play a role in accusations that many New Orleaneans who "knew" Oswald—in addition to CIA agents and Cuban exiles—had to be involved in the Kennedy assassination. Furthermore, because many of these individuals seemed to be protected from serious investigation after the President's death, the suggestion of a government-based conspiracy recurs like a leitmotif. Sadly, the one conspiratorial possibility that should have been pursued has been kept from public scrutiny since day one.

The government indeed protected certain individuals who had, or seemed to have had, access to Lee Oswald. The reason for this protection had nothing. to do with who shot the president, and everything to do with shielding the Kennedys' "secret war" from public scrutiny. The source of the problem was

Bobby Kennedy's habitual drive to go outside of the official intelligence apparatus in his zeal for quicker results. His enlistment of essentially uncontrollable agents into projects that required the strictest control and security invites the long unspoken possibility: the activities of Robert Kennedy's New Orleans agents inspired Lee Oswald, perhaps with Cuban instigation, to assassinate John Kennedy. New information reveals that this contention is, in fact, highly probable.

To make sense out of the confusion that was New Orleans, it is necessary to understand the main players, many of whom have been linked to Lee Oswald, and their agendas during the Kennedy years. But, to understand these players, one must first fathom the city in which such characters flourished. The situation that existed in New Orleans cannot appear believable to anyone not grounded in its peculiar history. Perhaps if Robert Kennedy had understood this history, he would not have depended so much on its residents for help in the Cuba Project.

"Laissez Les Bons Temps Rouler:" Politics as Jazz

From the days of Jean Laffite to today's era of the oft-indicted Governor Edwin Edward, New Orleans has nurtured a wicked reputation as floridly stylized as the wrought iron of the French Quarter. Some point to the Voodoo folkways of this humid place. It's a culture that allows for evil in the scheme of things, evil as a lesser god to be propitiated. When the air hangs like a blanket, impervious to the slack overhead fan, one can understand how sin could relax in a town like this.

God (or Satan) has given New Orleans much. The wharves teem with grain, cotton, iron and steel to be shipped to Latin countries or to the islands of the Caribbean. Cargo, meanwhile, is unladen from foreign ports to be loaded onto trucks and rail, then to be absorbed by that country called America, to which Louisiana, as if by roulette spin, has been joined.

The slave trade and cotton were the high points in New Orleans' early fortunes. The grand architecture of its early period expresses a wealth we associate with the city-states of Europe, or the Gulf states of the Arabian peninsula. The Civil War changed all that, but geography had blessed the town as a natural point of transit, and all the Yankees in New York were never able to change that.

One only requires a brief sojourn in "The City that Care Forgot" to appreciate one key fact: the Byzantine historic tangle created by a host of quirky characters is a direct result of the city itself—a city so unique that the atmosphere Lee Oswald stumbled onto in the summer of 1963 could only have existed there and then.

Louisiana had always been different—"outside the mainstream of American life," as a chronicler of Mafia activities described it[4]—and with good reason. Before its sale to the United States in 1803, it had been ruled by Spain and France. While all other major American cities had their cultural roots in the British common law/Protestant tradition, New Orleans descended from a

French/Italian/Catholic past. Everything about the city reflects that distinction: from its laws, which are based on the Napoleonic Code, to its emphasis on Catholic religious trappings.

The Napoleonic Code stresses property rights, thus giving the inhabitants an aristocratic feeling. Louisiana law is the only system of "codified" law in the United States.[5] ("Codified" refers to the fact that the laws are written by the legislature, rather than being derived by judicial precedence, as in British common law.) The result is that the inhabitants, having a hands-on, unchecked approach to lawmaking, are steeped in all the graft and corruption that can accompany such responsibility. New Orleans is a city of "political animals" second to none. It exemplifies what has become known as the "good ol' boy" system of government.[6]

In New Orleans, more so than any other U.S. city, connections mean everything. This legacy is a holdover from the time when pirates preyed on ships coming and going from the port. Successful businessmen thus fell in league with the rogues. It is illustrative that the "pirate" is revered in Louisiana, where, euphemistically, he is often referred to as "privateer." Many inhabitants developed a suspicion, disrespect, and distrust of the law and the courts. This attitude was natural considering that many Louisianans were immigrants from Sicily, a country whose population is not exactly known for respect for legal systems. When Louisiana became a state, its way-of-life remained overwhelmingly rural, relishing its reputation as a fun-loving, law-flaunting subculture within U.S. borders. "Laissez les bons temps rouler" ("Let the good times roll") is less a local slogan than a way of life.

Mardi Gras itself may best exemplify the roguish personality of the city's inhabitants. The event consists of a twelve day drunken revelry, ostensibly in celebration of religion. Although "Fat Tuesday" refers to the Catholic tradition that precedes the season of fasting known as Lent, one of the distinguishing features of the New Orleans custom is the parade of floats bearing images of pagan gods! The discrepancy between the huge numbers engaged in bacchanalia on Tuesday night and the many fewer who actually attend church the next day (Ash Wednesday) makes the point: in this city, religion is just another excuse to have a party.

Music also says much about a city's personality, and it is a musical truism that the birth of jazz could only have happened in New Orleans. Jazz was originally considered vulgar, lowdown, and sinful when it emerged in the late 19th century. The rest of the country was listening primarily to religious music, with New Orleans marching to the beat of a different drummer.

In 1963, New Orleans was a city of three-quarters of a million people, and served as the Gulf Coast's business center and transportation hub. It boasted America's second busiest port, and some of its most modern harbor facilities. It was a metropolis, famed for its French Quarter and Mardi Gras celebrations, which gives witness to its international flavor (one visitor referred to the city as a "tower of Babel"). But it remained a small town, especially in the tight overlapping of business and social connections and the near absolute need to know the right people in order to get things done.

The city's economy depended on trade with Latin America. Seventy percent of the imports unloaded on its harbor wharves originated from Central and Latin America.[7] And Cuba was the number one source of those imports. New Orleans historian Arthur Carpenter offers these supporting statistics:

> *That nation [Cuba] was one of the city's chief trading partners—typically ranking alongside Brazil as its leading source of imports...Almost all of its considerable sugar imports came from that Caribbean island: 92.8 percent in 1955... Because much of this Cuban sugar was refined locally, this trade also encouraged the city's hopes of industrializing by processing Latin American commodities.*[8]

Castro's revolution wrought major changes. And the transformation of Cuba's economy directly affected New Orleans' economy and attitudes. The conversion from laissez-faire capitalism (provided the government was handed its cut) to state socialism tightly controlled by Castro struck the city like a bomb. Rumors had the Mafia losing $70 million in shrimp boats alone when Castro took over (and much of that shrimp had previously been shipped directly to the markets of Louisiana, to eventually make its way into the dishes of such "creole" favorites as shrimp étouffée). Practically speaking, New Orleans was cut off.

The American boycott of Cuban imports formally terminated Louisiana's long relationship with Cuba, but the citizenry blamed Castro for that, and for everything else. There was a great deal at stake: not only the already-lost, sometimes highly profitable business with Cuba, but also the wider Latin American market. What would happen if communism spread to Central and South America? How great would the damage be if the Cuban model of revolution were exported to Guatemala and Brazil, two examples of then politically shaky countries of great concern at the time? How many trading partners were likely to be roped into the socialist orbit? New Orleans businessmen and city officials viewed Cuba's threat less ideologically than economically. Even more so than the rest of the country, New Orleans was in a state of financial panic over the events in Cuba.

The link between New Orleans and Cuba was not only a monetary one. There was an ideological component as well. This aspect was a function of the influx of new Cuban residents. But these two components—financial and ideological—did not always overlap.

The Americans' dislike of Castro was matched (in spades) by Cuban exiles' hatred for him. They had begun settling in New Orleans from the earliest days of Castro's victory, and now their numbers were climbing astronomically. "Many people forget that during the summer of 1961, subsequent to the Bay of Pigs fiasco, Cuban refugees were arriving in New Orleans at the rate of as many as five thousand per day," recalls Layton Martens, a young American volunteer in the Cuban cause. "This was a major crisis to the city of New Orleans," Martens says.

"People are not aware that there were as many as two hundred thousand Latin people in and around the New Orleans area. They didn't make a lot of fanfare, but they were a major segment of the metropolitan community."[9]

New Orleans was, in fact, second only to Miami as a center of Cuban exile activity. That activity, as well as the attitudes in which it was grounded, distinguished the Cubans from other immigrants. Those who had arrived earlier in the United States, as recently as World War II and the postwar period, quickly and invisibly merged into American life, often in communities of their ethnic brothers throughout the country. They embraced America as their new home. Few planned to return to their native countries. The Cuban immigrants during the Castro-era, by contrast, were closer to their native country—and they did plan to return—because they believed Castro would be overthrown, and very soon.

The exiles thus considered themselves temporary residents in America, and made few efforts to assimilate. They were always "exiles," not "refugees." Instead of joining the American mainstream, they wished a return to a "liberated" Cuba—for which their many militant organizations planned, plotted, and conducted terrorist raids, which were supported and supplied by civilian volunteers, clusters of right-wing financiers, the CIA, and the Kennedy administration. A local New Orleans writer described the Cuban community in the U.S. at that time:

> Because they expected to return to Cuba, the emigrants tended to settle within the Gulf States, especially in Miami and New Orleans. Rather than attempt assimilation into the melting pot, the more militant Cubans stuck together, maintained their political organizations, and plotted for their eventual return.[10]

Miami, where the largest CIA base in the world was located, remained the center of exile organization and operations. New Orleans was quieter. But beneath the surface, New Orleans' pre-occupation with Cuba was intense. The city may have seen wave after wave of immigrants from almost everywhere in the world, but it was now hosting and encouraging and supervising something new: a concentrated effort to return the Cuban exiles to their homeland, and the ensuing economic bounty to the United States.

For all the business community's desire to help liberate Cuba, the New Orleans locals, suffering from a depressed economy, had very little money to donate to the cause. At the government's urgings, William Dalzell, a retired CIA officer, was a founder of one of the fund-raising organizations, The Friends of Democratic Cuba (FODC). "New Orleans had long been the center of banana-republic war intrigue, and by the early 1960's the residents were tired of it," recalls Dalzell. "I was contacted by CIA officer Lloyd Ray—'Mr. Ray of the CIA'— prior to the Bay of Pigs invasion, wanting me to help the [Cuban] exiles. Thus began the Friends of Democratic Cuba. I got 2,000 empty cans to use for collecting contributions. But there was no interest. I think we made five dollars."[11]

Sergio Arcacha Smith, a Cuban exile leader and one of the intended recipients, agrees, "They [FODC] never gave me any money."[12] Julian Buznedo, who lived with the Arcacha's for a time while they helped him write a book on his Bay of Pigs experiences, remembers this period as rather stoic. "Very often," he says, "our dinners consisted of K-rations, right out of a tin can."[13] An internal CIA investigation by the Miami station later revealed that the FODC "was actually created for the personal gain of the promoters."[14]

Most of the non-governmental financial aid came from right-wing anti-communists, like the John Birch Society, and sympathetic religious groups, especially the Catholic Church. The church tried to make up for the lack of public donations in other ways: contributing clothes, medical supplies, rural property for homesteading, etc. The conservative groups tended to contribute large sums of money and weapons, used in training at the half-dozen "camps" established around the perimeter of the city, especially on Lake Ponchartrain. The Mafia also contributed weapons and money to the exile camps (expecting payback in the form of new casino licenses in liberated Havana).

As in Washington, the official policy in New Orleans was "hands-off Cuba," but the reality was far different. Virtually all of the government agencies that were represented in New Orleans were encouraging the exiles. A local magazine noted, "By closing their eyes to the activities of these anti-Castroites, the federal government was tacitly encouraging them to retake Cuba."[15]

In fact, the encouragement was far more than "tacit." Sergio Arcacha's organization, the Cuban Revolutionary Council, was cited in the records of the New Orleans Police Intelligence division as "legitimate in nature and presumably [has] the unofficial sanction of the Central Intelligence Agency." Arcacha himself proudly admits his close working relationship with the FBI's Special Agent in Charge in New Orleans, calling Warren DeBrueys "the nicest man I ever met."[16] DeBrueys would later testify that he contacted Arcacha "maybe six to ten times."[17]

Some prominent businessmen also came to the aid of the exiles. The founder of the renowned Ochsner Clinic, Dr. Alton Ochsner, for instance, had a wing of his hospital built solely to provide free medical treatment to Latin American patients. Ochsner was a prime contributor to anti-communist groups in New Orleans. Donations also derived from such high-profile right-wing contributors as oil tycoon H.L. Hunt of Texas. Thus, the exiles, backed by the government, churches, and business community, went about the business of planning the liberation of their homeland.

Friends in High Places

At the time of the Castro takeover, the mayor of New Orleans was a popular four-term incumbent, DeLessups "Chep" Morrison. Chep's reputation as a friend of the Cuban exiles, and of Latin American liberation in general, was widely known. Among his papers are Certificates of Appreciation from Sergio Arcacha Smith, leader of the local Cuban Revolutionary Council.

Mayor Morrison was also a good friend and ally of both John and Robert Kennedy. Their relationship dated back to the 1956 Democratic Convention, when Chep Morrison, then a delegate from Louisiana, introduced the young Senator from Massachusetts, a dark-horse candidate for the vice-presidential nomination, to the rest of the Louisiana delegation at a group breakfast. "My relations with the President were cordial and highly informal," Morrison has written. "He had been my guest in New Orleans several times; our paths crossed often."[18] When Kennedy became President, he appointed Morrison Ambassador to the Organization of American States, a highly important spot given the new administration's emphasis on Central and Latin America.

Morrison was closer to Robert Kennedy than John Kennedy. Among Morrison's papers at the New Orleans Public Library is correspondence between him, as Mayor, and the Attorney General; also, there are many notes of phone calls to and from Kennedy, often signed "Bob K."

When Lee Oswald arrived in New Orleans, official Washington's political interests pervaded New Orleans. Some of those interests involved secret government agendas, many of which were played out one block from where Lee Oswald would find work. The extent to which those agendas were actually the agendas of Robert Kennedy is previously unreported. The main actors in the Attorney General's mini-drama were, by tragic coincidence, part of the fabric of Oswald's neighborhood-to-be. Among them were Guy Banister, Sergio Arcacha Smith, David Ferrie, and Mike McLaney's brother, William.

Guy Banister

In 1955, Chep Morrison, the new "reform" mayor of "The Big Easy," wanted to give at least an appearance of tackling the problem of police corruption.[19] He hired Guy Banister to do the job.[20] Banister, a native of New Orleans, had just retired after a twenty year stint with the FBI, most recently as the Special Agent in Charge of the Chicago office. During World War II, he had served in the Office of Naval Intelligence. While in Chicago, he had founded the Anti-Communist League in the Caribbean (which assisted in the overthrow of the Jacabo Arbenz government in Guatemala).[21]

As Deputy Superintendent of Police (with the understanding that he would later become Superintendent), Banister was hired to investigate corruption in New Orleans, but fell from favor when his investigation came too close to some of Mayor Morrison's appointees.[22] Banister was suspended and soon fired, but remained on good terms with Morrison and with his successor, Mayor Schiro. They both would know and approve of his actions on behalf of the Cuban exiles (as well as those of Morrison's friend, Robert F. Kennedy).[23] Soon after Castro's declaration that his revolution was Marxist, Banister became one of the central figures in the New Orleans "underground" determined to topple him.

After his firing, the ex-ONI, ex-FBI stalwart founded "Guy Banister and Associates," a private detective agency. He was not much interested in acquiring private clients because he was kept busy, and presumably rewarded, by activities in aid of government agencies and government-sponsored endeavors. If he had sought clients, his looks would have been a considerable asset. He could have played a forbidding and sometimes remorseless—but essentially principled—football coach in a 1940's movie. Despite the edge of ruthlessness in his eyes, he could also have played the president of a university or the Director of the FBI, a distinctly handsomer one than the bulldog-like Hoover. Tall and relatively trim, Banister dressed for business in dark suits only, and always carried two guns, one a long-barreled .44. He was rarely seen without a jacket and tie, rarely called anything less formal than "Mr. Banister."

Banister was the picture of an extreme right-winger, a fervent segregationist, and an anti-communist who saw enemies under every bed. He was a member of the White Citizens Council that would contribute so much hate-filled opposition to the civil rights movement in the 1950's and 1960's.[24] Banister also worked for the Louisiana State Committee on Un-American Activities, while Guy Banister and Associates published a thin report called the "Louisiana Intelligence Digest." The first offering, in February, 1961, defined itself as "a militantly conservative publication...devoted to the exposure of the operations of the Socialist and Communist organizations in Louisiana, and the dupes, fellow-travelers, and do-gooders who give them aid and comfort."[25]

It is a fact that Banister disliked President Kennedy's politics—just as he hated the decisions of Chief Justice Earl Warren, another favorite target of abuse from the far right. Like many who occupied a position near the political fringe, Banister would have been happy for Kennedy to be out of office. But there is no credible evidence whatever—and none is likely ever to appear—that his dislike would express itself in the violence of November 22nd. When Banister's research assistant heard the news on the radio that day, she told him she was glad the President had been shot. "Don't let anybody hear you talk like that," he replied. "It's a terrible thing that someone could shoot the President." Banister was shocked. He closed his office early and kept it closed for several days, out of respect. "He didn't like the President, but he was a loyal FBI man," the research assistant would remember.[26]

But Banister's covert activities would play into the hands of conspiracy-minded writers. It is now known that his company was engaged in what would today be called "dirty tricks." These tricks would have scandalized at least part of the public: they were for the benefit, and under the supervision, of people high in the government who had the power to prevent a proper investigation. When many of Banister's most sensitive files were never found, some assumed that they contained information on Oswald and the Kennedy assassination, when in fact the missing material dealt only with sensitive local scandals.

In the years before John Kennedy's death, Banister was a key player in preparing the local Cuban exile contingent for the Bay of Pigs invasion, especially the *Santa Ana*, piloted by Nino Diaz. It is also known and documented that his office, and the building in which that office was located (the Newman Building) later became a "Grand Central Station" for the Cubans, through which arms were funneled to various Latin American concerns as well as Cuban exile groups. Banister's office was in the same building as Arcacha's CRC office, and it is known that he saw David Ferrie, Arcacha's assistant, with some regularity.

Banister never discussed any connection with Arcacha, but FBI files indicate that Banister was performing at least one critical function for Arcacha's group. Arcacha told the local papers that many New Orleans Cubans were recruited for the Bay of Pigs invasion force from local universities.[27] A future Congressional investigation would conclude:

> [Banister] ran background checks on those Cuban students at Louisiana State University who wished to be members of Arcacha's anti Castro group, ferreting out any pro-Castro sympathizers who may be among them.[28]

Today Arcacha denies Banister ever did this for his organization. Arcacha, however, had a more powerful ally in his corner: the Attorney General of the United States, Robert F. Kennedy.

Sergio Arcacha Smith

"Whenever we needed anything in New Orleans, I'd call Bobby Kennedy and he'd help us right away. He was always there for us. I stayed in touch with him until the end."
        —Sergio Arcacha Smith, May 14, 1994[29]

In pre-Castro Havana, President Batista appointed Sergio Arcacha Smith Cuba's ambassador to India. Arcacha had actually attended high school with controversial young Fidel Castro, whom he disliked. However, he held President Kennedy and his brother Bobby in high esteem. "Kennedy lacked experience, but he had charisma," Arcacha offers. "The proof of his charisma is that when he died, people in every country cried."

After the revolution, Arcacha went to Venezuela. "The original idea was to set up the Frente [Frente Revolucionario Democratico (FRD)] there. However, the Frente was formed in Mexico," Arcacha recalls. After a brief stopover in Miami, the Frente leadership sent him to New Orleans to oversee that city's outpost, an umbrella organization known as the Cuban Revolutionary Council (CRC).

Shortly before the April 17, 1961 Bay of Pigs invasion, the United States, attempting to coordinate the various exile groups, formed the CRC. It was an activist organization whose stated purpose was "to establish a democratic government in Cuba through the use of military force."[30] According to the CIA, which helped form the alliance, the CRC was "created...to coordinate and direct FRD activity... [It] had direct access to President Kennedy and top White House aides...Arcacha Smith became the [CRC] delegate in New Orleans."[31] On the CRC's board of directors sat such Bobby Kennedy exile intimates as Manuel Ray and Manuel Artime. This was not by accident. Prior to the Bay of Pigs invasion, the White House had called upon the Council to monitor pro-Castro activists who threatened to kidnap JFK's children. When the CRC opened its branch in New Orleans, it tapped Arcacha to be its delegate.

Arcacha is protective of his friends, and it is only now, three decades after the fact, that he made himself available for the first time to talk about certain aspects of his time in New Orleans. To newsmen in the 1960's, Arcacha used to claim he received funds from the State Department and say he was under the Department's thumb. That was in public; in private, he called it the CIA.[32] He even occasionally admitted he was working for the CIA.[33]

Arcacha's most important superior was Robert Kennedy. Arcacha is discreet when asked about Bobby Kennedy directly, saying only, "In 1961, I started working with the U.S. government." He would first acknowledge their relationship (off the record) to Dick Billings, former editor of *Life*, in April 1967. This magazine had long involved itself in anti-Castro operations. "Off the record," Arcacha insisted, "because I do not want to involve Mr. Kennedy and do not think it would be right, we used to call Mr. Bobby Kennedy whenever we had anything to report or ask advice. He knew what we were doing all the time. But please don't use this, as it's off the record. That's the way it was. We would call Mr. Bobby Kennedy and he would take care of it."[34]

How Arcacha became acquainted with the Attorney General is something that he is not yet ready to discuss, but one thing is certain: he was close to Bobby Kennedy, and their bond would strengthen as the years progressed.[35]

Whatever his relationship with RFK, it is well-known in the exile community that Arcacha was heavily involved in smuggling exiles out of Cuba. Public relations executive Ronnie Caire helped Arcacha to begin fund-raising, to set up bank accounts, etc. He testified that Arcacha attempted to purchase PT-boats for the Cuban invasion. In addition, Caire said, the *New York Times* reported one week before the invasion that Arcacha's New Orleans branch of the CRC coordinated the exile training camps around New Orleans.[36] Arcacha also smuggled spies into the Cuban underground, facilitated by his experience and contacts in Batista's secret police prior to the Castro takeover.[37]

As to his own role, Arcacha implied that the Cubans he was recruiting were to become part of the landing force, Brigade 2506.[38] Recently, Arcacha admitted that he also assisted the ill-fated Bay of Pigs mission of Nino Diaz, and coordinated shipments of supplies to the training camps in Latin America.

Arcacha still considers the details of his relationship with the Kennedys during this time as the equal of state secrets. However, some details have been recently revealed. "Whenever we needed a plane, for example to send arms to the camps in Nicaragua, I'd call Bobby. The next day it would be there," recalls Arcacha.[39] Robert Kennedy had vested interests in Latin American Cuban exile training camps *(about which much more will be seen)* and was giving Arcacha an open channel.

Regretfully, Arcacha says, his travails in New Orleans were in vain, as "Castro knew everything we were doing. He had people everywhere."[40] This observation was echoed by, among others, the CIA's Mexico City Station Chief, Win Scott, who said, "We're completely infiltrated by Castro's agents. All they have to do is get into Mexico and walk across the border."[41]

In truth, Castro didn't need "people everywhere," because the Cuban exiles were notorious for being their own worst enemies. Justin Gleichauf, the former chief of the CIA's Miami office, has put it this way, "To a Cuban, a secret is something you tell only one hundred people." Another CIA Cuba Project officer told author David Corn that, "A Cuban is someone who can't keep his mouth shut."[42] Arcacha himself admits, "Cubans talk too much."

CIA executive assistant Lyman Kirkpatrick wrote of this less-than-secretive atmosphere:

> *I heard one newspaper correspondent claim that he could spend a day in Miami visiting the gathering places of exiles and end up knowing everything that was being planned against Cuba....The loose talk was most unfortunate for those free-lance exiles who were running their own operations against Cuba, often using unsavory boats and whatever arms they could beg, borrow or steal. Many of these died needless deaths as their plans quickly reached the ears of Castro's agents in the United States, who then sent advance warning to the island.*[43]

According to some, Arcacha also was instrumental in arms procurement for the many raids on Cuba that were, after the Bay of Pigs, to become part of 1962's Operation Mongoose. But often, his proximity to the administration's plans (and his "Cuban big mouth") would cause trouble. Three months before the Bay of Pigs invasion, he was quoted in the local newspaper as predicting, "Cubans will launch an invasion in 1961 to overthrow the regime of Fidel Castro. The actual invasion will not be launched from U.S. territory."[44] One week before the invasion, Arcacha again spoke with the paper, saying, "Preparations are almost complete for an anti-Castro Cuban invasion...The invasion could begin this afternoon, tomorrow, anytime. We are just waiting for the signal."[45]

After the Bay of Pigs raid was launched, Arcacha told the paper of how he had waited by his short-wave radio for the coded signal: "Look to the rainbow. The sky is clear. The fish are ready." According to Arcacha, each sentence had its own important meaning.[46]

Not long after moving into his Camp Street office in New Orleans, Arcacha started to build a network with local activists, many of them connected to the detective agency housed around the corner, Guy Banister and Associates. They had bold ideas about liberating Cuba. Through Banister's FBI friends, channels were in place in the bureau. What Arcacha brought was the imprimatur of Robert Kennedy.

Arcacha adds to the narrative:

> *I rented office space at 544 Camp Street. My office was on the second floor above the restaurant [Mancuso's], and Banister's was downstairs and around the corner. I only met Banister three or four times. He was more interested in*

Central America than Cuba. Any contact with his office was through Dave Ferrie, whom I saw regularly.[47]

David William Ferrie

"If Oswald is an enigmatic character, and he is, David Ferrie is his soulmate."
   —G. Robert Blakey, HSCA Chief Counsel

"David was a wonderful man, who truly wanted to help our cause. He was a gentleman. He loved to play with my children. He was a good Catholic who only wanted to help."
   —Sergio Arcacha Smith, New Orleans exile leader

David Ferrie has long been portrayed on paper and in film as an American grotesque: a raving hater of President Kennedy, who threatened to kill the President. He was said to be angry at JFK for failing to help the Cuban exiles restore liberty to their land. It seems certain he made a celebrated statement after the Bay of Pigs fiasco on which much of the portrait has been based. That incident occurred in July 1961, when Ferrie was addressing the New Orleans chapter of the Order of World Wars. Ferrie became so critical of Kennedy's handling of the Bay of Pigs invasion that he was asked to discontinue his remarks.[48] But that was almost certainly taken out of context and misinterpreted.

A devout Catholic (who was, for a time, a seminarian), Ferrie voted for Kennedy in 1960 and was "elated" when he defeated Richard Nixon for the presidency that year. "Things are going to turn for the better now that a Catholic has been elected," a good friend would remember Ferrie saying.[49] Another friend elaborated, "After all, he was an Irish Catholic too. He was an enthusiastic supporter. Dave was a spokesman for the Kennedys. To him, the idea of a Catholic president was mind-boggling. He thought Kennedy was fabulous."[50]

Ferrie and the Cuban Exiles

"Dave was a man who honestly thought he could make a difference. Remember when Bing Crosby played a priest in the movies? That was Dave Ferrie."
   —Al Beauboeuf, a friend and student of Ferrie in the Civil Air Patrol (CAP)[51]

"Dave saw himself as a healer, a soother—truly trying to help out. He was anything but a killer of presidents. He has been taking the rap for Robert Kennedy, who was behind it all [the exile movement]."
   —Morris Brownlee, Ferrie's godson[52]

For a time, Ferrie worked as an investigator for the local detective, Guy Banister. Uniting the two was their virulent anti-communism, focused especially on Cuba. Ferrie's rage intensified because he personally supported Castro before "the bearded one" declared his attachment to Marxism.

"Dave got involved with the Cuban exiles through his work with the

Catholic Charities in early 1961," recalls Ferrie's godson, Morris Brownlee.[53] Brownlee's statements are credible given Ferrie's devout religious background. Through Ferrie's connections with the Catholic Church, he was able to help secure property on nearby Lake Ponchartrain. The property was owned by a local seminary, and used initially by the exiled homesteaders, but it later evolved into a full-scale military training base for Cuban exiles.

Ferrie used the power of his personality to encourage young Civil Air Patrol (CAP) cadets (whom Ferrie was instructing) to enlist in the cause. One such recruit was Layton Martens, who recently recalled, "One of the camps was on the property of a seminary. Just outside the seminary was a landing field. Dave used certain channels of the church, with which he was familiar."[54] Anti-Castro activist Gerry Hemming was one of the key organizers of early training activity on Lake Ponchartrain. Not only does Hemming readily admit to this, but he is backed up by recently-released CIA documents. "The Lake Ponchartrain activity was run by Gerald Patrick Hemming" was the wording of a February 1, 1977 CIA Memo.

Hemming told the author that his activities were sanctioned by Bobby Kennedy, via Miami-based exile leader Manolo Reboso. When Hemming flew over Covington, Louisiana (on Lake Ponchartrain's north shore) in the summer of 1962 looking for sites for training camps, Ferrie met him. "One of Ferrie's seminary friends, a bishop, had okayed the use of his seminary property for training," says Hemming. The idea for using the site as such was abandoned when the secret project was exposed in a local newspaper story.[55]

As Ferrie's involvement in the exiles' plight deepened, he teamed up with Guy Banister, who, as has been noted, helped the Cuban exiles prepare for the Bay of Pigs invasion. Thus, it was not surprising that Ferrie would soon come into contact with the local Cuban exile leader, Sergio Arcacha Smith, whose spare Cuban Revolutionary Council office was on the other side of the same building that housed Banister's office.

Arcacha remembers, "[Ferrie] had just shown up at my door one day offering to help."[56] Recalling Ferrie's bravery, Arcacha says, "He wanted to fly into Havana harbor and bomb the refineries. Ferrie had an idea to make two-man submarines, go in, and just blow [the refineries] up. We actually made two of them, but we were prevented from using them."[57] Layton Martens, who came with Ferrie to Arcacha's volunteer effort, also remembers the submarines. "Dave made them out of B-47 wing tanks," he recalls. "He kept one on his front lawn for a long time."[58]

Arcacha's relationship with Ferrie became very close. He grew to depend on Ferrie's help in the exile cause. On July 18, 1961, Arcacha wrote to Eastern Airlines Chairman Eddie Rickenbacker, asking that Ferrie be given a 90 day-leave with pay so that he could help with the Cuban problem—and help reinvigorate the Cuban underground in New Orleans. Arcacha's letter read, in part:

> [After the Bay of Pigs], the [morale] of the Cubans in exile and the underground within Cuba fell to zero. Then along came Captain Ferrie. He strongly

*prodded our whole organization until it was revitalized. Fund collecting
began. The underground was re-organized and the re-harassment of Castro
has begun. The reinvigorating of our program was the result of Captain Ferrie
and his associates here in New Orleans. Through him, we've been able to get
the best advice in affairs political, economic, and military. In addition,
Captain Ferrie has been assisting in obtaining needed equipment.[59]*

It is evident that David Ferrie brought to Arcacha's cause amazing charisma
and leadership abilities.[60] It was about this time that talk started to proliferate
about Ferrie's relationship with the federal government. "I remember I was discussing career plans with Dave," recalls Morris Brownlee, "and he suggested I
think about the CIA, who he said he had a long relationship with."[61] Ferrie's role
with the government was also assumed by his young CAP cadets whom he persuaded to volunteer in the Cuban relief programs. One of these volunteers,
Layton Martens, would become an assistant in Arcacha's office. Like Arcacha,
Martens is clear about who was giving support to the project run out of 544
Camp street. But Martens didn't just suspect a relationship—he knew of it:

*Ferrie at that time was essentially working for the Attorney General of the
United States. He was doing fund raising for the refugee assimilation here in
New Orleans. We did this under both Mayors of New Orleans—Schiro and
Morrison—and then subsequently directly for the Attorney General under the
aegis of President Kennedy.[62]*

Ferrie appeared proud of his new status, and made no secret of it. On one
occasion, Ferrie and Arcacha approached their friend, loan officer Herbert
Wagner. They told him they wanted to take out a loan to finance their exile
activities. Ferrie asked Wagner if he had ever heard of Operation "Mosquito" (he
probably meant Mongoose). Wagner said he had not, whereupon Ferrie told
him it was part of a sabotage operation against Castro. Wagner wanted no part
of it, telling Ferrie he was crazy—the government had radar everywhere. At that,
Ferrie replied, "The government knows what we're doing! As a matter of fact,
they're backing us."[63]

When Ferrie appealed his suspension as an Eastern Airlines pilot, he again
played the Kennedy card, writing the airline, "I have likewise been involved in
activities approved and encouraged by the President and the Attorney General—
helping to raise arms for the liberation of Cuba."[64]

Ferrie's godson Morris Brownlee elaborates upon the Ferrie/RFK connection:
"Dave was put in touch with the Justice Department, who gave him authorization to help mobilize the Cuban community in New Orleans."[65]

Ferrie seems to have interpreted this Justice Department link as a mandate
to step up his activities on behalf of the exiles. That would be understandable,
if the allegations of Layton Martens and others are accurate.

Layton Martens' Excellent Adventure

As a seventeen year-old CAP cadet, Layton Martens was one of those who answered Dave Ferrie's call to assist in the exile cause. By doing so, Martens put himself into an atmosphere of political activism, a vantage point from which he would observe some of the Kennedy administration's secrets first-hand. For over thirty years, he, like Arcacha, has absorbed the slings and arrows of those who have accused him of protecting fellow "conspirator" Dave Ferrie. Frightened by the excesses of the 1967 Garrison "probe," as indeed many New Orleaneans were, he has remained silent about what he witnessed in Arcacha's office. It is only now that he feels ready to reveal what actually occurred.

Martens spent the summer of 1961 in the service of Arcacha's Cuban Revolutionary Council, which, in the fall of 1961, would relocate to 544 Camp Street. His observations go a long way towards explaining what some have referred to as "the mystery of 544 Camp Street." Those same observations make understandable how the tragedy of Dallas must have been compounded for Bobby Kennedy when it was revealed that Oswald had stamped the infamous Camp Street address on his leaflets.

One of Martens' first assignments was soliciting contributions from local New Orleans businessmen. Although Martens and his associates had identification cards given them by Mayor Schiro, they still met resistance, with the potential contributors questioning the legality of Arcacha's operation. " I went to [FBI agent] Warren DeBrueys, our government liaison, " says Martens. DeBrueys had no answer for Martens, but promised to "kick it upstairs" to the Attorney General, Bobby Kennedy. At the CRC office a few days later, Arcacha and Ferrie told Martens that they had been in contact with Bobby and that he suggested obtaining an opinion from the local U.S. Attorney.

"So I went over to see the [U.S.] Attorney, but he said he wanted no part of it," Martens remembers. "A couple of days later, I saw Arcacha. He was smiling as he told me, 'In two weeks there will be a new U.S. Attorney, and he will tell you the law.'"[66] Martens then learned from a laughing Ferrie that the original U.S. Attorney was transferred to Bismarck, North Dakota. His replacement, when approached about the legality of the fundraising effort, responded to Martens, "It's OK."

"The next thing I know, I got a letter, I suppose because of DeBrueys, from Bobby Kennedy," remembers Martens. "It was typed on official Justice Department stationery."

The letter was brief, and Martens says he remembers it almost word for word. It read:

To Whom it May Concern,

> *These persons are acting legitimately on behalf of the United States government. Please extend to them any courtesy that you can in good faith.*

Thank You,
Robert F. Kennedy

Martens' boss, Arcacha, in a conversation with the author, recently admitted to being aware of the Robert Kennedy letter, although, typically for Arcacha, declined to discuss it in any detail. After using the letter throughout the summer to solicit contributions, Martens says, "My copy was eventually stolen from my briefcase when I left it at Ferrie's apartment."[67] Martens believes that, in fact, Ferrie took the letter, feeling Martens should not have any reason to keep this kind of material because, at the time, he was leaving the CRC and returning to school.

Collecting donations was only a small part of the CRC's role in New Orleans. The office at 544 Camp Street became a center not only for arms procurement for Bobby Kennedy's sabotage program, but for intelligence gathering from what remained of the Cuban underground back on the island. As one of the Camp Street volunteers told the author, "This office became a White House priority because of the information we were getting. We had the FBI at our disposal." This intelligence included information so sensitive that Arcacha and his associates were allowed to continue their pre-Bay of Pigs direct line to both the White House and Robert Kennedy. The White House wanted to know about missiles.

Missiles in Cuba

It has long been acknowledged that the earliest reports of Soviet missiles appearing in Cuba originated with Cuban exiles and their sources on the island. The reports predictably made their way to the exiles' CIA case officers in Miami and New Orleans. At the time, Miami-based CIA agent Ross Crozier was the liaison with the Miami headquarters of Carlos Bringuier's Cuban Student Directorate, or Directorio Revolucionario Estudiantil (DRE). Crozier says that the DRE "was the first to report the missiles in Cuba and have that information ignored. I was passing that information along, but it was like pouring water down a rat hole."[68] The CIA's Chief of the Miami JM/WAVE station, Ted Shackley, had also been told of the missiles by his Cuban sources. Shackley acknowledged as much when he later testified before Congress. Congressional investigator Gaeton Fonzi has written:

> His station knew, Shackley said, that there were missiles in Cuba long before the policymakers would accept that reality. He said Kennedy announced that fact only after receiving a U-2 aerial photograph of the missiles. An edge of cynicism in his tone, Shackley said if he had known what Kennedy meant by "hard intelligence" he would have gotten him a U-2 photograph much earlier.[69]

Layton Martens claims that the CRC office in New Orleans, as early as 1961, began receiving reports of small missiles, on portable launchers, arriving in Cuba. Both the Soviets and American governments agree that the first ICBM (inter-continental ballistic missiles) shipments of what the Russians called Operation Anadyr arrived on the island in mid-July, 1962.[70] Nonetheless, there are many who corroborate Martens' claim that smaller tactical weapons appeared much earlier.

Martens remembers the night Ferrie burst into Arcacha's office screaming, "They've got missiles! They've got missiles!" It was the summer of 1961, and "they" were Castro's Cubans. Arcacha's Cuban underground had reported that at least 10 portable tactical weapons, which they believed to be nuclear, had been observed on the island and were deployed along the perimeter of Mariel Harbor, where they had arrived. Morris Brownlee, Ferrie's godson, recalls, "Dave had early knowledge of the missiles in Cuba from his Cuban contacts. He had a map of the sites. I saw it. He sent this information to the Justice Department."[71]

Ronnie Caire, who worked with Arcacha and Ferrie, said in December 1961, "Cuba has missiles. And these missiles are twenty minutes away from New Orleans."[72] Joe Newbrough, a Ferrie friend and an investigator for Guy Banister, told the author, "I remember laying in bed, watching the crisis unfold on television [in October, 1962]. When Kennedy showed the U-2 reconnaissance photos of the missiles, I jumped out of bed and yelled to my wife, 'These are the same photos I've had for months!' I may have gotten it from Ferrie. He had a whole set of them."[73] According to Luis Rabel Nunes, Arcacha's successor at the CRC, "We heard about the missiles much before the crisis."[74] David Atlee Phillips, the CIA's Director of Covert Operations in Mexico City who oversaw Cuban operations, wrote in his autobiography, *The Night Watch*:

> The early fragmentary reports that Fidel Castro had agreed to Soviet missiles being installed secretly in Cuba began to arrive in Washington in late 1961. The very first, I believe, came across my desk before I left Washington for Mexico...[CIA Director] John McCone went to see President Kennedy in August of 1962 and told the President it was his belief that the Soviets were in the process of establishing missile bases in Cuba. He admitted that his estimate was not supported by hard intelligence. Nonetheless, he persisted.[75]

Ed Dolan worked at CIA headquarters throughout the Kennedy administration, in charge of disseminating Cuban photo analyses. "There certainly were SA-2 SAMs (surface-to-air missiles) in Cuba in early 1962," Dolan recently stated.[76] While these were clearly not nuclear weapons, they were nonetheless of strategic interest to U.S. policy planners. (Martens and others in the exile movement are adamant, however, that Cuba possessed tactical, or battlefield, portable nuclear weapons as early as 1961.)

Members of Castro's own government have also reported that small portable missiles were believed to be on the island in 1961. Rafael Nuñez, who served from 1960 to 1976 as one of Castro's diplomatic attachés, told the author, "In 1961, we often heard that missiles on trucks were moving around the island. I agree with the exiles about that fact."[77]

Layton Martens remembers how the information was handled in New Orleans:

> We reported what we heard to [FBI agents] Regis Kennedy and Warren DeBrueys. They set us up with a direct link to the White House and Bobby

Kennedy. I was given Geodetic survey maps of Cuba, and we were told to have the Cuban informants mark where the missiles were located, which we did. There were ten sites that I remember.

The White House wanted us to continue to explore this information, and by all means keep it coming. We were getting something he was not getting from the CIA. So the President, through his brother Bobby Kennedy, asked us to communicate with the FBI. The two agents assigned to me were Warren DeBrueys and Ernest Wall.[78]

All the fragmentary information of early missile reports leaves many nagging questions: Did the administration feel that the best way to confront the problem was to take Castro out quietly, avoiding a nuclear confrontation? Could the exile underground have observed not only non-nuclear surface-to-air missiles (SAMs), but portable nuclear weapons, as Layton Marten believes? If Kennedy did have early knowledge of the missiles, it could answer the questions posed by former CIA Cuba Project officers, who were perplexed by Kennedy's obsession to "go after the little guy [Fidel]."

As with President Kennedy's Vietnam policy, it is possible that the President ignored this problem, hoping it would go away. Kennedy biographers have written that the President wanted to avoid confrontation at all costs, and his administration suffered because of it.[79] Could this have been the case with the Cuban missiles? Some believe that Kennedy's lack of action on the early missile reports led to the Soviets' decision to up the ante with ICBM's in 1962. This embarrassment, some contend, explains a cryptic memo from Nixon aide Charles Colson to chief-of-staff H.R. (Bob) Haldeman, concerning a statement by the CIA agent who acted as liaison with the exiles, E. Howard Hunt. Colson wrote: "[Hunt] told me a long time ago that if the truth were ever known, Kennedy would be destroyed."[80]

The questions surrounding the missile reports may never be adequately answered, but the important point is that Layton Martens' allegations of a New Orleans Cuban exile pipeline to Washington certainly carry more credibility than might appear at first glance.[81] The fact remains that, in addition to their support for the Bay of Pigs operation, the exiles and their intelligence network on the island would clearly be of interest to the Kennedy White House.

The missile disclosure was but one phase of Martens' volunteer summer in the offices of the Cuban Revolutionary Council. On the heels of the missile episode, Dave Ferrie would ask Martens to participate in an arms transfer. This was to be carried out, according to the CRC volunteers, with the approval of Robert Kennedy.

The Houma Weapons Transfer

According to the CIA's own documents and its own admissions, one of the firms that co-operated with the CIA in its preparations to wage secret war against

Castro's recently-declared Marxist government was Schlumberger Wells Services Company. In fact, a 1967 CIA memo released in 1992 confirms that its Domestic Contact Service (DCS) "has discreet and continuing contact with the main Schlumberger office in Houston and branch offices in Minneapolis and elsewhere."[82]

Located in the little town of Houma, deep in the Mississippi River delta, and 50 miles southwest of New Orleans, Schlumberger served as a small arms depot for the CIA. It permitted a bunker it leased for storing blasting supplies to be used as a cache for ammunition, bomb casings and other military items, some of which were shipped abroad—presumably to CIA staging areas in Guatemala or areas elsewhere within striking distance of Cuba. The arms were shipped in crates bearing the markings "Schlumberger" and "machinery." Other weapons were earmarked for rebels in the French West Indies, but were never shipped. Some of the weaponry was to have been used in the Bay of Pigs invasion. The government's fumbling of the invasion upset the firm, which subsequently decided to terminate its contract with the CIA.[83]

According to Guy Banister's attorney, Guy Johnson, Banister learned that some of the munitions remained at the Houma depot after the invasion. He thought that they should be put to use in the post Bay of Pigs anti-Castro effort. Ever the straight-laced FBI man, Banister wanted to finesse the issue legally.

"Banister went to Washington, and saw a high official in the Justice Department," says Johnson. "Presumably it was RFK."[84] At this time, FBI agent Regis Kennedy—who had no blood relationship to the Kennedys in Washington—made one of his regular appearances in Banister's office.[85] According to Banister associate Jack Martin, "It was about this time that the 'letters of marque' and keys showed up."

A "Letter-Marque" is a legal device, generated by a high federal authority, that hasn't been employed since the time of Thomas Jefferson. Its purpose is to give legal license to someone who is about to commit a quasi-legal action. More importantly, it prevents prosecution should the person be apprehended by local authorities. Jack Martin recalled some of the wording of the alleged letter: "You are hereby directed to seize munitions or arms, the property of a foreign government, that are illegally located within the United States, using any and all means to do so."[86]

The Letter-Marque was on Justice Department stationery, signed by Robert Kennedy. It was allegedly observed by Jack Martin, Gordon Novel (who says he was involved in the Houma transfer), Guy Johnson, and Banister friend Kent Courtney. Banister and the local anti-Castro activists were thus given the go-ahead to "liberate" the weaponry.

When the weapons transfer was carried out that summer, it became clear that the CIA and the FBI were heavily involved. The transfer didn't happen overnight; in fact, military supplies were confiscated over a period of three months. In preparation for the transfer, says Jack Martin, Guy Banister (his boss) telephoned M. E. Loy, manager of Schlumberger Well Services Company. The point of the call was to make sure that the FBI or CIA would supply keys to the bunker where the weapons were stored. On another, earlier trip, the work party came armed with a pair of wire cutters in place of the promised keys, which had not been delivered.

"It was a CIA operation," says Arcacha's attorney, Frank Hernandez. "It was set up so that Schlumberger could report it [the weapons transfer] as a robbery, and be reimbursed by their insurance company. They went in at midnight and the material was waiting for them on a loading dock. We later verified that the CIA indeed reimbursed the insurance company."[87]

Layton Martens, participating in the transfer, remembers one of the trips to the bunker. For this excursion, keys to the depot were in hand and the munitions were delivered to the office of Guy Banister and Associates. "It seemed like there was a whole caravan there, led by Dave Ferrie," says Martens. The young participant "didn't know what the hell was going on," except for having heard that the transfers were conducted by order of David Ferrie, who participated, and, by inference, under orders of Sergio Arcacha Smith.[88]

Arcacha's attorney, Frank Hernandez, has long believed that Arcacha participated personally in the weapons transfer, but Arcacha denies this. Martens supports Arcacha's denial, saying, "I don't remember Sergio there." However, Arcacha did tell Ronnie Caire that on one occasion, Arcacha drove a truck-load of "plastic explosives" from Houma, Louisiana to New Orleans because no one else wanted to drive the truck.[89] Arcacha's good friend Carlos Quiroga also stated that he participated in the transfer with Banister, Ferrie, Arcacha, and a U.S. Marine named Andrew Blackmon.[90] He put the explosives in a U-Haul trailer to be sent to Miami, Quiroga says, but it stayed in New Orleans for a long time.[91]

One of the accomplices in the transfer—unwitting, he insists—was Luis Rabel Nunes, who replaced Sergio Arcacha Smith as New Orleans head of the CRC in 1962. Rabel supplied a laundry truck with which the weapons were transported—but he, like DeLaBarre, didn't quite know what was up. "I had a laundry truck I used to loan out to help re-settle Cuban refugees—just for humanitarian reasons," Rabel recalled recently. "The Catholic Church asked us to help out. We also helped the refugees find jobs. In that effort, we had the backing of both Mayors—Mayor Morrison and Mayor Schiro—Dr. Ochsner, and FBI agent Warren De Brueys. It wasn't until years later that I learned they had sometimes used the truck to transfer weapons."[92] Rabel gave a bit more information in Congressional testimony: "As far as I knew, they took them [the crates of munitions] to Lake Ponchartrain."[93] It will be seen that Lake Ponchartrain played host to exile training camps which operated in concert with a White House-backed anti-Castro invasion force training in Central America.

Guy Banister's office was the destination of many of the Schlumberger munitions. In fact, Guy Banister and Associates (the Cuban exile "Grand Central Station") often resembled a small freight depot for weaponry destined for use in the exile cause. Among the most enduring images of Banister's office—at least according to those who had access to it—was of crates of munitions, including grenades, land mines, and firearms, as well as of Banister's nonchalance about their presence there.

Delphine Roberts, Banister's research assistant, remembers a hidden panel in the ladies room where some of the armaments were stored.[94] The weapons were of such prodigious quantity that they spilled out into the rest of the office. And this would continue in spite of the Kennedy administration's promise, as part of the settlement of the Cuban Missile Crisis, to stop the sabotage raids on Cuba launched from the United States. Mary Brengel, Banister's secretary, would remember "rifles stacked all around his office up until the day of the assassination." Brengel added:

> There were 10 or 12 of them around, and groups of four or five men at a time would come in and speak in hushed tones. And they would pick up the rifles and heft them and sight them. Even if I were at my desk, I'd hear the jingling and jangling and I'd know what they were doing.[95]

A local newspaper, citing a reliable source, claimed that there were 50 to 100 crates of ammunition in Banister's office at about this time, all labeled "Schlumberger." The paper went on to say:

> Five or six boxes were open. Inside…were rifle grenades, land mines and some little missiles of a kind he [the source] had never seen before. The friend said he remonstrated with Banister because "fooling with this kind of stuff could get you in trouble." He added: "Banister said no, it was alright, that he had approval from somebody. He said the stuff would just be there overnight, that somebody was supposed to pick it up. He said a bunch of fellows connected with the Cuban deal asked to leave it there overnight."[96]

FBI documents would show that some of the material also ended up in Ferrie's apartment, where it was observed by a number of his CAP cadets.[97] It is not documented where all this material ended up, although most believe it was funneled by the Banister organization to various Latin American anti-communists, with some of it going to the Cuban exiles.[98]

By the end of 1962, the Cuban exiles were well-entrenched in New Orleans and seemingly encouraged by official Washington. New Orleans was the Cuban exiles' epicenter for weapons, their training ground for military leaders, and a likely launch point for another invasion. To stir the mix of a national nightmare, all that was needed was for a motivated, unhinged, pro-Castro activist to arrive.

CHAPTER SEVEN

THE KENNEDYS AND
THE COMMUNISTS, 1963

Immediately after learning definitively of the Soviet missile presence in Cuba, JFK snapped, "[Castro] can't do that to me!"[1]

But one month later, at a November 20, 1962 press conference, Kennedy pledged, "For our part, if all offensive weapons are removed from Cuba and kept out of the hemisphere in the future...and if Cuba is not used for the export of aggressive Communist purposes, there will be peace in the Caribbean."

With the missile crisis seemingly resolved through the president's expansive pledges, the fortunes of the Cuban exiles waned dramatically. First, they had been stung by Kennedy's "betrayal" at the Bay of Pigs. Then, Project Mongoose was dismantled. Now, President Kennedy was telling the world that Castro might remain in power in Cuba after all. Some exiles, like imprisoned Brigade Commander Pepe San Román, were beyond embitterment. "I hated the United States," he said, "and I felt I had been betrayed. Every day it became worse. Then I was getting madder and madder and I wanted to get a rifle and come and fight against the U.S."[2]

Until the missile crisis, Kennedy's "secret war" against Cuba—Operation Mongoose—had appeased the exiles' wrath, convincing them that Kennedy had not slipped in his commitment. But in the autumn of 1962, the exiles assumed that the discovery of missiles in Cuba would increase U.S. resolve to demolish Castro. Instead, they witnessed a U.S. pledge to the Soviets to leave the island alone—a "no invasion" agreement, in effect. The exiles, most of whom were out of the Kennedy loop, were incensed. One prominent exile called Kennedy's agreement with Soviet leader Khrushchev a violation of his famous pledge made three days after the Bay of Pigs to never abandon Cuba to communism. The exile leader wrote, "For the friendly Cuban people, allies of the United States, and for hundreds of thousands of exiles eager to stake their lives to liberate their native land, it was a soul-shattering blow."[3]

But John Kennedy's foreign policy was both less, and more, than what appeared on the surface. In fact, his Cuban policies after the missile crisis might best be described "dualism in the extreme." While the President had come to decide, no doubt as a result of the 1962 missile crisis, that it was time to be conciliatory towards the Soviet Union, he and his brother continued their relentless secret war against Castro. To make this delicate dichotomy successful, it became necessary to alter the style, though not the substance, of the Administration's Cuba Project. The result? The U.S. cracked down on some exile activities, and encouraged others.

By March 1963, the U.S. Coast Guard, FBI, Secret Service, and even the British police in the Bahamas were teaming up to arrest certain Cuban exiles.[4] To most observers, it seemed that the Kennedys had abandoned the exile cause. But that was not the case. Bobby Kennedy was merely tightening the reins, streamlining the Cuba Project to include only his most trusted exile friends.

Dan Kurzman, the *Washington Post's* Latin-American expert, wrote an August 1963 story that stated in part:

> *The United States is apparently trying to prevent independent exile organizations from engaging in parallel activities that might jeopardize its own...United States policy is to centralize the underground's control under the CIA. This agency is reportedly recruiting particularly trusted and competent members of individual exile groups into its service.*[5]

It is now known that JFK never intended to fulfill the U.S. side of the missile crisis agreement. In 1997, the State Department released a 934-page compilation of previously-secret missile crisis documents. On November 5, 1962, mere days after the crisis, Kennedy instructed Defense Secretary Robert McNamara that "we must operate on the presumption that the Russians may try again [to place missiles in Cuba]." The president proceeded to ask McNamara for suggestions.[6] That same day, JFK sent another memo to McNamara, this time remarking, "The plans for X seem thin" and "may thus require us to build additional divisions."[7] In this case, as footnoted in the memo, "X" was a quick-reaction plan for an airborne assault on Cuba, in the event of an internal civilian or military uprising. In early 1963, the Kennedy brothers would hit high gear trying to create such an uprising.

A worried Kennedy also told the State Department's George Ball that, missiles or no missiles, he felt he could not have his hands tied in dealing with Castro. Ball assured the president that he could break the "no invasion" pledge at any time under the provisions of the Rio Pact. Kennedy then addressed the National Security Council in December 1962, saying that he "was not going to rat on an agreement with the Russians, but we're not going to tie on to a no-invasion pledge which allows Castro to operate from an invulnerable base."[8] Thus, Kennedy maintained his resolve to deal with the upstart dictator. The President and his brother merely switched tactics.

Evidence of Kennedy's commitment to deal with Castro after the missile agreement is overwhelming. A retired CIA officer told the author, "Bobby wanted to deal with Castro in a way that wouldn't start a war with Russia. The 'crackdown' was for Khrushchev's benefit." In this light, the "crackdown" can be seen as a convincing ruse, the effect of which was to comb out the more roguish exile groups launching raids from U.S. soil. To plausibly maintain that the U.S. had no role in the anti-Castro efforts, the administration had decided that any raids would have to emanate from a third party country rather than the U.S.

At the same time, the action served the Kennedys' prestige and need for control. As former FBI agent William Turner would write, "The White House had its own Cubans, and its own plans for dealing with Castro. The rest of the exiles," in the words of one CIA operative, "'were told to stuff it,' but they weren't told why."[9]

The tragedy for Bobby was that his trimmed-down stratagem would again involve training camps and activists in New Orleans, all of whom were in close proximity to Lee Harvey Oswald. Bobby hinted at his real intentions for Cuba on April 23, 1963. When his Special Group met, the Attorney General proposed a study on how to cause "as much trouble as we can for Communist Cuba," and to culminate in "overthrowing Castro in eighteen months"—or in October 1964, one month before the U.S. presidential elections. One week after this directive, the Joint Chiefs of Staff would submit to the Kennedys just such a planned timetable. Robert Kennedy also wanted this proposed study to include "measures we should take following contingencies such as the death of Castro."[10]

With the political gains the Cuban crackdown was achieving on the Soviet front, John Kennedy was now able to offer his olive branch to Khrushchev.

The USSR and The "Peace Speech"

> "Recalling now President John F. Kennedy, I would like especially to note his speech at the American University...[which] can be called courageous and more realistic than what the Soviet Union...often heard from those shores. Although...[it] had some conflicting points and a tribute was unfortunately paid in it to the so-called policy of 'containment and pushing back of communism,' as a whole, however, it proceeded from acknowledgement of the inevitability and necessity of co-existence of states with different social systems...He said that 'peace need not be impracticable and war need not be inevitable.'"
>
> —Nikita S. Khrushchev, June 1964

At 10:15 a.m. on June 10, 1963, John Kennedy left the White House for American University, where he would make a major address at the institution's 49th commencement exercises.

Washington sweltered that morning, even by its own June standards. Just after 10:30, Kennedy flashed his winning smile in acknowledgment of his introduction and began his talk with familiar self-deprecation. "I have...chosen this time and place," said Kennedy, rocking slightly until he hit his stride, "to discuss a topic on which ignorance too often abounds and the truth is too rarely perceived—and that is the most important topic on earth: peace."

The "Peace Speech," as it would become known, would be the best-written and most lyrical of the President's life:

> *I am talking about genuine peace, the kind of peace that makes life on earth worth living, the kind that enables men and nations to grow and to hope and to build a better life for their children—not merely peace for Americans but peace for all men and women—not merely peace in our time but peace for all time... I speak of peace...as the necessary rational end of rational men. I realize the pursuit of peace is not as dramatic as the pursuit of war—and frequently the words of the pursuer fall on deaf ears. But we have no more urgent task.*

> *Too many of us think [peace] is impossible. Too many think it is unreal. But that is a dangerous, defeatist belief. It leads to the conclusion that war is inevitable, that mankind is doomed, that we are gripped by forces we cannot control. We need not accept that view. Our problems are man-made. Therefore, they can be solved by man...*

Historian David Halberstam called it "a landmark speech," and it was. As Halberstam noted, after seventeen years of hard line Cold War rhetoric and action, Kennedy had taken a bold first step towards thawing the relationship between the superpowers. Kennedy's speech continued:

> *I speak of peace because of the new face of war. Total war makes no sense in an age where great powers can maintain large and relatively invulnerable nuclear forces and refuse to surrender without resort to those forces. It makes no sense in an age when a single nuclear weapon contains almost ten times the explosive force delivered by all the Allied air forces in the Second World War. It makes no sense in an age when the deadly poisons produced by a nuclear exchange would be carried by wind and water and soil and seed to the far corners of the globe and to generations yet unborn.*

Two weeks after it publicly played out, Kennedy said the missile crisis may have been an important turning point in East-West relations.[11] Now, at the D.C. campus, he pursued the potential new course, delivering the text in his moderated Boston-Irish accent. Everyone knew Kennedy could turn on his great charm whenever needed. However, his "Peace Speech" was delivered as free of affectations as any he had ever given. He read straight, hard, and at a steady clip:

> *With such a peace, there will still be quarrels and conflicting interests, as there are within families and nations. World peace, like community peace, does not require that each man love his neighbor—it requires only that they live together with mutual tolerance, submitting their disputes to a just and peaceful settlement. And history teaches us that enmities between nations, as between individuals, do not last forever. However fixed our likes and dislikes*

may seem, the tide of time and events will often bring surprising changes in the relations between nations and neighbors...

So let us not be blind to our differences—but let us also direct attention to our common interests and the means by which those differences can be resolved. And if we cannot end now our differences, at least we can help make the world safe for diversity. For in the final analysis, our most basic common link is that we all inhabit this small planet. We all breathe the same air. We all cherish our children's future. And we are all mortal.

The President used his next breath to assert that no government or social system was so evil that its people must be considered so—and he hailed the Soviets for their courage, cultural achievements, and abhorrence of war. "No nation in the history of battle ever suffered more than the Soviet Union in the Second World War. At least 20 million lost their lives. Countless millions of homes and families were burned or sacked. A third of the national territory, including two-thirds of its industrial base, was turned into a wasteland—a loss equivalent to the destruction of this country east of Chicago."

The radical nature of this speech, replete with sympathy and praise for the putative enemy, is hard now to appreciate. It was daringly contrary to the preponderance of conventional wisdom at the time. Its emotional context was a blend of resolution, anger, dismay, and hysteria:

Some say that it is useless to speak of peace or world law or world disarmament—and that it will be useless until the leaders of the Soviet Union adopt a more enlightened attitude. I hope they do. I believe we can help them do it. But I also believe that we must re-examine our own attitudes—as individuals and as a nation—for our attitude is as essential as theirs. And every graduate of this school, every thoughtful citizen who despairs of war and wishes to bring peace, should begin by looking inward—by examining his own attitude towards the course of the Cold War and toward freedom and peace here at home...

Kennedy spoke without stopping for applause, which he seemed not to expect. In fact, his only substantial applause came after two dramatic announcements. The first was that no more American nuclear tests would be conducted in the atmosphere so long as other nations also refrained from testing.[12] The other was that the United States would join the Soviet Union and Great Britain at a high-level meeting in Moscow in another attempt to agree on a nuclear test ban treaty. Recent comments by Khrushchev slightly encouraged hope that progress on nuclear control might be possible (provided the Soviet Chairman's equally recent denunciations were ignored), and Kennedy thought his speech would be a good place to communicate his optimistic state of mind.

He also used it for other, more short-term political purposes. Norman Cousins, a U.S. writer and editor involved with American-Soviet exchanges, had seen Khrushchev two months before, and promptly afterward urged Kennedy to make some kind of dramatic approach to the Soviets before a forthcoming meeting of the Communist Party's Central Committee. Aware that the First Secretary was increasingly disparaged for weakness by Chinese Communist leaders and under pressure from his own hawks, administration advisors agreed it was worthwhile trying to lend support to the Soviet doves. Everyone knew Kennedy had forced Khrushchev to withdraw his missiles from Cuba.[13] If the belittled First Secretary could not boast of concrete results from that retreat, he would have to demonstrate his fortitude by denouncing the imperialist Washington warmongers who ignored his peaceful gesture. Hence, the conciliatory noises from Washington.

Kennedy felt very good about the speech. Evelyn Lincoln, who had been Kennedy's personal secretary for twelve years, said he considered it the speech of his life, and it "lit" him with passion well into the evening, when he enjoyed a long swim in the White House pool. Lincoln believed June 10th marked more than a fundamental policy change. "Kennedy became President that day," she wrote.

The full importance of Kennedy's initiative would be revealed only during the following weeks, when American representatives arrived in Moscow for negotiations on the test-ban treaty, and the first break in the glacial Cold War was followed by the crucial first agreement to limit it. But even at first hearing, the speech made a profound impression on Khrushchev, who called it "the greatest speech by an American president since Roosevelt."[14] Fidel Castro also praised the speech and Kennedy personally, although Havana's press insisted that American treatment of Cuba contradicted Kennedy's remarks about non-interference in other countries' affairs.

British newspapers were also generally favorable. *The Manchester Guardian* called it "one of the great state papers of American history." Prime Minister Harold MacMillan said, "Jack Kennedy's acceptance of Test Ban and of the policy of détente with Russia were really his own—I mean, were not shared by any except his most intimate advisers. He took great risks for them."

The American press was more subdued, and even antagonistic. After banner headlines on the afternoon of June 10th and the morning of June 11th, mention of the speech virtually disappeared. Kennedy's call for examination of attitudes that unnecessarily deepened animosity produced very little scrutiny or discussion, even of the superficial kind.

The public responded even more weakly. During the week following the president's seminal statement, 50,000 letters were mailed to the White House. Just under 900 were about the speech: 25 were critical. At the same time, 28,232 people wrote to discuss impending legislation on freight rates.

In Congress, the response was disapproving and directly hostile. Senate Republican leaders saw the proposed test ban talks as a dangerous double-cross by the Soviets—as "another case," according to Everett Dirksen of Illinois, the Senate Minority Leader, "of concession and more concession to Khrushchev."

As he concluded his 28 minutes at American University's sun-drenched podium, Kennedy quietly declared:

This generation of Americans has already had enough—more than enough—
of war and hate and oppression. We shall be prepared if others wish it. We
shall be alert to try to stop it. But we shall also do our part to build a world
of peace where the weak are safe and the strong are just. We are not helpless
before that task or hopeless of its success. Confident and unafraid, we labor
on—not toward a strategy of annihilation, but toward a strategy of peace.

For those who saw this as the new crux of U.S. foreign policy, the speech
was very moving. But few knew about America's hidden foreign policy. Even
fewer were aware of Kennedy's immense talent for compartmentalization which
allowed him to simultaneously embrace great moral dichotomies. In short, most
Americans did not know of the Kennedys' continuing obsession with, and secret
war against, Fidel Castro.

Cuba: Murder and Mayhem

"Kennedy's infatuation with paramilitary operations, counter-insurgency, and
inability to rationalize intelligence made a mockery of rhetoric that appealed
to reason."
—Herbert S. Parmet, Kennedy historian[15]

Only one month after the Peace Speech, Kennedy began publicly reducing his
lavish praise of the Soviet Union. In a July 17 press conference, the President
stated that the United States "cannot exist in a peaceful sense" with Cuba as
long as it remains a "Soviet satellite." Within four days, Castro, in a note to the
United States, protested Kennedy's statement, asserting that Cuba's ties to the
Soviet Union were "indestructible" and "unalterable." During the next month,
Cuba reported numerous sabotage bombings of fuel stockpiles, metal plants,
and factories, all originating, it alleged, in the United States. These reports came
as the Kennedy administration was orchestrating a public "crackdown" on exile
activities. The "crackdown" was nothing more than a cover for an intensified
super-secret program that promised to remove Castro once and for all.

New "Autonomous" Projects: Cuban Coordinating Committee

Many of the US's anti-Castro operations in 1963 have, historically, been referred
to as "autonomous," a term the Kennedys introduced to provide them a layer of
all-important deniability. But referring to these 1963 events as "autonomous"
fooled no one on the inside. Close observers were well aware that the Kennedy
administration was fully supportive of, and was, in fact, the driving force
behind, the covert activity. This new, more obfuscated strategy had its genesis
on June 19th, when President Kennedy approved "autonomous operations"
directed against Castro—operations designed to encourage continued harassment of Castro, while at the same time distancing the administration from the
efforts.

Soon after these operations were authorized, an Army Officer assigned to the CIA's Miami JM/WAVE Station had an encounter he would never forget. Captain Bradley Ayers, attending a bash thrown by the JM/WAVE officers at a swank Key Biscayne home in late June, was astonished when he was introduced to another guest—Robert Kennedy. "His presence reinforced my belief that the Cuban situation was a prime concern to the White House," Ayers later wrote. "With an election year just around the corner, the President had to continue to try to silence critics of his Cuban policy."[16]

As recently-released documents show, the President sought to encourage a program of sabotage directed at "four major segments of the Cuban economy," 1) electric power; 2) petroleum refineries and storage facilities; 3) railroad and highway transportation; and 4) production and manufacturing.[17] Operations under this program were to be conducted by CIA-controlled Cuban agents from a United States island off the coast of Florida and were intended to complement a similar effort designed to "develop internal resistance elements which could carry out sabotage." All these activities came under the aegis of Bobby's Kennedy's newest brainchild, the Cuban Coordinating Committee, or CCC. Other, even more sinister aspects of the new approach were deemed so sensitive that they were overseen by Bobby Kennedy himself.

The CCC was formed, ostensibly, to help assimilate Cuban Brigade members into American society. This agenda, however, provided a convenient front for the CCC's more important agenda—the coordination of anti-Castro aggression that would culminate in a coup, tentatively set for late 1963 or early 1964. This coordination involved the Cuban specialists at the State Department, Defense Department, Army, Navy, and the Joint Chiefs of Staff. With the CCC at the top of the pyramid, inter-agency memos were written planning the removal of Castro, then sent to Robert Kennedy and the National Security Council for approval.

As remembered by CCC staffer, General Alexander Haig, "The covert programs against Castro and the whole counter-insurgency program throughout the hemisphere was just amazing, and they were really the main line of work of the Cuban Coordinating Committee."[18]

After the Mongoose operation began in early 1962, the concerned agencies brainstormed repeatedly on the Castro problem. By May 1963, the CCC was handed a list of options from which to choose. Among them were:

Operation Free Ride—Free one-way airline tickets out of Cuba were to be air-dropped by the thousands on the island. Special note was made that the tickets would not bring the Cubans to the United States.

Operation Dirty Trick—Should one of the Mercury manned space shots fail, it would be blamed on Cuban sabotage, thus justifying a U.S. invasion.

Operation Bingo—A simulated attack on the U.S. forces at Guantanamo would likewise be used to justify a U.S. attack.

Operation Good Times—To be fabricated was a photograph of a fat Castro living lavishly with two "beauties." A suggested caption would say, "My ration is different." The Department of Defense author added, "This should put even a

Commie Dictator in the proper perspective with the underprivileged masses."[19]

Operation Invisible Bomb—Air Force F-101's would fly early mornings over Havana, creating sonic booms to blow out "all the windows" in Havana. The attack simulation would cause great apprehension among the populace, and cause "malicious damage."

In charge of filtering these reports for the CCC was Secretary of the Army Cyrus Vance, assisted by General Alexander Haig, and Vance's assistant, Joseph Califano. These men saw to it that the reports were forwarded to Bobby Kennedy for potential action. In Haig's view, the Kennedy brothers so disdained the bureaucracy that they felt the need to run the CCC directly. Haig later wrote:

> By reaching down into the government and setting up ad hoc operations, they were able to make certain that projects that were important to them were administered by one or more of the Kennedy loyalists who had been stationed at nearly every junction box in the government…In this case, the junction box was the office in which I worked under Vance and Califano.[20]

In a 1997 interview, Haig elaborated on Bobby's role:

> Bobby Kennedy was running it—hour by hour. I was part of it, as deputy to Joe Califano and military assistant to General Vance. We were conducting two raids a week at the height of that program against mainland Cuba. People were being killed, sugar mills were being blown up, bridges were demolished. We were using fast boats and mother ships and the United States Army was supporting and training these forces. This was after the Missile Crisis when the Cuban Coordinating Committee was set up [in 1963]. Cy Vance, the Secretary of the Army, was [presiding] over the State Department, the CIA, and the National Security Council. I was intimately involved. It was wrong-headed, I'm sorry to say. Weekly reports were rendered to Bobby Kennedy—he had a very tight hand on the operation. [21]

Recently, Haig was shown an organizational chart of the numerous Cuban committees at various government agencies. At the top was the President; nowhere on it did the Attorney General, Robert Kennedy, appear. Viewing the chart, Haig chuckled and exclaimed, "Bobby was the President. He was the President! Let me repeat, as a reasonably close observer, HE WAS THE PRESIDENT!"[22]

General Haig recalled that his tenure on the CCC was marked by "the impatient prodding of Robert Kennedy and the frequent invocation of the President's name." Clandestine activities, including acts of economic sabotage, always went to Bobby Kennedy's office for final approval. On October 3, 1963, the Cuban Coordinating Committee approved nine operations, several of which involved sabotage. On October 24th, thirteen major operations, including the sabotage of an electric power plant, an oil refinery, and a sugar mill, were approved for the period from November 1963 through January 1964.[23] Haig points out that CCC leaders reluctantly followed Bobby Kennedy's imperative. "Cy Vance was very unhappy with it. He's a decent human being—not a fellow who would ever be comfortable with operations that were covert. Califano the same."

Los Amigos de Roberto

Six months before JFK's eloquent Peace Speech directed at the Soviets, Bobby Kennedy lustily embraced not only his "bad cop" role in his brother's administration, but also his new friends in the Cuban exile community. The potential success of the Kennedys' plans to train Cuban exile soldiers for a second invasion hinged on the abilities of the "White House Cubans," so-named by the FBI's William Turner. According to the CIA, Bobby's Cuban allies, who would soon be massing in Central America, referred to themselves as "Los Amigos de Roberto" (friends of Robert), for a sort of secret password when traveling.[24]

The exiles' embrace of the White House was strongly encouraged when the Attorney General personally sought to finalize back-channel negotiations with Castro to release all the remaining Bay of Pigs hostages. Manolo Reboso and Roberto San Román also tell of Bobby's personal assistance in obtaining hospitalization for a child of a Brigade member who needed heart surgery. [25]

But other Bobby contemporaries claim his personal interests in Cuba's leadership radiated beyond anything that could be remotely referred to as "humanitarian." RFK often brought freed members of Brigade 2506 to his home in McLean, Virginia, or treated them to ski trips in New Hampshire, where a darker agenda began to be formulated. The key actors in this play included Harry Williams, Manuel Artime, and Rolando Cubela. Williams would recruit Cuban exiles for training, and Artime and Cubela would be useful later on (*as described in the next chapter*).

Enrique "Harry" Ruiz-Williams

Among the first Brigade 2506 members to be released from Cuban prison were those wounded in the Bay of Pigs invasion. One of these unfortunates, Enrique "Harry" Ruiz-Williams, was permanently crippled, courtesy of one of Castro's bombs. Williams had been riddled with more than 70 pieces of shrapnel, smashing both feet, and leaving one hole in his neck, and another near his heart.[26] In April 1962, the last man off the plane in Miami, Williams was said to have fallen into the arms of his former commander, Roberto San Román, who had become fast friends with Robert Kennedy after the invasion. Now San Román headed straight for the phone. He told the Attorney General, "I want you to meet this guy who can tell you what the hell is going on out there." Bobby Kennedy, who had been watching everything on TV, told San Román, "Bring him to me."[27]

Only three days after his release from a Cuban prison-hospital, a nervous Harry Williams arrived in Washington with his friend Roberto San Román, and met with Bobby Kennedy. Williams, a geologist by profession, had much in common with Bobby and they got on famously. Former FBI agent William Turner wrote:

Harry Williams was a Kennedy kind of man, tough and liberal, and ferociously anti-communist. Burly, round-faced and handsome, he combined the geniality of a Lions Club toastmaster with a tough-minded singleness of purpose.[28]

"We've selected you to be, let's say, the man we trust most in the exiles," Bobby told Williams. Bobby Kennedy later said of Williams, "He was very brave and had very good judgment."[29] Harry was thus drafted onto RFK's hand-selected Cuban team.

Williams recalls what happened next: "It was my idea to physically elimi-nate Castro. I suggested it to Bobby."[30] The Attorney General responded by telling Williams that their goals were the same—the elimination of Fidel Castro, and that when the President was ready, they would strike. He assured Harry not to worry, saying, "We're going to go."[31]

Thus began a series of meetings between Bobby and Harry Williams. After the Bay of Pigs, Williams, like many exiles, had been suspicious of Kennedy intentions. There was every reason, even now, to doubt that Bobby would fol-low through on his promises. Bobby, however, impressed Williams with his unceasing effort to free the rest of the Brigade members. By the time they were finally released on Christmas eve, 1962, Williams was won over. As their friend-ship grew, Williams was often invited to spend weekends at Bobby's Hickory Hill home, where he shared a guest room with Bobby's head of security, Rafer Johnson.

"I worked for Bobby. I was his number one man on Cuba," says Williams. "He was my friend. I got into a lot of trouble with the Cubans who hated the Kennedys. They called me 'Bobby's Boy.'"[32] Williams' contention is buttressed by a perusal of RFK's phone logs, which show 36 phone conversations between Williams and RFK at the Justice Department. These would be in addition to any calls from RFK's home in Virginia. According to Williams, the Cuba Project went into high gear when he became "Bobby's Boy":

Bobby called the shots in the Cuba Project. In my opinion, Bobby ran the CIA. Bobby's anti-Castro campaign continued right up until the assassination. We had camps in the Dominican Republic, in the jungles of Guatemala, in Costa Rica. What we wanted to do was keep the thing going. Everything was geared to eliminate Castro...At the camps, the CIA guys would try to give me orders, but I would just laugh and say, "I don't work for you. You work for me."[33]

Williams' CIA case officers were E. Howard Hunt and Bernard "Macho" Barker. For years, Hunt had functioned as the Agency's chief liaison to the anti-Castro Cuban exiles. He became particularly close not only to Williams, but to such other Kennedy confidantes as Manuel Artime and former CIA Director Allen Dulles. (Hunt's affection for Kennedy-loyal exiles like Artime strained rela-tions with many of his fellow CIA officers.) In addition, Hunt served as the Agency's advisor to the Kennedy-backed Cuban Revolutionary Council, with its headquarters in Miami and New Orleans.[34] It has been widely reported that Hunt was the first person to propose to Allen Dulles that Castro be assassinated.

Hunt's biographer, Tad Szulc, wrote of him, "His specialty was so-called covert political action...black propaganda...This was the kind of political groundwork the CIA laid in many instances for a coup d'etat in a foreign country."[35] A gifted writer, Hunt had played key propaganda roles in coups in Guatemala and Panama. (After Dulles left the CIA in the wake of the Bay of Pigs, Hunt assisted Dulles by ghost writing five chapters of Dulles' 1963 book, *The Craft of Intelligence*.) Former Batista aide and anti-Castro activist Frank Sturgis has said, "Howard was in charge of a couple of other CIA operations involving disposal, and I can tell you that some of them worked."[36] ("Disposal," in the CIA patois, meant assassination.) Years later, Richard Nixon's White House Counsel John Dean would testify that Hunt was hired by the White House to oversee the operation to assassinate Ambassador Moises Torrijos of Panama, because of Torrijos' opposition to the Panama Canal Treaty. (Dean also brought Hunt in to mastermind the infamous Watergate break-in.)[37] Now Hunt was asked to help bring about Castro's fall.

Starting in early 1963, Williams, Barker, and Hunt would hold dozens of meetings in Washington and New York. Attempting to unite the various exile factions at Hunt's direction, Harry Williams told Miami Cubans of an impending invasion, with initial infiltrations set to commence in December, 1963. Williams' recruitment efforts were reported in the Associated Press:

> *A new all-out drive to unify Cuban refugees into a single, powerful organization to topple the Fidel Castro regime was disclosed today by exile sources. The plan calls for formation of a junta in exile to mount a three-pronged thrust consisting of sabotage, infiltration and ultimate invasion...Seeking to put together the junta was Enrique [Harry] Ruiz-Williams, a Bay of Pigs invasion veteran, and friend of U.S. Attorney General Robert F. Kennedy. Cuban leaders said intensive sabotage and guerrilla activities inside Cuba might start in a month to spark a possible uprising. Hundreds of exiles, reported itching for action and resentful of U.S. imposed curbs against the anti-Castro raids, will be recruited to infiltrate Cuba, the sources added.[38]*

Williams added the detail that the invasion would be launched from Costa Rica. And anti-Castro CIA contract agent Robert Morrow recalls:

> *Williams claimed that the Attorney General had promised CIA assistance, arms, and money for the invasion...Guerilla warfare, sabotage, and infiltration of Castro's armed forces would be the means by which the Cuban exiles would prepare for the December 1963 operation.[39]*

The CIA's Morrow, at the time, was assisting Mario Kohly, the President of the Cuban provisional government-in-exile. Kohly had been involved with the original plans of former Vice President Richard Nixon to oust Castro. Morrow says that Kohly was also aware of the planned December 1963 invasion of Cuba, to be launched from Costa Rica.[40]

Researcher Lamar Waldron, who has developed strong sources both in the Kennedy sphere and the exile community, learned more about the coup from a

Cuban close to Bobby Kennedy. The source told Waldron that Bobby Kennedy personally authorized the source to plan for the violent overthrow of Castro, as a prelude to an American invasion. The source was promised that funds for the operation would be deposited by the Kennedy administration in the bank of a third party nation.[41]

One of these Cubans, who insists on anonymity, has told how in 1963 another senior Castro official, not Cubela, agreed that—for a large cash payment—he would organize the violent overthrow of Castro and key colleagues for a deposit to be paid into a foreign bank, and by November 22, the operation was imminent. Had the president's assassination not intervened, the exile go-between would have set off on a secret mission to Havana. The initial coup pre-infiltrations, to be followed by American support, were expected to occur within 10 days.[42]

The Cuban exiles Williams recruited for this invasion were training in a number of places, including the camps on Lake Ponchartrain, north of New Orleans—the same camps that Lee Harvey Oswald would later attempt to infiltrate. The exile trainees chose as their urban New Orleans hangout a city park two blocks from where Oswald was soon to find employment.

The purpose of all this exile activity in New Orleans was to provide a pipeline of equipment and able bodies to the operational headquarters of the re-invasion effort in Central America. There the plans were overseen by a personal emissary of Bobby Kennedy. His name was Dr. Manuel Artime Buesa.

CHAPTER EIGHT

YET ANOTHER INVASION PLAN

Dr. Manuel Artime

D r. Manuel Artime, the military leader of Brigade 2506, was known as the CIA's "Golden Boy." In fact, he was even more so Bobby's "Golden Boy." Imprisoned in Cuba for using his organization, the Movement for Revolutionary Recovery (MRR), to oppose the Castro regime in 1959, he escaped the island, and went to Miami, where he directed not only the Brigade, but the parent organization of Sergio Arcacha's CRC, the Frente Revolucionario Democratico (FRD). After being captured again in the Bay of Pigs invasion, Artime was imprisoned in Cuba.

Artime first met with then-Senator John Kennedy in July 1960, before the Democratic National Convention. The meeting in Kennedy's Washington Senate office was arranged by the CIA, its purpose shrouded in secrecy.[1] Also in attendance was Dr. José Miro Cardona, the president-to-be of the yet to be formed Cuban Revolutionary Council, the man who would later be Sergio Arcacha's superior. It is believed that Artime, Cardona, and the CIA wanted the Democratic frontrunner (and friend of CIA chief Allen Dulles) to be apprised of the invasion planned for the following spring. Colonel L. Fletcher Prouty, the Air Force's liaison to the CIA, recently recalled his role as the chauffeur assigned to transport the Cuban leaders from Kennedy's office to the Pentagon.[2]

Artime went on to become close friends with both Kennedy brothers, for reasons that now seem apparent. "Manolo was not only a revolutionary leader, but a Catholic revolutionary leader," says his comrade Bernard "Macho" Barker.[3] Another exile leader, Justo Carillo, says that Artime's mentor, a Jesuit priest named Father Posada, was a close friend of Allen Dulles' cousin Avery Dulles, who was also a Jesuit. According to Carillo, Artime and the Dulleses "created this thesis, followed by the CIA, to bring up [encourage] a young leader, who had been a revolutionary and who was also a Catholic [Artime], and of course, their future presidential candidate [Kennedy]."[4] This seems to explain the CIA-arranged meeting between Artime and the young Senator prior to his presidential nomination. Artime's deputy, Angelo Kennedy, recently recalled, "Everything was happening so fast during the Eisenhower administration. Artime visited Kennedy many times during this period, and I know he told him [Kennedy] of the invasion plans."[5]

Eight months after the release of Harry Williams, Artime and the remaining prisoners of Brigade 2506 were set free in December of 1962. For 20 months after the Bay of Pigs, Bobby Kennedy had worked tirelessly, negotiating with Castro, and raising the $53 million in pharmaceuticals and farm machinery (Castro's demand) to release the prisoners. On the day of the release, Williams called RFK at home. The Attorney General said, "You got it, Enrique. This is it. The guy with the beard has accepted."[6] Williams and the other Brigade members were understandably moved by RFK's efforts.

One wonders, however, how they would have felt had they seen documents, released by the CIA in 1996, which show that Castro had been anxious to complete the prisoner exchange by early September 1962. However, as CIA Director John McCone noted, RFK worried that the ransom issue might be seized upon by the Republicans in the upcoming November elections. The administration thus decided to hold off the exchange until after the balloting, effectively assuring that the prisoners would languish four more months in the infamous Cuban dungeons.[7] This was done despite horrendous inside reports of prison conditions. One article prominently featured in *Newsweek* magazine quoted letters from the prisoners, one of which stated, "We are experiencing such hunger. We often wonder if we can endure two or three more months...Tell the ones that can pay the ransom to do so now. If they delay it may be too late."[8]

After his release in December 1962, Artime met with President Kennedy, this time at the Kennedy compound in West Palm Beach, Florida. Also attending the late-December meeting were Pepe and Roberto San Román, and Harry Williams.[9]

Within days, the talks were re-convened in the White House. In his first-ever interview in 1997, Angelo Kennedy, a close aide to Artime and other exile leaders, recalled: "I was with Artime in early 1963 when the call came from the White House. Soon we were brought to Washington to meet with President Kennedy." Although Angelo would wait in the ante room of the Oval Office, he was well-aware what the topic of discussion would be between Artime and Kennedy: the authorization to train a new invasion force. "I remember Artime leaving Kennedy's office with a broad grin," recalled Angelo. "When we got outside, he gave me a huge hug, saying, 'We got it! We got everything!'" The President and Artime would become fast friends. "They were very close," remembers Angelo. "Artime used to tell me what a horny Irishman Kennedy is."[10]

The hands-on control of any Cuban initiative, as usual, would fall to the younger brother. JFK suggested to Artime, "Talk to my brother Bob."[11] By

January 1963, Artime and other exile leaders were being treated to ski vacations in New Hampshire with the Attorney General. Angelo Kennedy says of their relationship: "Bobby and Artime were very close. Artime stayed at his house so much I wouldn't be surprised if he had a set of keys." For a time, Artime's close associate, Manolo Reboso (also a confidante of RFK), even shared a girlfriend with the President. According to Gerry Hemming, Reboso dated longtime JFK mistress, Pam Turnure, Jackie's appointment secretary.[12]

Though many exile groups would soon come to feel the wrath of "the crack-down," one would have gotten an entirely different impression from the topics being discussed around the fireplace in January 1963. The talk revolved around finding new ways to get rid of "that guy with the beard." The secret meetings, from which Cuban Coordinating Committee member Al Haig was excluded, soon shifted to Bobby's home and office.

It was a tricky balancing act for Artime, because most Cuban exiles distrusted the Kennedy brothers after their Bay of Pigs performance. According to "Macho" Barker, "Artime was able to work with President Kennedy and not hate him, saying, 'Well, he's human. The important thing is that he makes restitution for the mistake.' And it sure looked like he was going to."[13]

At that time, Manuel Hernandez was Artime's Washington liaison.[14] In a 1998 interview, he recalled, "I used to drive Artime to these meetings at Bobby's office in early 1963. They also met at Bobby's home in McLean, Virginia." Like Hernandez, Artime's CIA case officer, Howard Hunt, received reports of Artime's "lunches at Hickory Hill [RFK's home]."

On April 2, 1963, Artime hand-delivered to Bobby Kennedy a message from Nicaraguan leader Luis Somoza. Its contents are unknown, but can be reasonably surmised by what soon happened. After he made the delivery, according to Artime's report to the CIA, Bobby told Artime "to come and see him when he had a specific plan of action." Artime further noted that Bobby had rented homes for Brigade leaders Roberto and Pepe San Roman on Chain Bridge Road (also Bobby's street) in McLean, VA.[15]

Cuban Coordinating Committee member Al Haig wrote that, like all those not considered Kennedy "loyalists," he was excluded from the secret planning sessions that took place in Bobby Kennedy's office.[16] One of those who did participate in the CCC's closed-door meetings was Harry Williams. "We had at least three or four big meetings at Bobby's office with leaders of the Brigade and [Cyrus] Vance and two or three others," Williams remembers. "Joe Califano, who was working with McNamara, was there too."[17] Knowing the bind he was in as a result of the restrictive missile crisis resolution, Bobby and his cadre decided that all domestic activity be focused towards funneling arms to training camps located outside the U.S. borders. It was at these meetings, also attended by Artime, that Robert Kennedy approved exile training camps in Latin America. "The general outline of the camps emerged from the meetings with Bobby," Hernandez recently recalled. The training and invasion operation was christened the "Second Naval Guerrilla."

According to Artime, Bobby Kennedy told him that if a Central American country played host to the invasion force, the liberators could technically avoid violating the chief provision of the missile crisis agreement: no raids against Cuba could be launched from within the United States. If Artime could negotiate the deal outside American borders, Bobby would see to it that the money flowed.[18] Artime's aide, Nilo Messer, explains, "Manolo had already spoken to Bobby Kennedy. And he told Artime that if military camps outside of the U.S., where American laws would not be broken, could be acquired, Kennedy would then promise to provide help."[19]

It wasn't long before Artime had negotiated agreements to use land in Guatemala, at Monkey Point in Nicaragua, and on the property of Colonel Vico Jimenez in Costa Rica to train for the upcoming invasion. "All those camps in Nicaragua were the result of Artime's meetings with Bobby Kennedy," remembers Manuel Hernandez.[20] A future Congressional interview with Artime summarized:

> He [Artime] stated he had direct contact with both President Kennedy and Robert Kennedy and, through them, was given full support by the CIA for his anti-Castro operations. He said he felt the death of President Kennedy marked the end of the U.S. government's attempts to liberate Cuba.[21]

Al Haig, the CCC coordinator excluded from RFK's secret pow-wows, later learned another important detail of what he had missed. "Under the personal leadership of Robert Kennedy," Haig later wrote, "at least eight efforts were made to eliminate Castro himself."[22] Artime later told Congressional investigators that "the plan was to eliminate Castro by taking over the Caco Peninsula while Castro was visiting, isolating him from the rest of his government."[23]

While all these plans were being developed and decided on, Cuban exiles left out of the RFK loop were demanding some answers. Shortly after the initial Kennedy-exile lunches at Hickory Hill, a group of Cubans in Miami wrote Bobby, sarcastically noting how Artime and his "cronies" recently "visited the offices of Robert Kennedy,...over a modest lunch of sandwiches, soup and pie." The letter-writers (Miami's Cuban Information Service, or CIS), made it clear that the Kennedy liaison with the chosen exiles left the rest of the Brigade members "seething with indignation."[24] The CIS, unaware of the elaborate plans being hatched, still believed the Kennedys to be traitors to the exile cause as a result of their betrayal at the Bay of Pigs.

Bobby Kennedy delivered on his promised financial support for the exiles. Artime was placed on a $1,500-a-month retainer, and allocated $225,000 a month to launch the Second Naval Guerrilla.[25] The CIA estimated the total sum allocated to Artime eventually came to $4,933,293.00.[26] The exiles put the figure closer to $9 million.[27] The funds were routed from Canada to banks in Switzerland, then to Costa Rican and Nicaraguan front companies.[28] The materials bought with the funds included two mother ships, eight small vessels, two speed boats, three planes, eighty tons of weapons, and $250,000 worth of electrical equipment.[29] Though most of the exile training was taking place in Central

American nations, some of Artime's commandos were also trained on the CIA's "Farm" in Camp Peary, Virginia.

"Bobby Kennedy was the creator of this operation," Artime's Deputy, Raphael Quintero, recently recalled. "It was much like Oliver North's operation—autonomous of the CIA, and run by the White House.[30] This operation was what [future CIA Director] Bill Casey later called a 'self-standing operation.' The CIA didn't want it that way. Bob Kennedy, it seems, was pushing the CIA and making them do it."[31]

Miami CIA Station Chief Ted Shackley agrees: "The training camps in Central America were funded by Washington."[32] Army Intelligence documents sent to Bobby Kennedy's Cuban Coordinating Committee, released in 1998, noted, "Shackley has not been given responsibility for the autonomous operations springing from Central America and he is personally skeptical about these operations. Shackley is a very knowledgeable and professional individual."[33] Shackley's biographer, David Corn, wrote, "To Ted Shackley... the Artime sideshow represented the indulgence of Bobby Kennedy."[34]

The facts that have emerged support Shackley's statement that the exiles' funding originated in Washington. Helping coordinate the CIA's Cuba Desk back at the Agency's Langley headquarters, Sam Halpern knew more than Shackley about where the re-invasion money was coming from, and on whose orders. "We provided the dough," says Halpern. "Bobby [Kennedy] knew everything we were doing. We were doing it under his orders. The Cubans got all the money they needed."[35]

Like many other young Cuban students, Raphael Quintero initially supported the revolutionary Fidel, only to leave Cuba in November 1959, at age twenty, after detecting Castro's turn toward dictatorship. Joining the exile Brigade forces, Quintero was one of the few to infiltrate Cuba before the Bay of Pigs invasion. As a student friend in the Cuban Agrarian Reform movement, Quintero spent the years with Artime, gaining a bird's-eye view of the Artime/RFK relationship. Quintero himself was brought to Washington twice to meet with Bobby Kennedy. At a 1996 Bay of Pigs seminar, Quintero described the atmosphere:

> I had the luck to become a good friend of Bob Kennedy...I was involved in the operation with Artime in Central America...Bob Kennedy was obsessed...He had to get even with Castro...He mentioned this often to me and was very clear about it: He was not going to try to eliminate Castro because he was an ideological guy... He was going to do it because the Kennedy name had been humiliated...He mentioned it clearly to me one day—we went to the circus together and he mentioned it to me.[36]

On June 22nd, three days after JFK had authorized "autonomous operations" against Cuba, Bobby met with Harry Williams, Erneido Oliva, and

Roberto San Román, telling them "what a good job Artime is doing," adding that their operations were anything but "autonomous." "Don't worry. All [your] forces, though outside the country, will be coordinated," Bobby advised. "Don't get the idea you will be working independently." In an attempt to cover his tracks, as well as those of the U.S. government, he asked that the group stop making personal calls to him "because of the frequency of rumors linking him with certain operations against Cuba."[37] However, three weeks hence, a State Department memo stated, "We support Artime's plans for sabotage and resistance against Cuba."[38]

Simultaneously, on July 19, RFK's closest exile ally, Harry Williams, traveled to Nicaragua to formally tell Artime something he already knew: "You are now being supported by the offices of GPIDEAL [President Kennedy]."[39]

Soon, Artime and Quintero journeyed to Fort Benning, Georgia to recruit leaders for the new operation. Fellow exile and CIA agent Felix Rodriguez was, at the time, part of Ft. Benning's Cuban Officer Training Program, which assimilated former Brigade members into the U.S. military. Long a friend of both Artime and Quintero, Rodriguez recalls Artime's first words: "We're going to overthrow Castro—this time we're really going to do it." Artime added that "the President himself was sponsoring the liberation movement" and the operation was being overseen by Robert Kennedy.

Before he would leave his Ft. Benning post, Rodriguez wisely demanded to see proof that the U.S. government had approved the Second Naval Guerrilla. "What assurance do you need?" Artime asked. Rodriguez suggested that they provide him special communications training at Fort Benning, right under the nose of the U.S. Army. "If that's what you want, OK," replied Artime. Shortly thereafter, two men showed up at the Army fort, and trained a suitably impressed Rodriguez and two others in how to clandestinely communicate during the Central American operation. "That [training] convinced me that Artime was planning a bona fide U.S. government-sponsored operation," says Rodriguez, "and I took steps to resign my commission." In November 1963, Rodriguez moved to Nicaragua.[40]

Artime accurately summed up the enterprise just before his death from cancer in 1977: "I was protected by Bob until his brother was assassinated. He met with me personally in the offices of the Attorney General. He kept in touch with the entire operation."[41]

All this Kennedy-Cuban intimacy did not sit well with those in charge of the CIA's official Cuba Project—an operation that was accustomed to not only running professional espionage operations, but to simultaneously providing deniability for the White House. A CIA memo added that "personnel at JM/WAVE possessed certain ill feelings towards Artime's operation," because, according to author David Corn, "it could do what JM/WAVE was no longer permitted to do: conduct sabotage."[42]

The CIA's JM/WAVE station chief, Ted Shackley, was particularly vexed. Artime's CIA liaison to JM/WAVE, Tom Clines, remembered Shackley's reaction.

"He couldn't stand it," said Clines. "He hated the idea that the Cubans had gotten to the Kennedys and convinced them that they could operate on their own."[43]

Shackley worried that the Kennedys' closeness to the exiles' actions could later be used against the White House. Once, when Shackley sent a Cuban confidante of Bobby on a raid of the island, the agent was captured and tortured. Shackley feared that Bobby's name would surface—just the kind of thing the CIA was supposed to prevent.[44]

At times, the exiles' coziness with the Kennedys was downright embarrassing to the CIA professionals. According to Corn, "When Clines in Miami had trouble requisitioning a boat for a mission, his Cubans crowded a pay phone and rang the President's brother. 'We got the boat,' Clines recalled, 'and [Station Chief Ted] Shackley was pissed at me.'"[45] Cuba Project Executive Officer Sam Halpern recently recalled, "It was insanity. If the exiles didn't like what their [CIA] case officers told them, they'd just pick up the phone and call Bobby. Nobody knew who was running the thing!"[46]

One of the few CIA officers who willingly participated in the Second Naval Guerrilla scheme was the Kennedys' close friend Des FitzGerald. On August 9, 1963, Des wrote to JFK's National Security advisor McGeorge Bundy to discuss what he called "the Somoza Plan." In the memo, FitzGerald worried that Nicaraguan head Somoza would be able to "keep out of the limelight of public curiosity a project which is essentially designed to rebuild an indigenous resistance movement inside Cuba."

The CIA officer further noted Somoza's concern that Cuba might retaliate against his country if sabotage raids were traced to Nicaragua. He therefore recommended that those components be shifted to Costa Rica, while the Nicaraguan forces concentrated on fomenting the internal Cuban revolt. FitzGerald also pointed out that Artime's operation, unlike other exile schemes, at least had a chance of succeeding.

Lastly, FitzGerald reported Somoza's statement that he had received the following assurances:

> /A./ The 'green light' to run anti-Castro raids and resistance operations [was] obtained in Washington discussions with President Kennedy and the Attorney General. /B./ [Artime was] asked by President Kennedy and the Attorney General to take four Brigade leaders to Nicaragua. /C./ [Artime was] appointed by President Kennedy to represent him in dealings with the five Central American presidents who are interested in overthrowing Castro. [47]

Rolando Cubela Secades

Manuel Artime testified not only to his direct contact with Bobby, but also with the President. According to Artime, it was the President who suggested, perhaps as a result of Harry Williams' suggestion to Bobby eight months earlier, the coup de grace for the Second Naval Guerrilla: an Artime associate, Rolando Cubela

Secades, should be enlisted to kill Castro.[48]

Rolando Cubela was a natural choice for the role of Castro's future assassin. A doctor and former student guerrilla leader in Cuba, Cubela was an experienced assassin, having murdered Batista's chief of military intelligence, Lt. Col. Antonio Rico. Cubela cut down Rico in a hail of bullets as he exited a Havana nightclub in 1956. After the murder, Cubela and his co-conspirator, Guillermo Riestra, escaped in a small boat to Tampa, Florida. From there, they were believed to have made their way to New Orleans.[49]

Cubela was thus considered a hero by Batista's enemy, Fidel Castro. As such, Cubela was given a high post in the Castro government, becoming a confidante of the new dictator, with direct access to "el lider maximo." Later, when Castro embraced Marxism, Cubela felt personally betrayed by the revolution.

As early as 1961, Cubela began making clandestine contacts with CIA agents. He recalls meeting a CIA officer in the Hilton Hotel in Mexico City. "This [CIA] officer, according to what he informed me, had the responsibility of infiltrating communism in the Caribbean area," Cubela recalls.[50] Over the next two years, the CIA would continue to meet with Cubela, now code-named AM/LASH. Cubela had expressed a desire to defect to the U.S., but his CIA case officers were instructed to keep him in Cuba, where he would "stay in place and report to us."[51] At the same time, Cubela also met with Artime and Quintero.

On September 3, 1963, Secretary of the Army Cyrus Vance, Bobby Kennedy's Army representative on the CCC, wrote a memo listing various options available to the administration in dealing with Cuba. The list included, "Bribing, embarrassing, blackmailing, assassinating, coercing and kidnapping leaders."[52] Four days later, a CIA agent in Porto Allegre, Brazil spoke with Cubela, at which time Castro's "confidante" said he was now prepared to attempt an "inside job."[53] Raphael Quintero remembers that the plan was to unfold on July 26, 1964, the anniversary of the start of Castro's own ascension to power. "Sixty men were to embark simultaneously, after Cubela had killed Castro. They were to take out the entire cabinet. Cubela had given us the impression that he had enough support in the military."[54]

This gambit was part of an elaborate, long-planned, super-secret effort to retake the island before the 1964 presidential election. In actuality, Artime's troop activity and Cubela's murder attempt were but two parts of a full-blown U.S. invasion known as OPLAN 380-63.

OPLAN 380-63: The Kennedys Plan an Invasion

"We never stopped going after Fidel. In fact, the pressure from the Kennedys became worse after the missile crisis."
   **—Sam Halpern, CIA executive Assistant to Cuba Desk directors
   Desmond FitzGerald and William Harvey**[55]

On October 18, 1962, two days after Soviet missiles were detected in Cuba, President Kennedy met with Andrei Gromyko, the Soviet Foreign Minister.

Kennedy emphasized a key point that he hoped Gromyko grasped clearly: The U.S. had no intention of invading Cuba.[56] Three weeks after resolving the missile crisis, John Kennedy further remarked at a press conference, "We will not abandon...efforts to halt subversion in Cuba...but these policies are very different from any intent to launch a military invasion of the island."

Recent disclosures, however, make clear that these remarks were intended more for Soviet consumption than the president's policy-making minions. It now appears that the administration was moving rapidly towards a full-scale assault on the Castro regime, with AM/LASH its capstone.

Details of the AM/LASH operation, as well as the invasion predictions of Bobby's Cuban exile allies, have been known for some time. However, until the CIA, Army, State Department, and the Cuban Coordinating Committee (CCC) were required to release their files in 1997, the true importance of those activities went unappreciated. It is now known that CCC actions—a well-planned U.S. operation to overthrow the Castro regime before the 1964 U.S. presidential election—were to have been coordinated with the operations of Artime, Williams, and Cubela in Central America. In fact, the CIA admitted that Cubela only agreed to meet and discuss assassination on the condition that the assassination would signal the prelude to a U.S.-sponsored coup.[57] Cubela's CIA case officer, in the presence of Bobby Kennedy's emissary, Desmond FitzGerald, gave Cubela "assurances that the United States would help in bringing about that coup."[58]

FitzGerald was referring to a top secret operation that had been in the planning stages since the Lansdale Mongoose days of early 1962. This was clearly the same operation that Nikita Khrushchev cited as his reason for the 1962 installation of nuclear missiles in Cuba. However, merely five weeks after the northern hemisphere was threatened with nuclear annihilation, the Joint Chiefs of Staff wrote in a memo to the President, "Our ultimate objective remains the replacement of the Castro regime."[59] One month later, the Coordinator for Cuban Affairs, in writing, suggested that the National Security Council support "the developments within Cuba that offer the possibility of replacing the Cuban government." The U.S. government, he wrote, should be prepared "to employ U.S. combat elements."

The use of U.S. combat forces was known as OPLAN 380-63, and it was the product of a year of planning by the State Department, Army, Navy, and the Joint Chiefs of Staff (JCS)—all under the control of the White House's Cuban Coordinating Committee. Often revised and refined, the plan for the U.S. instigation of a Cuban coup d'etat was nearing completion by May 1963. Documents now available denote that the operation would be overseen by the Commander in Chief of the Atlantic Fleet (CINCLANT), Admiral Robert "Denny" Dennison. A May 1, 1963 JCS Memo stated that the plan called for "a full scale invasion, if necessary." The end product was to be "the defeat of Castro's government and establishing the groundwork for the installation of a government compatible with the aims of the OAS [Organization of American

States] and friendly to the U.S. by 1 October, 1964."[60] The U.S. presidential elections would occur one month later.

The operational plans are well-detailed, with much thought given to coordinating the post-Castro provisional government. The timetable called for the introduction of Unconventional Warfare (UW), meaning sabotage and revolt-instigating agents, at least seven months in advance of U.S. conventional operations, which would occur "on or about July 15, 1964"—the same timeframe predicted by Quintero. August 3, 1964 was referred to as "D Day," when all-out air strikes (OPLAN 316) would commence. The progressively escalating actions would start "when authorized by the President." Based on what is known about U.S. operations in 1963, it appears that such authorization had indeed been given.

Although Robert Kennedy assumed the task of dealing with the nuts and bolts of policy implementation, this by no means implies that the younger brother was operating without JFK's implicit agreement. When Robert Kennedy issued his April 23, 1963 directive seeking studies aimed at overthrowing Castro in 1964, he was merely echoing the President's own words. Two months prior to the RFK directive, the President addressed General Maxwell Taylor, Chairman of the Joint Chiefs of Staff, regarding the "Cuban Invasion Plan." As he had in the wake of the missile crisis, Kennedy again stressed the need to develop plans for a quick-reaction invasion of Cuba.[61]

On April 29, 1963, President Kennedy wrote Defense Secretary Robert McNamara, asking, "Are we keeping our Cuban contingency invasion plans up to date?" Kennedy worried that new information showed the Cuban resistance to be stronger than originally anticipated. Kennedy added, "It seems to me that we should strengthen our contingency plans on this operation."[62]

One week later, McNamara responded: "I wish to assure you that our contingency plans for an invasion of Cuba have been and are being maintained up to date." McNamara noted the "planned employment" of U.S. forces, as well as the fact that more aircraft, heavy combat equipment, and troops had been added to the plan. "Through these measures, the weight of our early attacks will be increased and the probability of their success will be enhanced." The secretary closed the memo with a reminder to the President of the 1964 military timetable for the invasion.[63] Clearly, President Kennedy was thoroughly briefed on the continuing implementation of OPLAN 380-63.

Just as clearly, he had failed to take seriously the dangers implicit in invading a Soviet satellite nation. Most astounding, the U.S. planners appear not to have been at all chastened by the near holocaust of the missile crisis, and showed no fear of baiting the Soviet bear once again. In one bravado-laced memo, the JCS, the State Department, and the Army cited the "military inferiority of the Soviet Union in the Caribbean" as a reason to not fear its military intervention. The memo continued:

> Our air and ground forces would have to be given explicit instructions at the time on the conditions under which they would engage Soviet forces in Cuba.

This point should be made quite clear to the Kremlin. U.S. planning should include plans...for the possible neutralization or elimination of Soviet forces in Cuba.[64]

Bobby Kennedy tightly supervised the invasion-provoking coup, and only the most trusted Kennedy allies in the various federal agencies had access to its planning. Incredibly, its existence was kept even from then-Secretary of State Dean Rusk, who recently acknowledged that he only learned of the coup operation after the President's assassination.[65]

Phase one of the impending coup would be overseen by the CIA, and called for an insurrection by rebellious military officials in Castro's army. The operation carried the CIA code name of AM/TRUNK.

Operation AM/TRUNK

While the military handled large-scale logistical planning, the CIA undertook the "UW" (Unconventional Warfare) aspects of the plan. These operations were so sensitive that when the Church Committee investigated plots against Castro, the CIA code names for their related operations were not only withheld, but the entire program was relegated to a footnote. The footnote read:

During this period, the CIA also sponsored a separate operation to "penetrate the Cuban military to encourage either defections or an attempt to produce information from dissidents, or perhaps even to forming a group which would then be capable of replacing the then present government in Cuba." The case officers for AM/LASH were also involved in this second related program.[66]

At various times, the coup-related operations were given cryptonyms such as MH/APRON, and OPERATIONS PICADOR & TOREADOR. Inside Cuba, the upcoming revolt was known as OPERATION JUDAS. However, all came under the umbrella of a project code-named AM/TRUNK, whose inspiration came not from the government planners, but a well-connected newsman ("AM," when used to name a CIA project, specifically meant Cuba).

In February 1963, *New York Times* correspondent Tad Szulc learned through one of his Cuban contacts, Dr. Nestor Moreno, that dissension was rife in the higher echelons of Castro's Rebel Army. Moreno convinced Szulc, who had access to both the President and the Attorney General, that a program of Cuban infiltration and exfiltration should be proposed to the White House. Originally named "The Leonardo Plan," the strategy of encouraging an army revolt was indeed passed up the chain of command by Szulc. According to the CIA, Szulc "had had a standing invitation, since November 1961, for direct contact with President Kennedy, Attorney General Kennedy, or Mr. McGeorge Bundy, on matters concerning Cuba."[67]

When CIA Director John McCone heard of the plan, he presented the idea to Robert Kennedy at a Special Group meeting in March 1963. Bobby much preferred this proposal to that of advisor McGeorge Bundy, who at the same meeting proposed an accommodation with Castro. Bobby wrote a memo to his brother, who showed no immediate interest. A week later, Bobby again wrote the President, complaining that JFK had not moved on the idea.[68] Soon, JFK was persuaded to let the idea proceed. Szulc testified in 1975 about what happened next:

> *I was invited to lunch with Mr. [Robert] Kennedy at the Justice Department. We discussed in considerable length the situation in Cuba following the invasion, the pros and cons of some different possible actions by the United States government in that context. At the end of this conversation, the Attorney General asked me if I would have objections to meeting with his brother the President. I said I would of course be pleased to do so. The following day I received a call from the White House indicating that the President would like me to come in at 11 o'clock in the morning on that day in November, which I did.*

Much of the remainder of Szulc's testimony is still withheld. However, through various other sources, we can begin to piece together the ensuing activity.

After JFK's meeting with Szulc, Robert Hurwitch, the State Department's representative on RFK's Cuban Coordinating Committee was called in to meet with the President. "I've just had a meeting with a well-known journalist," Kennedy told Hurwitch. JFK proceeded to outline an aggressive plan aimed at ridding the world of Castro once and for all. As usual, Bobby was to be in charge, with Lansdale as the coordinator. As Hurwitch wrote in his unpublished memoirs:

> *I was speechless, and regrettably failed to object to what had seemed to me to be a doomed, romantic adventure...[Lansdale] obtained this assignment despite his total lack of experience in Latin America in general, and Cuba, in particular.[69]*

By February 9, 1963, Szulc was accompanied by Moreno and Hurwitch to a CIA safe house in Washington, D.C. to formalize the stratagem. Hurwitch recalled, "After the first meeting, I regretted more than ever not having objected at the White House meeting." To object, Hurwitch knew, was to doom his career. "What the hell do you do with the brother of the president of the United States?" Hurwitch recently lamented to journalist Seymour Hersh. "I've got four kids." Thus, the project proceeded, given the CIA code-name AM/TRUNK.[70]

Apparently, despite his nonmilitary background, Szulc remained a consultant on the project as it progressed. A note found on a September 23, 1963 CIA cover sheet written by Helms ("going back many months") instructs the CIA's Cuba Project officer Alfonso Rodriguez to *"maintain periodic contact with Szulc on Cuban matters at Presidential request."*[71] (Author's italics)

Hurwitch's assistant at the State Department's Cuba Desk, Robert Stevenson, recalled in 1996 a key facet of the program to which he was privy. "I remember hearing during the Kennedy term that there were plans afoot to kill Castro," says

Stevenson, adding that he most likely became aware of the plotting through his boss, Robert Hurwitch.[72] Raphael Quintero, a coordinator of the infiltration scheme, readily admits that "taking out" Castro was always part of the 1963 AM/TRUNK plan, further confirming that AM/TRUNK was indeed coordinated with AM/LASH.

It was quickly decided that the two key Cuban exiles to be used in the AM/TRUNK operation would be Jose "Ricardo" Rabel Nunes and Miguel Diaz Isalgue. Ricardo was the brother of Luis Rabel Nunes, who succeeded RFK confidante Sergio Arcacha as the CRC delegate in New Orleans. Luis supplied the laundry truck used by David Ferrie and others to transport munitions in the "Houma transfer." Ricardo had been raised in the U.S., but, like many Hispanic-American idealists, had moved to Cuba in the 1950s to aid the anti-Batista effort. He became the manager of the Havana Hilton hotel and, after the revolution, was appointed by Castro to lead the Agrarian Reform Movement. However, Castro retained suspicions about Ricardo, who had spent so much time in the U.S.

Similarly, Ricardo Rabel had grown disillusioned with Fidel Castro. In 1960, Ricardo entered into a long relationship with a CIA contact on the island. He spent the next two years collecting intelligence data for the United States. By 1962, Ricardo was tipped off that Castro was on to him and that his days were numbered. The CIA started to make escape plans for him and his wife, Sylvia. He was promised eventual passage to the U.S. in return for secreting Cuban government documents in his baggage.

Late one night, in December 1962, Ricardo, accompanied by his wife Sylvia, kept his rendezvous with a CIA escape plane at a dirt airstrip in the Cuban jungle. Sylvia, however, seized by fear and the possibility of never seeing her family again, refused to board the plane. Ricardo, Cuban documents in hand, had no choice, because he had received word that his execution was imminent. Amid tears and hysteria, Ricardo pleaded with his wife, but to no avail. Accompanied by Navy planes, with Castro's Air Force planes giving chase, Ricardo made his escape. Upon arriving in Miami, the CIA assured him that they would bring his family out. It never happened, and Ricardo Rabel never saw his wife again.[73]

Throughout 1963, Ricardo Rabel assisted the CIA in screening Cuban military leaders for inclusion in AM/TRUNK, as well as helping infiltrate exile spies back to the island. The other key AM/TRUNK exile, Miguel Diaz, was busy infiltrating the island, helping incite the forthcoming rebellion. Diaz told members of the Cuban Army that he was authorized by "Bob Kennedy" to offer a large sum of money if a Cuban pilot would fly a Russian MIG 21 to the U.S.

According to CIA documents, the CIA's Richard Helms and Seymour Bolten held secret AM/TRUNK meetings in the White House with, among others, JFK aide Ralph Dungan, whose name is reflected dozens of times in RFK's phone logs for the period. Still, the complete list of White House attendees can only be surmised.[74] When asked how preparations were going for the upcoming revolt, a

CIA officer who worked on both AM/LASH and AM/TRUNK told the author, "We were excited. Things were looking good, and it was beginning to look as though we had turned the corner on the Castro problem."[75]

The CIA's senior officials knew otherwise, and saw the folly of the AM/TRUNK operation. Ted Shackley, the Miami Station chief, recently recalled, "We didn't see any evidence that the military revolt would be successful. There was no proof of large numbers of Cuban officers interested."[76] At the "troop" level, Brigade leader, and RFK confidante, Raphael Quintero tended to agree, saying, "The underground was kaput in 1963." Certainly as an isolated action, AM/TRUNK would have failed, but in concert with AM/LASH and the invasion scenario of OPLAN 380-63, anything was possible (including another nuclear confrontation with the USSR.)

The fact that military planners had a "contingency plan" for invading Cuba means nothing by itself. Senior defense officials will describe hundreds of such contingency OPLANS, some fanciful, which are written regularly and never see the light of day. However, some do get implemented—and OPLAN 380-63 was clearly on the fast track to full implementation. The proof is in the context. Consider:

- *OPLAN 380-63 called for UW (Unconventional Warfare) elements to be carried out in Cuba by the CIA in the months before escalation. This is exactly what happened with AM/TRUNK, and was attempted with AM/LASH.*

- *The plan further called for the initial landings to involve Cubans trained in the U.S. and Central America. In fact, in 1963, the Cuban Officer Training Program was in full swing in places like Ft. Holabird, Maryland; Ft. Benning, Georgia; and other Army facilities. Also, Artime and associates had large camps functioning throughout Central America. These camps, secretly endorsed by the White House, were often supplied forces by camps near New Orleans.*

- *Cuban exile groups in Miami and New Orleans (especially within the Cuban Revolutionary Council) were talking openly about an imminent U.S.-supported invasion that would start in late 1963 and culminate in 1964— exactly the timetable described in the newly-released JCS papers. The very exiles making these predictions were meeting with continuing frequency in 1963 with Bobby Kennedy—whom they point to as having authorized the Central American camps. These meetings continued until the very day John Kennedy was assassinated on November 22, 1963.*

General Alexander Haig, assigned to the CCC, but excluded from the most secret sessions in Bobby's office, opined in 1998 that no unprovoked invasion would ever have been undertaken by the U.S.. However, when shown the recently-released OPLAN's call for a coordinated pre-invasion revolt, Haig said, "Now this certainly was something different. This would change the landscape." Haig conceded that this change of landscape could clearly be utilized to justify the 1964 invasion plan.[77]

In fact, the ongoing activity appeared to be slightly ahead of the OPLAN timetable and there is not the slightest reason to suspect, with all this investment, that the plan was not going forward. The heightened activity demonstrates that, "crackdown" notwithstanding, the Kennedys had big plans for Castro. An integral part of these plans concerned maneuvers that were occurring on the shores of a body of water north of New Orleans known as Lake Ponchartrain.

The Camps on Lake Ponchartrain

Para-military training camps were a fact of New Orleans life in the 1960s. From the days prior to the Bay of Pigs, when Nino Diaz, in violation of international law (but backed by the U.S. government), trained there for the invasion, New Orleaneans had made their land available to those engaged in the liberation of Cuba. The weapons in the Santa Ana's hold (Diaz's ship) were, it was later learned, packed in crates labeled "Schlumberger"[78]—the very company whose bunker Banister, Ferrie, et al, emptied after the invasion, allegedly under the Kennedys' aegis.[79] Through the efforts of New Orleans volunteers like Dave Ferrie, Cuban exiles, again citing Kennedy acquiescence, continued to occupy camps for training and homesteading for a number of years.

Because he had infiltrated the exile community, the Cuban dictator (unlike the American populace) knew what was going on from the start. A year after the Bay of Pigs invasion, in an exposé of the camp, a local newspaper would state, "As a matter of fact, only the Castro government ever formally named New Orleans as a Bay of Pigs training ground. And as a matter of fact, he was right."[80]

When Lee Oswald came to New Orleans from Dallas in 1963, there were as many as six Cuban exile training camps and weapons bunkers situated on and around Lake Ponchartrain. By far, the two most important were what came to be referred to as the "McLaney Camp" and the "MDC Camp" (Movemiento Democratica Cristiano, or, the Christian Democratic Movement).

The McLaney Camp

On July 31, 1963, the FBI, acting on a tip, raided the Lake Ponchartrain property of William McLaney. Kept in the dark about AM/LASH, AM/TRUNK, and OPLAN 380-63, the FBI agents confiscated more than a ton of dynamite, 20 100-pound bomb casings, fuses, napalm, and other assorted explosive paraphernalia.[81] Some of the material, according to one source, had been part of the Banister arms transfer at Schlumberger two years earlier.[82] As one investigator in New Orleans discovered, "The explosives had been found crated for shipment to Cuba."[83] FBI interviews in Miami also suggested that some of the explosives were to be loaded on two planes near the camp—B-25 aircraft slated for an imminent bombing run to Cuba.[84]

Mrs. McLaney told reporters that she and her husband had turned over their cottage as a "favor to friends" they had known from their days in Havana. What she didn't say was that her husband William was the brother of Mike McLaney, with whom he had worked at the Nacional Hotel-Casino in Cuba. She also neglected to mention that some of their "good friends" included the Kennedys. Six weeks earlier, in a similar raid in Miami, William McLaney's brother Mike was "detained, but not arrested," even after it was determined that he supplied the money and explosives for the operation.

The FBI briefly detained eleven men, none of whom was ever charged with a crime. This is a curious omission, given the amount of illegal weaponry confiscated and the fact that the McLaney's past history ostensibly connected the weapons with organized criminals such as Meyer Lansky. In addition, the Bureau was aware that the same individuals who, six weeks earlier had supplied the explosives to Mike McLaney, had also stocked William's cottage on the lake. It has now been accepted that both operations were overseen by Mike McLaney, and his brother was merely letting him use the cottage for storage after the Miami raid.

Ever since the raids, researchers have been confounded by the fact that no one was ever formally charged with a crime. Some have inferred that the FBI was in league with certain exiles to dilute the efforts of the Kennedy "crackdown"— a crackdown now known to be superficial in nature. Others suspected that it had more to do with the Kennedy/McLaney relationship.

In an attempt to determine if this played a role, the author made contact in 1994 with Mike McLaney, William McLaney, and Mike McLaney's aide, Steve Reynolds. Reynolds was the most direct: "The Kennedys got us off," he said. "They were aware of that operation from the start." William McLaney, measuring his words, would only say, "My brother and I both met Robert Kennedy many times. We did favors for him, and sometimes he'd return them."[85] William McLaney first met Bobby in Haiti on an occasion Reynolds remembered: "At the time, Mike owned the Royal Haitian Hotel. Bobby Kennedy used to come down with Peter Lawford."

If the FBI had pursued the tangled web, it would have discovered that those seized at the camp effectively implicated their highly-placed sponsors. Among those seized were:

Victor Espinoza Hernandez—Hernandez, it would later be determined by the Church Committee, was the lifelong friend of Rolando Cubela Secades (AM/LASH), the man who would, according to Manuel Artime, be suggested by the President as a likely candidate to assassinate Castro. The Church Committee left little doubt that Hernandez and Artime were in constant friendly contact with both Cubela and Robert Kennedy. And, the Cubela/AM/LASH operation was under the personal supervision of Robert Kennedy.

Sam Benton—Mike McLaney's lieutenant at the Nacional, who, according to Gerry Hemming, had cooperated with Robert Kennedy on a stolen securities investigation. Hemming has recently stated that Sam Benton introduced Johnny Rosselli to Robert Kennedy at the infamous Miami houseboat meeting with Michael McLaney.[86]

Rich Lauchli—Lauchli, an Illinois-based arms supplier, was the co-founder of the Minutemen, a fanatical right wing group. Lauchli was also the arms supplier for the provisional Cuban government led by Dr. Paulino Sierra, of Chicago. Sierra's contacts, like Benton's and McLaney's, went straight to Bobby Kennedy.

At the time of the raid, Sierra had expressed concern that the Nicaraguan training camps are "a political maneuver of GPFOCUS [RFK], to protect GPIDEAL [JFK] in the coming elections."[87] According to State Department records, two weeks after the raid, Bobby Kennedy's office contacted the State Department's Coordinator of Cuban Affairs, John H. Crimmins, advising him to meet with Dr. Sierra. Bobby's exile liaison Harry Williams then called Dr. Sierra in order to set up the meeting.[88]

Years later, Sierra noted that both he [Sierra] and Crimmins were mutual friends of "Bobby's Boy," Harry Williams.[89] At the meeting, Sierra said that he had recently visited Luis Somoza in Nicaragua, where "Somoza told him that he was heading a movement of the five Central American countries to overthrow Castro and that he had the blessing of the United States government." Somoza had been "telling Carribean notables [including another exile leader named Laureano Batista Falla] that he had received 'the green light'" directly from Robert Kennedy.[90] After Batista Falla "received the green light" from Somoza (who stated that he received it from Bobby Kennedy), his men "left Miami for the camp on July 23, 1963."[91]

The FBI would learn in 1967 that "the arms cache was an operation of the Directorio Revolucionario Estudiantil (DRE),"[92] which was created by the CIA in September 1960.[93] The DRE was under the wing of Dr. Paulino Sierra's provisional government, the Chicago Junta (approved by JFK), and in direct contact with Bobby. Most importantly, as the *New York Times* confirmed, the Louisiana camps had been conceived in 1961 by the Cuban Revolutionary Council,[94] whose local branch had been founded by Bobby Kennedy intimate Sergio Arcacha.

The MDC Camp

The Christian Democratic Movement (MDC) was an early underground movement in Cuba that split off from Castro when it detected his Communist leanings. The MDC's military chief was an independently wealthy young Cuban named Laureano Batista Falla. The HSCA referred to Batista's MDC as "one of the most active and effective underground groups in Havana in the early 1960's."[95] Like other underground groups, the MDC migrated to Miami after the Castro revolution.

When Artime set up his Latin American camps in 1963, he used part of the money Bobby Kennedy provided to, in effect, subcontract with the MDC the job of recruiting and training troops on the outskirts of New Orleans. According to company employee, Nilo Messer, the MDC's New Orleans operation used the "cover" of being a lumber business called Maritima BAM, with headquarters in Miami. "Funds from the U.S. government backed the company. It was a mobilization of hundreds of men, and it was expensive."[96]

Richard Davis, a Cuban exile and MDC leader living in New Orleans, had struck a deal with a wealthy right-wing geologist named David L. Raggio to assist Batista in training exiles. Raggio, who had ties to the John Birch Society, agreed to finance the training to the tune of $10,000 a month. The "cover" was Raggio's Guatemalan Lumber Company, which he co-owned with Gus DeLaBarre. The camp's public purpose (as told to DeLaBarre) was to train Cuban workers to log mahogany trees, then relocate the workers to Latin America. By this time, Somoza had approached Costa Rican President Francisco Orlich to go along with the Washington-approved plan. Orlich convinced his brother to supply the land.[97]

According to Maritima's treasurer, Luis Arrizurieta:

The Costa Ricans were told by their government that a group of Cubans had been given the opportunity to extract wood from the Sarapiqui River to Colonel Orlich's [the president's brother's] farm. That was our cover. We would chop down a few trees in the beginning to build the camp, but then we didn't chop down anymore. We created the image of a timber yard, where wood was cut and exported.[98]

Back in New Orleans, one of the camp managers (hereafter referred to as Juan) played his own role. He recently recalled, "Our camp was located four miles from Covington, on a 70 acre spread. The camp was in operation until right after Kennedy was killed."[99] Most estimates put the total number of trainees at between one and two dozen men. Gus DeLaBarre's nephew Frank DeLaBarre describes the camp as "a big lodge. They all had separate rooms in one large building. It had a large porch and a swimming pool."

Frank DeLaBarre remembers:

We [Frank and Gus DeLaBarre] were originally approached by Richard Davis on behalf of the Catholic Church. We thought we were offering land as homes for Cuban refugees. One day I heard gunfire out there, and I wondered if we had been duped.[100]

Juan, who readily admits that the camp was indeed used for military training, says, "Batista's military aide, Commandante Diego [Victor Paneque], was involved with the training. We stopped after the assassination, because it was no longer kosher to go after Castro." Another camp member, Angel Vega, testified that the men were put on a physical fitness program, and trained in rifle assembly and disassembly—hardly prerequisites for lumber cutting.[101] Carlos Quiroga, who admitted being involved with the Houma arms transfer (allegedly approved in Washington), told the New Orleans D.A. that some of the Schlumberger weapons "went to Richard Davis' MDC group."

Frank remembers asking his "Uncle Gus," "What the hell is going on out there?" Gus DeLaBarre responded by saying, "I already checked with the FBI. They know everything we're doing and they said just to forget about it."[102] Frank remembers, "The local sheriff reported that heavy armaments were being used on the property. [After the assassination,] I wondered if we had harbored, unknowingly, an assassination squad aimed at Castro by Kennedy." Frank says that after Kennedy was killed, he sought out the FBI, and was advised by an agent not to worry. "We know all about it," the agent said.[103]

During this time, Dave Ferrie was believed by many to have been involved in training Cubans at one of the camps. It was probably the MDC camp. Ferrie had once told Julian Buznedo, "I'm working with some wealthy people from the John Birch Society who are helping at the refugee camps."[104] Ferrie/Banister friend Joe Newbrough told the author in 1993, "I understand Dave was there [the camps] frequently. He had a daily involvement with the Cubans as a whole. He met with them at a place on Bienville Street almost nightly."[105] Ferrie's godson, Morris Brownlee, remembers, "There were often Cubans at Dave's apartment. They had maps of Cuba, and appeared to be in training for a re-invasion."[106]

Juan recalls an incident at the camp that would put the activists on constant alert: "It involved a pro-Castro infiltrator named Fernando Fernandez." The details of the Fernandez incident also corroborate the invasion planning underway in Central America.

On July 23, 1963, Batista Falla, in Venezuela, wrote a letter to the camp, partially in English "for security reasons." Fernandez, who spoke excellent English, was asked to translate. The letter gave specific details of the administration's plans:

> We have acquired the necessary financial resources as well as military bases so that we can now hit Castroland with everything we have. I have received a check for $9,575 from Mr. Davis and his friends with which we have paid for two Mustang's (P-51) and one B-26 bomber. All with their bombs and ammunition. [We will] hit the refineries of Bellot in Habana Bay and the Naramjito power station. The commandos…will cut all telephone communications, and proceed in 14 minutes to kill every Russian, [and] shall be immediately evacuated by the U.S. Navy submarine U.S.S. Barracuda…The men under your command will leave your base on August 1st, 0700 hours, and shall proceed to Nicaragua.[107]

By this time, for reasons not known, the exiles had become suspicious of Fernandez' true allegiance, and another camp member was assigned to monitor him. On August 1st, a letter Fernandez had written to the Cuban Ambassador to Mexico City, Carlos Lechuga, was intercepted and opened by his monitor.[108] The letter "reported his 'chance' infiltration of a 'serious operation' whose imminent attack 'is leaving from Central America.' He said he had 'detailed reports of this military plan.'"[109]

The letter went on to say that Fernandez wanted to return to Cuba. The letter's parting sentence advised, "In short, we await instructions."

Juan says consideration was given to taking "this Castro agent" (Fernandez) deep out into the bayou and drowning him. He was eventually driven out of Louisiana by Angel Vega and released. "But the guy made it back to Cuba and became high in the Cuban Secret Service," says Juan. Fernandez would tell Miami authorities that although he admitted that he was "Castro's spy," the MDC trainees had tortured him into the confession. A UPI story stated that Fernandez's chief assignment in New Orleans had been "to follow the activities of Manuel Artime, one of the leaders of the unsuccessful invasion of the Bay of Pigs, who is connected with the so-called "Central American Plan."

The Fernandez incident would greatly heighten tensions among the exile community in New Orleans, who, as a result, were constantly on the lookout for infiltrators.

Laureano Batista Falla later admitted under oath to the New Orleans District Attorney the true destination of the trainees: the Naval guerrilla base in Guatemala, under the direction of Bobby and JFK's confidante Manuel Artime,. He also said this was done with the approval of General Somoza of Nicaragua.[110]

The Kennedy administration's fingerprints were all over New Orleans and the surrounding environs—from 544 Camp street to David Ferrie to the training camps on the lake. The exile movement, which already "leaked like a sieve," also seemed rife with Castro spies. Clearly, the pot was boiling.

In the winter and spring of 1963, the FBI intercepted letters from Cuba to Miami that, if authentic, indicated that President Kennedy's Cuban agenda had placed his very life in danger. The intercepts stated that "there was a plan underway in Cuba to assassinate President Kennedy during his forthcoming visit to Costa Rica." An FBI memo of February 25, 1963 said that ten unidentified Castro agents "will be furnished with false passports, transported to Mexico and then flown to Costa Rica." In a separate intercept, the Bureau obtained a letter that "discussed a plan to assassinate the President of the U.S., and indicated there was a Cuban espionage group in the U.S." The intercepted letter was released in 1994, and said in part:

> I already told "your friends" in Miami and Passaic, as well as the people in Washington, the exact instructions for the attack we are planning on Kennedy. We must wound imperialism to the heart, a death blow. If we are able to kill President Kennedy, it would be an extraordinary success for Fidel...We would completely paralyze the future plans of the United States if we are able to kill Kennedy. Surely, after that, Vice President L. Johnson would not bother us for

a long time. Get in touch with your friends and tell them they can pass on the instructions they have received through proper channels...Specific and detailed instructions will be sent by the channel that is known to you. Answer me by the same channel. Fidel is anxious to know how the plans are going.

Best Regards,
Pepe[111]

It now seems inevitable that someone in the United States, loyal to Castro, would decide to take action against the president. It seems all the more likely that that "someone" would be in a city teeming with members of Castro's "espionage group" and the Kennedys' escalating anti-Castro operation.

That someone appeared in New Orleans on April 25, 1963.

CHAPTER NINE

KENNEDY AND OSWALD: COLLIDING OBSESSIONS

By the time Oswald arrived in New Orleans in the spring of 1963, Sergio Arcacha had long since vacated his Camp Street office. On the first day of the Cuban missile crisis in October 1962, he departed for Miami. Nonetheless, the network he established with Ferrie, Martens, Banister and others—with Robert Kennedy's blessings—was still in place, and well-oiled. Its focus shifted from fund-raising to military training at a half-dozen camps along Lake Ponchartrain, east of the city. At least two of these six camps had links to Robert Kennedy and his bold Central American plan.

RFK's new streamlined operations included preparing for a Cuban reinvasion while simultaneous assassination plots were planned. This new agenda was to be carried out by a group of Cubans that included Manuel Artime, Harry Williams, Dr. Paulino Sierra, and Rolando Cubela Secades. The group was predominantly composed of former members of Brigade 2506 and their associates whom Bobby had adopted into the Kennedy clan as they became more important to his plans.

Not only did the tentacles of this network extend into New Orleans, but they seemed to be everywhere Lee Oswald went. And virtually every New Orleans participant not only knew the network was penetrated by Castro's spies, but thought Oswald was one of them. The words of Arcacha ring again: "Castro knew every move we made."

Oswald in New Orleans

"How will it all end?"
> —**Marina Oswald, from New Orleans, in a letter to Ruth Paine**

On April 24, 1963 Oswald took an overnight bus from Dallas to New Orleans. Marina and their baby daughter June went to live, temporarily, with Ruth Paine in a Dallas suburb called Irving. The Oswalds planned to re-unite when Lee found work in New Orleans.

Upon arriving in New Orleans, Oswald called his aunt Lillian Murret, and she agreed to allow him to stay with her until he gained employment and had an apartment of his own. From his first days in New Orleans, Oswald began looking for work. He found it on May 9th, two weeks after his arrival. He became a maintenance man at the Reily Coffee Company, oiling and greasing the machinery. Landing the job initially delighted him, but actually performing it was something else again. As with school, the Marines, and his time at the Minsk radio factory, Oswald quickly lost interest.

On the same day of his hiring, he found a small apartment at 4907 Magazine Street. That day, Ruth Paine, with her two children, drove Marina and daughter June the 500 miles to New Orleans. Marina would later tell friends that her first weeks in New Orleans were the happiest times for her and Lee. For an instant, life seemed almost normal. However, it wasn't long before Lee reverted to form and began behaving erratically. He vacillated between wanting to return to Russia, and wanting to send Marina back alone. He had forced her to write to the Soviet Embassy asking to be readmitted, which she did. Lee Harvey Oswald had obviously reached another crossroad in his life. He hated his life and was desperate to change it. Marina's biographer Priscilla McMillan describes this period:

> Lee was having trouble in his sleep again—the first time since February [1963]. One night he cried, yet when he woke up he could not remember what his dream had been about. He started having nosebleeds. Once or twice he talked in his sleep, and one night toward the very end of June he had four anxiety attacks, during which he shook from head to toe at intervals of half an hour and never once woke up.[1]

Marina said that the last time Lee had experienced sleep problems was in the spring of 1963, before he went to New Orleans, indeed before his attempt on General Walker's life. Whenever Lee was going through a painful decision-making process, he seemed to have trouble sleeping.

And Lee was again becoming abusive. As in Texas and Minsk, neighbors were disturbed by the sound of loud fights coming from the Oswalds' apartment.[2] Marina's letters to Ruth Paine describe in painful detail the sorry state of her marital relationship. In one such letter, Marina wrote, "As soon as you left, all 'love' stopped...He insists that I leave America...And again he has said he doesn't love me...How will it all end?"[3]

Their landlady, Mrs. Jesse Garner, later recalled, "I tried to talk to Marina and the baby...[Marina] would put her hands over her eyes and start crying."[4]

Marina's own personality didn't help matters. A consummate "tease," she spared no energy in finding ways to emasculate Oswald, according to her biographer. For example, she constantly referred to an earlier love, Anotoly. He was Marina's partner in a Minsk tryst that had taken place when Lee was out of town. She would often compare Lee to Anatoly, telling Lee that if he spent his whole life trying, he could never learn to kiss as well as Anatoly. The stories of Anatoly and others would drive Lee to scream, "Stop it! I can't stand it. I don't want to hear about your boyfriends."[5]

Perhaps the worst insult was that Anatoly physically resembled President Kennedy. Marina even bought a picture of the president, and displayed it in the apartment to remind her of Anatoly. She told Lee of Kennedy, "He is very attractive—I can't say what he is as President, but, I mean, as a man." She knew just how to push Lee's buttons, and this kind of baiting blinded him with jealousy.[6]

Oswald let his personal hygiene deteriorate: not brushing his teeth regularly; bathing infrequently; shaving every second or third day; walking around the apartment stark naked. Later investigation located three neighbors who complained about a ghostly pale Oswald spending days in the apartment's backyard, clad in a yellow bathing suit and thongs, armed with bug spray, incessantly battling garden pests. The corner grocer recalled how Oswald often came into his store, argued about his prices, and left without ever making a purchase.[7]

The neighbors also complained that it was more than a little unsettling watching Oswald on his front porch at night, regularly "dry firing" his rifle as fast as he could, aiming at passing cars. Marina herself was horrified by Oswald's front porch displays of machismo.[8]

One evening, returning from a stroll with daughter June, Marina caught Lee on the porch, perched on one knee, aiming the rifle toward the street. Marina scolded him, yelling, "What are you doing, playing with your rifle again?"

"Fidel Castro needs defenders," came Lee's reply.[9]

Marina and her neighbors were not alone in their observations. Oswald's fellow employees considered him odd as well, especially his habit of pointing his index finger at them and saying "Bang," as if shooting them. Charles LeBlanc, who trained Oswald in his job at Reily Coffee, would later testify that Oswald seemed to care little about learning to perform his job tasks. He would lie about greasing machines he hadn't even touched.[10] Lee's 15-minute work breaks turned into 45-minute disappearances from the workplace. He would spend this time next door at the Crescent City garage, where he and the owner, Adrian Alba, would discuss guns, debating which ones were the most deadly. True to form, Oswald kept to himself at Reily, never associating with other employees. From the beginning, the personnel manager wanted to fire him, but because of a shortage of employees in Oswald's department, he was kept on. The situation was similar to the one in Minsk, where his manager had wanted to fire him but was prevented because of government fears that Oswald would stage another suicide attempt. However, by July 19th, the Reily manager had had enough, and Oswald was fired.

The firing may have been an immediate disappointment to Oswald, but there was one major benefit. His painful decision had been reached. He would devote no further energy to his job, or to thoughts of living in America or Russia. Lee was now free to devote all his energy to defending Castro and moving to Castro's Cuba.

Castro's Champion

"Fidel Castro needs defenders. I'm going to join his army of volunteers."
—Lee Oswald to his wife, Marina[11]

"Fidel Castro was his hero."
—Marina Oswald[12]

"The one thing we know from all the investigations of Oswald, from the Warren Commission's to Jim Garrison's to my own and to every other one conducted, was that when Oswald got to New Orleans, his central focus was Castro's Cuba. Almost everything he did concerned Castro. Whether it was to try to hand out leaflets in support of Castro or organize a Fair Play for Cuba Committee, his correspondence or his attempts to infiltrate the anti-Castro groups and even provoke fights with them, can be related to Cuba. This is also true of his appearances on radio and television—whatever he did during this period."
—Author Edward Jay Epstein[13]

There is no evidence that Oswald's employment at Reily was anything but coincidental. But if he had intended to penetrate the anti-Castro operations of the Kennedy administration, he couldn't have placed himself in a better location. In 1963, the Reily Company was located on Magazine Street, in the heart of the New Orleans intelligence community. The CIA, FBI, and Office of Naval Intelligence all surrounded Lafayette Square, a two-block walk from Oswald's place of work. The anti-Castro "Grand Central Station," 544 Camp Street, was a mere block away. That location, on one side of the Newman building, had formerly housed Bobby Kennedy's friend Sergio Arcacha Smith and his Cuban Revolutionary Council. The Lafayette Street side housed the offices of Guy Banister, the anti-Castro former FBI Special Agent in Charge. On the first floor corner, where the two streets—Lafayette and Camp—intersected, was Mancuso's restaurant, a hangout for the community of Cuban exiles. Some of them were volunteers being trained at the camps on Lake Ponchartrain, an extension of the Kennedy administration's "autonomous operations" aimed at retaking the island. Adrian Alba, with whom Oswald shared many an extended workbreak, reported that he often saw Oswald at Mancuso's.[14]

One of the first things Oswald did in New Orleans was to obtain a borrower's card from the New Orleans Public Library. The first book he took out was *Portrait of a Revolutionary: Mao Tse Tung*, by Robert Payne. He also withdrew a book on the assassination of Louisiana Senator and presidential candidate Huey Long. But another book may have played an even more significant part in Oswald's accelerated political activism—John F. Kennedy's *Profiles in Courage*. With chapter titles such as "Courage and Politics" and "The Meaning of Courage," Kennedy exhorted the reader to be bold enough to take decisive political action, in spite of public disapproval—to have the courage of one's convictions. "Always do what is right," Kennedy wrote, "regardless of whether it is popular."[15] Kennedy elaborated, "In the days ahead, only the very courageous will be able to take the hard and unpopular decisions necessary for our survival in the struggle with a powerful enemy."[16]

Whatever his inspiration, Oswald's pro-Castro activities greatly increased during his stay in New Orleans. An early example was Oswald's request to the pro-Castro organization, the Fair Play For Cuba Committee (FPCC), for permission to open a New Orleans chapter, explaining that he was going to rent an office for that purpose. There was little question that Castro's government was behind the organization. Cuban exiles interviewed in Miami and New Orleans reported that the FPCC received its funding from Havana, by way of Montreal, Canada. The FPCC was also known to work closely with the Cuban Embassy in Mexico City, a center for Cuban-sponsored espionage and terrorism.

The FPCC's National Director in New York, Vincent Lee, encouraged Oswald to start a New Orleans chapter, but tried to dissuade him from renting an office. It was about this time that the janitor of 544 Camp Street recalls a young man inquiring about renting an office in the building, but not following up on the inquiry. The man stuck out, the janitor noted, because hardly anyone came in desiring to rent space in the now run-down building, which was notoriously difficult to keep occupied with paying tenants. Of the handful of offices available, only two were occupied in 1963, with workers' unions.[17]

The correspondence with Vincent Lee initiated a steady stream of Marxist literature that Oswald began receiving, not only from the FPCC, but from other pro-Castro organizations. Many of these documents have been widely reported; however, one that has not received any attention is entitled "Cuban Counter-Revolutionaries in the United States" by Vincent Lee. The pamphlet is nothing less than a diatribe against Cuban exiles in the United States. Vincent Lee wrote that the Kennedy administration, using these exiles, had "created a subversive army" and that "evidence is piling up for another invasion of Cuba." The document went on to cite the two organizations to be used in these "crimes against Cuba": the Cuban Student Directorate (headed by Carlos Bringuier in New Orleans), and the Cuban Revolutionary Council (created by the White House, with Bobby Kennedy as liaison). Lee ended the pamphlet by singling out RFK confidante Roberto San Román, who led the Bay of Pigs invasion force and fought against Castro in the mountains before the revolution, as one of Cuba's most reprehensible turncoats.

If Vincent Lee's pamphlet were not enough to alert Oswald to the Kennedys' plans for Castro, surely word on the street would have been. "These Cubans were very public about what they were doing," says Dave Ferrie's godson, Morris Brownlee. "In fact, it was publicized—they were trying to enlist people."[18] Juan, who coordinated the MDC camp on Lake Ponchartrain, adds, "We Cubans have a bad habit of talking too much. There were no secrets."[19] Sergio Arcacha merely laughs when the subject of the exiles' lack of secrecy is mentioned. "Everybody, including Castro, knew every move we made," Arcacha says.

Without question, the combined preparations for AM/TRUNK, AM/LASH, and OPLAN 380 were among the Kennedy brothers' worst-kept secrets. The laughable lack of security was beginning to resemble the fiasco of the pre-Bay of Pigs planning.

The final words in the Vincent Lee pamphlet were "fight for HANDS OFF CUBA!!!"[20]

Lee Oswald adopted the FPCC's motto "HANDS OFF CUBA" as his own, and soon had 1,000 leaflets *(see photo spread)* made announcing meetings of his New Orleans "chapter." As Lee explained to Marina, "These papers will help people be on the side of Cuba. Do you want them attacking little Cuba?"[21] In the space under "Location," Oswald hand stamped some of the handbills with his newly acquired Post Office Box number, and others with the address "544 Camp Street," the very center of anti-Castro exile activity in New Orleans. As one of Arcacha's co-workers at Camp Street told the author, "The plans were in place for a second invasion of Cuba. What we started at Camp Street was strategically coordinated with Washington." Although Arcacha, by this time, had left for Miami, the building, still housing Ferrie, Banister, and Mancuso's, continued as a virtual clearing house for anti-Castro Cuban exile activists, especially those training at the MDC and McLaney camps on Lake Ponchartrain. The Kennedys' encouragement of the New Orleans exile movement logically excluded movement participants from conspiring in a Kennedy assassination. However, due to a post assassination coverup of Washington's links to these New Orleans exiles, some concluded—quite erroneously—that they must have been in league with Kennedy's killer.

Guy Banister himself got caught up in this conspiracy talk; the rumors about his alleged involvement began when Warren Commission investigators seemingly excluded him from their probe. His former Bureau colleagues conducted a mere five-minute phone chat with Banister, and in that call to the private detective, the FBI investigator never even mentioned Oswald. The discovery of this fact increased the rumors that Banister had conspired with the FBI in the Kennedy assassination.

After much contention, it has become clear that Banister had nothing to do with Oswald or any Kennedy assassination attempts. The author has seen some of Banister's so-called "secret files"—supposedly detailing his links to Oswald. In fact, the files contain salacious surveillance photographs of prominent New Orleaneans. Banister, it turns out, was part of a typical dirt-gathering operation that FBI Director J. Edgar Hoover had no intention of disclosing or compromising for the sake of the post-assassination investigation. Banister never exploited the file material for blackmail, but according to his assistants, it was funneled to Hoover, infamous for his desire to maintain the upper hand with potential political enemies.

The question remains: Why did Oswald claim Banister's address as his own? The answer is—he didn't. A thorough investigation reveals that, like so many other conspiracy allegations, the "shared address" claim was without merit. In fact, Banister's address, around the corner, was technically on Lafayette Street, and locals never even thought of it as a Camp Street address, so the Banister-as-Oswald's-partner allegation was misplaced from the beginning.

It got started, it seemed, because most people outside New Orleans could not understand the physical layout of the place. Few offices in the Newman building had entrances on both 531 Lafayette Street and 544 Camp Street. Banister's office entrance was on the Lafayette Street side, which served only his first floor operation. *(See photospread.)* The Camp Street side consisted of a small lobby and stairs which led up to the few offices on the second floor, and only two were occupied (with trade unions) in 1963. Previously, and until February 1962, the second floor had also housed the offices of Arcacha's Cuban Revolutionary Council, but these offices were unoccupied in 1963. The use of the 544 Camp Street address certainly didn't imply a relationship with Banister, as the building was partitioned in such a way as to make it impossible to gain access to the detective agency on Lafayette Street from the Camp Street side. Banister investigator Joe Newbrough recently recalled:

> *If you entered 544 Camp Street, the only way you could have gotten to Banister's office was to go out a window....The Camp Street entrance went strictly to the second floor of the building. You had to exit the second floor to the sidewalk, walk around the corner, and go into Banister's office. Banister never even considered his office to be part of the Newman Building.[22]*

But the question still lingers. If neither Banister nor Arcacha's CRC were involved with Oswald, then why would Oswald stamp his leaflets "544 Camp St."? Guy Banister's explanation was simple and echoed that of many others at the time. "Oswald did it [used the address] to embarrass me," the anti-Castro Banister told his brother Ross Banister before his death in 1964.[23] Sergio Arcacha agrees. "Of course that's why he did it. Is there really any doubt?" he asked incredulously. More pointedly, Oswald, the childhood fan of *I Led Three Lives*, may have been relishing the role of provocateur—causing the exiles to doubt each others' true loyalties. Who, they would have wondered, was the true turncoat?

Oswald's intention to embarrass the anti-Castro community is certainly a possibility. It was widely known on the streets of New Orleans that anti-Castro activities were centered in the Newman building. Lafayette Square, on whose edge the Newman building was positioned, was the epicenter of Cuban exile activity, which included fund-raising and leafletting. Oswald, known to lunch at the exiles' hangout, Mancuso's, which was in the Newman Building, could not have been unaware of the thick anti-Castro fervor that enveloped him.

Thus, the possibility is strong: Oswald was again demonstrating his ability to unintentionally establish a trail that would confuse and confound historians long after he had died. This talent would force the government to initiate coverups that seemingly implied the government's own involvement in the Kennedy assassination. After Oswald was arrested for JFK's murder, and his use of the 544 Camp Street address was publicized, those in the know quickly grasped the implication: like everyone else in Lafayette Square, Oswald had learned of the sabotage and invasion plans, and using an exile hangout as his address was Oswald's way of embarrassing the exiles and their supporters—Robert F. Kennedy chief among them. RFK did not learn of the leaflets until the aftermath of Dallas, and at that time, embarrassment was the least of Bobby's problems.[24]

Oswald's attempts to build up the FPCC chapter in New Orleans, through leafletting, were a failure. He was made to leave the Dumaine Street Wharf for handing out the fliers and other FPCC literature in front of the USS Wasp because he lacked a proper permit. Oswald constructed other "membership" cards inventing a member named "A. J. Hidell"—the same imaginary person who ordered the Mannlicher Carcano rifle months earlier. When teased by Marina that Hidell sounded like the name of his hero, Fidel, he was embarrassed, but nonetheless admitted that no such person existed. "I have to do it this way. People will think I have a big organization," was Oswald's explanation.[25]

Marina told the local FBI, "Oh, he like [sic] Fidel and thought Hidell rhymes with it...No, he [Hidell] didn't exist."[26]

There is no evidence that Oswald's leafletting attracted even one recruit.

Lee Harvey Oswald, Spy

What Oswald saw on New Orleans' streets verified what Vincent Lee's literature had been telling him: Oswald's revered Castro was in trouble. For a brief period, Oswald seemed to harken back to his childhood spy fantasies, attempting to infiltrate the exiles' movement. Ernesto Rodriguez, who ran a Spanish language school not far from Lafayette Square, remembers Oswald coming to his office and introducing himself:

> He came here asking about Cubans and Cuban training camps and the like. He offered to help...Seemingly he was already aware that there was a training camp across the lake from us, north of Lake Ponchartrain. And he wanted to get into that. But that was supposedly top secret at the time. He seemed to know. But then you know, the Cubans were very indiscreet, so I wouldn't be surprised if he picked it up someplace on the street. I told him that I wouldn't be the party to help him. And I directed him to Carlos Bringuier.[27]

Oswald proceeded directly to Casa Roca, the clothing store owned by Carlos Bringuier—the local delegate to the exile group, the Cuban Student Directorate (DRE). It was August 5th, four days after the McLaney Camp raid made front page news in New Orleans. It is a virtual certainty that Oswald, a compulsive newspaper reader, read the article. Indeed, the raid was a major topic of conversation among the exiles in Lafayette Square at the time.

Upon arriving at the storefront, Oswald inquired of two young American teenagers, "Is this the Cuban exiles' headquarters?"[28] Oswald then assured Bringuier that he was opposed to Castro. He bragged to Bringuier and the two teenage boys that his Marine training had made him proficient in guerrilla warfare. Oswald then volunteered to help train Cubans in the fight against Castro. The teenagers were impressed with Oswald's technical knowledge. He claimed to know how to make a homemade gun. He claimed to know how to make gunpowder, and to derail a train. And, he said, he knew the art of sabotage, offering them specific advice on how to blow up the Huey Long bridge.[29]

Bringuier, because of several recent events, was suspicious of new faces in the community. First, he had just been told that the Miami headquarters of the DRE was involved with the McLaney Camp, and was worried that "the crackdown" would soon be cracking down on him. Second, the Fernandez infiltration incident was a fresh wound. Bringuier wrote:

> On August 2, 1963, I received in the store that I manage in New Orleans the visit of two friends of mine who informed me that there was a training camp a few miles outside of New Orleans...They also informed me of the fear they had that a Castro agent could be infiltrated into that training camp...The agent was a former Cuban newspaperman called Fernando Fernandez Baroenas...Notice the special interest of Oswald in helping me to train Cubans at a time when there was a secret training camp just a few miles from New Orleans...I did not trust Oswald.[30]

Bringuier was further put on alert by recent confrontations with other pro-Castro groups. In all that's been written about Oswald's time in New Orleans, very little attention has been given to these other groups, and many perceive Oswald as the lone pro-Castro activist in New Orleans. This is far from the truth. If fact, there was an active pro-Castro network, which could very easily have been aware of, or in touch with, Oswald. "Before Oswald, we had a lot of confrontations with pro-Castro supporters," says Bringuier. "Not long before he came into my store, we had a fight with a group called the New Orleans Council for Peaceful Alternatives. This is another reason I was suspicious of Oswald."[31]

The suspicious Bringuier told Oswald that he wasn't interested in his assistance. Oswald left the Casa, but returned the following day, leaving behind for Bringuier his Marine Corps training manual, which Bringuier retains to this day. Soon Oswald composed a ten-page document he had hoped would ingratiate him with pro-Castro officials.

Found among his possessions after his arrest for Kennedy's death, the document states in part, "I infiltrated the Cuban Student Directorate [DRE] and then harassed them with information I gained including having the N.O. [New Orleans] City Attorney General call them in and put a restraining order pending a restraining order pending a hearing on some so-called bonds for invasion they were selling in the New Orleans area."[32] Like most others who frequented the Lafayette Square vicinity, Oswald had become aware of the administration's re-invasion plans.

Three days later, on August 9th, one of Bringuier's friends, Celso Hernandez, came running into the store, upset at having seen an American on Canal Street handing out pro-Castro leaflets and holding a sign that proclaimed, "Viva Fidel.

Hands Off Cuba!" The two grabbed their own poster saying "90 miles away Cuba lies in chains," picked up their friend Miguel Cruz, and went hunting for the young activist. It took some searching, but eventually the protester was located at the corner of Canal and St. Charles. Bringuier was astonished to see that the young man was the very individual who had offered him help three days earlier, Lee Harvey Oswald.

The ensuing shouting match has been well documented over the years. For the record, Bringuier played Oswald like a violin, his well-known smirking grin in full display. Bringuier and his friends grabbed Oswald's leaflets and threw them in the air. Bringuier recalls what happened next:

> When he recognized me, he smiled at me. He even tried to shake hands with me. I refused to shake hands with him and I started insulting him and curs-ing him in English. When I saw that there was a group of Americans that gathered over there, I turned to the Americans and told them that Oswald wanted to destroy the United States in the same way that they have destroyed Cuba. The Americans start[ed] insulting Oswald then.[33]

A shoving match followed, and Bringuier felt Oswald was taunting him into throwing the first punch. Realizing how a foreigner would be perceived striking an American citizen, Bringuier regained enough self-control to refrain from hit-ting Oswald. However, the shouting continued until all four men were arrested.

Oswald was the only one of the four who couldn't initially make the $25 bail, and thus was the only one to spend the night in jail. In jail, he was inter-viewed by the local FBI (at Oswald's request), and by a New Orleans policeman, Lt. Francis Martello. The reports they filed are replete with Oswald's lies about his local "chapter" of the FPCC, its meetings and membership. Oswald also gave both FBI Agent Quigley and Lt. Martello copies of his pro-Castro fliers with the "544 Camp Street" address stamped on them—quite possibly in an effort to expose the threat to Castro posed by the anti-Castro Cubans who frequented that building. After initially contacting his cousin Joyce Murret, who refused to post bail, Oswald eventually secured his release through his aunt Lillian, with a loan from a family friend.

Oswald clipped and attached a small news article about the incident, and sent copies to the FPCC headquarters, and to the American Communist Party. He wrote, "I am doing my best to help the cause of new Cuba."[34]

Juan, the MDC camp manager, recently made a claim as to what happened next. "One day Lee Oswald knocks on my door," Juan recalls. "I have no idea how he found out about me or where I lived." Oswald said he was aware that Juan was involved in training Cubans on the lake. "I knew in my bones that Castro was behind Oswald," Juan says. "What I saw was a shitty-looking guy who was trying to finagle something. He was a lunatic hillbilly with B.O.—a casualty of life."[35] Juan then discussed with other camp members whether they should burn down Oswald's house. They decided against it because Oswald obviously didn't own the house he was living in, and the aggression would only harm his landlord. Instead, Juan accompanied Carlos Quiroga (a friend of both

Arcacha and Bringuier) to Oswald's apartment.

Arriving in the evening, Juan remained in the car while Quiroga went in to speak with Oswald. They spoke for approximately 45 minutes on the screened-in front porch. During this time, Quiroga became convinced that Oswald was a committed Communist. At one point, Oswald's daughter June came running out to the porch, and Oswald addressed her in Russian. Quiroga asked him where he had learned the language and Oswald replied, "I'm studying Russian at Tulane University."[36] Oswald also told Quiroga, "Cubans in the United States are all criminals." If the U.S. invaded Cuba, Oswald said, he would fight with Castro.[37]

Local FBI Special Agent in Charge Warren DeBrueys, who had started monitoring Oswald a month earlier, now stepped up his interest. Oswald had been called to his attention after a New York informant alerted him to Oswald's correspondence with the FPCC and other communist groups located there. As he had with Arcacha in 1961, DeBrueys sought out the current CRC and its members for information. He utilized Arcacha's successor, Frank Bartes, as well as Carlos Quiroga, Carlos Bringuier, and others.[38] When no evidence could be found of Oswald's network, the FBI lost interest in him. Bartes, who briefly met Oswald at his sentencing trial (Oswald was fined $10), advised DeBrueys that "Oswald was a potentially dangerous man"[39]—an astute conclusion that obviously wasn't taken very seriously.

Leaving the courtroom, Oswald was briefly interviewed by a local TV station. But the increasingly self-absorbed Oswald, who relished the notoriety, was in a quandary. He had no TV on which to watch himself on the news. He decided that with a little better planning, he could actually arrange to see himself on television. Three days later, he called all the local stations and advised them that on the following day, Friday, August 16, he could be seen demonstrating in front of the International Trade Mart. Two stations accepted his invitation. When the Friday demonstration was filmed for TV, Oswald was elated. He also had ideas about where he would view the coverage. That evening, he raced to the same corner grocery store where he had made himself a nuisance. The owner, Henry Cogreve, refused to let Oswald turn on his TV, whereupon Oswald left and followed Plan B: he would visit his Aunt Lillian.[40] Marina, by now sick of Lee's posturing, refused to accompany him, saying, "I see you all day at home in all forms. I don't want to see you on TV."[41]

The climax of this series of events was Oswald's participation in a radio debate with Bringuier, journalist Bill Stuckey, and Ed Butler. Bringuier had brought Oswald to Stuckey's attention after the trial, and Stuckey asked the all-too-willing Oswald to participate. Butler was the head of an anti-Communist organization known as the Information Council of The Americas (INCA).[42] Bringuier remembers first seeing Oswald at the radio station on the evening of the debate, Saturday, August 17:

> *Before the debate, we were talking over there for about 15 minutes and first I*
> *told him that if at any time he changed his mind and he wants to come to the*

right side, he can come to me and that I would try to help him. He said no,
that I was on the wrong side and that he was on the right side and he saw my
guidebook, the guidebook for Marines, that he had left for me. He said to me,
"Carlos, please don't use that guidebook because it's obsolete, you're going to
get killed."[43]

Butler recalls that Oswald arrived at the station in a heavy black wool suit on a typical New Orleans August day—incredibly hot and humid. "Yet he was as cool as a cucumber—didn't sweat a drop." Describing Oswald's appearance, Butler remembers, "Oswald had the face of a parrot on the neck of a bull! He had not a perpetual smirk but a sort of a fleeting sneer that would come over his face every once in a while."

For a while, the thirty-five minute debate went well for Oswald, who held his own against three well-informed opponents. Ed Butler remembers that "he was a total Castrophile. He wanted to promote Fidel Castro and did everything that he could in the debate, prior to it, and afterward."[44]

However, Oswald soon became unnerved when Ed Butler blind-sided him with information he had received from friends in Washington. Quiroga had already reported to Butler that Oswald spoke Russian. Both Butler and Quiroga were suspicious. A couple of phone calls later, Butler learned of Oswald's defection to Russia. Butler remembers, "The information came from the House Un-American Activities Committee files. I requested it and they sent it." Some have assumed that Butler had a CIA connection because of his ability to so quickly learn of Oswald's past. But as Butler explains, "They got it from the newspapers, the open press. That's basically what they sent me—clippings that Oswald had defected to Russia and so forth. Got it by special delivery, and as soon as I got it, I knew that I had a serious guy on my hands."[45]

Oswald's problem was that he had been informing the radio audience that he was a pure ideological Marxist, not a Russian Communist. When it was exposed on the air that he had once lived in the Soviet Union, as a Soviet citizen, he immediately lost his credibility and composure. Oswald began noticeably stammering at that point. Carlos Bringuier says, "My last memory of Lee Harvey Oswald during the debate … was Oswald becoming red and redder in his face because he was angry that it had been discovered that he had tried to defect to the Soviet Union and he had been exposed in the debate. I could still see his face becoming red and redder and redder."[46] Bringuier was overjoyed at the turnabout. "After the debate," he said, "I thought Oswald was destroyed."[47]

Oswald was not only embarrassed, but furious at Ed Butler. Butler recalls:

The last thing that I remember was Oswald taking out a notebook, glancing
up at me, fixing me with a gaze of hatred, asking for my name and address
and phone number, writing it down in the notebook, and snapping it shut.
Then he looked up and gave me that Oswald sneer. I went one way and he
went the other. I saw it as a threatening act and I think it was [so] intended.
Nobody knows what's going on in another person's head, but I think it was a

very calculated threat. "Alright, you got me on the air, but I'll take care of you later." I immediately went to the television media, the other media, and did what I could to warn them about Oswald and say that this guy is a danger. I was surprised when he killed President Kennedy, but I wouldn't have been a bit surprised if he had killed Ed Butler.[48]

When Oswald went home after the taping, he said to Marina, "Damn it. I didn't realize they knew I'd been to Russia…I wasn't prepared and I didn't know what to say."[49]

Carlos Bringuier summed up the entire series of events this way: "In my opinion, when he approached us—when he approached me here in New Orleans—he was trying to gain information about what the Cuban refugees were up to here in New Orleans. I don't know who sent him to me, but he was trying to gain information for the Communist cause."[50]

Oswald, considering himself "exposed," wrote to the Central Committee of the Communist Party, saying, "I feel I may have compromised the FPCC." He inquired if he should go "underground," and signed off, "Please Advise."[51] A response came from the Party secretary, Elizabeth Gurley Flynn, in which she discouraged him from going "underground," but advised him that the Party might find a way to get in touch with him later.[52]

Oswald then made his next major life decision: he would go to Cuba. He had already told Marina to return with June to Russia. He now told her that he would only join her there if he didn't like Cuba. His problem was that the State Department had forbidden U.S. citizens from traveling to Cuba. But Lee had the solution: he'd hijack a plane to the island. "I'll be needing your help," he announced to his startled wife.

"Of course I won't help," was Marina's response. She could not contain her laughter, saying, "The whole thing is so funny, it even makes the baby laugh." She then turned to baby June and said, "Junie, our papa is out of his mind."[53]

Lee was not in the least bit dissuaded by Marina's response. He embarked on an exercise regimen, training to subdue the pilot. He obtained maps and flight schedules determining which flights had sufficient fuel to make the trip to Cuba. He then composed the scenario, which he forced the laughing Marina, now pregnant again, to rehearse with him. Priscilla McMillan, Marina's biographer, wrote:

> *He would sit in the plane's front row. No one would notice when he got up and quietly moved into the pilot's cabin. There, he would pull his pistol and force the pilot to turn around…[Marina] was to sit in the rear of the plane. Once Lee had subdued the pilot, she was to rise, holding June by the hand, and speak to the passengers, urging them to be calm.*[54]

When Marina reminded him that she hardly spoke any English, he amended the script. The new version had her drawing a pistol, ordering, "Hands up and don't make any noise!" It was still too much English for Marina to master, she said.

The very pregnant Marina also objected, "Do you really think anybody will be fooled? A pregnant woman, her stomach sticking way out, a tiny girl in one hand and a pistol in the other?"

It was during this same period that Lee decided on a new name for their unborn baby, whom he hoped would be a boy. Up until this point, Lee and Marina had agreed that a son's name would be David Lee. Now, Oswald had a new suggestion: "Fidel—Fidel Oswald." Marina reached down to her Russian roots, and firmly responded, "There is no Fidel and there will be no Fidel in our family."[55]

After many days of planning, exercising, and rehearsing, the whole hijacking idea was abandoned. Lee came bounding into the apartment, exclaiming, "Guess what, Mama? I've found a legal way. There's a Cuban Embassy in Mexico. I'll go there." Oswald's plan involved acquiring a Cuban visa from the Cuban Embassy in Mexico City, and spending the rest of his days in Cuba, fighting for Castro's cause. According to Oswald's own writings, he intended to inform the Cuban Embassy officials of what he had learned in Lafayette Square about the Lake Ponchartrain camps and the U.S. re-invasion plans for Cuba. On September 25th, after sending Marina and June back to Texas to live with Ruth Paine, Lee Oswald boarded a bus bound for Mexico City.

Oswald's Connections

Although rarely explored, circumstantial evidence exists that Oswald was in contact with pro-Castro Cubans, not only in Los Angeles during his Marine stint, but in New Orleans as well.

If Oswald was supported by a pro-Castro network in New Orleans, he could have transmitted to Havana what he was learning in Lafayette Square, as well as his suspicions about the "bonds for invasion," and "the camps on the lake." This raises the spectre of an assassin who was not only inspired by the Kennedys' Cuba Project, but possibly encouraged by Havana. Of course, given Oswald's new-found celebrity and the general description of New Orleans as a city where "everybody knows everybody else," it is certainly possible. While there is no firm evidence of Oswald contact with Havana during his New Orleans period, there are nonetheless some teasing and intriguing anecdotes.

On the subject of whether a pro-Castro network in New Orleans could have existed, Sergio Arcacha says, "Of course, it's possible. Why there was a pro-Castro man who had a bar on the same block as Carlos' [Bringuier's] store. His name was Pena." Two doors from Bringuier's Casa Roca on Decatur Street was the Habana Bar, owned by Orest Pena. Pena and a number of his employees and patrons admitted to the FBI that Oswald had been in his bar, accompanied by "Mexicanos."[56] Although a Cuban, Pena was not an exile fleeing the Castro regime. "He came before the revolution," says Bringuier. Although Bringuier has no evidence that Pena was working for Havana, he says, "I always suspected him."[57]

An FBI report discloses two reasons for the exiles' suspicions about Pena. An

FBI informant in the Cuban community told agent Warren DeBrueys that Pena had been heard to say in the Habana bar, "Castro should have been notified about that as soon as possible." What *that* was is unknown. The report also cited three different exile sources as saying that Pena had mentioned plans to travel to England, Europe, and Moscow.[58] Bringuier finds it equally suspicious that Pena applied for a passport for this travel at the same time and place as Oswald. Indeed, around this time, Oswald also noted his desire to travel to England, Europe, and Moscow.[59] Further, Pena was a potential source of information for Oswald regarding the Kennedy Cuba Project. For Pena knew David Ferrie very well, referring to him as "Captain Ferrie." According to author Harold Weisberg, who interviewed Pena in 1968, Pena met Ferrie when they both attended meetings of Arcacha's Cuban Revolutionary Council. Pena even took flying lessons from Ferrie.[60]

There are several other reasons it seems likely that Oswald had still-unknown Cuban allies in New Orleans. Of note is the testimony of New Orleans attorney Dean Andrews, who told the Warren Commission that Oswald had come into his office attempting to secure U.S. citizenship for his wife, Marina. Andrews said that Oswald did not come alone. He was accompanied by what Andrews referred to alternately as "Mexicanos," "Latinos," or "Cubanos."[61]

Further, Oswald's leaflets have potential significance exclusive of the stamped address. Oswald had leaflets made at two different print shops. Myra Silver, who worked for Jones Printing (directly across the street from Reily Coffee), testified that on May 29th, a man working for Reily placed an order for 1,000 FPCC leaflets. However, the man used the name "Osborne" and she could not identify him after being shown Oswald's picture. If someone else had been working with Oswald in New Orleans, it most logically would have been another pro-Castro Cuban (or someone masquerading as such).

Finally, according to Oswald's Russian friend, Pavel Golovachev, at the height of Oswald's frenetic New Orleans odyssey, the Russians unexpectedly renewed their interest in him. Golovochev, as previously explained, was one of Oswald's many acquaintances the KGB enlisted to keep tabs on the mysterious defector. Golovachev disclosed 30 years later that he had stopped his Oswald-related reporting to KGB superior Alexander Kostikov when the Oswalds left Russia in May 1962. He did not hear again from the KGB for 15 months. Then, in August 1963, KGB superiors instructed him to deliver to headquarters all correspondence from Oswald in the USA, and anything Oswald had left behind in Minsk. Golovachev delivered the material, which was carefully inspected, then returned to him. He was never told the reason for this inspection.

After the assassination, the KGB would again contact Pavel Golovachev, confiscate everything pertaining to Oswald, and subject him to a hostile interrogation, which was dominated not by talk of Oswald, but by Russian fears that Marina might be a security risk. The KGB even pressed Golovachev as to whether he personally had slept with Marina, and demanded to know the names of all her lovers.[62]

Regardless of Oswald's potential for pro-Castro Cuban contact in New Orleans, it is a matter of historical fact that he made such contact when he arrived in Mexico City in September 1963. Although there is no proof that Oswald had prior contact with anyone in Mexico City before his arrival there, one of his statements on arriving in that city could lead one to infer a prior communication. Over the phone (which was monitored by the CIA), Oswald informed a Soviet Embassy employee of his contacts at the nearby Cuban Embassy, saying, "I went to the Cuban Embassy to ask them for my address because they have it."

Nobody knows what address Oswald meant. His statement, made just weeks before Oswald murdered Castro's nemesis, JFK, triggered a 30-year debate among investigators over the precise meaning of Oswald's relationship with the Castro outpost in Mexico City.

The extreme sensitivity of Oswald's Mexican contacts were known to a few key officials. Those contacts sent paroxysms of fear through official Washington.

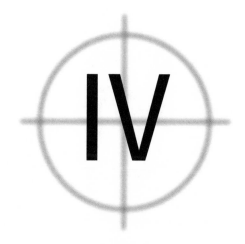

THE FALL OF CAMELOT

CHAPTER TEN

MEXICO CITY:
THE PARALLAX VIEW[1]

"Mexico City is like another world."
   —Donald Fagen, songwriter (from his song "Maxine")

"Mexico City was the only place in the Western Hemisphere where every communist country and every democratic country had an embassy, and it was a hotbed of intrigue."
   —Gaeton Fonzi, former HSCA investigator[2]

"The Mexican capital is a huggermugger metropolis of cloak-and-dagger conspirators."
   —David Atlee Phillips, CIA Chief of Covert Operations in Mexico City, 1962-1964[3]

In unraveling the truth behind the Kennedy assassination, understanding the peculiar characteristics of Mexico City is indispensable. By the time of Oswald's visit, this megalopolis had become the most spy-infested in the Western hemisphere, if not the world. Oswald's presence among these Cold Warriors was one of the initial reasons the investigation whitewashed the facts behind the President's death. It is now clear that, even at the time of his visit, the assassin-to-be jeopardized sensitive aspects of Kennedy's Cuba Project by meeting with Soviet and Cuban informants (called "targets" in the espionage business). A thorough investigation, at the least, could have exposed hard-won and well-placed double agents.

In addition, Oswald's unwitting contact with these CIA sources threatened the Agency with mortifying embarrassment after the assassination. Behind the government's zeal to protect these secrets was a dreadful possibility: a concern, shared alike by senior American intelligence officers and politicos, that Oswald had received illicit encouragement for a murderous mission during his seven-day Mexico City stay.

It seems inevitable that a man as intriguing as Oswald would gravitate to locales such as New Orleans and Mexico City, arguably the two most intriguing cities in the Americas.[4]

A City of Dichotomy

By all rights, Mexico City should not exist. It would be hard to find a more inappropriate site for one of the world's largest cities. The city is flung on a 7,000 ft. volcanic plateau landlocked by the Sierra Nevada mountains, which ring it on all sides. No rivers feed it. No coasts serve it. The details of its founding are lost in myth, but there can be little doubt the site was originally used by the Aztecs as a center for human sacrifices aimed at appeasing the gods of the volcano.

For much of the year, the Mexico City sun blazes with a special, unremitting, malevolent force. The altitude, far from being invigorating, clutches at the visitor like a fist, making any movement a dizzy effort.

Mexico City, it has been said, pounds the senses like a metal climbing staff. The deafening noise, putrid smells, eye-stinging smog, poverty, and crowding rival that of Cairo or Calcutta. Traffic creeps like a slow-motion junkyard. Honking horns, broken mufflers, and the put-put of motorbikes rattle the nerves. Diesel and smog choke the lungs and make the eyes tear. But the magnitude and cacophony of the crowd dwarfs all else to mere annoyance.

To a first-time observer, it seems as if the entire population of Mexico has emptied, village by village, into Mexico City. An accurate population tally is impossible, but estimates run as high as 20 million people. The resulting swarm is engaged either in selling something or begging. Cobblestone alleys become makeshift marketplaces where everything becomes a negotiable commodity—including "intelligence."

Against this backdrop are set splendid monuments, statues, and the ever-present bougainvillea flower. The city thus defines the word "dichotomy." Author Dick Russell has written that Mexico City "seems to epitomize double images." The city blends the "splendid and the squalid," pyramids and sky-scrapers, statues of Christian gods alongside pagan ones.[5] Though recurrent volcanic activity insures occasional urban renewal, this 4,000 year-old city appears otherwise impervious to change, and even immortal.

Intelligence in Mexico City

Drawn by the cover this maelstrom provides, consulates, embassies, and their requisite spies proliferate like mushrooms. With antennas pointed north, they hunker down, embracing anonymity with a professional's admiration. In 1963, the United States and its Cold War adversaries were prime examples of this phenomenon. Mexico City was then the Lisbon of the North American continent, a mecca for eastern-bloc spies, a KGB locus for operations radiating throughout Latin and North America.[6] One expected to find the Blue Parrot just around a corner, with Sidney Greenstreet grinning in a smoky back room negotiating for the carnet internationale. *The New York Times* referred to Mexico City as the "Casablanca of the West, where the American [CIA] and Soviet [KGB] intelligence services did battle for the hearts and minds of Latin America."[7]

The leading actors—Cuban, American, and Soviet—were hard at work in this sprawling arena, trying to "turn" each other's agents, and to gain the huge prizes this brought. In the convoluted business of intelligence-gathering, a "pretender" reports first-hand information from behind enemy lines. As importantly, he has the ability to create an analytical nightmare by controlling the information fed to the enemy's intelligence-gathering machine. A double agent can muddle authentic material or lead the other side off-track entirely.[8]

In 1963, the CIA's Mexico City Station, located in the American embassy, was the Agency's largest permanent station in the Western Hemisphere. The outpost employed more than 25 full-time agents, who blended into the thousand-plus employees of the embassy. The FBI, which likewise had a permanent presence in the embassy,[9] deployed a Legal Attaché, or Legat, for the purposes of locating American communists hiding across the U.S.-Mexican border, and more importantly to monitor Soviet intelligence activity aimed at the United States.

The Soviet embassy in the city was the base for spying operations against the United States. Melvin Beck, a CIA case officer assigned to Mexico City at the time, recalls that the station's efforts against the Soviets had long emphasized double agent operations.[10] Beck further describes the conditions:

> I monitored the activities of Soviets all over Latin America. Mexico was unquestionably the most important target. Mexico hosted the largest contingent of the Russian Intelligence Service in Latin America, quite understandably because both the KGB and the GRU used Mexico as a third-party base for running operations against the United States.[11]

David Atlee Phillips, who was the Chief of Covert Operations in Mexico City at the time, summed up the location's strategic value:

> The CIA station in Mexico is one of the most important in the world...The reason for the large CIA contingent...[is that] Mexico City has been the main outpost of Soviet Intelligence for its activities throughout Latin America and, since 1959, for the support of Cuban skulduggery in the Western Hemisphere...Mexico is an exile haven for Latin Americans of whatever conviction who are waiting, and often trying to abet, a change of government in their countries...All of this has spawned a conglomeration of intelligence officers, agents, spies, provocateurs, and shadowy figures...Each intelligence service in Mexico City plays the cat-and-mouse game of attempting to penetrate each other's organization.[12]

For the Americans, the man in charge of directing this maddening traffic was CIA Station Chief Winston "Win" Scott. Scott typified the atypical—the early generation spymaster/renaissance man. Known as a workaholic, he was sufficiently charming to captivate the Mexicans, who were ever-cautious about befriending "gringos." Scott had a distinctly personal disadvantage to overcome—more than one hundred years earlier, an American general named Winfield Scott (no relation) had invaded and captured Mexico City.

By any definition, the CIA's Scott was brilliant. A mathematics professor by age nineteen, he attained his Ph.D. in matrix theory mathematics (and had turned down a major league baseball contract in order to further his studies). Serving in the Navy in World War II, Scott broke the Germans' coded messages in the Caribbean. He also spent time with the FBI. He joined the CIA at the time of its inception in the late 1940's. During Lee Oswald's visit in Mexico City, Win Scott would witness events so disturbing that he would come to suspect, as he later wrote, a possible foreign conspiracy in Kennedy's death.

Like the U.S., the Soviet Union's largest intelligence operation was its Mexico City contingent. Over half of its 35 intelligence agents were also known to be in league with Castro's spy apparatus, known as the DGI (or its military equivalent, the G-2).

Likewise, Cuba had a powerful espionage presence in Mexico City. According to former CIA officer Phillip Agee:

> *The only Cuban diplomatic mission in Latin America is in Mexico City. They have thirteen diplomatic officials and an equal number of non-diplomatic personnel. Over half the officers in the mission are known or suspected intelligence officers. The main Cuban target is penetration of the Cuban exile communities in Mexico and Central America, but they also have operations in Mexico City designed to penetrate the exile communities in the U.S., particularly Miami.*[13]

"Castro's best intelligence agents were in Mexico City,"[14] emphatically states Brigade leader and Bobby Kennedy confidante Raphael Quintero. Those agents operated out of the Cuban embassy. In addition, the Cuban embassy had a curious procedure of providing travelers with pseudonyms for international travel, and of making no entry on their passports, according to what Bobby Kennedy's Cuban Coordinating Committee learned in 1963. "This procedure," the report advised, "is obviously designed to impede any effort by other Latin American governments to identify the travelers and control their movements."[15] Lastly, and perhaps most important, the Cuban embassy was believed to serve as headquarters for Cuban terrorists operating throughout the western hemisphere.

The permutations of suspicion seem limitless in Mexico City. Life is best accepted on this high altitude stage through the parallax view—nothing is what it seems.

Oswald in Mexico City

"For me, it's all going to end in tragedy!"
> —Lee Oswald to an official of the Soviet Embassy in
>   Mexico City[16]

Lee Oswald arrived in Mexico City at 10 a.m. on September 27, 1963. He had traveled by bus for almost two days, journeying from New Orleans by way of Houston and Laredo, Texas.[17] He proceeded to check into the Hotel del

Commercio at the daily rate of 16 pesos ($1.28). The hotel was just a few blocks from the focal point of Oswald's journey: the Cuban embassy. If his preoccupation had been with Cuba during his entire stay in New Orleans, this was also true of his much shorter stay in Mexico City, but to an even greater degree. On the Trailways bus, and on a Mexican bus to which he transferred at Nuevo Laredo, he announced to fellow passengers that he had been the secretary of the Fair Play for Cuba Committee in New Orleans and that he was on his way to Cuba—through Mexico—because Americans were prohibited from traveling directly to Cuba. He hoped, he said, to see Fidel Castro in Havana.[18]

In Mexico City, Oswald would not, of course, see Fidel, but he did meet a number of people who, by their natures and positions, deserve close scrutiny. The Warren Commission would state unequivocally that, in Mexico City, Oswald "was seen with no other person either at his hotel or at the restaurant"[19]—a small, cheap restaurant near the hotel, where he often ate. This conclusion is flatly wrong, but the Commissioners were largely kept in the dark about all things Cuban, including the Cuban component to Oswald's Mexico City foray.

Soon after checking in at the hotel, Oswald went to the Cuban Embassy, which, together with the Soviet Embassy, he marked on a map. A young Mexican woman named Sylvia Duran was working in the consular office as secretary to the Consul. At great length, Oswald told her that he was travelling to the Soviet Union but wanted to stop in Cuba on the way, and would need a transit visa quickly because he wanted to leave in three days, on September 30th. He informed Duran, who spoke English, that he was "a friend of the Cuban revolution," in support of which he showed her his membership card in the Fair Play for Cuba Committee, newspaper clips about his arrest in New Orleans while distributing FPCC leaflets (with a photograph of himself flanked by policemen), proof of his Soviet residence and work experience, and correspondence with American socialist and communist organizations. Impressed by this and by Oswald's intensity, Duran asked her boss, the consul, whether he might shorten the ordinary process of visa application, which began with filling out a long application form. The consul, Eusebio Azcue, said that he could not. Oswald, said Azcue, would have to go through the usual procedure, and his application would have to first be approved in Havana. Azcue, on his own, could not do that here in Mexico City.

With Duran's help, Oswald began filling out the regular application form. After photographs were added and attached to the completed application, Duran suggested, Oswald might speed its approval by getting his Soviet visa first. He hurried out to a nearby shop to get the requisite passport photographs. However, while he was doing so, Duran called the Soviet Embassy, only to learn that Soviet acceptance of a visa application might take months. Upon Oswald's return, Duran gave him the bad news.

No doubt upset by not having been greeted as a socialist comrade or hero, Oswald protested the bureaucratic delay and claimed he had a right to get a

Cuban visa quickly—especially since his Mexican tourist visa was valid only for several days. "That's impossible," Oswald shouted. "I have to go to Cuba right now because I have permission for only three or four days in Mexico City. So I have to go quickly."[20] In his Cuban fantasy, Lee had never considered being frustrated by such an imbecilic delay. Couldn't these people see the obvious? Hadn't he traveled on his own time and at his own expense to donate his considerable expertise to the Cuban cause? And didn't his work for the FPCC entitle him to a sliver of special consideration?

Oswald's angry complaints became louder and drew Azcue out from his office. The consul confirmed to Oswald that he would have to go through regular procedures for a Cuban visa, which could take several weeks. But if Oswald had a Soviet visa, said Azcue, he could grant him a 15-day visa to Cuba on the spot, without having to contact Havana.

Oswald's reaction to this suggestion was not pleasant. He wanted an instant visa, he said, and believed he deserved it. His demeanor upset Azcue enough for him to complain, during lunch with his wife, about the American's "very, very bad manners," his "nastiness," and his "arrogance." The Cuban even wondered whether the applicant who "screamed and shouted so violently" and "wanted to draw attention to himself" was a provocateur.[21] Meanwhile, Oswald himself hurried to the Soviet Embassy, two blocks away, arriving there at about 12:30 p.m.

At the Soviet compound, he told a sentry in Russian who he was. Led to the consul's office, he was received by a consular officer named Valery Kostikov. Telling Kostikov of his Russian wife and his wish to return to the Soviet Union, Oswald showed him the same collection of documents and supporting items as evidence of his dedication to the socialist camp. He also claimed that the FBI kept him under constant surveillance in the United States. The Russian consulate was staffed by three men, all actually working under consular cover while carrying out their main duties as KGB officers in foreign intelligence. Kostikov called for a comrade, Oleg Nechiporenko, to come to his aid in this strange case. Nechiporenko's specialty was foreign counterintelligence. His first impression of Oswald was of aloofness. "He seemed to be looking beyond me, absorbed in his thoughts, and did not even react as I approached him...[He] appeared to be in a state of physical and mental exhaustion."[22]

Well before the end of the hour or so he spent with Oswald, Nechiporenko concluded, with professional instinct, that although the KGB had surely kept watch on Oswald during his residence in the USSR, it would not have had any "operational contact" with him. "From my first impression of him, it was clear that he was not suitable agent material."[23]

Nechiporenko noted that Oswald's mood went from discomfort to "a state of great agitation, creating the impression of a high-strung, neurotic individual."[24] Applications to travel to the Soviet Union, Nechiporenko explained to Oswald, were handled by the embassies in the countries where the applicants lived. In Oswald's case, he could make an exception and send the necessary applications to Moscow, but the reply would still be sent to the Washington Embassy and would take four months at the least. Oswald, now distraught and "extremely agitated," leaned forward across the desk and virtually shouted in Nechiporenko's face: "This won't do for me...For me, it's all going to end in tragedy." The interview had ended, but the Soviet officers decided to contact Moscow, just in case KGB headquarters had some reason to grant Oswald an immediate visa.

Oswald returned to the Cuban consulate. It was closed—for siesta time— until the early evening, but the guard could not make that understood to Oswald, and admitted him to wait. Oswald told Duran there was "no problem" and he wanted a Cuban visa because he already obtained a Soviet one. When she asked to see it, he refused. "No, no, no," he answered. "You can call the Soviet Consul. They're going to give me the visa."

Duran felt a kind of sympathy for the young man so eager to go to Cuba. She did call. The Soviet official who answered said that he remembered Oswald, but that it was impossible for Oswald to get a Soviet visa in less than three or four months. The Soviet official said he couldn't understand why he was claiming otherwise now.

On his first visit to the Cuban embassy, Duran had noticed that Oswald was "very nervous, very anxious." Now, having had his bluff called, Oswald was flushed out. When Duran told him that things did not appear to be as he claimed at the Soviet Embassy and repeated the procedure he would have to abide by, he became angry and "anguished." "Impossible!" he shouted. "I can't wait that long!" Duran would remember him as both white and "very red" in the face at the same time—simultaneously sad, on the point of tears, and "furious." "He was very, very excited. He started shouting. And I started to get—well, he was a thin man and I didn't think he could kick me or something like that, but anyway I was afraid."[25]

Duran went to Azcue's office to ask for help with "this man out there." In 1993, Duran recounted for Frontline what she told Azcue about Oswald:

> I think he's becoming crazy...So Azcue says [to Oswald], "If you are a friend of the Cuban revolution, you don't have to be like that—you harm the Cuban revolution, you don't help with this attitude." And his [Oswald's] answer is, "I have to, to, I need that visa, I have to go to Cuba." But he already explained to you: If you go to Cuba and you're in transit, and soon as you get the visa from the Soviet Union, you will have your Cuban [visa] without any problems...And then the man become more and more angry, so that Azcue becomes also excited because he didn't want to understand and he try [sic] and explain some with passion and so he got excited also and he said, "Listen, if you continue like this, I'm going to kick you out."

With that, Oswald left the Embassy. The following morning, Oswald returned to the Soviet Embassy. Although it was a Saturday and the consular office was closed, the consul, Captain Pavel Yatzkov of the KGB, told the sentry to admit Oswald. Soon, Valery Kostikov and Oleg Nechiporenko joined Yatzkov, and the three consular/KGB officers heard Oswald's plea. Disheveled, rumpled, and unshaven, he looked "hounded" to Kostikov—"much more anxious" than the day before.

Speaking warmly of his wife and child, and apparently willing to say anything to get him quickly to Cuba, Oswald told the Soviet officials that he "dreamed" of returning to the Soviet Union, resuming his former job there and living "quietly" with his family. But he himself was anything but quiet.

Though Oswald was extremely agitated and clearly nervous, especially whenever he mentioned the FBI, he suddenly became hysterical, began to sob, and cried through his tears, "I am afraid…they'll kill me. Let me in!" Repeating over and over that he was being persecuted and that he was being followed even here in Mexico, he stuck his right hand into the left pocket of his jacket, pulled out a revolver, and placed it on the desk, saying, "See? This is what I must now carry to protect my life."[26]

Kostikov, who was startled, recalls, "It was strange to see a man who protected himself from such an organization [the FBI] with the help of a gun."[27] The consular/KGB officers had no trouble taking possession of the revolver and removing the bullets from its cylinder. But the officers did not quite know what to do with Oswald. What they did do was notice—as they could hardly help noticing—his profound emotional distress. Oswald sobbed and sobbed. Later, he "began to droop. Most likely the peak of his tension had passed, but his eyes were wet with tears and his hands shook…His state of extreme agitation had now been replaced by depression."[28]

The Soviet officers escorted him to the door. Oswald left. Raising his jacket collar to conceal his face and to prevent being clearly photographed, he dissolved into Mexico City. The three officers, in his absence, discussed Oswald. Pavel Yatzkov would write that they decided they "could not take Oswald seriously." Yatskov said recently, "Oswald produced the impression of an insane person…he looked wan, a worn-out person."[29]

> His nervousness during the conversations, his rambling and even nonsensical speech at times, his avoidance of answering specific questions, and the shifts from strong agitation to depression gave us reason to believe that his mental state was unstable or that, at the very least, he suffered from a serious nervous disorder.[30]

They also remember a promise Oswald made after stuttering about the impossibility of living any longer in the United States. His revolver returned to him, Oswald vowed, "If they don't leave me alone, I'm going to defend myself."[31]

If this were the full story of Oswald's stay in Mexico City, it would only serve to elaborate on Oswald's emotional problems. Oswald's near breakdown in both embassies—especially his prolonged sobbing and seeming detachment from reality in the presence of the Soviet officers—could legitimately be taken as further evidence of a man "prepared for anything," as he had written to *The Militant* when he sent the newspaper a print of his backyard photograph with the guns. By this time, less than eight weeks before the assassination, Oswald had clearly come to a point where his frustration and depression, mixed with a propensity for violence in the service of a political goal, indeed prepared him for anything. If he was not a lone nut, he was clearly a man obsessed enough to do anything to gain entry into Cuba.

But there is much more to the story, for if Pavel Yatzkov and his KGB friends "could not take Oswald seriously," there is evidence that someone did. This evidence centers around what Oswald said to the Cubans, not the Russians. It also explains what the CIA's Melvin Beck referred to as his agency's reliance on double agents, some of whom functioned as triple agents.

Oswald and the Cubans in Mexico City: Echoes of Conspiracy

Between Saturday, September 28th, when he left the Russian Consulate, and Wednesday, October 2nd at 8:30 a.m., when he boarded a bus back to Texas, Lee Oswald had four days with essentially nothing to do. And that is exactly what he did, according to the U.S.' official government findings. Perhaps the dejected Oswald visited the pyramids, or sipped margueritas at some brightly-painted cantina. Denied full access to the complete record of Oswald's stay, the Warren Commission was provided with what a higher authority deemed necessary. All told, enough evidence exists to safely assume that Lee Oswald didn't just buy a sombrero and go on burro rides during those four days.

The truth is that Oswald disappeared into what David Phillips referred to as the "conglomeration of intelligence officers, agents, spies, provocateurs, and shadowy figures" that is Mexico City. What happened to Oswald during the remainder of his trip was not so mysterious as it was dangerous. The mystery was manufactured because American intelligence lied and covered up what it knew. What did the CIA have to hide?

There was evidence that Oswald had one additional conversation with the Soviets, and that he spoke with the Cubans about much more than just a visa. Oswald's trail also points to surreptitious meetings with Cubans judged to be not only dangerous to top secret American operations, but to President Kennedy specifically. And Win Scott, the CIA Bureau Chief, was aware of all of this, if not immediately, then shortly after the assassination.

First, there may have been more Oswald contact with the embassies than has been officially revealed. The CIA had extensive surveillance on the Soviet and Cuban embassies, both visual and audible. Cameras were hidden in storefronts across the street, and phone lines were tapped. It has been accepted that Oswald made no more than two phone calls to the Soviet embassy. However, in 1979, the HSCA interviewed three new witnesses, including a senior CIA officer in Mexico, a later Station Chief, and the translator who worked on transcribing the telephone conversations. They all testified that there was a third call to the

Soviet embassy. The contents of the mysterious third call have never been made public. However, testimony now available makes it possible to at least start piecing together the puzzle of that call, and of Oswald's unaccounted-for time in Mexico City.

It is now known that, after Kennedy's assassination, U.S. intelligence received alarming reports that went undisclosed to the Warren Commission. Some of this material was withheld by the CIA, some by President Johnson, and some by Robert Kennedy. From the CIA's perspective, the reports they received could have given the public the misperception that the Agency had a relationship with Oswald—a perception that, from the CIA's perspective, would have added nothing to the investigation, while possibly incurring the public's wrath toward the already beleaguered unit. It would have also brought to light the ongoing, much-planned, super-secret Cuba Project that the CIA did not want compromised, especially for little or no good reason.

From LBJ's standpoint, the information was so explosive that its disclosure would have brought about a public outcry for a post-assassination retaliation against Cuba—something he strongly opposed. Robert Kennedy, ever the loyal younger brother, merely wanted to keep the family name, and his brother's myth, intact. A full disclosure of Mexico City matters would have bared the Kennedys' plans to murder Fidel Castro, and to barrage and invade his nation. Such a disclosure would certainly have diminished JFK's mystique as an innocent martyr.

What follows are some of the more intriguing stories of Oswald in Mexico City. They were never fully investigated and never disclosed to the Warren Commission.

Story One: Lee, Sylvia and Elena—Twisting the Night Away

First, there is the question of Sylvia Duran. As secretary to the Cuban Consul, Duran, with one important exception, has been consistent in her story that her contact with Oswald was brief and innocent. However, evidence has been accumulating over the years that indicates she may have been less than candid about her role in the events surrounding Oswald's visit. The initial stories revolved around the allegations of a Duran friend named Elena Garro.

Elena Garro De Paz, the cousin of Sylvia Duran's father Ruben, tells of a "twist party" at Ruben's home to which she and her daughter Elenita were invited. To the best of her recollection, the party occurred on either September 30 or October 1st—two of Oswald's four "missing" days in Mexico City. Party guests included numerous Cuban Embassy employees, including Consul Azcue. At one point, Azcue and Emilio Carballido, a pro-Castro writer (and Castro agent), became involved in a heated discussion about President Kennedy. They "came to the conclusion that the only solution was to kill him."[32]

Elena's cousin Sylvia Duran attended the party and brought three Americans with her. When Elena attempted to speak with one of them, Sylvia stepped in. To Elena, it was clear that Sylvia had romantic designs on him. Two months later, on the day Kennedy was killed, both Elena and Elenita recognized the assassin as the man at the party—Lee Harvey Oswald.[33] (Duran's name and home address were later found in Oswald's address book.)

Garro first told her story on October 5, 1964, eleven days after the Warren Commission findings were released.[34] She told it to June Cobb Sharp, an occasional contact of the U.S. Embassy. According to Sharp, Garro had come to the conclusion that "the party must have been set up by those Cuban individuals involved, and [by] some of their Mexican friends, so that they could provide an underground for Oswald after the assassination, in which there would be people who would recognize him and assist in his escape."[35]

Sharp passed the story along, and as a result, on November 24th Garro told the story to FBI LEGAT Clark Anderson. She told Anderson that she had attempted to give her account directly to Robert Kennedy a week earlier (November 14, 1964) when he was visiting Mexico City.[36] On Christmas Day, 1965 she repeated the story to the American Embassy's Political Action Officer Charles Ashman. This time, however, she added one new detail she had learned in the interim: "Sylvia Duran had been Oswald's mistress while he was there [in Mexico City]."[37]

In the atmosphere of official "lone nut" conclusions, there was no desire to follow this information up with an interview of Sylvia Duran. In fact, Duran's first official interrogation by the U.S. government occurred when the HSCA contacted her in May 1978. Garro's allegations were ignored for 14 years, in spite of an important phone call Sylvia Duran herself made in 1967. Duran called an old friend (and unknown to Duran, a CIA contact viewed as very reliable by the agency), and essentially verified everything Garro had said, seemingly without knowledge of Garro's prior testimony. According to the report filed by the contact, "Duran admitted that she had had intimate relations with Oswald, but insisted that she had no idea of his plans."[38] Subsequently, the Mexico City Station filed the following report to headquarters:

> That Sylvia Duran had sexual intercourse with Lee Harvey Oswald on several occasions when the latter was in Mexico is probably new, but adds little to the Oswald case.[39]

It is not known who authored the report to headquarters, but whoever it was clearly reached the wrong conclusion, whether on his/her own, or because of pressure from above. Others in the CIA Station knew that Duran was a double agent, and that piece of information would certainly add a great deal to "the Oswald case."

Story Two: Sylvia Duran, Double Agent

Fifteen years after the assassination, David Phillips, the CIA's Cuban specialist in Mexico City (and later Chief of the Western Hemisphere), told Congress of his belief that "Duran was possibly an agent or a source" for the U.S.[40] Phillips allegedly told more to *Houston Post* reporter, Lonnie Hudkins, with whom he was friendly. According to Hudkins, Phillips told him of a meeting attended by three people: Lee Harvey Oswald; a CIA undercover man; and Sylvia Duran, posing as a prostitute. Phillips admitted to Hudkins that, in Mexico City, he had often bought information from Duran.[41]

All this corroborates what New Orleans attorney Dean Andrews told the New Orleans District Attorney's office. After the assassination, he claimed to have learned that Oswald had "befriended a CIA whore" in Mexico City.[42] A confidential source told the HSCA that "all that would have to be done to recruit Sylvia Duran, whom he referred to by using the Spanish word for 'whore,' would be to get a blond, blue-eyed American into bed with her."[43] The HSCA received many other reports of Duran's promiscuity.

An internal CIA memo dated June 13, 1967 seems to lend weight to the possibility of a CIA relationship with Duran at the same time she was trysting with Oswald. The memo was prepared for "Willard C. Curtis" (Win Scott), by the same CIA agent/asset who had received the call from Sylvia Duran admitting her relationship with Oswald. The agent stated that he was "doing his best to keep active certain contacts...on the periphery of the official Cuban circle."

According to the document, one of those contacts was Sylvia Duran, who is "well-known to headquarters."[44] Laurence Keenan, the FBI agent sent to Mexico City after the assassination to coordinate the investigation, has said "Sylvia Duran was possibly a source of information for the Agency [CIA] or the Bureau [FBI]."[45]

Lastly, a Congressional investigator, Edwin Lopez, told author John Newman, "We saw an interesting file on Duran. It said that the CIA was considering using her affair with Carlos Lechuga [Cuban Ambassador to the U.N. and former Ambassador to Mexico City] to recruit her."[46] As damaging as this would be to the CIA—the assassin of President Kennedy having met with a CIA contact in Mexico—one can only imagine the damage to the Agency if Duran had been a triple agent, whose ultimate loyalties belonged to Havana.

Story Three: Sylvia Duran, Triple Agent

Barney Hidalgo, a CIA officer in Mexico City, told the HSCA that "he thought Duran was a Cuban intelligence agent."[47] The CIA apparently had more evidence that connected Duran to Cuban Intelligence, but revealing this information to the official investigators of President Kennedy's death would have jeopardized the still-ongoing, top-secret administration plans for a new Cuban invasion.

At the time of the Oswald visit to Mexico City, an important part of the Cuba Project was being run directly out of Mexico City. This operation seems to have been part of the AM/LASH-AM/TRUNK coup that was in its final planning stages. A recently-declassified CIA memo describes the mandate: "Pursuant to instructions from the 303 Committee of the Kennedy Administration [another name for Bobby Kennedy's Cuban Coordinating Committee], the CIA established among its objectives against Fidel Castro's Cuba the fragmenting of its governing coalition and the undermining of its relations with the USSR."

According to this same memo, a sensitive operation in Mexico City involved Teresa Proenza, the Cuban Cultural Attaché, known to be a long-standing Cuban Communist and a contact of Soviet intelligence in Mexico. In addition, Proenza had highly-placed confidantes in Havana, including the Vice-Minister of Defense. Thus, Proenza became the target of a complicated CIA scheme.

The details are still sketchy. However, it is clear that the CIA used Proenza, whom it believed was a lesbian, to mount a clever campaign of slander against the pro-Moscow Cuban Vice Minister of Defense. Through a CIA asset in the Cuban Embassy, false papers were planted on Proenza implicating the Vice-Minister of Defense as a CIA spy. The object was to drive a wedge between Moscow, which could be expected to rise to the minister's defense, and Havana. Apparently the scheme worked, for CIA documents state that the minister was arrested by the Cubans on charges of treason. The operation was so sensitive that the CIA, in 1978, was still refusing to turn over its Proenza file to HSCA investigators.

At that time, the CIA sent the investigators a memo that concludes with the following mysterious language:

> This is but the barest outline of a highly complex operations system that made use of a wide variety of techniques which have not been revealed to the public. The story would make the juiciest of headlines if it became known...In short, this file is a Pandora's Box, the opening of which would not only expose the cryptonyms of other operations of this type, but would attract unfavorable publicity for the Agency in certain quarters, and would expose hitherto secret techniques and assets [that] would make their employment in the future very difficult.

Although this operation had nothing to do with the Kennedy assassination, it hints at the reasons the CIA concealed Proenza's involvement in the Oswald case. According to another document, Proenza was Sylvia Duran's best friend. She, in fact, had recommended Duran for the job at the Cuban Consulate. When later interviewed by the HSCA, Proenza's brother Alvaro told the investigators that Teresa admitted that one of Oswald's "acquaintances" had contacted Proenza in the Cuban Embassy.[48] FBI documents show that Teresa Proenza told a close friend that she was the first person to speak with Oswald when he entered the Embassy.[49]

In other words, protection of intelligence secrets, an investigation of which could have shed light on Proenza's knowledge of Oswald (or her relationship with the lover of Lee Harvey Oswald), was given a higher level of importance than the investigation of President Kennedy's assassination. These revelations help explain why, the day after JFK's murder, the Mexico City Station received a phone call from CIA headquarters in Washington instructing them to stop Duran's arrest by Mexican police.

Story Four: Oswald and the Cuban Embassy Officials

Some of the most explosive reports that were never fully investigated deal with possible clandestine meetings between Oswald and Cuban embassy officials. Salvador Diaz Verson, a former newspaperman and Chief of Cuban Military intelligence under former Cuban President Carlos Prio, was regarded by the FBI as "of highly reliable character." He told a story that, he said, had been related to him by Dr. Eduardo Borrell Navarros, an exiled Cuban newspaperman.

According to Prio, on the day after Oswald arrived in Mexico, Oswald went with Sylvia Duran to the Caballo Blanco restaurant near Chapultepec Park, on the outskirts of the city, "where they met an official of the Cuban embassy." That official was supposedly the Cuban Ambassador to Mexico, Joaquin Hernandez Armas. They had an extended conversation. Then Oswald and the ambassador left in the ambassador's car "for a talk without being overheard."

According to the FBI report, this information was brought to the FBI's attention by the White House.[50] In the wake of the assassination, monitored phone calls in Mexico City seemed to give this story credibility.

Navarros initially denied to the FBI that he was the source of this information. This is understandable: with so many Castro spies in its midst, the Cuban exile community was gripped by fear after the assassination. However, when interviewed in 1993, Navarros made it apparent that he had not been candid with the investigators, and now gave the following details:

> My main sources were Cubans...ex army officials under Batista. I learned about his [Oswald's] activities through Conrado Peres Mundriera, who was a high Cuban official at one time...It was through him that I learned about Oswald's visits to the Embassy, to the consulate, and that it was also said at the time that he paid a visit to the Caballo Blanco, a very well-known Mexican restaurant...that he had contact with Cuban diplomats.[51]

Still wary of divulging too much, Navarros abruptly ended the 1993 interview, saying, "I really have little more to tell you—I'm limiting myself to what I can tell you."

The testimony of Pedro Gutierrez confirmed reports of Oswald's secret Embassy liaisons. A credit investigator for a Mexican department store, Gutierrez told a CIA contact that he saw an American leaving the Cuban Embassy in the company of a tall Cuban. He later identified the American as Lee Harvey Oswald. The two men, Gutierrez recalls, got into a car and drove off together. When the FBI later traced the car described by Gutierrez, a Renault, it turned out to be owned by the family of Sylvia Duran. Duran's car had Texas license plates, and was known to make frequent trips to Texas.[52]

Is it plausible, though, that a Cuban ambassador could be personally involved in planning the assassination of a foreign leader? Consider the story of the former Cuban Ambassador to Morocco, Walterio Carbonell. Carbonell, a Castro friend since his law school days, was advised in 1960 that Castro, before making ambassadorial appointments, demanded that each ambassadorial candidate promise him that he would assassinate U.S. leaders if called upon to do so. According to the *Miami Herald*:

> *Cuban Premier Fidel Castro had arranged the assassinations of several U.S. ambassadors in the event any suspected CIA plots to kill him during his early days in power were successful...The assassinations would be carried out by various Cuban ambassadors and Carbonell had to agree to be one of them if he wanted the post.*[53]

In addition, the CIA's JM/WAVE station in Florida was told by an informant that Cuba "employs killers and assassins...Two persons [were] killed in Mexico by Robert Coronevsky who received three hundred dollars for the deed from Embassy [in] Mexico."[54] This echoes an FBI report of October 25, 1962, which stated that the Bureau had information that a former Cuban ambassador to Panama, named Jimenez, had teamed with a Castro "repression" agent named Humberto Rodriguez Diaz for the purpose of assassinating the President of Panama, Roberto Chiari.[55] And, as will be seen, pro-Castro terrorists belonging to the Fair Play For Cuba Committee were known by the FBI to be under the control of Cuban Embassy officials.

Story Five: An Offer the Cubans Couldn't Refuse?

If Oswald had secret meetings with Cuban Embassy officials already prone to use "executive action," one huge question is raised: Did the potential murder of Castro's nemesis, John Kennedy, become a subject of discussion? There is evidence that it did.

Ernesto Rodriguez was a CIA contract agent in Mexico City at the time of Oswald's visit. In 1975, he told a news reporter that Oswald disclosed to the Soviets and the Cubans that he had learned (no doubt on the streets of New Orleans) of a CIA plot to assassinate Fidel Castro. According to Rodriguez, Oswald also unmasked this plot to members of the Fair Play for Cuba Committee in Mexico City.[56] It was at this point, according to Oswald's FBI case officer, Jim Hosty, that Oswald made an offer to Cuban intelligence that he hoped they couldn't refuse.

According to Hosty (and corroborated by government documents), FBI Director Hoover, after the assassination, dispatched two undercover agents to Havana to carry out a "vetting" —to feel Castro out.[57] The agents, officially designated "Solo Source," were, it has been revealed, Morris Childs, treasurer of the U.S. Communist Party, and his brother Jack Childs, editor of *The Daily Worker*.[58] "Solo Source" represented at the time the U.S.' most significant penetration into the international Communist Party. What Castro told the agents goes far beyond what the premier has said publicly. According to Hosty, the Cuban leader confided that Oswald had offered to kill President Kennedy because Kennedy was threatening Castro. Castro claimed that the Cubans turned down Oswald's offer.

In another version of this story, according to a document withheld until 1995, Castro told "Solo Source" that he was informed by Embassy officials in Mexico City that Oswald's exact words were: "I'm going to kill that bastard. I'm going to kill Kennedy." Castro further stated that he was told of the remarks immediately, but they were considered a madman's rantings, and not an offer.[59]

Even this version is ominous. If true, Castro allowed Oswald to proceed without warning U.S. authorities. Castro apparently repeated the story again in July 1967 to British writer Comer Clark, who said Castro told him a story similar to the one he told "Solo Source." According to Clark, Castro explained:

> I was told he [Oswald] wanted to work for us. He was asked to explain, but he wouldn't. The second time [Oswald came to the embassy], he said he wanted to "free Cuba from American imperialism." Then he said something like, "Somebody ought to shoot that President Kennedy. Maybe I'll try to do it."[60]

According to award-winning TV journalist Daniel Schorr, the Cuban Ambassador to Mexico relayed this offer to Havana.[61] Castro later admitted, according to Clark, "Yes, I heard of Lee Harvey Oswald's plan to kill President Kennedy. It's possible that I could have saved him, but I didn't."[62]

Some have sought to disparage the Comer Clark story, citing his connection with tabloid journalism, and pointing to Castro's expected denials that he met with Clark. However, the HSCA believed differently:

> The committee was informed that the substance of it [the Comer Clark story] had been independently reported to the U.S. government. A highly confidential but reliable source reported that Oswald had indeed vowed in the presence of Cuban Consulate officials to assassinate the President.[63]

Houston Post reporter and regular CIA contact Lonnie Hudkins claims that he learned from a high-ranking minister in Castro's government that Oswald returned to the Cuban Embassy after October 1st. At this secret meeting, according to Hudkins, Oswald was given explicit details of the Kennedy assassination plots against Fidel Castro. Oswald became infuriated and decided then and there to do away with Kennedy.[64]

Story Six: The Story of "A-1"

Still more evidence seems to show that Havana knew of Oswald's intentions, and that the FBI and the CIA knew also, but never turned this information over to the Warren Commission.

In 1964, a Cuban defector and former Cuban intelligence officer, described as a "well-placed individual, who has been in contact with officers of the Cuban Directorate General of Intelligence (DGI)," told of sensitive Oswald contacts in the Cuban embassy. The defector, code-named AM/MUG-1 or "A-1," claimed that Oswald "was in contact with three Cuban agents before, during, and after" his visit to the Embassy. The Cuban agents were identified as Cuban Consulate employees Luisa Calderon, Manuel Vega Perez, and Rogelio Rodriguez Lopez. According to A-1, Castro knew of these contacts in advance of the assassination, and of Oswald's offer to kill President Kennedy. The source further stated that, after the assassination, the DGI took extraordinary security precautions to cover its tracks.[65]

During the second week of November 1963, Oswald worked on drafts of a letter that, on November 12th, he would send to the Soviet Embassy in Washington. The letter is replete with Oswald lies and exaggerations about his time in Mexico, Hosty, etc. However, the letter's most intriguing aspect is its closing sentence, which refers to the "stupid" Cuban Consul (Azcue), and how Oswald was "glad he had been replaced by another."[66] Azcue would be replaced at the Cuban Embassy on November 18. The obvious question is: How did Oswald know of this personnel change (and a week before it took place)? Was this common knowledge among young warehouse workers in Dallas?

The answer is that A-1's allegations were correct: Between the time of his visit to Mexico City and the time of the assassination, Oswald maintained contact with someone in the Cuban Consulate. According to "A-1," that person was Luisa Calderon. After the assassination, this highly sensitive lead was never investigated.

In the wake of the assassination, CIA Counterintelligence executive Raymond Rocca was especially concerned that Vega and Rodriguez may have been involved in Kennedy's murder. According to Rocca, both men were known to have been Cuban intelligence officers (DGI) and to have run assassination operations in Nicaragua. Rocca further stated, "Vega, it is established, was on post in Mexico City during Oswald's stay there...All individuals going to Cuba, legally or illegally, had to pass through him first. He took the biographical data [of Oswald] and sent it to Cuba for name checking," along with Oswald's application, which Oswald filled out in the Cuban Embassy. In addition, Rodriguez was known to have run into V.T. Lee, the Fair Play for Cuba leader, in Cuba on numerous occasions in 1962 and 1963 (Lee Oswald had been in regular contact with V.T. Lee in 1963).[67]

In 1978, the HCSA interviewed "A-1," whose bona fides were strongly vouched for after he defected to the United States in late 1963. According to A-1, Consulate employee and alleged Castro agent Luisa Calderon had a relationship with Oswald that went "beyond her capacity as secretary in the Mexico City Consulate." A-1 also knew of a letter—presumably intercepted by another of Castro's Mexico City agents—sent to Calderon soon after Oswald's visit. The letter was from an American (Calderon had been seen in Mexico City with a young American) whose name sounded like "Ower"—conceivably Oswald after mouth-to-mouth communication in two languages.

Immediately after the assassination, Calderon was recalled to Havana. On the day Kennedy was killed, she was asked if she had heard the news. A reliable source quoted her as saying, "Yes, of course. I found out almost before Kennedy."[68]

CIA transcripts of the conversation support the source. But they reveal even more detail. The conversation is punctuated by so much laughter, and such joyous disbelief, that the two parties appear giddy. Calderon, through her laughter, said that she couldn't believe the news of Kennedy's death, and continually remarked on how great it was. When the caller said that Kennedy was "shot three times in the face," Calderon exclaimed, "Perfect!"

She went on to call Kennedy "degenerate, unfortunate, an aggressor." Calderon then phoned another Embassy employee named Nico to pass on the good news. Again, both parties laughed, then Nico said, "Okay. What time will the plane arrive?" Calderon replied: "At 4, and at 4:30 they must be at the airport."[69] (This "airport" conversation will take on added significance after the assassination. *See Chapter 14*.) The CIA, in reviewing its assassination file in 1975, concluded that, in hindsight, Calderon "could very well have known something that would make what she said less a matter of boastful self-indulgence than was assumed at the time."[70]

HSCA Chief Counsel G. Robert Blakey wrote, "We decided the [Calderon] allegations raised suspicions of the most sinister sort."[71] As part of its investigation, the Committee traveled to Havana to conduct interviews with, among others, Fidel Castro and Luisa Calderon. In the interim, the HSCA obtained a CIA memo verifying that all three of Oswald's alleged Cuban contacts in Mexico City were indeed in the employ of the DGI (Cuban Intelligence).[72] The HSCA interview of Fidel Castro took place, but permission to interview Calderon was refused because of "illness."

The HSCA wisely concluded that Castro intelligence operatives, by the fall of 1963, had penetrated the Kennedys' assassination plots, including that of Rolando Cubela Secades (AM/LASH). HSCA Counsel Robert Blakey later wrote:

> *The HSCA was uneasy about the timing of the unmasking of Cubela and the allegations about Calderon...[We were] inclined to believe that Oswald had uttered the threat attributed to him in the Cuban consulate...Therefore we believe that the Cuban government withheld important information...We also believe that the Cuban government kept a careful eye fixed on its own best interests. Here that interest—as the Cubans saw it—warranted not telling us the truth.*[73]

Further Allegations

The HSCA unearthed another alleged Oswald/Havana link from a Cuban named Autilio Ramirez Ortiz. Ortiz, who hijacked a plane to Cuba in 1961, was ostensibly sentenced to a prison term in Cuba. In actuality, he was given a job at an intelligence facility. While there, he entered the G-2 (Cuban Military Intelligence) file room and attempted to locate the file on him in order to learn why he had been refused a visa. As he was searching, he noticed directly behind the Ortiz file a file labeled "Oswaldo-Kennedy." It contained a passport photo of Oswald, with a KGB notation:

> *This individual was recommended to us through the Cuban G-2. Oswald is an eternal adventurer. We have instructions to communicate with him through our embassy in Mexico. If this individual is to be utilized it has to be very careful.*[74]

It is not clear how the HSCA evaluated the Ortiz testimony, but apparently he told the story consistently for many years. John Martino, who worked for the Mafia-owned casinos in Havana, and was subsequently imprisoned in Havana during the early 1960's, had long claimed that Oswald was working for the Cubans. Curiously, when asked how he knew this, he said he learned it from a Cuban named "Ortiz."[75]

The "Oswaldo/Kennedy" file story recalls the allegations of Dr. Herminio Portell-Villa, a professor of history at the University of Havana before leaving the country with other exiles in 1960, after the revolution. Villa told the FBI that via reliable sources inside Cuba, he had learned of another file sent from Moscow to "the Castro brothers" in Havana two days after the assassination. The notation on the file read:

> *File of Oswald with Concheso (Cuban Embassy in Moscow) from files of MARIN HERRERA (Ministry of Foreign Relations, Havana), today handed to the CASTRO brothers.*[76]

According to Portell-Villa, the file documented that Oswald, during his stay in the Soviet Union, had made contact with Cuba's Ambassadors in Moscow, Faure Chomon and Carlos Olivares. This confirms a rumor reported in the usually unreliable *Police Gazette* in June 1967. The paper stated:

> *What is not generally known is that in Minsk at the time [Oswald was there] were several hundred Cuban students sent by the Castro regime to Russia for training in schools there. Oswald became friendly with one key man in the student group—a man known to have been an intelligence officer for Castro.*

Not long after the assassination, the FBI and the Secret Service briefly investigated a story making the rounds on Miami streets: While in Mexico City, Oswald was put in contact with Quinton Pino Machado, a known strongarm in Castro's Diplomatic Service. Castro had previously appointed him Cuban Ambassador to Nicaragua, where he was subsequently declared persona non grata for teaching Nicaraguan youth groups how to carry out sabotage. After his expulsion, Pino was sent by Castro to Mexico City, where he was assigned to investigate activities directed against the Castro regime. Allegedly, Pino cut a deal whereby Oswald would be taken to Cuba after the assassination. Pino himself crossed the border from Mexico into Texas for the purpose of escorting Oswald back to Havana. However, according to a Secret Service informant, "the plan went awry because Oswald had not been wearing clothing of a prearranged color and because of the shooting of Dallas Patrolman J.D. Tippit." Pino returned to Havana.[77] Fifteen years later, when reviewing the official investigation into the President's death, a Congressional Committee would state, "The Committee could find no record of follow-up action [on the Machado reports]."[78]

That Cuban hit men were able to slip through the Mexican-U.S. border is not an entirely new story. Eight months before the events of Mexico City, the *Boston Record-American* newspaper, citing two sources, reported that two Cubans, "said to have been especially trained," entered the U.S. from Mexico with the intent of killing Richard Cardinal Cushing, a longtime friend of the Kennedy family. The *Boston Globe* said it had received similar information. Cardinal Cushing declined a Boston police offer of a 24-hour guard, and was not harmed. Earlier in the year, similar threats had been made against the Kennedy children by Cubans entering the country through Mexico.[79]

Simultaneous with the Cuban threat to the Kennedy family, distinguished UPI reporter Edward McCarthy was informed by UPI national news editor Bill Sexton that New York cops had recently picked up reports of Cubans planning to assassinate JFK. Assigned to the story because of his great sources in the federal government, McCarthy immediately checked with Peter Esperdy, head of the Immigration and Naturalization Service in New York. What Esperdy confirmed to McCarthy points out not only the pro-Castro threat to Kennedy, but also the use of Mexico as a conduit for the treachery:

> *We know from more than one quarter that Fidel has sent four hit teams of assassins—three to four men to a group—into the United States. The killers illegally entered our country through Mexico with orders to go underground in Cuban or Hispanic-dominated communities such as those in south Florida, New Jersey, and elsewhere, even Brooklyn, and then, at the right moment, they are to go into action and murder the president.[80]*

Stressing the sensitivity and seriousness of the threat, Esperdy implored McCarthy to sit on the story, lest the Cubans involved go deeper underground. McCarthy assented and would not divulge the information until he wrote his autobiography 35 years later.

By early October 1963, the CIA had determined that one of the persons it had monitored darting between the Cuban and Soviet embassies was a former American defector to Russia named Lee Harvey Oswald. But for reasons that may be a combination of colossal ineptitude and a compulsive need to protect its "sources and methods," virtually nothing was done about it. Although the CIA knew that Oswald met with the KGB's Valery Kostikov, believed to be involved in "wet operations" (assassinations), the Agency felt it was unnecessary to so inform the FBI or the Secret Service.[81]

In the aftermath of the assassination, the CIA has maintained an impenetrable silence when it comes to details of how many double agents it had on the inside of the Cuban Embassy, although it is agreed by all parties that it had them. Additionally acknowledged is that the Cuban Embassy was electronically bugged, phone-tapped, and photo-surveilled.

Because it knew that the Calderon document had been placed in Oswald's file before the assassination, and because of the testimony of numerous Mexico City "assets," the HSCA would later state that it disbelieved the CIA's official stance that it was ignorant of Oswald's visit. The HSCA thus concluded:

> *The Agency maintained that prior to the assassination, its field sources had not actually linked Oswald [to] the person who visited the Cuban consulate in October 1963. Testimony obtained directly from these sources, however, established that this connection had in fact been made in early October, 1963.*[82]

It is not difficult to speculate about the myriad of problems in store for the CIA if it made a complete disclosure of the Cuban Embassy affair. Chief among these difficulties:

- *The CIA would have to give up years of hard work establishing "assets" (like Proenza and Duran) in the Cuban Embassy (arguably the most critical CIA operation in the Western Hemisphere). This would have been unthinkable, considering the Kennedys' preoccupation with Cuba, the imminent commencement of OPLAN 380-63, and the position Mexico City held as a center of espionage.*

- *The disclosure of photos and tapes would give away valuable sources of future infiltration and intelligence.*

- *The disclosure of CIA agents in the Cuban Embassy could very well show them to have been in contact with President Kennedy's assassin—a guaranteed fatal blow for the beleaguered CIA. Perhaps these agents were even photographed with Oswald.*

- *Most damaging would be the possibility that the CIA was contemporaneously aware of just who Lee Oswald was—a psychopath who had defected to Russia—and that, though it was fully informed of his threat/offer to kill Kennedy, did nothing. At a recent Bahamian conference attended by former Cuban intelligence personnel, more evidence surfaced that the CIA may have heard Oswald's threat at the time he made it. Arturo Rodriguez, a former security officer at the Cuban Embassy in Mexico City, described the atmosphere at the consulate after the assassination. According to Rodriguez, security personnel "tore the place apart" searching for "bugging" microphones. What they turned up astonished them: microphones believed to be American were found in the arms of chairs, window frames, light fixtures, and elsewhere. Some of the bugs could be remotely turned on and off. Others appeared to be permanently "open." If those monitoring the Cuban Embassy didn't take the Oswald threat seriously at the time, one can only imagine their horror when they heard the news a month later that Oswald had indeed killed the President. Those in a position to know thus held the power to both destroy the CIA and possibly to start a nuclear confrontation between the world's two superpowers.*

When David Phillips was asked to characterize the CIA's performance in the Mexico City affair, he replied with possibly the most profound understatement in the entire Kennedy assassination oeuvre: "At the very best, it [was] not professional."[83]

At 8:30 a.m. on October 2nd, 1963, Lee Oswald left behind the labyrinthine intrigue of Mexico City, boarding a bus bound for Texas. He crossed the border at Laredo at 1:30 a.m. the next day, and arrived in Dallas at 2:30 p.m. on October 3rd. It was the last long-distance trip in the much-traveled life of the twenty-three year-old.

On the same day, back in Washington, Bobby Kennedy's Special Group Augmented (SGA) met and approved nine operations in Cuba, several of which included sabotage.[84]

In Miami, Cuban exile businessman Jose Aleman, considered a reliable source by the FBI, informed the Bureau that three Cuban agents had recently appeared in Miami, and then proceeded to Texas. "I advised the FBI in long conversations that I thought something was going to happen," Aleman later testified. "I was telling them to be careful."[85]

CHAPTER ELEVEN

TWO TRACKS TO OBLIVION

"Cuba is Kennedy's bone in the throat."
—**Nikita Khrushchev, Chairman of the Soviet Communist Party in 1963**

By the fall of 1963, Cuba had become the sine qua non of the Kennedy administration. After the president's numerous foreign policy disasters—the defeat at the Bay of Pigs, his weak performance at the Vienna Summit with Khruschev, and the embarassing erection of the Berlin Wall in Germany— JFK knew that his prospects for re-election in 1964 would be greatly enhanced by a resolution of "the Cuba problem." If Kennedy couldn't control Cuba, ninety miles away, why would the country entrust to him the simmering quagmire of Laos and Vietnam? And, if that weren't bad enough, polls showed the president's other political weakness: by 4 to 1 margins, Kennedy was "pushing [civil rights-related] integration too fast."

With each new poll, the possibility of a Kennedy mandate in 1964 dwindled. From a high of 82 percent approval rating after the Missile Crisis, the president's popularity had plummeted to 55 percent—a staggering 27 point decline.[1] Furthermore, if a Republican other than Senator Barry Goldwater was nominated, Kennedy feared he could lose altogether. (Goldwater was considered a soft opponent, easily portrayed as trigger-happy and kooky.) Governor David Lawrence of Pennsylvania had said that the President confided to him his fears of defeat. James Reston of the *New York Times* wrote about "doubt and disappointment" among the voters, adding, "People don't quite believe in him [the president]."

Particularly worrisome for the Kennedy camp were the recent attacks of a GOP presidential hopeful, New York governor Nelson Rockefeller. Rockefeller had been hitting Kennedy hard on the Cuban issue, calling it Kennedy's "Achilles' heel." He accused JFK of allowing the Soviets to maintain a secret force in Cuba after the Missile Crisis resolution. "This will raise hell as it increasingly comes out," Rockefeller remarked at the time. According to Kennedy aide

Roswell Gilpatrick, Kennedy was obsessed with Rockefeller's attacks.[2]

Although the polls predicted a slim Kennedy victory against the likely Republican opponent, Senator Barry Goldwater, Kennedy needed a heftier margin, and maybe a landslide, in 1964 to build political capital with Congress. Such a mandate would allow him to accomplish the lofty goals he had set for himself. Only strong public confidence would allow him to increase or decrease U.S. involvement in Southeast Asia.[3]

Kennedy's civil rights stance was more than a little troublesome. JFK was viewed in the South as a federal meddler from the North; his political support in the South was virtually non-existent. His only chances for victory in "the Bible belt" were, it was said, in Texas and Florida. To win Florida, he would have to appeal to the Cuban exile community, then politically dominant in Dade County.[4] In Texas, Kennedy's problems revolved around fallout from the "Peace Speech." He was now seen by many Texans as "soft on Communism." When Kennedy arrived in Houston the day before the assassination, he would observe a streamer towed by a biplane which read: "COEXISTENCE IS SURRENDER."

Indeed, to many, nothing was more dangerous than the president's overture to "the Reds." Ted Dealey, the Kennedy-bashing publisher of the *Dallas Morning News*, believed that Kennedy had endangered America with his displays of gullibility and weakness. Less than two years earlier, in the autumn of 1961, Dealey was among a group of Texas publishers invited to a White House luncheon. Startling his fellow guests with a prepared diatribe, he attacked his host with a slashing statement, first about attempts (such as that luncheon's) to "soft soap" others to the president's side, then about his larger failure.

The publisher fumed, "You and your administration are weak sisters...We can annihilate Russia and should make that clear to the Soviet government." The nation, Dealey asserted, needed a "man on horseback" to lead it, "and many people in Texas and the southwest think that you are riding   Caroline's [Kennedy's daughter's] tricycle."

Politically, Kennedy wasn't faring much better in the North. His rollback of steel prices, and his desire to deprive the oil industry of its lucrative 27 percent oil depletion allowance, had alarmed big business. In his first 30 months as President, Kennedy's domestic initiatives remained largely bogged down in Congress. Some wondered whether Kennedy was simply a pampered, ineffectual scion—and doubted that he was the reformer he professed to be. Others saw him even less charitably, as just an opportunistic son of a latter-day robber baron, installed to do his father's bidding.

The polls revealed that both North and South agreed on one point: everyone had Cuba on their mind. A recent book by Montague Kern superbly described Kennedy's dilemma:

> *The administration was acutely aware of the Cuban issue and kept track through polls ever since the Bay of Pigs in the knowledge that Cuba was, in Theodore Sorenson's apt phrase, President Kennedy's "Achilles' heel." The*

polls that the administration solicited and picked up from newspapers showed the same thing: a public acutely aware of Cuba and eager for the government to "do something" about it. [Pollster] Louis Harris, who studied attitudes on the Cuban issue in Florida for the administration in December 1961, concluded that "the vast bulk of public opinion favors doing everything possible short of armed intervention." [5]

A poll clipped from the San Francisco Chronicle and sent to Sorenson in early 1962 indicated that on Cuba, alone among foreign policy issues, the administration received a 62 percent negative rating. By September 1962, many Americans clearly were in an angry mood: A Gallup poll of September 18 reported that 71 percent of those having opinions wanted action against Cuba, and that many respondents used words like "bomb," "invade," or "starve them out."...[In the 1962 elections,] Cuba became the Republicans' number one campaign issue...The initiative belonged not to the president, but to the Republicans and the Cuban exiles. [6]

The poll results on Cuba clearly reflected hard-hitting press coverage of Republican attacks on Kennedy. GOP Senators Homer Capehart of Indiana and Kenneth Keating of New York were demanding action, with Capehart saying, "The U.S. has every right to land troops, take possession of Havana, and occupy the country."[7] More distressing were Democrats such as Strom Thurmond of South Carolina, and Kennedy's friend George Smathers of Florida, who broke party ranks and demanded military action.

Usually loyal to the administration, the liberal press took up the Cuban exiles' cause, praising their efforts to overthrow Castro. *The New York Times*, the *Washington Post*, and the British press often ran uncritical pieces about exile raids on the island, referring to them in heroic language.

In retrospect, the Kennedy administration's actions in the fall of 1963 make it clear that the president considered a victory over Castro in 1963-64 to be politically crucial. Yet, practically speaking, an all-out American invasion of the island was out of the question unless and until three components fell into place: the Cuban exiles' initial involvement; a revolt by the Cuban military; and the assassination of Castro himself. At least one powerful man in the CIA doubted the pieces would come together to permit that sort of major action. "Kennedy wasn't going to invade Cuba, for goddamn sure," Richard Helms has said.[8]

Effective action had to take the form of a Cuban insurrection, followed by U.S. support—the essence of OPLAN 380-63. As one CIA officer concluded recently, "Kennedy wanted to deal with Cuba in a way that wouldn't draw in the Soviet Union." This explains part of the thinking behind "the crackdown" on exile operations considered uncontrollable. There was no desire to return to the Cold War terror of the Cuban Missile Crisis. As a bragging point on the campaign stump, Kennedy couldn't afford to forget the fact that relations were warming ever so slightly with the USSR. As has been noted, the origins of the thaw can be traced to Kennedy's speech on June 10, 1963 at American

University. Many scholars point to this initiative as John Kennedy's most visionary accomplishment. And Kennedy knew it. However, the obsession with Cuba continued unabated. And as historian Herbert Parmet implies, Kennedy operations like AM/LASH and AM/TRUNK "made a mockery" of the eloquent "Peace Speech."

Thus in late 1963, the Kennedy brothers decided to pull out all the stops in dealing with the Castro problem. They even considered, briefly, making peace. Finally, a simple plan evolved: Remove Castro or get him to make peace on U.S. terms, whichever came first—with both scenarios having to play out before the 1964 presidential elections. Ironically, Kennedy was now handcuffed by secrecy, much as Richard Nixon had been in the 1960 elections. Unable to counter his critics by revealing his secret anti-Castro operations, he needed results. The resulting strategy would become known as the "two track" approach. In fact, the energy devoted to the peace overtures was dwarfed by that devoted to killing and overthrowing the dictator Castro.

Track One: Peace

> *"How can you figure him out?"*
>
> —**Fidel Castro, October 1963, speaking of President Kennedy and his simultaneous peace and sabotage policies** [9]

Not only did Kennedy develop a simultaneous two-track policy (peace and sabotage), but the peace gambit itself was two-pronged. The prongs consisted of overtures by an American broadcast journalist, Lisa Howard, and a French journalist, Jean Daniel, with the same U.S. diplomat, William Attwood, facilitating both entrées.

In September 1963, William Attwood, the special advisor for African Affairs at the U.S. Mission to the United Nations, began receiving hints from fellow U.N. associates and a press correspondent that Castro might be willing to enter "détente" talks with the United States. The Guinean ambassador to Cuba, Sékou Touré, told Attwood he had reason to believe that Castro was prepared to make "substantial concessions" to the United States in order to achieve a normalization of relations. Around the same time, according to Attwood, "Lisa Howard, an ABC correspondent, told me she'd recently interviewed Castro in Havana and was convinced he'd like to restore communications with the U.S."[10]

Often referred to as a "spirited" news reporter from New York, Lisa Howard was the perfect American-Cuban peacemaker. She was a strong admirer of President Kennedy, and on friendly terms with the Cuban dictator. Besides all that, Howard was an attractive and talented newsperson. As the only woman in the country with her own network news show, she had scored many journalistic coups, including interviews with such "untouchables" as the Shah of Iran, Nikita Khrushchev, and Fidel Castro, with whom she spoke several times. In addition, she had long pursued a personal quest to help normalize the Kennedy-Castro relationship.

At a cocktail party Lisa Howard arranged to explore the subject, William Attwood approached the chief Cuban delegate to the U.N., Dr. Carlos Lechuga Hevia, who authenticated the offer. "He said Castro had hoped to establish some sort of contact with Kennedy after he became president in 1961," remembers Attwood, "but the Bay of Pigs ended any chance of that." Lechuga said Castro was intrigued by "the Peace Speech." The U.S. Ambassador to the U.N., Adlai Stevenson, passed the response along to the administration. Kennedy agreed in principle to pursue the overture, but insisted that any meeting with Castro would have to be secret and occur outside of Cuba (possibly in Mexico). The meetings, JFK also suggested, should be brokered by a third party unaffiliated with politics.

The next move along this track involved the editor of the French socialist newsweekly *L'Observateur*. Jean Daniel had been scheduled to interview Fidel Castro in November. In early October, he was drafted to perform a simultaneous diplomatic mission. Daniel, as the chosen "third party," was briefed by his old friend Attwood that Castro might be receptive to a gesture of peace from President Kennedy.

Attwood, through his friendship with JFK confidante Ben Bradlee, arranged for Daniel to meet with Kennedy before going on to Havana. On October 24th, Daniel met with the President, who expressed his lack of confidence in Castro, and complained that Castro had betrayed the revolution.[11] Nonetheless, Kennedy instructed Daniel to determine if Castro's recent positive response to a Kennedy peace overture was genuine.

Daniel was to meet with Castro in the third week of November—the same week Kennedy was to be in Dallas on his first campaign stop for the 1964 election.[12] In fact, on November 22nd, Daniel was with Castro when he received the news of Kennedy's assassination. At first, Castro seemed dismayed, but upon hearing the news that Lyndon Johnson had been sworn in as Kennedy's successor, quickly asked Daniel, "What authority does he [Johnson] exercise over the CIA?"[13]

On October 31, 1963, Lisa Howard telephoned a Castro aide, Major Rene Vallejo, attempting to set a secret summit in motion. According to a friend, Howard arranged for Attwood and Robert Kennedy to meet clandestinely with Castro. Vallejo called Howard, affirming that Castro would go along with any secrecy provisions President Kennedy required. On November 19th, Presidential aide McGeorge Bundy informed Attwood that the President would be available to pursue the rapprochement after "a brief trip to Dallas."[14]

That would appear to be the end of the episode, except that after one of Howard's meetings with Castro, her opinion of the Kennedys, especially Bobby, changed drastically. When Bobby ran for the Senate in New York in 1964 against Republican incumbent Kenneth Keating, Lisa Howard (considered a kingpin in the Lexington Democratic Club) joined with Jacqueline Kennedy relative Gore Vidal to form an organization called "Democrats for Keating." She had come to detest Bobby Kennedy, describing him at the first meeting as:

The very antithesis of his brother, the late President. He is ruthless, reactionary, and dangerously authoritarian. We feel he must be stopped now…if you feel strongly about something like this, you can't remain silent—you have to show courage and stand up and be counted.[15]

Debating pro-Kennedy lawyers two weeks later, she expanded on the theme, sniping, "Brothers are not necessarily the same. There was Cain and Abel."

The question lingers: Why did Lisa Howard turn against Bobby Kennedy? Former FBI agent William Turner offers a possible explanation: "Friends said she had learned from Cuban sources that all the while she was talking peace to Castro for the Kennedys, the morally flexible brothers were indulging in invasion and assassination plans against him."[16]

It has been posited that Howard obtained her information about the plots from either Lechuga, at the cocktail party mentioned earlier, or from Castro himself. Either is plausible. Recall that Lechuga was the alleged recipient of the letters of Fernando Fernandez, who had penetrated the exile operations in New Orleans. Fernandez admitted to the FBI that Lechuga ran a pro-Castro terrorist network, adding, "The subversive and espionage activities are directed by the Cuban ambassadors in the United Nations and in Brazil."[17]

This assertion seems valid when one takes into account the arrest one year earlier of a pro-Castro terrorist cell operating in New York City. The three arrestees possessed huge quantities of explosives they intended to use against large department stores such as Macy's, Gimbel's, and Bloomingdale's when the stores were clogged with Christmas shoppers. One of the terrorists was an aide to Lechuga, while another traveled to New York with Cuban President Osvaldo Dorticos, a friend of Rolando Cubela (AM/LASH). Even more disturbing, these terrorists belonged to the Fair Play for Cuba Committee, of which Lee Oswald claimed to be a member, and with whom he maintained a continuing correspondence.[18]

Also of note is the fact that Lechuga had an affair with none other than Sylvia Duran, who admitted—to a CIA plant in the Cuban Embassy—to being Lee Oswald's Mexican lover as well.[19] This relationship opens up a myriad of intriguing possibilities, given the many possible directions for the potential flow of information:

• *Was Oswald linked to a pro-Castro network which had links to the Fair Play for Cuba Committee, Carlos Lechuga, and the Cuban Embassy in Mexico City?*

• *Because Rolando Cubela (AM/LASH) was known to frequent the Cuban Embassy in Mexico City, where he was originally contacted by the CIA, could Duran have obtained sensitive information about that operation from her lover Lechuga and passed it on to Oswald? Likewise, could Lisa Howard have learned the same details from Lechuga (who attended the original Lisa Howard cocktail party)?*

• *Had Oswald learned of AM/TRUNK or AM/LASH in New Orleans (where these two operations were known about in certain circles) and informed Duran, who then informed Lechuga and other Embassy personnel?*

The point here is that the official investigators of Kennedy's assassination had no inkling that all the critical elements intersected in the Cuban Embassy.

Two weeks after her anti-Kennedy lambast, Lisa Howard was fired by ABC News, ostensibly because she had "chosen to participate publicly in partisan political activity contrary to long-established ABC News policy."[20] Eight months later, she was found dead, the victim of a barbiturate overdose that many consider suspicious. Her friend and colleague Craig Karpel said, "Lisa just wasn't the type to kill herself. She was too dynamic, too dedicated, too sure of herself ever to admit defeat in that ultimate way."

Whatever her source on the administration's plotting, it was clear that Lisa Howard had stumbled onto "Track Two."

Track Two: Invasion and Assassination

"It [our Cuban policy] was just an either/or situation. That went on frequently," Kennedy's Secretary of State Dean Rusk said recently. Rusk admitted that, with Cuba, the Kennedys were "playing with fire."[21]

In Congressional testimony, the CIA's Richard Helms clarified Kennedy's policy, terming the accommodation efforts with Castro a "feint," saying, "Like most two-track policies, try everything." In implementation, stated Helms, the administration's "real energy" on Cuba was channeled into covert action.[22] The disclosures of the last thirty years have proven Helms correct (witness AM/LASH. AM/TRUNK, OPLAN 380-63, and Artime's Second Naval Guerrilla).

A Naval Intelligence officer stationed in Guantanamo in the fall of 1963 remembered firsthand the Kennedys' frustration with the lack of success in their secret war against Cuba. The officer recalled, "In 1963, the Kennedys sent down Joseph Califano—the head of Bobby Kennedy's Cuban Coordinating Committee—and he fired everybody."[23] In September 1963, the administration's aggression went into higher gear. Between October 3rd and October 24th, twenty-one more acts of Cuban sabotage were approved.[24]

"We were making more of an effort through espionage and sabotage in August, September, and October," Robert Kennedy himself later confirmed. "It was better organized that it had been before and it was having quite an effect. I mean, there were ten or twenty tons of sugar cane that were being burned every week through internal uprisings."[25]

The Kennedys' commitment to these sabotage attempts, more extensive than their interest in peace with Cuba, was clear even to the men and women directly involved in the "secret war" effort. One of those at the troop level, Army Captain Bradley Ayers, was deep in the Florida Everglades shortly after the October sabotage authorizations, planning for the newest raid—an oil refinery attack. When night had fallen, Ayers heard the distinctive whirr of a helicopter.

The copter sported a West Palm Beach air service name on its tail boom. Soon, two men emerged from a Quonset hut. One of the men was the JM/WAVE assistant Chief, Gordon Campbell. The other was Robert Kennedy. Recall that this was the second time Ayers had seen RFK in Florida. The first was right after the June 19 "autonomous operations" authorization by JFK.

"Kennedy had apparently come over from the family compound in West Palm Beach to inspect preparations at the Everglades camp," Ayers later wrote. As Campbell escorted Kennedy to his waiting chopper, the Attorney General passed Ayers, shook his hand, and wished him luck on his mission.

"If the President felt strongly enough to send his brother, something very big was being planned," Ayers reasoned. Campbell explained to Ayers, "Everybody from the President on down has his eyes on this one...If we can hit Castro a couple of good blows like this, he'll fall right on his ass...and that's what the President wants." Ayers soon learned that "the down-to-the-last details were approved by Bobby Kennedy."[26]

Ayers concluded the obvious: "The President and his brother were tough, smart politicians, and the elections were getting closer."

Also in the fall of 1963, Harry Williams and Manuel Artime, coordinating with Bobby Kennedy, were hard at work training a new Cuban invasion force in Guatemala, Costa Rica, and Nicaragua, under the auspices of the Second Naval Guerrilla contingent. AM/TRUNK and OPLAN 380-63 were all timed to commence in the coming months, despite the fact that Castro had heavily infiltrated these operations with his own spies. The frenzy of operations was aimed at settling the Cuba problem before the 1964 presidential election. To guarantee success, the coup de grace known as AM/LASH was now placed on the front burner.

AM/LASH Reactivated

"AM/LASH was a product of Bobby's pressure on Des [FitzGerald]. The CIA was there to take the rap for the President."
—**Jim Flannery, CIA officer stationed in Mexico City and Tokyo**[27]

"The objective as I understood it—why we were doing all this—was in order to foment a military coup, internal coup, against Castro."
—**Nestor Sanchez, AM/LASH's CIA case officer**[28]

On September 7, 1963, Cuban Army Major Rolando Cubela Secades, a Castro insider, met two CIA agents in Porto Alegre, Brazil. One of them was Nestor Sanchez, a career CIA officer, who had been working closely with such CIA luminaries as Seymour Bolton, Bill Harvey, and Des FitzGerald, and who had worked in the propaganda section of the Cuba Desk (Task Force W). Sanchez would later testify that his role at Task Force W was "to develop assets inside Cuba that could be used in a coup against Castro."[29] The Spanish-speaking Sanchez traveled to Brazil, on Des FitzGerald's orders, to meet Cubela. It was thought that he might gain rapport with Cubela while functioning simultaneously as a translator. He would later become Cubela's CIA case officer.

Cubela informed Sanchez and his fellow CIA agent that he was ready to perform an "inside job" against Castro. This offer was communicated to CIA Headquarters the same day. AM/LASH, the operation that, according to Harry Williams and Manuel Artime, was initially proposed by JFK (and coordinated by Kennedy friend Des FitzGerald), was back in stir.[30]

After Bobby Kennedy's Cuban Coordinating Group met on September 12, 1963, clandestine meetings between Sanchez and Cubela escalated. Cubela told Sanchez that he would assassinate Castro, provided it was in conjunction with a coup d'etat. Sanchez, known to Cubela only as "Nicolas Sanson," assured him that such a coup was under consideration at the "highest levels." Cubela made two other requests: he had specific ideas about which weapons should be used in the hit (he wanted rifles and explosives), and he wanted to meet with Bobby Kennedy (given the CIA code name "GPFOCUS") to obtain his pledge of U.S. support. Sanchez/Sanson cabled this request to CIA headquarters on October 11.[31]

On the very day that Cubela cabled FitzGerald with his request for Kennedy's authorization, Des FitzGerald called and spoke with Robert Kennedy at the Justice Department. The topic of their conversation is not noted on paper, but can be easily surmised. It was the only call (at least recorded on paper) that Kennedy took from FitzGerald during the fall of 1963.[32] Soon (Oct. 29) FitzGerald, using the pseudonym "James Clark," was off to Paris with the "high level" assurance Cubela had requested.

In 1994, FitzGerald's planning memo for the Paris meeting was released. It states, in part, that FitzGerald "will represent self as personal representative of GPFOCUS [Robert Kennedy] who traveled [to] Paris for specific purpose [of] meeting AM/LASH/1 and giving him full assurances of United States support if there is a change of the present government in Cuba."[33] As shall be seen, this and subsequent memos omit the more sinister subjects that were to be discussed at the meeting. Cubela told the HSCA, "I didn't know this man was FitzGerald, but due to the [Church Committee] Final Report, I realized that it was. He told me that he came representing [Robert] Kennedy."[34]

FitzGerald readily admitted in 1967 that he told Cubela of Bobby Kennedy's imprimatur on the plan. Cubela himself recalled:

> He [FitzGerald] offered me on behalf of the U.S. government the support, the political support of the United States…[This support was] for being able to carry out either the plot attempt against the Prime Minister of Cuba or any other activity that will put in danger the stability of the regime.[35]

Cubela's version is corroborated by Sanchez/Sanson, who acted as the translator. He later testified, "FitzGerald gave assurances that the United States not only would support the government which emerged after a successful coup, but also gave assurances that the United States would help in bringing about that coup."[36]

FitzGerald later claimed that he didn't actually speak with Kennedy about this matter. Instead, he told CIA investigators that he and Richard Helms together decided "it was not necessary to seek approval from Robert Kennedy for FitzGerald to speak in his name." Helms, however, recalled no such conversation with FitzGerald. Further, Helms (and other believers in "plausible denial"—the concept that political leaders are shielded from responsibility for their actions) have always contended that they would never undertake anything as serious as an assassination of a foreign leader without the White House's approval.

In later years, some CIA officials claimed that there was a misunderstanding on Cubela's part—that he was not authorized to kill Castro, only to antagonize him. FitzGerald's assistant, Sam Halpern, recently refuted that assertion unhesitatingly, "My boss at the time, FitzGerald, decided that we would give Cubela something to use to, if possible, assassinate Castro."[37] FitzGerald's Cuba specialist on his Special Affairs Staff (SAS) agreed when he testified, "The AM/LASH operation, at all times during its existence, was characterized by senior SAS officers, including Helms and FitzGerald, as an assassination plot sponsored by the CIA."[38] It should be noted that Helms later finessed the subject when testifying that AM/LASH was not an assassin per se, but a "political action agent" who might coincidentally murder Castro.[39]

Three weeks after the Paris meeting of October 29, the CIA equipped Cubela with a poison pen device designed for use on Castro.[40]

In 1975, Senator Richard Schweiker of Pennsylvania chaired a subcommittee looking into just this question: How much did RFK know about Cubela's assassination plot? Because Robert Kennedy's and Des FitzGerald's deaths precluded their testifying, the official Senate report concluded that it was impossible to determine the depth of Robert Kennedy's knowledge of the AM/LASH operation. However, by 1994, Richard Schweiker was ready to divulge more than the Committee's 1976 report.

"I was told in executive session by a high-ranking CIA official that, in fact, Des FitzGerald was acting on behalf of Bobby Kennedy," Schweiker admits. "We had a witness confirm it. It was either Helms or one of his associates. I'm fairly certain it was Helms."[41] When questioned if he would like to go further now that time had passed, Helms recently told the author, "The Church Committee went into it as far as I'm willing to go."[42] (One is left with the inference that there is more to go into.) It would later be learned that Helms had no such reservations when he spoke to his friend Henry Kissinger, then serving as President Gerald Ford's National Security Advisor (*details to follow*).

Senator Schweiker's recollections are buttressed by the statements of a high CIA official who worked closely with FitzGerald and AM/LASH. Speaking with the author in 1995 on conditions of anonymity, the officer pulled no punches. "The Kennedys were trying to play every kind of card in the deck," the officer recalled. "The CIA was definitely not operating as a rogue elephant. The idea that Des was operating on his own is a bunch of rubbish. The Kennedys knew everything."[43] Another agency official who worked closely with FitzGerald on the Cuba Task Force, as well as AM/LASH, summarized the situation for the author. "One thing is certain: Des was no 'rogue.' He was a true professional. The Kennedys were aware of all operations, including AM/LASH."[44] Bobby's CCC staffer General Alexander Haig agrees. "No question but that Bobby knew of the plots. It was John Kennedy and Bobby, not the CIA."[45]

The Mafia: Continuing Plots

As if all this activity were not enough, the Kennedy administration continued its contacts with the criminal underworld, as it had years earlier with the likes of Norman Rothman, Johnny Rosselli, and Sam Giancana, and sometimes with the assistance of the CIA's Charlie Ford.

Although many of the Kennedys' contacts with organized crime were terminated during the "crackdown" on Cuban exiles, Johnny Rosselli has testified that he was never told to end his Mafia-based Castro assassination project, which continued on a track parallel to the AM/LASH plot. Documents released in 1994 show that, in official testimony, Rosselli recalled meeting some of his fellow Cuban plotters in Washington in 1963. Rosselli told a congressional committee that he would reveal the name of only one of the Cubans, because he was dead: Castro's first Prime Minister and Brigade leader Dr. Jose Miro Cardona (Miro). Although he would not reveal the other name, Rosselli made it clear that both men had been involved in the Phase One assassination attempts that allegedly had been terminated two years earlier.[46]

"They [the Cubans] said they were there meeting with the Attorney General [in Washington], and that they were waiting for an appointment to the White House," Rosselli recalled.

A Miro meeting with RFK would not be surprising. Miro was the president of the Cuban Revolutionary Council, the same group run out of 544 Camp Street in New Orleans by Robert Kennedy confidante Sergio Arcacha Smith. Miro also was one of the participants in the secret meeting with Senator John Kennedy in July 1960. He later attended private White House meetings with JFK, after one of which Miro announced that he and the President "had formalized a pact which called for a new invasion."[47]

By the late spring of 1963, Miro fell victim to the exile "crackdown," resulting in a much-publicized split with the Kennedy administration. Kennedy aide/protector Arthur Schlesinger, Jr. advised the President in writing that his comments on Miro should be "restrained" lest the CRC leader be "goaded into giving away Kennedy's most secret operations with the exiles." Schlesinger added:

Miro has not told all he knows, and if driven into a corner, could do us a lot more damage...If goaded, Miro could give a hopelessly squalid picture of our covert dealings with the exiles.[48]

But, even without Miro, the plots by select Kennedy loyalists in both the exile community and within organized crime continued after the crackdown. The bottom line, according to Rosselli, was that "there was never a time a halt [on the assassination plot] was called."[49] He would later tell journalist Jack Anderson that he sent three sharpshooters into Havana in March 1963. This time, like all the previous attempts, Castro was forewarned—his troops were waiting to arrest the men upon their arrival. As Rosselli later recounted, the assassination team was "captured and tortured until they told all they knew about our operation, which they said was ordered by the White House."[50]

By this time, Bill Harvey had been removed from the Rosselli assassination project, and sent packing to the CIA station in Rome. However, the Kennedys had their own network in place with numerous direct links to Rosselli with which they could keep the plots alive. First, Rosselli was a close friend of JFK's lover Judy Campbell. Second, the Kennedy family had a historic relationship with Rosselli's close associate, Sam Giancana, who had assisted Papa Joe Kennedy in Jack's 1960 electoral effort. Third, Rosselli was a close friend of JFK/RFK lover, Marilyn Monroe.[51]

Fourth, the man who originally enlisted Rosselli's help in the plots, Robert Maheu, shared his private investigating office with the Kennedy family investigator, Carmine Bellino. Bellino, who started with the Kennedys as RFK's investigator on the McClellan Investigating Committee on Labor Racketeering in the late 1950's, was often referred to as the "Kennedy family spook." Investigative journalist Jim Hougan accurately described Bellino as a "zero-cool, behind-the-scenes figure in the Kennedy organization."[52]

The Open Secret

> "The AM/LASH plot was known to Castro. We believed Cubela was a double agent."
> —Grayston Lynch, CIA agent in Florida[53]

> "Among the things [the Cuban exiles] said—undoubtedly reported to Castro by the Cuban Intelligence service, which had penetrated the emigré community—was talk of plans against Castro himself...The fact must be accepted that such information was reported to him."
> —Scott Breckinridge, CIA Deputy Inspector General[54]

Not the least of the Kennedys' problems was the fact that Castro's extensive intelligence apparatus had made inroads into every component of the U.S.-Cuban operations. The dictator had already demonstrated that he was aware of U.S.-sponsored terrorism. He had penetrated the Central American training sites for the Bay of Pigs invasion, the Guantanamo-based assassination plots, and the New Orleans training camps. According to Al Tarabochia, of Florida's Dade County sheriff's intelligence unit, "The exile community was penetrated to the fullest degree."[55]

Castro was also aware of Artime's Central American camps, if only by his partisans' monitoring of the Miami newspapers. On July 14, 1963, not long after

Artime had solidified the RFK/Somoza deal, reporter Hal Hendrix wrote an article in the *Miami News*. The piece, entitled "Backstage With Bobby," noted Bobby's "hip pocket plans with the exiles and Somoza" in mounting a new invasion.[56]

Fabian Escalante, Castro's counterintelligence chief, disclosed in 1994, "We had several agents, not only there [in Miami], but also in other places."[57] However, as the CIA's Miami Station Chief Ted Shackley remembers, "Castro didn't need to have a lot of agents. The Cubans not only talked a great deal, but Castro monitored their phone calls and mail back to the island. He would have learned the most through these methods."[58]

In May 1975, Fidel Castro sent South Dakota Senator George McGovern (the 1972 Democratic nominee for president) a list of operations the Cubans had penetrated. Twenty-four incidents were described, and the list did not profess to be all-inclusive. The sheer detail of Castro's knowledge was stunning. The document included not only key names and dates, but the identities of the CIA case officers, operatives, sites of planning meetings, etc. McGovern stated, upon receiving the documents, "I have no way to verify these allegations. But if they are true, the CIA has engaged in the most shocking, murderous, and un-American behavior against the leaders of a neighboring state. I find such behavior a complete contradiction of the principles on which our nation was founded."[59]

What McGovern didn't say, or didn't know, was that at least one, if not most, of the plots had been instigated by the Kennedys themselves, and not by the CIA. One of the twenty-four listed, complete with his assistants and backups, was "Rolando Cubela Secades"—known to Bobby Kennedy and Des FitzGerald as AM/LASH.

Details are beginning to emerge of just how the Cubans penetrated the AM/LASH plot. In 1992, the Chief of Cuban Counter-Intelligence, Israel Behar, told BBC filmmakers:

We started to notice that Cubela attended different cabarets every evening— the Tropicana, the Capri. He spent all the time with the same group of people, chattering suspiciously. They used to drink to excess, and spent enormous amounts of money. We knew he was capable of doing it [an assassination] because he had already eliminated a torturer in the Batista regime. So we infiltrated his group and delayed the execution of the plan for longer than the Americans wanted. I knew of at least 26 CIA-backed assassination plots. But we penetrated them, again, and again, and again.[60]

In November 1993, Cuba released more details on how the AM/LASH operation was penetrated. In 1963, the man responsible for coordinating these penetrations was the Cuban head of counterintelligence, General Fabian Escalante. In the Brazilian-Cuban TV documentary ZR/RIFLE, which had Escalante's assistance, a Cuban agent named Juan Felaifel gave his version of the story behind AM/LASH. Together with the released Cuban intelligence documents, the agent's interview was powerful.

Felaifel says he was told of the AM/LASH plot by his brother, who was described as an intelligence chief planted in the exile organization of Bobby Kennedy intimate (and Cubela friend) Manuel Artime. Felaifel's brother later helped Artime craft a silencer for the 7.62 FAL rifle which Cubela intended to use in an attempt on Castro.[61] This attack was to take place from an apartment building located directly in front of the university where Castro often spoke. Obviously, this attempt was also thwarted.[62]

The AM/LASH operation was so insecure that between July 1962 and October 1963, street informants in Miami reported the CIA/Cubela contact to the FBI. One such report states that the "CIA is aware of subject's reported plans."[63]

At least two of FitzGerald's associates were prescient enough to go on record against the FitzGerald-Cubela liaison. "Joseph Langosch" (pseudonym) was the Chief of Counterintelligence for the CIA's Special Affairs Staff, which was responsible for coordinating the Cuban operations, as well as participating in Bobby Kennedy's Cuban Coordinating Committee. Langosch suspected Cubela was a "dangle"—a double agent. He warned FitzGerald against meeting with Cubela, but FitzGerald ignored him. Langosch issued this assessment:

> The AM/LASH operation might have been an insecure operation prior to the assassination of President Kennedy because it was highly possible that as of 1962, the Cuban intelligence services had knowledge of the CIA's association with persons involved in the AM/LASH operation, including AM/LASH.[64]

Langosch later testified that he thought the operation was "nonsense" and "counterproductive" and that AM/LASH's bona fides were subject to question. "I basically disagreed with the whole thrust of the AM/LASH operation," recalled Langosch. "My disapproval of it was very strong. Des FitzGerald knew it…and preferred not to discuss it anymore with me."[65]

Ted Shackley, Chief of the CIA's JM/WAVE Station in Florida, also advised FitzGerald against meeting Cubela, but for different reasons. He later testified that "if anything went wrong, an individual as prominent in Washington both within the agency and in the social world in Washington [as FitzGerald] would be exposed in the press. That would create a flap that I thought was not worth what would be gained from the meeting."[66] Shackley told Des Fitzgerald that the only thing he'd get from such a dangerous meeting was "the satisfaction of saying you saw the guy. [But] Des shrugged and went on his way."[67]

"The problem," recalls FitzGerald's executive assistant Sam Halpern, "was that Des had been photographed at Georgetown parties so often that his cover was blown."[68] As history records, however, FitzGerald made the October 29th appointment with Cubela. "It wasn't the first time Des went on a gut feeling," says Sam Halpern.[69]

Shackley's suspicions about Cubela's true loyalties persisted, however, and he is far from alone among CIA operatives and contacts in Florida (Grayston Lynch, for example) who were (and are) convinced that Cubela was reporting back to Fidel. They point to the fact that when Cubela was finally arrested by Castro's police in March 1966, instead of being executed, he was given a jail term that Castro himself eventually commuted.

In a final sexual linkage, the CIA was aware that a one-time mistress of Cubela was believed to be working for Cuban intelligence, and her brother was definitely working for Cuban intelligence.[70]

Cubela in Doubt

Still other things about Cubela were, or should have been, worrisome for security reasons, including, notably, his alleged connections to organized crime. In the midst of the Kennedy "crackdown," organized crime figures did not amicably view the American president. By late 1962, most members of organized crime had been cut out of the Kennedy sphere generally, and Kennedy's Cuba Project in particular. They were in fact being hounded by Robert Kennedy's Justice Department, and feared that they would never do business again in Havana. Threats against the President were soon being overheard in underworld circles.

One oft-cited threat was voiced in September 1962 by Florida underworld boss Santos Trafficante, Jr., who was dangerously close to Cubela. Trafficante had worked with Meyer Lansky in the Batista era as manager of Havana's Sans Souci Casino. After the Castro takeover, Trafficante was imprisoned briefly by Castro before being allowed to leave for Florida. Soon, he was attending meetings with the CIA and Johnny Rosselli, where the early assassination plots against Castro were hatched. These plots were ignominious failures, and it has been the conclusion of many that Castro had inside information of their plans.[71] Some believe Santos Trafficante might have been Castro's "mole."

In September 1962, an exile businessman named Jose Aleman, considered a highly reliable source by the FBI, approached Trafficante for a loan. The conversation turned to Robert Kennedy's harassment of the mob. At this point, Trafficante told Aleman not to worry: "He is going to be hit." Aleman's story has been repeatedly interpreted by researchers to mean that the mob was going to kill President Kennedy.

That, however, may have been a serious misinterpretation. Aleman himself was convinced that Trafficante was tied to Cubela, and that both Cubela and Trafficante were agents of Fidel Castro. Given his connections to Castro, the possibility must be considered that Trafficante was aware of a different Kennedy assassination plot—one which involved Cuba, not JFK. Aleman would later testify that Cubela was among those who attempted to secure Trafficante's release from a Cuban prison immediately after the revolution.[72] Several members of Cuban counterintelligence have since corroborated Aleman's suggestion that both were Castro agents. At a 1995 conference on the Kennedy assassination held in Nassau, Cuban officers Arturo Rodriguez and Fabian Escalante stated that Cubela intervened on Trafficante's behalf in 1959 when he was imprisoned in an interment camp.[73] Trafficante would himself later admit meeting Cubela "after the revolution in Cuba," but claimed it was "just a hello and good-bye."[74]

Aleman said that he had long known Cubela to be a "closet communist." He was also aware that after the revolution, Trafficante ran a Havana-based numbers racket, with part of the skim going to Castro's secret agents. Aleman felt in his bones that, as far as Trafficante and Cubela were concerned, "something was wrong in some way."

Aleman's suspicions were echoed by many others, including agents with the Federal Bureau of Narcotics. A Bureau memo of July 21, 1961 reported the possibility that Castro's brief imprisonment of Trafficante was a ruse designed "to make it appear that he [Trafficante] had a personal dislike for Castro, when in fact, Trafficante is an agent of Castro." The memo also verified Aleman's suspicions about Trafficante's ties with Castro's numbers racket (bolita). "Fidel Castro has operatives in Miami making heavy bets with Santos Trafficante Jr.'s organization," the Bureau confirmed.[75]

Famed undercover detective Joe Shimon, who had extensive underworld contacts, was likewise concerned. "Suddenly, Trafficante is released [from jail in Cuba] with all his assets. The thought ran through my mind: Trafficante is working for Castro, or he is working through Castro's agents here. He's the contact [Castro's contact in Miami]."[76] Anti-Castro activist Gerry Hemming believes Trafficante "sold out the CIA plots to Castro in exchange for a heroin trafficking route through Cuba."

Johnny Rosselli also voiced his suspicions about Trafficante. Referring in 1966 to the assassination plots against Castro, Rosselli told Shimon, "This whole thing has been a scam. Santos [Trafficante] never did anything but bullshit everybody. All these fucking wild schemes the CIA dreamed up never got further than Santos. He just sat on it, conned everybody into thinking that guys were risking their lives sneaking into Cuba, having boats shot out from under them—all bullshit."[77]

In 1967, the CIA conducted its own internal review of the assassination projects. Its "Inspector General's Report" noted that Trafficante's lawyer, Rafael Garcia Bongo, had been aware not only of the Phase One attempts against Castro, but the Phase Two AM/LASH operation.[78] A congressional investigation would point out that attorney Bongo made trips to Cuba in 1962 to represent Trafficante's Capri Hotel interest in Havana. The committee speculated that "Bongo was involved in approaching the Castro government in 1962 on Trafficante's behalf for permission to reopen the Capri casino."[79] Two years later, Bongo went to the CIA to say he was aware of the AM/LASH plot. The congressional committee theorized that:

> Bongo's real purpose in contacting the CIA was to act as a double agent for Castro in ascertaining the nature and scope of the AM/LASH operation...Given the extent of Trafficante's high-level contacts within the exile community and the low-level security in the CIA exile operations, it is therefore logical that Trafficante and other members of the underworld knew,

*in some fashion, part or all of the AM/LASH plot...If Trafficante was a dou-
ble agent, working for the CIA, but actually supplying information to Castro,
then another scenario emerges. It is logical to assume that Castro knew of the
AM/LASH   and   CIA-organized   crime   operations   from   their
inception...Trafficante could have received a sanctuary and assistance in
smuggling contraband for such information.[80]*

This conclusion jibes with the conclusions of anti-Castro activist Gerry
Hemming, who states uncategorically, "I know that Trafficante traded intelligence with Castro in exchange for a protected heroin trafficking route." If true,
the Trafficante connection would go a long way to explaining why the Rosselli
and AM/LASH plots came up so short.

William Harvey, who coordinated the Rosselli attempts, later testified,
"Given the capabilities of Castro's security apparata and the general sieve-like
character of the Cuban community-in-exile... it was quite conceivable that it
[the Rosselli plot] had been penetrated."[81] There is no evidence that these warning signs were relayed to either Bobby Kennedy or Des FitzGerald. It was on such
shaky ground that U.S. plans involving Rosselli and Cubela were allowed to proceed.

As for Cubela's demand for a coup, just such an undertaking had already
been in the planning stages. A future investigation would locate at least four
secret government documents referring to the upcoming event.[82] Those findings
were buttressed by the newly-released material on the Artime operation,
AM/TRUNK and OPLAN 380-63. Unknown to the Kennedys, Juan Felaifel and
his Cuban associates had penetrated even the Kennedys' coup plans. Felaifel
told the Brazilian filmmakers in 1993:

*Cubela had the assassination planned...The plan had two phases. Following
the assassination, in case there was no immediate supporting coup, they were
planning to start an uprising in the Escambray with the support of approximately 1,000 mercenaries Artime had in Central America. They were planning to bring them through Punta Icacos, dividing the road and establishing
there a beachhead in order to create a government supported and approved by
the Organization of American States. To that end, Artime had already contacted several Central American governments that were going to support them.
Now the time came to put together the final information...We were able to
dismantle [the plan] practically before it was conducted.[83]*

But if the AM/LASH operation was compromised, the fallout quite possibly
jeopardized the other anti-Castro initiative, AM/TRUNK, which was so key to
OPLAN 380-63. According to the CIA, Cubela was closely associated with
Commandante Ramon Tomas Guin Diaz (Guin), an important early recruit in
the AM/TRUNK project. In 1966, Guin was arrested simultaneously with
Cubela, by Cuban police, and was a co-defendant at Cubela's trial.[84]

Author David Corn has written that the planned increase in U.S. sabotage
operations came as "no secret to Castro, or anyone who bothered to listen to

him." Corn points out that on October 30, 1963, Castro publicly charged that the Agency was using a 150-foot long ship called the "Rex" in operations against Cuba and that the vessel was berthed in Palm Beach, Florida."[85]

Newly released CIA documents disclose that on September 30, 1963, U.S.-backed exiles blew up the Marabi, a Cuban lumber mill. On October 22, 1963, more U.S.-backed exiles blew up two Cuban patrol boats and two oil-storage tanks. In retaliation, one week before President Kennedy's fateful Dallas trip, Cuba executed thirteen Cubans accused of spying for the CIA. Cuba had concluded, rightly, that the U.S. "peace initiatives" had been a ruse.

Castro's Ultimatum

A CIA operative who by his own admission participated in three Castro assassination attempts, former Castro ally Frank Sturgis had a good perspective on Castro's psyche. In 1993, he explained, "Kennedy made his attempts with double agents to try and kill Castro." As to Castro's response, he said, "You think for a minute they're going to sit on their ass and not do anything to retaliate?"[86]

Rafael Nuñez, a career diplomat who served in Castro's government for eighteen years, said of Castro, "He is a psychopathic person. He hates everybody who ever acted against him—presidents, anybody." This intensity, according to Nuñez, led Castro to become obsessed with U.S. activities aimed at Cuba. "I knew many in the counterintelligence sections, and I know of no other leader in the world as updated on U.S. intelligence as Castro," says Nuñez. "He was pathologically obsessed with what was happening in the U.S. government, and personally read every intelligence report."[87] Even former Soviet Premier Nikita Khrushchev, who eventually concluded that Castro was a "hothead," still was stunned when Castro proposed a preemptive nuclear strike against the U.S. during the missile crisis blockade.[88] Author Georgie Anne Geyer, who has conducted a number of interviews with Castro, wrote in her book *Guerrilla Prince*:

> Castro in truth hated John F. Kennedy. In his speeches, Castro made Kennedy
> into a monster. Billboards all over Havana derided and abused Kennedy…It
> was part of the long play of hatred between Cuba and America.[89]

Fidel Castro had never been easily fooled. Finally, in the Fall of 1963, in response to American actions against him, Castro all but threatened Kennedy's life. On September 6, 1963, the Cuban Armed Forces Ministry reported one dead and three injured in an air attack on Santa Clara, Cuba, and charged the United States with responsibility. The next day, while Cubela made his assassination offer to the CIA in Brazil, Castro appeared at the Brazilian Embassy in Havana, and gave an extemporaneous speech to the receptive press. This was not a typical Castro harangue, however. Prominent in it was this threat:

> We are taking into account…the Caribbean situation, which has been deterio-

rating in the last few days due to piratical attacks by the United States against the Cuban people...Kennedy is a cretin...the Batista of our times...If U.S. leaders are aiding terrorist plans to eliminate Cuban leaders, they themselves will not be safe. Let Kennedy and his brother Robert take care of themselves since they too can be the victims of an attempt which will cause their death.[90]

This warning was reported in most metropolitan newspapers in the U.S., including the *New Orleans Times Picayune*, where it was prominently displayed with a three-column headline. Compulsive newspaper reader Lee Oswald, still living in New Orleans at the time, certainly read about the speech. It was three weeks later that Oswald made his appearance at the Cuban embassy in Mexico City, talking about killing "that bastard" Kennedy.

That Castro's threat at the Brazilian Embassy and Cubela's offer to kill Castro occurred on the same day, and also in Brazil, is a coincidence that has not gone unnoticed. Historians have pondered the possibility that both events were orchestrated by Castro, with Cubela acting, as suspected, as a witting double agent for Cuba.

In any case, Castro's threats were consistent with what the Childs brothers (Solo Source) had been reporting. As leaders of the Communist Party USA, the Childs were trusted confidantes of all the world's Communist luminaries: Castro, Khrushchev, Brezhnev, and Mao. Although these leaders regularly denounced the ideology of the United States, Castro's rantings were unique in that they were clearly personal—and this latest threat was aimed directly, and forebodingly, at President Kennedy himself.

On October 7, 1963, Carlos Lechuga, the Cuban U.N. representative with whom William Attwood had been discussing normalized relations, let it be known that his country would not be tricked. Lechuga declared that Cuba would not sign the nuclear test-ban treaty so long as the United States continued to wage an "undeclared war" against the Castro regime. The U.S. Ambassador to the U.N., Adlai Stevenson, replied that Cuba had "declared war on the Western Hemisphere by its program of infiltration, subversion, and terrorism."

On that same day, just three weeks after his very public threat against U.S. leaders, Castro again rattled the sabre. After a typical marathon speech in Havana in which he chastised Kennedy for his "undeclared war" of sabotage against Cuba, Castro warned, "They [Kennedy and his administration] are our enemies, and we know how to be their enemies."[91]

John Kennedy had long been aware of the possibility that his Cuba Project could backfire on him. As early as 1961, Kennedy remarked that if U.S. officials were ever linked to the plotting, "we would all be targets."[92]

Castro's threats also became a major point of concern for Bobby Kennedy's Cuban Coordinating Committee. CCC staffer General Alexander Haig recalls:

We were getting warnings. During the covert operation program, there were messages—arriving at the lower level, but always drifting to the top: "Castro says if this goes on, he was going to take action." And it did go on, right up until the day Kennedy was killed.[93]

Three days after Castro's first threat, on September 12, 1963, the Cuban Coordinating Committee met at 2:30 p.m. at the Department of State to assess the U.S.' "contingency plans" for Cuba. The minutes of that meeting demonstrate that the Committee unanimously agreed: "There was a strong likelihood that Castro would retaliate in some way against the rash of covert activity in Cuba."[94]

On September 27, the same day that Oswald made his declaration/offer to the Cubans in Mexico City, the Cuban Coordinating Committee directed its subcommittee on Cuban Subversion to submit, by October 4, papers discussing the possibility that there might be increased assassination attempts on American officials or citizens.[95] According to *New York Times* reporter Tad Szulc, this was no ordinary subcommittee. It "was created by Robert Kennedy, presumably out of concern that Castro might retaliate against CIA attempts on his life," Szulc wrote in 1976.[96] As a highly regarded investigative journalist, Szulc never divulged his sources for this information. Confronted with the question again in 1994, he told the author, "I got it from sources close to Bobby. It was as close as possible, fair enough? That's all I will say."[97]

Szulc, it must be recalled, was working closely with the White House on the AM/TRUNK operation.

Countdown to Invasion

"If JFK was not shot, Castro never would have continued to exist."
—**Manolo Reboso, exile coordinator for Robert Kennedy**[98]

"Castro knew Kennedy had to do something before the [1964] election, so Castro had to act first."
—**Carlos Bringuier, Cuban Student Directorate delegate**[99]

Despite the administration's fears and Castro's threats, the anti-Castro enterprises only escalated. On September 3rd, the Special Group was told, "Artime is ready to go in November or December." Des FitzGerald noted in his report of that meeting that "considerable pressure exists in the Special Group at this particular moment for intensification of our raiding program." On September 23rd, in a futile effort to give RFK some measure of deniability, the U.S. Ambassador to Artime's host country, Costa Rica, was advised "to state [that] RFK knows nothing of Artime's plans."[100]

On October 4, 1963, in Washington, the Joint Chiefs of Staff, coordinating with the Departments of Defense and State, submitted its most up-to-date revision of OPLAN 380-63. The new document included the exact timetable for the invasion of Cuba and related goings-on:

- *By January 1964, infiltration into Cuba by Cuban exiles (as per AM/TRUNK).*

- *On July 15, 1964, U.S. conventional forces would join the fray.*

- *On August 3, 1964, which was designated as "D Day," an all-out U.S. air strike would commence.*[101]

- *By October 1, 1964, "a full-scale invasion, with a goal the installation of a government friendly to the U.S.," would be launched.*

The Kennedys' planned victory over Castro would thus conveniently occur one month before the November 1964 Presidential election.

About a month after the new timetable arrived, Des FitzGerald placed a friendly wager with Michael Forrestal of the National Security Council staff. The November 13 bet, according to a memo in his files, had FitzGerald predicting the downfall of the Castro regime "during the period 1 August 1964 and 1 October 1964."[102] The wager further stipulated that removal of Castro had to occur during that two-month window. Considering FitzGerald's inside knowledge of the AM/LASH and OPLAN 380-63 timetables, he may have had an unfair advantage.

The day before placing the wager with Forrestal, FitzGerald attended a Special Group meeting at the White House. In attendance were Robert Kennedy, his CCC leader Cy Vance, and the CIA's Richard Helms and Ted Shackley, among others. FitzGerald took the occasion to apprise the group of Artime's progress in Nicaragua and Costa Rica. He sweetened the outlook by adding that "it was also hoped that the autonomous group under Manolo Reboso [another RFK confidante] would soon get itself established in a working base, possibly Costa Rica." He added that "much could be accomplished by those autonomous groups once they get established."[103]

After so many fits and starts—the Bay of Pigs, Executive Action, Operation Mongoose, and fragmented exile group efforts in both New Orleans and Miami—the administration's Cuba Project had seemingly turned the corner. With the impending invasion planned, manned, and financed, with AM/LASH on board, and with the continuing activity of Rosselli & Co., it now appeared that the Kennedy brothers would finally get their wish: a pre-election victory over Fidel Castro. The march toward victory could have started within weeks, but the President insisted on one quick trip to Dallas to stock the war chest for the upcoming presidential campaign.

CHAPTER TWELVE

THE EYE OF THE HURRICANE

*"Observing the steady fall of the barometer, Captain McWhirr thought,
'There's some dirty weather knocking about.'"*

—Joseph Conrad, Typhoon

O ne of the many myths surrounding John Kennedy's assassination is that the
president would not have journeyed to Dallas that day if Lyndon Johnson
and other Lone Star politicians had not asked him to come and patch-up internal party squabbles. This interpretation was most widely promulgated by
William Manchester in his 1967 book *The Death of a President*. Upon reading
Manchester's manuscript, Lyndon Johnson told Attorney General Nicholas
Katzenbach, "Ninety-five percent of Manchester's book is completely fabricated."[1]

To be sure, there was party dissension in Texas. However, the White House
dispatched aide Bill Moyers, not the President, to attend to it, which he did.[2] The
fact is that the only person who wanted the trip to go forward was John
Kennedy. On this, all the principals agree. The trip was, pure and simple, an
effort to fill the party coffers and to improve the president's standing in Texas.

By the fall of 1963, the Democratic National Committee was $4 million in
debt. In spite of the size of the state and Johnson's place on the national ticket,
Texas was one of the smallest contributors to the national committee. "If we
don't raise money in another state, I want to do so in Massachusetts [his home
state] and Texas [Johnson's home state]," Kennedy told Texas Governor John
Connally. "If we don't carry another state next year, I want to carry Texas and
Massachusetts."[3] Kennedy's friend and Air Force aide, General Godfrey McHugh,
recalled that the Texas trip "wasn't so much for votes as it was for money,
because Texas is where the money is."[4]

Kennedy aide Kenny O'Donnell wrote, "[Kennedy] had been pressing the
reluctant Governor Connally for months to stage a fund-raising event for the
party, and Connally, who had no desire to be branded a Kennedy supporter in

Texas, had been stalling him off."[5] According to Connally, for over a year and a half, Kennedy had been pressuring both him and Vice President Johnson to set up the trip. But both were less than enthusiastic. Johnson later told aide Robert Kintner:

> *Kennedy did not come at my request. That's a great myth. He came down here because he wanted to raise a million dollars and to improve himself. I put him off several months and Connally put him off several months. I didn't want him to come—told him it was a mistake to come...Connally agreed.*[6]

The Kennedy-Johnson ticket had barely squeaked to victory in Texas in 1960. The same pairing now appeared a straw dog in 1964, and Connally felt political risk in associating with the President, who was anathema to his "power base" in oil and other sources of Texas wealth. Some affluent Connally backers even hoped the governor, a Democrat, would gain a vice-presidential spot on Goldwater's Republican ticket. In any event, the Governor supported Kennedy's policies as little as possible.

Connally had still more reasons for stalling the President: he had his own legislative and electoral problems to take care of, and no time to devote to the planning of such a trip.

Finally, in June of 1963, on a Kennedy trip to El Paso, Texas, Connally was summoned to the Presidential hotel suite, where he found both the President and Vice President. Addressing Johnson (but intending to reach Connally), Kennedy asked sarcastically, "Well, Lyndon, do you think we're ever going to have that fund-raising affair in Texas?"

Connally resignedly took the hint, responding, "Mr. President, fine—let's start planning your trip."[7] Although the date wasn't yet set, both Johnson and Connally let the word leak to the press that Kennedy was coming to Dallas in the fall. By September 26th, the *Dallas Morning News* broke the story that the President would visit several Texas cities on November 21 and 22. A potential sniper would only have to stand by for further details to be announced.

On October 4, 1963, Connally was in Washington and met with the President to iron out the details. Although Connally had figured on one fund-raising dinner, Kennedy, to Connally's dismay, pressed for four. Not only did Connally think that this would leave a bad taste in Texans' mouths, appearing as a financial rape of the state, but he also knew he had no time to mount such an offensive. It was mutually decided that the president's campaign trip would consist of unspecified events in Houston and San Antonio, a breakfast in Fort Worth, a fund-raising luncheon in Dallas, a dinner in Austin, then a fund-raising steak cookout at the LBJ Ranch in Austin on Friday night—all in a whirlwind two days.

The Security Problem

"Politics and protection don't mix."
—Kenny O'Donnell, JFK aide to Secret Service man Jerry Behn[8]

"Keep those Ivy League charlatans off the back of the car."
—JFK, speaking November 18, 1963 to Agent Floyd Boring about Secret Service men assigned to the Dallas motorcade[9]

From the very start, the Texas trip was replete with security problems. Not only would Kennedy insist on the trip, but he would also insist on a motorcade through Dallas, over the objections of Connally and Texas State Democratic Party executive secretary Frank Erwin. Kennedy used motorcades as political campaign tools, convinced the visibility they offered had helped him win the 1960 election. Kennedy instructed the Secret Service and the Dallas Police to relax security: he didn't want motorcycles riding alongside his limousine, partly because the noise would impede conversation within the car. He didn't want Secret Service men bracketing the limousine, because he wanted the crowds to "see Jackie."

Local Democrats argued against publishing the motorcade route in the newspapers. But again, the decision was made by the President's people. Presidential assistant Bill Moyers informed the Dallas coordinators, "[Kennedy's] not coming down here to hide. He's coming down here to get a public reaction, and the decision is to print the route of the President's procession." Or, as Kennedy himself said, "If you want the people to turn out, they have to know where to find you."[10]

The President's Lincoln limousine was equipped with a removable protective bubble-top, but its use was similarly vetoed by JFK. Advance man Marty Underwood remembered Kennedy saying, "This is Jackie's first trip, and the people love her, and I'm going to keep it down." Kenny O'Donnell, John Connally, and even Jackie herself, Underwood remembers, wanted the top up, but JFK prevailed. Finally, Bill Moyers instructed the Dallas contingent to "get that God-damned bubble-top off unless it's pouring rain." Thus, the critical decisions of November 22nd were made by the White House, and not by a gang of government conspirators luring Kennedy into what has been referred to as "the kill zone."[11]

On November 14, the White House, in effect, determined that the downtown route in Dallas had to traverse the "insecure" Dealey Plaza. Kennedy's aide Kenny O'Donnell concluded that the day's luncheon should be held at the Trade Mart, as opposed to the Women's Building on the south side of Dallas.

It was not the only time Kennedy would drive through Dealey Plaza. In a startling coincidence, the summer before the assassination, Kennedy visited House Speaker Sam Rayburn, then on his deathbed at Baylor University Hospital, just east of downtown Dallas. Kennedy proceeded to the hospital, where a Secret Service officer spied a man with a gun-like bulge under his coat.

The mysterious man seemed to be giving orders. The Secret Service detail thought he belonged to the press. Members of the press assumed he was with the Secret Service. The man lost himself in the crowd. Even then, Dallas seemed haunted with mysterious figures who posed a threat to Kennedy's life.

Oswald Returns from Mexico City

Oswald spent his first night back in Dallas at the YMCA. To avoid paying for the room, he lied about still being in the Marines.

The next day, he applied for a job as a typesetter, but when the firm called Oswald's references, they refused to vouch for him—calling him "an oddball." Oswald didn't get the job. He then hitch-hiked to Ruth Paine's home in Irving, where Marina and daughter June were staying. This pattern of staying in Irving only on weekends would continue until a week before the assassination. Lee told Marina of his frustration in Mexico City, and Marina was convinced that Oswald had completely dropped the idea of going to Cuba. The couple decided that, for financial reasons, Oswald should live in Dallas alone while he searched for work. After spending that first weekend in Irving, Oswald took a bus to Dallas, where he found a room-for-rent at $7 a week. However, the landlady, Mary Bledsoe, considered him odd, and evicted him by the end of the week.[12]

On October 14, while Lee was in Dallas looking for work and lodging, Ruth and Marina visited with neighbor Linnie Mae Randle. The women were commiserating on the young couple's financial plight, especially with Marina now due to deliver their second child. Randle said that her brother knew of a job opening at his place of employment, the Texas School Book Depository in downtown Dallas. Later that night, when Lee called, he accepted Ruth's suggestion that he pay a visit to the Depository.

In Dallas, Lee had already found a new room, just large enough for a single bed and dresser, in a rooming house for single men at 1026 N. Beckley Street. This time the rent was $8 per week. By sheer luck, the location was a direct, four-mile bus ride to and from the Depository. Oswald, now worried that the FBI had queered things with his previous landlady, registered under the name of "O.H. Lee."[13] One of his co-tenants, Leon Lee, remembered the day of Oswald's arrival.

"Isn't that interesting?" housekeeper Earline Roberts remarked to Leon Lee. "We have another Mr. Lee who just moved in." Leon Lee remembers Oswald:

> *He rarely smiled, and always seemed preoccupied. The other tenants used to walk up the street and have an occasional dinner. Oswald only joined us once. He just stayed in his room all night while the rest of us would be in the living room watching television. I remember that he only came out to watch "The Fugitive," which he loved.*[14]

The owner of the house, Mrs. A.C. Johnson, recalled: "That man [Oswald] never talked. That was the only peculiarity about him." Like Leon Lee, Johnson also remembered Oswald spending his evenings alone in his room, except for an occasional TV program.[15] He only seemed to emerge from his social shell when in the company of children. Johnson's daughter, Mrs. Fay Puckett, says that "Mr. Lee" became very close with her children, often playing catch with them in the front yard. Buell Frazier would have similar memories. Fay Puckett remembers Oswald as a frugal man who seemed to subsist on apples, cheese, and milk, which he kept in the refrigerator..[16]

Oswald started working as an order-filler ("a picker and packer") for Scott-Foresman Books at the Depository on Wednesday, October 16, 1963. Two days later, at Ruth Paine's home, he celebrated his 24th birthday. By Marina's account, it was one of the most pleasant nights of their family life. Oswald was happy and considerate of his pregnant wife, rubbing her ankles, and following her around the house like a puppy dog at her beck and call. He seemed enthusiastic about the future.

That night, Marina dozed with her head in Lee's lap as he watched two movies on television, both of them involving assassinations. In the 1954 movie "Suddenly," Frank Sinatra played a sniper attempting to assassinate a U.S. president by shooting him from an open window with a rifle. In the second film, "We Were Strangers," John Garfield starred as an American in Cuba who attempts the assassination of a corrupt dictator. Although the Garfield character died before seeing the success of the revolution, his cohorts were successful. Marina woke up in time to see the end of the Garfield film. She recalled the scene for her biographer, Priscilla McMillan:

People were dancing in the streets, screaming with happiness because the president had been overthrown. Lee said it was exactly the way it once happened in Cuba. It was the only time he showed any interest in Cuba after his return from Mexico.[17]

Two days later, on Sunday, Marina went into labor. Lee stayed home to babysit June, while Ruth drove Marina to the hospital. When Marina was taken into the labor room, Ruth Paine returned to Irving to care for her own family. Two hours later, Marina, with no family or friends present, gave birth to Audrey Marina Rachel Oswald (had it been a boy, the two had settled on naming the baby David Lee). When Ruth arrived home, she found Oswald, a father now for the second time, asleep—amazingly uninterested in the welfare of his wife or newborn child. She didn't wake him. Before he went to work on Monday morning, Ruth told him the news.[18]

Bureaucracy and Tragedy

"What do you think about Oswald being in touch with the Russians in Mexico City?" The question startled FBI agent Jim Hosty. It was early in October 1963, shortly after Oswald's visit to Mexico City, and Hosty had been visiting the Immigration office on another case when the INS officer posed the question to him. Hosty had already been informed by the FBI's New Orleans bureau that

Oswald's mail was being forwarded to the Paine house in nearby Irving. He had also planned to speak with Oswald in the future. This new information, although incomplete and revealed through informal channels, changed everything. "Whoa! That's news to me," said Hosty.

It was in this roundabout manner that the man responsible for the Oswald file in Dallas learned about his subject's Embassy visits. Further, due to a combination of bureaucratic regulations and, ostensibly, bungling, neither Hosty nor the Secret Service had been informed of the sensitivity of Oswald's contacts in the Russian Embassy. The disclosure of these facts clearly would have flagged Oswald's case workers to watch him closely at the time of the president's Dallas visit.

It was known as the Third Agency Rule, and had it not been in effect in 1963, Lee Harvey Oswald would have never been allowed to get near the President when he came to Dallas. (In fact, when the tragic potential of this rule was recognized after the Kennedy assassination, it was promptly replaced by a rule requiring the sharing of information.) In essence, this federal regulation prevented the dissemination of information beyond those agencies and offices specifically addressed in writing. Thus, neither Jim Hosty nor the Secret Service would be informed of the seriousness of Oswald's liaisons in Mexico City. Hosty, specifically, was not informed that Oswald met KGB officer Kostikov, allegedly a KGB assassination specialist. (Note: this allegation, although believed at the time, has never been proven.)

"Here's the big hullabaloo," said Hosty. "I did not know who Kostikov was. Headquarters probably knew who he was, but they didn't tell either New Orleans or Dallas." If Hosty had known these facts, if the work and information of several different government agencies on Oswald had been compiled and shared, the matter would have been dealt with more seriously. But government regulations prohibited the agencies from even reporting individuals to the Secret Service, the president's protector, unless they had made specific threats against the President. Anything else would have been viewed as an invasion of privacy and a violation of a person's civil rights. And as far as Hosty knew, Oswald had uttered no such threats.

Former FBI Director Clarence Kelley summed up the situation:

> Had our intelligence communities pooled their information on Oswald, had the Oswald-Kostikov-Mexico City information been distributed among the various agencies (assuming the facts about Kostikov were as explosive as they appeared to be), had the Secret Service Protective Research Section been aware of all the Oswald data, and had the information been distributed to the New Orleans and Dallas FBI field offices in time for them to act, then, without doubt, JFK would not have died in Dallas on November 22, 1963.[19]

Perhaps most disturbing is the fact that when the CIA notified the FBI and the U.S. Department of State of Oswald's Soviet Embassy visit, it omitted any reference to Oswald's Cuban Embassy visit. The CIA later maintained publicly that it wasn't aware of that visit until after the assassination, although the evidence is convincing that it knew well before. That omission demonstrates the extremely sensitive nature of both the CIA operations in that Embassy and of Oswald's contacts there. It was still another bureaucratic decision that may have contributed to the tragic events of November 22, 1963.

Even if he had known of Kostikov, or of Oswald's Cuban Embassy visit, Hosty was aware of the risk he would run in interviewing Oswald. With even this cursory knowledge of Oswald's Mexico visit, Hosty was now hamstrung—his own government's regulations kept him from contacting Oswald. Hosty recently recalled the situation:

The reason I didn't interview Oswald was because I couldn't. It was forbidden. The regulations said that if a person had been in touch with an embassy, he could not be interviewed without first clearing it with the agency developing this information.

You have got to understand that if I had gone out and asked him what he was doing talking to the Russian Embassy, that would have given away a very, very secret operation that the CIA had in Mexico City; that they had this capability of determining this. This could have had serious repercussions on the international scene. I doubt very much whether the CIA would have ever granted permission to interview him, and I don't think based upon his previous interviews that I would have even requested an interview. I just don't think that interviewing Oswald would have been productive, and certainly if we had interviewed him, we would have given away a very, very vital secret [the nature of CIA operations in Mexico City].[20]

Hosty decided, however, that it might be worthwhile to visit Marina Oswald and Ruth Paine when Lee wasn't home. After learning from neighbors that Lee wasn't living with Marina at the Irving home during the week, Hosty dropped in twice, on November 1 and 5. Although Marina, who associated all law enforcement with the authoritarian KGB, was initially frightened, Hosty calmed her down with his manner, even winning her over. "I gave her the basic 'we-are-here-to-help-you' talk and it lasted only fifteen minutes." Hosty told Marina the FBI would protect her from any Soviet agents who might use threats to recruit her.

Marina's biographer wrote, "Marina was delighted. She liked this plumpish, pleasant-looking dark-haired man who was talking to her about her rights and offering to protect her. No one had given her so much attention in a long time, much less offered to protect her rights."[21] A week after this second Hosty visit, Oswald, during a lunch break at the Depository, walked the four blocks to the Federal building, which housed the local FBI offices. Oswald left Hosty's secretary Nanny Lee Fenner an envelope for Hosty that contained an unsigned note. Typical of his FBI paranoia, Oswald asserted in his note that Hosty had "bothered" Marina. Hosty remembers the note as containing one or two sentences along the lines of, "If you have anything you want to learn about me, come talk to me directly. If you don't cease bothering my wife, I will take appropriate action and report this to the proper authorities."[22]

Hosty, however, assumed that the unsigned note had come from a right-winger named Jimmy George Robinson, "one of my klansmen," whom he was investigating. He put the note aside and dismissed it. Years later, his secretary Nanny Fenner claimed that the note contained violent threats. She also claimed never to have opened the envelope, but that the note fell out of the unsealed envelope.[23] Hosty says that the note was folded in such a way that Fenner never could have read it. Fenner consistently refuses to be interviewed on the matter.

When the Warren Report was released in 1964, it asserted that the FBI (meaning Hosty) should have reported Oswald to the Secret Service, in spite of the Third Agency rule. As a result, Hosty became one of FBI Director Hoover's scapegoats, agents who were suspended or transferred after JFK's death. Hoover promptly suspended Hosty without pay and transferred him to the FBI equivalent of Siberia—Kansas City.

Hosty's fellow agents knew better. Robert Gemberling, the agent who headed the Oswald investigation after the assassination, says that Hosty's fellow agents took up a collection for Hosty and his family. "Hoover would have been pissed if he knew," laughs Gemberling. "But the fact is that Jim Hosty was a terrific agent, who did as much or more than any other agent."[24]

Hoover knew Hosty had done nothing wrong, but someone had to be blamed for the heat the Bureau was taking over the handling of the Oswald case. Typically, Hoover was more concerned with the reputation of his beloved FBI than the rights of any one individual, including Jim Hosty.

Oswald's activities thus far in Dallas give no hint of an offer or deal made with anyone (in Mexico or elsewhere) to kill the President. However, that possibility is not unsupported by Oswald's future actions. Indeed, on the very day Hosty met with Marina (November 1), Oswald rented a post office box near his job in Dallas. Among those Oswald listed as being entitled to receive mail at his box was the group belived so dangerous by the CIA and the FBI—the Fair Play for Cuba Committee.

Other curious activity concerns Oswald's apparent planning for the assassination, as witnessed by a number of Dallasites. While it is true that many Oswald "sightings" are based on mistaken identification, some clearly are not. For a time, it was alleged that someone impersonated Oswald in order to later frame him for the assassination. That now appears not to be the case. Witnesses over the years attest to a pattern of Oswald activity, clearly suggesting his premeditation. One set of witnesses make a strong case that Oswald spent much of his last month honing his rifle-shooting skills.

The Shooting Range

"Of course we engage in subversion, the training of guerrillas, propaganda! Why not? This is exactly what you are doing to us."
—Fidel Castro, November 1963[25]

"Just wait, and you will see what we can do. It will happen soon. Just wait. Just wait."
—Ricardo L. Santos Pesa, the Cuban Third Secretary to the Hague, November 7, 1963, after being asked to comment on recent exile raids against Cuba[26]

"There's no doubt it was Oswald," gunsmith Howard Price told Dallas newsman Hugh Aynesworth. After the assassination, Price came forward to say he saw Lee Oswald practicing with his rifle at the Sportsdrome Gun Range in Grand Prairie, thirteen miles from Oswald's Beckley Street apartment. Price said that he witnessed Oswald there starting on October 26, then on November 9 or 10 (Saturday or Sunday) and again on Sunday, November 17—five days before Kennedy was killed. More importantly, according to Price, "Other people were with him [Oswald]."[27]

Mrs. Price recalls her (now deceased) husband's reaction when Lee Oswald's face first appeared on the television screen on the day of the assassination: "Howard jumped out of his chair, and before the suspect's name was mentioned, said, 'That's Oswald! He comes to the rifle range. I sighted his scope.'"[28]

When the FBI later interviewed Howard Price, he didn't tell them that he knew Oswald's name as well as his face. "Howard only allowed the FBI to interview him for fifteen minutes. He didn't want to get involved," says his widow. Price, however, did say he recalled Oswald's 7.30 rifle with a 4X Japanese scope.[29] Oswald owned a 6.31 rifle, but the two are very similar in appearance. Oswald's Mannlicher Carcano was, in fact, equipped with a 4X Japanese scope. Price told newsman Aynesworth that Oswald was not alone, recalling that someone passed a wrapped-up rifle over the five-foot fence to him.

Also at the range on the second Oswald visit (Sunday, November 17) was Garland Slack, who fired from the stall next to Oswald's. Slack remembered Oswald well because he got into a shouting match with him. Oswald was shooting, rapid-fire, at the targets assigned to other shooters, including Slack's. Slack affirmed Oswald's proficiency with the rifle, saying, "I think he centered them all." Slack, like Price, remembered that the person with Oswald, a man "25 years old or younger," passed a rifle over the fence to Oswald wrapped in "rags or something."[30]

Another credible witness saw Oswald come to the shooting range on November 16. Dr. Homer Wood, at the range that Saturday with his 13 year-old son Sterling, recalled his reaction on seeing Oswald on television the day of the assassination:

As soon as I saw Oswald on TV, I said to my wife, "He looks like the man who was sitting in the next booth to our son, out at the rifle range." ...When my son came home from school, I purposely didn't say anything to him. Well, he also looked at the television and he spoke to me quickly, saying, "Daddy, that looks just like the man we saw at the range when we were sighting in our rifles." [31]

Although a youngster, Sterling Wood was quite the rifle buff, and, to the episode's recounting, added a professional's eye-for-detail. He told the FBI that while he was at the range, another shooter attracted his attention. Each time the man shot, he said, the rifle spit fire from the barrel. To Wood, this meant that the shooter was using bullets with an extra-heavy powder charge (Oswald's 160 grain bullets were almost double the charge of the average rifle bullet). Young Wood remarked to his father, "Daddy, it looks like a 6.5 Italian Carbine." He asked the shooter if that was the case.

The man responded, "Yes, it is." Sterling thought he recognized the Japanese four-power scope, and again asked the man if he was correct.

Again the man responded, "Yes." Sterling also remembered that each time the man fired, he retrieved the spent shells and placed them in his pocket. Wood counted 13 shells spent during the session. Oswald was, far and away, the best marksman at the range that day, said young Wood. At 100 yards, Oswald hit 8 of 10 bullseyes, with the other two only four inches off. Wood told the FBI he was positive that the shooter was Lee Harvey Oswald. He also recalled that Oswald was accompanied by another man of the same height (5'9").

Dr. Homer Wood told Frontline's W. Scott Malone in 1993, "This guy, if he was Oswald, and I think he was, was an incredible shot with that old junky rifle—incredible!"[32] Wood also told Malone that the FBI interview of his son Sterling made the young boy cry. Sterling told his father, "I don't want to go back with them [the FBI agents] anymore."

Accompanying Sterling Wood to the range that Saturday was his friend Ken Longley, also 13 years-old. Longley recently recalled that he also saw the man with the old "bolt-action" rifle, and also remembered him as about 5'9", although he didn't recall the man's face. "I was watching the result, not the shooter," said Longley. "The man I saw shooting could have done it [the assassination]."[33]

In the years immediately following the assassination, those doubting Oswald's guilt pointed to the rifle range episode as evidence of an Oswald double sent out to set up the innocent "patsy." The doubters claimed that Oswald was a poor shot, and therefore, they asserted, the gifted shooter seen at the range could not have been Oswald. However, not only could it have been Oswald, it most assuredly *was* Oswald.

In 1993, following up on a tip from Dallas resident Dave Perry, who had recently spoken with Sterling Wood, the author contacted one of the rifle range witnesses. Now a successful dentist sharing an office suite with his podiatrist father (Dr. Homer Wood), Sterling Wood was reluctant to meet, let alone repeat the story he had told Perry. "Do you really think that what I have to say is that important to history?" he asked. He was assured that what he had told Perry would help put a key myth to rest—one that some had used to exonerate Oswald.

After many weeks of haggling, Wood tentatively agreed to talk to the author. He had avoided interviews, he said, because, within a year of the assassination, he had been attacked and hospitalized—and almost died—with the permanent physical result being the implantation of a metal plate in his skull. It should be realized that in the wake of the assassination, paranoia gripped Dallas even more than the rest of the country. Every act of violence in Dallas was viewed initially as connected to the violence of that tragic weekend.[34]

Finally agreeing to the interview, Wood stated, "I'll be bringing some things that will blow your mind. Do you know that Marina later contacted us so that we might help forward letters to her family in Minsk? Do you know about 'the ride'?"

As it turned out, Wood backtracked on his decision to be interviewed. His family, especially his father, was dead set against it. In order to keep family peace, Wood, offering his apologies, begged off. However, the salient points of his conversation with Perry and others are known: Sterling and his father had another reason to be certain that the talented shooter they saw was Lee Oswald—a reason they failed to tell the Warren Commission.

On one occasion, they drove Oswald home from the range. And not only did they drive him to Oak Cliff, where Oswald's Beckley Street apartment was located, but they spoke to him of Minsk, where the Wood family had relatives. After the assassination, the Woods received letters from Oswald's widow, hoping the Wood family would forward them to Minsk. That Marina knew of the Woods and their family in Minsk establishes the credibility of the son's allegation.

But if the son is to be believed on this point, the question remains: Who was the second man at the range with Oswald?

The fact that Oswald was practicing with his rifle is unremarkable, considering what he was going to attempt in a few weeks when Kennedy rode through downtown Dallas. Most important about these sightings are the questions raised about a second man seen with Oswald, and the mysterious movements of the Mannlicher Carcano rifle (and the contradictions implicit in the Warren Commission on the subject). Neither of these points necessarily implies conspiratorial allies in Dallas. Rather, it now seems that there has been a concerted effort to protect someone whom the Dallas Police determined had nothing to do with the assassination, but may have been innocently involved with Oswald.

Buell Wesley Frazier

After the assassination, the *Dallas Morning News* reported that the man who had driven Oswald to the rifle range had been located. The newspaper's source, an investigator within the police department, said, "A man who knew Oswald stated he drove the 24 year-old suspect to the range area."[35] There was never a follow-up to this story, and if the police had such a man, they never spoke another public word about him. It was later determined that the police source claimed Michael Paine drove Oswald. Paine, however, denied that he was the man.[36] One of Oswald's roommates at the Beckley Street house, Leon Lee, adds to the mystery, saying:

> I remember that Lee used to occasionally get picked up and dropped off by someone who would park his car on the street and wait out there for Lee to join him. That wasn't all that unusual, though, because few of the tenants had cars, and we always had friends give us rides.[37]

It may not seem unusual to Leon Lee, but it certainly does to anyone attempting to characterize Oswald as a total "loner." So who was the mystery driver? There is at least one known suspect. When Garland Slack's wife, Lucille, was interviewed by the FBI in 1964, she volunteered that her husband told her that Oswald was driven to the range by a man named "Frazier."[38]

The descriptions of the rifle range "mystery man" as a young man about Oswald's height and age, and according to one witness, driving an old black Ford hardtop narrows the field of possibilities. The addition of the name "Frazier" realistically reduces the field down to one: Buell Wesley Frazier. "B.W." was the 19 year-old brother of Ruth Paine's neighbor Linnie Mae Randle. B.W., who worked at the Depository, had told his sister of the job opening there. She relayed the information to Ruth and Marina, and that resulted in Oswald's employment. In addition to having the same name, Frazier matched the description of the "mystery man" right down to the model of car he drove.

In the years since the assassination, Buell Frazier has rarely made himself available for interviews. During those few interviews, he limited the questions to Oswald's personality, and the size of the package that Oswald took to work when Frazier drove him there on the morning of the assassination. The author's own meetings with Frazier, beginning in 1987, revealed a man very nervous about discussing the subject.

At the first meeting, Frazier spoke through a crack in the door for over an hour before being coaxed outside. Eventually, more meetings were held over lunches throughout the Dallas area. Frazier told of how he lost "dozens" of jobs as a result of his association with Oswald. He was constantly uprooting himself to remain hidden from the press, and maintained an unlisted phone number. Frazier always spoke highly of his friend Lee. "He was wonderful with kids and animals," Frazier remembered. "I used to sit on my porch in Irving and watch him play catch with the neighborhood children down the street [by Ruth

Paine's house]." Although he never socialized with Oswald (he denies driving him to the rifle range), Frazier said that he felt closer to him than any of the other co-workers at the Depository:

> He liked me because I was the only one who didn't make fun of him. He used to use big words, and the other workers used to kid him about it. I used to go home and look the words up in the dictionary. Even though he was only a little older, he was like a big brother. I always felt that Lee wouldn't stay long at the Depository. He was different. He was thin, not muscular like other [lifelong] warehouse workers. His hands weren't callused. I always felt he was just passing through.[39]

Three things emerge from encountering Frazier: One, he had true affection for Lee Oswald. Two, he continues to be frightened. And, three, he comes across as a genuinely nice person, unsoliciting of fame, and wishing to be left alone. His matter-of-fact disingenuousness resists the most imaginative portrait of an accomplice to assassination (he is a volunteer little league baseball coach, who has achieved remarkable success with a group of youngsters who worship their beaming instructor).[40] Still, one is left with the distinct impression that Frazier is withholding something.

The questions linger:

- *If Frazier was just an unwitting 19 year-old kid, why the fear and withdrawal?*
- *How could he have been duped into apparent involvement in the assassination?*
- *Was he the man the newspaper referred to as knowing Oswald, and who "stated he drove the twenty-four year-old suspect to the range area"?*
- *Was he, in fact, the man at the range whom Garland Slack remembered as "Frazier"?*

Either these questions were never pursued by authorities, or they were swept under the rug to protect an innocent boy spending a day shooting with a friend. Similar to the authorities' treatment of Sterling Wood, this was another case of an important witness, who may have added key detail about Oswald's preparation for the crime, getting overlooked, purposely, for a personal reason.

More Mysterious Sightings

Not only did Oswald appear to be honing his shooting skills, but by the third week of November 1963, he was making appearances in downtown Dallas that were unforgettable to those who encountered him.

On Saturday, November 16, the *Dallas Morning News* reported the first concrete details of the Kennedy motorcade, scheduled for the following Friday. Although the turn in front of the Depository on Elm Street was not mentioned, the paper noted that the parade would traverse Main Street. Oswald spent that day at the shooting range.

Later that night, indeed late in the evening, a man named Hubert Morrow was approached by a stranger he would never forget. It was late in the evening and Morrow was on duty as the night manager of the Alright Parking Garage in downtown Dallas. For thirteen years, he had worked for the garage, which was located next to the FBI headquarters in the Federal building. During that time, Morrow had become quite friendly with many of the local FBI agents. He recently recalled what happened that November night:

> *I was working here at night. It was 'round ten o'clock when he came into the garage and he asked me if he could see Main Street from the top of the roof. I said, "You probably can, but you're not allowed up on that roof." Nobody was allowed on that roof at that time. He asked me about the motorcade—would the motorcade be going down Elm Street or Main Street? I said it would be going down Main Street. He asked if you could see Main Street from the roof [you could in 1963]. He was carrying a long item that appeared to be about as long as a rifle. But it was wrapped up in a brown paper or canvas sack. It was completely wrapped up. Only the muzzle was sticking out of the end. But he turned around and walked back out of the garage. The next time I saw him was when he'd assassinated the President.*[41]

Undeterred by Morrow's rejection, Oswald apparently returned to the garage to try again. Mrs. Viola Sapp, a garage cashier who was not on hand for the alleged confrontation with Morrow, remembers a separate Oswald encounter. "You know, he came to me asking about a job at the Commerce Street garage," recalls Sapp.[42] She was so struck by the oddness of her conversation with Oswald that she claims to be able to reconstruct it from memory:

> *Oswald: "Hello, my name is Mr. Oswald. I'm new in town and I'd like to see about a job here."*
>
> *Sapp: "Have you had any experience?"*
>
> *Oswald: "No."*
>
> *Sapp: "I'm sorry, we're full up. However, we have some openings at our other garages if you're interested."*
>
> *Oswald: "No. I've been walking around here at night, and I really love this building and location. I like how all the floors are open to the street and you can see the people on the street below. Tell me, does the top floor have a roof?"*
>
> *Sapp (not oblivious to the strange turn the conversation had taken): "No."*
>
> *Oswald: "Do you think I could go up? I just love Dallas, and I'd like to see the sights."*
>
> *Sapp: "Absolutely not. No one is allowed up there."*
>
> *Oswald: "But I sure would like to—*
>
> *Sapp: "No!"*

With that, Oswald left the premises. Both Morrow's and Sapp's later statements to the FBI reveal none of this detail. When asked about the discrepancies, Sapp would only suggest that her supervisor advised her against providing additional detail. "Just keep it to yourself," he had told her. Under no circumstances was she to reveal his name. After a period of time, however, Mrs. Sapp was persuaded to reveal that her supervisor was Claude Hallmark, presently a national executive in the Alright Parking Corporation.

Reached for comment, Hallmark told the author, "Mrs. Sapp is level-headed in all respects, good common sense, steady as a rock. She rates an A+." He himself distinctly remembers that on the day of the assassination, Mrs. Sapp told him, "That crazy Oswald was in here looking for a job." When asked about Sapp's allegation that he advised her against speaking with the FBI, Hallmark replied, "It is quite possible that I advised Mrs. Sapp not to talk to the FBI."[43]

Oswald lived in the suburb of Oak Cliff, and, according to the official report, was not known to spend his evenings in downtown Dallas. However, the garage employees were not the only witnesses to Oswald's late night wanderings in downtown Dallas. Six weeks earlier, on October 10, an exchange student named Cristobal Espinosa was taking an evening stroll in Dallas. He was in town to attend the Texas-Oklahoma football game. At about 11:30 p.m., he met a stranger near the Baker Hotel who identified himself as Lee Oswald. Espinosa would remember the name because he had difficulty with English and asked the man to write the name in a notebook. Espinosa would re-copy the name "Oswald" next to the date.

As the two men walked along the street at night, they chatted mostly about Espinosa's native Ecuador. Oswald was curious about what the living conditions would be like for an American. Oswald seemed very familiar with Dallas' downtown buildings, Espinosa told the FBI, and pointed out which night clubs had the best shows.[44]

Oswald's rejection at the parking garage left him undeterred in his quest to land a job in the heart of downtown Dallas. According to the manager of Dallas' famous Adolphus Hotel (also on Commerce Street), Oswald applied there for a job as a bell hop. Again, he was turned away.[45]

If Hubert Morrow and the witnesses at the rifle range are accurate on the dates they encountered Oswald with a rifle, another important question arises: How and when did Oswald retrieve the rifle from the Paine's house where his things were stored? The official investigation would later conclude that Oswald went to Ruth Paine's house on November 21, the eve of the assassination, for the express purpose of retrieving his rifle from her garage. But if the above accounts of the shooting-range are accurate, Oswald already had the rifle in his possession the previous weekend, one of the few times he did not go to Paine's home in Irving. There is no evidence that he visited her between the 17th and the night of the 21st, when he could have returned the rifle, only to retrieve it again on the eve of the murder.

Buell Frazier also owned a rifle (a British Enfield .303). The possibility exists that if Frazier was the "mystery driver," he could shed light not only on Oswald's movements, but also the rifle's. When interviewed by the author in 1987, Frazier was firm in his belief that Oswald did not bring the rifle to work with him on the morning of the assassination. The package he carried was just too small. Frazier suggested, however, "He could have brought the rifle in to work at an earlier date, or in one piece at a time over several days." Indeed, this latter possibility was not given adequate consideration by investigators.

Compounding the rifle mystery is the testimony of others who claim to have seen Oswald lugging a rifle-like object around Dallas, when his Mannlicher Carcano was supposedly wrapped in a blanket in Ruth Paine's garage.

Another Beckley Street tenant, Jack Cody, recalls that on the morning of either November 20 or 21, he had an encounter with a man he recognized as a new tenant—a man who occupied the room in the center of the first floor, right off the common living room (the known location of Oswald's room).

> I was living in the basement at 1026 North Beckley. It was Wednesday or Thursday, the week Kennedy was assassinated. It was about seven o'clock in the morning. I was waiting on the bus. A man came off the front porch of the place where I stayed. [He] got on the bus after me and sat down on the other side of the bus. When he got on the bus, I saw he was carrying a package, a newspaper-wrapped package. It was about six inches thick and a foot wide and about two foot long.[46]

When shown a photo of Lee Oswald, Cody was firm in his identification of him.

Another report of Oswald with a long package came from Ralph Leon Yates. Five days after the assassination, Yates told the FBI the story of his encounter with Oswald. He was driving near Beckley Street on Wednesday the 20th of November, when he picked up a young man hitchhiking into downtown Dallas. During their brief trip, the young man, who was carrying a long package that he said contained curtain rods, asked Yates questions about the President's upcoming motorcade. He wanted to know two things: Was the route changed, and did Yates believe a person could take a rifle and shoot the President from the top of a building or from a window? Yates replied that he believed it could happen if the man was a good enough shot and had a scope. Yates dropped off his passenger at Elm and Houston Streets, the site of the Texas School Book Depository. After this strange encounter, Yates returned to his place of work and related the incident to a co-worker, Dempsey Jones.[47]

If Oswald's encounters with Morrow and Sapp were predicated upon his need to locate a sniper's perch along the then-known motorcade route (Main Street) by Tuesday, November 19, it became a moot point. On that day, the *Dallas Morning News* published the exact motorcade route, showing the turn in front of Oswald's place of work on Elm Street. Oswald's quarry was handed to him on a silver platter.

Until now, there has been no proof of how Oswald learned the exact route of the motorcade. Some who have championed Oswald's innocence point to other published versions of the route, showing no turn in front of the Depository. If Oswald had seen these maps, they say, he wouldn't have shot Kennedy. It is now known that Oswald did indeed learn the exact route of the motorcade, and in plenty of time to finalize his plans.

As mentioned, Oswald rarely socialized with his housemates at Beckley Street. However, one of those tenants, Hugh Slough, has one and only one lingering memory of Oswald. On Wednesday evening, November 20, Slough was sitting in the living room of 1026 North Beckley, watching television with four other tenants. Typically, Oswald was alone in his tiny room, which adjoined the living room. Jerry Duncan, employed at the service station directly across the street, had come over to the house to socialize with Slough and others. Duncan told Slough that he had met the new tenant, "Mr. Lee," and would introduce them if Lee ever came out of his room. Slough remembers what happened next:

> On television, they were announcing that they were about to show the final plans for Kennedy's parade route on Friday. Suddenly, Oswald came out of his room, stood behind the couch, staring intently at the television set. They were showing the exact parade route, the turns—where it was going to go right past the School Book Depository. Jerry kept trying to introduce me to Oswald, and frankly couldn't get his attention. He was just completely absorbed by the news. Nothing else seemed to matter. And when it was over—it didn't last over five minutes—Oswald just turned around and went straight back into his room. I never got a chance to be introduced to him.[48]

There are some indications as to what Oswald may have been doing back in his room. After the assassination, the *Dallas Morning News* published a report based on a piece of information leaked by the Dallas police. An anonymous source described a map of Dallas found in Oswald's room. The paper reported, "Oswald had placed marks at all major intersections along the motorcade route—three or four as I recall. There was also a line from the Texas School Book Depository Building to Elm Street. This was the trajectory of the bullets which struck the President and Governor Connally."[49]

The original Oswald map, stored in the National Archives, is too faded to be of any use. In addition, the map, after-the-fact, was laminated, which obliterated the faint pencil markings on it. Prior to the lamination, Dallas-based Kennedy archivist Mary Ferrell made a photocopy which retains some of the markings. At least twelve Oswald markings are still visible. Dealey Plaza is prominently marked. Eight of the marked sites provide a direct line of sight to the motorcade route. Elmo Cunningham, of the Dallas Police Intelligence Division, found the map in Oswald's room. He told the author, "The map definitely had the President's route on it. It was in pencil, very faint—but it was definitely there. It extended all the way from Love Field to the Trade Mart [the beginning and end of the motorcade route]."[50]

On Thursday, November 21, according to Buell Frazier, Lee Oswald approached Frazier at work and asked if he could ride back to Irving with him to pick up some curtain rods. At 5 p.m., Oswald arrived unannounced at the Paine house, his first visit there on any Thursday since moving back to Dallas. Marina, who had not seen him for two weeks, later described him as looking lonely. But Marina was in no mood to be sympathetic. Earlier, she had been upset to learn that Oswald had used a fictitious name when registering at the rooming house. She was not ready to let him off the hook.

Whatever intrigue Oswald had planned for the following day—whether inspired by Cubans in Mexico City, or by Bobby Kennedy's anti-Castro allies in New Orleans—this trip to Irving was a last desperate attempt at self-preservation. It now seems clear that Oswald was hoping Marina would give him an excuse to not jump into the maelstrom on Friday. It was his last attempt at salvaging a normal life.

Although she later claimed she was inwardly happy to see Lee, Marina, ever the strong-willed Russian coquette, also admitted that she did everything she could to not let him know it. Her biographer wrote:

> Marina saw Frazier's car stop at the house and Lee get out. She did not go to greet him. She looked sullen as he entered the bedroom...He took her by the shoulder to give her a kiss. Marina turned her face away and pointed to a pile of clothes. "There are your clean shirt and socks and pants. Go in and wash up."[51]

"He tried to start a conversation with me several times, but I would not answer," Marina later told her biographer. He also tried to kiss her several times, but each attempt was rebuffed. Four times that night, Lee asked Marina to move with him to a nicer apartment in Dallas. Each time, she refused.

"I was like a stubborn little mule," Marina recalled. "I was maintaining my inaccessibility, trying to show Lee that I wasn't easy to persuade. If he had come again the next day and asked, of course I would have agreed. I just wanted to hold out one day at least."[52]

Lee then went outside with his daughter Junie (Junie was his pet name for June). He played with her longer than ever before, until dark. Marina would later wonder if he was saying goodbye to her.

After helping to put June to sleep, Oswald himself went to bed around 10 p.m. Marina avoided him, soaking for over an hour in the bath while Lee lay on the bed. She later said that Lee was awake most of the night, finally dozing off around 5 a.m.

The morning of the 22nd, Oswald's late night took its toll. When the alarm went off at 7 a.m., he failed to rouse. Marina had to wake him. He arose and got ready for work, saying, "Mama, don't get up. I'll get breakfast myself." He then went and kissed his two sleeping children, uncharacteristically not doing the same to Marina. Approaching the bedroom door, he turned around and said to his wife, "I've left some money on the bureau. Take it and buy everything you and Junie and Rachel need. Bye-bye."

When Marina later arose, she would find $170, practically all of Lee's savings. Had she noticed something else, she says she would have been alarmed. The next evening, after Lee had been arrested for murdering John Kennedy, Marina would make another discovery on the bureau that made her heart sink: Lee had left his wedding ring in a small demitasse cup. He had never taken it off before.[53]

For those who subscribe to the theory that even the most complicated human events can be distilled down to the basic human desire for security and companionship,[54] they need look no farther for verification than the assassination of John Kennedy. Certainly there are political dimensions to the murder, with the likelihood that Lee Oswald's murderous act was encouraged by shadowy figures in Mexico City and concrete plans discerned in New Orleans. But just as the Washington Senators' scout, Joe Cambria, could have altered the future by signing young Fidel to a baseball contract, so could Marina Oswald have changed the shape of history the night before the assassination.

"The Other Assassin"

"The greater the U.S. support for the overthrow [of Castro], particularly in terms of military force, the greater the U.S. influence on the new government."

>—State Department memo to Robert Kennedy's CCC head, Joseph Califano, November 7, 1963[55]

"I think maybe we've got him now."

>—President Kennedy, November 19, 1963, referring to Fidel Castro, as related by the CIA's Richard Helms[56]

As the middle of November rolled around, events seemed to gather speed, and all of the omens pointed towards success for the Cuban plan about to unfold. On November 15, 1963, Artime's commando leaders, who had been training with the CIA in Virginia, embarked from Norfolk, Virginia. On November 19, the Second Naval Guerrilla, commanded by another exile friend of Bobby's, Brigade hero Pepe San Román, received over one-half million dollars for weapon purchases.[57] The former President and strongarm leader of Nicaragua, General Luis Somoza, was so convinced the invasion would begin soon and succeed that he predicted, "In November, strong blows will begin against Cuban Prime Minister Fidel Castro by groups we are training."[58]

On Tuesday, November 19, Rolando Cubela (AM/LASH) told his CIA case officer "Nicolas Sanson" (Nestor Sanchez) that if he didn't receive immediate assurances of backup support from Washington, he would break off and return to Cuba. Later that day, impromptu meetings were held at the White House. Those present were the President, Bobby Kennedy, the CIA's Deputy Director of operations Richard Helms, and Herschel Peake of the CIA's Technical Services Division (among other things, this department was responsible for designing the exotic assassination devices referred to earlier).[59] The CIA officers in attendance claim that while Cuba was the topic of the meeting, AM/LASH was not discussed.

Also on November 19, exile leader Tony Varona, training in the Cuban Officer Training Program at Ft. Holabird, Maryland, received a phone call from fellow exile (and Bobby Kennedy friend) Erneido Oliva. Oliva requested that Varona come immediately to Washington to attend a meeting with Bobby Kennedy.[60] According to Miami Station Chief Ted Shackley, Oliva had Bobby's private telephone number and used it regularly to discuss the Cuban situation.[61]

On this same day in Havana, AM/TRUNK infiltrators in Castro's Army were advised by their CIA contacts to monitor the Voice of America radio network on the coming night for an important message: a program was planned that would "inspire the rebel army to unite and rise [up] in a coup against Fidel." The broadcast would also "carry two major guarantees from the U.S. Government."[62]

On Wednesday, November 20, Cubela received a telephone call from "Sanson" (Sanchez), who told Cubela that the meeting he had requested seeking express Kennedy approval for his mission would take place on November 22 (at that meeting Cubela would be provided with the weapon that Herschel Peake's division had designed). The Church Committee later summarized, "At earlier meetings with the CIA, AM/LASH had only received general assurances of U.S. support for a coup plan, and thus the November 20 telephone call was the first indication that he might receive the specific support he requested."[63]

Later that same day, Robert Kennedy wrote a memo to National Security advisor McGeorge Bundy concerning Cuba, the contents of which remain secret. Only Bundy's response is known: "The Cuban problem is ready for discussion now... so we will call a meeting as soon as we can find a day when the right people are in town." The right people were clearly the Cubans Bobby had alerted the previous day: Oliva and Varona, along with Harry Williams and Manuel Artime.

Thus, the same day that Oswald watched the November 22 motorcade proceed along the route previously detailed on television, "the other assassin" was assured that the Kennedys would give him not only their support, but a custom-made weapon to use against Castro. It was to be delivered to him on November 22nd in Paris.

CHAPTER THIRTEEN

DIE BY THE SWORD

"I've created such a can of worms for myself with my Cuban policy that, yes, something could happen to me."
— **President Kennedy, to author John Davis, September 1963**[1]

"I don't want him to go."
— **Robert Kennedy, referring to his brother's scheduled trip to Texas, Nov 20, 1963**

"Dallas is a very dangerous place. I wouldn't go there. Don't you go."
— **Senator William Fulbright pleading to President Kennedy in October 1963**

The letter arrived like so many others at Robert Kennedy's Hickory Hill home. However, this one was different. It was not a request for a photograph or autograph, nor was it congratulations on the birth of the latest Kennedy child. In this letter, an anonymous writer from Texas was warning RFK not to let the President go to Dallas because "they" would kill him there. It is not clear who "they" were. And the letter would never again see the light of day. Thirty-five years later, it, like most of Bobby Kennedy's personal papers, is unavailable to historians, its whereabouts unknown.[2]

On November 20, the day of his 38th birthday, Bobby informed Ramsey Clark of his misgivings about his brother's trip to Texas. Kennedy's fears were not merely based on anonymous letters or intuition. For not only were warnings being received at Hickory Hill, they were also being monitored at the White House, the FBI headquarters, and the Secret Service. Responding to the September threat by Castro, Bobby's Cuban Coordinating Committee's secret unit was casting a wide net, collecting information implicating not only pro-Castro activists, but anti-Castro exiles left out of the Kennedy loop.

Bobby Kennedy was not alone in his reservations about the president's upcoming trip. Senators were prominent among those who, in turn, urged Kennedy not to go to Texas, and especially not to Dallas. William Fulbright,

Chairman of the Senate Foreign Affairs Committee, made it plain that Kennedy should go nowhere near the city, especially after the *Dallas Morning News* fiercely attacked the president for his supposedly insufficient opposition to communist aggression. The editorial's vehemence reflected the depths of loathing Kennedy could expect, Fulbright told the White House. Seven weeks earlier, on the day before Kennedy's final trip-planning conference with Governor John Connally, Fulbright, of the neighboring state of Arkansas, virtually pleaded with the President to skip Dallas. Any political gain in the city wasn't worth it, he urged.

On U.N. Day, October 24th, almost exactly a month before the trip's Thursday morning take-off, Adlai Stevenson, the U.S. Ambassador to the U.N., had urged a fundamental reconsideration of the trip after right-wing extremists in Dallas had struck and spat at him. Stevenson was stunned; the malevolence in Dallas surpassed even what he had anticipated.[3]

A week later, on November 4th, Byron Skelton, a sober Democratic National Committeeman from Texas, asked Robert Kennedy to earnestly consider dropping Dallas from the president's itinerary. Skelton cited a prominent Dallas resident's recent pronouncement that Kennedy was "a liability to the free world." That, in addition to what the Committeeman had seen in the city while making preparations for the trip, convinced him that Dallas simply wasn't safe. Skelton wrote Bobby Kennedy directly:

> *I am worried about President Kennedy's proposed trip to Dallas…A man who would make this kind of statement ["Kennedy is a liability to the free world"] is capable of doing harm to the President. [I would] feel better if the President's itinerary did not include Dallas… [Cancellation of the stop] should receive earnest consideration.[4]*

Bobby knew and trusted Skelton. He therefore took the letter seriously, forwarding it to JFK aide Kenny O'Donnell, who didn't treat it the same way. Skelton then wrote LBJ's right-hand man, Walter Jenkins, urging the same course. Skelton felt so passionately about bypassing Dallas that he flew to Washington to plead his case.

Even Governor John Connally intervened, asking Kennedy to re-consider the stop in Dallas, where people, he warned, might be "too emotional." Private citizens echoed these admonitions throughout October and November. Anne Brinkley, wife of newscaster David Brinkley, delivered her warning the evening before the trip, at a birthday party for Robert Kennedy. That happy gathering was otherwise noteworthy because Ethel Kennedy, Robert's wife, dropped her usual bantering toasts for a solemn request that guests drink to the President of the United States.

None of these people had access to the voluminous record of threats against JFK's life. Secret Service files were spilling over with warnings, almost all issued by crackpots, but a dozen or so by men who thirsted for vengeance and consorted with professional killers. Kennedy's friends and associates knew nothing about those potentially real threats, which should have been investigated with all possible means. They recognized only that Dallas was a dangerous place. The menace lay not in an uncounted number of lone, unknown Marxist assassins, but in known radical conservatives whose passions included a love of guns and a regular use of them.

This belief in the possibility of danger was not the product of prejudice against the city. Many Dallas residents agreed with the assessment. Natives and residents of varied backgrounds, including members of the civic leadership and federal judges and attorneys, urged planners of the trip to call it off. The city harbored too much malice toward Washington in general and the Chief Executive in particular, they said. The danger couldn't be exaggerated. That fact was driven home again and again, often just days before the Dallas trip.

Early in November, the president's visit to Chicago to attend the Army-Navy football game was dropped, ostensibly because the president needed the time to deliberate about the increasingly worrisome war in Vietnam. In fact, Secret Service officers had gotten wind of an assassination plot, soon traced to Cuban exiles excluded from the Kennedy-exile loop. Their plan had been to kill the President in Chicago Stadium.

On November 9th, just two weeks before Kennedy arrived in Dallas, a right-wing militant in Miami specified how the presidential killing would be accomplished: from a high building during a motorcade in a city of the south or southwest, using gunfire from several locations, and channeling blame to a patsy. A FBI informant taped the eerie prediction. The threat was particularly vexing, because President Kennedy was scheduled to arrive in Miami in just over a week.

The Kennedy trip to Florida nine days later, on November 18, was not cancelled. However, Kennedy's planned time in the city was shortened and security was reinforced, especially at the airport, after more talk was overheard about an attempt to damage Air Force One. The Miami leg of the trip was complicated by a number of security problems, including more threats on the President's life. During the Miami stopover, Harry Williams, the Cuban exile known as "Bobby's Boy," was assigned to handle a potentially dangerous situation. Williams recalled the incident in 1993:

> I was given a list by the Secret Service with the names of five people on it. They were members of the [2506] Brigade who said they were going to kill President Kennedy. I didn't know the guys. I got into a car, picked them up, and took them to Key West, where we rented a motel and kept them there while Kennedy was in Miami. The Kennedys were definitely worried about the Cubans in Miami.[5]

While in Miami, Kennedy delivered a speech in which he all but encouraged an overthrow of the Castro government, which he severely criticized and termed a "barrier" to any improvement in relations between Washington and Havana. The *Miami Herald* headlined its coverage of the speech, "Kennedy Invites Coup."

When AM/LASH's case officer, Nestor Sanchez, met with AM/LASH four days later, he informed the potential assassin that the speech was, in fact, written by the CIA's Desmond FitzGerald. The article and headline, planted in the paper via CIA source Hal Hendrix, were meant to signal not only Cubela (AM/LASH), but also internal Cuban dissidents, that the U.S.-supported coup was imminent.[6] According to CIA officer Seymour Bolton, President Kennedy personally approved the secret-encoded message to Cubela. A decade after the fact, Bolton told a congressional investigator that he personally carried the key paragraph from CIA headquarters to the White House for Kennedy's approval. Bolton told the investigator in the strongest terms that there was "no difference between Kennedy's policy and the CIA's policy."[7] (As he had so often, JFK was again following Eisenhower's precedent. In advance of the 1953 coup in Iran, CIA Director Allen Dulles worked with White House speechwriters to insert a message in one of Ike's speeches, providing a signal to their co-insurgents in Iran.)[8]

Bobby Kennedy had begun to worry about his brother's forays into hostile U.S. cities, but his older brother John, a politician to the last, was undeterred. He didn't like this aspect of the job, but he knew it to be a necessity, and accepted the attendant risk.

Kennedy and Death

> "It [death] didn't really concern him. He never thought he was going to live to be an old man anyway."
>
> —An anonymous JFK aide to *New York Times* reporter Tom Wicker[9]

To his confidantes, Kennedy openly expressed distaste for his Texas chore. He told Senator George Smathers of Florida that he wished he could escape the "pain in the neck" trip to Texas. But it was more the inconvenience of having to raise money than the death threats that bothered the President. Kennedy was a legendary fatalist (some even ventured that he had a "death wish"), whose disdain of security protocols had given the Secret Service a three-year headache.

It wasn't unnatural for John Kennedy to have occasional thoughts of expiring before he left office. Two of his six siblings had died well before their prime, and one had been lobotomized to near mental-death. The family that was uncommonly lucky in the procurement of great wealth kept getting the worst rolls of the dice on airplanes and in other personal matters.

Kennedy dwelled on death more than occasionally—often enough to say it seemed sometimes to preoccupy him. Decor in his office included lines from one of his favorite poems, which concerned death. Jackie would later describe him as haunted by "the poignancy of men dying young."

Kennedy's aides, always alert to the boss' whims and moods, remembered his moments of reflection as much as the incidents that threatened him: the times when the President would observe that it could be all over now if the man at the back of the crowd were a fanatic or if the fan in the bleachers had a gun in his hand instead of a score card or beer can.

More than anything, they remembered his tendency to joke about the danger, as about so much else. When a California admirer tossed a little gift into the president's car, Kennedy quipped to Dave Powers, his longest-serving aide, confidante, and crony, that he, Powers, wouldn't be around if that "admirer" actually had wanted to get rid of Kennedy. When another car sped past Kennedy's in Virginia shortly before his Texas trip, he observed to another old friend: "They could have shot you, Charlie." That was among the weaker demonstrations of Kennedy's wit, but it displayed both his attention to the possibility of death at any time and his natural tendency to jest about everything. Except in extremis, he could not be solemn even about the most serious subjects.

Returning from a trip, Kennedy would often remark that he'd been lucky enough, "Thank God," not to have been killed that day. He said this with his customary conversational buoyancy, but psychological expertise is not required to suspect that dark thoughts prompted his black humor. JFK's private conversations with friends and cronies were known to have included his queries about how they would like to die. When one of them thought to turn the tables and ask his preference, he answered without hesitation: in an airplane. Why there? Because it would be quick, replied the president.

Even less avid readers of history know that Presidents are, in a sense, an endangered species. Two assassination attempts on his predecessors had failed; three had succeeded. Kennedy spoke of the act often enough for mystics to speculate that he had a premonition of being the next to die. He even composed a scene of how it might happen.

In September 1963, he had, in fact, written and acted in a brief home movie about his assassination—not the imminent one, but a fictional episode, shot for amusement on Labor Day weekend, 12 weeks before his Texas trip. Following his own script while a White House photographer's camera rolled for several takes, Kennedy disembarked from the "Honey Fitz," the family's yacht, and walked down a pier at the Rhode Island estate of his wife's parents. Suddenly, he clutched his chest and fell to the boards. Jackie and a visitor casually stepped over him, as if he weren't there. Paul Fay, an Undersecretary of the Navy and Kennedy's buddy from World War II, then fell on the body, sending a gush of red liquid spurting from the President's mouth. The few lines of dialogue were never revealed—for 20 years, the film's existence was kept secret as well. Reporters and Secret Service agents who observed its production respected Kennedy's wish for privacy.

Kennedy's attitude toward the security designed to protect him was a mixture of nonchalance and resignation, flavored with a pinch of morbidity and self-mockery. Given how aware he was that his life could easily be threatened or taken, his behavior, at times, had to be called cavalier, especially when considering his extraordinary sexual libido. He would often ignore all precautions and violate all rules in the pursuit of a "skirt." On other occasions, he would be exasperated by what he termed overzealous measures, as when teams of Secret Service agents patrolled empty beaches. Sometimes, he even sent the agents away—U.S. law permitted him to at the time.

Ordinarily, however, he tolerated the very burdensome precautions—which had Secret Service personnel all but accompany members of the family to the toilet—with passable humor, even while doubting that the most elaborate, expensive protection could save him against a truly determined killer. "If they're going to get me, they'll get me even in church," he liked to say to Evelyn Lincoln, his personal secretary. Jackie's attitude was even more fatalistic than her husband's. "Oh shit," she would say. "They'll get us one day."[10]

Kennedy was only partially right: he could indeed be killed even in church—but only if the killer had out-thought the meticulous security apparatus of the presidency, or was willing to die himself. There was no right way to balance the demands of politics, which required mixing with people, and of protection, which required keeping a distance from them; between living as the energetic, uncommonly inquisitive President liked to live, and existing in a cage.

About 25,000 threats were reportedly logged during Kennedy's 34 months as President (actual figures have not been released): again, the vast majority were made by crackpots, but some came from potentially real assassins. In 1976, the Secret Service released a report indicating that its "Security Index" listed one million people as potential threats to Kennedy at the time of his death.[11]

The Fateful Trip

"Oh God, how I wish we could change places."
> —President Kennedy to Secretary of the Treasury Douglas Dillon
> on November 20th, as Dillon began a trip to Japan

Jacqueline Kennedy's decision to accompany her husband on the Texas tour surprised the President's advisors. Jackie disdained the posturing good politics required. Campaigning smacked of favor-mongering, which ran counter to her boarding school concept of good manners.

Jackie's upbringing had been amidst old money. There, she was taught that her duty lay in setting style and culture. Her milieu was the drawing rooms of Europe and the American Northeast. She observed the forms—as a well-trained political wife must—but when she volunteered to go into deepest, darkest Texas, where the gauche flower of new money could be found in its most pristine state, more than a few eyebrows were raised.

There was no mystery behind her decision. Jackie had recently given birth to a premature infant. His death had reawakened both spouses' human sensitivity, and the Kennedy marriage.

During the Houston leg of the Texas trip, the presidential advance man in charge, Marty Underwood, observed, "They were all over each other...crazy about each other."[12] They made more public displays of affection than was typical of their relationship. Underwood, like others, attributed the warming of their tumultuous marriage to Patrick's recent death. "It was the first time Kennedy knew love," Underwood says.

During the San Antonio leg of the trip, President Kennedy helped dedicate the Air Force School of Aero-Medicine. At one point, he turned to a scientist involved in oxygen chamber research. Kennedy asked him if his space-related work might lead to improved oxygen chambers for premature babies. "The death of his infant son Patrick Bouvier Kennedy was still weighing on his mind," wrote aide Kenny O'Donnell.[13] In Houston, Jackie pledged to her husband, "I'll go anywhere with you this year."[14]

The President's delight about Jackie's decision was obvious to all. "Jackie will show those Texas broads a thing or two about fashion," Kennedy remarked.[15] If Jack saw her as an ornament on this trip, it was a precious one. Revealing the importance he attached to it, he took unusual pains to please her so she would look and feel her best. Ordinarily, he did not involve himself at all in her choice of clothes. This time, before their departure, he reviewed her wardrobe and stressed the importance of looking splendid—in particular, "as marvelous" as any of the "rich Republican women" of Dallas, in their furs and jewels. "Be simple," he prompted. "Show these Texans what good taste really is."

President Kennedy's helicopter took him (and travel companions) from the White House grounds to Andrews Air Force Base in less than five minutes. Nine minutes after that, at 11:05 on Thursday morning, November 21st, Air Force One revved its engines and took off. Tanned from a brief visit to the Florida family compound earlier in the week, toned by two long swims in the White House pool the previous day, Kennedy looked ready and fit. Few knew how much he looked forward to the return flight four days later—just in time to celebrate young John, Jr.'s birthday.

Once having decided to travel, Kennedy assumed his outwardly insouciant form. The presidential Boeing 707, designed by the celebrated Raymond Loewy, featured a comfortable double bedroom, with a bathroom in the suite. Forward of the bedroom, in the quiet, finely-appointed stateroom, the Chief Executive read from the five newspapers and 15 magazines to which Air Force One subscribed, scanned secret military and intelligence reports, and studied a briefing book for a state visit by West German Chancellor Ludwig Erhard, scheduled to arrive in Washington on Monday, four days hence. He also got up from his desk to talk with Secret Service agents and members of the White House press pool. Four veteran newsmen represented dozens of others in a chartered plane following closely behind. In the plush presidential plane, Kennedy was his usual off-stage self, exchanging wise-cracks with reporters, most of whom adored him.

However, speaking at the huge Houston Coliseum later that evening, the President would be so nervous that his hands, which he had learned to conceal from sight, trembled violently.

Texas

"Don't let the President come down here... I think something terrible will happen to him."
—A Dallas woman to Pierre Salinger, Kennedy's Press Secretary

"If I did see him [Kennedy], I'd just spit in his face."
—A Dallas schoolteacher explaining to her students why, the next day, they wouldn't be excused, as promised, to see the presidential motorcade

Air Force One landed in San Antonio, Texas at 2:30 p.m. Vice President Johnson and Governor Connally were there on the tarmac to greet it. The airport crowd roared, especially for "Jackeee!" Behind the scenes,the atmosphere was unpleasant. The feud between Texas Senator Ralph Yarborough and Governor John Connally showed signs of worsening rather than healing. When a Yarborough admirer in the welcoming committee warned the senator that Johnson was Connally's ally in the vendetta against him, the prickly Yarborough refused to ride in Johnson's car.[16]

There would be just two-and-a-half hours in San Antonio—essentially happy hours because this was a relatively liberal city, its press and political establishment attuned to the instinctive Kennedy constituency of the Latin poor. But the his-and-her Kennedy charisma produced a far greater reaction than expected in a huge, excited turnout on the streets. With the temperature even higher than predicted, the presidential couple were drenched with sweat, but exhilarated. Like politicians before and after him, Kennedy thrived on large crowds because they generated momentum for victory, especially when replayed on television.

Then it was on to the next stop, from a different airport to which Air Force One and the other planes had transferred. The presidential party landed in Houston at 4:37 p.m., local time. The temperature there was even hotter, and the banners and signs were less welcoming (reflecting Houston's distinctly less liberal leanings). Still, the airport crowd was enthusiastic, and Jackie actually waded into it until she felt a frightening surge towards her. Desire to see Jackie—how she looked, what she was wearing—would continue to swell crowds at all of the stops in Houston.

To rest before the evening activities, the President and First Lady were installed at the Rice Hotel, Houston's most prestigious, in its sumptuous International Suite. Kennedy was pleased by the First Lady's remarks in Spanish to a full, cheering audience of Hispanics in the hotel's ballroom, although he didn't understand a word she said "What did you say?" he asked her. Teased Jackie, "I'll never tell you."[17] (The good feeling continued the following morning, when Jackie told her husband she would accompany him on a trip to California two weeks later.) Next, Kennedy delivered a speech at the Houston Coliseum.

Later that night, the President had dinner in his hotel room with his wife and Marty Underwood, while the advance man briefed the President on the remainder of the Houston itinerary. JFK complimented Underwood on another great turnout. To that, Underwood replied, "It wasn't because of me, it was because Mrs. Kennedy was there."

"Great, I'll never live this down," Kennedy joked. The First Couple were clearly in a playful mood, and soon Marty was shown the door so the couple could be alone.

Later, Underwood accompanied the couple to the airfield for the flight to Fort Worth. He recalls that before Kennedy flew from Houston, the president, against the advice of the Secret Service, went out to "work the fences," shaking hands with admirers in the dark. Underwood was concerned. Threats to Kennedy had been picked up and relayed to him. He told the president, "I'm worried about tomorrow."

When the President climbed the staircase to the plane, he turned before entering the cabin and surveyed the crowd. Eager to show Underwood that he had made it safely, he yelled in his best Boston accent, "Where's Maahty?" Then Kennedy turned to an aide, saying, "Marty worries too much."

"I had been hearing from different agencies that the Dallas trip might be the site for an attack on the President," Underwood recently recalled.[18] One of his sources was his good friend, CIA Mexico Station Chief Win Scott. Although Scott may not have been specifically referring to Oswald, he clearly was aware of Cuban agents who had a history of operating out of the Mexico City Embassy and were known to move easily across the Texas-Mexico border.

Beyond these threats, Underwood had other reasons to worry. On arriving in Texas two weeks prior, Underwood had sensed the hostility himself. He even phoned Washington to demand that Kennedy's limousine have the bubble-top on hand, though he knew Kennedy would probably not be convinced to use it.

The presidential entourage left for Fort Worth, landing after midnight and arriving at the Hotel Texas just before 1 a.m. Because of the motorcades between each stop and the endless solicitations of support, it had been a grueling day. The First Couple was exhausted.[19] Johnson, too, was exhausted, but in a very different way, and for a very different reason.

The Running Mate

"Nixon Predicts Kennedy May Drop Johnson"
—**Headline of story in Dallas Morning News, November 22, 1963**

For some Washington insiders, it was a fait d'accompli that JFK would jettison Lyndon Johnson from the ticket in the fall. Rumors of kickbacks had been nipping at Johnson's heels to the point where he was now the target of a Senate Rules Committee investigation. The alleged key players with Johnson were Bobby Baker, Billie Sol Estes, and Don Reynolds. All the signs portended a major feeding frenzy, indeed a major scandal.

Kennedy, however, delayed acting, just as he did on other important matters such as Vietnam. The Chief Executive asserted that he had no plans to replace Johnson on the 1964 ticket. During the next five months, he would repeat that assurance, with greater and lesser enthusiasm. His last assurance was on the morning of November 22 in Dallas, with Johnson riding two cars behind him in the motorcade. But the assurances had begun to sound weak.

Kennedy most likely delayed aborting Johnson because, for all LBJ's baggage, he still represented a tenuous connection to the South—which was virtually another country in terms of Kennedy's political viability. Plus, the president was relying on Texas to feed a demanding campaign war chest. The hide-worn Johnson, the politician's politician, knew how to stall and dissemble with the best of them. Reassurances notwithstanding, he was convinced that Kennedy was biding his time and would drop him at the moment most convenient for the president.

Johnson had hoped for much more when joining Kennedy three years earlier. Over the past months, he had been excluded from both White House meetings and 1964 campaign planning sessions. Johnson's political intelligence network, which was as legendary as his powers as Majority Leader had been, told him what he already knew: his place on the 1964 ticket was anything but assured. For him, the final Kennedy humiliation was leaving him out of the planning for the Dallas trip. Even reporters saw the storm clouds, and believed the President, at the very least, had plans to review the matter of Johnson's position on the ticket. The reporters were correct.

As longtime Johnson friend and aide Horace Busby remembers, "In the summer of 1963, Kennedy began consulting with Democratic Party Chairman John Bailey. He asked Bailey to draw up a list of [vice-presidential] replacements."[20] Busby's knowledge makes it apparent that Johnson, too, knew the score. A number of Johnson friends have also confirmed that Johnson knew he was in trouble. For example, LBJ military aide Air Force Colonel Howard Burris said, "I was concerned in the summer of 1963 that LBJ was off the ticket in 1964. The Kennedy crowd didn't want to hear our opinions on anything."[21] Burris, a fellow Texan and an LBJ friend since 1937, was told by a high-ranking Kennedy insider (whom he still declines to name), "Johnson served his purpose in 1960. He's not going to be on the ticket." Then-Senator and future vice-president Hubert Humphrey knew that a Kennedy administration group was holding secret meetings on the subject. "I got a full report on the meeting, and they were going to dump Johnson," Humphrey later said. "I know [Presidential Special Assistant] Arthur Schlesinger was one of them. They had a meeting out in Georgetown."[22]

According to JFK's secretary Evelyn Lincoln, not only had Kennedy reviewed the situation, but he had made up his mind. "Who is your choice as running mate?" Lincoln asked Kennedy just prior to the Dallas trip. "At this time I am thinking about Governor Terry Sanford of North Carolina," came Kennedy's answer. "But it will not be Lyndon."[23]

Lincoln's allegation has never been corroborated, and remains controversial. However, the recollections of a former investigator for the FBI add weight to Lincoln's recollections.

Walt Perry, an investigator for the Internal Revenue Service at the time, says that Bobby Kennedy was attempting to use Johnson's legal problems as leverage, should Johnson not agree to leave the ticket voluntarily. Perry was brought in by William Webster (later to become the FBI director) to assist in the Billie Sol Estes investigation. He befriended Estes, who, in the course of things, told Perry that he had funneled $10 million in bribes to Johnson. He also related an anecdote about Bobby Kennedy. Perry recalls, "Estes told me that in 1963, Bobby Kennedy contacted him in prison. Bobby made him an offer: 'If you testify against Johnson, you're out [of prison].' Billie declined the offer, saying, 'If I testified against him, I'd be dead within twenty-four hours.'"[24]

Johnson himself remarked to Bobby Baker, "Jack Kennedy's as thoughtful and considerate of me...as he can be. But I know his snot-nosed little brother's after my ass, and all those high-falutin' Harvards, and if I give 'em enough rope they'll hang me with it."[25] Johnson may have been overly kind to the President. Bobby Baker would write that the President himself seemed to desire leverage against his Vice-President:

> *I was leaving the Oval Office after the conference with the President [when] JFK said to me in a hearty and jovial manner, "Bobby, how about this damned Texas tycoon, what's his name? Billie Sol Estes? Is he a pal of yours?" I sensed that the President was on a fishing expedition, attempting to find out what I might know of any connections between his vice-president and the Texas wheeler-dealer who'd just been charged with any number of crimes."[26]*

At the time of JFK's Dallas trip, according to a high Justice Department source developed by author John Davis, Robert Kennedy had a thick file on his desk detailing Johnson's alleged bribery by a bagman for New Orleans Mafia don, Carlos Marcello.[27] Documents recently released by the FBI show that throughout 1962 and 1963, Bobby Kennedy sought to obtain a list of the Texas politicians compiled by Jack Halfen, a legendary payoff man. For two years, Bobby had been interested in an investigation of Halfen, which, he determined, could lead to dozens of organized crime convictions, and some juicy material on Johnson. This material was RFK's chief aim.

According to information developed by Mike Dorman in his 1972 book *Payoff*, Kennedy first became interested in Halfen in 1961. His Assistant Attorney General at the time, a tough racket-buster named Edwyn Silberling, was given the go-ahead to launch an investigation. Halfen was serving his second year of a ten-year sentence—actually three years in Texas and ten in Oklahoma, running concurrently—for passing forged money orders, the core of a scheme to defraud the Las Vegas Western Union office of $500,000. At the time of the Siberling investigation, Halfen was 49 years old, having spent 34 of those 49 years in crime, beginning at the age of 15. He had been arrested many times, and had hinted that he might be willing to reveal incriminating information about high-ranking politicians who had landed him in jail.

When the pertinent FBI documents were released in 1998, Halfen's politicians list was one of them, but of the forty names cited, thirty-seven were blacked out. The three names visible were all close friends of LBJ: Tom Clark , former U.S. Attorney General and U.S. Supreme Court Justice; Albert Thomas, U.S. Congressman from Harris County, TX; and a former Texas Deputy Sheriff named Jake Colca.[28] (As will be seen, RFK would revisit this allegation in the coming years.) In 1998, a high government official, on condition of anonymity, confirmed that Robert Kennedy had in fact instructed his Justice Department to initiate a "criminal investigation of Lyndon Johnson."

Burkett Van Kirk, the minority counsel on the Senate Rules Committee in 1963, recently detailed Bobby's disposition of the "dirt" he collected on Johnson. "Bobby gave the material to [Republican] Senator John Williams of Delaware," who passed it on to Van Kirk. Williams kept the material in his Senate safe. "He told me it came from Bobby." Other LBJ "dirt" began to be delivered "continuously" to Van Kirk by courier from a Department of Justice lawyer. Van Kirk explains that Johnson controlled the Committee's Democratic majority (through his long association with the Committee's chief investigator, Senator Everett Jordan of North Carolina), that he had "greased" the Democratic contingent on the Committee, and that Bobby was thus forced to deal with the Republicans to politically go after Johnson.[29]

Johnson's Secret

> "You don't really have any idea how unhappy I am now."
> —Vice President Lyndon Johnson to his friend Bobby Baker[30]

> "He was really down. 1963 was the beginning of the end for Johnson. He was cut out; they were not giving him anything, and the message was basically: 'We don't want you and we don't want your opinion.' He knew that he was going to be thrown off the ticket and that was going to be the end for him."
> —Colonel Howard Burris, Johnson's Military Aide (1992)[31]

Although some still debate LBJ's future with Kennedy, most insiders agree that Kennedy was at least reviewing his options. But what of Johnson's plans? Little attention has been given to what he planned for 1964.

Oft-reported is the fact that Johnson had grown to hate the Vice-Presidential role, but few knew of his intentions for the future. The earliest rumblings were heard by Minnesota Governor Orville Freeman. Freeman remembers, "He hinted on a number of occasions that he was thinking seriously of doing something else. He had apparently some offers from colleges that he was interested in, that were asking him if he might be a president."[32] As far back as July 1963, Johnson had opened up an office in Austin to explore a possible bid for reelection to the Senate in 1964.

According to longtime friend and aide Horace Busby, Johnson had also contacted his friend Harry Provence, editor of the *Tribune-Herald* in Waco, Texas. "I'm going to look into the newspaper business," Johnson told Busby. Johnson had strong opinions about his next career move. Busby recalled, "He said what he thought he wanted to do was become a publisher of a progressive, forward-looking Texas daily [newspaper]. He said he'd be the publisher and I'd be the editor. He got very excited about the whole thing. He was going to reform the state."[33] Provence agrees that Johnson had put out such feelers, adding, "He was completely unhappy as Vice President, no question about that."[34]

It is now clear that Lyndon Johnson was, like Kennedy, reviewing his options. But, unlike Kennedy—and probably unknown to Kennedy—Johnson had made his decision. The timing suggests that the secret October meeting between JFK and Connally, the one in which they planned the Texas trip without the vice-president's aid, was, for LBJ, the final insult.

"I'm withdrawing from the 1964 ticket," a weary Lyndon Johnson told Horace Busby. Busby recalls the night in October when Johnson dropped the bomb:

> We all were aware of Schlesinger's secret meetings with John Bailey. Johnson had also come to feel that he had just played out his string. He had thought about it [his decision] during most of the year and had decided. He felt he had accomplished more than he ever dreamt possible for a boy from a small town in Texas. He felt it was time to move on. He was going to tell the President when they got to the ranch in Austin that Friday night [November 22, 1963].[35]

Colonel Howard Burris recently added, "I was to be there at that [Friday night] meeting. Johnson had asked me to prepare a briefcase full of 'Eyes Only' documents for the meeting." According to Burris, the documents were to buttress a Johnson confrontation with the President on foreign policy issues, especially Vietnam and Cuba.[36]

Friday, November 22

The day dawned in Cuba with AM/TRUNK infiltrator Modesto Orozco posting a "Secret Writing" message to his CIA contact. The message stated:

> Castro recently expressed fear of the possibility of "Commando insurrections." ...So as to negate this possibility, Castro was undertaking an intensive propaganda campaign to give confidence to his troops and to limit the occurrence of any internal uprising.[37]

In Madrid, Spain the CIA reported hearing from a Cuban journalist who claimed to have received a letter "stating that GPIDEAL [President Kennedy] would be killed today."[38]

By the early morning hours, the streets of Dallas were festooned with 5,000 handbills headlined: WANTED FOR TREASON. The text declared that "This man is wanted for treasonous activities against the United States." Among the charges were betraying the Constitution, surrendering American sovereignty to the "communist controlled" United Nations, betraying Cuba, promoting the Test Ban Treaty, upholding the Supreme Court's "Anti-Christian rulings," and

telling "fantastic LIES to the American people" (including personal ones denying a previous marriage and divorce). The wanted man, the President of the
United States, was pictured in full face and profile, as on sheriffs' posters.

At 5 a.m., in nearby Irving, Texas, Lee Oswald was just dozing off after a fit-
ful night of tossing and turning.

Less than 40 miles away, John Kennedy arose, showered, and prepared for
his breakfast speech before the Fort Worth Chamber of Commerce. In his haste,
the President committed one dramatic oversight: he took off his Saint Jude and
Saint Christopher Medals and left them hanging on the shower head. When
"sweeping" the room later, Secret Service agent Ron Pontius found the medals
and put them in his pocket, with intentions of returning them to the President
after the Dallas motorcade. Pontius eventually gave the medals to Marty
Underwood, who still retains them.[39]

Just before nine o'clock in the morning, Kennedy addressed a gathering in
the parking lot of the same Hotel Texas. It was composed chiefly of blue-collar
working men. The talk was a last-minute concession to liberals, who had persuaded the President that union members and supporters of his policies would
be all but excluded from the one public event of his Fort Worth stay, the breakfast sponsored by the Chamber of Commerce. The size of this outdoor audience
far exceeded all expectations, despite a steady drizzle. Kennedy was delighted—
in contrast to Johnson, whose mood was brooding.

The president began by thanking his listeners for being there, despite the
weather. When someone shouted out the question of where Jackie was, the president joined the general laughter. "Mrs. Kennedy is organizing herself. It takes
longer but, of course, she looks better than we do when she does it." The
President was using a microphone. Through her bedroom window, Jackie heard
this beautifully delivered compliment, followed by whoops and cheers, . She
wished the rain would continue so that the Secret Service would rig the bubble-
top to the presidential Lincoln, saving her hair in the motorcade and perhaps
hiding her tired eyes.

Jack and Jackie then appeared at the Chamber of Commerce's breakfast for
2,500 guests in the hotel's Longhorn room. As distinguished visitors, the president and First Lady were presented with gifts: ornate, hand-tooled boots that
Jackie would never wear; a five-gallon cowboy hat that Jack declined to put on
even for a moment because he had contempt for what he liked to call "baloney
pictures" of presidents demeaning themselves in outlandish costumes. It took
skill to finesse the moment of not donning the hat despite Texan calls for him
to do so. Kennedy promised to wear his gift back in the White House.

The President's speech followed: an undistinguished paean to Fort Worth
for its historic and current contribution to the nation's defense, together with a
plug for the importance of American global commitments and the growth in
military spending and strength. Defense appropriations, especially for aircraft,
was vital to the economy of this city, which had its origins as a military outpost.
Though Kennedy had little hope the Chamber of Commerce stalwarts would

vote for him next November, he would highlight, in boldface, the very profitable Pentagon procurement orders, which were a boon to local banks and businesses. At a stop in the Houston Space Center the day before, his tongue had Freudian-slipped when he spoke of the world's largest "payroll" instead of the world's largest "payload." Speaking to the business people that morning, he would return to the same point almost as bluntly.

First among the contemporary weapons he championed was "the Iroquois helicopter from Fort Worth, [which] is a mainstay in our fight against the guerrillas in South Vietnam." With this segue, he went on to claim credit for increasing, under his presidency, the number of counterinsurgency forces engaged in Vietnam by 600 percent.

There was almost an hour between the end of breakfast and the departure for Dallas. Back in his suite on the hotel's eighth floor, Kennedy was shown a page he had missed earlier when scanning the local newspapers. What he had noticed in that day's *Dallas Morning News* was the hostile coverage: two front-page stories devoted to the Yarborough and Connally-Johnson troubles, and an inside third one headlined, "PRESIDENT'S VISIT SEEN WIDENING STATE DEMOCRATIC SPLIT."[40]

Now aides pointed to a full page advertisement entitled, "Welcome Mr. Kennedy to Dallas." In case a reader might miss the morbid sarcasm, the page was bordered in thick black, suggestive of mourning. "What kind of journalism do you call the Dallas Morning News?" Kennedy later asked an aide.[41] The message in the advertisement was only slightly less crude than the "Wanted For Treason" handbills. The charges, couched as twelve rhetorical questions, were roughly the same: contributing to communist Cuba's slavery, approving the sale of wheat to America's communist enemies, ordering his brother, the Attorney General, to "go soft on Communists, fellow-travelers, and ultra-leftists in America, while permitting him to persecute loyal Americans who criticize you, your administration and your leadership." The ad continued:

> *WHY has Gus Hall, head of the U.S. Communist Party, praised almost every one of your policies and announced that the party will endorse and support your re-election in 1964?...WHY have you scrapped the Monroe Doctrine in favor of the "Spirit of Moscow"?... Mr. Kennedy, WE DEMAND answers to these questions, and we want them NOW.*

Kennedy did not know that Nelson Bunker Hunt, son of millionaire H.L. Hunt, was among the moving forces behind "The American Fact-Finding Committee," the organization identified as the ad's sponsor. However, Kennedy had long been concerned with the radical right's militant opposition to him. Earlier that fall, he had commissioned a top-secret report on the dangers his presidency faced from such arch-conservatives as the Hunts.[42] And this ad infuriated him. His ire was deepened by knowledge that the *Dallas Morning News*, the oldest newspaper in Texas, enjoyed wide circulation and substantial influence. "Can you imagine a paper doing a thing like that?" he murmured.[43]

Perhaps to distract himself or his disbelieving wife, he voiced speculation about being assassinated—this time, setting his imagination in the previous evening's rain and jostling. He called it "a hell of a night to assassinate a President... Suppose a man had a pistol in his briefcase."

He pantomimed the killer using his revolver and suggested he could have melted into the crowd. To Jackie, whose comfort on this trip still concerned him, he spoke with disgust barely softened by humor: "We're heading into nut country now." [44]

"Nut Country"

At 7:15 a.m., Lee Oswald walked one block east from the Paine house, and poked his head into the back door of Linnie Mae Randle's home, looking for her brother Buell Frazier for a ride to work. Both Randle and Frazier later agreed that they observed Oswald place a package in the backseat. Both were adamant that the package was far too small to be even a broken-down Mannlicher Carcano rifle—34 inches long. Buell Frazier told the author that both he and his sister were badgered by Warren Commission investigators to reconsider their memory of the object's length. Frazier recalled:

> They had me in one room and my sister in another. They were asking us to hold our hands apart to show how long the package was. They made me do it over and over—at least ten times. Each time they measured the distance, and it was always 25 inches, give or take an inch. They did the same with my sister and she gave the same measurement...But I don't understand what the problem is—Lee could have taken the rifle in on another day and hidden it in the warehouse. Why did he have to take it in on Friday?[45]

Indeed, this is one of many unanswered questions regarding the movements of Oswald's rifle. One possible answer to this conundrum: if Frazier had been the "mystery driver" at the rifle range, it could be that, in the Friday package, Oswald was simply returning Buell Frazier's British Enfield rifle, which he might have borrowed from him, either with intent to purchase it or to test it as a possible murder weapon. If that were the case, few could fault the 19 year-old Frazier for withholding this information, to prevent being implicated in the crime.

For his part, Oswald later told authorities that he had merely taken his lunch with him to work that morning. Frazier said Oswald told him the package contained curtain rods for his apartment. The Warren Commission located only one employee who saw Oswald enter the depository after leaving Frazier's car. That employee, Jack Dougherty, testified, "I'll put it this way, I didn't see anything in his hands at the time."[46]

It is possible that Dougherty missed the rifle—34 inches long, broken down—but not probable. But is it likely that Lee Oswald, the same man who so meticulously snuck his rifle to the Walker shooting site, burying it nearby days earlier—would attempt the murder of the century by openly carrying the rifle, even wrapped up, to the sniper's nest in full view of the other employees?

Whatever the modus operandi, Oswald's rifle was at the ready by the southeast sixth floor window when the President passed by on Elm Street below.

The ride to work in the morning rain, according to Frazier, was unremarkable. Lee wasn't particularly quiet or talkative, and gave absolutely no hint that anything was out of the ordinary.

Washington

In the nation's capital, Bobby Kennedy was occupied at the Justice Department in meetings with his organized crime task force. However, documents released in 1997 show that Bobby was also scheduled to meet secretly this day with Manuel Artime, Roberto San Román, and Harry Williams, "Los Amigos de Roberto."[47] It is not known if this meeting had in fact occurred when the news of JFK's death arrived. However, Bobby's secret Cuban allies were known to have been closeted in planning sessions in Washington on the morning of the 22nd. The man referred to by the Cuban exiles as "Bobby's Boy," Cuban exile coordinator Harry Williams, recalled the scene for former FBI-agent-turned-author William Turner:

> Harry Williams told the authors...that, on that day, he was meeting in a CIA safe house in northwest Washington with Richard Helms, Howard Hunt, and several other CIA agents. It was, Williams would say, "the most important meeting I ever had on the problem of Cuba." He was buoyant. Plans for his invasion from the Dominican Republic were crystallizing. Manuel Artime was "ready with his things in Central America," and he and Williams were about ready "to do a whole thing together.[48]

Across town, the Senate Rules Committee was threatening the future of Lyndon Johnson with its ever-tightening investigation of Bobby Baker. Baker, a former Secretary to the Senate Democrats, was one of Johnson's right-hand men throughout his Senate career and LBJ's 1960 national campaign. He had also run a number of scams, allegedly peddling Johnson's influence. For example, LBJ reportedly lined up friends on Capitol Hill to purchase insurance policies from D.C. insurance broker Don Reynolds. In exchange for the business, Reynolds alledgedly would kick back a percentage of the commission to the purchaser, and then to LBJ for arranging the transaction.[49]

The talk about Baker seemed to augur a major, unstoppable scandal. Indeed, to many, Baker's influence peddling had become so flagrant that the term "payola" re-entered the lexicon as the investigations unfolded. Yet to be established was the depth of Johnson's complicity in Baker's various schemes. But the influence being peddled, after all, was Johnson's—the former Senate Majority Leader. And even if no legally damaging relationship could be established, Johnson's reputation would never fully recover. On the basis of "where there's smoke, there's fire," the reading public would never believe that LBJ had been ignorant of Baker's wholesale milking of Washington's legislative supplicants.

A second looming stormcloud for the Vice President involved his Texan crony Billie Sol Estes. This time, the payments—in the form of government contracts—turned out to be for the storage of fictitious grain and for other fraudulent schemes. Some of the proceeds were said to have gone directly to Johnson and were rumored to be substantial. Johnson knew these allegations were also being investigated.

Washington insiders whispered about imminent disaster for the Vice President. It could reach as far as impeachment proceedings, they said, and possible criminal liability that could end, as Johnson himself believed, in a prison term. And on this very day—at the very moment of the assassination—Don Reynolds was testifying before the Senate Rules Committee, perhaps only hours away from implicating Vice-President Johnson in the Baker scandal. Rules Committee Counsel Burkett Van Kirk recently opined, "There is no doubt in my mind that Reynolds' testimony of November 22 would have gotten Johnson out of the Vice-Presidency."[50] However, Reynolds' testimony was cut short when the news from Dallas arrived, and it would never resume.[51]

Paris

It was evening in Paris now and Cubela (AM/LASH) was meeting with his CIA case officer, Nestor Sanchez, and others. Cubela remembered the evening thus:

> There were many officials there—several of them, three, four...Among the things they pointed out to me, there was a pen that could shoot a bullet...He [Sanchez] did not give it to me, but actually he showed it to me. I did not accept it...It seems to me there was a kind of syringe which I was told contained poison.[52]

According to CIA documents, the agency recommended that Cubela fill the pen with the deadly poison, Black Leaf 40. The pen itself (a Papermate) had a protruding, micro-thin needle imperceptible to Fidel Castro as it pricked his skin. Cubela, however, balked. He had requested rifles and explosives. The CIA's AM/LASH file contains the following entry: "The case officer assured AM/LASH that the CIA would give him everything he needed (telescopic sight, silencer, all the money he wanted)."[53]

When later investigating the CIA's AM/LASH file, the Church Committee concluded, "AM/LASH intended to kill Castro, and the CIA knew his desire and endeavored to supply the means that he needed."[54]

As President Kennedy entered his limousine at Dallas' Love Field airport, the Kennedy brothers' Cuban plans were accelerating. But in a few moments, Lee Oswald would achieve the only major success of his life. Using a $13 rifle, in an act taking just nine seconds, he would prevent the imminent implementation of OPLAN 380-63 and, perhaps, save Fidel Castro's life.

Dallas: One Hour To Live

"President Kennedy should be awarded the Purple Heart just for coming to Dallas."
  —A Dallas resident who watched the Presidential motorcade

"We're nothing but sitting ducks in a shooting gallery."
  —Jacqueline Kennedy, to a member of the Secret Service[55]

"Jackie, if somebody wants to shoot me from a window with a rifle, nobody can stop it, so why worry about it?"
  —President Kennedy to his wife, in Fort Worth, 8 a.m.,
  November 22, 1963

The presidential plane touched down in Dallas at 11:38 a.m. following a 13-minute flight from Fort Worth. At Love Field, the city's outcast band of liberals was determined to be seen and heard—to demonstrate its loyalty to Kennedy and gratitude for his presence. But even amidst this good will, the ominous symbolism was manifest. Bobby had received the letter of warning about the Dallas visit. Jack had read the black-bordered ads (and left his protective religious medals behind). Now, it was Jackie's turn. At every stop on the Texas trip, the First Lady was presented with a bouquet of yellow roses, the official state flower of Texas. Now, however, upon descending from Air Force One at Dallas' Love Field, that tradition suddenly changed. "In Dallas they gave me red roses," Jackie would recall a week after the assassination. "I thought how funny, red roses—so the seat was full of blood and red roses."[56]

As the motorcade set out on its 11-mile route to the city's center, the frightening predictions about the day seemed exaggerated. Early that morning, Dallas Police Chief Jesse Curry had declared on television that the police department would tolerate no nonsense during the President's visit. Without mentioning recent death threats received by his office, Curry made it clear that Dallas would be free of incidents and demonstrations by "extremists." But what passed elsewhere as extremism was no more than an exercise in common sense and honest patriotism to some in Dallas. In their opinion, all politics and politicians to their left were traitors to a sacred nation under siege by communists. They believed the threat to be an inside one, and the President its proxy, especially because he had not only appeased the Kremlin, but even joined with the "Negroes" pressing for equality. (Dallas extremists tended to concentrate more on the enemy in Washington than the one in Moscow.)

As the Kennedys began their trip to downtown Dallas, some of the posters held up to the passing motorcade expressed outrage at the civil-rights movement. Some spectators—the sullen more ominously than the boisterous—waved Confederate flags. But the menace in the air seemed to come from something more substantial than the hisses of high school students and the ugliest of the posters and signs: "KENNEDY GO HOME!" "IN 1964, GOLDWATER AND FREEDOM." "HELP KENNEDY STAMP OUT DEMOCRACY." "MR. PRESIDENT,

BECAUSE OF YOUR SOCIALIST TENDENCIES AND...SURRENDER TO COM-
MUNISM I HOLD YOU IN COMPLETE CONTEMPT." And "YOUR [sic] A TRAI-
TOR." The anger in the air seemingly distilled all the resentment the people of
Dallas, Texas harbored towards the young President.

Although such hostility later became more intense in the memories of some
spectators than in reality, it was not invented. Seasoned observers, including
Texan politicians who had joined Kennedy's party, winced at what they saw in
the streets and felt in the atmosphere.

The weather had improved, and the President's car proceeded without its
bubbletop, which, when screwed and bolted to the car, covered almost the
entire passenger section, from the back of the rear seat to the windshield.
Together with Jack and Jackie, Governor and Mrs. Connally rode in the open
dark blue Lincoln. It was followed by a large Secret Service car carrying agents in
sunglasses, some of whom had spent much of the night before drinking at the
Cellar, a late-night bar in Fort Worth. The third car was another Lincoln, this
one rented for the Vice President and Lady Bird Johnson. (Senator Yarborough
was, at last, ensconced with Johnson.)

Midway between the city's limits and its heart, an increasingly cheerful
Kennedy saw small children behind a sign asking him to stop and shake their
hands. He complied, prompting shrieking delight, then stopped a second time
to greet a company of nuns. In between, throngs responded to every wave of
Jackie's hand, gloved in impeccable white. "Jackeee!" Far more aware than she
of the vote-power of being seen in person, the President twice asked her to
remove her sunglasses.

Kennedy's gloom had clearly begun to lift. The turnout for the motorcade
was increasingly large and enthusiastic. The city's official reception committee
consisted of nine Republicans, two conservative Democrats, and a sole liberal
from the Justice Department. This defiant assemblage was a calculated demonstration of conservative interests, purposely lacking sympathetic representation.
Evidently, the city fathers wanted their message delivered loud and clear, but
they had not counted on the Kennedys' ability to capture a crowd. His charisma,
and hers, appealed to the grass roots of Dallas, bypassing the civic leaders.

It was magic. To those predicting riots, everything seemed backwards. Dallas
was swept up in the glamour of the moment. A reporter in the press bus behind
the limousines referred to the turnout as "a whale of a lot of people." The
reporter's colleagues concluded that Kennedy would surely be re-elected next
year. Even Governor Connally, riding in the Lincoln, surprisingly conceded to
the President that he could probably carry Texas in 1964.

At 12:21 p.m., the procession took a sharp right turn at the Dallas City Jail
and began the last leg of the inner-city route, along 13 blocks of Main Street.
Again, the size and warmth of the crowd was startling. Main Street was a prover-
bial sea of humanity, a canal seemingly filled by most of the city's 750,000 residents. Cheering, roaring throngs were packed ten deep, from the gutters to the
buildings.

In the windows of those buildings, some of the faces were hard. A stone-faced H. L. Hunt watched the tumult from his seventh-floor office in the Mercantile Building, which could have been a model for "Dallas," the later television series. But the street—at this point, flanked by banks and expensive shops; further down, by pawn shops and other cheaper establishments—belonged to Kennedy, even more than in the three previous cities. His "thank you, thank you" as he and Jackie waved could not be heard, even by the others in his car. Nellie Connally, the Governor's wife, called to him. "You sure can't say Dallas doesn't love you, Mr. President."

"No, you can't," Kennedy smiled. Farther back in the procession, Evelyn Lincoln remarked with delighted surprise that they had come through all of Dallas without even a single demonstration.

The motorcade's lead car, driven by Police Chief Curry, reached the end of Main Street just before 12:29. It turned right onto Houston Street, the eastern border of a triangular area named Dealey Plaza, named after E. M. "Ted" Dealey, founder of the *Dallas Morning News*. In the offices of that newspaper, Ted's son Joe—the man who had published the black-bordered ad—permitted secretaries to watch the proceedings on his television set. The young women were glued to the screen. In a moment, the motorcade would be at a triple underpass that marked the end of the route, then pick up speed—perhaps a little more than planned, for the party was behind schedule—on the Stemmons Freeway leading to the Trade Mart, where Kennedy would make another speech, this one featuring a full salvo at his right-wing critics. Aides and Texas Congressmen, who had an advance copy, wondered whether the president would consider toning the speech down. He would not.

Arrival at the Trade Mart was scheduled for 12:30. After lunch, there would be another short hop to much-less-hostile Austin, then a weekend at the Johnson ranch—not an entirely pleasant prospect with the current tension between the President and Vice President.

After a cloudy morning, the Texas sun beat down. It was so bright Jacqueline Kennedy kept slipping on her sunglasses despite the President's reminders that one reason for their trip was to show themselves, to win crowds for next year's presidential election. Waving and smiling in the Lincoln was hot, hard work, especially for a First Lady who had not packed the right clothes and could not quite conquer her disdain for what she considered the vulgar aspects of politics.

But relief was in sight. The motorcade was nearly over. A few more blocks and they would arrive at the luncheon site, the new, air-conditioned International Trade Mart on the city's north side.

The lead car traveled one block on Houston Street, the eastern border of Dealey Plaza, then swung left onto Elm Street. The second turning, which was wider than 90 degrees because Elm Street ran on an angle rather than perpendicular to Houston Street, was regarded as a minor security concern. But it would slow the President's car, making him an easier target for

assailant, the Secret Service had decided on this route because only Elm Street provided access to the freeway that led to the Trade Mart. In order to reach the freeway directly from Main Street, the motorcade would have had to jump a low curb.[57]

The Killing

"I fight for communism... In the event of war, I would kill any American who put on a uniform in defense of the American government—any American."
—Lee Harvey Oswald in a letter to his brother Robert[58]

"Castro knew Kennedy had to do something before the election, so Castro had to act first."
—Carlos Bringuier, Cuban Student Directorate delegate[59]

"Personally, I consider Kennedy responsible for everything."
—Fidel Castro in an interview, November 22, 1963, minutes before he heard the news of Kennedy's death[60]

The motorcade slowed to a crawl as it made the 110-degree turn from Houston to Elm. The northwest corner of that intersection was occupied by the seven-story Texas School Book Depository. On the sixth floor, Lee Oswald crouched against a windowsill. Dealey Plaza, the triangular-shaped park bordering the western edge of the city, lay in the palm of his hand from his sixth-story vantage point. Rifle accuracy is usually measured in distances of hundreds of yards. In this case, the distance to a car on Elm Street below was slightly over 100 feet, almost point-blank in target-practice terms.

Oswald waited. He had been alone for at least fifteen minutes, and most likely thirty-five. One employee vacillated as to whether she had seen Oswald in the lunch room at 12:15, while the rest were unanimous that he wasn't there. Other workers clearly remember leaving Oswald alone on the sixth floor at about 11:55 a.m. when they took the elevator down to lunch. Oswald therefore had plenty of time to stack book cartons around the window and to reassemble the two-piece rifle (an FBI man later did it in six minutes, using only a dime— two minutes with a screwdriver.)[61] Co-worker Harold Norman remembers seeing Oswald:

At approximately ten o'clock that morning, Junior Jarman and myself were on the first floor looking out towards Elm Street. Oswald walked up and asked us, "What is everybody looking for? What is everybody waiting on?" So we told him we were waiting on the President to come by. He put his hand in his pocket and laughed and walked away. I thought maybe he's just been happy that morning or something. He was glad the President was coming through. He acted as though he didn't know, but I kind of think he did know. I don't know where he went—if he went upstairs or downstairs or whatever. I didn't see him any more till late that afternoon when they captured him on TV.[62]

This strange reaction has always stayed with Norman, who now suspects that Oswald's was a knowing laugh.

By 12:30, the Presidential limousine had turned onto Houston street, and was coming directly toward Lee Oswald and the Book Depository. Through the four-power scope, Kennedy must have appeared to be inches from Oswald. Two things might have kept him from shooting at this point: first, hundreds of eyes on the street below were now facing Oswald's building as they watched Kennedy approach it—too many potential witnesses. If he just waited until the car made the turn down Elm Street, Oswald may have decided, these same potential witnesses would all have their backs to him as he shot. Secondly, Oswald had already decided to employ a classic military firing strategy known as "downwind shooting"—it is much easier to track a moving target "going away" from a high perch than approaching it. If Oswald had attempted a shot on Main Street, he would have had to constantly lower his rifle in order to follow the target as it neared his building. Going down Elm, Kennedy would appear as a relatively stationary target.

The moment Lee Oswald had long-prepared for had at last arrived. Even though he probably hadn't chosen his target while living in New Orleans, he had started practicing there to shoot someone. (As previously mentioned, Marina and her neighbors were often disturbed in the evening by his rapid-fire "dry runs" on the screened-in porch.) He had continued to hone his skills at the Dallas shooting ranges, impressing witnesses with his ability at 200 yards. Step by inexorable step had delivered him to this juncture. Now, as Kennedy's limousine turned below his window, the target distance was a mere 30 yards, referred to by rifle enthusiasts as "shooting fish in a barrel" distance. However, Oswald initially resisted the temptation to shoot "the fish"—his arm-rest boxes were aligned for a later shot. (In addition to constructing a four-foot high wall of boxes behind him, Oswald had arranged three boxes against the half-opened windowsill.) The boxes were angled to allow him a rifle rest, affording a "downwind" shot into the middle of Elm Street. Oswald assumed his crouch, resting the rifle on its perch.

On the street below, fifteen-year-old Amos Lee Euins, standing on a concrete pedestal across from the Depository, noticed something protruding from the sixth floor window. "I could see everything. I saw what I thought was a pipe. I saw it ahead of time... I never realized it was a gun until the shooting started."[63]

Also on Elm Street was a man with extraordinary distance vision, Howard Brennan. Brennan would later testify that he could read license plates on cars over 200 feet away, and that God had allowed him to be the main witness to the shooting because of "my gift of super eyesight." Before the shooting started, Brennan saw Oswald pacing around inside the southeast corner window of the sixth floor. He later recalled: "As I looked at the man, it struck me how unsmiling and calm he was. He didn't seem to feel one bit of excitement. His face was almost expressionless... He seemed preoccupied."[64] The Lincoln Presidential limousine had just turned below Lee Oswald's perch.

—◇—

"It's always better to take advantage of your chances as they come along."
—Lee Oswald, in a letter to his brother Robert (March 1963)

"I would describe Lee Oswald at the time I saw him as being potentially explosive."
—Dr. Renatus Hartogs, court-appointed psychiatrist, assigned to the adolescent Lee Oswald[65]

What follows involves some obvious speculation about Oswald's thought processes. However, it is speculation derived from over twenty years of research into what considerations Oswald had to deal with in those crucial moments:

When the President's back first appeared to Oswald, he could resist no longer. Without waiting for Kennedy to clear a tree and arrive in the planned "target zone," Oswald made the impulsive mistake of attempting a quick "shot from the hip." This was a tendency first observed by Oswald's Russian friends. When in Minsk, he had joined a hunting club. On one occasion, a fellow rabbit hunter, Leonid Tsagoika, noticed this quirk:

Suddenly a shot rang out. I asked Oswald, "Why are you shooting?" He said, "Look, look, a hare!" The others fired too but missed. And then we all stopped and discussed why he had shot too soon. He explained that, because the hare had started from underneath his feet, he was startled and shot.[66]

Now, Oswald was again startled by the closeness of his prey. He pulled out of his military shooting crouch, and took a step back from the window to gain a reasonable chance at the severely-angled target below. Even though he had to remove the rifle from its armrest, and even though this unplanned-for shot was probably obstructed by the upper frame of the half-opened windowsill, Oswald fired his first shot. It missed badly, with its final resting place never determined (most likely it buried itself deep in the middle section of turf within the triangular-shaped plaza).

Because Oswald had taken a step back into the building, the building itself absorbed much of the sound of the first shot, thus sounding muffled to the motorcade participants and observers—like a firecracker, as they later testified.

With his adrenaline now pumping ferociously, Oswald ejected the spent shell and placed his rifle back in its planned armrest. He had to wait five seconds, which must have seemed an eternity, for the limousine to emerge from the partial obscurity of the tree. He would thus fire his second shot from the military crouch in which he had proved so proficient while in the Marines.

Amos Euins looked back up at the "pipe" extending from the sixth-floor window. This time he saw more detail—he saw the shooter. Later, he recalled seeing "the rifle laying across his hand, and I could see his hand on the trigger part."[67]

Nineteen-year-old James Worrell was also standing on Elm Street, directly below Oswald's sixth floor lair. "I looked up—just straight up," he recalled. "I saw the rifle, about six inches of it. I saw about four inches of the barrel...but it had a long stock...I saw about two inches [of the stock]."[68]

When Oswald regained sight of his target, the President was still a mere 60 yards away. Kennedy appeared stationary as his driver took the car directly away from Oswald at a snail's pace—9 miles per hour. If Oswald had decided to sight in the target with his four-power scope, the President's head would have filled his field of view. But at this distance, even using only the fixed iron sights on the rifle barrel, it was an easy shot. For a trained shooter like Oswald, this was a "gimme." Again he squeezed the trigger.

James Worrell was still looking at the rifle as the shot rang out. Like the witnesses at the shooting range the previous weekend, Worrell saw "what you might call a little flash of fire" as the bullet escaped the rifle barrel.[69]

The extremely dense Mannlicher Carcano bullet hit the President at the junction of the neck and back, just to the right of the spinal cord. Experts believe that the pressure exerted by this spinal cord blow so severely injured the President as to render him a quadriplegic. The President's physical reaction to the shot—the involuntary raising of his arms known as "Thorburn's response"— indicated to many experts that the shock to Kennedy's mid-brain was severe. Conceivably, the injury could have prevented this area of the brain from performing its breathing control function. In short, this injury alone could have proved fatal. The trauma to the nervous system also mercifully left Kennedy unconscious to the horrible shot yet to come. Encountering no hard bone, the bullet traversed the President's neck unscathed, exiting at the base of the front of the neck.

The slowed-down bullet tumbled erratically. Sitting in the lower seat in front of and slightly to the left of Kennedy, Governor Connally was next in line for the projectile, which hit him lengthwise just below his right armpit. Coursing through his chest, the back end of the bullet shattered five inches of rib bone, leaving the base of the bullet flattened. This collision also forced the full metal-jacketed bullet to extrude some of its inner lead core out of the rear portion. These lead fragments would later be removed from various parts of Connally's body.

Now traveling much more slowly, the bullet exited Connally's chest, only to find his waiting wrist. One of Connally's wrist bones was fractured in this encounter. The bullet ricocheted, hitting Connally in the thigh, moving far too slowly to penetrate the flesh. The bullet would later be recovered at Parkland Hospital, having fallen down Connally's pants leg onto a stretcher.

By this time, the Secret Service, who had mistaken the first shot for a backfire or a firecracker, realized what was happening. Emory Roberts of the Secret Service shouted "Go!" and Jack Ready (assigned to the President) and Clint Hill (assigned to the First Lady) finally left the Secret Service backup car ("The Queen Mary") and raced to the Presidential limousine. Hill looked over his shoulder for Ready, who had stumbled. As Hill approached the rear bumper of the limousine, the impossible happened—Kennedy's driver, agent Bill Greer, slowed down the car.

With three advance cars and eight motorcycles in front of the Presidential limousine, and none of them aware of what was happening, Greer had no place to go. Regardless of what Greer did next, Oswald was sure to find his mark again three seconds later—with the president still only 88 yards away. But Greer made an easy shot virtually unmissable when he stepped on the brake pedal in order to turn and try to observe the President. Thus, the car was almost brought to a standstill, with Greer looking directly at "Lancer," Kennedy's Secret Service code name.

With his target positioned perfectly, Oswald squeezed the trigger and achieved his best result. This bullet was a direct hit, striking Kennedy in the cowlick area of his head. Because it was a "clean hit," the bullet did not dramatically force Kennedy forward. But it did slightly push him ahead nonetheless. Immediately thereafter, other forces took effect. As the bullet traversed the right side of Kennedy's brain, the area behind the bullet created a pressure cavity that literally caused the inside of his head to explode. Seeking to exit the area of least resistance in the skull, this pressurized brain matter then located the bullet exit wound just above Kennedy's right ear. The explosive force of the exiting brain matter created a "jet effect," jerking the President's head violently to the rear. This reverse head snap would be the hook upon which dozens of conspiracy theories were hung—the theories that a shot had been fired from the front, thus refuting the lone gunner conclusion. *(For more on these details, see Appendix A: The Shooting of the President.)*

The President died instantly. As one of the attending physicians at Parkland Memorial Hospital told the author, "He was dead before his car went under the triple overpass [50 feet from where Kennedy was shot]." By now, Clint Hill was ready to jump onto the rear bumper, where Jackie had crawled out to meet him. Hill had long been assigned to Jackie, during which time they had become extremely close. "She depended on him for everything," recalls Mike Howard, a fellow agent and close friend. "She always ran to him as her protector."

Hill would later tell Howard that when Jackie realized that the President was hit, she instinctively turned, looking for him, and screamed, "Clint!"[70] Hill, approaching the now-accelerating limousine, later told Marty Underwood that he yelled back at Jackie, "Tell him to slow down!" The plea went unheard, and driver Greer stepped on the gas. With his first attempt, Hill missed his foothold, barely hanging on. It is a wonder more fatalities didn't occur under the circumstances. Both Hill and Jackie could have easily fallen off the trunk as Greer hit the gas, and, if they had, they might have been run over by the accelerating back-up car, the "Queen Mary." Also, when the limousine made it under the triple overpass, it nearly collided with its forward motorcycle escorts, which hadn't yet accelerated. Witnesses have said that in the shadows of the overpass, there came a cacophony of screeching tires and swerving vehicles.

For a third and final time, Amos Euins looked up at the sixth floor window and watched, this time as the shooter "pulled the gun back in the window." Reporters and cameramen riding in the convertible cars in the motorcade also saw the rifle. Among them were Malcolm Couch and Bob Jackson. They also saw the gun being drawn back into the Depository.[71]

At the time of the shooting, the people closest to Oswald's position were three Depository workers, all of them watching the motorcade from the window one floor directly below the assassin. Bonnie Ray Williams, Junior Jarman, and Harold Norman's recollections were clear and consistent about what happened. Norman repeated them in 1993:

> *At the time of the shooting, James Jarman and myself were on the fifth floor. Somehow he [Bonnie Ray Williams] lost us. But he did come down to find us just before the motorcade came through. So he joined us and we pulled up some cartons, standing in the window waiting on the motorcade. And as the motorcade came by, we started looking and we had a good view. And all of a sudden, we hear something. "Boom, ack, ack, boom, ack, ack, boom." I told Jarman, "I believe somebody's shooting at the President." And he said, "Yeah, that certainly sounds like it." And then by this time we looked over and there was some debris or dirt or something fell on top of Jarman's head. And that was three of the shells I heard on the floor. And when the police officer asked about it, we told them about it and they went up there and that is what they found up there on the sixth floor. Three empty shell cartridges up there.[72]*

Norman was thus the first person to deduce that the shooter was not only in the sixth floor window of the Depository, but that he was using a bolt-action rifle (making the "ack-ack" sound). He summed up his experience: "I could hear the sound of the click, I could hear the shells hitting the floor, I could hear everything. Three shots. No doubt in my mind."[73]

After the shooting, Norman and his friends walked out into the street in front of the Depository. Watching them emerge, Howard Brennan instantly recognized the men he had seen watching from the fifth floor window. Brennan saw them just as clearly as he saw the man shooting one floor above. But unlike Norman and his friend, Brennan had actually seen everything that they correctly deduced was happening. Brennan later wrote of his experience of staring directly at Lee Oswald as he killed the President:

> *What I saw made my blood run cold. Poised in the corner window of the sixth floor was the same young man I had noticed several times before the motorcade arrived. There was one difference—this time he held a rifle in his hands, pointing toward the Presidential car. He steadied the rifle against the cornice and while he moved quickly, he didn't seem to be in any kind of panic...Then came the sickening sound of the second shot...I wanted to cry, I wanted to scream, but I couldn't utter a sound...He was aiming again and I wanted to pray, to beg God to somehow make him miss the target...The sight became so fixed in my mind that I'll never forget it for as long as I live...Then another shot rang out. To my amazement, the man still stood there at the window. He*

didn't appear to be rushed. There was no particular emotion visible on his face except for a slight smirk. It was a look of satisfaction, as if he had accomplished what he set out to do… [Then] he simply moved away from the window until he disappeared from my line of vision."[74]

Brennan reported what he saw to Dallas police inspector Herbert Sawyer, whom he met outside the Depository. As a result of this encounter, an accurate description of Oswald was quickly dispatched on police radios all over Dallas. That night at the police lineup, Brennan refused to positively identify Oswald. It was, however, a calculated refusal. Oswald could have accomplices at-large, and Brennan, fearing for his family's safety, worried that word would get out that he was the only man who could identify the killer. Why invite difficulty, he decided, "since they already had the man for the murder, that he wasn't going to be set free to escape and get out of the country immediately, and I could very easily…get in touch with [the FBI] to see that the man didn't get loose." Brennan later admitted to the official investigators, "But with all fairness, I could have positively identified the man." As he wrote in his autobiography, "I knew I could never forget the face I had seen in the window on the sixth floor of the Texas School Book Depository."

By the time Brennan encountered police inspector Sawyer outside the Depository building, Oswald had stashed his rifle between some boxes on the far side of the sixth floor, and had left the building weaponless. He proceeded to walk east on Elm Street for seven blocks, where he caught a bus heading in the direction of his Beckley Street room. He asked for and received a bus transfer slip—it's unclear where the transfer was to. It was 12:36 p.m., six minutes having elapsed since Oswald had shot off the right side of President Kennedy's head.[75]

President Kennedy arrived at Parkland Memorial Hospital in a matter of minutes. Emergency procedures were performed at a frenetic pace, although Kennedy had arrived in what physicians refer to as an "agonal state"—no blood pressure, and a rather meaningless sporadic cardiac sputter. He was clinically dead. But in the frenzy to do something, the attending medical staff, busy performing a tracheostomy and "cutdowns" for liquid replenishment, were too preoccupied to sort through Kennedy's shock of hair and see what they were up against.

Baltimore-based emergency room physician Dr. Robert Artwohl says he understands what the Dallas doctors were thinking. "We all have the same response," says Artwohl. "Some deaths are just harder to accept—a five-year-old child, for example—and certainly a President of the United States. So you proceed, hoping this case will be the one in a million where a miracle takes place."[76] William Manchester later wrote of the scene:

Everything Parkland had was going for Kennedy now. Ringer's solution, hydrocortisone, and the first pint of transfused blood were entering his vessels through the two catheters. A nasogastric tube, thrust through Kennedy's nose and fitted behind his trachea, was clearing away possible sources of nausea in his stomach. Bilateral chest tubes had been placed in both pleural spaces to suck out chest matter through the cuffed tube and prevent lung collapse. Now, in a treatment older than the invention of the most primitive medical device... [Dr.] Perry was stroking and palpitating the tough, well-muscled flesh over the President's rib cage, trying to coax a single beat from the heart until his own sinews ached and begged for relief.[77]

After some twenty minutes of this futile activity, the chief physicians, Drs. Malcolm Perry, Pepper Jenkins, and Kemp Clark, finally scrutinized the President's head and realized the hopelessness of their task. It was then that Jenkins declared, "We have no way of resuscitating him." Jenkins later recalled, "That was the first time anyone looked at it [the head wound]."[78]

In later years, the Parkland doctors would give descriptions of Kennedy's head wound that differed from the description on the autopsy protocol. The Dallas description, placing the large wound more rearward, seemed to indicate a shot from the front, exiting the rear. These statements fed the suspicion that there had been multiple shooters in Dealey Plaza.

When these statements are read in toto, however, one sees that the Dallas doctors often prefaced their statements with phrases like "I really didn't get a good look at it, but...," or "I could be wrong, because we never lifted his head...,"or "I was at the other end of the table, but I glimpsed out of the corner of my eye..." Critics never include these qualifications in their accounts of the Dallas statements. One of the attending physicians, Dr. James Carrico, recalls, "Everyone in that room was trying to save a life, not figure out forensics...We were trying to save a life, not worrying about entry and exit wounds." Dr. Pepper Jenkins told the *Journal of the American Medical Association (JAMA)* in 1992:

I was standing at the head of the table in the position the anesthesiologist most often assumes—closest to the President's head. My presence there and the President's great shock of hair were such that it was not visible to those standing down each side of the gurney where they were carrying out their resuscitative maneuvers.[79]

The bottom line is that the overwhelming majority of those in the crowded trauma room agree with the Bethesda autopsy findings of a rear-entering shot.[80]

While the President's medical attendants were coming to grips with the impossibility of their task, Governor Connally's physicians were hard at work in the next room. His "sucking" chest wound and collapsed right lung were serious, but not critical if given prompt attention, which they were. After two hours of surgery, his lung and torn muscles were repaired, and his condition stabilized.

Although Dr. Kemp Clark pronounced John Kennedy dead at 1 p.m., the official announcement was delayed for one hour. During that hour, JFK was given the last rites of the Catholic Church, and his body was prepared for transport to Air Force One. Before the lid was closed on his coffin, Jacqueline Kennedy placed her wedding ring on her husband's finger.[81]

Hickory Hill

"There's so much bitterness. I thought they'd get one of us, but Jack, after all he'd been through, never worried about it…I thought it would be me."
—**Robert F. Kennedy to Ed Guthman, November 22, 1963**[82]

"J. Edgar Hoover's calling," yelled Ethel Kennedy. Her husband Robert was home at Hickory Hill for a working lunch with two of his Justice Department assistants, Robert Morganthau and Silvio Mollo. The men were sitting by the pool eating clam chowder and tuna fish, the luncheon having started in a typical RFK manner—with a swim.

At that moment, Bobby Kennedy suspected that something was wrong because "he wouldn't be calling me here."

"I have news for you," Hoover said. "The President's been shot."

"What? Is it serious?" Bobby responded.

"I think it's serious. I'll call you back when I find out more."

Hoover sounded matter-of-fact, Bobby later recalled—not a bit upset or sympathetic. He was, Bobby stated, "not quite as excited as if he was reporting the fact that he found a Communist on the faculty of Howard University."[83]

Robert Morganthau watched as Bobby turned away, a look of horror on his face, clapping his hand to his mouth. He then turned to his aides and screamed, "Jack's been shot! It might be fatal." Bobby then went back to the main house, walking around in a state of shock. Later, followed by Ethel, he went up to their bedroom to try calling Dallas. He was simultaneously preparing to pack for an emergency flight to Texas.

Eventually, RFK's call to Parkland Memorial Hospital was put through—he wasn't sure to whom, though he believes it was to Secret Service agent Clint Hill. Bobby remembered the conversation:

They said that it was very serious. And I asked if he was conscious, and they said he wasn't, and I asked if they'd gotten a priest, and they said they had… Then, I said, will you call me back, and he said yes, and then he—Clint Hill called me back, and I think it was about thirty minutes after I talked to Hoover…and he said, "The President's dead."[84]

"Oh, he's dead!" Bobby cried.

In his traumatized state, Bobby proceeded, as if on auto-pilot, to call family members, friends, and Air Force One. He also called CIA director John McCone at Agency headquarters, which was only a short distance from Hickory Hill. McCone came over immediately. When he arrived, Bobby asked him if any CIA people could have been involved in the shooting. McCone, a fellow Catholic, assured him, in a way that convinced the Attorney General, that there had been no CIA involvement. Then Hoover called back.

The FBI director was, for once, not on top of the news. He was calling to tell Bobby that the president's wounds appeared critical.

"You may be interested to know," Bobby said, "that my brother is dead!"

With that, he slammed down the phone.[85]

The next day, while the rest of the world mourned in front of their television sets, and a vast team of investigators pursued a still-hot trail, J. Edgar Hoover went to the race track.[86]

Washington

In Washington, when the news from Dallas arrived, the participants in Bobby Kennedy's "secret war" were still hard at work at the CIA safe house. At the same time, RFK's appointed exile leader, Harry Williams, was ensconced at the Ebbitt Hotel on H Street, NW, with journalist Haynes Johnson. Johnson had been hand-picked by Bobby Kennedy to chronicle the Bay of Pigs story; the Ebbitt was the CIA's hotel of choice for lodging exile partners in the Cuba Project.

Soon the phone was ringing. Answering the call, Harry Williams immediately recognized the Boston accent on the other end. It was his friend Bobby Kennedy, who by now had gotten it into his head that one of his plots against Castro may have boomeranged. Kennedy asked Williams to pass the phone to Haynes Johnson. Johnson later recalled, "Robert Kennedy was utterly in control of his emotions when he came on the line, and sounded almost studiously brisk as he said, 'One of your [Cuban] boys did it.'"[87]

Safely distanced from the exile meetings, Desmond FitzGerald was at lunch at the City Tavern Club in Georgetown when the call came. His executive assistant, Sam Halpern, remembered that the usually ruddy-cheeked FitzGerald emerged from the call "white as a ghost."

"The President's been shot," FitzGerald said.

"I hope this has nothing to do with the Cubans," said Halpern as they raced across the Potomac to CIA headquarters. The two were silent for the rest of the ride. Nothing needed to be said: Both men were thinking the same thing. Both knew that Bobby and FitzGerald had ignored Castro's threat of September 7, and both had proceeded full steam with the AM/LASH plot. And FitzGerald had been warned that Castro might be wise to the plot. Castro most assuredly was aware of the planned-for coup, which had been exposed in Miami newspapers. The question now crystallized: Had Castro struck first? Both men knew what was then underway in Paris, and how devastating it would be to all involved if it became known.[88]

The next day, FitzGerald went to see Director McCone's assistant, Walt Elder. He confessed to meeting with Cubela regarding a future shipment of weapons, but withheld the most explosive information—that, at Bobby's request, he had had his agents furnish Cubela with a poison pen at the very moment Kennedy was driving through Dallas. However, Elder sensed that FitzGerald was not revealing all that was troubling him. Years later, Evan Thomas wrote:

> *"Des was normally imperturbable, but he was very disturbed about his involvement," recalled Elder. The director's assistant couldn't understand why*

FitzGerald seemed so distraught, wringing his hands and shaking his head. "I thought Des was overreacting," says Elder.[89]

Elder, like most everyone else, was unaware of the troublesome linkages of Oswald, Cubela, Mexico City, and Bobby's New Orleans-based exiles.

Paris

It was evening in Paris when President Kennedy was shot. AM/LASH's all-important meeting with the Bobby Kennedy/Des FitzGerald envoy, Nestor Sanchez, was progressing smoothly. They were going to change history.

But just moments earlier, Lee Oswald had beat them to the punch, had stopped them dead in their tracks. The CIA AM/LASH file reflects the instant effect the shooting had on the meeting: "The situation changed when the case officer left the meeting to discover that President Kennedy had been assassinated. Because of this fact, plans with AM/LASH changed and it was decided that we could have no part in the assassination of a government leader (including Castro)."[90]

Cubela recalls, "[The meeting] ended in a hurried abrupt manner because of a telephone call received by the CIA person [Sanchez] and it said that President Kennedy had been killed."[91]

Sardinia, Italy

Bill Harvey, the CIA's former Mongoose coordinator, was unconscious. His drinking had progressed from habit to disease after his excile to Italy a year earlier. When the telex noting Kennedy's murder was received by his deputy, Harvey had to be awakened from a late-day martini stupor. The man who hated the Kennedys, both for their treatment of him and for their naive directives regarding Cuba, staggered to his feet.

What he said to his deputy should be taken with Harvey's condition in mind, and the fact that there is only one witness to his comments, but that witness was so stunned that he wrote it down for posterity. "This was bound to happen," blustered Harvey, "and it's probably good that it did." Soon, when Harvey discovered that his deputy was spending time helping local officials with condolences, he sent the deputy packing for the U.S. "I haven't got time for this kind of crap," Harvey told him.[92]

Love Field/Dallas

Aboard Air Force One, chaos reigned. Lyndon Johnson, the new president, understandably, feared a wide foreign conspiracy, and wanted the presidential plane to take off quickly. But he was in a quandary. He refused to leave Dallas without Jacqueline Kennedy, and she wouldn't leave without her dead husband's body aboard the plane. Johnson thus ordered the Secret Service to bring the body immediately from the hospital, local ordinances notwithstanding.

Robert and John Kennedy 1959

The Cuban Adversaries

These previously unpublished
CIA photos provide a glimpse
into the life of the young
Cuban revolutionaries.

CIA/Ross Crozier

Che Guevara 1959

Fidel Castro taking time off from guerrilla warfare for a smoke break.

Drilling Fidel's tooth using Singer Sewing equipment.

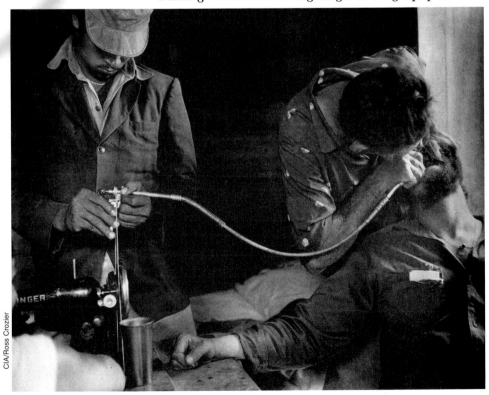

KENNEDY AND DULLES

November 28, 1961

JFK escorts longtime friend Allen Dulles to the dedication of the CIA's new headquarters in Langley, Va.

CIA

Kennedy then surprises Dulles with the National Security Medal.

Dulles Collection, Princeton University

Later, inside the new building, Robert Kennedy beams in the background.

Dulles Collection, Princeton University

TWO YEARS LATER, RFK MADE CERTAIN DULLES PLAYED A KEY ROLE IN THE PANEL INVESTIGATING JFK'S DEATH.

William King Harvey

"Robert Kennedy was knowledgeable of the operation...and is in a very vulnerable position"

regard to the

(1) Testimony

A FLAT LIE

next said

McCone testified... Cuban leaders aros... ploring the alterna... MONGOOSE. (Mc... this suggestion, but ... "strong exception" to ... states:²

I took immediate exceptio... completely out of bound... concerned and th... papers, ...

I seriously doubt it

(6–7, 17), and that if he had ever been asked al... have disapproved. McCone testified:

I had no knowledge of any authorized plan or plan... request for authorization. Of course, during those da... for one person or another to say, "we ought to dispose ... no time did anyone come to me, or come to other auth... with a plan for the actual undertaking of an assassi... p. 3)

McCone also testified:

Senator Hart of Colorado: Did you ever discuss the s... with your predecessor, Mr. Dulles?
McCone: No, I did not.¹

(ii) *Testimony of Helms, Bissell, and other S...
Employees.*—Bissell was DDP under McCone for t... November 1961 until February 1962. Helms assu... DDP from Bissell and served throughout the bal... terms as Director.

Bissell testified about McCone's knowledge as follo...

Q. Your testimony is that you never discussed assass... McCone?
A. That is correct.
Q. * * * [D]id you tell McCone anything about that conv... Harvey in which you at least told him to take over the rela... criminal syndicate?
A. I don't remember so doing. (Bissell, 6/11/75, p. 19)

But Bissell is an honorable man.

Helms testified that he did not recall ever having ... assassination plots with McCone while the plots wer... When asked whether McCone was aware of the assas... against Castro, Helms testified:

No, it isn't my impression that I told him, at least I don't have a... unfortunately * * *. Mr. McCone is an honorable man. He has ... testifying, and all I can say is that I do not know specifically w... aware or not. (Helms, 6/13/75, pp. 90, 101–102)¹

Helms further testified:

Senator MONDALE: I believe Mr. McCone testified that he never i... of these attempts when he was Director. Would you have any reaso... with his testimony?
HELMS: Sir, I have always liked McCone and I don't want to get int... tion with him. He had access to Harvey and everybody else just the ... and he had regular access to the Attorney General.

*   *   *

Senator MONDALE: If you were a member of this Committee wouldn... sume that Mr. McCone was unaware of the assassination attempts w... were underway?
HELMS: I don't know how to answer that, Senator Mondale. He was ... in this up to his scuppers just the way everybody else was that was in i... just don't know. I have no reason to impugn his integrity. On the oth...

¹ Walt Elder, McCone's Executive Assistant, testified that Dulles gave McCone a... to twelve informal briefings between September and November 1961. He also ... Dulles and McCone travelled together on a briefing trip to Europe to enable Mc... get "up to speed" on CIA activities. (Elder, 8/13/75, p. 13)
² Helms testified that he first informed McCone about the plot using underworld ... in August 1963. See discussion *supra* at p. 107.

...informed of any activity that he thought was ser... and indeed under all circumstances you can imag... the exception of a situation in which Helms had ... him." (McManus, pp. 32–34)

McManus told the Committee that he had had ... prior to reading about them in the newspaper. ... stated in 1967 that McManus was aware of such ... ² In August 1963 Helms gave McCone a copy ... to the Attorney General. See discussion *infra* at ...

1. O'Connell & Edward... *have been close...* '65 (Possibly re O'C'... the little...

McCone that no such k... knowledge ... a Castro assassination." (Mc...

Like hell! did it he knew I was McNamara's idea!

nor do I, but... agreed he was not unthing disavow... and East officially chargeable with knowledge & approval...

In his own hand, Harvey criticizes the Church Report.

Documents courtesy Harvey family member.

"MONGOOSE was the most frustrating damn thing I've ever tackled."

General Edward Lansdale

Sam Halpern
"It was the Kennedy brothers demanding 'boom and bang' all over the island."

J.C. King receives the National Security Medal from Richard Helms.

KING, WHO PROPOSED THE ELIMINATION OF CASTRO, MAINTAINED A PRIVATE PHONE LINE TO JFK THROUGHOUT HIS PRESIDENCY. HE WAS ALSO IN TOUCH WITH RFK. THIS PHONE RECORD OF ONE CALL FROM KING TO RFK CONCERNS CUBANS BOBBY ASKED HIM ABOUT. ACCORDING TO JOHN GORDON, IT TOOK PLACE WHILE RFK WAS DIRECTING A CASTRO MURDER PLOT CENTERED IN GUANTANAMO, CUBA.

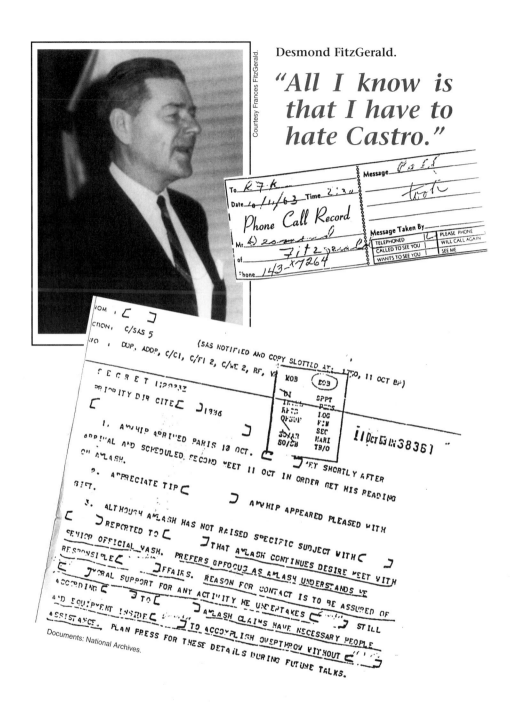

Courtesy Frances FitzGerald.

Desmond FitzGerald.

"All I know is that I have to hate Castro."

Documents: National Archives.

On October 11, 1963 AM/LASH informed Des ("C/SAS")
that he demanded GPFOCUS' (RFK's) approval for the
Castro hit. It was the same day Des called and spoke
with RFK. Two weeks later, Des met with AM/LASH in
Paris and told him he had RFK's support.

LEE HARVEY OSWALD

As a child in New York, Oswald often played hooky and went to the Bronx Zoo.

National Archives

National Archives

IN THE MARINES, OSWALD BEGAN MEETING MYSTERIOUSLY WITH OFFICIALS FROM THE CUBAN CONSULATE NEAR LOS ANGELES (PREVIOUSLY UNPUBLISHED PHOTO).

In Minsk

Oswald, pictured here wearing shades and surrounded by fellow radio factory workers, liked being a celebrity, but it soon wore off.

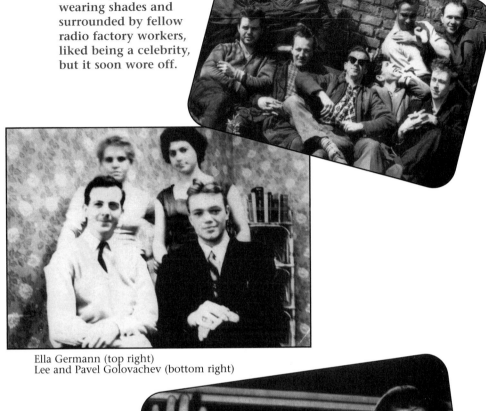

Ella Germann (top right)
Lee and Pavel Golovachev (bottom right)

All photos National Archives.

Lee and Marina on the train leaving Minsk, May 1962.

"Castro needs defenders"

Photo taken March 31, 1963.

In 1993, FBI Special Agent James Hosty revisits
the site of the famous backyard photos.

National Archives

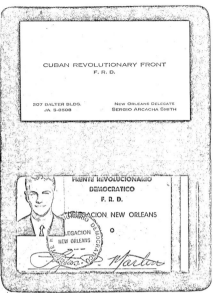

CUBAN REVOLUTIONARY FRONT
F. R. D.

207 BALTER BLDG.   NEW ORLEANS DELEGATE
JA. 5-8508   SERGIO ARCACHA SMITH

FRENTE REVOLUCIONARIO
DEMOCRATICO
F. R. D.

DELEGACION NEW ORLEANS

A page from Martens' 1967 letter to Arcacha discussing "the letter from Robert Kennedy."

–5–

I wanted to tell you this and I almost forgot. Remember the letter from Robert Kennedy, the one that said it was OK for us to do what we were doing? It was stolen with my briefcase in 1961 from Ferrie's house. Garrison is looking for that letter. I think he will use it to hurt us and Senator Kennedy if he finds it. I think I know who has it, but I cannot find him.

REPRODUCED AT THE NATIONAL ARCHIVES

Sergio Arcacha Smith
"Whenever we needed anything in New Orleans, I'd call Bobby Kennedy and he'd help us right away. He was always there for us."

Courtesy Sergio Arcacha Smith.

412

David William Ferrie

Ferrie at St. Mary's Seminary in Cleveland (previously unpublished).

Courtesy Julian Buznedo.

Ferrie with Bay of Pigs
veteran Julian Buznedo.

Ferrie's friends reunite in 1993 to share
"Big Easy" memories. (Left to right:
Layton Martens, Al Beauboeuf,
Morris Brownlee, Allen Campbell.)

Author's photo

The New Orleans delegation of the Cuban Revolutionary
Council posed with Ferrie's plane (previously unpublished).

Courtesy Julian Buznedo.

"THE WHITE HOUSE CUBANS"

With JFK at Palm Beach, December 1962 (previously unpublished).

Left to right: Alvaro Sanchez, Pepe San Roman, John Kennedy, Manuel Artime, Erneido Oliva, Enrique "Harry" Ruiz-Williams.

Left to right: Roberto San Roman, Manuel Artime, Ramon Ferrer, Robert Kennedy, Enrique Ruiz-Williams, Pepe San Roman, Erneido Oliva.

"LOS AMIGOS DE ROBERTO"

ON THE DAY OF THE BAY OF PIGS PRISONER RELEASE, HARRY
WILLIAMS CALLED RFK AT HOME. KENNEDY SAID,"YOU GOT IT
ENRIQUE.THIS IS IT.THE GUY WITH THE BEARD HAS ACCEPTED."

Courtesy Eleanor Rollo.

Left to right: Robert Kennedy, Enrique Ruiz-Williams, and James B. Donovan.

Cuban Coordinating Committee leader Cyrus Vance, presents Legion Merit
Medal to fellow CCC staffer General Alexander Haig. Mrs. Haig looks on.

Department of Defense

National Archives

Oswald's notes. On the streets of New
Orleans, he was learning of the White House
plans for a reinvasion of Cuba. He intended
to inform the Cubans in Mexico City.

V.T. LEE FURTHER ALERTED OSWALD TO
THESE PLANS. THE CIA BELIEVED V.T. LEE
WAS NOT ONLY ASSOCIATED WITH CUBAN
ASSASSINS, BUT WAS FUNDED BY HAVANA.

Photo: CIA

Oswald, the provocateur, stamped his fliers with the address of the Cuban exiles' "Grand Central Station"—544 Camp Street.

HANDS OFF CUBA!

Join the Fair Play for Cuba Committee

NEW ORLEANS CHARTER MEMBER BRANCH

Free literature, Lectures

LOCATION:

L. H. OSWALD
544 CAMP ST.
NEW ORLEANS, LA

EVERYONE WELCOME!

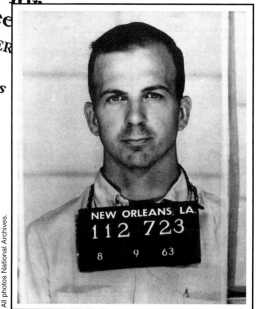

NEW ORLEANS, LA.

112 723

8 9 63

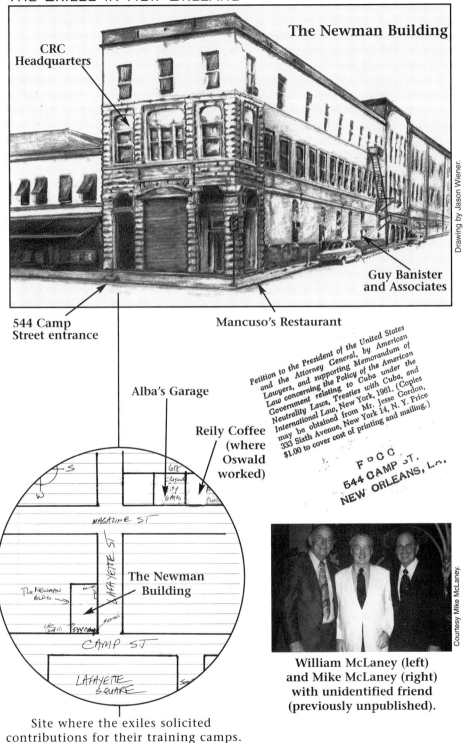

The Newman Building

CRC Headquarters

Guy Banister and Associates

544 Camp Street entrance

Mancuso's Restaurant

Alba's Garage

Reily Coffee (where Oswald worked)

Petition to the President of the United States and the Attorney General, by American Lawyers, and supporting Memorandum of Law concerning the Policy of the American Government relating to Cuba under the Neutrality Laws, Treaties with Cuba, and International Law, New York, 1961. (Copies may be obtained from Mr. Jesse Gordon, 333 Sixth Avenue, New York 14, N. Y. Price $1.00 to cover cost of printing and mailing.)

F□C C
544 CAMP ST.
NEW ORLEANS, La.

The Newman Building

Drawing by Jason Wiener.

Courtesy Mike McLaney.

William McLaney (left) and Mike McLaney (right) with unidentified friend (previously unpublished).

Site where the exiles solicited contributions for their training camps.

Dear Lemay,

These are important. Please put in a *very* safe place. Then forget until asked for them. BY <u>US</u> NOT U.S.

DO NOT READ or mention to Siox, or anyone

EDNA & John.

7810 4th Ave S

(over) St Petersburg Fla

**Lt. Commander
John Gordon, USN**

```
12.   Benes
13.   "Estrella"
14.   Sr. Balart
15.   Glassman
16.   ——  Pepa?  } 2 ex-Batista cops
17.   ???           }
18.   Bob Spohr
19.   Jose Maldonado *
20.   Jack Hodessett
21.   Capt Crepella
22.   Dave Lasher
23.   Tom Ewald
VI.   ── the veterinarian
      During ──g ones'
Intelligence ──── ' base in trailers
thoroughly briefing preparatory for ass ──── USN)
made Op 922H13).        ────
I can corroborate Officers certain activities in O
that there was an individual identified in key 1
number 10 key list who was competent and 45
assassination of either Fidel Castro and prepar
I did not know his identity already on the base
informed that he was identity and did not positively Cast
he was the Cuban introduced to him by number 4
shooting.        National Champion in both skeet and
```

```
I  37.
F  38.   Tony ──
G  39.   Airplane fr ──
H  40.   Boat from Jamaica
I  41.   Water plant manager, b ──
J  42.   Sgt Duggan
   43.   Capt USMC - Capt Yanochek
K.
L.
M.
N.
O.
P.
Q.
R.
S.
T.
U.
V.
W.
X.
```

Gordon, Lowery, Thomas, Hern
*Aces, Maldonado,
CASTROdad, SUAREz

* click key

Will explain many years later. Thanks, Tom!

Johnny

Tom,
Do not use a safe deposit box — or any place that can be quickly ordered open or searched by officials. Please do not leave in any spot that can be inadvertently discovered by anyone.

JG

"Duran was possibly an agent or source for the U.S."
–David Phillips, CIA, Mexico City

HSCA

Sylvia Duran

Courtesy Michael Scott (previously unpublished).

Win Scott

Oleg Nechiporenko

Author's photo

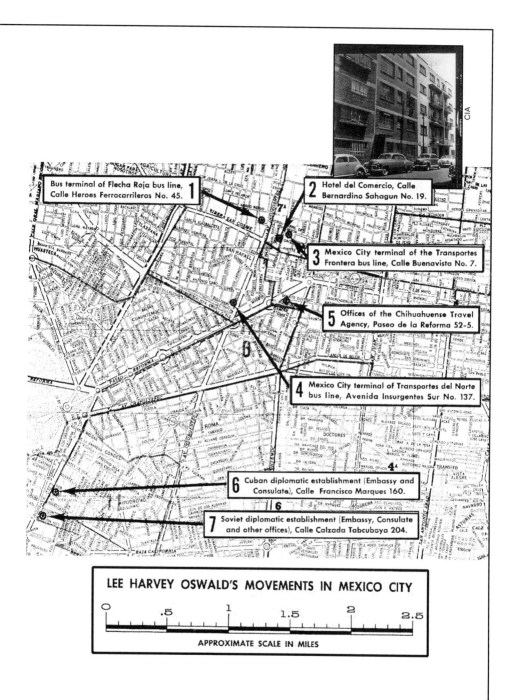

CIA

Bus terminal of Flecha Roja bus line, Calle Heroes Ferrocarrileros No. 45. **1**

2 Hotel del Comercio, Calle Bernardino Sahagun No. 19.

3 Mexico City terminal of the Transportes Frontera bus line, Calle Buenavista No. 7.

5 Offices of the Chihuahuense Travel Agency, Paseo de la Reforma 52-5.

4 Mexico City terminal of Transportes del Norte bus line, Avenida Insurgentes Sur No. 137.

6 Cuban diplomatic establishment (Embassy and Consulate), Calle Francisco Marques 160.

7 Soviet diplomatic establishment (Embassy, Consulate and other offices), Calle Calzada Tabcubaya 204.

LEE HARVEY OSWALD'S MOVEMENTS IN MEXICO CITY

0 .5 1 1.5 2 2.5

APPROXIMATE SCALE IN MILES

"We thought Oswald might be a dangerous potential defector...We kept a special watch on him and his activities [in Mexico City]."— **Win Scott**

"Track One"
Lisa Howard with Fidel Castro.

"Track Two"
AM/LASH (Rolando Cubela, left), with his intended victim Fidel Castro.

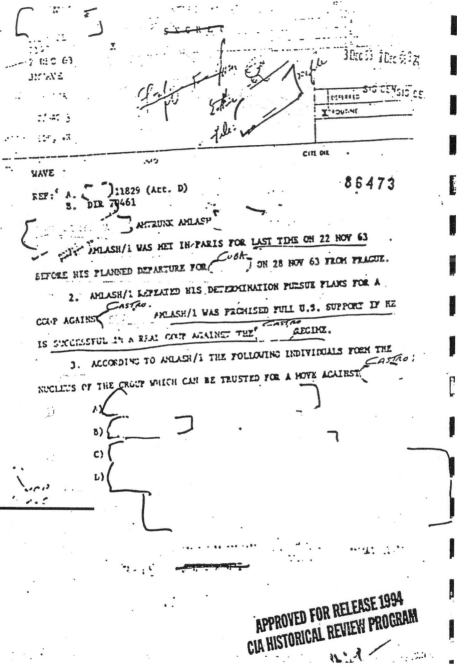

WAVE

REF: A. [   ]:1829 (Att. D)
     B. DIR 79461

86473

[   ] ANTRUNK AMLASH

1. AMLASH/1 WAS MET IN PARIS FOR LAST TIME ON 22 NOV 63
BEFORE HIS PLANNED DEPARTURE FOR [CUBA] ON 28 NOV 63 FROM PRAGUE.

2. AMLASH/1 REPEATED HIS DETERMINATION PURSUE PLANS FOR A
COUP AGAINST [CASTRO]. AMLASH/1 WAS PROMISED FULL U.S. SUPPORT IF HE
IS SUCCESSFUL IN A REAL COUP AGAINST THE [CASTRO] REGIME.

3. ACCORDING TO AMLASH/1 THE FOLLOWING INDIVIDUALS FORM THE
NUCLEUS OF THE GROUP WHICH CAN BE TRUSTED FOR A MOVE AGAINST [CASTRO]:

A) [   ]

B) [   ]

C) [   ]

D) [   ]

AM/LASH's CIA CASE, OFFICER NESTOR SANCHEZ, FILED THIS MEMO OF HIS NOVEMBER 22, 1963 MEETING WITH AM/LASH. SANCHEZ LATER DELETED ANY REFERENCE TO THE POISON PEN, AS ORDERED BY DES FITZGERALD.

Oswald's view from the Depository

The Motorcade

Taken the night of the assassination, this previously unpublished photo of the president's limousine, clearly shows the relationship between JFK's and John Conally's positions *(For details see Appendix A).*

All photos National Archives.

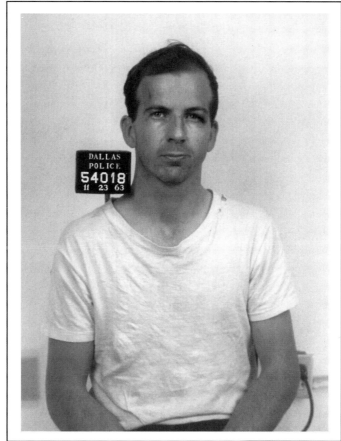

Dallas Municipal Archives

National Archives

LIKE OSWALD, GILBERTO LOPEZ WAS LINKED TO BOTH V.T.
LEE AND THE CUBAN CONSULATE IN LOS ANGELES. THIS
CIA DOCUMENT NOTES HIS CROSSING FROM TEXAS INTO
MEXICO HOURS AFTER THE ASSASSINATION.

1. Attached are copies of a photograph of Gilberto LOPEZ, U.S. citizen, Subject of reference. This photograph was taken the night of 27 November 1963 at the Mexico City airport by Mexican authorities.

2. As previously reported, Subject secured a fifteen day Mexican tourist card (FM-8-#24,553) at Tampa, Florida, on 20 November 1963. Subject entered Mexico on this document at Nuevo Laredo on 23 November 1963 - the day after President Kennedy's assassination in Dallas, Texas.

3. Subject checked into the Hotel Roosevelt, Avenida Insurgentes 287, Mexico, D.F., at 1600 hours (Mexico City time) on 25 November 1963. He stayed in room 203 at this hotel. At 1900 hours (Mexico City time) on 27 November 1963, Subject checked out of the Hotel Roosevelt and at 2100 hours on 27 November 1963 Subject departed Mexico for Habana.

4. Subject was listed on Cubana Flight #465 of 27 November 1963 as the only passenger. A crew of nine (9) Cubans was listed. On departure from Mexico, Subject used U.S. passport #310,162 which contained a Cuban "Courtesy" visa.

(continued)

Attachment:
 Photograph (3)

Distribution:
 3 - WH, w/att

GROUP 1
Excluded from automatic
downgrading and
declassification

Dup of
308-9

Gilberto Lopez

CIA (previously unpublished)

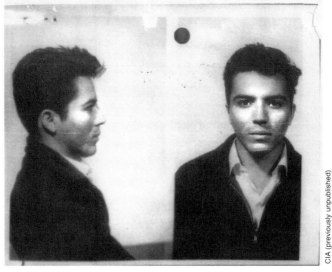

CIA (previously unpublished)

Gilberto Alvarado (above), like Pedro Gutierrez, gave an account of seeing
Oswald accept money in the Cuban Embassy in Mexico City.

the Dallas Police

of the many tricks
and ruses that
were played on me
during my incar-
ceration here at
the county jail
you will find on
a future date t.
what I am stated
here will be true
you must believe
me, that the only
reason I committed
that horrible crime,
because of my love
for the president,
and his wife.

...every adversary and
to have someone that
him from behind.
This broke the little
pieces that were left
of my heart!

Pages from the Ruby Diary (previously unpublished *[see Appendix C]*).

Left to right: Gerald Ford, Hale Boggs, Richard Russell, Earl Warren, John Sherman Cooper, John McCloy, Allen Dulles, and counsel Lee Rankin.

Warren Commission

US Senate

Senator Frank Church:

"I will have no part in pointing a finger of guilt at any former president."

The Kennedy Re-Interment, March 14, 1967 (6 pm–midnight)

Left to right: Senator Ted Kennedy,
Senator Robert Kennedy, Richard Cardinal Cushing,
and Defense Secretary Robert McNamara.

According to RFK's press aide, Frank Mankiewicz—
"The President's brain is in the grave.
LBJ, Ted, Bobby and maybe, McNamara,
buried it when the body was transferred."

FOLLOWING AND ABOVE ARE EXAMPLES OF
SEVENTY-FIVE PREVIOUSLY UNPUBLISHED
PHOTOGRAPHS TAKEN BY THE DEPARTMENT
OF THE ARMY THAT NIGHT.

"I found out something I never knew. I found out my world was not the real world."

—Senator Robert F. Kennedy

Although Texas law required that an autopsy had to be performed locally in a homicide case, both Lyndon Johnson and the Kennedy entourage demanded otherwise for the dead President. After a heated argument, the Texas officials relented, and Kennedy's body was delivered to the waiting Air Force One at Love Field.

When Kennedy's body finally arrived, Johnson's O.K. was needed for the take-off. Because Johnson's belongings were being transferred from Air Force Two to Air Force One, no one dared give the order without consulting the new President. Aides boarded Johnson's plane to secure his take-off command. However, Johnson couldn't be found. President Kennedy's Air Force Aide, Brigadier General Godfrey McHugh, commenced a frantic search for the new chief executive. McHugh boarded the Presidential jet—no Johnson. McHugh searched the Presidential bedroom—still no Johnson. Finally, McHugh opened the door to the tiny toilet area, where he discovered Johnson, "hiding in the toilet...muttering, 'Conspiracy, conspiracy, they're after all of us!'" McHugh spent the next few minutes calming Johnson down.[93]

Soon, Johnson was his functioning self again, and by all accounts he handled the rest of the traumatic day and weekend with great aplomb. After phone consultations with Robert Kennedy, it was decided that a local judge could perform the official Presidential swearing-in. The ever-present, ever-prepared Marty Underwood jotted down the oath on two 5" x 7" index cards and handed them to his old friend Judge Sarah Hughes, who swore Johnson in as president. Afterward, Underwood took the cards and put them in his coat pocket. (He has kept them ever since.) By phone, Robert Kennedy instructed Underwood to destroy all remaining copies of the speech JFK was to give that night in Austin.[94]

CHAPTER FOURTEEN

THE SUBURBAN NET CLOSES

Escape to Oak Cliff

Lee Oswald, his bus mired in the gridlock of downtown Dallas, hopped down and grabbed a cab (the first known use of such an extravagance by the poor, penny-pinching Oswald). He asked the cab driver to leave him off at the 500 block of North Beckley, five blocks from his Oak Cliff rooming house. Oswald ran home to fetch his pistol and a jacket in which to conceal it.

The suburb of Oak Cliff was gripped by fear. Only a five-minute car ride away, an assassin (or assassins) had just shot off part of the head of President John Kennedy, and severely wounded Texas governor Connally. A half an hour had gone by, and still no one had been arrested. Were the killers now in one of these Dallas suburbs? Although the rest of the country was in shock, little attention was paid to what Dallasites were experiencing: they, too, were shocked, but they were also in abject fear for their lives.

Elcan Elliott, who by coincidence lived just a few blocks from Oswald's rooming house, was slowly driving the streets of Oak Cliff, searching for his 14-year-old daughter. Elliott, who spoke of his experiences for the first time in 1994, was worried about his daughter's safety. "There was no one on the streets," recalls Elliott. Residents, either caught up in terror or curiosity, or both, shut themselves inside, glued to their television sets or radios. Anyone walking around stuck out in this vacuum of inactivity.

At about the 700 block of North Beckley, Elliott saw a suspicious looking character "relieving himself" on some bushes, in full view of anyone who might venture out. "That's what first attracted me to him," says Elliott. Curious and concerned, Elliott followed the young man, circling around streets, to catch up with him.

"I watched as he would walk down a block, stop, look around, and reverse direction," says Elliot. "He did this three or four times. He looked lost, bewildered."[1] At one point, Elliott was less than 10 feet from the man as he approached Lancaster Road. Coming face-to-face with Elliott, the man again reversed direction. When Oswald's face flashed on national television later that day, Elliot instantly recognized him as the man he had encountered. "There's absolutely no doubt about it," Elliott insists.

A disoriented Lee Oswald was once again calling attention to himself. Had he missed a promised rendezvous—a ride to a private airstrip, as alleged by various sources in Mexico City? Did Cuban agents in Mexico City make him promises they never intended to fulfill? Was he searching for a bus that would carry him to the Mexican border? Oswald had once told fellow Marine Nelson Delgado that if he were ever running from the law, he would attempt to enter Mexico, and from there travel to Cuba or Russia. "That's the way I would go about it," Oswald had said.

The Warren Commission would later check the bus schedules and verify that a bus route traversed Lancaster Road, near where Elliott saw Oswald, which would have eventually taken the assassin to the United States-Mexico border at Laredo, Texas. The bus transfer Oswald had asked for when he first boarded in downtown Dallas would have been accepted on such a bus.[2] Warren Commission attorney David Belin has written, "It is likely Oswald was fleeing to Mexico City."[3]

Oswald had barely enough cash on him ($13.87) to pay for a bus ticket to the border. However, as Belin queries, "Is it not reasonable to assume that he would have taken cash with him unless he were in league with someone who could provide funds for him when he reached his destination?"[4]

As Washington began to react to Kennedy's murder, mysterious events were occurring in the Dallas area. These incidents indicate three possible connections between Oswald and a shadowy net of conspiracy. Whether any or all point toward definite Cuban involvement in the assassination may never be known. It is known, however, that none of these incidents, or those in the following chapters suggesting possible Cuban involvement, were sufficiently looked into during the investigation of the President's murder. These dark events, seen in bits and pieces through the filter of witnesses of undetermined reliability, nevertheless hint that Oswald had somewhere he was planning to go after shooting President Kennedy and returning to Oak Cliff.

Redbird

The first example is a "getaway" plane Oswald might have been planning to escape on—if he had gotten there in time after the assassination. "There was a plane revving up at Redbird," remembers the FBI's Jim Hosty. "It was disturbing people's TV reception. It took off around 3 p.m. [November 22, 1963]. We did an investigation on it. We ran it out but it got nowhere."[5]

Redbird Field was a private airstrip located four miles to the south of Oswald's Beckley Street apartment. Over the years, a number of allegations, emanating particularly from the Cuban community, have maintained that Oswald was to have been flown out of this tiny private airstrip by his fellow conspirators. Cuban exile activist Dr. Fernando Penebaz, for example, alleged that "the head of Castro's Air Force" had flown into Dallas to meet Oswald.[6]

This recalls the story of Quinton Pino Machado, a strong-arm in Castro's Diplomatic Service, who allegedly cut a deal with Oswald to bring him to Cuba after the assassination (*See Chapter 10*). Certainly if some sort of deal was made in Mexico City between Oswald and the Cubans, an escape plan from a private airstrip would have been logical.

What elevates all this beyond speculation is that there were, in fact, mysterious goings-on at Redbird, on November 22 and days before—strange events that were never sufficiently explained.

Wayne January, an employee of Redbird in 1963, remembers an incident that took place on Monday, November 18—four days before the assassination:

I was visited by three men who asked about renting a plane for a trip to Mexico on November 22. The types of questions they asked made me suspicious—they wanted to know about fuel consumption, vectors, distances— things a pilot should know. That's why I later reported it to the FBI. As I recall, the men wanted to go to a village on the Pacific coast of Mexico. When Lee Harvey Oswald was arrested, he instantly reminded me of the man who stayed in the car.[7]

The air traffic controller at Redbird on November 22, 1963 was Louis D. Gaudin. He told the author (and the FBI) that on the day of the shooting, he saw a green and white Comanche-type aircraft being serviced at the airport's Texair facility. Gaudin spoke with the plane's three well-dressed occupants. "They said they were headed southbound," recalled Gaudin in 1994. "The plane took off between 2:30 and 3 o'clock. Forty minutes later, it returned with only two occupants. It was met by a part-time employee who was moonlighting from the Dallas Police Department. The plane then took off again."[8]

Texair's owner, Merritt Gobel, is reluctant (and apparently frightened) to discuss the matter. In 1994, he said, "[The flight] was common knowledge. That's all I can say."[9]

The Redbird allegations, if true, correspond neatly to what Senate investigators later referred to as "The Cubana Airlines Incident." According to CIA documents released in 1977, two Cuban men (on the night of JFK's murder) arrived at the Mexico City airport from Dallas, via Tijuana, on a twin-engine aircraft. The CIA received "highly reliable" information that the men were met at the Mexico airport by Cuban diplomatic personnel from the Cuban embassy. One of the men boarded either a FAR (Revolutionary Armed Forces) or Cubana Airlines plane, avoiding customs, and traveled to Cuba in the cockpit to avoid mixing with the passengers.[10]

Congressional investigators concluded that the Cubana schedule made available to them eliminated that airline as the culprit in the transfer. However, the FAR flight remains a possibility.

The passenger on-board was identified as Miguel Casas Sayez ("Miguelito"), a well-known Cuban gangster. Further investigation revealed that Casas was an agent of the G-2 (Cuban Intelligence). Casas' background was that of an ardent revolutionary who idolized Raul Castro. Known as a strong-arm himself, he often "went beyond what was required of him to get the job done." A source close to Casas reported:

> *Miguelito has just arrived from the U.S. He was in Dallas on the day of the assassination of Kennedy, but managed to leave through the frontier of Laredo; already in Mexico a FAR plane brought him to Cuba. You know that he is one of Raul's men [referring to Raul Castro]. Miguelito is very brave, very brave!*[11]

The arrival of these mysterious men in Havana is underscored by other curious arrivals in Cuba, according to a Cuban informant of undisclosed location. The source stated that a well-known Cuban scientist friend of his witnessed peculiar activity at the Havana Airport on November 22, 1963. The scientist related that at approximately 5 p.m., he saw a plane with Mexican markings land and park at the far side of the field. Two men, whom he recognized as Cuban "gangsters," alighted, entered the rear entrance of the administration building, and disappeared, bypassing mandatory customs procedures. His curiosity aroused, the scientist was able to learn that the plane had arrived from Dallas via Mexico City. (Recall that the Cuban Embassy in Mexico City was known to occasionally allow passage without the requisite passport stamps.)

The CIA purposely did not follow-up on the information. By the time it received the information in 1964, it said, its source had died. Attached to the CIA report is a routing slip with the following handwriting by an unknown CIA officer: "I'd let this die a natural death, as the Bureau is doing."[12]

FBI agent Jim Hosty was also aware of the mystery flight. "I was told by an FBI agent who was sent to Mexico to investigate," recalls Hosty, "that the CIA agents in Mexico City were investigating the possibility of Castro's involvement. They picked up information about a mysterious person flying in from the United States, and then departing under mysterious circumstances on an airplane for Cuba, when all of a sudden they received orders to cease and desist their investigation."[13]

It should be noted that the address and phone number of Cubana Airlines was found in Oswald's addressbook, just below that of Sylvia Duran. CIA transcripts of Cuban Embassy wiretaps reveal a flurry of phone conversations between the Embassy and Cubana Airlines on November 22, asking about flight arrivals. One call reveals that "the ambassador went to the airport to receive some passengers."[14] Also, calls were monitored that day between Luisa Calderon, Oswald's alleged contact in Havana, and Cubana Airlines.

Saturday: Border Crossing

If Lee Oswald was headed for Cuba via Mexico City in the hours after the assassination, he was not the only suspicious person with that intent. The border between Texas and Mexico was closed immediately after Kennedy's murder, but when it was reopened the next day at noon, a Cuban-born American named Gilberto Policarpo Lopez was among those lined up in cars and on foot awaiting entry into Mexico from Laredo. (The border shut-down was so thorough that busloads of school children were trapped on both sides.)[15]

On November 17, prior to his arrival in Texas, Lopez had spent a night in the Tampa, Florida home of the president of that city's chapter of the Fair Play For Cuba Committee (FPCC). The Tampa branch had been personally formed by FPCC's president, V.T. Lee, with whom Oswald had corresponded while living in New Orleans. Lee had written to Oswald on May 29, 1963, advising him against forming his own New Orleans chapter of the FPCC, and had also recommended that he work instead through the Tampa branch. Tampa was V.T. Lee's home before he moved to New York. He would eventually move back to Tampa and retire there. V.T. Lee was also known to have been smuggled into Cuba by the Cuban Embassy official in Mexico City (Rogelio Rodriguez) whom the CIA believed was an assassination specialist.

Not only was Lopez linked to the same FPCC branch as Oswald, but previously he had worked with pro-Castro groups in Los Angeles, where Oswald had first made contact with pro-Castro Cubans.[16] Friends would later testify that Lopez was decidedly pro-Castro, and had in fact been attempting to return to Cuba for over a year. Manuel Artime's secretary, Nilo Messer, heard from good sources in Cuba that Lopez's brother held a high rank in Castro's military.[17]

On November 23, Lopez arrived in Mexico City, where he seemed to receive special treatment. Congressional investigator Jim Johnston would later write, "The Cuban government appeared too eager to get Lopez out of Mexico. It cut through red tape and gave Lopez a Cuban courtesy visa, ignoring the fact that his U.S. passport had expired."[18] It would later be determined that Lopez flew on to Havana on November 27 aboard Cubana flight #465, the only passenger on a flight manned by a crew of nine.

By December 5, the CIA's Mexico Station had been advised of Lopez's "suspicious" activities and sent a classified message to headquarters requesting "urgent traces" on Lopez. The FBI also had gathered details about Lopez which it considered suspicious, specifically that Lopez, in Havana in 1964, was not working, and was seen spending his time in the leisured pursuit of dominoes and other games. By March 19, 1964, the "suspicious" activity became more focused: a CIA source in Mexico City advised the Station that "Gilberto Lopes [sic] was involved in the Kennedy assassination."[19]

Taking all this into account, the House Select Committee on Assassinations concluded in 1979 that the Lopez reports "all amount to a troublesome circumstance that the committee was unable to resolve with confidence."[20] Could

Lopez, Miguelito, and the other men on the Redbird and Cubana Airlines flights have been Oswald's "Latin friends"? Were the four of them supposed to act as Oswald's escorts to Cuba? Just like "The Cubana Airlines Incident," the Lopez lead was never sufficiently investigated. But other facts came to light in the days after the assassination reinforcing the idea that Oswald might have been counting on help.

New York

Just before midnight on the day of the assassination, Clare Booth Luce and her husband, wealthy Time-Life publisher Henry Luce, were in their New York apartment. Like the rest of the nation, they were watching TV coverage of the assassination. When the phone rang, the Cuban voice on the other end was a familiar one, but the information he was conveying was shocking, if true. For years, Clare Booth Luce had been giving financial assistance to the Cuban exiles who operated out of Miami and New Orleans, including the "renegades" who operated outside of the Kennedy loop. The caller told her that he feared for his life and swore Luce to secrecy. Fifteen years later, testifying before a Congressional investigation, Luce finally divulged the facts that the call had originated in New Orleans and that the caller's name was "something like Julio Fernandez."

"Fernandez" told his benefactor that he and two of his "comrades" had encountered Oswald in New Orleans, where Oswald had attempted to infiltrate their anti-Castro cell. Suspicious, the Cubans monitored Oswald, later tape recording him at a secret pro-Castro meeting. On this occasion, Fernandez alleged, Oswald had boasted that he was "a crack marksman and could shoot anybody—including the President or the Secretary of the Navy." Fernandez went on to say, "There is a Cuban Communist assassination team at-large, and Oswald was their hired gun."

Of course, all this information could be seen merely as a self-serving attempt to rally influential citizens to the exiles' cause. However, Fernandez's story was elevated beyond the expected hyperbole with the final bit of information he passed on to Luce: through his network of contacts, Fernandez was aware that Oswald had traveled to Mexico City, where he came into a large sum of money. As will be seen, the rumor that the Cubans, in Mexico City, gave Oswald money for Kennedy's assassination made the rounds in many cities (including Mexico City itself) and was never sufficiently investigated. In any case, the statement is significant—on the night of the assassination, no one in the public-at-large knew of Oswald's Mexico City visit.

Luce instructed her friend, "Go at once to the FBI, give them your tapes, give them your photographs. Tell them everything you know." Luce forgot the incident until 1967, when one of the Cubans called to tell her that, in 1963, the three had complied with her suggestion to give the material to the Bureau. The FBI agents, he told her, took both the photos and tapes, then "roughed them up and told them to scram and keep their mouths shut and disappear or they would all be deported."

Years later, at the behest of Senator Richard Schweiker (R-PA), who was then investigating the Kennedy murder, Luce herself contacted "Fernandez," who by then was a successful attorney in Miami. "I told him he could testify in secret if he wanted," Luce recalled in 1979. "But he said he would just as soon broadcast from the top of the Empire State Building as testify before a Senate investigating committee. He begged me not to reveal his name because he would then be on the Cuban [Castro] hit list." Luce honored his request, and never divulged the attorney's name. Luce later determined that the second of Fernandez's comrades was deported, while the third was murdered in Miami.[21]

If the murder in Miami was, indeed, performed by pro-Castro Cubans, was it intended to frighten Fernandez into silence? If so, it accomplished its purpose. Perhaps the three anti-Castro Cubans had stumbled into Oswald, Lopez, Miguelito, and his friend secretly meeting to plan the Kennedy assassination. Perhaps Oswald met with a different group of Cubans assembling for the same end, or towards a different end. Or perhaps the Fernandez story is made up, an attempt to profit from the controversy surrounding Oswald's past.

In any case, the preceding leads were never investigated any further. They were not reported to the Warren Commission any more than the Cuba Project was. In fact, the Warren Commission was deliberately steered away from any Cuban connection, preferring to focus on aspects of the assassination that were inconsequential or irrelevant to Oswald's motivation. This was the very beginning of the government's coverup of the Kennedy assassination, which has grown to be the abiding mystery of the twentieth century.

Meanwhile, Oswald would reach his apartment in the Oak Cliff suburbs, but would never reach whatever escape route he had planned. He might have been betrayed by confederates who did not mean to or were unable to spirit him away (recall the "Machado" allegation that Oswald missed his appointed rendezvous.) There might have been a chance accident on someone's part. Or he might have betrayed himself in Oak Cliff. However, the chance is slim to none that Oswald, after rigorously planning his escape from the Walker attempt, did not bother to plan his escape from the Kennedy assassination.

Whatever Oswald's plans, they were rendered meaningless when he encountered Dallas Police Officer J.D. Tippit on the streets of Oak Cliff at approximately 1:15 p.m.. The man who had just murdered the 35th President of the United States, and had, amazingly, escaped the immediate vicinity of Dealey Plaza undetected, had one more murderous hurdle to jump. And he almost made it.

The Murder of J. D. Tippit

"Attention all squads. Attention all squads. The suspect in the shooting at Elm and Houston is reported to be an unknown white male, approximately thirty, slender build, height five feet, ten inches, weight one hundred and sixty-five pounds, reported to be armed with what is though to be a 30 caliber rifle...No further description at this time or information 12:45 p.m. KKB-364, Dallas."

As a result of Howard Brennan's description, the entire Dallas police force was now alerted to the first details of the killer's appearance. Dozens of police cars headed straight for Dealey Plaza, leaving the outskirts unprotected in the simultaneous event of a robbery or accident. With this in mind, Police dispatcher Murry Jackson contacted Officer J.D. Tippit and told him to remain in his suburban precinct of Oak Cliff, instructing him, "You will be at-large for any emergency that comes in."

Thirty-nine year-old Tippit, an eleven-year veteran of the force, had just returned from lunch with his wife. He initially proceeded to an Oak Cliff service station, where he remained for a few minutes. According to witnesses, Tippit suddenly raced off at a high rate of speed. He was seen at approximately 1:11 p.m. in the Top Ten Record store on Jefferson Boulevard, where he asked several patrons to move aside and let him use the phone. He then placed a call, letting the other end ring several times, but getting no answer. He then hurried out of the store. It has never been determined whom Tippit was attempting to contact.[22] Except by his killer, the officer was not seen alive again.

Oswald had left his rooming house a few minutes after 1 p.m. It is not known how he traversed the nine-tenths of a mile to Tenth and Patton in the intervening 15 or 16 minutes. It is also not known for certain if Elcan Elliott witnessed Oswald's strange movements before or after the Tippit encounter. However, it can be deduced that, due to the police dispatch describing the killer and Oswald's erratic back-and-forth movements on foot in Oak Cliff, Tippit had good reason to pull over and speak with the young man walking along Tenth Street.

Witnesses to the encounter differ on which direction Oswald was walking when Tippit stopped him. An equal number claim he was walking east as walking west. They may both be right. If Elcan is correct regarding Oswald's constant changing of direction, it is possible that Oswald, walking east, saw the westbound Tippit approaching, and turned to walk west.

Some have claimed that, from his rooming house nine-tenths of a mile away, Oswald didn't have time to reach the Tippit murder scene by 1:17 p.m. The fact is that he could have easily reached Tenth and Patton by then, and with time to spare. Reconstruction of Oswald's cab ride from downtown showed that he would have arrived at the apartment around 12:55. Oswald's landlady, Earlene Roberts, testified that Oswald ran into the Beckley Street house just after she heard a bulletin on the President's shooting. The bulletins had started as early as 12:45. Roberts testified that Oswald was in his room for a couple of minutes, then dashed out again.

Reconstructions show that, going at a fast walk, one could reach the Tippit slaying site in 11 minutes. But consider that almost everyone in Dallas that day was at home glued to the TV set. In that case, as one writer has stated, "Oswald could have run a four-minute mile naked and no one would have seen him." As it was, most of the witnesses to the Tippit slaying were on their way to or from their places of employment, supposedly going to or returning from lunch. The rest had to tear themselves away from their TVs when they heard the shots.

When Tippit parked his police car, Oswald exchanged a few words with him through the passenger window vent. Tippit got out of the car and started to walk around the front of it towards Oswald. The closest witness to the entire event was Jack Tatum, the chief medical photographer at Baylor University, who happened to be in the neighborhood on business. In 1963, Tatum volunteered to tell the Dallas police what he knew, but the police never called him. His first official statement did not come until the House Select Committee on Assassinations (HSCA) interviewed him in 1978. Located by the author in 1993, Tatum was persuaded to grant a series of rare interviews. He described what he saw:

> I was preparing to turn on Tenth Street and I noticed a squad car coming in my direction and a young man walking on the sidewalk toward my direction. As I approached the squad car, I noticed that he was bending over talking to the officer through the passenger window. He had both hands in the pockets of his light windbreaker jacket. As I passed the squad car and looked forward, going into the intersection, I heard three, maybe four shots. I stopped my car and looked and saw the officer laying in the street.[23]

Tatum was the only direct witness to what happened next—Oswald's coup de grace:

> The person with a gun in his hand walked from the passenger side around behind the car, up to the officer, and shot him again in the head as he lay in the street. He then surveyed the situation, looked around. He looked in my direction and started a slow run in my direction. I was only several feet from him. I saw him direct on. The man I saw shooting the officer was average height, five eight or nine, black hair, had on a light-colored zipper jacket and darker colored pants. I saw him very clearly. I was very close to him—got positive identification. Also, he has a very unusual mouth that turns up—kind of like he's smiling maybe—and I could not mistake that. He had dark hair. I put my car in gear and went forward, watching in the side view mirror ... He turned left and ran down Patton Street. At that point, I backed up, [and] went back to the scene to see if I could be some help.

> I didn't know who that man was at the time. That evening I saw him appear on TV as the suspect of the assassination of JFK. That was Lee Harvey Oswald—the same person I saw shoot the officer, no doubt.

> I still see that face and I was very, very close to him. I still see that scene also.

Oswald was heard by another witness to say "poor damn cop" or "poor dumb cop" as he left the shooting scene. (Interestingly, Lee Oswald's brother Robert recounts an occasion in 1957, when Lee was home on leave from the Marines. Robert, who was driving, received a citation for running a red light. As the cop pulled away, Lee, a passenger in the car, muttered, "Poor dumb cop."[24])

Oswald then made his way to Jefferson Boulevard. Tippit's encounter with Lee Oswald on Patton Street, just west of Tenth, took place at approximately 1:17 p.m. (Witnesses who called police estimate that they waited 30 seconds to a minute before calling in. The call was recorded at the police headquarters at 1:18 p.m.,[25] placing the murder at 1:16 or 1:17.)

By 1:22, police had broadcast a description of the Tippit killer. Squad cars descended on the area and proceeded to shake down all the buildings in the vicinity to locate the cop-killer. A number of Dallas police have candidly admitted to the author that they were more disturbed and angry over the slaying of Tippit than they were over the death of Kennedy. "The President was one thing," one officer observed, "but this was one of our own."

In addition, most of the experienced cops automatically linked the two murders. One officer on the scene, Gerald Hill, recalls, "I made the statement that the two incidents were awfully close together. Although Dallas is a big town now, it wasn't that big at that time. You didn't have two major incidents like this going on that close together. It would automatically make you suspicious."[26] Former Assistant District Attorney Bill Alexander shared this professional's gut feeling, recalling, "We all knew the same man that killed the President had killed Tippit. We had made up our minds by the time we got there."[27]

When police cars screamed down the street toward the Tippit murder scene, shoe store manager Johnny Brewer saw Oswald staring into the recessed window of his storefront, just a few doors from the Texas Theatre on Jefferson Boulevard. Brewer told the FBI, "His hair was sort of messed up and it looked like he had been running, and he looked scared, and he looked funny....The man looked over his shoulder toward the street as the police car headed away."

When Brewer later walked to the street to see what the police were doing, he again noticed Oswald as he snuck into the theater while the ticket-taker, Julia Postal, was looking the other way. Brewer alerted Postal, who called the police, saying, "I know you all are very busy, but I have a man in the theater who is running from you for some reason." Within minutes of determining that Postal's description of the non-paying customer matched their suspect in the Tippit killing, the police swarmed the Texas Theater. Entering the theater, one officer was heard to remark, "I'll get that son of a bitch if he's in there."

When the lights went up, Brewer pointed out Oswald. There was a ferocious struggle. It took seven policemen to subdue the assassin. Oswald even attempted to get off a shot, but his pistol trigger became wedged between the thumb and index finger of one of his captors. By the end of the battle, Oswald's face was battered, Detective Paul Bentley had a broken ankle, and Officer Nick McDonald was cut on the face. In typical Oswald fashion, he was heard to yell, "I am not resisting arrest!"

By the time the police dragged the kicking and screaming Oswald out to the street, a crowd of over 150 had gathered. The mob was screaming, "Kill the son of a bitch," and, "Give him to us, we'll kill him!"

On the ride to the Dallas police station, Oswald pleaded his innocence. In the police car, Officer C.T. Walker told Oswald that he was a suspect in the murder of a police officer. Oswald replied sarcastically, "Police officer been killed?" Officer Gerald Hill, also in the car, recalls Oswald saying, "I haven't done anything I'm ashamed of." Hill told the author, "Oswald was very surly—very cocky. He was the kind of person that had it been under different circumstances, you would have wanted to hit him."[28]

After a brief period of silence, Oswald said, "I hear they burn for murder." Walker replied, "You just might find out."

"Well, they say it just takes a second to die," came Oswald's retort.

Detective Bentley, a third officer in the car, then perused Oswald's wallet and observed both his "Oswald" ID's and his fake "Hidell" cards. Oswald refused to say which was his real name. Like numerous others who had come into contact with Oswald, Paul Bentley remembers "the smirk" permanently affixed on Oswald's face. While Officer Hill radioed to Captain Fritz at headquarters, giving him the two names, Fritz shot back, "You may have a suspect in the Kennedy shooting." With that, Paul Bentley asked the suspect, "Did you kill our beloved President?"

"You find out your own way," came Oswald's icy reply. It was, Bentley remembers, the last thing he said on the ride in. The rest of the trip took place in total silence—at least inside the car. Outside was a different story altogether. "On the way downtown, cars—mostly containing women—pulled up alongside, yelling, 'Kill the bastard,'" Bentley remembers.[29]

Upon arriving at the police station in downtown Dallas, Oswald was led through a phalanx of reporters. Lonnie Hudkins was among those in attendance. He recently recalled the scene:

> I was in the hallway with all the other reporters when [Captain] Fritz came out and asked me if I'd come in and sort of be the token reporter inside for a few minutes. I went in to see Oswald and the only thing Fritz said is, "Please don't ask him about the President," and so I didn't. The first question I asked was—"Was he being treated all right?" He said "yes," and I asked him about his eye and he said that he was punched out and knocked down—you know, wrestled down. And then I asked him, "Why did you kill officer Tippit?" and he said, "Someone get killed? Policeman get killed?" At that time, he had this little smirk on him. I wanted to hit him but I didn't. Then all of a sudden it dawned on me he wasn't sweating—not a drop of sweat on him. He said something to the effect that he hadn't done anything that he was ashamed of.[30]

There is every reason to believe that Lee Oswald was, for once, telling the truth—for he probably was not in the least bit ashamed of murdering John Kennedy, an act with far-reaching implications for Oswald's hero, Fidel Castro, and quite possibly one of the most successful revolutionary strikes of the 20th century. If Lee Oswald's motivation was to halt the Kennedy attempts on Castro's life, and the prevention of another invasion of a sovereign country he admired, one can imagine how he himself regarded the deed.

The Dallas police assembled the evidence and put two and two together: Lee Oswald, the Tippit suspect, was the only employee missing from a roll call at the Book Depository, where the sniper's nest had been located. In addition, Oswald's appearance seemed to match the descriptions of those who saw the sniper in the Depository window. While the Dallas police settled in for a long series of fruitless interrogations of the suspect, government functionaries struggled with the implications of what had occurred.

The question remains: Was Lee Harvey Oswald en route to a clandestine rendezvous on the afternoon of November 22—at Redbird or elsewhere? If Mexico was Oswald's destination, and if he intended getting there on his own— or missed a rendezvous—then the bewilderment Elcan Elliott witnessed is understandable: the next bus to leave Lancaster Road for Loredo was due at 3:15 p.m. It was approximately 1:10 p.m. when Elliott observed the disoriented assassin, who may have been pondering where to hide for the next two hours.

That Friday night, the trail was still fresh. Oswald had missed whatever escape might have been planned for him, but his "Latin friends" had not yet scurried back to Cuba. The CIA, hampered by the slow cognitive processes of a bureaucracy, would not realize the event's full implications in time to detain the Cubana Airlines flight in Mexico City or Lopez at the border. However, once the principals had escaped to Cuba (if that in fact happened), why did the CIA not investigate these possible Cuban connections to the Kennedy murder? The answer is that they were prevented from doing so by Washington officials who feared what they might find out.

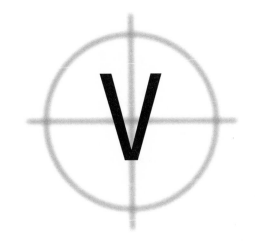

A COVERUP

CHAPTER FIFTEEN

THE AFTERMATH

O n Air Force One, Lyndon Johnson was now fully recovered from his uncharacteristic bout with hysteria, and comfortably in charge again. The man famous for wielding the telephone as an excalibur took it up once more. He placed his first calls to his attorneys and business associates, and to Robert Kennedy. The details of the call to Bobby are still withheld. We do know that Johnson wanted an update from his attorney, Abe Fortas. Fortas, a politically savvy attorney later to be named to the U.S. Supreme Court, had successfully led Johnson through many potentially scandalous quagmires and now was serving as Bobby Baker's lawyer. From Fortas, Johnson most wanted to know if the insurance salesman Don Reynolds, in testimony that day before the Senate Rules Committee, had given up Johnson's name. The new president was greatly relieved to learn that the news of the assassination had halted the inquiry, preempting Reynolds just before he could disclose his most famous client.[1]

Johnson's next call was to J.W. "Waddie" Bullion, a Dallas lawyer and Johnson business crony. One of Bullion's former associates, requesting anonymity, has alleged that Johnson called, in part, for advice on what to do with his stocks in light of the market's almost certain plunge on news of the assassination.

Most now saw in Johnson a sober political pro masterfully doing what needed to be done. Yet, his success in these first few hours moving a paralyzed, fearful nation forward was viewed by Kennedy loyalists as insensitive. New York Times reporter Tom Wicker, traveling with the president's press entourage, wrote: "In the terrible hours of Kennedy's assassination, Lyndon Johnson had found himself reprieved from political oblivion…His whole life, in a sense, had been resurrected and Johnson meant to make the most of it."[2]

Observing Johnson's activity, JFK aide Kenny O'Donnell was heard to say, pointing at the new President, "He's got what he wants now. But we take it back in '68." The Kennedy brother whom they hoped would recapture the presidency five years hence had more immediate concerns. Back in Washington, Bobby Kennedy put his grief on hold to perform important favors for his dead brother.

The Coverup Begins

"Bobby's a lawyer, he's savvy, he knows all the political ins and outs, and he can protect you."
> **—Joe Kennedy to JFK, bolstering his insistence that he appoint Bobby as Attorney General**[3]

"For Bob, the important thing was now the memory of the President, and he wanted it to be pure and golden."
> **—Ramsey Clark, former U.S. Attorney General**[4]

Robert Kennedy immediately grasped the fact that his role had changed. An hour earlier, he had been consumed with furthering his brother's career and policies. Suddenly, without any warning, he had become the protector of his older brother's legacy. As his close friend, former Assistant Secretary of State Averell Harriman, recalled, "Bobby's value was in his most extraordinary loyalty, his understanding of his brother's objectives, and his fierce instinct to protect him in every way he knew."[5]

Thus, before he could allow himself time to grieve, Bobby had to clamp down all threats to his brother's legacy. Placing his sorrow on hold, Bobby Kennedy took the steps necessary to protect Jack's place in history. Before making plans to meet Air Force One, then carrying his brother's corpse to Washington, Bobby dispatched Jack Miller to Dallas to be his eyes and ears and to determine what had happened. Miller was an Assistant Attorney General in the Justice Department's Criminal Division.[6]

Bobby then called the Secret Service at the White House and demanded the Oval Office tapes. White House conversations had been taped since July 1962, but only a handful of people were aware of the taping: JFK's personal secretary Evelyn Lincoln, the two Secret Service agents who installed the system, Bobby Kennedy, and a few others.[7] Those tapes are, as of this writing, still withheld from historians. In fact, the tapes made after November 8, 1963 are missing.

Years later, Bobby would summon George Dalton, a young Naval aide, to the Executive Office Building to undertake the task of transcribing some of the tapes he was given. Dalton had attracted the attention of the Kennedy family in September 1963. He was then responsible for launching helicopters to and from Hyannis and Squaw Island, where Jackie was staying just before the premature birth and death of Patrick Bouvier Kennedy. When he left the Navy, Dalton went to work for Senator Edward Kennedy and performed odd jobs for Bobby. During the 1970's, he reportedly removed tapes, and other family records, from a family vault in a National Archives warehouse in Waltham, Massachusetts. Dalton has consistently refused comment on all these matters.[8] Recently, however, more was learned of the disposition of the Oval Office tapes.

The issue surfaced again in 1973, when the Kennedy family was preparing material for the newly-constructed John F. Kennedy (Presidential) Library in Boston. At the time, Kennedy family attorney Burke Marshall informed Senator Ted Kennedy's aide Rick Burke, "We're erasing the tapes." A stunned Burke learned that "countless sensitive" conversations had been deleted by Marshall, Dalton, and Kennedy family key advisor (and brother-in-law) Steve Smith. In a few days, Marshall called to reveal some of what had been heard on the tapes: "Marilyn [Monroe] was on the phone with the President. Boy the things they talked about...." In the coming weeks, Rick Burke was assigned to ship all of JFK's files, now locked in storage in Ted's inner office, to Steve Smith, who would then send them to the library. Burke discovered a 3-inch thick folder of telephone transcriptions of the tapes. He quickly scanned the conversations, reading steamy dialogue between the President and Monroe, and others such as Judy Campbell.[9]

Not yet finished his efforts at protecting his slain brother, Bobby took immediate steps to conceal other Presidential artifacts. Bobby quickly placed a call to Presidential aide McGeorge Bundy, directing him to change the combinations on White House safes containing John Kennedy's personal files, which he did.[10]

Finally, Bobby was ready for the drive to Andrews Air Force Base to meet the Presidential party. After his brother's legacy, the next thing on Bobby's mind was his sister-in-law, Jackie. Together, they might get through the terrible days that lay ahead.

The Kennedy Autopsy

In the cramped quarters of the presidential jet, Jackie Kennedy spent the trip to Washington sitting by her husband's coffin. John Kennedy's personal physician, Dr. George Burkley, knelt in the aisle, and delicately broached the practical decisions that had to be made. Foremost in Burkley's mind was the choice of an autopsy site. Burkley explained that, for security reasons, the autopsy venue should be a military facility. The only ones in the immediate area of Andrews Air Force Base, where the plane would land, were Bethesda Naval Hospital and Walter Reed Army Hospital.

"Of course, the President was in the Navy," whispered JFK aide Godfrey McHugh. "Of course. Bethesda," came Jackie's decision.[11] She would later inform Bobby, "I don't want any undertakers. I want everything done by the Navy."[12]

In November 1963, Dr. James Humes was the lab director at the Bethesda Naval Hospital. In the wake of the presidential assassination, Humes, who was home early that day, was busy calling invitees to cancel a dinner party he and his wife had scheduled for that evening. The assassination had hit the Humes like many other Americans—like a loss in the family—and clearly that evening was an inappropriate time to go ahead with a party. As Humes' wife Ann was telling one friend of the party's cancellation, an emergency operator broke through with a call for James. The caller, at 5:15 p.m., was Admiral Edward Kenney, the Surgeon General of the Navy. "Jim, you'd better hurry over to the hospital," said Kenney.

Dr. J. Thornton Boswell was Bethesda's Chief of Pathology. On the afternoon of November 22nd, he was going over autopsy slides with pathology residents when he received a similar call. Like Humes, Boswell was informed that the president's autopsy was to be performed at Bethesda. In 1992, Boswell gave a rare interview to the *Journal of the American Medical Association* (JAMA), in which he described his reaction:

> I argued, "That's stupid. The autopsy should be done at AFIP [five miles away at Walter Reed Army Medical Center]." After all, the AFIP was the apex of military pathology and, perhaps, world pathology. I was told, "That's the way it is. Admiral Burkley [the president's personal physician] wants Bethesda."...I was told that Jackie Kennedy selected Bethesda because her husband had been a Navy man.[13]

It was an inconsolable Bobby Kennedy who at 7:30 that evening met the incoming Air Force One carrying his dead brother and his grieving sister-in-law, Jackie. Given what is now known about the practical consequences of the day's tragedy, Bobby could well have been experiencing brain-numbing inner turmoil—if, in the farthest recesses of his grief-stricken consciousness, he considered them for only a microsecond. That weekend was supposed to have been so much different: by mutual decree, the Lyndon Johnson so despised by the younger Kennedy would soon be wrapping up his final year in the Kennedy administration; with Cubela on his way to Havana, and Artime in Central America, the equally despised Fidel Castro seemed to be even more endangered.

Instead, Bobby was now addressing Johnson as "Mr. President." The realization may have begun to creep in that El Presidente Castro would outlive them all. Worst of all was the unthinkable possibility that this was all Bobby's fault—that one of his schemes had backfired. It was against this real world backdrop that Bobby, accompanied by Jackie, rode in the ambulance transporting Jack's body to the Navy's medical facility just outside Washington. The oft-considered October 1964 election now seemed to belong to another universe. Bobby's world had been turned upside down in every way imaginable.

Bobby Continues To Protect His Brother

> "The Kennedy who was really in charge in the [autopsy] tower suite was the Attorney General."
> —William Manchester, author, The Death of a President[14]

> "It is true that we were influenced by the fact that we knew Jackie Kennedy was waiting upstairs to accompany the body to the White House and that Admiral Burkley wanted us to hurry as much as possible."
> —Dr. James J. Humes, 1992[15]

While President Kennedy's body was taken to the autopsy suite, the Kennedy entourage was escorted to a 17th floor suite in the hospital tower. Dr. John Walsh, Jackie's obstetrician, arrived, and quickly noticed the unmistakable signs of nervous exhaustion in the widow. She turned to him saying, "Maybe you could just give me something so I could have a little nap." Walsh proceeded to inject her with 100 milligrams of Visatril. The formidable dose had absolutely no effect. Walsh thought, "I might just as well have given her a shot of Coca-Cola."[16]

In addition to choosing the autopsy venue, the Kennedys also attempted to limit the extent of the autopsy, and to rush those performing it. From their 17th floor room, where they were in phone contact with the autopsy suite, Bobby and Jackie Kennedy exerted their influence over the proceedings.

There were still other components to the Kennedy family's "presence" at Bethesda. In 1993, Dr. Pierre Finck, who assisted in the autopsy, described the president's autopsy as only "adequate," and "not as complete as some other autopsies I have done." When pressed for details, Finck stated that neither the abdominal cavity nor the organs of the neck were examined. In addition, no mention was made of adrenals, pituitary, thyroid, parathyroid, larynx, trachea, ureters, urinary bladder, testes, prostrate, gastrointestinal tract, or spinal column. Finck explained that the Kennedy family did not want a "complete" autopsy, adding (contradictorily, it seems), "The Kennedy family did not want us to examine the abdominal cavity, but the abdominal cavity was examined."

Dr. Robert Karnei was present and assisting at most of the autopsy. In 1991, regarding the internal organs that were not dissected, Karnei stated flatly:

> They [Boswell and Humes] were not allowed to do that...Robert [Kennedy] was really limiting the autopsy...We had to get permission all the time from Mrs. Kennedy to proceed with the autopsy...Jim [Humes] and Jay [Boswell] were really handicapped that night with regards to performing the autopsy.... I think it was as complete as they were allowed to do.[17]

Karnei later testified that two days after the autopsy, the Kennedy family circulated a statement that he and all others present were asked to sign. The statement was a pledge that no one would discuss the details of what they saw at the autopsy for twenty-five years. Like everyone else, Karnei obliged.[18]

Complicated homicide autopsies have been known to last for two days. But when John Kennedy's autopsy had been in progress for just two hours, Bobby Kennedy, in his suite on the 17th floor, began growing impatient. It was 10 p.m. and he was ready to leave with his brother's body. Godfrey McHugh spoke with Bobby by phone and assured him the doctors would be finished by midnight.[19]

In his later testimony, McHugh stated that Bobby Kennedy frequently phoned the autopsy suite, inquiring "about the results, about why the autopsy was taking so much time, and about the need for speed." McHugh said that even after informing Kennedy that the autopsists would need a few more hours, Bobby called frequently to ask why it was taking so long.[20] According to Captain John Stover, the Commander of the Bethesda Naval Medical School, Bobby went so far as to periodically visit the autopsy room during the procedure, further heightening the pressure on the investigators.[21]

Dr. Boswell testified that JFK's physician, Dr. Burkley, made it clear that he didn't want a report on the adrenals. Burkley was in constant phone contact with Bobby and Jackie.[22] An FBI agent present confirmed that, to this point, there was "no question that Burkley was conveying the wishes of the Kennedy family."[23]

The above accounts, taken together, demonstrate a family's abnormal concern over the details of a murder autopsy. There is little doubt about the reason for the Kennedy family intrusions. It was indeed a coverup, but not of the assassination.

During the 1960 primary campaign for president, questions about JFK's health had been raised from many quarters, including that of Lyndon Johnson, then a Democratic rival for the party's nomination. The American public, traditionally sensitive about the health of their candidates, was assured that Kennedy was in fine shape. They were further assured that rumors of his having Addison's disease, about which the voters were particularly concerned, were incorrect.

In fact, the assurance was entirely false. In recent years, it has been learned—from Kennedy's own autopsists—that Kennedy's adrenals had atrophied to the point where they had practically evaporated, leaving only a few trace cells behind.[24] The *Journal of the American Medical Association* summarized the importance of this finding:

> *The Nixon vs. Kennedy presidential election of 1960 was extremely close; a scant 0.17% (114,673) of voters separated the victor from the loser. The mental and physical health of a presidential candidate in 1992—or in 1960—is of great political concern to the electorate. But had the American people been told that one candidate had suffered for more than 13 years from an incurable, potentially fatal, although fully treatable disease and that there were potential serious adverse effects of treatment, would the election results have been different?[25]*

When asked about Kennedy's adrenals in 1992, Dr. Finck curtly cut off this line of questioning, saying, "Don't even ask. There were no wounds in the abdomen; the adrenal glands have nothing to do with the wounds and the assassination of the President."[26] Asked the same question, Dr. Humes answered, "I am not prepared to answer this question now...At some time in the near future, Jay [Boswell] and I will have to sit down and write for history our report on the condition of the President's adrenal glands."[27] In 1996, Boswell admitted to the Assassinations Record Review Board that Humes in fact promised the Kennedy family attorney, Burke Marshall, "that we would not discuss the adrenals until all the members of the Kennedy family were dead."

Of even more potential embarrassment was the fact that JFK suffered from severe and persistent venereal disease—gonorrhea, specifically. Long-rumored, this fact became conclusive when the notes of JFK's physician, Dr. William Herbst, were made available at the Kennedy Library in Boston in 1992. Those notes clearly reveal his treatment of Kennedy's massive "gonococcal infections."

Herbst was originally called in 1950, after the renowned Lahey Clinic of Boston had failed to halt Kennedy's VD infection. Not only did the clinic admit failure, but so did Herbst, who treated JFK for 10 years before passing the baton to Dr. Janet Travell, the new President's personal physician. The available medical record shows that Kennedy continued to receive massive doses of penicillin (600,000 units at a time) throughout his presidency, including one injection on the very day of the Bay of Pigs invasion.[28]

Thus, on the evening of November 22, decisions were made by Robert Kennedy to perpetuate the lie of JFK's health history—a move that also served to consolidate the myth of Camelot. For years, this secrecy fed the flames of rumors about a government-based conspiracy. In 1998, after an exhaustive review of the events, the Assassinations Record Review Board concluded that, "[in] protecting the privacy and the sensibilities of the president's family—the legacy of such secrecy has caused distrust and suspicion."

Before leaving the autopsy suite, Dr. Finck was specifically instructed by the Surgeon General of the Navy not to discuss the case without first coordinating with Robert Kennedy.[29] That directive was bolstered two weeks later, on December 6, when Bobby Kennedy directed JFK's personal physician, Dr. Travell (over her strong objections), that "all correspondence which deals with a personal medical matter should be regarded as privileged information, and should not go to the Central Files."[30]

The Flawed "Autopsy of the Century"

It was under these extreme pressures that the overwhelmed autopsists proceeded. Political realities and personal considerations dominated. Much of the controversy that would later surround the JFK autopsy focused on the competence of Drs. Humes and Boswell. In fact, given what they were charged to determine, they were competent. "My orders were to find the cause of death," Humes later recalled. And therein lies the crux of the controversy.

There is a fundamental difference between a pathological autopsy (as performed by Humes and Boswell) and a legal-forensic autopsy performed in murder cases. Although Humes and Boswell determined the cause of death, a bullet to JFK's head, they were not precise enough for medical-legal standards—which they weren't told to consider. (In truth, the doctors should have been prescient enough to undertake this type of autopsy without being so directed.) As a result, the President's head was not shaved, and the brain not sectioned. These procedures would have determined the exact point of entrance and trajectory of the fatal wound.

The doctors made at least two other clear mistakes: First, they attempted to track the angle of Kennedy's back wound with their fingers. Considered an unpardonable breach of medical protocol, this action made the wound impossible to accurately describe. Secondly, the Bethesda staff didn't consult with the

Dallas doctors prior to the autopsy. If they had, their initial impressions about the wound to Kennedy's back, and their subsequent investigation, would have been very different. The Dallas emergency crew, in performing a tracheotomy, had obliterated the exit wound in the front of Kennedy's throat. Therefore, those given the job of describing Kennedy's wounds didn't see even one of them. It wasn't until a discussion the following day with Dallas that the Bethesda doctors realized their oversight.

Dr. Michael Baden, a former New York Medical examiner, recently summarized the performance of the Bethesda physicians. "In 1963, there was little appreciation for the difference of the two very different types of autopsies available," explains Baden. "There was the usual hospital one, which is what the President received, and there was the forensic one. Most people mistakenly thought a pathologist was a pathologist."[31]

Years later, when Dr. Pierre Finck testified about the disconcerting presence of the military at the autopsy, another conspiratorial thread was woven. According to some, Finck's testimony is evidence of military control of the autopsy. What Finck may not have realized was that the military men were all aides to the dead President.

In 1992, Dr. Humes recalled the scene: "The President's military aides from the Air Force, Army, and Navy were all present, and they were all in dress uniforms, but they weren't generals and their influence on the autopsy was zero," Humes recalled. "The only high-ranking officer was Admiral Burkley [JFK's personal physician] and he left shortly after the autopsy began to join Jackie and Bobby upstairs."[32] Dr. Finck recently expressed his agreement with Humes, saying, "I saw generals, but they did not interfere with the autopsy. There was no military interference."[33]

One final aspect of the Bethesda episode created an enduring mystery in the minds of many—another example of conspiracy talk that could have been quickly dispelled had Bobby Kennedy been interested in doing so. At the autopsy's conclusion, President Kennedy's brain, as well as tissue samples, were given to Dr. Burkley, who told Doctors Humes and Boswell that the president's family intended to give it all to Bobby Kennedy for subsequent burial. In fact, the brain would move from one location to another, and finally, in 1972, was declared missing (*as is discussed later, in Chapters Seventeen and Eighteen*). Later, it would be alleged that "conspirators" made off with the brain in order to hide the fact that Kennedy was shot from the front, when, in fact, it was simply a matter of Robert Kennedy taking control of an unusual and somewhat chaotic situation.

The Mysterious File

Back at the Vice President's Washington home, the new President, Lyndon Johnson, received a visit from CIA Director, John McCone. Former LBJ speechwriter Leo Janos relates what happened: "When Lyndon got back from Dallas,

McCone briefed him" on the cause of the assassination, allegedly saying: "It was the Castro connection." The information was contained in a file McCone brought with him to LBJ's vice-presidential residence. In the days to come, more secret files on the possible "Castro connection" would be viewed and destroyed in Washington corridors of power.

According to Janos, Johnson immediately called Senator Richard Russell, relayed to him McCone's conclusion, and asked, "What do we do?" Russell replied, "Don't let it out. If you do, it's World War III." Johnson swore Russell to secrecy, and proceeded to destroy McCone's file.[34] This would not be the last reference to a mystery file suggesting possible Cuban involvement in Kennedy's murder.

Under heavy guard, Lyndon Johnson was later observed off in a quiet corner of the first floor living room. He was staring at a painting of his deceased idol, and fellow Texan, former Speaker of the House, Sam Rayburn. Johnson raised his glass of carbonated orange soda and said, "Oh, Mister Sam, I wish you were here now. How I need you."[35]

New Orleans

Dave Ferrie, one of the foot soldiers in Bobby Kennedy's secret war, was in court when news of the assassination reached New Orleans. Ferrie had been working in recent years as a legal assistant to attorney G. Wray Gil. "Dave had a photographic memory," remembers friend Layton Martens. "Gil used him both in researching and pleading cases. Ferrie was very successful, winning over twenty cases for Gil."[36] On the morning of November 22, 1963, Gil was working for the local Mafia don, Carlos Marcello. Marcello was in the midst of fighting a series of deportation hearings instigated by Bobby Kennedy.

After winning the court case, Ferrie met up with two young friends, Al Beauboeuf and Melvin Coffey. For three weeks, the three men had been planning a car-driving vacation into Texas. Much has been made about the conspiratorial possibilities of such a trip: Ferrie, the pilot, with links to 544 Camp Street, may have been preparing to fly the assassins out of Texas, the thinking went. The truth is far less suspicious.

"Ferrie had said that if he won the case, he might be interested in purchasing a skating rink," says friend Layton Martens, who stayed at Ferrie's apartment while Ferrie and friends made the trip to the closest skating facility in Houston, Texas. "I was a former roller skating champion with dozens of medals," says Al Beauboeuf. "I wanted to see how good I'd do on ice. I had convinced Dave that ice skating was going to be the next big thing—like disco became in the seventies. We had been planning the trip for a couple of weeks."[37] It should be noted that on May 10, 1967 Al Beauboeuf, like Layton Martens, took and passed a lie detector test on these issues.[38]

"When Dave returned from the trip, he was in shock and disbelief over the assassination, as we all were," says Martens, "but he had more pressing concerns—[D.A] Jim Garrison was after him." By this time, District Attorney Garrison had spoken with local adventurer Jack Martin, who spun his tale that Oswald and Ferrie were acquainted. Although Martin eventually recanted much of his story, Garrison would continue to pursue Ferrie until Ferrie's death in 1967. To many locals, it had the appearance of a vendetta. It may have been.

"For years, Ferrie had been trying to put Garrison in jail," says Martens. "Dave had helped Guy Banister compile 'the bomb' on Garrison. Garrison never forgave him for it." According to Martens, "Banister and Dave Ferrie had 'the goods' on [D.A. Jim] Garrison, among other people. Banister called his file on Garrison 'the bomb.' He used to carry it around with him in his briefcase. It was almost a foot thick."[39] All former Banister employees interviewed agreed that the files contained political dynamite.

But "the bomb," however explosive, would never be used, because Garrison got his hands on it first. Martens recounts how the "bombshell" file came into Garrison's possession. Ray Comstock of Garrison's office entered Ferrie's apartment after midnight on Sunday, November 25, 1963, "with no search warrant," with Ferrie kept outside, forbidden from entering. "I was a witness to Garrison burglarizing Dave's apartment," says Martens. "[Police Officer] Ray Comstock had a gun pointed at my face. They arrested me on 'suspicion,' and held me incommunicado for three days."[40] Martens says the Kennedy assassination provided a convenient pretext for the true purpose of the raid: "They wanted Dave's file on Garrison—'the bomb,'" Martens says adamantly.

Ferrie was furious, according to his godson Morris Brownlee. Brownlee recalls, "Dave said Garrison's allegations were 'Goddamned ridiculous. Garrison's people act like gestapos.'"[41]

After Ferrie calmed down, the talk turned to the assassination. Brownlee recalls the discussion: "Dave thought it was a terrible thing. Dave was a very religious man, and very much into the idea of order. He equated the assassination to a high crime and anarchy."[42]

Like many others who had even minimal contact either with Bobby Kennedy's secret war or with Lee Oswald, Dave Ferrie was about to begin a personal nightmare.

Dallas: The Shooter in Custody

> *"Honest people don't hide anything, but you're a deceiver. You're always deceiving. You deceive everyone."*
> —**Marina Oswald to Lee (in Russia), from a KGB surveillance tape**[43]

> *"I could see by his eyes that he was guilty."*
> —**Marina Oswald, after visiting Lee in prison**

The Dallas Police Department's interrogation of Lee Oswald started immediately. That weekend, he would be interviewed five times for a total of 12 hours. Both federal and local authorities participated in the process, but Oswald divulged next to nothing.

Even before police realized that their Tippit murder suspect was the same man missing from the Depository, Homicide detective Jim Leavelle was alone with Oswald, asking routine questions. "He was sitting very quietly and didn't seem outwardly perturbed about anything," recalls Leavelle. "He answered my questions, but he didn't tell me the truth...He said, 'I didn't shoot anybody.'"[44]

Based on Oswald's behavior when arrested at the theater, police were already fairly certain they had the man responsible for the Tippit slaying. Leavelle informed Oswald that the police could run a ballistics test on the pistol to prove Oswald killed Tippit—Leavelle was trying for a quick confession. Oswald countered, "Well, you'll just have to do it."

Soon, however, it was determined that Oswald was the man missing from the Book Depository, and Leavelle removed his prisoner. The subsequent interrogations would be conducted under the direction of Dallas' homicide chief, Captain Will Fritz.

Will Fritz was a legend among local cops, especially revered for his prowess in conducting interrogations. Jim Leavelle remembers, "I once heard him get a confession on the telephone from a man in Cincinnati, Ohio—on a murder!" Leavelle says that Fritz embodied the "good cop" style of interrogation. He would use his good 'ol boy charm to soften up his suspects, just before he blindsided them. "He would let you know that you could trust him and he would do what he could to help you," says Leavelle.

The Cincinnati confession is a good example. Leavelle says the suspect consistently denied any involvement. Fritz switched to inane topics like hunting and baseball. Then, when the conversation was rolling, Fritz slipped in, "By the way, was this the first time you killed anybody?"

The man responded without thinking, "Oh, yes, but—" The line went dead. But it wasn't long before Fritz had his all-important signed confession. Most observers felt Fritz's style would eventually work on Oswald as well.

Years later, critics would cite the lack of a stenographer, and the failure to tape record the interrogation sessions as proof of a police coverup. The fact is that the Dallas police had no taping system in 1963. Further, a stenographer would have been useless because Oswald wasn't doing much besides nodding his head.

Finally, according to the Assistant District Attorney at the time, Bill Alexander, "[The tapes] would have been inadmissible in any court."[45] (Although the landmark *Miranda vs. Arizona* decision, which mandated the reading of rights and the presence of an attorney, was not rendered until June 13, 1966, Texas law already contained similar provisions. Oswald had no lawyer present.) In the end, all that mattered was a signed and witnessed confession. Leavelle summarized:

We did it the hard way. After we broke a man down, he would confess, then we had him reduce it to writing and sign it in front of witnesses, usually newspaper people—then he can't go to court later and claim he was coerced.

Besides, what's the use of keeping a thousand words of conversation that you're never going to be able to use? Another purpose of the interrogation was to indicate to police if they should be fanning out for accomplices.[46]

One of those present for the interrogation was Frank Ellsworth, a local agent from the federal Bureau of Alcohol, Tobacco and Firearms (ATF). He recalls that Oswald, with a "smug look on his face," was "surrounded by 14 agents and officers and he didn't even seem disturbed. He had the 'cat-that-ate-the-canary' look on his face the whole time."[47] Police Officer Elmo Cunningham found Oswald "a very arrogant young man."[48] Cunningham's impressions were shared by everyone else present. Ellsworth confirms that Oswald denied everything and "kept trying to change the subject." Ellsworth remembers Oswald as looking "self-satisfied."

When Oswald did speak, he rarely even flirted with the truth. "I couldn't get a direct answer from him about the gun. I tried twice and gave up," Ellsworth remembers. Oswald's constant and characteristic lying seems to have unnerved a number of those present. He lied, for example, about owning a rifle and pistol, about his "Hidell" alias, about the backyard photos showing him with his weapons, even about where he lived. His manner while delivering these falsehoods was consistently calm—with one glaring exception. Jim Hosty, who was also present, explained:

> *Now I kind of stuck my neck out. I figured with the President being killed, I'd better go ahead and press the issue on this, and I said, 'Have you ever been to Mexico?' And Oswald said, 'Yes, I've been to Tijuana when I was in the Marine Corps.' And I said, 'Have you been to Mexico City?' And at that he blew up and he said, 'How did you know? I—I—I didn't—I've never been there.' He started to admit it and then, quickly changed, and said, 'No, I've never been there. How'd you know about that?' And it was obvious that I had startled him. It was the only time he ever became unglued.*[49]

Hosty recalls the suspect's other admission. When Hosty asked Oswald how he had received the bruises to his face, Oswald replied, "I resisted arrest and I had it coming." This was a far cry from his earlier protestations of total compliance in the Texas Theater.

Meanwhile, the case against Oswald was mounting exponentially, with or without his cooperation. At lineups, he was identified as the Tippit murderer. His rifle as well as dozens of his fingerprints were found in the sniper's nest, precisely where witnesses in the plaza below had seen someone who looked just like Oswald shoot. One of the chief "indicators" to the professionals was the fact that Oswald alone had fled the Depository, gone home, gotten a pistol, and killed a cop. Flight from a crime puts up red flags for any investigator.

While the interrogation dance with Oswald proceeded, other members of the Dallas police force collected evidence in other parts of the city. Investigators learned that Oswald had stored his meager possessions in the garage at Ruth Paine's home. The materials they confiscated gave an early indication of

Oswald's links to pro-Castro groups. Listed among the pamphlets the police collected were the following titles:

- *"The Crime Against Cuba"*
- *"Fidel Castro Denounces Bureaucracy and Sectarianism"*
- *"The Socialist Workers Party"*
- *"The Coming American Revolution"*
- *"Cuban Counter Revolutionaries to the U.S."* by the Fair Play for Cuba Committee (FPCC)
- *A list of Communist and Russian publications*
- *"The Revolution Must Be a School of Unfettered Thought"* by Fidel Castro
- *An FPCC catalogue*
- *"The Road to Socialism"*
- *"Speech at the U.N."* by Fidel Castro

At 7 p.m. on Friday, November 22nd, roughly five hours after being taken into custody, Oswald was charged in the Tippit slaying. Six and one-half hours later, at 1:30 a.m. on Saturday, he was charged with the President's assassination. By now, the police had collected the damning pro-Castro material from the Paine garage, and been advised both of the Cuban Embassy aspects of Oswald's background, and his defection to the Soviet Union.[50] Assistant D.A. Alexander leaked the fact that he intended to formally charge Oswald with committing the assassination "in the furtherance of a communist conspiracy."

When the press reported this, Alexander was telephoned by a very irate D.A. Henry Wade. Jim Hosty remembers, "When President Johnson found out about this [Alexander's "conspiracy" charge], he had somebody from the White House—it was either Clark Clifford or Cliff Carter—call down to the District Attorney Henry Wade and demand that he immediately remove that from the complaint."[51] "What the hell are you trying to do, start World War III?" Wade screamed at Alexander. The offending language was quickly removed.[52]

New Orleans

By Saturday morning, November 23, U.S. investigators had obtained copies of the fliers Oswald had stamped with the address 544 Camp Street. Early that day, Secret Service agents visited the building and were told that Oswald was not a tenant, but that the building had been a headquarters for an anti-Castro exile group, the Cuban Revolutionary Council, run for a time by Sergio Arcacha Smith.[53] However, neither the Secret Service nor the later investigators were informed that the CRC and Arcacha were linked directly to the Kennedy brothers' White House. Neither were they told about OPLAN 380-63, the full-scale assault against Cuba that the brothers had planned for the coming weeks. And neither did they know that New Orleans was acting as one of many staging points, helping to supply the Cuban exile camps in Nicaragua and other Central

American countries.

Two days later, the FBI made a cursory phone call to Guy Banister, whose New Orleans office was around the corner from the CRC, and also in the Newman Building. Because the Bureau had an ongoing relationship with Banister, the agents were well aware that the straight-laced former Special Agent in Charge was no presidential murderer. Thus, during their five-minute chat, Oswald's name was never brought up. Banister was merely asked if he had any knowledge of young men associated with the 544 Camp Street address. He replied that he had a passing acquaintance with Arcacha years ago, who once was in the company of a young man—who could have been any of a number of CRC volunteers like Layton Martens.[54]

Years later, this brief interview would be seized upon by conspiracy theorists as evidence that the FBI was in on Kennedy's murder, and had helped cover up Banister's role as an accomplice. These theorists had no inkling of the sensitive nature of Banister's ongoing Bureau contacts. He was, in fact, a small cog in J. Edgar Hoover's dirt-gathering machine, supplying the director with the goods on local pols. And Hoover wasn't about to expose that.

Washington

Much to Robert Kennedy's dislike, he and Jackie had to wait until almost 4 a.m. Saturday, November 23rd, to accompany Jack's body from Bethesda Naval Hospital to the White House. Later that morning, the Attorney General tried to get some sleep in the Lincoln Bedroom of the White House. He was heard sobbing and crying out, "Why, God, why?"[55]

On Saturday morning, the family viewed the open casket of President Kennedy in the East Room of the White House. A major debate was then raging over whether the general public should also be allowed to view the open casket of the deceased President. Jackie was adamantly against it from the start. When pressed that the public would want to see a head of state, Jackie replied, "I don't care. It's the most awful, morbid thing; they have to remember Jack alive."[56]

After polling those who observed the body, Bobby came to agree with Jackie that the public viewing should be of a closed coffin. Besides, Bobby had said, "It doesn't look like him." The face was described as "waxen" and "rubbery." Later, Jackie would confide, "It wasn't Jack. It was like something you would see at Madame Tussaud's."[57]

Saturday night, after midnight, Bobby and Jackie returned to the open coffin to place personal mementos inside. Jackie had already placed her ring on her husband's finger. Now, she added three letters, a pair of Jack's cufflinks, and a piece of scrimshaw, which JFK had collected as a hobby. She then removed a lock of his hair. In his brother's coffin, Bobby placed his PT 109 tie clip, an engraved rosary,[58] and a lock of his own hair.[59]

The Death of Lee Harvey Oswald

Oswald's detention at the city jail was supposed to be temporary. In Dallas, the city jail is considered merely a holding facility, where prisoners typically are booked, held for three or four days, then transferred to the more secure county jail, located a few blocks away and, coincidentally, overlooking Dealey Plaza..

The members of the Dallas Police force seem to have been unanimous that Oswald should be moved secretly in the middle of the night. However, the decision of when to move him was neither Fritz's nor Curry's to make.

Detective Paul Bentley recently recalled, "Curry wanted to move Oswald at 2 a.m. [Sunday], but Elgin Crull [the city manager] overruled him." Crull had promised the press that they could see Oswald one more time, in part to prove that the police had not roughed him up after his arrest.[60] (FBI agent Jim Hosty adds that, three years later, Crull was quietly fired as a result of this decision. According to Hosty, when Hoover learned of Crull's decision, the FBI Director pressured Chief Curry into dismissing him.)

That Sunday, the new plan was to move Oswald at 10 a.m., but before that was to happen, several unexpected delays occurred. The suspect, still on the third floor of headquarters, expressed a desire to go back to his cell to select a different sweater to wear to his new jail location. (In what would turn out to be a fitting decision, he chose a black one.) After a last minute unscheduled interrogation, Oswald began his journey at about 11:18 a.m.

As Oswald was finally led into the third floor elevator, he was flanked on his right by Detective Jim Leavelle, to whom he was handcuffed, and on his left by L. C. Graves. Leavelle remembers talking with the prisoner:

> I said, more in jest, "Lee, if anybody shoots at you, I hope they're as good a shot as you are," and he kind of laughed and said, "Oh, you're being melodramatic—nobody's gonna shoot at me." I said, "Well, in case they do, you know what to do, don't you?" And he said, "Well, Captain Fritz told me to follow you out—I'll do whatever you do." I said, "In that case, you'll be on the floor very quickly."[61]

According to Leavelle, when the trio exited the basement doors to the garage, they encountered a blinding bank of press floodlights. When his eyes finally adjusted, one of the first things Leavelle discerned was a local nightclub owner, well-known as a police hanger-on. Leavelle recalled, "I couldn't see anything...I was momentarily blinded by those lights...As I walked through the double doors, I saw Ruby in the crowd out of the corner of my eye...I could see the gun in his right hand down at his side."

Jack Ruby, who had arrived at Oswald's transfer only seconds before, screamed: "You killed my President, you son of a bitch!" He got off only one shot, but it was one in a million.[62] Army wound expert Dr. John Lattimer put it this way:

> It's pretty hard to imagine a bullet doing more damage than that. It perforated

*the chest cavity, went through the diaphragm, spleen, and stomach. It cut off
the main intestinal artery, and the aorta, and the body's main vein, as well as
breaking up the right kidney. That wound was definitely fatal.[63]*

Leavelle recalls, "Oswald just groaned when he was shot—that's the only
sound he made." Within seconds, he slipped into unconsciousness. Riding with
him in the ambulance, Leavelle observed, "He groaned and stretched a little bit,
and then just went completely limp, and actually that's when I think he expired,
because I never saw him make another move at all."

As the police dragged Jack Ruby away to a holding cell, he kept yelling, "I
hope I killed the son of a bitch! I hope I killed the son of a bitch!" Hyped-up,
Ruby bragged to the cops about how he had just saved them a lot of trouble,
avenged his beloved dead President, and honored his Jewish heritage (his birth
name was Rubinstein) all in one stroke. He was, at least momentarily, very
proud. Later that day, having had time to reflect, Ruby told Jim Leavelle, "All I
wanted to do was be a hero, but it looks like I just fucked things up good."[64]

An example of the kind of confusion and paranoia rampant that weekend
is the way the Ruby news was received at the White House. Kennedy's deputy
press secretary, Malcolm Kilduff, recently recalled, "There was a White House
employee named Jack Rublee. The staff initially thought he had killed Oswald
in a state of hysteria."[65]

Numerous interviews with those who had contact with Ruby on that weekend in November, combined with the author's discovery of Ruby's diary (kept in
jail), make the motivation of Oswald's killer clear. Ruby, apparently a manic-
depressive, revered, among other things, the city of Dallas, the Dallas Police,
President Kennedy, and his Jewish heritage. When Ruby learned that the infamous black-bordered anti-Kennedy newspaper ad appearing in the Dallas papers
was paid for, in part, by a Jew (Bernard Weissman), he feared the worst. As Ruby
anticipated, Dallas was now awash with rumors that Kennedy's death resulted
from a Jewish conspiracy.

It was all too much for a man who, according to his friends and employees,
had been crying like a baby all weekend. With many in Dallas, and indeed the
nation, whispering that Oswald should be killed, Ruby knew what he had to do.
(For more on Ruby, see Appendix C: "Who was Jack Ruby?")

Inn of the Six Flags

Before the events of that Sunday morning, Marina Oswald had already assured
herself of Lee's guilt. In 1964, Marina would spend six months with writer
Priscilla McMillan (*Marina and Lee*), giving the author her story, including her
impressions of this day:

> *Marina was now certain that Lee was guilty. She saw his guilt in his eyes.
> Moreover, she knew that had he been innocent he would have been screaming
> to high heaven for his "rights," claiming he had been mistreated and demand-
> ing to see officials at the very highest levels, just as he had always done before.*

For her, the fact that he was so compliant, that he told her he was being treated "all right," was a sign that he was guilty.

Marina's biographer summarized her feelings:

Was he sorry for what he had done? Marina's impressions were mixed...She thought that he was glad he had succeeded, and yet at the same time sorry...In spite of his obvious satisfaction, it seemed to her that he was also carrying a burden of regret heavier than he, or anyone, could bear. He was on the edge of tears all the time they were together and was barely holding them back...He had looked at her altogether uncharacteristically, with supplication in his eyes...He knew this was the end.[66]

This was Marina's state of mind on Sunday morning when she heard the news that Lee had just been shot. Secret Service agents Mike Howard and Charles Kunkle were assigned to locate Oswald's surviving family (mother, brother Robert, Marina and the two babies) and transport them to sequestered protection at the Inn of the Six Flags motel, halfway between Fort Worth and Dallas. Priscilla McMillan later wrote that:

Word had come from the Attorney General, Robert Kennedy, and the new President, Lyndon Johnson, that the Secret Service was to protect the Oswald family. Within an hour the inn was an armed camp, with men patrolling outside armed with carbines. "All we need is to have one more of you killed," one agent said, "and we're in real trouble."[67]

Agent Mike Howard remembered a call from Johnson himself, ordering, "Nobody talks to those people, not even Washington. Nothing is to happen to that family."[68] At one point, Howard instructed one of the local police guards to remain outside the motel as a "final line of resistance." Howard handed the cop a submachine gun and ordered him, "If anyone comes up that walk, you take care of 'em one way or the other."[69]

The protective entourage remained at the inn for five days, during which Mike Howard developed a friendship with Lee's brother Robert, as well as with Marina, whom Howard assured wasn't headed to a U.S. prison camp. (Howard remains friendly with Marina to this day.)

The assassin's mother, Marguerite, was another matter altogether. Howard remembers her as being "nutty as a fruitcake." Marguerite grew "angrier and more abusive by the hour," at one point demanding to know why her son—who had served in the Marines, after all—would not be buried in Arlington National Cemetery with Kennedy.

During the five days of sequestration, Howard would interrogate the Oswalds. The recorded conversations, by his estimate, comprised over 1,000 feet of recording tape. In one of their conversations, Howard asked Marina about a piece of evidence he had recovered among Lee's possessions the day after the assassination. It was a little blue memo book which belonged to Lee. Howard read Oswald's scribblings in the book and hoped Marina could shed light on them. According to Howard, Oswald noted his intention to kill General Edwin Walker, Governor John Connally (a former Secretary of the Navy), and Vice-President Lyndon Johnson. In a notation referring to FBI agent Hosty, Oswald had written, "I will kill this son of a bitch." Up until this time, the Walker shooting had remained an open case, with no suspects. Marina now closed the case, admitting to Howard that Lee told her of his murder attempt the previous spring.

In a few days, the FBI took over the interrogation of the Oswald family. Howard reluctantly surrendered the blue memo book to the FBI. He didn't tell them that he had read its entire contents into his tape recorder, although he also had to hand those recordings over. Howard suspected that the tape, including Oswald's assassination threat, would vanish and, in fact, neither ever surfaced.

Years after the assassination, Howard was assigned to Lyndon Johnson's security detail, and brought up the topic with LBJ. At the time, Johnson appeared stunned that a page was missing from Oswald's recovered memo book. When he heard the page's contents, he told Howard, "That wasn't in there."

"It was when we saw it," Howard said. "It's on the tape." According to the *Houston Post*, "The pair speculated that FBI Director J. Edgar Hoover could have had those pages removed. Or that maybe they had disappeared somehow between the FBI and the [Warren] Commission."[70]

In 1993, Frontline investigator Scott Malone, unaware of the Howard story, was given access to Oswald's addressbook at the National Archives. Malone recalls that the book was "blue-black," consistent with Howard's description. At that viewing, Malone became the first person to discover that one page of the notebook had been removed by a precise "razor-cut."[71]

CIA Headquarters, Langley, Virginia

Just when Des FitzGerald and the CIA thought the news could get no worse, it did. On Sunday, November 24, while Oswald was meeting his maker, CIA headquarters received a cable from the Mexico City Station. The station had been compiling a list of individuals recently seen in the Soviet Embassy with Oswald's contact there, KGB agent Valery Kostikov. One name on the list was Rolando Cubela Secades, known to Bobby Kennedy and Des FitzGerald as AM/LASH.[72]

A second cable arrived that day with still more frightening information: Cubela was acquainted with Theresa Proenza, the first person to meet Oswald in the Cuban Embassy, and a counter-intelligence target of the CIA. She functioned as the Cultural Attaché for the embassy, and in this capacity had arranged press conferences for Cubela when he visited Mexico City. Sinister implications were unavoidable: Proenza's close friend Sylvia Duran admitted to having affairs with both Oswald and Cuban Delegate to the UN Carlos Lechuga. Lechuga was the focus of the Kennedys' "Track One" initiative, linked to a pro-Castro terrorist cell, and the recipient of warning letters from Fernando Fernandez, who had infiltrated the New Orleans bases of the Cuba Project.

FitzGerald thus became consumed by the possibility that Castro, through any number of contacts, had found out about AM/LASH—and that many of these contacts had also met with Lee Harvey Oswald. Now FitzGerald, presented with a list of Cuban Embassy visitors that included Cubela, was asked for any information he could add to the investigation of Kennedy's death. Did, for example, anyone in the Agency know Cubela?

Although RFK's friend FitzGerald knew of the implications, and in fact knew Cubela, he didn't say a word. The scene was described by Evan Thomas of *Newsweek:*

> *FitzGerald kept silent. Technically, he did not have to answer. His super secret Special Affairs Staff was exempt from queries from the Counterintelligence staff...A decade later, when the CIA official who was assigned to oversee the Agency's investigation of the assassination learned about Cubela, he stated, "That would have become an absolutely vital factor in analyzing the events surrounding the Kennedy assassination."*

> *At lunch on Sunday, FitzGerald was at home watching television when Jack Ruby shot Oswald...[His] wife Barbara was shocked to see her husband burst into tears. She had never seen him cry before. "Now," said FitzGerald, "we'll never know."*[73]

Years later, an undated memo from FitzGerald would surface that clearly conveyed his fears about the AM/LASH operation: "The AM/LASH circle is wide and each new friend of whom we learn seems to have knowledge of the plan," FitzGerald wrote. "I believe the problem is a more serious and basic one. Fidel reportedly knew that this group was plotting against him and once enlisted its support. Hence, we cannot rule out the possibility of provocation."[74]

Continuing the coverup, on Monday, November 25, 1963, Nestor Sanchez, Cubela's case officer, drafted a routine "contact report" of his Paris meeting with Cubela on November 22. The report conveniently omitted the passing of the poison pen to Cubela. Sanchez later told the Church Committee that FitzGerald ordered him to drop that detail from his report.[75]

The night after the murder, the Secret Service brought over to the CIA a copy of an 8mm home movie taken of the murder, the "Zapruder film." Now, in another part of the CIA's headquarters, the National Photographic Interpretation Center, the Agency's top photo analyst, Dino Brugioni, watched in horror as the top of the president's head exploded in a shower of crimson. Brugioni recently recalled:

> *There were six or seven of us at the meeting. We were asked to time it, which was difficult because the camera was spring-loaded. We also developed still frames, which we enlarged and mounted on a large board which [Director] McCone took over to President Johnson. Later, we had the U-2*

photograph Oswald and Marina's residences in Minsk. We gave the photos to Richard Helms.[76]

Cuba on Their Minds

Official Washington assured itself early that the Soviets had not been involved in the assassination. Top secret wiretaps and intercepts by the National Security Agency made it clear that Moscow was clearly surprised and alarmed over the killing—Khrushchev appeared downright frantic. Cuba, however, was a different matter. Hal Hendrix, the Miami-based Scripps-Howard reporter known for his Agency contacts at the JM/WAVE (Miami) Station, wrote on November 24 that, "Federal investigators are probing reports that Oswald...may have been in touch with Castro's G-2 or espionage agents in this country."[77] Outside of Oswald's connection to the Fair Play for Cuba Committee, it has never been revealed which Cuban agents the government considered to be likely contacts for Oswald.

Even though most in the CIA were unaware of the AM/LASH-Des FitzGerald connection, thoughts of a Castro-based plot dominated the Agency's thinking immediately after the murder. A perusal of the record reflects a constant theme: Cuba.

Consider the following CIA activity:

Saturday, Nov 23—CIA Director John McCone meets with LBJ to discuss information from the CIA in Mexico City; the CIA cables AM/LASH's case officer, telling him to break off contact with AM/LASH because of the president's assassination. The Agency also wants the planned arrest of Sylvia Duran called off, saying, "The arrest could jeopardize U.S. freedom of action on the whole question of Cuban responsibility."

Sunday, Nov 24—McCone meets with LBJ, this time concerning the CIA's operational plans against Cuba.

Monday, Nov 25—The Mexico City Station sends a dispatch to CIA headquarters reminding them of Castro's September 7 statement threatening U.S. leaders.

Tuesday, Nov 26—U.S. Ambassador to Mexico Thomas Mann sends a cable to the State Department, expressing his fears that Cubans were involved in the assassination. (He initiates his own investigation, but is stopped by the White House.)

Monday, Dec 2—CIA Director McCone meets at 10 a.m. with LBJ and national security advisor McGeorge Bundy; McCone's calendar reveals that, at 3 p.m., he has a still secret meeting to discuss Cuba in the CIA's conference room.

Wednesday, Dec 4—The CIA receives a report from one of its Cuban agents that he had met Oswald in Cuba, Mexico City, or the United States. This agent believes that the Cuban government employed assassins and carried out at least one assassination in Mexico.

Sunday, Dec 8—*CIA Headquarters cables the Florida Station ordering it to halt two planned operations against Cuba—one of which was to deliver weapons to the assassin AM/LASH.*

Monday, Dec 9—*A memo to McCone notes that dissident anti-Castro Cubans in Cuba want assurances that they will not be liquidated and will be protected following the planned plot and imminent coup in Cuba. (The fact that even people in Cuba were preparing for the coup provides further evidence that it was imminent, and likely would have occurred had the Kennedy assassination not intervened.)*

Tuesday, Dec 10—*McCone again meets secretly on Cuba in the CIA conference room.* [78]

Across the Potomac at the White House, concerns about Cuba mirrored those at the CIA. Army General Alexander Haig, who had been assigned to Robert Kennedy's super-secret Cuban Coordinating Committee, was now busy supervising the late president's funeral arrangements at Arlington National Cemetery. On Sunday morning (Nov 24), Haig was at the White House when he witnessed his CCC superiors Cyrus Vance, Robert McNamara, and others headed into a closed door meeting with President Johnson. At the time, Haig paid little heed to the meeting, but in the coming days, it would take on added significance. Haig later wrote:

Very soon after President Kennedy's death, an intelligence report crossed my desk. In circumstantial detail, it stated that Oswald had been seen in Havana in the company of Cuban intelligence officers several days before the events in Dallas, and that he traveled there by way of Mexico City...I walked the report over to my superiors, some of whom had attended that Sunday morning meeting with President Johnson. Reading it caused their faces to go ashen.

"Al," one of them said, "you will forget, from this moment on, that you ever read this piece of paper, or that it ever existed." The report was destroyed.[79]

Haig was impressed with the report's detail—"locale, precise notations of time, and more." He recently confirmed to the author that the report was hand-delivered to him by a CIA officer, and added that the report was read by both CCC leaders, Vance and Califano. "To this day, I'm convinced that Oswald not only visited Mexico City, but also Havana."

It is possible that Haig was reading the report filed by "Jeremy Ryan" (pseudonym), a CIA Chief of Station posted in Latin America. Recently, Ryan recalled to the author the day Kennedy was killed—a day when Ryan was attending a pre-arranged lunch meeting with a communist source he had developed. "This man was the best recruitment I had made in my thirty years with the Agency. He was very close to both Fidel and Ché [Guevara]." As the recruitment was

reconstructing recent conversations with Fidel and Che, in broke a Ryan intermediary with the news of Kennedy's murder. "On hearing the news from Dallas,
he [the source] broke down in tears, and said, 'Oh, my God. They said they
weren't going to do that.'"

Ryan immediately filed a report of this conversation with headquarters.
"When I reported that discussion, everything came down on me like a thun-
derstorm. Headquarters wanted me to develop more information. The most I
got was that my source had met Oswald in Cuba. Based on this source's known
reliability, I'm convinced to this day that Oswald was in Cuba."[80] We are left to
wonder: Are the Haig and Ryan "file" stories connected to McCone's briefing of
Johnson on the night of the assassination?

The reliability of the Oswald-in-Havana allegation was further bolstered by
sources for the CIA's Miami JM/WAVE Station. According to one such source,
Oswald was seen in Havana sometime during the first week of October in the
company of "Comandante Miranda," cited as an officer in the Cuban Navy.[81]

A source close to the CIA's Mexico Station Chief Win Scott likewise recalled
information about Oswald making a quick back-and-forth hop from Mexico
City to Havana, saying, "It had something to do with luggage that was found at
the airport."[82] This might be a reference to what Warren Commission staffers
referred to as the "two suitcase problem." During the official investigation into
the President's death, it was learned that Oswald had left New Orleans with two
suitcases, but was seen in Mexico City with only one.[83]

It should be recalled that Oswald spent four largely unaccounted-for days
during his trip to Mexico City. In addition, after returning to Dallas, Oswald's
whereabouts are unknown during the three days between October 7 and
October 11. Either of these gaps could have easily afforded him the time for a
plane trip to Havana. Also, recall that the Cuban Embassy was known to issue
false identifications, and to allow travelers to cross borders without stamping
their passports. Thus, there might be no record if, as Haig and others suspect,
Oswald had journeyed to the island.

The meetings delineated above—between November 23 and December 10—
represent only some of what the CIA and the White House were doing about
Cuba. A complete list of the Cuba-oriented activity would require many pages.[84]
A CIA memo later uncovered by Congressional investigator James Johnston
underscored the obvious reason for the meetings. Generated within the first
twenty-four hours after the assassination, the memo stated, according to
Johnston, that "there was reason enough to believe that Oswald was part of a
foreign plot."[85]

It is difficult to ascertain the extent to which Bobby Kennedy was informed
of the drama being played out over Cuba and Mexico City at CIA headquarters—the shroud of secrecy over his papers is so total. However, given the fact
that Bobby practically ran the CIA from 1961 through nearly end of 1963,
and had trusted allies like Des FitzGerald, Allen Dulles, and Richard Helms in
key CIA positions, he probably was aware of everything.

In a memo, Win Scott indicated that RFK's friend, Deputy Attorney General Nicholas Katzenbach, was being kept informed of the Mexico City developments.[86] It seems unlikely that Katzenbach had no discussions with his boss, RFK, on issues such as Oswald's link with "544 Camp St." and the Kennedys' trusted CRC. In addition, the U.S. Ambassador to Mexico in 1963, Thomas Mann—appointed by JFK—later gave a statement regarding Bobby Kennedy's involvement.

Mann had been conducting his own investigation of the killing through his contacts inside the various agencies and embassies in Mexico City. He had convinced himself that there was a Cuban component to the crime. Washington was, rightfully, concerned that Mann might jeopardize its own investigation. In 1993, Mann recalled what happened next:

> *I received this instruction to drop the investigation…It was the only time in my career that I was ever told to stop investigating. I still think it was strange…I had this suspicion that our intelligence community, which included Win Scott, knew much more about it [the assassination]…[Later] I got death threats, quite often in envelopes slipped under the embassy gates.*[87]

Mann would later add, "The message I received from Hoover…was, 'We don't want to hear any more about this case. And tell the Mexican government not to do any more investigating. We just want to hush it up.'"[88] When asked in 1976 why he didn't challenge the order to cease his investigation, Mann replied, "If the President's brother thought Oswald did it entirely on his own, I didn't see why I should be more Catholic than the Pope."[89]

Mann wasn't the only one receiving the "cease and desist" orders. Oswald's FBI case officer, Jim Hosty, soon became aware of Bobby Kennedy's direct control of the CIA's Mexico City investigation. Hosty later befriended Michael J. DeGuire, an FBI official stationed in the American embassy in Mexico City at the time of the assassination. According to DeGuire, "President Johnson and Robert F. Kennedy ordered intelligence agents in Mexico to stop pursuing a possible Cuban or Soviet connection."[90] Hosty recalled that DeGuire added, "There was a near mutiny on the part of the CIA agents when they were told this. It wasn't until they received word that Attorney General Robert Kennedy concurred that they finally agreed to cease and desist."[91]

Mexico City—The Day After Kennedy's Murder

Meanwhile, the reverberations of Dallas had hit Mexico City like a nuclear firestorm. On the day after the assassination, CIA headquarters in Langley received a cable from the Mexico City Station informing them that the Mexican Police were detaining and planning to arrest Sylvia Duran, the suspected triple agent with whom Oswald had been in contact, to interrogate her about Oswald. Headquarters immediately telephoned the Mexico Station ordering them to prevent the arrest. If Cuba was involved in the president's assassination, the CIA wanted to find out before the Mexico City police did. Considering that Duran was the CIA's occasional asset, and a close friend of CIA target Theresa Proenza, a Mexican police interrogation of Duran might be disastrously compromising, even if she knew nothing of the assassination.

Thomas Karamessines, Deputy to Richard Helms, the CIA's Deputy Director for Plans, has testified that "the CIA feared that the Cubans were responsible [for the assassination], and that Duran might reveal this during an interrogation." The Mexico Station cabled back that the arrest could not be stopped. Karamessines replied, saying that the arrest "could jeopardize U.S. freedom of action on the whole question of Cuban responsibility."[92] The CIA was also aware that automobiles owned by Duran's family bore Texas license plates, and, as stated before, that members of the family were known to make frequent trips into the state from Mexico.

The CIA was unsuccessful, however, in preventing the arrest, and was forced to settle for assisting Mexican authorities preparing their Duran interrogation questions. At this time, the CIA was clearly very interested in the possibility of a Cuban conspiracy. Among the questions it submitted on a written list were:

- *"Was the assassination of President Kennedy planned by Fidel Castro...and were the final details worked out inside the Cuban Embassy in Mexico?"*

- *"Who were Oswald's contacts during the period 26 September 1963 to 3 October 1963?"*

- *"If Castro planned that Oswald assassinate President Kennedy, did the Soviets have any knowledge of these plans?"*

Though these were, and remain, the three most critical questions surrounding the assassination, the CIA held out little hope that the Mexicans would pose them to Duran—relations between Mexico and Cuba were sensitive, and Mexico was one of the only countries in Latin America to maintain diplomatic ties with Havana. The Agency was forced to sweat it out, wondering how many secrets Duran was privy to, and worrying that her divulging of those secrets might compromise CIA operations inside the Cuban embassy. As expected, Duran's Mexican interrogators chose not to ask the critical questions about possible Cuban or Soviet complicity.[93]

Also on this day after the assassination, Duran's friend Elena Garro and her daughter, outraged at what they felt to be Cuban complicity in the crime, visited Duran at her place of work. As Garro herself later admitted, the two proceeded to cause a ruckus by pointing fingers at Cuban Embassy employees and screaming, "Assassins!"[94] Afterwards, a close friend, Manuel Calvillo, contacted Elena Garro.[95] An undercover agent for the Mexican Government, Calvillo had contacts both in the Cuban Embassy and with local police sources used by the CIA's Win Scott. Calvillo warned Garro that she was in danger from the "Communists." He proceeded to take Elena and her daughter—presumably with their consent—to a hotel to get them out of sight for a week.[96]

Havana

The CIA wasn't alone in its consuming interest about the Duran interrogation. Officials in Havana were burning up the phone lines to Cuban representatives in the Mexico City consulate. The Mexico City Police might be the first to know if there would be another world war, but Havana wanted to be second.

In a flurry of calls, all tapped by the CIA, Cuban President Osvaldo Dorticos phoned his representative in Mexico City, Ambassador Joaquin Hernandez Armas, wanting to know what Duran had told the police. In his call on Tuesday, November 26, Dorticos asked, "Had the police threatened [Duran] so that she would make a statement that the [Cuban] Consulate gave money to that man—that American?" The Cuban President repeated the question numerous times, just to make sure Hernandez understood. Hernandez said he had debriefed Duran, and the answer was "no."[97]

The CIA had been aware since at least 1960 that Cubela accompanied Dorticos on foreign trips *(CIA Memo of Dorticos' Uruguay Trip, June 20, 1960)*. Recall also that Dorticos, also a known friend of AMLASH/Cubela, traveled to New York in 1962 with a member of a Cuban terrorist cell linked to the Fair Play For Cuba Committee.

President Dorticos may have been interested in the Duran interrogation because of the appearance in the U.S. Embassy in Mexico City the previous day of Gilberto Alvarado. Alvarado, a young Nicaraguan, had told the U.S. officials that in mid-September, 1963, when he was in the Cuban Embassy to secure a visa, he saw Lee Oswald there. According to Alvarado, Oswald was in the company of a white man and a red-haired black man. Alvarado also claimed that, in the Cuban Embassy, Oswald's alleged lover, Sylvia Duran, gave Alfredo Mirabal, Consul Azcue's assistant, a total of $6500 in cash. Mirabal, in turn, handed it to Oswald. Accepting the money, Oswald commented, "You're not man enough [to kill him]. I can do it."[98]

At the same time, the CIA was being advised of rumors circulating in Mexico "that Oswald made a bank deposit of five thousand dollars in the United States after he got back from Mexico." Knowing of no such deposits, the CIA quickly disregarded this potentially corroborative piece of information.[99] Also, about this time, President Johnson received a letter from a Mexican credit investigator named Pedro Gutierrez. Gutierrez stated that he too had seen Oswald receive a large wad of money in the Cuban Embassy.

Although Gutierrez was viewed as a reliable witness, his story was never corroborated, and the big questions it raised were left unresolved; the Warren Commission's allocated research time had elapsed.[100]

Alvarado's original statement about an embassy money-exchange had set off a frenzy of activity in Washington and Mexico City. Eventually, Alvarado insisted that he had invented the story, then retracted his retraction, saying the story was true all along, but he had been pressured to retract it by the Mexican Police.

There was never any proof that President Dorticos knew of Alvarado. In discussing the subject, he may have been referring to the allegation (by Verson) linking Oswald to Cuban Ambassador Hernandez, or to any of the numerous other sinister possibilities linking Oswald to the Cubans. In any event, even if the Alvarado story is fiction, the persistence of Dorticos' calls remains striking.[101] He called Hernandez back twice that night, at late hours, still demanding to be assured that Sylvia Duran had said nothing about "money" and an offer to Oswald. Ambassador Hernandez seemed unsuccessful at easing Dorticos's worries. In closing their last conversation that night, Dorticos again asked if Duran had been questioned about money. Hernandez again said no.

It is worth noting that, at the time of this writing, virtually all of the Warren Commission documents ("Commission Documents or CDs") have been released, with a few exceptions, most involving personal tax records. One of the other exceptions is CD 1551. Parts of this document are still withheld by the CIA on the grounds that their release may endanger national security interests. As of this writing, it has been thirty-five years since the assassination, and one wonders what could still be of national security interest. Perhaps the subjects of the document, which are known, offer a clue. CD 1551 contains references to both Dorticos and Hernandez, and most likely concerns their telephone conversations.

The day after these conversations, Sylvia Duran attempted to flee Mexico City for Havana, but she was caught in the act and re-arrested by Mexican authorities.[102] Duran's friend, Theresa Proenza, however, did return to Cuba. She was relieved of her post in Mexico City within a month of the killing, and sent back to Havana, where, according to her brother, Alvaro, she was appointed Director of the Federal Public Library.[103]

By December 1963, the CIA would receive a report from a "very good source," stating:

Fidel Castro reportedly extremely concerned with persistence of investigation into President Kennedy's murder and with possible disclosures that could result...Dozen people in know have been jailed...Close friend [of source], Celia Sanchez, [claimed] plot organized by Castro...No Soviet participation...contact men in Dallas are [DELETED], and Fernandez Feito.[104]

There is no further information on the name "Feito." According to a reliable Cuban Intelligence Officer who defected to the U.S. after the assassination (known as A-1, or AM/MUG), Havana sent out instructions to sort and box all DGI documents according to secrecy classification. Travel by DGI officers, and the transporting of all DGI pouches, were suspended.[105] Through its UN Ambassador, Havana was sending out word to its various delegations "to cease looking happy in public" about President Kennedy's demise.

Oswald's Secret Life

Oswald's secret life is as key to unraveling the mysteries of the Kennedy assassination as his propensity to violence, his willingness to kill. "The question is not,

'Did Lee Harvey Oswald shoot the President?' The question is, 'Did he have help?'" stated Robert Blakey, former Chief Counsel for the House Select Committee on Assassinations, in 1993. "Within 30 hours of the assassination, that was the question. Thirty years later, that remains the question." Between that Saturday night and Monday morning, the question of whether there was a conspiracy to help Oswald was on the minds of Bobby Kennedy, Lyndon Johnson, and top officials in the CIA and FBI. All of these men would satisfy their curiosity in their own ways, but none of them would allow their conclusions to go on the record. And the historical record is far worse for it.

Due to these sadly incomplete investigations and the slow pace of investigation technology, the question of whether or not Oswald committed the assassination has dominated the discussion for 35 years. In the decades since the assassination, many genuinely puzzling questions have arisen: about ballistics, about echoes of gun fire in Dealey Plaza, about other possible shooters there, and about seeming contradictions in the medical and autopsy evidence. It took a range of scientific capabilities and tests developed after the late 1970's to lay the suspicions to rest: to confirm that the bullets that killed Kennedy came from Oswald's rifle and no other weapon; to demonstrate conclusively that there had been no other shots; and to prove that the "magic bullet" that traveled from Oswald's perch in the Texas School Book Depository through President Kennedy and through Governor John Connally had behaved quite normally, given its composition, path, and obstacles.

Still, Lyndon Johnson, Bobby Kennedy, and top-ranking government officials, for their own disparate reasons, obfuscated and clouded the issue, and the muddle they created has survived for thirty-five years. Skeptics would point to the "dark areas" in the case, the places the official investigations ignored, as evidence that each of these investigations had been subverted by a laughably huge conspiracy. In fact, these dark spots did represent a coverup—but not of a conspiracy to assassinate the President. This coverup was actually the effort of these "great men" who realized that to uncover the truth, whatever its shape, would possibly precipitate a nuclear war, and certainly destroy the memory of "Camelot."

The assassination of John F. Kennedy was a classic example of "blowback," as some in the intelligence profession call it: a disastrous backfire on a covert operation. Either Lee Oswald had found out what the Kennedys were up to, or someone loyal to Fidel had so informed him, and this information led to the tragic event of November 22, 1963. Evidence would be uncovered in the early investigations. The Redbird and Cubana Airlines incidents, Gilberto Policarpo Lopez's Saturday border crossing, "Julio Fernandez" and his associates' overhearing of an Oswald pro-Castro meeting, the Dorticos phone calls, the Alvarado story, the Calderon evidence and transcripts—all implied a Cuban conspiracy to kill the American President. And these aforementioned leads are only those publicly acknowledged in the case, not the information from the results of the private queries of Bobby Kennedy, Lyndon Johnson, Allen Dulles, Win

Scott (CIA Mexico City Station Chief), and numerous others in sensitive posts who never went on the record—leads which are now nearly impossible to pursue.

This evidence certainly seems to imply that Cuban agents were either pushing Oswald's buttons or helping him with money, equipment, or a means of escape. But these leads would not be followed. Unfortunately—and perhaps fortunately— they were left unresolved. The coverup prevented the discovery of the true facts about the President, and may have prevented a world war in retaliation for the Kennedy assassination.

For reasons both patriotic and selfish, America's "great men" of the times shielded from view both the secret war against Castro and the hints of a Cuban conspiracy to assassinate the President. These details became "The Big Secret." For three decades, Kennedy loyalists would fight tooth and nail to perpetuate the "lone nut" hypothesis and to keep the lid on the Kennedys' attempts to murder Fidel Castro. In their extreme efforts, the knights of Camelot allowed all sorts of other conspiracy theories to flourish. All that mattered was that "The Big Secret" not be revealed. From Lyndon Johnson to Bobby Kennedy, to members of the Warren Commission, they would all say that Oswald acted alone with no clear motive. They lied, or in the case of the Warren Commission, were kept out of the loop.

Bobby Kennedy did not want his culpability in his brother's murder to become a matter of public scrutiny. Castro had his own reasons to hide Oswald's Cuban connection. And Lyndon Johnson (and others like him) knew the feeling of the American public for Kennedy and against Castro. As the nation's new leader, he realized that if it were uncovered that the assassination may have been the result of Castro's success in the Kennedys' private feud, it could begin World War III. Thus, he hid the truth, and refused to follow suspicious, yet promising leads. LBJ, Bobby Kennedy, and others would help to clamp down the dirt on Kennedy and Oswald's graves, leaving a trail of doubt and unanswered questions lasting 35 years.

"William Bobo"

On Monday morning, November 25, while the nation was watching the lavish tribute and burial of John Kennedy at Arlington National Cemetery, Lee Oswald was buried in Rose Hill Cemetery in Fort Worth.[106] The two gravediggers were told that they were preparing a plot for a "William Bobo."[107] When Oswald's cheap moleskin-covered pine coffin arrived with over one hundred policemen in tow, the grave-diggers deduced whose hole they were digging.

Lee's brother Robert had assumed the difficult task of arranging for the funeral. As Marina's biographer Priscilla McMillan wrote, "One cemetery after another refused even to countenance the suggestion that they sell Robert a plot for his brother's body...The same thing happened with ministers. Four of them turned Robert down."[108]

The Lutheran minister who ended up presiding was practically forced to do so by the National Council of Churches in Dallas. At the proceedings, his hesitation and reluctance were not lost on the grief-stricken family.

Robert Oswald accompanied Marina and Marguerite to the burial, helping to carry Lee's daughters June and four-week-old Rachel. That was the extent of Oswald's mourners. The family was surrounded by FBI, Secret Service, and members of the press. Many of the press managed to reach a new low in insensitivity, even for members of the fourth estate. Conscripted into acting as pall-bearers, some of the journalists were photographed laughing and joking as they carried the coffin past the grieving family.

One of the journalists so conscripted was Jerry Herald, a free-lance photographer working now for the French magazine *Paris Match*. "It was pretty gruesome," remembers Herald. "There weren't very many volunteers to help carry the body so that might give you an idea of the anger—I would say there were not a lot of sad faces for Lee Oswald," says Herald. Just before the coffin was to be lowered into the ground, the FBI instructed that the casket be opened for final identification by Oswald's survivors. When this was done, Marina placed her wedding ring on the finger of her deceased husband, just as Jackie had days before.[109]

Upon returning to the motel sanctuary, federal agents Kunkle and Howard resumed their debriefing of the Oswalds. By this time, New Orleans D.A. Jim Garrison had finally spoken with Dave Ferrie, who had voluntarily surrendered himself to Garrison's office. Garrison had no reason to hold Ferrie, so he turned him over to the FBI for more questioning. Like Garrison, the FBI, many of whom knew Ferrie, also found no reason to hold him. According to Mike Howard, word of this reached the Justice Department in Washington.

Suddenly a phone call came to Howard from Robert Kennedy's Justice Department. "They wanted us to ask Marina if she had ever heard of Dave Ferrie," remembers Howard. "We did—she didn't."[110]

By February 1964, Robert Kennedy would personally authorize the FBI to place bugs and wiretaps on Marina Oswald's residence. No conspiratorial contact was ever overheard.[111]

CHAPTER SIXTEEN

THE INVESTIGATIONS

"Looking back, I feel a certain amount of shame. I think the FBI can look back and feel that this one investigation disgraced a great organization."
   —FBI Supervisor Laurence Keenan, who conducted the Mexico City portion of the FBI's investigation[1]

"I personally believe Oswald was the assassin... As to whether he was the only man gives me great concern; we have several letters...written to him from Cuba referring to the job he was going to do, his good marksmanship, and stating when it was all over, he would be brought back to Cuba and presented to the chief. We do not know if the chief was Castro and cannot make an investigation because we have no intelligence operation in Cuba."
   —J. Edgar Hoover, December 12, 1963[2]

"The Warren Commission relied on the intelligence agencies for investigation and analysis, but unfortunately, the agencies failed the Commission and the American public. The most notable intelligence failure related to the investigation of possible complicity by the Cuban government. The CIA...had ample reason to suspect Cuban involvement."
   —James H. Johnston, counsel to the Senate Select Committee on Intelligence (the "Church Committee"), 1993

The Early Investigations

The investigation of the assassination, predictably, fell to the CIA and the FBI, with the Justice Department directing. After reviewing international intercepts and NSA surveillance of the Kremlin, the CIA had assured itself that there was no Soviet complicity in the crime. Given the CIA's foreign purview, and its knowledge of the Kennedys' provocative Cuban policies, the other principal suspect was Cuba.

The day after the assassination, Richard Helms assigned "John Scelso" (pseudonym) of the CIA's Special Affairs Staff (SAS), which contained the largest concentration of Agency experts on Cuba, to oversee the initial investigation. Scelso, assisted by Birch O'Neal, stated that "Helms gave me broad powers."

One month later, Helms announced that the investigation was being turned over to James Angleton and Ray Rocca. In his brief tenure, however, Scelso had deduced one of Oswald's true motives for the murder—of which the official investigators (the Warren Commission) could have no inkling. As Scelso testified in 1978, "Oswald was a genuine pro-Castro nut and he was excited about what he read about our attempts to knock off Castro."[3]

But in 1976, the Church Committee concluded that the SAS, which was run by Des FitzGerald, had contributed next to nothing tangible to the investigation. The Committee's findings stated:

> There is no evidence whatsoever that SAS was asked or ever volunteered to analyze Oswald's contacts with Cuban groups...The CIA investigation into any Cuban connection, whether pro-Castro or anti-Castro, was passive in nature...In view of Oswald's preoccupation with Cuba, and his visit to Mexico City to obtain visas to Cuba and the Soviet Union, it would appear that potential involvement with pro-Castro or anti-Castro groups should have been investigated.[4]

The CIA's Coverup

Further compromising the investigation was the CIA's desire to shield Oswald's Cuban Embassy visit from official scrutiny. In 1963, Boris and Anna Tarassoff were a husband and wife team employed by the CIA to translate from Russian the Agency's surveillance tapes of the Soviet Embassy in Mexico City. Anna Tarassoff later testified that they translated Oswald's phone call to the Soviet Embassy when he told the Soviets of his visit to the Cuban Embassy. Boris Tarassoff added that at the time of Oswald's visit, the CIA was "very hot about the whole thing." He said, "It was possible that Oswald first came to the Station's attention through Oswald's contact with the Cuban Embassy." Anna added that the CIA's order to learn what they could about Oswald "was marked as urgent."[5]

Even Station Chief Winston Scott, in his manuscript, *Foul Foe*, wrote:

> In fact, Lee Harvey Oswald became a person of great interest to us during this 27 September to 2 October, 1963 period...[In] the Warren Commission Report [pg. 777] the erroneous statement was made that it was not known until after the assassination that Oswald had visited the Cuban Embassy!...Every piece of information concerning Lee Harvey Oswald was reported immediately after it was received...These reports were made on all his contacts with both the Cuban Consulate and the Soviets.[6]

A CIA internal memo discovered years later states flatly that "it was the combination of visits to both the Cuban and Soviet Embassies which caused the Mexico City Station to report this to Headquarters."[7] When confronted with the abundance of damaging evidence in 1995, former CIA Director Richard Helms said of the CIA's official denials, "I think probably the answer is that they didn't want to blow their source."[8] According to an undated internal CIA memo, the Agency had successfully developed sources within the Cuban Embassy—sources who could possibly shed light on Oswald's contacts and conversations, but *to this day* have not been made available to official investigators of JFK's death.[9]

The surviving CIA officer who could clear up the mystery of what the CIA really knew regarding Oswald in the Cuban Embassy is Ann Goodpasture. According to Allan White, the Mexico Deputy Chief of Station, Goodpasture worked hand-in-glove with both key decedents, David Phillips and Win Scott, and "her main responsibilities were to handle the surveillance operations."[10] In addition, before his death, David Phillips nominated Goodpasture for the Career Intelligence Medal, in part because "she was the case officer responsible for the identification of Lee Harvey Oswald in his dealings with the Cuban Embassy in Mexico."[11]

When contacted by the author, Goodpasture refused to be interviewed. When interviewed by the staff of the HSCA on March 13, 1978, Goodpasture denied all knowledge of photos, wiretaps, sources, and tapes that might bear on Oswald. Goodpasture's 1963 fitness report notes that she was connected to the CIA's most secret compartment at headquarters, Staff D, the agency's designation for the office run by William Harvey. As has been seen, Harvey's office controlled the ZR/RIFLE and AM/LASH assassination projects. In her position, Goodpasture might have been privy to both the AM/LASH plot and Oswald's threat/offer in the Cuban Embassy.

When the author interviewed the HSCA investigators who compiled the Mexico City Report, they agreed that Goodpasture withheld key details from them. One Congressman stated flatly, "She lied to us."

An examination of Luisa Calderon's alleged foreknowledge of the Kennedy murder further suggests that the CIA had early, untapped information about Oswald. After his defection to the Soviet Union, Oswald had been the subject of a "201" or "Personality" file that tracked his movements whenever they were brought to the Agency's attention. One document placed in his file, after the Mexico City trip but before the assassination, was a memo detailing a tapped phone conversation that took place on July 19, 1963 between Cuban Embassy employee Calderon and an American about to relocate to Dallas.[12] When queried by a Congressionally-appointed investigator, Russell Holmes, who was the custodian of the Oswald 201 file (and assistant to CIA Director Richard Helms), verified that the document was added to the file before the assassination.

Russell Holmes' admissions present a major problem for the Agency. Not only did he admit the existence of the Calderon material in Oswald's pre-assassination file: it was included, he said, because Calderon was a contact of Oswald in the Cuban Embassy. When Holmes was reminded of the CIA's claim that it did not know of Oswald's Cuban Embassy visit until after the assassination, he merely smiled sheepishly.[13]

The CIA's conundrum is clear: its professed lack of knowledge of Oswald's Cuban Embassy visits was the excuse it offered for not informing the FBI and Kennedy's security detail about this portion of Oswald's Mexico City escapade. An admission that it knew and purposely did not pass along the information to the FBI would brand the CIA as tragically negligent.

So, despite the evidence that the CIA knew of Oswald's Cuban embassy visits at the time they occurred, the Agency tried to make it appear otherwise. Two months after the assassination, the CIA wrote the Warren Commission that in the days after the tragedy, it learned for the first time from its Mexico City sources that Oswald had visited the Cuban Consulate and had met with Sylvia Duran.[14] Although this memo to the official investigators is at odds with the document trail and the memories of many other agency personnel in Mexico City, it served a clear purpose: to clear the CIA of negligence in connection with Kennedy's death.

In later years, CIA executives admitted that their investigation was seriously deficient. Miami Station Chief Ted Shackley said that he conducted no follow-up with his sources on the Oswald case. Shackley explained that because the CIA had not penetrated Castro's spy apparatus, the Agency "couldn't pursue the possibility of Castro's involvement."[15]

Raymond Rocca, James Angleton's assistant, was in a position to observe the CIA's investigation of the assassination, known in the Agency as "GPFLOOR." Rocca would later tell a Congressional investigator that the CIA provided no name traces on Cuban agents operating in Mexico City. Further, he commented that the Cuban diplomatic and intelligence personnel in Mexico City should have been more carefully examined. Rocca was also concerned about Castro's penetration of the New Orleans-based exile activities. He pointed out that Castro agent Fernando Fernandez was sending Castro intelligence about New Orleans via a mail drop in Mexico City.

In sum, Rocca believed that Cuban leads should have been pursued much more aggressively.[16] His superior, counterintelligence chief Angleton, agreed that "the Mexican phase of the investigation was unsatisfactory." Angleton expressed worry over reports that Castro, years earlier, had been photographed in Mexico City with a KGB official. Again raising the specter of a Cuban plot originating with a KGB faction—a guaranteed nuclear trigger—Angleton would later testify that he was opposed to "ever closing the case of the assassination."[17]

The FBI: "A Poor Investigation"

It was not long before the Justice Department and the FBI assumed total control of the assassination investigation from the CIA. As far as the Justice Department was concerned, Nicholas Katzenbach would handle things by proxy for Bobby Kennedy, who, after his frenetic "cleanup" on the heels of the assassination, removed himself from the scene altogether. As RFK's Deputy Attorney General, Katzenbach was Kennedy's close ally and trusted friend.

Within three days of the assassination, Katzenbach issued a now infamous memo to the Johnson White House which made the Justice Department's position clear. It stated: "The public must be convinced that Oswald was the assassin; that he did not have confederates who were still at large...Speculation about Oswald's motivation ought to be cut off."[18]

Thirty years later, Katzenbach would explain that "there was fear that the Soviets could be responsible. And that could be a major problem."[19] George Ball, an undersecretary who was then running the State Department in the absence of Secretary of State Dean Rusk, would agree, saying, "We were just scared to death that this was something bigger than the act of a madman."[20]

In practical terms, it was a wise decision to prune away any speculation, especially considering the sensational range of rumors that were circulating. However, the directive to convince the public of Oswald's guilt not only was prejudicial in the other extreme, but helped create an atmosphere in which Oswald became the investigators' sole agenda. Proof of this can be seen in Hoover's conversation with Katzenbach the day after the memo was issued. One of Hoover's assistants wrote that Hoover interpreted Katzenbach's directive as asking for a quick FBI memo for RFK that would "settle the dust, insofar as Oswald and his activities are concerned, both from the standpoint that he is the man who assassinated the President, and relative to Oswald himself and background."[21]

In light of these three things—the CIA's activity, the agenda set by RFK's Justice Department, and the blessing given it by Johnson's White House—the narrow investigation that followed was, in retrospect, predictable. Thirty years later, Nick Katzenbach, whose memo effectively set the tone for the investigation, said it was not his intention to produce a whitewash. However, he euphemistically conceded, "The memo is not as artfully worded as I would like it to be."[22] (Notwithstanding that, it's virtually impossible to interpret his words any other way.)

The FBI's investigation was run by the Domestic Intelligence Division, under the leadership of William Sullivan. FBI agent Harry Whidbee is one of the few agents to have spoken openly about the deficiencies of the Sullivan strategy. As an agent based in California, Whidbee was directed to investigate Oswald's Marine buddies—the ones who served with him at El Toro. In 1988, Whidbee told an interviewer:

> It was a hurry-up job. Within three weeks, a letter of general instruction came to the field divisions. We were effectively told, "They're only going to prove he [Oswald] was the guy who did it. There were no co-conspirators, and there was no international conspiracy." I had conducted a couple of interviews and those records were sent back again and rewritten according to Washington's requirements.[23]

One of the investigation's supervisors later testified, "Our investigation was primarily concentrated on Lee Harvey Oswald: Was he the assassin? And to get

November 25, 1963

MEMORANDUM FOR MR. MOYERS

It is important that all of the facts
surrounding President Kennedy's Assassination be
made public in a way which will satisfy people in
the United States and abroad that all the facts
have been told and that a statement to this effect
be made now.

1. The public must be satisfied that
Oswald was the assassin; that he did not have
confederates who are still at large; and that
the evidence was such that he would have been
convicted at trial.

2. Speculation about Oswald's motivation
ought to be cut off, and we should have some basis
for rebutting thought that this was a Communist
conspiracy or (as the Iron Curtain press is saying)
a right-wing conspiracy to blame it on the Communists.
Unfortunately the facts on Oswald seem about too pat--
too obvious (Marxist, Cuba, Russian wife, etc.). The
Dallas police have put out statements on the Communist
conspiracy theory, and it was they who were in charge
when he was shot and thus silenced.

3. The matter has been handled thus far
with neither dignity nor conviction. Facts have been
mixed with rumour and speculation. We can scarcely
let the world see us totally in the image of the
Dallas police when our President is murdered.

I think this objective may be satisfied
by making public as soon as possible a complete and
thorough FBI report on Oswald and the assassination.
This may run into the difficulty of pointing to inconsistencies between this report and statements by
Dallas police officials. But the reputation of the
Bureau is such that it may do the whole job.

105- 82555

ENCLOSURE

ENCLOSURE

the complete background investigation of him…It was an investigation of Lee Harvey Oswald, the man."[24] This same supervisor further stated that the Bureau never conducted an investigation to determine whether the Cuban government was responsible for the assassination of President Kennedy.[25]

In his book *The Bureau*, Sullivan admitted, "There were huge gaps in the case, gaps we never did close. For example, we never found out what went on between Oswald and the Cubans in Mexico."[26] The leading Cuban experts within the Bureau resided in the Nationalities Intelligence Section. The supervisor of this department testified that he never received memoranda or instructions to contact Cuban sources about possible Cuban involvement in the assassination. In addition, this supervisor was never informed of Castro's September 1963 warning of possible retaliation against U.S. leaders.[27]

Laurence Keenan: The FBI in Mexico City

"The most vivid memory I have is that of Ambassador [Thomas] Mann telling me 'The missiles are going to fly.'"

—Lawrence Keenan, the FBI Agent in charge of the Mexico City investigation[28]

J. Edgar Hoover may have sent an FBI supervisor to Mexico City, but to describe his resulting investigation as cursory would be exceedingly generous to the FBI. He spent all of five days there, barely enough time to unpack his bags. This FBI supervisor would later testify that his main purpose in visiting was to discredit the Gilberto Alvarado claim that Oswald was seen accepting money in the Cuban Embassy. He further testified that he never even had the opportunity to question Alvarado. He merely accepted the Mexican Police's word that Alvarado had recanted.[29] Consequently, the supervisor spent the bulk of his visit observing the FBI's attempts to trace Oswald's bus companions on his border crossings.

This supervisor's name was not included in the 1976 Congressional report of his interrogation. However, it is now known that the man was Laurence Keenan. Prior to 1963, Keenan served as the FBI's Legal Attaché (LEGAT) in Madrid. In the fall of 1963, he was back at headquarters, assigned to the Foreign Liaison Desk, under the supervision of William (Bill) Sullivan. At the time of the assassination, Keenan was at the FBI's Quantico training facility, undergoing the periodic retraining (known as "in-house" work) required of all Bureau agents.

Keenan recalled, "Two days after the assassination, Bill Sullivan handed me a memo asking me to go to Mexico City." The memo was signed by the entire Bureau triumvirate—Hoover, Alan Belmont (Hoover's assistant), and Bill Sullivan. Keenan, they thought, would be suited to the role because, as a result of his Madrid stint, he was fluent in Spanish. Furthermore, he was well-acquainted with Mexico City's LEGAT, Clark Anderson, who had served with Keenan in Spain.[30]

Keenan recently sat down for a series of interviews and was extremely candid about his feelings toward not only the FBI's post-assassination agenda, but his Mexican investigation specifically. "The memo [from the FBI's top officials] was ambiguous," Keenan says. "It stated that I would have the complete cooperation of the Agency [CIA], which didn't happen."

That is an understatement. According to Keenan, he was initially met by CIA's Win Scott and Dave Phillips. "My briefing consisted of them listening to my resumé. They never said a word to me," Keenan remembers. This stony silence continued for the duration of Keenan's stay. Such treatment, however, was not surprising to the FBI man. He is quick to point out that the inter-agency rivalry was total and unrelenting during those years. "There was an impenetrable wall between the CIA and the FBI. There was not enough trust to coordinate the investigation," Keenan points out. "There was absolutely no conversation between myself and [Win] Scott. It just wasn't done. There was no support."[31]

Keenan adds that he was given little support from Washington to follow his investigative instincts. "I had the feeling that we didn't want to broaden the investigation," Keenan says. "The strings were being pulled at a higher level." It was in this atmosphere that Keenan attempted to do his work. In 1993, he told Frontline:

> *It was surprising how fast things developed. We had the information later that afternoon [of the assassination] that an ex-Marine was involved. I think the name was pronounced to us even then: Lee Harvey Oswald. He was described as a loner, a kook. The information at the time was definitely that it was no conspiracy. The crime was already solved. There was definitely a feeling that there was not going to be any investigation pursuing this. Within a few days...[it was confirmed that] this was a single assassin and there was no thought of any further investigation. The idea was to wrap this thing up as soon as possible...We could say that the investigation was over, and there was no feeling that there was any conspiracy. In fact, this was discouraged. Any idea that Oswald had a confederate or was part of a group or a conspiracy definitely placed a man's career in jeopardy.*[32]

Keenan did not feel it necessary to explain why an unauthorized question could jeopardize an FBI career. Every agent knew that any little thing he did that might irritate J. Edgar Hoover could get him fired or sent to a highly undesirable post. Imagine the fear generated by utterly disagreeing with Hoover about who had killed the President. Keenan did not need sensitive antennae to deduce that the despotic, supremely self-promoting Director had already made up his mind about the killing. Of his specific activities in Mexico City, Keenan recalled, "We had the feeling that the Cubans would have pulled out all the stops to assassinate the President, if given the opportunity...to isolate themselves—without any definite information or evidence tying them to the assassination."[33]

His concern notwithstanding, Keenan readily admits that the FBI did next to nothing to ameliorate suspicions that the Cubans had been involved. "I had the feeling that Duran was a CIA source. We knew of her scandalous reputation within a day. I wanted to interview her, but that was off-limits. I wanted to interview Alvarado, but was told that he was unavailable."[34] He continues:

It was a very subtle affair…The idea was to wrap this thing up as soon as possible…I was in somewhat of a paradox. I had the authority, in fact you might say the jurisdiction, to conduct this investigation, yet having telephone contact with Washington, I realized that these orders were somewhat "paper" orders—that they were not to be taken literally. My desires to continue the investigation were frustrated from day one…I was blocked…I requested to see Sylvia Duran. However, I wasn't getting the support either from my own Legal Attaché office or from the CIA. This was a very tender, very sensitive moment. We're talking about nuclear engagement—nuclear war…We had to be very careful on whose toes we were stomping…

We'd call it [the investigation] window dressing. There was not an attempt, really, to take charge of the investigation, and delve into it the way we should have…Again, it was a window dressing, paper investigation. Looking back, I feel a certain amount of shame. I think the FBI can look back and feel that this one investigation disgraced a great organization.

Most damning, Keenan says, was the fact that "I went down there with no knowledge of Kennedy's anti-Castro plots."

The Warren Commission

"So-called Presidential Commissions do not work. They never will. Such commissions, in my opinion, are not a valid part of the American system."
   —Senator Charles Keating, a member of The President's Commission on Obscenity and Pornography[35]

"The Warren Commission wasn't trying to get to the bottom of it. They were trying to prevent World War III."
   —Jim Hosty, 1993 interview

"You can imagine what the reaction of the country would have been if this information [of Cuban involvement] came out. I was afraid of war."
   —Lyndon Johnson, to columnist Drew Pearson[36]

"The U.S. government not only has the right but the obligation to lie if it means the prevention of an atomic war."
   —Arthur Sylvester, Asst. Secretary of Defense in the Kennedy administration[37]

"We don't send in a bunch of carpetbaggers. That's the worst thing we could do right now."[38]

Using these words three days after the assassination, President Lyndon Johnson informed columnist Joseph Alsop that Texas Attorney General Waggoner Carr would conduct the investigation into the president's death. Johnson feared an uproar in the south over "states' rights" if the inquiry was not conducted by Texas state officials. Within four days, however, the suggestions of others would prevail. RFK's number two man in the Justice Department, Nick Katzenbach, was insistent: The public must be convinced of Oswald's sole guilt, and so he told Johnson and everyone else within earshot.

Eventually, President Johnson came to agree that because so few trusted the FBI, the investigative groundwork would need to be done by someone other than Carr (a young, unknown southerner). Thus, on November 29, 1963, LBJ signed into law Executive Order 11130, establishing a blue ribbon Presidential Panel to report on the assassination. Johnson's next problem was convincing trustworthy, prestigious citizens to sit on the new commission. Consulting again with his trusted attorney, Abe Fortas, Johnson determined that there would be six panelists and a Chairman. The first two, as will be seen, were chosen for him.[39]

To draft the remaining four members, Johnson thought it would help if he obtained the most respected person possible to chair the panel. In Johnson's mind, that cut the list to one: The Chief Justice of the United States Supreme Court, Earl Warren. The problem was Earl Warren wouldn't hear of it, feeling that it might breach the important principle of "separation of powers."

It was a constitutionally valid argument—a member of the Judiciary should not sit on an Executive branch panel. The imperial Johnson cared little for the subtleties of the *Federalist Papers*. He wanted, in fact needed, Earl Warren. Johnson implored the reluctant Chief Justice:

> *You'd go and fight if you thought you could save one American life...Why, if Khrushchev moved on us, he could kill 39 million in an hour...I'm asking you something and you're saying no to everybody when you could be speaking for 39 million people.*

Recalling Warren's reaction, Johnson said that "tears came in his eyes...You never saw anything like it. He said, 'I just can't say no.'"

Warren described Johnson's arm-twisting thus: "The President told me he was greatly disturbed by the rumors that were going around the world about a conspiracy and so forth. He thought that, because it involved both Khrushchev and Castro, it might even catapult us into a nuclear war."[40]

In order to fulfill his simultaneous responsibilities to the Supreme Court and the Commission, Warren put in seven-day work weeks, rising at 4 a.m., and working until midnight. Some members of his family feared he wouldn't survive the ordeal. "Physically, it almost killed him," says grandson Jeffrey Warren. Earl Warren, Jr. said, "It was taking ten pints of blood a day from him." His son Robert recalled that the work "did more to age him than anything I've ever seen."[41] Earl Warren would later look back on this period and call it "the worst nine months" of his life.[42]

Although controversial, Warren was revered by liberals for the way he had handled some of the most controversial court cases in U.S. history, including *Miranda*, and *Brown vs. Board of Education*. (Eisenhower had called his appointment of Warren the "biggest damn fool mistake" of his presidency, for Warren turned out to be the liberal's liberal.)

Warren was also a good friend of John Kennedy. As shall be seen, it is thus a possibility that the chief inadequacy of the Warren Commission—the failure to search for Kennedy provocation of the assassin—stems in part from the fact that a trusted friend of the martyred President chaired the hearings. Kennedy friends and loyalists kept popping up in successive investigations that likewise failed to point the finger of guilt at Kennedy's own programs.

"Earl [Warren] and John Kennedy had a sort-of 'love affair,'" says Warren's grandson, Jeffrey Warren. "My grandfather saw JFK as the great hope of the court," says Jeffrey Warren. "It was a mutual admiration society."[43] Warren's son, Earl, Jr., later said that his father and Kennedy "were always tremendously cordial to each other." The son pointed out that John Kennedy would "call [Warren] up in regard to certain judicial appointments, and asked his counsel and so forth."[44] Two days before the assassination, JFK feted Warren at a White House dinner in Warren's honor. When he heard the tragic news from Dallas, tears came to his eyes. "It was like losing one of my own sons," Warren remarked.[45]

Warren's relationship to the Kennedy family was so close that his appointment as head of the Commission was personally approved by family members.[46] That friendship was so special that on the day after the assassination, Jackie Kennedy personally called Warren to ask him to deliver the eulogy for her husband, which he did two days later at the Rotunda. On that occasion, Warren called his friend "a believer in the dignity and equality of all human beings, a fighter for justice, an apostle of peace." He added prophetically, "What moved some misguided wretch to do this horrible deed may never be known to us."[47]

Warren's biographer concluded that the Chief Justice "placed very little pressure on the investigative agencies to cooperate with the Commission," and that his principal function, as Warren saw it, was to "allay doubts."[48] Jeffrey Warren disputes this, saying "Earl would have checked everything. He was fond of using 'back channels.' That was his style. The fact that it doesn't appear in the paper record means nothing."[49]

Johnson's choices for the remainder of the Commission were so intentionally disparate as to render laughable any future discussion of panel collusion. The Commission already possessed a representative from the left—Warren—and Johnson's second choice was so far to the right that the invitation was initially declined solely on the basis of Warren's presence. Johnson's old friend and mentor, Senator Richard Russell of Georgia, the feisty Democratic Chairman of the Armed Services Committee, responded to Johnson's invitation with, "Well, now, Mr. President, I know I don't have to tell you of my devotion to you, but I just can't serve on that commission…I couldn't serve there with Chief Justice Warren. I don't like that man, and I don't have any confidence in him." And the feeling was mutual. Warren, for his part, would later ask rhetorically, "What possible set of circumstances could get Dick Russell and me to conspire on anything?"[50]

But much as he had with Warren, the new President got Russell on the

Commission by applying the screws, Johnson style:

> Johnson: *"Well, this is not me, this is your country. You're my man on that commission, and you're going to do it, and don't tell me what you can do and what you can't, because I can't arrest you, and I'm not going to put the FBI on you, but you're goddamn sure going to serve, I'll tell you that."*
>
> Russell: *"I'm at your command and I'll do anything you say—"*
>
> Johnson: *"Well, you're damned sure going to be at my command—you're going to be at my command as long as I'm here."*[51]

Rounding out the Commission were Democratic Congressman Hale Boggs of Louisiana (Democratic Majority Leader), and two Republicans, Senator John Sherman Cooper of Kentucky, and Congressman Gerald Ford of Michigan. These men, combined with two others from the intelligence establishment, held their first organizational meeting on December 5, 1963.

Even before the Commission heard its first witness, Johnson hinted that he was about to dismantle the Kennedys' anti-Castro initiatives. At a December 19, 1963 meeting between Johnson and the Army Chief of Staff, General Earle Wheeler, the new President "expressed reluctance" at continued sabotage in Cuba.[52] Within weeks, the operations would come to a complete halt.

RFK Stacks the Deck

> *"As for the makeup of the rest of the Commission, I appointed the two men Bobby Kennedy asked me to put on it, Allen Dulles and John McCloy— immediately."*
> **—President Lyndon Johnson**[53]

> *"Only Johnson, obviously, the Chief Justice [Warren], Allen Dulles, and Bobby Kennedy knew about the CIA plots against Castro. Its disclosure would have had very important implications. It might have allowed us to say something reasonably definitive about Oswald's motive. It would have put a new dimension on his Cuban activities and opened up new areas of exploration."*
> **—Judge Burt Griffin, Warren Commission staff lawyer**[54]

In a 1966 phone conversation with Abe Fortas, Johnson told his advisor how the other two members of the Commission were chosen. "We even asked the Attorney General to name the people he wanted," said the President. "He named Allen Dulles and John McCloy." When he spoke with the publisher of his memoirs at the LBJ ranch years later, Johnson confessed surprise at Bobby's suggested nominees for the new commission. "I could never understand why Bobby tried to put some CIA people on the Warren Commission," LBJ admitted to his publisher, Lord George Weidenfeld.[55] "I had Dick Helms here not long ago and I asked him point blank, but he refused to be drawn [in]," Johnson said.

Although Johnson, through his own sources, had known of the Mongoose and assassination plots, he may not have been privy to the long history shared by the Kennedys and CIA leaders such as John McCloy and Allen Dulles. LBJ was probably also unaware that Dulles had authorized the initial J.C. King assassination proposals in 1959, and that two key staging areas for Bobby Kennedy's secret war were Mexico City and New Orleans: cities that shared a history with Lee Oswald.

John Kennedy once described John McCloy this way: "[He is a] diplomat and public servant, banker to the world, and Godfather to German freedom...He has brought cheerful wisdom and steady effectiveness to the tasks of war and peace."[56] In addition to being the Chairman of the World Bank, McCloy was a former diplomat, advisor to Presidents, Wall Street insider, and an early architect of the post-war U.S. intelligence community. Kennedy so admired McCloy that he had offered him his choice of Cabinet posts, all of which McCloy declined. The banker/diplomat eventually agreed to serve as Kennedy's advisor on disarmament. McCloy also was Kennedy's point man in crafting the details of the missile removal from Cuba during negotiations with Russia after the Cuban Missile Crisis.

On December 6, 1963, JFK was to have presented McCloy with the nation's highest civilian honor, the Freedom Medal.[57] Given JFK's admiration for McCloy, Robert Kennedy's choice of him for the Warren Commission comes as no great surprise.

His other choice, Allen Dulles, was also no surprise, at least to those in the Kennedy inner-circle. But selecting Dulles served a purpose far more important to Bobby Kennedy. It would guarantee that Kennedy interests were served on the panel. And that meant a coverup. Robert Kennedy would later tell "Track One" representative, William Attwood, that a heavy lid must be kept on the investigation "for reasons of national security."[58]

The Warren Commission and the Dulles Connection

"I am personally shocked and feel betrayed that such coverup activities have occurred. I still believe that the Commission, with the possible exception of Allen Dulles, did not participate in any coverup."
—Judge Burt Griffin, Warren Commission staff attorney, 1976[59]

"The CIA withheld from the Commission information which might have been relevant...in light of the allegations of conspiratorial contact between Oswald and agents of the Cuban government."
—David Belin, Warren Commission staff attorney, 1975[60]

"I was outraged to learn [in 1975] of the CIA/Mafia plots. Certainly it [the Warren Commission investigation] would have bulked larger [in] the conspiracy area [had this been known in 1963-64]."
—J. Lee Rankin, Warren Commission Chief Counsel, 1978[61]

The appointment of Allen Dulles to the Warren Commission can be pointed to as the single most important occurrence in the history of the Kennedy assassination whitewash. For it was Dulles, alone among the Commissioners, who knew of a potential Cuban motive to encourage Oswald. He knew of White House plans to kill Fidel Castro and he kept it from the other investigators. Hiding the Cuban intrigue was not the first major favor Dulles had performed for his friends in the Kennedy family. His new exercise of discretion recalls the manner in which he dealt with the explosive Arvad file at the time of JFK's 1960 election. In 1963-64, Dulles once again would keep the family's darkest secrets from seeing the light of day.

Of course, Dulles could have had a dual motivation. In addition to his closeness with the Kennedys, the former CIA director might have harbored the same fears as LBJ: a full disclosure of the U.S.'s anti-Castro intrigue could have resulted in a nuclear war.

Dulles' contributions to the Warren Commission are best considered for what he didn't add, rather than for what he did. When asked, Dulles assured the Warren Commissioners that the CIA had submitted all pertinent information to the Commission. Paradoxically, Dulles admitted that he felt obliged to tell the truth only to the President—and only if asked for it. Speaking with a colleague on a later occasion, he widened the circle by one: "I'll fudge the truth to the oversight committee. But I'll tell the chairman the truth—that is, if he wants to know."[62]

Dulles even admitted to his fellow Commissioners that a CIA man, under certain circumstances, "ought not tell [the truth] under oath."[63] Dulles elaborated, "I would tell the President of the United States anything, yes, I am under his control. He is my boss, [but I] wouldn't necessarily tell anybody else, unless the President authorized me to do it."[64] On a different occasion, Dulles added, "I have always felt that the [CIA] Director should naturally assume full responsibility...and whenever he could shield or protect the President, he should do it."[65]

Dulles' philosophy mirrors that of another key CIA player in the Cuba Project—Deputy Director of Plans, Richard Helms. When convicted of perjury for concealing information about CIA operations in Chile, he stated, "I wear this conviction as a badge of honor... I don't feel disgraced at all. I think if I had done anything else, I would have been disgraced."[66]

Helms was also the recipient of an internal CIA memo which seems to demonstrate the Agency's resolve to stall the Warren Commission. Helms directed James Angleton's Counterintelligence Division to function as liaison with the Warren Commission. When weighing how much of the CIA's Mexico City operation to divulge to the Commission, Helms was advised, "Unless you feel otherwise, Jim [Angleton] would prefer to wait out the Commission on the matter."[67] That is exactly what the CIA did. The Commission knew next to nothing of the CIA's counter-intelligence activities in Mexico City, and nothing of the CIA's Castro plotting for the Kennedy brothers.

What Dulles Knew

"I don't know of any member of the Commission, other than Dulles, that knew that the CIA had been involved [in the plots against Castro], and I have specifically discussed this with some of the living members."
—David Belin, Warren Commission Assistant Counsel, 1975[68]

"At no time did the CIA disclose to the Warren Commission any facts which pertained to alleged assassination plots to kill Fidel Castro...which might have been relevant...in light of the allegations of conspiratorial contact between Oswald and agents of the Cuban government."
—David Belin, Warren Commission Counsel

"As far as I know, all phases of this [Castro assassination] operation were approved by Allen Dulles and President Eisenhower. Well, you know, Dulles was a member of the Warren Commission and I don't remember hearing him say anything about it. And I don't remember Eisenhower coming forward either. So what was I supposed to think? Maybe President Johnson wanted to keep the lid on."
—Johnny Rosselli, 1966[69]

At a meeting of the National Security Council on August 18, 1960, President Eisenhower angrily ordered his intelligence agencies to "dispose of" Patrice Lumumba of the Congo, and CIA Director Dulles became personally involved in planning the assassination. Lumumba had frightened Washington with his cozy new relationship with the Soviets. The Church Committee would take testimony from a number of those present at NSC meetings that summer of 1960. Many were convinced that Eisenhower had given the go-ahead to murder Lumumba.[70] One NSC staffer, Robert Johnson, told the Committee that not only did he hear Eisenhower order the assassination, but Eisenhower was "looking right toward the Director of Central Intelligence [Dulles]" when making the statement.[71] Johnson recently reaffirmed this contention, adding that he was anything but naive, but nonetheless was surprised to learn assassination was an instrument of U.S. policy.[72] Writer Darrell Garwood summarized:

The record showed that immediately after the meeting in which Eisenhower uttered the words "dispose of," Dulles authorized $100,000 for a full-scale assassination attempt against Lumumba...Dulles...told Station Chief Lawrence Devlin that "we wish to give you every possible support in eliminating Lumumba from any possibility of resuming governmental position."[73]

Likewise, scholars are virtually unanimous in their belief that Allen Dulles knew about the plots against Castro, even those that continued after his term as CIA director. It has already been seen that Dulles approved J.C. King's memo suggesting the "elimination" of both Fidel and Raul Castro. In addition, CIA officers Richard Bissell and Sheffield Edwards indicated in testimony that Dulles knew of the 1961 CIA/Mafia plots.[74] Edwards later testified, "The plan was approved by Allen W. Dulles...I personally briefed him."[75] When once asked what the CIA would do if U.S. national security were threatened by a foreign agent, Dulles himself answered, "We'd kill him."[76]

After hearing from numerous associates of the by-then deceased Dulles, the 1975 Church Committee concluded it likely that "Dulles knew about and authorized the actual plots that occurred during his tenure."[77] That committee's predecessor, the Rockefeller Commission, was told by the CIA's Inspector General, Donald Chamberlain, "As far as we can tell from all the materials at our disposition, no one discussed with the Warren Commission any alleged plan to assassinate Castro."[78]

Dulles' biographer, Peter Grose, wrote of Dulles' performance on the Warren Commission:

Allen systematically used his influence to keep the commission safely within bounds, the importance of which only he could appreciate....And from the start, before any evidence was reviewed, he pressed for the final verdict that Oswald had been a crazed lone gunman, not the agent of a national or international conspiracy.[79]

In another passage, Grose wrote, "Allen's top priority throughout the ten months of the commission's study was to press for endorsement of the FBI's conclusion that Kennedy was murdered by a lone assassin; a finding of any international or domestic conspiracy might compromise all of America foreign policy."[80]

After the assassination, Secretary of State Dean Rusk summoned Dulles to the State Department and asked the question outright: Was the CIA aware of any foreign government that might have had a motive to kill Kennedy? Dulles said they had no such information. Rusk later said of the Dulles lie, "I find that unforgivable."[81] There can be little doubt that the Kennedy family felt otherwise.

The CIA and the FBI: On the Warren Commission

For his part, FBI Director Hoover led the Warren commissioners to believe that the Bureau had conducted a thorough investigation of the assassination. He also wrote the Commission a letter assuring them that Oswald had not fulfilled the requirements to place him on the Security Index of dangerous persons. Both contentions were lies. As pointed out earlier, the FBI had already prevented supervisor Lawrence Keenan from performing his investigation of Oswald in Mexico City. Hoover knew that if the significance of the Mexico City developments were known, the FBI would be destroyed. Furthermore, during the Commission's work, a Hoover-ordered internal probe by the FBI concluded that Oswald should have been on the Index and that his passport should have been revoked. In private, Hoover agreed with this conclusion. He even insisted, over strenuous objections, that seventeen agents, including Jim Hosty, be censured. The cited agents "could not have been more stupid," Hoover wrote. Regarding the responsible agents, Hoover added:

> *They were worse than mistaken. Certainly no one in full possession of all his faculties can claim Oswald didn't fall within this [Security Index] criteria...Such gross incompetency cannot be overlooked nor administrative action postponed.*[82]

When Bureau officers objected to the censures, citing the restrictions of the Third Agency Rule, Hoover was adamant: "We were wrong," he wrote. "I do not intend to palliate actions which have resulted in forever destroying the Bureau as the top level investigative agency."[83] This was, however, Hoover's private position. His public stance, dictated by his overriding desire to protect the Bureau's image, had to be that the FBI agents in charge of Oswald's case had done nothing wrong.

In fact, J. Edgar Hoover was too concerned with the reputation of his FBI to be overly concerned with a thorough investigation of the crime itself. And the best way to protect its reputation was to focus the entire investigation, and fix all the blame, on Lee Harvey Oswald alone. Hoover's man in charge of the investigation, William Sullivan, candidly admitted, "Hoover's main thought [regarding the Kennedy investigation] was always how to cover, how to protect himself."[84] Clearly, Hoover wanted to stop any speculation that Oswald was someone whose murderous impulse could have been predicted. Anything the Director could do toward this end, he did, including narrowing the investigation before it got started in November 1963 and supervising a woefully inadequate investigation for the Warren Commission.

Not only had the CIA and FBI backed away from investigating the Cuban angle, but now their chief officers met in secret to coordinate their responses to the Warren Commission. The Church Committee later located a memo from the CIA's head of Counter-intelligence, James Angleton, to the FBI's William Sullivan. In the memo, Angleton suggests that both agencies coordinate their replies to questions posed by the Warren Commission. The memo included a list of questions that the Commission would ask CIA, along with the CIA's replies. This way, neither agency would suffer potential embarrassment.[85] Senator Richard Schweiker, who chaired the Committee's investigation of the Kennedy assassination, later stated, "That was one of the most shocking things we learned—that the CIA and FBI rehearsed and coordinated their Warren Commission testimony."[86]

With J. Edgar Hoover, Lyndon Johnson, Robert Kennedy, and Allen Dulles in agreement that not only would there be no investigation of Cuban complicity, but the Kennedys' provocation of Castro would not be divulged, the Warren Commission set about its work. Within these parameters, the result was a foregone conclusion.

The Workings of the Commission

Although the Commission held its first meeting on December 5, 1963, it didn't actually hear its first witness until February 5, 1964. By then, the Commission had set up shop in the old VFW Building near the Supreme Court. At one of the Commission's first meetings, Allen Dulles opened the session by passing out copies of a ten-year-old book discussing seven previous attempts against U.S. presidents. The thesis of the book was that assassins are typically loners and misfits. Dulles pointed out to his fellow commissioners that "you'll find a pattern running through here that I think we'll find in this present case."[87]

The Commission's original deadline of June 30, 1964 was determined to be unreasonable, and the report was finally delivered three months late on September 24, 1964. Despite the extension, the overwhelming impression left by a close read of the Commission's work is of leads left unpursued because of time constraints. A typically disturbing example occurred when a Commission attorney was asked in May 1964 to follow up on an allegation that disputed Oswald's timeline and contacts made en route to Mexico City. The attorney responded, "We're closing doors, not opening them."[88]

Of the $1.2 million allocated to the investigation, a staggering $608,000 went to the cost of printing the report and the 1500 copies of its 26 volumes. In the interim, the Commissioners personally heard only 94 witnesses of the 25,000 questioned by its investigative arm, the FBI. Official meetings were poorly attended. Commissioner Russell, still seething with hatred for Warren, attended only 15 out of 244 hours of hearings, and heard only 6 percent of the testimony. Although the staff attorneys themselves heard more than 500 witnesses, the ensuing work suffered from the fact that neither the Commission members nor their staff were professional investigators.[89]

In 1992, in an article about the inner workings of the Warren Commission, *U.S. News and World Report* stated:

> *Warren never considered hiring anyone outside the legal profession for the main staff. In some ways, that decision was crucial. Lawyers, by inclination and training, were drawn to unified explanations for the assassination. Accustomed to ordering vast universes of facts, they found it difficult to imagine the murky conspiracy theories that might have come more easily to private investigators.[90]*

The commissioners were further hampered by the fact that they were all successful professionals with careers that couldn't be abandoned for almost a year while the Commission did its work. In 1992, *U.S. News and World Report* summarized:

> *These busy men ignored most day-to-day operations. The retired Dulles dropped by, often merely to shoot the breeze. Russell drafted a letter of resignation to LBJ, furious at not being notified of an early meeting. Even when he was notified, he came to fewer meetings than any other commissioner.[91]*

All the foregoing difficulties led to a dismally truncated investigation.

The Commission's oversights (and those of its investigative arm, the FBI) would fill many pages. Consider the following examples:

- *The FBI found time to note Jack Ruby's mother's dental records, but neg-lected to interview Sylvia Duran, Teresa Proenza, and other Cuban Embassy employees.*

- *The Bureau compiled life histories of everyone who rode on the bus to Mexico with Oswald, but deemed it of little interest to take formal testimony from the CIA's Win Scott and David Phillips, or critical witnesses such as Pedro Gutierrez, Gilberto Alvarado, Luisa Calderon, and Gilberto Lopez.*

- *The investigators interviewed owners of printing shops in New Orleans to determine where Oswald had his FPCC leaflets printed, but when it came to the address on the leaflets, "544 Camp Street," key figures who had worked in that building (like Sergio Arcacha) were never interviewed, or were dealt with in a brief and cursory phone call (like Guy Banister).*

- *The Bureau obtained information on the Socialist Party connections of the grandfather (born in the 1870s) of the estranged husband of the woman with whom Marina Oswald lived, but never determined the name of the man whom the police said drove Oswald to the Dallas rifle range.*

- *Although Oswald was clearly obsessed with Cuba, and was known to be in proximity to staging areas for the government's "Cuba Project," the man who ran that project with an iron fist, Robert Kennedy, was not required to testify, and the Commission didn't press the issue.*

On April 8, 1964, three Warren Commission attorneys traveled to Mexico City, where they would spend four days. They essentially met with the U.S. Embassy's CIA and FBI staff, and retraced Oswald's movements. They interviewed none of the witnesses or possible suspects cited earlier. In their memo summing up the trip, staffers wrote, "We did not want any appointments made at this time...We wanted to leave the entire problem open"—a curious decision, given that the actual writing of the Warren Commission's report would commence in a few weeks.[92]

On June 11, 1964, Earl Warren made a last-ditch attempt to get Robert Kennedy to contribute to the investigation. In a letter to the Attorney General, Warren asked whether RFK knew of "any additional information relating to the assassination of President John F. Kennedy which has not been sent to the Commission." Warren also asked the Attorney General about "any information suggesting that the assassination of President Kennedy was caused by a domestic or foreign conspiracy."

In his book, *Final Disclosure*, Warren Commission attorney David Belin wrote, "Robert Kennedy did not respond until August 4, nearly two months later, when he wrote that 'all information relating in any way to the assassination of President John F. Kennedy in the Department of Justice' had been referred to the Warren Commission."[93] According to Belin, the RFK letter went on to say:

> I would like to state definitely that I know of no credible evidence to support the allegations that the assassination of President Kennedy was caused by a domestic or foreign conspiracy. I have no suggestions to make at this time regarding any additional investigation which should be undertaken by the Commission prior to the publication of its report.[94]

Attorney Belin queries, "Why did it take Kennedy so long to reply?" Predictably, JFK aide/sycophant Kenny O'Donnell tried to put the most benign spin on RFK's silence, telling former Speaker of the House, Thomas P. "Tip" O'Neill, "Tip, you have to understand. The family—everybody—wanted this thing behind them."[95] Others, however, sensed a darker agenda. David Belin postulates: "Perhaps Robert Kennedy could not decide whether to tell the Warren Commission about the assassination plots against Castro. He eventually decided to withhold the information." Bobby Kennedy's continued pattern of stonewalling the Commission (he also wanted to withhold the autopsy material) brought Belin to the brink of resigning.[96] Close friend and aide to both JFK and RFK, Senator Harris Wofford, concluded:

> There was nothing Robert Kennedy could see to do or say about it. There was no way of getting to the bottom of the assassination without uncovering the very stories he hoped would be hidden forever. So he closed his eyes to the coverup that he knew (or soon discovered) Allen Dulles was perpetrating on the Warren Commission, and took no steps to inform the Commission of the Cuban and Mafia connections that would have provided the main clues to any conspiracy...In this situation, he was putting his brother's and the country's reputation above the truth...Robert Kennedy was his brother's keeper.[97]

And although Bobby would provide the Commission no information on his classified Cuban operations, he clearly spared no energy in trying to determine what the Commission was uncovering on its own. In a confidential interview in 1997, a senior Justice Department official, known to be assigned to the Commission staff, admitted he was planted there to be Robert Kennedy's eyes and ears. The attorney stated that other staffers and members, including Redlich (norman), Rankin, Warren, and Willens (Howard), were aware of his subterfuge. Bobby's aides, Jack Miller and Jack Cassidy, were also aware.

Bobby's mole continued, "I'm undercover there. Everybody on the Commission isn't supposed to know that I'm a plant, but it was understood...We go to lunch and they [other staff members] ask me how I got there. I never told those guys. I'd go and come from the offices and they'd ask: 'What are you doing?' I spent three hours a day at the committee—no secretary. My function was simply to read....I thought [Kennedy's assassination] was [the result of] a foreign plot—Cuba."

When Jackie Kennedy testified before the Commission, RFK was not only allowed to look on, but, incredibly, was given permission to have Nick Katzenbach edit the transcript to Bobby's liking.[98] The Attorney General told Nick Katzenbach that he wouldn't even read the [Warren Commission] report, saying, "I don't care what they do. It's not going to bring him [my brother] back."[99]

As a final insult, the Commission never called the man who would have been the repository of the most sensitive intelligence reports: the new President, Lyndon Baines Johnson.

The Non-Consensus

"Judgments were made back then that seemed rational and reasonable. Today, with a totally different atmosphere, those judgments might seem improper."
—**President Gerald Ford, former Warren Commission member, 1995**[100]

"We were wrong, in my opinion, in issuing the statement that 'there was no evidence of a conspiracy.' That was the wrong statement...Statements, like that sweeping 'no conspiracy' one, [do] a disservice to our overall work."
—**Judge Burt Griffin, Warren Commission staff lawyer, 1992**[101]

"Hale felt very torn during his work on the Commission. He wished he'd never been on it and wished he'd never signed it [the final report]."
—**Lindy Boggs, the widow of Warren Commission member, Congressman Hale Boggs**[102]

"I think someone else worked with [Oswald]...There were too many things— some of the trips he made to Mexico City, and a number of discrepancies in the evidence that caused me to doubt that he planned it all by himself."
—**Senator Richard B. Russell, Warren Commission member, 1970**[103]

LBJ received the Warren Commission's Report on September 24, 1964. One might infer that the deliverance of the report to Johnson meant that the signees agreed with its conclusions. That is not the case. The Commissioners and their staff expressed dissatisfaction from the beginning, and their doubts only increased with later revelations, especially those concerning the U.S.-sponsored assassination plots. The Commission members who most vocally disagreed with its conclusion were Senator Richard B. Russell, and House Majority Leader Hale Boggs. Senator Cooper was troubled by the events of Dealey Plaza. Even future President Gerald Ford expressed misgivings about the Commission's treatment of the conspiracy possibility. The only two members who remained silent were RFK's appointees from the intelligence community, Dulles and McCloy.

In a handwritten note found among Senator Russell's papers in the Russell Memorial Library at the University of Georgia, Russell seemed to express his fears of a coverup within the Warren Commission. During a discussion with Warren, Russell (the chairman of the Armed Services Committee, which oversaw the CIA) had been surprised to learn that Warren already seemed to know about the Alvarado story. Russell wrote, "[Warren] knew all I did and more about CIA. Something strange is happening—Warren and Katzenbach know all about FBI and they are apparently through psychiatrists & others planning to show Oswald only one who even considered—This to me is an untenable position—I must insist on outside counsel—'Remember Warren's blanket indictment of the South.'" (Warren was outspoken on the cause of civil rights.)[104]

Russell became so convinced that the Warren Commission wasn't obtaining all the intelligence needed to make a thorough report, he indeed did secure "outside counsel," secretly commissioning his own private investigation. According to his assistant, Colonel Philip Corso, who conducted the inquiry, no records of it were to be kept on paper. All briefings of the Senator were to be oral. Corso, a twenty-year Army Intelligence veteran, had been on loan to the CIA in the 1950's and was later named a National Security Advisor to the Eisenhower White House.

The first thing Corso did was to contact an old friend, CIA officer Frank Hand. Hand was the CIA's liaison to the Operations Coordinating Board. He later was assigned to Mongoose chief Edward Lansdale's office. In 1967, when the CIA Inspector General wrapped up his report on the assassination plots, Hand's name appears (p. 114) as Lansdale's aide, and it is Hand who, according to the Inspector General, had removed the phrase "liquidation of foreign leaders" from a sensitive CIA report. Hand was clearly a well-placed source.

Over the years, Russell's associates have expressed their certainty that the senator, because of his Congressional position as CIA overseer, was privy to the Castro assassination plots. This would explain why, in a November 29, 1963 phone conversation, Russell is heard telling President Johnson, "I wouldn't be surprised if Castro—" At that point, Johnson cuts him off, saying, "Okay, okay, that's what we want to know." Regarding Russell's possible knowledge of the plots, his biographer wrote that because the Senator "possessed secret information others [on the Commission] did not have, he may have had reason to suspect some kind of conspiracy. Whatever he knew, if anything, he took to his grave"[105] when he died on January 21, 1971. According to Corso, Russell told him, "You know, we can't publish this. They'll never believe it and they'll never put it in print."[106]

But Russell was so troubled that he, along with fellow commissioners Cooper and Boggs, demanded an eleventh-hour, pre-release, executive session to air their disputes. At that session, held just six days before the report was handed over to President Johnson, the dissenting Commissioners had their say. The meeting remains the only executive session for which no transcript can be found, although one was known to be kept. Rumors abound that the meeting was a no-holds barred shouting match. Russell said he made known his objections to numerous Warren conclusions, delivered a written dissent to the Chairman, and received Warren's guarantee that it would be included in the final report. The concluding words of Russell's written dissent are worth reproducing in full:

There are several bits of evidence that have raised questions in my mind that are not answered by any evidence the Commission could procure. Among these are the extent of Oswald's associations with the large number of Cuban nationals who were students in the educational institutions in Minsk during his residence there; the nature and extent of his relationship with foreign nationals who may have had a purpose in wishing to kill the President of the United States; the scope and number of communications he may have had with such persons after his return to the United States, and a detailed account of all of Oswald's movements, contacts and associations on his secret visit to Mexico a few weeks before the assassination of the President. The inability to gather all evidence in these areas as well as a number of suspicious circumstances, deduced from the record as made, to my mind preclude the conclusive determination that Oswald and Oswald alone, without the knowledge, encouragement or assistance of any other person, planned and perpetrated the assassination.

Corso remembers that, even with his dissent noted, Russell had to be "arm-twisted" by Johnson into signing the Report. Russell was later shocked to learn that despite Warren's guarantee, his dissent was not published with the rest of the report, nor mentioned in it. For years, Warren Commission critics wondered about the contents of the Russell dissent.[107] It was only recently discovered among Russell's papers at the University of Georgia.

Fellow Commissioner (and future president) Gerald R. Ford (R-Michigan) shared Russell's suspicions. In a secret meeting with Hoover's assistant Cartha DeLoach shortly after the Commission's first meeting, Ford voiced his suspicions of a foreign conspiracy, and his fears of a narrow investigation. DeLoach wrote of his meeting with Ford:

Ford told me that he was currently having problems inasmuch as a majority of the members of the Commission desired to go along with the recommendation made in Deputy Attorney General Katzenbach's letter to the Commission dated 12-9-63. In this letter, Katzenbach recommended that the Commission make an immediate press release pointing out that the FBI clearly showed that there was no international conspiracy and that Oswald was a loner.[108]

The memo went on to say that Ford disapproved of such an early rush to judgment. When CIA Director John McCone told Ford that the Cubans may have paid Oswald, "Ford stated this excited him greatly inasmuch as it definitely tended to show that there was an international connection involved in the assassination." Like Russell, Ford may have had some inside knowledge that encouraged his suspicions. In a 1995 interview with the BBC, Ford revealed:

I had been on two committees in the Congress that had responsibility of our overall intelligence community and secondly, a committee that had jurisdiction over all money for the Army, Navy, Air Force, Marines, etc...As a member of those two committees, I had certain background information that at least gave me the understanding that our government was doing whatever was needed in order to make a change in Cuba.[109]

Although Ford asserted publicly that this knowledge did not color his thinking about the assassination, he was to become, as President, a key force behind the eventual leaking in 1975 of the CIA-Mafia plots that some insiders believe resulted in JFK's death. As Ford told his White House Counsel Phil Buchen in 1975, "I do not recall this information being furnished to the Warren Commission...As I remember, those of us on the Commission got the impression the Agency had not engaged in activities against Castro. I would be interested in any information you can give me on this subject."[110] Papers from the Ford Presidency indicate that his National Security Advisor, Brent Scowcroft, continually updated Ford on the later Congressional investigations into possible Cuban complicity.

Warren Commission member Hale Boggs, from Louisiana, was known to have had strong disagreements with the Commission's official conclusion. As has been noted, Boggs told his wife, Lindy, that he'd wished he'd never signed on to the report. It has been known for years that Boggs, like much of the public, was suspicious of stonewalling by the FBI and CIA. What has not been known is that Boggs, like Ford, may have been apprised of the plots to kill Castro.

Boggs' Louisiana colleague in the House, Gillis Long, was one of Boggs' closest friends. Long had known of the Castro plots since their inception. He was a lifelong friend of Robert Maheu, the acknowledged go-between in the early Castro plots, and had himself once worked for Howard Hughes as a Maheu aide. Maheu had told Long about the early Castro plots when they first started.

In the early 1960s, Long began retelling—to colleagues—Maheu stories about assassination plots. For example, Wayne Thevenot (now a D.C. lobbyist) accompanied Long on a trip to meet Maheu in Las Vegas in 1965. Maheu had contacted Long when Hughes lost ownership of TWA and wanted to vent about banking corruption. At that time, Long was a member of House committees regulating banking and business.

Thevenot, who had disbelieved Long's "keystone cops" story of the plots against Castro, was seated directly across from Maheu at the Desert Inn, when Long said to Maheu, "Go ahead, tell him what you told me. I want him to hear it from the horse's mouth." Maheu proceeded to tell his story, exactly as related previously.

What is most important is that Long, who had heard the story long before the Kennedy assassination, would undoubtedly have relayed these stories to Warren Commission member Hale Boggs. As Thevenot recalls, "Gillis and Hale were as close as you can get. They had no secrets from each other."[111]

The Warren Commission legal staff also had doubts about the "Oswald alone" conclusion. In 1993, staff attorney Burt Griffin said of his work on the commission, "We spent virtually no time investigating the possibility of a conspiracy. I wish we had."[112] Commission senior attorney Lee Rankin also voiced concern that the murder had a Cuban component. When Congressional investigators contacted Rankin in 1978, he asked them, "Are you looking into the [anti-Castro] plots on the basis of whether they were covered up by the CIA because some of the very people involved in them could have been involved in the President's assassination?" When answered in the affirmative, Rankin exhorted them:

> Good. Good. You have to look at it that way...I've been afraid that it was all true...You've got to go after that. Helms' role in the plots and his concealment of them from the Commission would just have been unconscionable. [That information] would have changed so much back then.[113]

Earl Warren and the Report

> "Earl never closed the door on the possibility of a conspiracy."
> —Jeffrey Warren, Earl's grandson, 1994[114]

Earl Warren is not known to have made public statements about the Commission's conclusions, even after the Castro-plotting revelations of the Church Committee in 1976. Jeffrey Warren believes that his grandfather was content with the Commission's work and would not have protected his friend John Kennedy at the cost of getting to the truth of the murder. Nonetheless, Jeffrey Warren concedes, "Earl knew everything. I'm sure he knew about Operation Mongoose." Earl himself, while saying that he had seen no concrete evidence of Cuban complicity, nonetheless added, "I am quite prepared to believe that Castro wanted to kill Kennedy, and may have sent some teams here to do it."[115]

This belief is buttressed by a statement made by a staff member of the Church Committee, which eventually made Mongoose public, and which unearthed the assassination plots. The aide was asked about how the committee initially learned of the Kennedy Administration's anti-Castro plotting. He responded, "You can bet one thing: if it hadn't been for Drew Pearson, [Earl] Warren, and LBJ pushing the thing, we never would have been told about it."[116]

Jeffrey Warren's opinion notwithstanding, it strains credulity to believe that a man of Warren's ability, knowing of the Kennedys' provocation of Castro, would not have been more interested in Oswald's Cuban contacts in New Orleans and Mexico City. There is evidence that he was.

Warren Commission Staff counsel William Coleman has spoken privately about being sent to Havana by Warren to investigate possible Cuban complicity in the crime. When asked about the trip recently, Coleman admitted to making the journey, but would say nothing else. "I can't talk. It was top-secret," Coleman said. He offered a "No comment" when asked if he was successful in meeting with Castro.

Although Coleman has stated that he came away from the Cuban trip convinced of Cuba's non-involvement in the assassination, it's hard to imagine that his findings were conclusive. It seems doubtful that one young, lone attorney could locate the pro-Castro functionaries who may have met with Oswald in Mexico City, and then persuade them to confess.[117] In sending this young attorney, Earl Warren may have made a decision not to air the dirty laundry of his friend John Kennedy.

Johnson and the Official Conclusion

"I never believed that Oswald acted alone."
  —Lyndon Johnson, 1969[118]

"LBJ saved the day…With one masterful hand, he clamped the lid down tight with the Warren Commission…thus saving the 'genius' RFK who, blinded by his own foolish stupidity, accompanied by a host of 'friends,' all murdered his own brother."
  —Jack Martin, New Orleans associate of Guy Banister and
    David Ferrie[119]

It has long been known that Lyndon Johnson privately disagreed with the Commission's conclusions. Evidence given secretly to Johnson as the years progressed only served to validate his beliefs.

Lyndon Johnson was the man who commissioned the Warren Commission report, and who accepted it when delivered to him on September 24, 1964. Yet only four days later, Johnson told Senate Majority Leader Mike Mansfield what he really believed. "There's a good deal of feeling that maybe the Cuban thing…" Johnson mused. "Oswald was messing around in Mexico with the Cubans."[120]

In fact, the Commission's report and Johnson's imprimatur on it were merely an attempt to reach a socio-political closure so the nation could move forward. Johnson had been against the Kennedys' Cuba policy of assassination, and his statements suggest a man who felt that Kennedy and Castro had been engaged in an irresponsibly dangerous game that Kennedy lost with his life. Deciding that 39 million lives should not be jeopardized because of the prideful actions of two men of privilege—John Kennedy and Fidel Castro—could have been Johnson's finest moment. Former FBI Director Clarence Kelley has written:

The withholding of that information from the public was thus complete—all because the White House seemingly considered the risk of a confrontation with the Soviet Union over the Kennedy assassination too great.[121]

Marty Underwood, Johnson's most-trusted advanceman and close friend, agrees. "Johnson had to set that thing up. We had to whitewash it," says Underwood. "Christ, with the mental state of the country—if they had thought for a minute that Castro or anybody was behind it, they would have gotten after them."[122]

General Alexander Haig, who not only worked on Bobby Kennedy's Cuban sabotage program, but later became a close friend of Lyndon Johnson, adds another possible component to Johnson's motivations, saying, "Johnson believed that if it were ever suggested that Castro had a hand in the assassination of Kennedy [and the U.S. did not retaliate], there would be a right-wing uprising marking the end of the Democratic Party's domination of the contemporary scene."[123]

Johnson's suspicions of an international component to the Kennedy killing never wavered. His initial behavior on board Air Force One bordered on the hysterical. The Warren Commission notwithstanding, everything Johnson would learn in the coming years only reinforced his beliefs. Even as the Warren Commission finished its work, Johnson initiated his own investigation into Kennedy's death. It was an initiative he would repeat in 1968, with dramatic results. Historian Michael Beschloss was briefed by the CIA's Richard Helms about Johnson's special investigation. Beschloss wrote:

> *Richard Helms found Lyndon Johnson distracted well into 1964 by his worry that Kennedy had been assassinated by a conspiracy. As Helms recalled, the Agency "was very helpful to Johnson on this" and met the new President's request for an independent CIA study.*[124]

According to LBJ Chief of Staff Bob Hardesty, Johnson also asked Nick Katzenbach and Ramsey Clark to investigate the Oswald-Castro connection.[125] LBJ's press secretary, George Reedy, noted, "[LBJ] frequently made statements that the Cubans must have been involved. The whole idea that the Cubans—meaning Castro—might have had something to do with it was linked to the CIA's attempt to assassinate Castro. That was the root of Johnson's concern."[126]

In his oral history, Robert Kennedy bitterly recounted a remark Johnson supposedly made to someone else after the assassination. "When I was young in Texas, I used to know a cross-eyed boy," Johnson said. "His eyes were crossed, and so was his character...That was God's retribution for people who were bad—and so you should be careful of cross-eyed people because God put his mark on them...Sometimes I think that what happened to Kennedy may have been divine retribution." JFK himself had slightly-crossed eyes.[127]

Over the years, Johnson continued, albeit quietly, to pound away at the same theme. Joseph Califano, Jr., an LBJ confidante and former director of RFK's Cuban Coordinating Committee, would recall in 1975 that "on more than one occasion" LBJ expressed "a very strong opinion, almost a conviction," that Kennedy's death was a "response and retaliation" by Castro. Califano remembers Johnson telling him, "In time, when all the CIA activities are flushed out, then maybe the full story of the assassination will become known."[128] Johnson told news anchor Walter Cronkite in 1969 that soon after taking office, he had learned that "we had been operating a damned Murder Inc. in the Caribbean." In 1967, Johnson told ABC newsman Howard K. Smith, on the condition that he was off-the-record: "I'll tell you something [about Kennedy's murder] that will rock you. Kennedy was trying to get Castro, but Castro got to him first...It will all come out one day."[129]

Johnson's conclusion never wavered. In retirement at his ranch in Austin, he continued his pronouncements of Castro culpability. In 1971, one year before his death, Johnson told White House reporter Marianne Means, "Oswald acted either under the influence or the orders of Castro."[130] That same year, Johnson told the publisher of his autobiography, "I think I know who killed JFK. I can't prove it yet, but one day I will. Goddammit, I know it…it was Castro. You see, the Kennedy brothers liked playing cops and robbers for the CIA and they sent people into Cuba to git Castro, but they failed and Castro git Kennedy…Oswald was a Communist agent…One day I will prove it."[131]

In addition to CIA and FBI reports made available to LBJ, foreign sources may have played a role in his suspicions of Cuban involvement in Mexico City. Sharing the American Embassy in Mexico City with the CIA in 1963 was the U.S. Ambassador, Thomas Mann. In 1990, Mann recalled, "Lyndon Johnson had lines into Mexico that I knew nothing about. I knew he had information, he had his own sources, and I didn't know who they were. [Johnson] was an amazing man. He didn't speak Spanish, but he was a good friend of [Gustavo] Diaz Ordaz, who became president of Mexico."[132]

The very week the Commission handed in its report, panel member Richard Russell phoned Johnson to say of the official conclusion, "I don't believe it." To that Johnson responded, "I don't either."

The Shortcomings of the Warren Commission

In later years, the Warren Commission's work would be evaluated by two official government investigations. In the first, the Church hearings of 1976, the committee concluded:

> The evidence indicates that the investigation of the assassination was deficient and that facts which might have substantially altered the course of the investigation were not provided to the Warren Commission or those individuals within the FBI and the CIA, as well as other agencies of Government who were charged with investigating the assassination…The FBI investigation, as well as the CIA inquiry, was deficient on the specific question of the significance of Oswald's contacts with pro-Castro and anti-Castro groups for the many months before the assassination…Senior Bureau officials should have realized the FBI efforts were focused too narrowly to allow for a full investigation. They should have realized the significance of Oswald's Cuban contacts…The possibility exists that senior officials in both agencies made conscious decisions not to disclose potentially important information.[133]…Neither the Warren Commission as a body nor its staff was given details of CIA Cuban operations…In any event, the Warren Commission did not pursue with the CIA the questions of Oswald's pro-Castro and anti-Castro contacts. Of the thirty-four requests to the CIA from the Warren Commission…only one deals with information on a Cuban matter. That is a request for the CIA to furnish information about Jack Ruby's alleged visit to Cuba in 1959.[134]

Three years later, the House Select Committee on Assassinations (HSCA) likewise evaluated the Warren Commission's performance. It concluded, "The Warren Commission failed to adequately investigate the possibility of a conspiracy to assassinate the President." Further, the HSCA pointed out, "the Commission overstated the thoroughness of its investigation...in particular, that of the conspiracy investigation...The report left the impression that issues had been dealt with more thoroughly than they had."[135] The Commission's inadequacies, the HSCA Report stated, stemmed not only from severe time constraints, but from "failure by the CIA and FBI to provide it with all relevant evidence and information."[136]

Among the specific areas pointed to as deficient by the HSCA were:

- *Oswald's activities and associations during the periods he lived in New Orleans.*

- *The conspiratorial and potentially violent climate created by the Cuban issue in the early 1960s, particularly the possible consequences of CIA/Mafia plots against Castro.*

- *The full nature and extent of Oswald's visit to Mexico City two months prior to the assassination, including not only his contact with the Soviet and Cuban diplomatic offices there, and the CIA's monitoring of his activities there, but also his possible associations and activities outside those offices.*[137]

The HSCA concluded, "It is a reality to be regretted that the [Warren] Commission failed to live up to its promise."[138]

Although it has not been widely publicized, the CIA in 1975 reviewed its file on the Kennedy case and also reached a conclusion critical of the Warren Commission report:

> *The belief that there was Soviet or Cuban (KGB and/or DGI) connection with Oswald will persist and grow until there has been a full disclosure of all elements of Oswald's handling and stay in the Soviet Union and his contacts in Mexico City. The Warren Commission report should have left a wider "window" for this contingency. That was the opinion of the counterintelligence component in the CIA in 1964...CIA would continue to regard this aspect of the Oswald case as still open.*[139]

All of these shortcomings could have been avoided if Robert Kennedy, Allen Dulles, Lyndon Johnson, or Earl Warren had desired it. They didn't. Robert Kennedy biographer Lester David wrote:

> *Robert Kennedy knew what had gone on since 1961. At the very least, the Warren Commission should have had the opportunity to pursue the Cuban link. It did not, because Bobby, deciding he wanted the entire horrible, painful story wrapped up and forgotten, participated in a coverup of essential evidence.*[140]

In this context, Robert Kennedy bore much responsibility for the seriously incomplete work of the Commission, and consequently set the stage for decades of condemnation to be hurled at both the commissioners and the federal government. It also triggered a catastrophic collapse of public faith in official government pronouncements of all kinds.

Senator Richard Schweiker, who investigated the Kennedy assassination in the 1970s, recently summed things up: "The Warren Commission was set up at the time to feed pabulum to the American people for reasons not yet known, and one of the biggest coverups in the history of our country occurred at that time."[141]

With hindsight, it is now apparent to most observers that the Warren Commission's work was undermined by its hidden agenda to "dispel rumors." There is no hint of a desire to examine every clue. Allen Dulles, Robert Kennedy, J. Edgar Hoover, and Lyndon Johnson had no qualms about telling the American people who shot JFK, but telling them why was out of the question. As Warren Commission attorney Burt Griffin would later testify, "We frankly ducked, I think. Everybody who has read the report knows we ducked the question of motive."

When asked how things would have been different if the intelligence community (which included Commissioner Dulles) had informed the Commission of the anti-Castro plots, Griffin responded, "I do not think we could have ducked the question of motive under those circumstances...It becomes very important that something that perhaps the U.S. government did is what supplied the impetus to select President Kennedy rather than some other target."[142]

The fact that this information was kept secret from the Commission protected the Kennedy myth, the reputation of the United States government, and the world from the possibility of nuclear war. But because so much of the government's investigation of the assassination and Cuban operations became shrouded in secrecy, speculation filled the vacuum. The result was 35 years of misdirected allegations leveled at many of those who were foresworn to keep "The Big Secret:" that there may indeed have been a conspiracy instigated by Jack and Bobby's "secret war." In the years to come, however, the theory of Castro retaliation would come within a whisker of blowing wide open on a number of occasions. And while LBJ pondered how to exploit this tragic Kennedy misadventure to his political advantage, Bobby Kennedy dealt with that horrible reality in his own very personal way.

CHAPTER SEVENTEEN

BOBBY ALONE

"I have...wondered at times if we did not pay a very great price for being more energetic than wise about a lot of things, especially Cuba."
  —**Robert Kennedy in 1968**[1]

"I found out something I never knew. I found out that my world was not the real world."
  —**Robert Kennedy, weeks before his own death in 1968**[2]

The day of the assassination, a devastated Bobby Kennedy remarked to his Justice Department assistant Edwin Guthman, "I'd received a letter from someone in Texas last week warning me not to let the President go to Texas because they would kill him. I sent it to Kenny O'Donnell." This warning, coupled with his knowledge of Castro's threatened reprisals and Oswald's pro-Castro obsessions, clearly weighed heavily on the mind of JFK's brother.[3]

In the wake of Jack Kennedy's death, only firebrand Black Muslim leader Malcolm X had the temerity to pronounce what many savvy political insiders secretly suspected: "The chickens have come home to roost." Harris Wofford, aide to both Jack and Bobby Kennedy, later wrote that Malcolm X's taunt "caused more pain to Robert Kennedy than any of us could have imagined at the time." The reason, Wofford explained, was that Bobby believed he was "to some significant extent, directly or indirectly responsible for his brother's death."[4]

Bobby had feared for some time that his policies were inviting reprisals—from prosecuted mobsters who felt double-crossed after dealing with Joe Kennedy during the election, or from right-wing hatemongers objecting to Kennedy policies on civil rights. But there was that third, more probable explanation, which surfaced soon after the assassination as the only clear conclusion. After the pro-Castro Lee Oswald was arrested, Bobby's relentless pursuit of Castro now appeared to be the trigger.

The Guilt-Ridden Brother

"Bobby felt responsible for his brother's death. One day he said to me, 'What do you think [about the assassination]?' I said I thought that Castro had gotten to Oswald. He just gave me a look that indicated it was possible."
—**Enrique "Harry" Ruiz-Williams**[5]

John Davis, author and cousin of Jackie Kennedy, was among those in the inner circle paying their respects at the White House that awful weekend. In the blur of the somber occasion, one memory stands out for him. "All of the Kennedy family were stalwart at the White House after the assassination," Davis recalled recently. "But Bobby was destroyed. He mumbled, walked in circles and, in my opinion, seemed consumed by guilt."[6]

After waiting a week, Sergio Arcacha Smith called to offer his condolences to the man who had offered so much hope to Arcacha's volunteers in New Orleans. "Little was said," Arcacha recalls. "Bobby was a broken man."[7] RFK's assistant on civil rights, William Vanden Heuvel, described the impact through an analogy: "What polio did for Roosevelt, the assassination did for Robert Kennedy."[8]

"It was as though someone had turned off his switch," said friend Dave Hackett.[9] Journalist and RFK friend Jack Newfield recalled that Bobby was "in the deepest kind of mourning" he had ever seen in anyone. Although he was still Attorney General, Bobby didn't appear at the Justice Department for more than a month. William Vanden Heuvel, Bobby's special assistant on civil rights, recalls, "I never saw anyone so grief-stricken over anything as Bobby was after the assassination. His face was all pain, filled with an anguish that never left him for the rest of his life."[10] A friend visiting after the assassination described Bobby as "desolate, bleak, a vacuum—crushed beyond hope, mentally, spiritually, and physically."[11]

G. Robert Blakey, who later became the Chief Counsel for the House Select Committee on Assassinations, was a young attorney for the Justice Department at the time. He recently recalled, "Bobby was traumatized to the point of total paralysis. He could no longer function. In fact, Nick Katzenbach ran the Justice Department after the assassination."[12]

When Bobby finally returned to work, he created a miniature shrine to his brother in a hidden corner of his office. An RFK biographer described it:

It was an obscure place, and only a few of his closest friends were even aware it existed. Bobby placed photographs, books, and small reminders there. He would go there many times during the day and stand in front of it, lost in thought. He would try to work, but within minutes of his arrival, associates would find him staring out a window. He would get up suddenly, go downstairs, and stride in the great courtyard of the block-square building. His eyes were always red from weeping.[13]

For many months thereafter, Kennedy exhibited the symptoms of clinical depression—unable to sleep or concentrate on work, given to long bouts of brooding. His eyes were frequently red from crying. One member of his Secret Service contingent remarked, "Bobby was so undone by the assassination he could barely speak to his wife."[14] After interviewing numerous RFK friends, Lester David wrote that Bobby Kennedy "became preoccupied with the idea of death...He was engulfed by feelings of sadness, hopelessness, and discouragement."[15]

One of Jack and Bobby's closest and oldest chums, Lem Billings, concluded, "When Jack died, a large part of Bobby died, too. I saw that life extinguished...When they buried Jack Kennedy in that grave at Arlington, they buried much of Bobby, too."[16]

All the observers saw a melancholic, vastly less energetic RFK. The only exception was when he protested Lyndon Johnson's immediate possession of the Oval Office. The Secretaries of State and Defense had advised Johnson to assert swift authority in his new office in order to demonstrate, nationally and internationally, that the American government would proceed without interruption or dislocation.

But when Johnson approached the Oval Office on the morning after the assassination, Bobby, seemingly half-deranged, spread his arms at the doorway and shrieked to the new President that he could not enter. "Don't come in here! ...You should not be here! You don't deserve to be here."[17] Although Johnson himself is the single known source for that story, he apparently repeated it often enough to give it validity. Bobby later explained, more convincingly, that he wanted to keep Johnson out only until his brother's belongings were removed. In any event, he confirmed that a confrontation did take place.[18]

The coming winter of 1963-64 was a spiritually desolate trial for RFK. His insomnia had deepened to the point where he would leave home in the middle of the night, driving at high speeds in his convertible in the freezing cold. He often would not return until dawn. Kennedy refused to allow Secret Service agents to accompany him on these rides, so no one ever knew where he had gone, although many suspected he went to his brother's grave.[19]

LBJ speechwriter Leo Janos was told by Johnson's personal secretary, Juanita Roberts, that Bobby was incoherent, "and found wandering around cities shortly after his brother's death, not just because of the loss of his brother, but because RFK felt personally responsible due to his involvement in the anti-Castro activities."[20] By all indications, Bobby Kennedy's now-legendary melancholia stayed with him until his own death-by-assassination four and a half years later.

When the Warren Commission report was released in the fall of 1964, Bobby told intimates that he didn't accept its conclusions. This was no surprise, considering Bobby knew secrets to which most of his friends weren't privy. In 1966, RFK would admit to historian Arthur Schlesinger his misgivings about the Commission's findings. Schlesinger wrote:

On October 30, 1966, as we talked until 2 a.m. in P.J. Clarke's saloon in New York, he wondered how long he could continue to avoid comment on the report. He regarded it as a poor job but was unwilling to criticize it and thereby re-open the whole tragic business.[21]

In the days after JFK's murder, Manuel Artime visited with his grief-stricken friend. Bobby Kennedy told his exile ally, "The Kennedy family has two big enemies, the Mafia and Castro. One of them killed my brother."[22] Bobby also told Schlesinger, just two weeks after the murder, that he was uncertain whether Oswald had acted alone "or as part of a large plot, whether organized by Castro or gangsters."[23]

RFK's brooding led him to an abrupt change in character. Writer Jack Newfield concluded that the "assassination punctured the center of Robert Kennedy's universe.... It made Robert Kennedy, a man unprepared for introspection, think for the first time in his life what he stood for."[24] In his search for meaning, he immersed himself in the brooding, existential writings of philosopher Albert Camus, which considered the fundamental questions: Why are we here, and what is the meaning of life?

Kennedy proceeded to read every Camus novel, play, and essay. Camus' published works were soon filled with RFK's marginal notes. The result was the rebirth of Robert Kennedy. He became not merely a fatalist, but a tireless worker for global peace, and a beacon of hope for the underprivileged. All the manic energy he had poured into the violent and ill-conceived "Cuba Project" now seemingly was channeled toward his new, loftier goals.

There was no in-between for Bobby Kennedy. He had changed 180 degrees. As one friend recalled, "His transformation was total. He changed as much as any human has the capacity to change." For all his energy though, Bobby Kennedy now suspected—no doubt thanks to Camus—that, in the long run, all his efforts were for naught. "I don't know that it makes any difference what I do," he once told his advisors. "Maybe we're all doomed anyway." When an aide was discussing how a certain recent occurrence might affect his political hopes in 1972, Kennedy replied, "Who knows whether I'm going to be alive in 1972?"

His new-found fatalism even became the butt of some dark humor. When arriving in Indiana during his 1968 bid for the Presidency, Kennedy was greeted by signs proclaiming: "KENNEDY AND CAMUS IN 1968."[25] Followers began to speak of the old "Bad Bobby" and the new "Good Bobby."

Robert Kennedy's friends have always maintained that RFK had no interest in the details of his brother's murder, or, for that matter, who committed the murder. In fact, this lack of interest has been a Kennedy family mantra for the last three decades, most recently uttered, almost to the word, by John Kennedy, Jr., when interviewed in 1992 by ABC's Sam Donaldson. The journalist asked the President's son who he thought had killed his father. Young Kennedy responded, "I frankly haven't given it much thought. All that matters is that my father is dead."

More than a year after the tragedy, journalist Oriana Fallaci suggested to

Bobby Kennedy that the memory of Jack "persecutes you, doesn't it?" Bobby dodged the question. "For a long time now, I have refused to speak of it...Please do not ask me. Let us forget the question."[26] He essentially repeated the same refusal almost three years after the assassination. In July 1966, Richard Goodwin, formerly of Jack Kennedy's inner circle, became convinced that the Warren Commission's investigation had been seriously flawed. Because he was well aware of Bobby's "still-unhealed vulnerability," he cautiously raised the subject in private—and received the response of a man still in pain. Goodwin wrote:

> *Bobby listened silently, without objection, his inner tension or distaste revealed only by the circling currents of scotch in the glass he was obsessively rotating between his hands, staring at the floor in a posture of avoidance. After I completed my brief presentation, he looked up: "I'm sorry, Dick. I just can't focus on it."*[27]

To some, such devastation, even given the special circumstances, was not only puzzling but suspicious. It seemed a grief of a different order than that felt by the other Kennedys. Friends portray Bobby as unable or unwilling to say why he was so overwhelmingly stricken. More than that, he seemed to be hiding something. CIA Director John McCone had worked intimately with Bobby on many intelligence matters and felt they had a close relationship. McCone sensed in Bobby's reaction to the assassination "something troubling [him] that he was not disclosing."[28] Later, McCone would state his belief that Robert Kennedy "had personal feelings of guilt because he was directly or indirectly involved with the anti-Castro planning."[29]

McCone's intuition was probably right, but not even he, the Director of the CIA, knew all the details of the most dangerous, potentially most explosive secrets. Those darkest secrets concerned plots and plans to eliminate Fidel Castro, an aspiration about which the Kennedy brothers were "hysterical," according to later testimony from Robert McNamara.

In one sense, Bobby's avoidance of the subject of Jack's death seems an understandable emotion, often referred to as a trait typical of the family's Irish heritage. Yet, one has to wonder if the "ruthless," sometimes "vengeful," side of Bobby Kennedy so easily gave in to this emotion. Did he, in fact, not care that his beloved brother's murderers might have escaped to a beach in Brazil? Although it is not certain, there have long been rumors that Bobby Kennedy did indeed take an interest, albeit a very discreet one, in ascertaining the details of his brother's assassination.

Considering the early data filtering back to Washington that weekend following the assassination, Robert Kennedy must have shared the same interpretation of events as Desmond FitzGerald: Had Castro, in fact, struck first? To recap:

- *Oswald had ties to Cubans in New Orleans, where Bobby Kennedy had numerous staging operations (involving the likes of Sergio Arcacha Smith, David Ferrie, and Nino Diaz), many of which were penetrated by Castro's agents. In fact, Oswald had used Arcacha's previous address on his fliers.*

And New Orleans D.A. Jim Garrison suspected that Oswald had contact with Ferrie.

• *Oswald had just returned from the Soviet and Cuban Embassies in Mexico City, where Bobby's own Castro assassin, Rolando Cubela, was known to frequent.*

And there was more. In early December 1963, Bobby Kennedy received a letter from Havana that had to hit him like a heat-seeking missile. The letter, dated November 27, 1963, indicated that Oswald had been hired and paid off by an agent of Fidel Castro. Although later determined by the FBI to be fictitious, the note nonetheless had to ignite Bobby's legendary thirst for revenge. In a second letter sent to a Cuban newspaper in New York, the same writer said that the contact with Oswald was made in Mexico City.

The letters bore an eerie resemblance to the allegations of Gilberto Alvarado, which already had official Washington in a tizzy. Recall Alvarado's claim that Oswald had been paid $6,500 by a Castro agent in Mexico City. These letters used the figure of $7,000—a great similarity that may have seemed too close for comfort.

Still other letters, like that from Ernesto Luna, were sent directly to Bobby. On January 17, 1964, Luna wrote RFK that he was in Mexico City at the time of Oswald's visit, and that he knew Oswald had spent time in the Tapachula, Mexico home of Victor Cohen, a pro-Castro agent and former Castro treasurer.[30]

In the face of these disquieting revelations, is it reasonable to conclude that RFK's infamous wrath demanded no answers? In fact, RFK's alleged "disinterest" was just another fiction. Behind the scenes, he was demanding answers.

Bobby's Private Investigations

In the assassination's immediate aftermath, before Lee Oswald's New Orleans/pro-Castro connections were revealed, Bobby suspected that the Chicago mob had carried out a vendetta against the president. Early in the evening of November 22, Bobby called a trusted National Labor Relations Board member—Julius Draznin—then living in Sam Giancana's Chicago. Knowing that Draznin had sources in "the outfit," Bobby asked him to see what they knew, and report back to Bobby directly. In four days, Bobby had his preliminary answer.

"There's nothing here," Draznin told Bobby, formalizing his conclusion in a memo to Bobby dated November 26, 1963. After several more weeks of checking, Draznin was convinced the mob played no role, either in Kennedy's or Oswald's murder. Draznin recently told writer Seymour Hersh, "I picked up nothing at all tying it to the Chicago mob."[31] Regarding Ruby, Draznin says, "Ruby was intent on taking care of the guy who killed his beloved president. I believe it to this day. I told that to Bobby face-to-face, in a private meeting."[32]

Another glimpse of Bobby's private inquiry came from Dallas itself. After thirty years of silence, Al Maddox, Deputy Sheriff of Dallas County, recently related the following episode :

> *I saw Robert Kennedy [a couple of weeks] after the assassination [in Dallas].*
> *I drove Sheriff Bill Decker to the Adolphus Hotel and went to the front door.*
> *When the door swung open, Robert Kennedy was standing there. Decker told*
> *me, 'You didn't see anything,' and I didn't see anything.*[33]

According to Maddox, Decker verified the obvious—that the mysterious visitor was indeed Bobby Kennedy. "At that time, Decker ran the city of Dallas," recalls Maddox, "and if he told you to jump off a ten-story building, you jumped…I never did read about it [Bobby's visit] in the papers and no one knew anything about it…It was never discussed after that."

FBI agent Vincent Drain verified that RFK indeed visited Dallas on a number of occasions before and after the assassination. Drain was the agent assigned to pick up and drop off the Attorney General at Dallas' Love Field airport whenever he came into town. "He used to like being dropped off at the Executive Inn [one mile from the airport] and jog to Love Field."[34] Drain, however, claimed to know of no "secret" RFK visits. Precisely why Bobby visited Dallas is not known.[35]

After the mob theory died, all that was left, it seems, was the possibility that the "Cuba Project" attempts on Castro's life had backfired. It may have been too difficult for Bobby to contemplate, and certainly not something he would have wanted JFK's adoring public to know.

The question of Bobby's "private" interest in the assassination will be difficult, if not impossible, to ever resolve. However, it is now clear that his abiding interest in looking out for his brother's interests continued unabated throughout the 1960's. That protection occasionally bordered on the macabre.

Bobby Kennedy and The Mystery of the President's Missing Brain

After Robert Kennedy's own murder in 1968, the Kennedy family's veil of secrecy was pulled back ever so slightly. Under the aegis of family attorney Burke Marshall, qualified members of the medical establishment, interested in scholarly review, were occasionally granted access to John Kennedy's autopsy materials. One such professional made front-page news in 1972 when he emerged from the National Archives and announced that President Kennedy's brain was missing. The clear implication (not discouraged by this doctor) was that the brain was removed in order to prevent an accurate tracking of the wounds—tracks that might lead to the infamous grassy knoll.[36]

The doctor's statements further inflamed public opinion about the government and completely misdirected those interested in learning the truth. The truth, in this instance had nothing to do with a conspiracy to kill John Kennedy. It had everything to do with Bobby's unceasing devotion to his brother. But the result was the same—it continued to feed the fires of domestic-based rumors and theories about possible assassination conspiracies.

In point of fact, staffers at the National Archives had known since October 1966 that the President's brain was missing. However, because they had a good idea of what had happened to it—a benign explanation, it turns out—they decided against making it public, fearful of inciting just the kind of public out-cry that occurred in 1972. What follows is the actual chronology of events that generated the controversy, compiled using the most recent releases of House Committee interviews and interviews by the author.[37]

On the night of the assassination, autopsist James Humes gave the President's brain and tissue slides to Kennedy's personal physician, Admiral George Burkley. Humes later said, "He (Burkley) told me that the Kennedy family wanted to inter the brain with the President's body. I don't know what happened to the brain, but I do know that Admiral Burkley was an honorable man."[38] Boswell agreed, saying, "I believe that it was buried with the body...I personally handed it over to Dr. Burkley and he told me that the family intended to bury it with the body. I believe Admiral Burkley."[39]

Two weeks later, the brain, however, by now fixed in formalin, was re-examined by Humes, and returned to Burkley.[40] Burkley then transferred it for storage to the Secret Service locker at the Executive Office Building, under the custody of Secret Service Agent Robert Bouck. There it remained for the next two and one-half years.

On April 22, 1965 Robert Kennedy sent a letter to Dr. Burkley directing him to transfer the material to JFK's former personal secretary, Evelyn Lincoln, whose office was by now in the National Archives. The letter also stated that Mrs. Lincoln was being instructed that the material was not to be released to anyone without the written permission of Robert Kennedy.

Three days later, Kennedy family attorney Burke Marshall, acting as executor of John Kennedy's estate, relinquished control of the materials to Robert Kennedy. They were then transferred for safekeeping to Mrs. Lincoln in the Archives. An inventory taken at the time indicated that nothing was missing.[41]

One month later, as Mrs. Lincoln later recalled it to the HSCA, Bobby Kennedy called, saying he was sending over his personal secretary, Angela Novello, along with Presidential archivist Herman Kahn and his deputies to take the trunk away to some undisclosed location. Mrs. Novello was out of town when the HSCA later attempted to interview her. Her attorney told the Committee that she knew nothing about the sequence of events.

In 1994, Mrs. Novello, in a phone interview with the author, said she only recalls moving "some papers," and to the best of her knowledge these papers were still in the Archives. The next question would have been, "Where in the Archives were these 'papers' taken?" At that point, however, Novello abruptly ended the conversation[42]— again proving that the secretaries of the world are the true keepers of secrets. In Novello's case, she not only functioned as RFK's personal secretary, but after his death, assumed the same function for the "ultimate insider," power attorney Edward Bennett Williams—the man who represented RFK's longtime nemeses Jimmy Hoffa and Sam Giancana.[43]

According to Lincoln, Bobby's driver and personal assistant, Master Sergeant Joseph Giordano, carried off the trunk.[44] According to Dr. Burkley, "Giordano moved the material to the JFK Library in Boston and knows something about the brain."[45] Giordano, however, told the HSCA that he did not move it, and had "no knowledge" of what happened to it. He suggested that George Dalton, who also worked for Bobby, might know. Dalton was no stranger to performing "secret" missions for the Kennedys—he had transcribed the Oval Office tapes at Bobby's request *(as mentioned in Chapter Fifteen)*. Neither Dalton nor Giordano would respond to the author's requests for an interview.[46]

On November 2, 1965, Public Law 89-318 was enacted. Among other provisions, the law made it clear that the Kennedy autopsy materials were evidence, and that it rightfully belonged to the government. Further, the materials had to be returned within one year of the law's enactment. At that point, Attorney General Ramsey Clark initiated discussions with Kennedy attorneys, who clearly wanted to stall Clark indefinitely.

By the fall of 1966, as the deadline neared, Clark approached Bobby Kennedy directly for the materials. Kennedy was not sympathetic to the government's position. Heated discussions ensued with family lawyer Burke Marshall. On October 29, 1966, an agreement was reached whereby the Kennedys donated the trunk back to the Archives. Deputy Archivist Trudy Peterson witnessed the material's return to the building, and suggested that Bobby, Novello, et al, had removed it from the building in May 1965 to a location Robert Kennedy himself designated.

National Archives General Counsel, Harry Van Cleve, receiving the transferred trunk, took an inventory and became the first person to discover that JFK's brain and other "gross material" were missing. Concluding that the Kennedy family had taken possession of the material, Van Cleve later noted that "we were borrowing trouble in exploring it any further."[47] He further cautioned against approaching Joseph Giordano.[48]

There is very little doubt that Robert Kennedy took control of the "missing" material. This was the finding of the HSCA, as well as many of the Archive employees. The only mystery remaining is exactly how Bobby disposed of the material. And even that mystery is finally starting to fade.

In 1976, RFK's former press aide, Frank Mankiewicz, told HSCA Counsel Blakey he thought that the "President's brain is in the grave. LBJ, Ted, Bobby, and maybe McNamara buried it when the body was transferred. Ted seemed to confirm it later."[49]

JFK's body was, in fact, reinterred in Arlington in March 1967, upon completion of a memorial structure.[50] HSCA Chief Investigator Robert Tanenbaum related to the author a comment that Mankiewicz allegedly made to him in 1978—that RFK, in an earlier phone call, said that the brain "is being put back in the coffin. Do not leak this or you'll be in big trouble."[51] Mankiewicz denies saying this, but acknowledges being on guard at the perimeter for the reinterment.[52] Evelyn Lincoln told the Committee that she would continue to investigate the matter on her own.

In 1992, in a final attempt to determine the whereabouts of the material, the author enlisted a close friend who is also a confidante of Mrs. Lincoln to put the question to her: After she told the HSCA that she would conduct further inquiries into the matter, did she indeed learn anything about the disposition of the President's brain? According to the intermediary, Mrs. Lincoln became quiet, looked her friend in the eyes, and said simply, "It's where it belongs."

Johnson and Cuba

"People just don't realize how conservative Lyndon really is. There are going to be a lot of changes."
> —Robert Kennedy to Ed Guthman, one hour after the assassination[53]

"Lyndon Johnson says he doesn't want to hear another thing about those goddamn Cubans."
> —E. Howard Hunt to "Harry" Williams, shortly after the assassination of President Kennedy[54]

"If Jack Kennedy had lived, I can assure you we would have gotten rid of Castro by last Christmas. Unfortunately, the new President isn't as gung-ho on fighting Castro as Kennedy was."
—Des FitzGerald, March 1964[55]

The assassination of President Kennedy, long considered an act of a disturbed man with no clear political motive, wrought major policy changes, just as many had predicted. On November 23, 1963, one day after the Dallas tragedy, CIA headquarters cabled JM/WAVE chief Ted Shackley, ordering, "Postpone [sabotage] ops indefinitely. Rescheduling will depend upon consultations with appropriate officials." The appropriate officials consisted of Lyndon Johnson and his administration.[56]

Soon after the assassination, Johnson directed the Joint Chiefs of Staff (JCS) to formulate new policy recommendations for Cuba. On March 21, 1964, the Kennedy-appointed JCS proposed OPERATION SQUARE DANCE, which called for the total destruction of Cuba's sugar crop. The result would have been not only the collapse of the Castro regime, but untold hardship on the general Cuban population. Johnson refused to back the proposal.[57]

On April 7, 1964, five months after the assassination, President Johnson discontinued all sabotage and raids against Cuba. One CIA officer who was present at that Special Group meeting remembered Johnson saying, "Enough is enough." The OPLAN 380-63 coup plans were allowed to die a natural death, with absolutely no misgivings from the Johnson White House.

The massive JM/WAVE CIA station in Florida was eventually disbanded, and AM/LASH was put out to pasture. The only known CIA objection to these changes was from the Kennedy-appointed Director, John McCone, who complained about the sabotage cutoff in an April 1964 memo, the day after Johnson's major policy shift. As David Corn writes, McCone knew that Johnson was "throwing in the towel." Nowhere else is there evidence that any other CIA official objected to these changes. In fact, many agents were relieved that the project had ended.

In Central America, Artime's camps were likewise disbanded. Nilo Messer, Artime's secretary, quotes Artime as saying, "This is the end for us."[58] Raphael Quintero, another Artime aide and RFK confidante, recently stated, "We were just really getting started with our [Central American] operation when President Kennedy got assassinated. After that, there were big problems."[59] Bobby Kennedy echoed the lament, when he later commented about the Cuba Project, "Since November [1963], we haven't really done anything."[60] Artime's Chief of Naval Operations for the Central American stratagem, Rene Cancio, agrees, saying, "I'm almost sure that the Central American project ended because Kennedy died and Johnson assumed power. And that project was not Johnson's idea. It was Kennedy's."[61]

General Alexander Haig, Jr., former Secretary of State, and one of the coordinators of Bobby Kennedy's Cuban Coordinating Committee, recently stated, "When John Kennedy was killed—and I'm not so sure that [the Cuba policy] didn't have a role in that as well—clearly everything stopped." Haig continued, "But I know that until the day he died, President Johnson was convinced that Castro retaliated by assassinating President Kennedy—retaliated against those covert operations."[62]

Bobby's protection of his brother's legacy would succeed for three years following the assassination. However, as a consequence of Bobby's vicious feud with Lyndon Johnson, and the political ambitions of a New Orleans District Attorney, the dam of concealment threatened to break in 1967.

CHAPTER EIGHTEEN

ASSAULT ON CAMELOT

In 1964, the Warren Commission produced a report with numerous loose strings and a single conclusion—that Oswald, a "lone nut," was President Kennedy's sole assassin, and that he lacked a clear motive. And that conclusion might have remained in the history books, undisturbed, had FBI director J. Edgar Hoover not returned to the scene on a seemingly unrelated matter.

In the spring of 1966, to assist in an ongoing investigation, Hoover wanted to put a spy inside Los Angeles' Mafia syndicate. The FBI director had learned—through immigration records—that Johnny Rosselli, a member of the Los Angeles mob, was an illegal alien living in the United States under a false identity.[1]

Ever the resourceful purveyor of intelligence, Hoover dangled the threat of deportation above Rosselli, reasoning that the mob's "Mr. Smooth" would see Hoover's side of the deal and be coerced into turning on his brethren. Rosselli was definitely feeling the heat.

Giancana associate Joe Shimon wisely informed Rosselli that the first "hood" that the Bureau would want Rosselli to turn on would be his longtime friend Sam Giancana. Shimon told Rosselli, "You wouldn't last twenty minutes" [if you talk to the FBI]. Rosselli then turned to his attorney, Edward Bennett Williams, and announced his decision: "Number one, I'm not going to snitch on anybody; number two, I want some way to keep those guys off my back; number three, I want the name of the prick that turned me in."[2]

Luckily for Rosselli, he had some leverage. As one of the key participants in the anti-Castro murder plots, Rosselli realized that he held one hell of a trump card. He also remembered that another key player in the plots, Robert Maheu, had escaped prosecution by playing the same card five years earlier.

On May 12, 1966, Rosselli met with his old CIA contact, the former Deputy of Security, Sheffield Edwards. He told Edwards about Hoover's threat, reminding Edwards in the process that he, Rosselli, knew about a few skeletons in the CIA's closet. Rosselli also expressed his fear that gangsters would kill him for "talking."[3] Rosselli wanted the CIA to intercede with the FBI on his behalf, as it had for Maheu. Immediately after this meeting, Rosselli visited his old friend William Harvey, the former head of the "Executive Action" program. Retired from the CIA, Bill Harvey then ran a Washington law firm. Over the next five years, Rosselli and Harvey met numerous times. At these sessions, Harvey expressed his "concern that Senator Robert Kennedy knew all about the operation." Rosselli agreed.[4]

As a result, the CIA intervened on Rosselli's behalf with the Immigration and Naturalization Service. A CIA memo dated February 26, 1971 admitted that the CIA had initiated contact with INS, and that "the purpose of this effort was to intercede with INS on behalf of Mr. Johnny Rosselli in the action being initiated for deportation."

But the CIA's intervention in 1971 was, for Rosselli, too slow in coming. In the meantime, he decided to light a few fires of his own under official Washington. Although he would not divulge all the details, he would give out enough, he hoped, to persuade the CIA to take him seriously. With his well-connected Washington lawyer, Edward Morgan, Rosselli decided to leak his story through two distinct channels.

Channel One: Jack Anderson

Syndicated columnist Jack Anderson was a close personal friend of Rosselli's lawyer, Edward Morgan. Anderson, along with his boss, Drew Pearson, wrote the weekly "investigative" news column entitled *Washington Merry-Go-Round*, and this was the kind of political intrigue that kept the syndicated column revolving.

In January 1967, Morgan forwarded to the columnists the first details from his (unnamed) source. He told them that Bobby Kennedy had supervised assassination plots against Fidel Castro that resulted in retaliation against his brother on November 22, 1963. According to Rosselli, as passed along to Anderson and Pearson, an underworld figure, "planted" close to Castro, gained Castro's confidence during the early 1960s. Allegedly this "plant" was present when Castro learned of the administration's plotting. According to the same source, Castro became infuriated and remarked, "If this is the way they play the game, I will play the same way."[5] Before publishing the material, columnist Pearson sought counsel from a couple of close friends, Earl Warren and President Lyndon Johnson.

Warren advised Pearson to report the information to the authorities (as he himself would later do to the Church Committee). On January 31, 1967, Warren took the initiative and contacted Secret Service Director James Rowley. Rowley would later testify:

> *The way he [Warren] approached it, was that he said he thought this was serious enough and so forth, but he wanted to get it off his hands. He felt that he*

had to—that it had to be told to somebody, and that the Warren Commission was finished, and he wanted the thing pursued.[6]

During the Kennedys' anti-Castro plotting, Johnson had been kept out of the loop, able only to obtain rumors of the policymaking. After the assassination, past Kennedy policies were apparently kept from President Johnson. His knowledge of possible Cuban complicity in the assassination, and the reports given him by McCone and others after November 22, are not known to this day. Now, in 1967, he finally learned the details of the Kennedy plots during a meeting with Pearson. Afterward, according to Johnson phone tapes released in 1996, the president called Attorney General Ramsey Clark, exclaiming:

It's incredible!...They have a man that was...instructed by the CIA and the attorney general [Robert Kennedy] to assassinate Castro after the Bay of Pigs....So he [Castro] tortured [the would-be assassins] and they told him all about it. [Castro] called Oswald and a group in and told them...Go...get the job done."

For Lyndon Johnson, the opportunity to embarrass Robert Kennedy couldn't have come at a better time. In the early 1960s, the enmity between Johnson and RFK was legendary, ameliorated briefly by their mutual desire for a limited investigation of President Kennedy's death. Bobby's motive had been personal— to protect his brother's name and the family legacy. Johnson's rationale had been patriotic—he wanted to avert a catastrophic war. It was a fragile coalition at best, and by January 1967, it had totally disintegrated.

"That Little Shitass" vs. "That Cornponed Bastard"

"You Johnson people are running a stinking damned campaign, and you're gonna get yours when the time comes."
——**Robert Kennedy, to Bobby Baker at the 1960 Democratic National Convention**[7]

Originally, Johnson aimed his anti-Kennedy vitriol directly at John Kennedy, his chief rival for the 1960 Democratic nomination for president. Referring to his inexperienced opponent as "young Jack" or "the boy," Johnson went out of his way to allude to JFK's health problems and privileged background. Though Kennedy's sickly youth and bouts with Addison's disease were widely known in Washington circles, they did not become public knowledge until years later. It wasn't because Johnson didn't try.

Johnson's "enmity and hostility" towards Kennedy dominated an interview that Peter Lisagor, of the *Chicago Daily News*, conducted of LBJ. Lisagor wrote, "He referred to Kennedy as a 'little scrawny fellow with rickets' and other diseases. 'Have you ever seen his ankles?' Johnson asked. Making a small circle with his fingers, he noted, 'They're about so round.'"[8]

That was just the beginning. Johnson became known to journalists for the viciousness of his attacks. He told President Eisenhower that Kennedy was "dangerous," alleging that "old Joe Kennedy" would run the country if Jack were elected. At the Democratic National Convention, Johnson had his campaign manager India Edwards spread rumors of Kennedy's impending death from Addison's disease. Johnson also attacked Kennedy's Catholicism, saying, "I wouldn't be caught dead running on a ticket with that goddamned Roman Catholic."[9]

Perhaps the lowest blow—and the one that Bobby never forgave him for—was his reference to Papa Joe's isolationist stance during World War II. While scrambling for last-minute votes from convention delegates, Johnson told one state delegation, "I wasn't any Chamberlain-umbrella policy man. I never thought Hitler was right."

When the remark filtered back to him, Bobby hit the ceiling. Encountering Johnson aide Bobby Baker, he became utterly livid:

You've got your nerve…Lyndon Johnson has compared my father to the Nazis, and John Connally and India Edwards lied in saying my brother is dying of Addison's disease. You Johnson people are running a stinking damned campaign, and you're gonna get yours when the time comes.[10]

Kennedy aide Kenny O'Donnell recalled, "I've seen Bobby mad, but never as mad as the day he heard what Johnson said about his father." Bobby was overheard remarking that he would rather lose the election than have "that cornponed bastard" on the ticket.

Nonetheless, a truce was eventually arranged, and, for a complex variety of political reasons, Johnson was offered the vice-presidential spot. After Johnson's acceptance, the Kennedy camp, according to Bobby, realized its huge mistake in making the offer. Bobby made a trip to Johnson's suite to thank him for accepting. However, he later recalled, he wanted LBJ to reconsider. Tears came to Johnson's eyes, but, in a move that shocked Bobby, Johnson stood firm. "I want to be Vice-President. I'll fight for it," affirmed Johnson. After Bobby left, Johnson and his camp were furious. RFK had already earned a terrible reputation on Capitol Hill, but it was on that night that Johnson's favorite nickname for him finally crystallized—"that little shit-ass."

Although Johnson grew to resent his isolation as Vice-President, he didn't blame John Kennedy for excluding him from important meetings. According to Johnson's Press Secretary, George Reedy, "he blamed it on Bobby." When the press first jumped on the Bobby Baker scandalwagon in 1962, Johnson was certain that Bobby Kennedy was leaking the information that got the coverage started. Johnson's paranoia reached such a height that he believed "that little son of a bitch" had wiretapped his telephone, not only during Kennedy's term, but during his own presidency!

After his brother took office, Bobby's dislike of Johnson similarly deepened to loathing. "He tells so many lies," Bobby said of Johnson, "that he convinces himself after a while he's telling the truth. He just doesn't recognize the difference between truth and falsehood."[11] Bobby described Johnson as "mean, bitter, vicious—an animal in many ways." Just prior to the Dallas trip in the fall of 1963, Bobby's aides gave the Attorney General a voodoo doll made in Johnson's likeness.

There is no shortage of Washington anecdotes highlighting the RFK-LBJ feud. Some are tinged with humor. At the end of 1966, for example, Johnson was sitting in the private box of Washington Redskins owner Edward Bennett Williams. According to Williams' biographer Evan Thomas: "As Williams and LBJ watched the game, Robert Kennedy knocked on the door of the box to get in. 'Let him pound,' ordered the President. Williams had to apologize [to Kennedy] the next day."[12]

In 1964, political expediency again became the great arbiter. In spite of his hatred of the new President, Bobby deduced that the vice-presidency offered him the best stepping-stone to the presidency itself. Although he never said it publicly, friends were convinced that Kennedy wanted to be the vice-presidential nominee. With the cooperation of Bobby's aides, pressure was applied to Johnson to offer his VP spot in 1964 to Bobby. The press started referring to Johnson as merely a "caretaker" while the heir apparent, Bobby, was waiting in the wings to assume his rightful place in the Oval Office.

For Johnson, the idea of any Kennedy on the ticket—and especially Bobby—was practically unthinkable. Johnson feared the obvious—with John Kennedy now assuming martyr status, Johnson would never be able to crawl out from beneath the long Kennedy shadow. Johnson possessed too much pride for that. He had long dreamt of a Johnson presidency, not a Johnson-Kennedy presidency. In addition, his ego dictated that he could win the presidency on his own, and he wanted to prove it. He told presidential biographer Doris Kearns Goodwin, "With Bobby on the ticket, I'd never know if I could be elected on my own." When polls showed that Bobby was a potential political liability, especially in the South, Johnson was elated. "I don't need that little runt to win," Johnson said. "I can take anybody I damn please."[13]

The Democratic National Convention was to be held at the end of August 1964 in Atlantic City. Up until the last minute, Kennedy partisans continued pressuring Johnson. The irony surely was not lost on Johnson: after Bobby's performance at the convention in 1960, and many months of rumors of a "Dump Johnson" movement in the last year of JFK's presidency (largely circulated by Bobby's faction), it was payback time.

Johnson called a July 29 summit meeting with Bobby in the Oval Office. Instead of the usual fireside chat, Johnson stayed behind the imperious Presidential desk and informed the crestfallen Attorney General that for "political" reasons, Bobby was unacceptable as Vice-President. In a single session, Johnson thus commenced and concluded his own "Dump Bobby" movement. Johnson remembered Kennedy as saying, "I'm sorry that you have reached this conclusion, because I think I could have been of help to you."[14]

Johnson's worries were not entirely over. He knew that Bobby was going to address the convention before the showing of a filmed tribute to his slain brother. It was bound to be emotional, and custom-tailored to ignite a groundswell of floor support for "the heir apparent." He expected a Kennedy-led attempt to take over the convention.

Figuring he needed some additional security, Johnson turned to an old Bobby Kennedy nemesis—J. Edgar Hoover—for assistance. The Director only too willingly provided it. He dispatched aide Cartha DeLoach and an FBI team of thirty agents and wiretappers to Atlantic City—the convention site. Arthur Schlesinger, Jr. chronicled the event:

> The ostensible purpose was to gather intelligence "concerning matters of strife, violence, etc." The real purpose, according to William Sullivan of the FBI, was to gather political information useful to President Johnson, "particularly in bottling up Robert Kennedy—that is, in reporting on the activities of Bobby Kennedy....DeLoach instructed...that the FBI squad was not to be disclosed to the Secret Service, and especially not to the Attorney General."[15]

DeLoach instructed Bobby's personal FBI escort to abandon the Attorney General if his faction tried to overtake the convention. DeLoach explained, "If he does that and he's got an FBI agent by his side, the President will not be too happy, so you're to immediately leave Atlantic City."[16]

As it turned out, Bobby's partisans did not attempt to storm the convention. Nonetheless, when Bobby reached the podium to give a two-minute introduction to a film paying tribute to John Kennedy, the convention gave him a 22-minute ovation that left his eyes filled with tears.

Three months later, Robert Kennedy quietly left the Johnson administration, and ran successfully for the Democratic Senatorial seat from New York—despite the opposition of Lisa Howard, Gore Vidal, and "Democrats for Keating." Over the next four years, Kennedy distanced himself from Johnson, and began quietly courting the eastern press, referring frequently to his now-sainted brother. People began referring to Bobby as a one man "government-in-exile." Johnson's camp was not oblivious to the goings-on. "It's impossible to separate the living Kennedys from the Kennedy legend," one aide stated. "I think Kennedy will be regarded for many years as the Pericles of a Golden Age. He wasn't Pericles and the age wasn't golden, but that doesn't matter—it's caught hold."[17] And it affected Johnson. The president would make public appearances, only to be greeted by "Where's Bobby?" placards.

Kennedy became increasingly critical of Johnson's Vietnam policies, placing the President in a delicate quandary. Knowing he needed the support of the Kennedy liberals in 1968, when he planned to run for another presidential term, LBJ had to bite his tongue when word of Bobby's criticisms reached him. However, Bobby became involved in two episodes in 1966 that pushed Johnson over the edge.

In late 1966, William Manchester, chosen by the Kennedy family to be the official chronicler of Camelot and its tragic end, was granted exclusive access to Kennedy family members, including Jackie and other members of the inner circle. Bobby and Jackie were to retain final editorial control over Manchester's book. In his role as the Kennedy in charge of "damage control," Robert Kennedy was once again putting out brush fires.

When Bobby and Jackie read Manchester's manuscript, they were appalled by its intensely personal nature—and very upset that it didn't always further the "Kennedy myth." Indeed, it made the Kennedys appear human. They smoked, they had aches and pains, and they even complained occasionally. Bobby and Jackie were so upset with Manchester's draft that they threatened a lawsuit to halt its publication. Manchester, completely surprised that they would attempt to censor his work merely to protect Bobby Kennedy's reputation and political interests, carried on his side of the battle in public. The Kennedys were seen to be what they hadn't seemed before—mean-spirited and manipulative: "For the first time since the assassination, Jacqueline Kennedy's stature was diminished," one historian noted. "A February [1967] Harris poll indicated that 20 percent of the public 'thought less' of Robert Kennedy because of the controversy."[18]

Although the rancorous episode ended when Manchester agreed to excise 1600 "offensive" words, the material left in the book took Lyndon Johnson to the brink with Bobby Kennedy.[19]

In December 1966, Johnson was given an advance copy of Manchester's book, *The Death of A President*. The Kennedys, it turned out, had no objections about Manchester's downright salacious portrayal of Johnson. The book portrayed the new president so negatively that even Kennedy loyalists feared accusations of character assassination. Manchester depicted Johnson as a power-hungry, insensitive hillbilly. In private, Johnson hit the roof, telling Nick Katzenbach on December 15, "Ninety-five percent of Manchester's book is completely fabricated. It makes Bobby look like a hero and me look like a son-of-a-bitch." When Jackie sent him a hand-written apology, the president responded icily.

Satisfied that the controversy had raised the veil of truth behind the Kennedy personae, Johnson said nothing publicly. Some in the press called this silence one of LBJ's finest moments. Nonetheless, it was obvious that no one's pride, least of all Johnson's, could take another hit without fighting back. When the next hit came one month later, coincidentally at the same time as Rosselli's leaks to Drew Pearson's and Jack Anderson's *Washington Merry-Go-Round*, Johnson was ready to act—and had the material to do so.

In January 1967, while on a trip to Europe, Bobby Kennedy double-torpedoed Johnson. First, while answering questions at Oxford University, Kennedy expressed "grave reservations" about LBJ's renewed bombing of North Vietnam. The remark was perceived in Washington as irresponsible. Next, Bobby met with the North Vietnamese peace delegation in Paris. He told the members he would relay their new peace terms to Washington. Because the Paris negotiations had not yet begun, Bobby was seen as presumptuous—as trying to force Johnson's hand for his own political gain. Johnson would bite his tongue no more.

The final confrontation with Bobby came on February 6, 1967, in the Oval

Office, and, because it had percolated for what seemed like forever, it was quite a doozy by all accounts. The combatants arrived bristling and exited screaming. Johnson blamed Kennedy for leaks to the press. Bobby denied responsibility, telling the president that the leaks had come "from your State Department."[20] To that, Johnson screamed, "It's not my State Department, goddamnit. It's your State Department!"[21] (Upon taking office after the shock and trauma of JFK's assassination, Johnson refrained from the traditional "purge" of administration officials, citing the public's need for a smooth transition after the trauma of Dallas. He was later to regret keeping the holdovers, blaming Kennedy administration officials, among other things, for encouraging him to escalate American involvement in Vietnam.[22])

Johnson next lectured Kennedy about his unilateral call for negotiations, claiming that the military could end the Vietnam war by the summer. Johnson bellowed, "I'll destroy you and everyone of your dove friends in six months. You'll be dead politically in six months." Johnson informed the recent convert to existentialism that RFK was, in fact, prolonging the war. He roared, "The blood of American boys will be on your hands. I never want to hear your views on Vietnam again. I never want to see you again!" After an hour and twenty minutes of confrontation, the equally enraged Bobby reportedly called the President a "son-of-a-bitch." He then got up and left the room, saying, "I don't have to sit here and take that shit."[23]

Twelve days later, Johnson put the White House's full weight behind an investigation into Johnny Rosselli's allegations that Bobby Kennedy had gotten his brother killed.

On February 18, 1967, LBJ informed Attorney General Ramsey Clark of the Pearson/Rosselli story, and ordered him to investigate it. In a March conversation with Texas Governor Connally, who had also picked up the story, Johnson said, "It's pretty hard to see how we would know exactly what Castro did....We will look into it....I think it's something we have to be aware of and watch."[24] When Clark reported back, Johnson, desperate for dirt on Bobby, was not happy with the half-hearted investigation. Johnson later told writer Leo Janos:

> "I asked Ramsey Clark to quietly look into the whole thing. Only two weeks later, he reported back that he couldn't find anything new." Disgust tinged Johnson's voice as the conversation came to an end. "I thought I had appointed Tom Clark's son—I was wrong."[25]

Although these initial leads were not successfully followed, Rosselli and Johnson set off a Washington firestorm with their allegations. This was in stark contrast to the reception given the story by Morgan's choice for a second channel. The New Orleans District Attorney had recently opened an investigation into Kennedy's death, but before he had even heard Morgan's story, he had already solved the presidential murder, he thought.

Channel Two: The Jolly Green Giant

"You gag at the smallest gnat in the Warren Report, but here in the Garrison-Shaw thing, you're swallowing an elephant."
—James Phelan, writer, to Mark Lane, a Garrison "investigator"[26]

"Well before Garrison's Kennedy investigation, Justice Department attorneys were all aware that he was a fraud—or slightly nuts."
—William Hundley, Chief of the Organized Crime Division in RFK's Justice Department[27]

Rosselli's attorney, Ed Morgan, also leaked his client's Castro allegations to Senator Russell Long of Louisiana. Long most likely passed the story on to "channel two"—Long's close friend, New Orleans' District Attorney Jim Garrison.[28] The way New Orleans D.A. Jim Garrison told the story, his interest in the Kennedy assassination was rekindled after a chance conversation with Long, when the Louisiana Senator remarked, "Those fellows on the Warren Commission were dead wrong. There's no way that one man could have shot up Jack that way."[29]

If Morgan or Long or Rosselli expected Garrison to aggressively pursue Rosselli's story, however, they couldn't have been more wrong. Garrison launched a legal inquiry into a Kennedy assassination conspiracy, but, immersing himself in the 26 published volumes that supplemented the Warren Commission report, his conspiracy theory was far different from Rosselli's.

The six foot, six inch Garrison had a reputation perfectly suited to the colorful city that he served. Although he was elected as a "reform" candidate, that distinction, as observed by writer James Kirkwood, has a (predictably) different definition in "The Big Easy." According to Kirkwood, "A reform candidate [in Louisiana] is someone on the outside looking at all the graft and trying to get in on the inside—to grab his share."[30]

In a city where the prosecutor's pen was often mightier than the sword, all that was needed to charge someone with a crime was the DA's signature on a bill of information. By all accounts, Garrison went through a lot of pens. Those unfortunate enough to be brought to trial were usually found not guilty. In Garrison's zeal to court public opinion, he often neglected one chief legal requirement—evidence.

On one occasion, Garrison charged the city's eight criminal court judges with racketeering. The charges were, as usual, found to be baseless, and the judges sued the D.A. for libel. Garrison was fined $1,000—the Supreme Court later overturned the judgment, not because Garrison was right, but because it was impossible to prove if his malice was intentional.

Despite his checkered record in court, Garrison was popular with the public, which responded enthusiastically to his adopted persona—that of a lone white knight battling the corrupt government. When Long piqued his interest in the Kennedy assassination, Garrison could only wonder how high his popularity would soar if he could gain a national constituency: If his white knight took on a dragon as huge as the federal government? Many New Orleaneans are convinced that Garrison, all along, had set his sights on national office, and saw this Kennedy investigation as his ticket.

Rosselli's account of the Kennedy assassination was of little appeal to Garrison. Indeed, by the time he heard Rosselli's story, Garrison—in his own mind at least—had already cracked the case. Before he heard from Morgan, one month after becoming newly interested in the assassination, Garrison called in an old nemesis—someone who, years earlier, had the nerve to help Guy Banister compile an investigative file on Jim Garrison's vices. His name was David William Ferrie.

When he first started his investigation, Garrison seized on the government's clear lack of interest in the offices at 544 Camp Street. Was it true, he wondered, that the Feds were protecting Oswald's co-conspirators? On December 15, 1966, Ferrie, who years earlier had worked out of the Camp Street address with Bobby Kennedy's friend Sergio Arcacha, appeared under subpoena in Garrison's office. Ferrie repeated what he had told Garrison immediately after the assassination in 1963—he had no idea what Garrison was talking about. Garrison was unimpressed that Jack Martin had long ago recanted his assertions that Ferrie knew Oswald. Ferrie, much like the "corrupt government," was a straw target. And, as an odd-looking man of dubious sexuality, Ferrie was no match for Garrison.[31] At least that's what Garrison hoped.

David Ferrie may be the only "assassin" in history to report directly to the FBI. The day after Garrison had a subpoena served on him, Ferrie went to the local FBI office and advised them of his scheduled appearance before the District Attorney.[32] As Attorney General Ramsey Clark informed President Johnson, "Ferrie wanted to know what the Bureau could do to help him with this nut [Garrison]."[33] Ferrie's New Orleanean friends agree that he was looking for protection from a D.A. known for destroying innocent people.

On February 22, 1967, just two months after his appearance in Garrison's office, David Ferrie died of a burst brain aneurysm. Because two notes of farewell were left behind—both seemingly forecasting his death—some suspected suicide. Garrison, of course, suspected murder. In fact, if Ferrie had been murdered, the murderer was Garrison himself—because he had turned up the pressure on him.

"Dave had been sick for a long time," remembers Layton Martens. "He had such high blood pressure. I remember him having spontaneous nose-bleeds all the time. His pressure was over 200. With the Garrison thing, his health deteriorated rapidly. He wrote those notes because he knew he was dying. Besides, Dave wasn't a coward. He'd fight rather than kill himself."[34]

After Ferrie's autopsy, Dr. Nick Chetta's phone rang off the hook for several days. Chetta was the coroner who had autopsied David Ferrie, and the press queried him extensively for details. One call, however, stood out.

Teenager Nicky Chetta, Jr. answered the phone for what seemed like the thousandth time. The voice on the other end intoned, "Hello, this is Robert Kennedy. May I speak with Dr. Chetta?"

"Yeah, and I'm the Lone Ranger," came young Chetta's sarcastic reply before slamming down the phone.

A minute later, the phone rang again. "This is Robert Kennedy, and I insist on speaking with Dr. Chetta." At this point, Nicky's father entered the room, noticed his son's look of exasperation, and asked what was wrong.

"There's this guy on the phone who's claiming to be Bobby Kennedy." The elder Chetta took the phone from his son, and conversed with the caller in hushed tones for several minutes. After hanging up, the coroner informed his son that the caller was indeed Bobby Kennedy. He had wanted to know the details of Dave Ferrie's death.[35] On March 3, 1967 Drew Pearson finally published his story (including Rosselli's leak and Garrison's investigation) under Jack Anderson's by-line. The article practically jumped off the page:

> *President Johnson is sitting on a political H-bomb—an unconfirmed report that Robert Kennedy may have approved an assassination plot which backfired against his late brother. Top officials, queried by this column, agreed that a plot to assassinate Cuban dictator Fidel Castro was "considered at the highest levels of the Central Intelligence Agency...One version claims that underworld figures were recruited to carry out the plot...One source insists that Bobby, eager to avenge the Bay of Pigs fiasco, played a key role in the planning...*

> *Some sources consider Robert Kennedy's behavior after the assassination to be significant. He seemed to be tormented, they say, by more than the natural grief over the murder of his brother...For weeks after the tragedy, this column was told, Bobby was morose and refused to see people. Could he have been plagued by the terrible thought that he had helped put into motion forces that indirectly may have brought about his brother's martyrdom? Some insiders think so.*

> *This report may have started New Orleans' flamboyant District Attorney on his investigation of the Kennedy assassination, but insiders believe he is on the wrong trails.*

Kennedy and Johnson: At War

Robert Kennedy reacted to the Anderson article swiftly. The next day, March 4, 1967, he had his secretary, Angela Novello, call Hoover for the express purpose of retrieving the May 7, 1962 memo—originally generated as a cover—that conveyed the clear impression that Bobby had been against the Castro plots.[36] Simultaneously, Kennedy contacted Richard Helms, now Director of the CIA, and had Helms retrieve his copy of the memo. Helms later lunched with Kennedy, at which time they discussed the memo.[37] With the death of David Ferrie, Robert Kennedy had no way of knowing if Garrison would follow up on the Rosselli tease. However, after the recent blowup with Johnson, Kennedy feared the President would find a way to leverage the issue, thus putting the kibosh not only to "the Kennedy myth" but to the slain president's "heir apparent."

And Johnson was indeed salivating. He was keeping track of the developments in Garrison's investigation through his aide Jack Valenti, whose cousin Judson James was married to a New Orleans reporter covering the story, Rosemary James.[38] Texas Governor John Connally also had sources in Garrison's office, and likewise kept LBJ informed.

On March 17, 1967, unhappy with Ramsey Clark's report, Johnson had his assistant, Marvin Watson, contact the FBI, instructing the Bureau to follow up on Rosselli's scenario. Five days later, Johnson met with CIA Director Richard Helms and asked Helms to look into assassination allegations involving Castro.[39] The next day, Helms instructed the CIA's Inspector General to submit to him a report on the CIA's assassination plots. (The subsequent revelations of this report would become the starting point for the Church Committee inquiries of 1975.)

Helms, however, had already conferred with his former boss in the Cuba Project—RFK. Two months later, when Helms read Johnson several portions of the Inspector General's report, some plotting was admitted to, but there was no mention of any Kennedy approval of the plots. All indications are that Johnson never saw the full report. CIA historian Thomas Powers described what happened next:

> After his meeting with Johnson, Helms held on to the Inspector General's Report for a couple of weeks, then returned it to Jack Earman [the CIA Inspector General] with a written order. Earman was to keep the draft, but that was all he was to keep. The IG's working papers were to be destroyed. Every scrap. Every transcript of an interview, every memo, every note made by the investigators. The draft which Helms had read went into a safe, his briefing notes neatly attached to the front, and it stayed there until William Colby [his CIA successor] learned of its existence in 1973.[40]

Convinced that the paper trail was in order, Bobby next made inroads into the New Orleans investigation to determine just what Garrison had. With the power of the Justice Department no longer at his disposal, Kennedy now relied upon trusted friends to (as the British might say) "suss out" Jim Garrison. But first Bobby had to attend to family matters.

Incident at Arlington

Although the official re-interment would not begin until the following day, a work crew was already making ready to excavate the old grave. The date was March 14, 1967, and the body of John Kennedy was to be moved to a new site. Permanent landscaping had been completed, including new stonework quarried on Cape Cod in the early 19th century, and a tasteful plaque in the walk declaring the dates of JOHN FITZGERALD KENNEDY (1917-1963). The U.S. Army Band would arrive for the solemn ceremonies early the next morning, then members of the Kennedy family and President Johnson.

Forty-four months earlier, on November 24th, 1963, President Kennedy's lot in the Arlington National Cemetery had been set aside "in perpetuity"— reserved forever in the honor of his memory, as Cemetery officials would inform visitors. He was buried in Lot 45, Section 30 on the afternoon of the following day, November 25th, when the "eternal flame" was lit. Work on a permanent site 20 feet away began soon thereafter, and would be completed four months after the re-interment—in July 1967.

Now it was time to re-bury the 35th President in that new site, together with the bodies of his two infant children. But, as if the absence of mystery could not be tolerated in any aspect of the Kennedy family history, something puzzling occurred.[41]

Before the workmen started their excavation, they were startled to witness what had all the appearances of a paramilitary operation. Some 300 military personnel arrived and closed Arlington National Cemetery to the public, clearing it of all unauthorized persons. An Army road-block shut down Arlington Memorial Bridge. The Military District of Washington established a command post at the guard house near the grave sites. A 50-man reserve troop stood by for summoning on short notice. Meantime, troops ringed the area, which was screened by canvas and open to only "key personnel" with "a specific job."

The detailed paperwork for these maneuvers was reminiscent of a minor military operation—which, in fact, it was. A handwritten note from the Army's General Counsel to a Deputy Secretary of the General Staff noted that Secretary of Defense McNamara wanted an "hour by hour detailed schedule" of what was to take place in the Cemetery. It also included an order that the crane, trucks, and other equipment of the firm responsible for the work bear no identifying markings. And memorandum after memorandum repeated the order that "all public will be clear of the cemetery prior to re-interment."

The March afternoon had been cool. By 6 p.m., it was growing dark. Ten minutes later, the mystery deepened: cemetery workers were startled to see two members of the official party arrive. Why now? Surely these movers and shakers, Senator Robert F. Kennedy and Secretary of Defense Robert McNamara, hadn't come merely to check on the preparations for the following day?[42]

Minutes after the powerful Senator and Secretary reached the site, the puzzled work crew was directed to break ground. A tractor and crane moved into position inside the canvas, where the tractor driver switched to his backhoe levers. Actually, the crew consisted of only two men—the tractor driver and a skillful crane operator. The commander of the 1st Battalion of the 3rd Infantry Division, who was in charge of the operation, was much impressed by the skill of the workmen, who "seemed like artists with their equipment." With a single swoop, the backhoe operator scraped to within an inch of the vault, without touching it. Soon, the crane operator lifted it up "as if it were a precious cargo," and transferred it from the old grave site to the new.[43]

Senator Robert Kennedy and Secretary of Defense Robert McNamara watched the funeral ballet in silence. At 7 p.m., Senator Edward Kennedy arrived, accompanied by Richard Cardinal Cushing of Boston and a priest named McGuire—both of whom were scheduled to bless the graves of the President and his two children the following day.

Considering that future researchers would note the disappearance of President Kennedy's preserved brain from the National Archives, the proceedings possibly take on an added significance. Recall that virtually all the evidence points to Bobby's control over this material, in spite of conspiracy theorists' claims. With Bobby in control of the material, and the brain still inventoried in 1965, the re-interment became the prime opportunity for a simultaneous re-burial of JFK's brain. Interestingly, in several newly-surfaced photos of the late-night operation, a small box appears by the Kennedy graveside, at the feet of Cardinal Cushing (see photo spread).

Just before the first shovel of earth was thrown on the vault in its new setting, Bobby Kennedy took a Kennedy half-dollar from his pocket, used it to scrape some earth from the concrete vault, and tossed the coin into the new grave. At 8:45 p.m., the mourners departed the property. But by 11 p.m., they returned—this time, RFK was accompanied by his wife, his brother Ted, Warren Billings, and Jacqueline Kennedy. They remained at the site until just before midnight. They would return in the morning for the actual re-interment proceedings.

Bobby and Garrison

After the re-interment, Robert Kennedy continued to monitor and react to the potentially troublesome Garrison "probe." As Bobby well knew, it could turn up connections between Oswald and Cuba. And it was just two short conceptual steps from Cuba to the Cuba Project, and from the Cuba Project to him. In fact, Garrison would eventually try to implicate Bobby, but on the wrong counts, and with little success.

"When the Garrison investigation started, Bobby asked me if he had anything," recalls RFK press secretary Frank Mankiewicz. "I said I didn't know. He asked me to learn everything I could about it. He said to me, 'I may need it in the future.' I read everything there was. A photo expert came to my home with huge blow-ups of the grassy knoll."[44]

Robert Kennedy also solicited the advice of his former right-hand man at the Justice Department, Walter Sheridan. Sheridan had worked at the National Security Agency (NSA), the super-secret agency in charge of electronic surveillance. He had played a key role in Kennedy's prolonged crusade against Jimmy Hoffa. He was now an investigator for NBC News, though some said he never severed his professional ties to Robert Kennedy. In 1961, three other veterans of RFK's "Get Hoffa" squad formed an investigative agency known as the "Five Eyes," taken from the five "I's" of its acronym—International Investigators

Incorporated, of Indianapolis, Indiana. According to rumor, the Five Eyes spied privately for the Kennedy family over many years.

According to sources developed by veteran investigative reporter Jim Hougan, the Five Eyes also received subcontracts to perform investigations and place wiretaps (of dubious legality) for such agencies as the Justice Department and the CIA. Otto Otepka, a former State Department Security Chief, told Hougan, "There's no question that they [Five Eyes] carried out wiretaps—not only against Hoffa and organized crime, but here in Washington, against government employees." Hougan's sources describe Sheridan as "the chief contact" between RFK and the Five Eyes, adding that Sheridan had presided "over the personnel and currency of whole units of the Central Intelligence Agency" while working out of the White House.[45]

In 1967, NBC News sent Sheridan to New Orleans to produce a TV special on the Garrison case, and thus Bobby Kennedy and the Five Eyes were provided an excellent earpiece in New Orleans. However, "Big Jim" Garrison did not take kindly to Bobby Kennedy's intrusion into an investigation of his own brother's death. When Sheridan tried to interview one of Garrison's "star" witnesses, Garrison promptly charged Sheridan with bribery. Bobby Kennedy immediately came to his friend's aid, issuing the following statement:

> *I have been fortunate to know and work with Walter Sheridan for many years. Like all those who have known him and his work, I have the utmost confidence in his integrity, both personal and professional. This view was shared by President Kennedy himself, with whom Mr. Sheridan was associated for many years in a relationship of utmost trust, confidence, and affection.*
>
> *His personal ties to President Kennedy, as well as his own integrity, insure that he would want as much as, or more than, any other man to ascertain the truth about the events of November, 1963. It is not possible that Mr. Sheridan would do anything which would in the slightest degree compromise the truth in regard to the investigation in New Orleans.*[46]

Like most of Garrison's "charges," this one against Sheridan was eventually dropped. But RFK's efforts could mean only one thing in the mind of "The Jolly Green Giant:" the conspiracy was even bigger than he thought. Garrison told a United Press International (UPI) reporter that Bobby Kennedy had made "very positive efforts" to obstruct his investigation. An incredulous ABC News reporter asked Garrison, "What you are saying, then, is that Senator Kennedy, by not cooperating, is, in effect, letting the murderers of his brother walk the streets!?" To which Garrison responded, "Well, yes, that's a fair statement."[47]

Within days, the FBI picked up word from New Orleans media sources that Garrison would soon issue a subpoena to Senator Kennedy himself. It never occurred. Kennedy later told Arthur Schlesinger, "Walter Sheridan is satisfied that Garrison is a fraud."[48]

In addition to getting the insights of Mankiewicz and Sheridan, Kennedy also sought out the opinions of a Garrison investigator, William Gurvich, who had had the good sense to bail out when he realized that the D.A. was on a witch hunt. He was brought to New York to meet with Kennedy. "Through one of his [Bobby's] emissaries, I was asked if I would see the Senator," Gurvich later recalled. "Basically, what I told him was, the exact words were, 'Senator, Mr. Garrison will never shed any light on your brother's death.' What he wanted to know most was, and I'll quote him, 'Then why is he doing this?'...I just simply said, 'I don't know. I wish I did.'"⁴⁹ Garrison promptly accused Gurvich of being a "double agent."⁵⁰

For Jim Garrison, 544 Camp Street retained one last lead, one final opportunity to ruin a life (Guy Banister was already dead by this time). Sergio Arcacha Smith had followed the Kennedy flag since the early days of 1961, when he did his bit to further the Cuba Project from a dusty office at 544 Camp Street. Now his ties to RFK would suffer a trial by fire, as the Camp Street connection made him the next unfortunate person caught in Garrison's net.

The Loyalty of Sergio Arcacha

With the death of David Ferrie, Garrison's next target became Ferrie's boss at the 544 Camp Street—Sergio Arcacha Smith of the Cuban Revolutionary Council (CRC). Arcacha, Garrison now concluded, had worked with the assassination "ringleader," David Ferrie, and together they "set up" the innocent Lee Oswald, who must have worked for them. This would conveniently explain Oswald's use of their address on his leaflets. What Garrison never learned, or chose to ignore, was that Sergio Arcacha (and by extension, David Ferrie) were working in concert with the President's brother, Bobby.

Thus, two weeks after the death of his chief suspect, David Ferrie, Garrison had his staff serve an arrest warrant on Ferrie's former boss, Sergio Arcacha Smith, then a manager for an air conditioning firm in Dallas.

"Garrison's warrant contained two counts," recalls Arcacha's Dallas attorney, Frank Hernandez. "The first count stated that he was involved in a burglary at the Houma munitions depot, and the second count was concealing information on the conspiracy to kill Kennedy."⁵¹ Garrison had been told by local Cubans of the weapons transfer, and, true to his style, determined that he could arrest Arcacha by referring to the transfer as a burglary.

On Monday, April 3, 1967, Arcacha was arrested at home, in front of his family. He wisely refused to speak with Garrison's officers, who insisted that Arcacha speak with them alone, without his attorney present. After posting $1,500 bail, Arcacha was released.⁵² This touched off a five-month battle in which Garrison sought to extradite Arcacha from Texas to Louisiana. The other Kennedy assassination victim, Governor John Connally, befriended Arcacha and refused to sign extradition papers within the required 90 days.

Meanwhile, Garrison called a press conference to announce that he had identified the men involved in the conspiracy. Clearly implying that Arcacha was one of them, Garrison told the UPI that most of the participants "are in

Texas and Dallas particularly where they are protected—one, by the Dallas law enforcement establishment and two, by the federal government."

With Garrison making so much noise about the 544 Camp street "assassins," Sergio Arcacha worried that the real truth of that operation might surface, forever making him and Robert Kennedy's secret war—in the public's mind at least—the reason Lee Harvey Oswald assassinated John Kennedy. In late March, Arcacha wrote U.S. Attorney General Ramsey Clark, asking for support in his fight against Garrison. On April 6, 1967, Assistant Attorney General Fred Vinson, Jr. replied, writing that "it would not be proper for us to comment in a case pending before a state court." However, Bobby Kennedy, as was his wont, would soon take things into his hands in his own way, showing his personal solidarity with Sergio Arcacha Smith.

Layton Martens, Arcacha's former volunteer, had the same worries as Arcacha. Now a high school teacher, Martens remembered something that he hoped would help his friend. He wrote Arcacha on June 20, 1967, informing him that he was searching for a copy of the letter Bobby Kennedy wrote sanctioning their operation *(see photo spread)*. In his letter to Arcacha, Martens expressed regret that someone had stolen the original of the letter from David Ferrie's apartment.[53] (A year later, Martens was interviewed by a Garrison investigator. Garrison's recently-released files show that Martens readily admitted his possession of the Robert Kennedy letter and that it was stolen from Ferrie's apartment. Martens has given the same account consistently for thirty years.)[54]

On March 28, 1967, Martens had visited the FBI in a last-ditch attempt to get Garrison off Arcacha's back. Bureau records show that Martens told them the same story he had repeated for four years. According to the FBI memo, "Martens stated that Senator Robert Kennedy had approved this activity and he feels Garrison may bring Senator Kennedy's name into the case."[55]

Just when things were their most bleak for Arcacha, he received a telephone call from Bobby Kennedy's secretary, Angela Novello. The Senator had made arrangements for Arcacha to fly to Washington and put his story on film. Walter Sheridan would make him part of his NBC News special, but agreed not to air Arcacha's segment without his permission.

Arcacha and Hernandez were met at the airport by Sheridan. "As we drove through the city," recalls Arcacha, "Sheridan pointed out the places where he had bugged Jimmy Hoffa for Senator Kennedy. When we did the film, I told them everything about my work in New Orleans, but I never gave them permission to use it." Not long afterward, Arcacha placed a call to Kennedy in Washington. After all these years of communicating only by phone, it was time to meet face-to-face.

Arcacha is still very protective of the most private aspects of his friendship with the man he refers to simply as "Bobby." When pressed for more details, Arcacha would often say, "I've already said too much...Maybe someday." Years earlier, Arcacha had incurred the wrath of the New Orleans Cuban exile community when he refused to go public about his relationship with RFK. In order to recruit more donations and volunteers, exiles wanted him to divulge the extent of the Kennedy commitment. "They wanted me to talk, but I wouldn't do it," recalls Arcacha. "Castro already knew too much about our plans. He knew about [our training bases in] Guatemala—everything. Cubans talk too much."[56] Again in 1967, Bobby's trusted friend and ally remained silent about their relationship even though its revelation most assuredly would have taken the heat off the exile leader, transferring it directly to Robert Kennedy.

Here is what Arcacha would say later about his meeting with Robert Kennedy in Washington. "We met in Senator Kennedy's office. Bobby had put me up in a penthouse for a week. He said to me, 'Sergio, I know none of your people killed my brother. Why is Garrison doing this [i.e., pursuing Cuban exiles]? You know that there is nobody in the world who wants to find out who killed Jack more than I.'" With that, Bobby Kennedy produced from his desk one of the coveted PT-109 tie-clips, bestowed only upon close friends. "Here, Sergio, this is for being a friend of the Kennedy family," said Bobby. Arcacha retains the clip to this day.[57]

But Arcacha was clearly disappointed. He had expected more than a tie-clip from the man with whom he believed he shared an important bond. A word to the public from RFK would have eased Arcacha's suffering, but it was not to be. "It would appear like I was covering up Garrison's investigation. I can't do that," said Bobby. Disillusioned and saddened, Arcacha left the meeting thinking, "He's just another politician after all."[58]

During his legal battle with Garrison, Arcacha took a polygraph test in which he admitted his friendship with David Ferrie, and his work with the Cuban Revolutionary Council. He, of course, denied any knowledge of a conspiracy to kill John Kennedy. He was not asked about his relationship with Bobby Kennedy. His responses were determined by the examiner to be one hundred percent truthful.[59] Layton Martens also took and passed a polygraph test during this period.

As with so many others who had been frivolously charged during Garrison's tenure, Sergio Arcacha suffered lasting harm. He lost his job at the air-conditioning company in Dallas. Both he and his attorney Frank Hernandez received numerous death threats. "It was horrible," says Arcacha. "It was very rough on our families." Hernandez recalls, "We met our kids' principals and teachers in order to work out special arrangements for their safety. Cops patrolled our neighborhood every 15 minutes." But compared to Ferrie, and to Garrison's next victim, Arcacha got off easy.

Over the next two years, Garrison, relying on the largest collection of impeachable witnesses ever assembled, built his "case" against another Dave Ferrie "accomplice," New Orleans businessman Clay Shaw. Garrison charged that Shaw and Ferrie had entered into a conspiracy with Lee Oswald to kill Kennedy. According to Garrison's case, the conspiracy was hatched at Ferrie's apartment.

Garrison's star witness, who had "observed" the assassination planning, was a cab driver named Perry Russo (no relation to the author of this book), whom Garrison paid $3,000 for "expenses," as Russo himself confessed. Russo may be one of the only star witnesses ever to openly admit that he "did not know the difference between fantasy and reality." Garrison considered neither the payoff incentive nor Russo's derangement to be material to his case.

In fact, it is questionable whether Clay Shaw even knew Dave Ferrie. "Between Morris [Brownlee], Al [Beauboeuf], and Alan [Campbell], one or more of us were at Dave's apartment practically every night that year [1963]," says Layton Martens. "And none of us heard any talk of killing Kennedy, none of us ever saw Clay Shaw, and none of us remember a Perry Russo." When interviewed by the author, Brownlee, Campbell, and Beauboeuf heartily concurred. Typically, Garrison wouldn't let a detail like that stop his persecution of Clay Shaw. He tried to bribe all three into railroading both Shaw and their deceased friend, Dave Ferrie.[60] The indictment Garrison needed to take Shaw to trial was handed down by a grand jury stacked with Garrison's friends and fellow members of the New Orleans Athletic Club.

"I know that he [Garrison] actually paid Russo $5,000," says Layton Martens. "He offered $10,000 to Al [Beauboeuf]. One day, Garrison called me at the school where I was teaching. He had me driven to his home, where he greeted me in a flowing silk robe. 'Here's what I want you to say,' he told me. 'You saw Ferrie and Oswald. If you play along, you can have money, a good job, cars...'"[61] Like the others (except Russo), Martens refused the offer. Unbeknownst to Garrison, Beauboeuf's attorney secretly taped the bribe by one of Garrison's staff.[62] Beauboeuf retains a copy of the taped conversation to this day.

Clay Shaw was, in fact, anything but an assassination conspirator. As the president of the International Trade Mart, he mixed comfortably with the city's elite liberal class. Considered a pillar of the New Orleans community as well as a gifted playwright and poet, Shaw was in the forefront of a group of local businessmen spearheading the restoration of the historic French Quarter. What put him at risk was the fact that he was also a homosexual at a time when that lifestyle, if known, could obliterate all his other accomplishments. Those who knew Shaw's secret (which included Garrison) worried that the out-of-control D.A. would threaten Shaw with public exposure.

When first questioned by Garrison's assistants, the bemused Shaw had no inkling of what lay ahead for him. Thinking he was merely being asked whether he had seen Oswald leafleting in front of his office at the Trade Mart, Shaw told the investigator he hadn't, and in fact had no memory of ever seeing Oswald in New Orleans, or elsewhere. After the interrogation, Shaw innocently wrote in his diary, "It was perhaps unfortunate that I did not [know Oswald], because then I might possibly have been a tiny footnote in history."

On the witness stand, Russo identified Shaw as the "white-haired, distinguished-looking" man he had seen at Ferrie's apartment with "Oswald." Off the stand, however, Russo admitted the possibility that the man who resembled Shaw could have been Guy Banister. If Perry Russo indeed crashed one of Dave

Ferrie's parties, there exists the possibility that through his own peculiar haze, he confused Shaw with Banister, who looked little like Shaw except that they were both "distinguished" and had white-gray hair.

Layton Martens admits to the potential for such confusion. "I saw Banister at Ferrie's apartment every year at Dave's annual Civil Air Patrol (CAP) party," recalls Martens. "Guy was one of Dave's best friends."[63] At other times, Russo admitted that "Oswald" could have really been Ferrie's roommate, James Lewallen. When he finally met Layton Martens on the evening of August 15, 1967, Russo said that, come to think of it, he was not even sure whether "the assassination talk" was about killing Kennedy or Castro.[64] If this weren't bad enough, Garrison's other witnesses made Perry Russo seem like Albert Einstein.

One of Shaw's attorneys, Sal Panzeca, concluded that "Garrison picked Shaw because he had to give the press something. He felt that Shaw wouldn't defend himself, that he might commit suicide."[65]

The obvious contradictions implicit in the indictment of Shaw left Garrison undeterred:

- *Clay Shaw, a well-known philanthropic liberal, had never associated with the kind of right-wing extremists Garrison had placed at the core of the "assassination conspiracy." Shaw's best friend was Edith Stern, known for her tireless work in the cause of civil rights—a cause for which the Kennedys had been in the forefront.*

- *Not only was Shaw a good friend of Bobby Kennedy's friend, Mayor "Chep" Morrison, but Shaw greatly admired John Kennedy. A close friend said, "Clay voted for Kennedy, he adored him. Kennedy was a builder, just like Clay was. Why would he want to harm him?"[66]*

Over a two-year period, Garrison held press briefings wherein he made statements like: "We solved the case weeks ago," or, "We know the names of the shooters." When all the briefings were taken into account, this was Garrison's bottom line: the President was murdered by a conspiracy whose members included oil moguls, members of the military-industrial complex, the Dallas police, Jack Ruby, anti-Castro Cubans, homosexual thrill-seekers, CIA and FBI agents, Nazis, White Russians, and Lyndon Johnson. It was all coordinated by ardent Kennedy admirer Clay Shaw, with meetings held at the modest Louisiana Parkway apartment of Arcacha's Cuba Project assistant, David Ferrie. (Possibly Perry Russo supplied the hors d'oeuvres.) Accessories-after-the-fact included virtually all the broadcast and print media, the FBI, the CIA, and, incredible as it may seem, Robert Kennedy. The right-wing plot was made possible by the coverup engineered by John Kennedy's close personal friends: Earl Warren, one of the most left-wing Supreme Court Justices in history; and CIA Director Allen Dulles, another close friend of the Kennedy family.

Writer Milton Brener summarized the feelings of many locals:

"Certainly," said many in New Orleans, "Garrison must have something." A man in his position would be stupid, indeed, to make such statements with-

out some solid evidence—and Garrison certainly was not stupid. Overlooked by many who so reasoned was the clear possibility that the man was stark, raving mad. [67]

On March 1, 1969, two years after Shaw's arrest, the jury quickly wrapped up the six-week trial. It took all of 45 minutes to reach a not-guilty verdict for Shaw. A juror said later that they could have taken half the time, except that several of the jurors had to use the bathroom.

In many ways, however, Clay Shaw lost. "I had planned my retirement so carefully," Shaw wrote in his diary. "This case will change all that." Indeed it would. His legal fees bankrupted him of his life savings—$200,000—and the accusations left him emotionally devastated. Like many others before him, Clay Shaw filed an abuse-of-office suit against Garrison. But in 1974, before it could come to trial, Shaw died of cancer.

In 1971, Garrison and nine others were indicted by federal prosecutors for accepting bribes to protect illegal pinball machine gambling, believed controlled by mobster Carlos Marcello. Garrison's nine alleged accomplices either pled guilty or turned states' evidence for a plea bargain. But once again, Garrison's popularity saw him through. When the case came to trial in 1972, Garrison conducted his own defense and the jury found him, and him alone, not guilty.

In the years that followed, Garrison was buoyed by supporters who found two 1949 photos of Shaw with a group of men dressed for Mardi Gras. One of the men in the photos, the supporters claimed, was Dave Ferrie. Although Garrison knew it wasn't, he told no one. When Garrison's personal papers were opened in 1997, a copy of the photos had captions with names. The "Ferrie" individual was in fact a fellow named Bob Brannon.

The flamboyant D.A. went on to earn over $1 million for the use of his version of the Shaw story in the 1991 movie, "JFK." Hollywood heartthrob Kevin Costner would give the overbearing, arrogant, and often obnoxious Garrison a quiet, Jimmy Stewart-type persona. Native New Orleaneans found the portrayal virtually unrecognizable.

As for Garrison's implication that Robert Kennedy was obstructing the investigation of his brother's murder, only RFK himself would have believed it. It was true, but in a way Garrison could never have imagined.

Bobby's Next Volley: The LBJ/Marcello Connection

"Here lies what remains of the man who stole everything."
—Jack Halfen's proposed epitaph for his tombstone

In his next offensive against President Johnson, Bobby Kennedy and his Senate aides tried to help a young investigative journalist revive an old payola scandal, the same alleged LBJ-mob link that had almost implicated Lyndon Johnson before JFK's death. The allegations held the potential for linking Johnson to one of the most powerful Mafia families in the United States—the Carlos Marcello family of New Orleans. The conduit for this information was a colorful Marcello "bagman" named Jack Harold Halfen. Bobby Kennedy didn't know it, but LBJ was aware of Kennedy's gambit from its start.

"In early 1968, I was researching a piece on LBJ for *Ramparts* magazine, which was in financial trouble," remembers investigative journalist Mike Dorman.[68] The article was to include an examination of Jack Halfen's influential connections. Halfen was a legendary "confidence man" from Texas whose native intelligence for the scam, combined with polished discretion, promoted him through the ranks to (never-recognized) national importance. These traits enabled him to work his way up to the diplomatically delicate position of liaison between some of the country's leading Mafia chiefs—Frank Costello and Vito Genovese in New York, Santos Trafficante in Florida and, most significantly, Carlos Marcello in New Orleans—and the politicians those chiefs needed to control. "The Big Fix," as Halfen was known, became a reliable bagman who carefully paid key legislators for their services.

Halfen's disbursements totaled in the millions of dollars. They were for protecting Mafia-operated rackets, especially gambling. The Mafia gained government protection by paying off local and federal law enforcement, buying the decisions of local and state judges, and bribing legislators to oppose bills that sought to restrict or regulate gambling. In the late 1950's, the payments escalated dramatically to stop or deflect Congressional investigations and hearings. The payments—some made on Capitol Hill, others in carefully-chosen hideaways—were in cash and disguised as campaign contributions.

Both payers and payees trusted Jack Halfen with the extremely sensitive work of transferring the "compensation." His self-cultivated intellect and discernment allowed him to move comfortably back and forth between the ordinarily disparate worlds of organized crime and statecraft. Mike Dorman believed Halfen was "perhaps the most accomplished payoff man organized crime has ever produced—the Johnny Appleseed of political corruption." For many years, Mafia financing was crucial to many political campaigns. Sometimes, it was the deciding factor.

Robert Kennedy first came to know Jack Halfen in 1961, as Attorney General, when he grew interested in rumors that Halfen could provide juicy material on Bobby's nemesis, then-Vice-President Johnson. He even dispatched a DOJ investigator to visit him in prison when Bobby sought to leverage Johnson off the 1964 ticket. Reluctantly, Kennedy had to quash an initial federal investigation when wiretaps turned up indiscretions not only on Johnson's part, but by important Democratic supporters of John Kennedy in New York and Indiana.[69] (Halfen had his hooks into everyone.) Although the probe was halted, Bobby never forgot Jack Halfen. In 1968, with Jack dead, Bobby decided it was time to take a fresh look at the Halfen-Johnson linkage. In fact, it became one of his strategies for removing Johnson from the presidency.

The appearance on the scene of Mike Dorman, already researching this Johnson-Halfen connection, was welcomed by the Senator from New York. Halfen had freely admitted to Dorman that he had "bought off" Senator Lyndon

Johnson to look out for Marcello's interests in federal gambling legislation. The pay-offs to Johnson, he would state, began well before he became the youngest Senate Majority Leader in history in 1954. Johnson's campaigns to both the House and Senate, Halfen elaborated, benefited greatly from Mafia money—and he had documentary evidence to prove their connection.[70] He had passed $100,000 a year—for ten years—to LBJ, he said.

"In return," says Mike Dorman, "Johnson helped kill in committee all anti-rackets and gambling legislation that could have harmed the interests of Carlos Marcello and Jack Halfen."

Soon, Dorman sought help in investigating Johnson's legislative record, which, he figured, would dovetail if the allegations were true (they were, and it did). The young reporter had to look no farther for help than Robert Kennedy. "I was using Robert Kennedy's aide Joe Dolan to research LBJ's Congressional record with respect to Marcello's interest in having LBJ kill gambling legislation," remembers Dorman. Dorman received RFK's personal attention, meeting with the Senator in his office. "Senator Kennedy was enthusiastic about the article," Dorman says. At one point, Kennedy asked if he, Dorman, thought *Ramparts* would survive long enough to publish the article. Kennedy further wondered, "Do they have the balls to publish it?"

Documents obtained from the LBJ Library in 1992 demonstrate that Johnson was aware of Bobby's interest in his Halfen connection. One hand-written memo of a 1968 phone conversation (written by LBJ aide George Christian) states that the Johnson White House had read Dorman's manuscript. Another memo asserts that the Kennedys helped Dorman write his book, *Payoff*, and that, as far as Halfen goes, "the Kennedys pushed him for info on LBJ."[71]

On March 31, 1968, as the *Ramparts* article went to press, LBJ announced that he would not seek re-election. It is generally agreed that the strain of Vietnam, and his perilous decline in the polls, precipitated the president's decision. The impending Halfen disclosures in print certainly may have tipped the scales of an otherwise difficult choice. Johnson may have further decided that the sensational disclosure that Bobby Kennedy had inadvertently instigated his own brother's demise paled in comparison to Johnson's colorful Texan past.

When the *Ramparts* article was published, the editors prefaced the piece by saying that they believed that "the disclosures in the following article warrant a federal criminal investigation of Lyndon Johnson's activities as a congressman and senator from Texas." There was scant chance of that happening. One of those Halfen allegedly bribed was associate Supreme Court Justice Tom Clark,. Clark's son, Attorney General Ramsey Clark, was the man who would have had the job of investigating and prosecuting.

Two months later, Robert Kennedy, like his beloved brother, was killed by an assassin's bullet. Foreign policy advisor Walt Rostow called President Johnson with the news at 3:30 a.m. One of the earliest to propose a "professional" Cuba Project with a contingency plan "to eliminate the [Castro] regime by U.S. force" (April 24, 1961), "[72] Rostow had also been a prime sponsor of General Lansdale's

White House appointment and, according to Richard Bissell, was aware of the ZR/RIFLE assassination project.

In early June, twenty-seven minutes after the shooting, Johnson called Rostow back with questions. According to Johnson's handwritten notes of the conversation, it is clear that the President, perhaps sparked by something Rostow said, was still consumed with the Cuban plots—perhaps he thought they had something to do with RFK's death as well. The sketchy notes contain the following words: "Burke Marshall [the Kennedys' lawyer]...Ed Morgan...Cosa Nostra...Send in to get Castro...Planning" *(See photocopy at chapter's end).*[73]

Robert Kennedy had lived just long enough to obtain a modicum of victory over Lyndon Johnson—he helped drive him from office. Bobby had also performed his duty of keeping the assassination plots, and the secrets of New Orleans and Mexico City, from surfacing.

Bobby and Jack were much more than "brothers in arms." They were brothers in fact, and Bobby performed his brotherly duties until his last breath. Robert Kennedy's family now would be responsible for shielding the secrets he had spent his life concealing. Three years later, the real answers to the events of Dallas were further buried, with the death of Mexico City Station Chief, Win Scott. His files, which likely could have provided important pieces to the puzzle of John Kennedy's murder, were soon spirited away, never to be seen again.

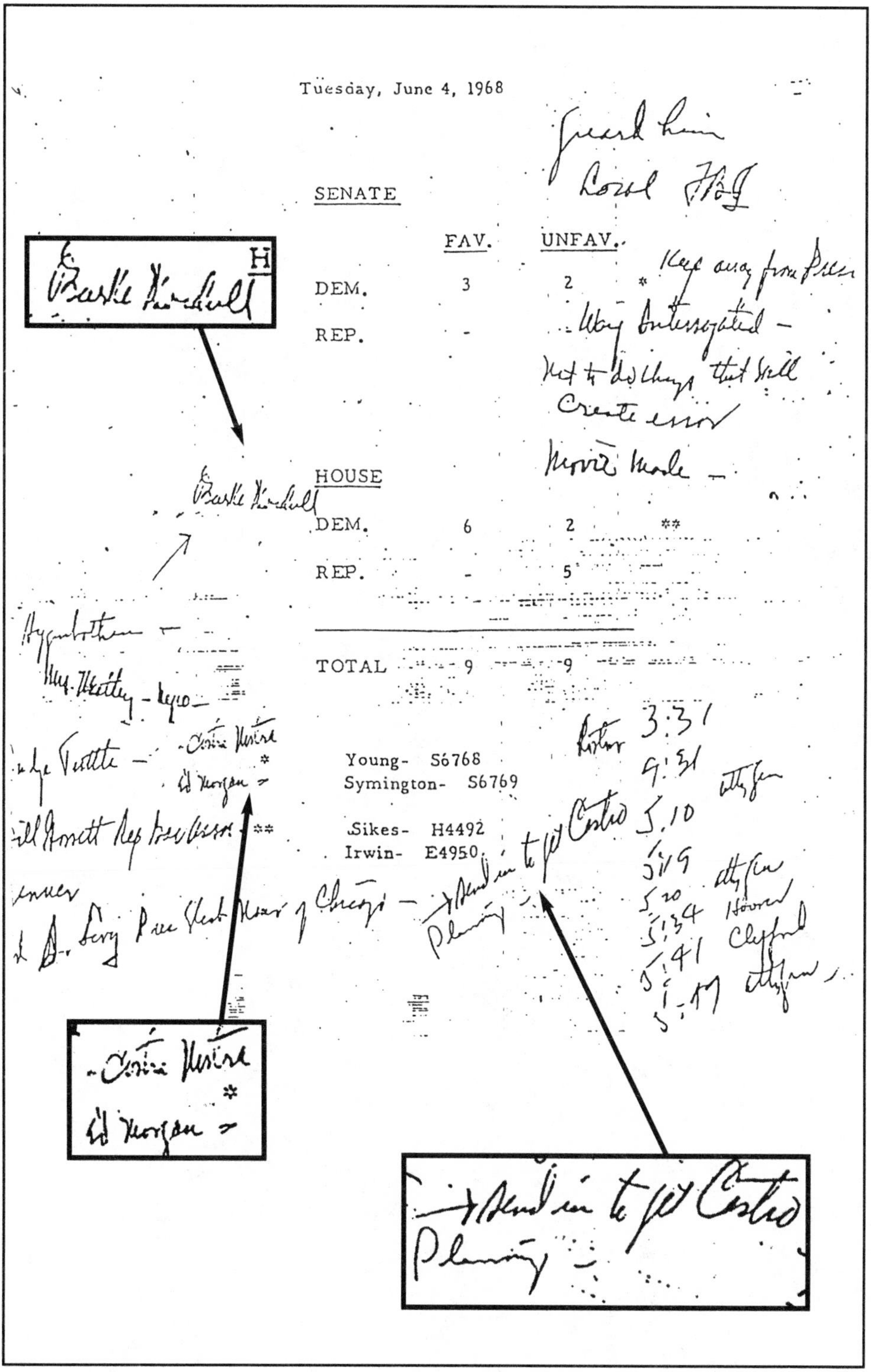

Tuesday, June 4, 1968

SENATE

	FAV.	UNFAV.
DEM.	3	2
REP.		

HOUSE

	FAV.	UNFAV.
DEM.	6	2
REP.		5

TOTAL   9   9

Young- S6768
Symington- S6769

Sikes- H4492
Irwin- E4950

CHAPTER NINETEEN

THE MYTH UNRAVELS

O n April 26, 1971, Win Scott suffered a fatal heart attack while eating breakfast. Within the hour, the CIA's counterintelligence chief, James Angleton,
caught a plane to Mexico City. Angleton, who had headed the CIA's limited
investigation of John Kennedy's death (and who had overseen the Agency's
rehearsal with the FBI of its Warren Commission testimony), was not going to
Mexico to pay his respects. His was a more urgent mission. Always suspicious of
Oswald's Mexico City contacts, Angleton left for Mexico City in such a mad
dash that he neglected to take along his visa or passport, and was consequently
delayed at Mexican Customs upon arrival.

"He finally arrived pretending to be there for my father's funeral," recalls
Michael Scott, Win's son. "But he had really come to get at his files." Angleton
eventually admitted to the son that, among other things, he wanted the auto-
biographical manuscript that Scott had been writing. Angleton went so far as to
warn a family member, "We have ways of getting it from you." Angleton threatened, for instance, that the CIA would rescind plans for a plaque honoring Scott
at CIA headquarters.[1]

Family members recall that the CIA "loaded cratefuls of stuff" from Scott's
Mexico City study. A CIA team was dispatched to locate the Mexican woman
who helped Scott type his manuscript, entitled *Foul Foe*. Scott's widow, Janet,
later stated that the CIA personnel also removed Scott's most sensitive papers
from his safe.[2] This material, with one slight exception—half the manuscript —
hasn't surfaced since. The loss of the Scott files is a major blow to historians of
the Kennedy assassination. Robert Krandle, a CIA aide to Scott in Mexico City,
later testified that Scott maintained a "bulky but foolproof filing system."[3]

Theories abound regarding the contents of the Scott "cratefuls." In
Congressional testimony, CIA officers said that Scott possessed photographs and
sound recordings of Oswald in Mexico City. A vigorous search was undertaken
to locate where the photos and tapes of Oswald's activities were stored. The CIA
informed Congressional investigators that they had routinely destroyed the

audio tapes prior to the assassination, and that their automatic "pulse" cameras were not in operation on the days of Oswald's visits. The House Select Committee on Assassinations, however, obtained photos from the Cuban government showing the CIA's cameras in operation at the time—the spies were indeed being spied upon.[4] New research indicates that not only were photos taken of Oswald, but that the photos and tapes both survived for a number of years, and perhaps still do.

The HSCA interviewed a number of CIA officers working at the Mexico City Embassy in 1963. Three of the officers claimed to have seen a photo of Oswald, and two others had heard of it.[5] In 1994, Scott's assistant station chief, and two Warren Commission attorneys, joined the chorus of those who had screened both the photos and tapes well after the assassination. The attorneys, William Coleman and David Slawson, told journalists Robbyn and Anthony Summers that they inspected the materials on a trip to Mexico City in the spring of 1964.

Robbyn and Anthony Summers corroborated the Coleman/Slawson statement by interviewing the assistant station chief at the time, who "absolutely" remembered giving the attorneys the material from Scott.[6] Coleman, in fact, remembered comparing the typed transcript of the Oswald tapes to the tapes themselves.[7] It is widely believed that these were among the materials confiscated by Angleton, who, until his own death in 1987, championed the possibility of a Cuban conspiracy in Kennedy's death.

Rumors persist that the photos have been withheld because they show Oswald in the company of Cuban agents.[8] After devoting thousands of man-hours to the search for the Oswald photos, the HSCA concluded: 1) "that it is probable that the camera was in operation on the days that Lee Harvey Oswald visited the Cuban Consulate," 2) "It would have been unlikely for the photo-surveillance operations to have missed ten opportunities to have photographed Oswald," leading to 3) "A photograph of Lee Harvey Oswald was probably obtained by CIA photosurveillance in Mexico."[9] Three decades after the assassination, neither the tapes nor photos of Oswald have surfaced.

However, thirty-two years after the event, the first serious crack appeared in the CIA's wall of secrecy. On September 20, 1995, the CIA begrudgingly complied with the orders of the Clinton-appointed JFK Review Board to release everything in its vaults pertaining to the Kennedy murder, including Oswald's Mexico City visit. The Board was the result of an uproar following the 1991 release of the movie "JFK," which featured sensational charges of a government-based conspiracy. The Board was granted unprecedented powers to force all federal agencies to comply with its directive of total disclosure.

In the 200-page September 1995 release of documents, two stand out. CIA memos dated December 10 and December 12, 1963, leave no room for doubt that the CIA inadvertently discovered copies of the Oswald "intercepts" after the assassination.

When author Edward Epstein was approached in 1975 by *Reader's Digest* to write an Oswald biography (*Legend*, 1978), the tape issue resurfaced. Epstein told

writer Dick Russell that as an inducement to write the book, the *Digest's* influential Washington Bureau senior editor, John Barron, promised him access to
the "non-existent" recordings from Mexico City. Barron, a formal Naval
Intelligence officer, was a close personal friend of (and literary agent for) Win
Scott. In fact, Barron was in Mexico City visiting Scott when the CIA officer died
in 1971, making the tape transfer at that time a distinct possibility. Epstein,
however, was never given the promised recordings.[10]

Considering that Scott was known to keep voluminous, yet meticulous files,
the question is raised as to what chance there might be for the surveillance transcriptions to be stored with his missing papers. In addition to the afore-men-
tioned Scott aide (Robert Krandle), both CIA security specialist "John Scelso"
(pseudonym), and former officer Phillip Agee have pointed out the importance
of the material missing from Scott's filing system, which they termed "legendary."

In the late 1970s, the CIA released a copy of Scott's manuscript (a highly-
sanitized autobiography of his entire intelligence career) to a Congressional
investigation. One chapter is devoted to Oswald and Mexico City. Two points
are of interest. First, it is clear by Scott's admissions that Oswald's "missing days"
were probably not missing after all. Scott wrote: "Because we thought at first
that Lee Harvey Oswald might be a dangerous potential defector from the USA
to the Soviet Union, he was of great interest to us, so we kept a special watch on
him and his activities."[11]

As to the Oswald photo, Scott stated firmly that "persons watching these
embassies photographed Oswald as he entered and left each one, and clocked
the time spent on each visit." But not one scrap of paper has surfaced from this
surveillance.[12]

Scott's conclusion about the assassination is stated in the form of a rhetorical question:

> *Aren't the contacts made in Mexico by Lee Harvey Oswald in the five day
> period he had in that city and what took place during his visits to and con-
> versations with communist embassies in September-October 1963, quite
> enough to cause a suspicion of Soviet involvement in the murder of President
> Kennedy?*[13]

Though distinctly a minority view, potential Soviet involvement is not
inconsistent with at least one key fact. Cuban intelligence agents were trained,
of all places, in Minsk, where Oswald once lived.

1972: The Game is Up

Another Washington notable also became interested in the important untold
story of American-Cuban intrigue during the Kennedy years. Like Johnny
Rosselli and Sam Giancana years earlier, this individual also hoped to parlay his
knowledge of the "hidden history" to avoid criminal prosecution. In 1972,

President Richard Nixon clearly needed some leverage.

With the CIA and the FBI breathing down his neck for his alleged complicity in the Watergate coverup, Nixon attempted to blackmail the government agencies that might investigate his Watergate involvement. It was a desperate ploy, but in 1972 Richard M. Nixon was a desperate man. Frantic to avoid connection to the Watergate break-in, the beleaguered President hit upon his plan, deciding to elevate the term "coverup" to gargantuan proportions. In a bold and elegant stroke, he would use his knowledge of one coverup to help him create another. The basis for his leverage was what he referred to as "the whole Bay of Pigs thing."

The first part of the coverup was quite simple: the White House would pay off the architect of the Watergate break-in, thus guaranteeing his silence. But it was part two that could only be defined as brilliant. Nixon knew what had gone on during the years of the Kennedys' secret war, and the proof of it could simultaneously mute presidential aspirant Ted Kennedy and remove the weight of Watergate from the president's shoulders. And it just might have worked had Congress never found out that Nixon's "obstruction of justice" sessions were being taped.

Knowing that the logistical architect of the break-in was none other than former CIA propagandist E. Howard Hunt, Nixon saw a way out. Hunt and the Cuban burglars he had employed were exceedingly connected to "The Big Secret"—the hidden history—a secret that Nixon, Lyndon Johnson, the late Robert Kennedy, and a few other insiders shared. They were key players in the ill-fated Cuba Project—the one that most likely resulted in the act of retribution that cost John F. Kennedy his life.[14]

Hunt had served as the liaison to Arcacha's CRC and as the case officer for Bobby Kennedy intimate Harry Williams. When Watergate erupted, Nixon would suggest that the CIA, not the FBI, investigate the White House. After that, Nixon would simply remind the CIA what he knew about its culpability in the plots against Castro.[15] If anything would enable Nixon to control the investigation, that should do it. Even more propitious was the fact that the CIA director in 1972 was none other than Richard Helms. In 1963, Helms, as then-Director of Covert Operations, was one of the key participants in the ill-fated Castro assassination plots. Nixon may not have realized it, but in 1963 Hunt and Helms were only following Bobby Kennedy's lead. Indirectly, it was Bobby Kennedy's legacy that might now get Nixon off the hook.

The first hint of Nixon's strategy came in a June 20, 1972 phone call to aide H.R. Haldeman.[16] Nixon told Haldeman what to pass on to another aide, John Ehrlichman, who was up to his ears in "damage control." "Tell Ehrlichman this whole group of Cubans is tied to the Bay of Pigs," Nixon instructed.

Puzzled, Haldeman responded "The Bay of Pigs? What does that have to do with this?" Nixon answered, "Ehrlichman will know what I mean."

As recounted by Haldeman, and verified by the "Watergate tapes," the subsequent strategy sessions are stunning. Speaking with Haldeman on June 23,

1972, Nixon muses on how to deal with a hoped-for CIA investigation:

Well, we protected Helms from one hell of a lot of things..Hunt will uncover a lot of things. You open up that scab, there's a hell of a lot of things...This involves these Cubans, Hunt, and a lot of hanky-panky that we have nothing to do with ourselves.

Haldeman had no idea what "hanky-panky" the president meant. It didn't matter. Nixon instructed his aide, "When you get the CIA people in, say, 'Look, the problem is that this will open up the whole Bay of Pigs thing again...and for the good of the country, don't go any further into this case, period.'" At a meeting later in the day, the president elaborated, "Tell them that if it gets out, it's going to make the CIA look bad, it's going to make Hunt look bad, and it's likely to blow the Bay of Pigs, which we think would be very unfortunate for the CIA."

In his autobiography, Haldeman concludes, "In all those Nixon references to the 'Bay of Pigs,' he was actually referring to the Kennedy assassination." Haldeman sums it all up in the following passage:

And when Nixon said, "It's likely to blow the whole Bay of Pigs thing," he might have been reminding Helms, not so gently, of the coverup of the CIA assassination attempts on the hero of the Bay of Pigs, Fidel Castro—a CIA operation that may have triggered the Kennedy tragedy, and which Helms desperately wanted to hide.[17]

Ever since his inauguration in 1969, Nixon had been pushing Richard Helms for information on the Castro assassination attempts. But Helms and the CIA's General Counsel, Lawrence Houston, worried that an untrustworthy Nixon might make the sensitive information public to foster his own personal/political agenda. On October 8, 1971, after years of stalling, Helms gave Nixon three thin files on CIA operations. Nixon, and everybody else, knew there was much more, but Helms never delivered. Such intransigence would apparently lead Nixon to fire Helms in 1973.

Helms' response was but another in a series of CIA refusals to divulge secret operations, or "snitch" on previous presidents for whom it had worked. President John F. Kennedy, in particular, owes a posthumous thanks to a long list of CIA executives who bit their tongues when they had the opportunity to disparage his memory.

If Nixon was correct about the importance of the Bay of Pigs to the CIA, he could only imagine what it had meant to the Kennedys. Unlike Rosselli, Giancana, and untold others, however, Nixon came up short when he dangled "the Cuba thing." The strategy might have worked had incriminating tapes not been divulged by one of his own staffers. When Nixon's own recordings forced him from office, it fell to his successor, former Warren Commission member Gerald R. Ford, and a former Warren Commission attorney, David Belin, to finally expose the sordid assassination plotting to the light of day.

The Rockefeller Commission

Until the mid-1970s, the U.S. government had never responded officially to the Jack Anderson/Drew Pearson story of Castro assassination plots. That stony silence would be broken as a result of a series of events that commenced in 1973.

On May 9, 1973, while attempting to ascertain if the CIA had any involvement in the Watergate break-in, new CIA Director James Schlesinger commissioned an internal report on all potential CIA abuses during the CIA's entire existence. The resultant 693-page report became known as "The Family Jewels." When a small portion of it was leaked to *New York Times* investigative journalist Seymour Hersh in 1974, the floodgates were opened.

Hersh, who had been developing the story for more than a year, disclosed a massive domestic CIA mail-opening operation known by the cryptonym MH/CHAOS. This operation, like so many other illegal operations that presidents routinely demanded of the CIA, began with a president's orders. It seems that LBJ, at the height of his Vietnam travails, had grown convinced that the anti-war movement was funded by the International Communist Party. Johnson demanded CIA action. The trouble lay in the fact that the CIA was only chartered for foreign, not domestic, spying operations. If it existed as alleged, the MH/CHAOS operation represented a major abuse of power.

The story broke in the *New York Times* on December 22, 1974. President Gerald Ford, who succeeded Nixon when he resigned in August 1974, responded quickly. On January 4, 1975, Ford met with his Secretary of State, Henry Kissinger, who reported to Ford on a recent conversation with friend and former CIA Director Richard Helms. As he would with no one else, Helms pulled no punches. "These stories are just the tip of the iceberg," he told Kissinger. "If they come out, blood will flow." Then the much-experienced CIA hand cut to the chase: "Robert Kennedy personally managed the operation on the assassination of Castro."[18] This was a bombshell, especially when coming from the man who was the CIA Director of Operations during the AM/LASH era.

The very next day, January 5, 1975, Ford appointed a commission to be chaired by Vice-President Nelson Rockefeller to investigate the alleged abuse of power. At a White House luncheon a week later, Ford made an off-the-cuff remark so sensational that it had to be read as intentional. While talking about the upcoming "Rockefeller Commission," according to one witness, Ford said that:

> He needed trustworthy citizens who would not stray from the narrow confines of their mission because they might come upon matters that could damage the national interest and blacken the reputation of every President since Truman.

> "Like what?" asked the irrepressible New York Times managing editor, A.M. (Abe) Rosenthal.

> "Like assassinations!" President Ford shot back, quickly adding, "That's off the record!"[19]

It was clear that Ford was well versed on the contents of the "Family Jewels."

In 1964, as a member of the Warren Commission, Ford publicly declared himself dissatisfied with the Commission's investigation of a possible foreign conspiracy. By being kept in the dark then, Ford may have seen the creation of the Rockefeller Commission as an opportune time to finally force the issue.

Like other presidential commissions, Rockefeller's was doomed from the start. Given its appointees' close ties to the intelligence community, it began its efforts with a major, built-in limitation, and, for that reason, was widely criticized in the press. Tom Wicker of the *New York Times* wrote:

> The "blue ribbon" commission appointed by President Ford to protect the public against domestic spying by the CIA looks suspiciously like a goat sent to guard a cabbage patch. Having the CIA investigated by such a group is like having the Mafia audited by its own accountants.[20]

When the Rockefeller Commission hired former Warren Commission attorney David Belin as its executive officer, it probably didn't know he was a stickler for public disclosure and would consequently be a thorn in the side of both the CIA and the Commission itself. Belin's tenacity single-handedly forced the CIA to give him access to the "Family Jewels" manuscript. "It was hard to believe," Belin later wrote, "page after page of confession."

However, Belin soon noticed that one section of the report was blank. The CIA liaison explained that "those pages pertain to foreign matters and are not within your jurisdiction, because the commission's jurisdiction only pertains to CIA activities within the United States." Belin hit the roof, saying that the commission would determine what was relevant, not the CIA.

Belin was reluctantly granted access to the missing section, but only if he would read it at CIA headquarters, which Belin agreed to do. Belin wrote:

> What I found was a sordid chapter in the history of our country—a chapter in which what we think of as the greatest democracy in the history of mankind adopted the philosophy of communism that the ends justify the means. The family jewels contained references to CIA consideration of plots to assassinate Cuban Premier Fidel Castro, Dominican Republic dictator Rafael Trujillo, and possibly Premier Patrice Lumumba of the Congo. By far the most extensive plans were directed against Premier Castro.[21]

Former Warren Commission counsel David Belin now became the second person outside the Kennedy/CIA loop (the first was Ford) to learn that, on the very day John Kennedy was shot, the CIA, with Robert Kennedy's imprimatur, was passing a poison pen to Rolando Cubela for Castro's own demise. Incensed at what had been withheld from him when serving the Warren Commission, Belin became consumed by a desire to expose what he had learned. Predictably, the Rockefeller Commission vetoed Belin's desire to go public with the information. Belin was stonewalled when he attempted to gain access to the minutes of the National Security Council meetings from 1960 through 1964— Rockefeller's old friend, NSC advisor Henry Kissinger, denied the request.

Similarly, the investigators were to obtain no cooperation from White House officials who served under Kennedy.

Behind the scenes and well off the record, Rockefeller was hotly pursuing another quest: to determine if Castro had retaliated against JFK for the murder plots. During the course of this secret investigation, Rockefeller located a still-unreleased document that seemed to point to Cuban involvement in JFK's death. "We got this information and we put it together and it was hot," Rockefeller later said. He decided to approach the last surviving Kennedy brother, Ted, to show him the document in question.

"Look, Teddy, this is being looked into informally," Rockefeller told him. "Can you remember your brother talking about this?" Kennedy replied, "I only have vague recollections about this document. I talked about this maybe once or twice up at Hyannis Port." There the matter was dropped. Rockefeller was content to have Congress pick up the ball if it so desired.[22]

McNamara's timely case of amnesia

When he testified before the Rockefeller Commission, former Secretary of Defense Robert McNamara claimed total amnesia. He stated that his work on the Vietnam War was so consuming that he "had lost virtually all memory of what took place in the Kennedy administration."[23]

The Rockefeller Commission pushed McNamara on the subject, but, still pleading amnesia, he said, "I have no notes—I did not take any notes of any meetings I attended with rare exceptions, and I have no other basis for refreshing my memory, and my memory of those years is very bad."[24] McNamara copped the classic Washington plea, adding, "I am sorry to say I cannot help you much with details about it because I can't fish them out of my memory, but I could not exclude [the possibility] that there were contingency plans, and a contingency capability of some sort, or plans for such a capability at some time."[25]

McNamara's testimony before a Congressional committee one year later made it abundantly clear that the man was conflicted. He knew the plots had not originated with the CIA, but couldn't say why he knew it. The former defense secretary stated:

> The CIA was a highly disciplined organization, fully under control of the government...I believe with hindsight we authorized actions that were contrary to the interests of the republic...I don't want it on the record that the CIA was uncontrolled.[26]

Rockefeller Commission Counsel Belin cited a damaging August 14, 1962 memo (prepared by William Harvey, the head of "Executive Action," for the Deputy Director of Plans, Richard Helms) which more than makes up for McNamara's memory lapse. The Special Group (Augmented), which included RFK and McNamara, had met on August 10th, 1962, and Lansdale wrote a highly sanitized August 13 memo about the meeting. Harvey's August 14th memo filled in the blanks:

> Reference is made to our conversation...Attached is a copy of that memorandum, excised from which are four words in the second line of the penultimate paragraph on page one. These four words were "including liquidation of leaders."

> ...The question of assassination, particularly of Fidel Castro, was brought up by Secretary McNamara...It was the obvious consensus of that meeting... that this is not a subject that has been made a matter of official record...

> Upon receipt of the attached memorandum, I... pointed out to Frank Hand the inadvisability and stupidity of putting this type of comment in writing in such a document. I advised Frank Hand that, as far as CIA was concerned, we would write no document pertaining to this and would participate in no open meeting discussing it. I strongly urged Hand to recommend to Lansdale that he excise the phrase in question from all copies of this memorandum, including those disseminated to State, Defense, and USIA...[27]

Ironically, Harvey's own memo about the dangers of express disclosure ultimately disclosed what he told everyone else to keep secret.

McGeorge Bundy's testimony was also peppered with "I can't recall" and "I don't remember" responses. At one point, during testimony before the Rockefeller Commission, the one-time Kennedy advisor admitted having "a vague recollection of the existence, or the possible existence, of contingency planning in this area." Des FitzGerald, who had died in 1967, could have given more information from the grave.[28]

In 1988, Richard Helms provided a possible explanation for these lapsed memories: "A lot of people probably lied about what had happened in the effort to get rid of Castro...There are two things you have to understand: Kennedy wanted to get rid of Castro, and the agency was not about to undertake anything like that on its own."[29] Helms would add that, "If President Kennedy had not been the motivating force, it [the Cuba Project] wouldn't have taken on the size and character it did."[30]

The Lansdale Admissions

In 1975, Edward Lansdale, in a two-part revelation, exposed what the Kennedys knew of the assassination plots, but it went largely unnoticed. In a newspaper interview in May 1975, the General said that he was acting under presidential orders, delivered through an intermediary, to develop plans for assassinating Fidel Castro. "On that project, I was working for the highest authority in the land," he said—but refused to provide the intermediary's name. When asked if it was McGeorge Bundy, President Kennedy's Assistant for National Security Affairs, Lansdale told the newspaper, "No, it was someone much more intimate."[31]

Lansdale would later deny under oath that he used the term assassination with the reporters. The reporters, also under oath, stood by their story.[32]

Should there be any doubt as to who the "more intimate" intermediary was, Lansdale would clear that up when he testified before the Rockefeller Commission later the same year. The general testified that, as the intermediary, the president "appointed his brother, who was the Attorney General."[33]

To David Belin, who served as Counsel to both the Warren Commission and to the Rockefeller Commission, the conclusion was obvious:

> Top officials inside the Kennedy administration were directly aware of the assassination plots against Fidel Castro; moreover, some of those officials were actively encouraging his liquidation. I believe that Robert McNamara was one of those parties. I also believe Robert Kennedy was another. And, if Robert Kennedy knew, I believe it is reasonable to assume that his brother, President John F. Kennedy, also knew and approved of the plans.[34]

Both Richard Bissell and Richard Goodwin agree with Belin. Bissell recently said that "there was never anything undertaken without presidential approval." Prior to the Bay of Pigs invasion, JFK had instructed Bissell to form a permanent assassination squad (Executive Action). According to Bissell, Castro's death was an integral part of the planning for the 1961 invasion. Richard Goodwin, JFK's assistant in Latin American affairs, admitted in 1994 that "Robert Kennedy would never have done anything important without his brother's OK. He was his brother's chief assistant."[35]

For a time, Belin considered calling a national press conference to air the dirty laundry. Instead, he decided, on November 22, 1975, to call for a formal reopening of the Kennedy assassination investigation. He vowed to make certain that a new committee investigating foreign assassinations, chaired by the Democratic Senator from Idaho, Frank Church, was apprised of the contents of the documents.

When Nelson Rockefeller was later asked who he believed instigated the Castro murder plots, he responded, "I think it's fair to say that no major undertaking by the CIA was done without the knowledge and/or approval of the White House."[36]

The Church Committee

> "There is no doubt in my mind that John Fitzgerald Kennedy was assassinated by Fidel Castro, or someone under his influence, in retaliation for our efforts to assassinate him."
>
> —Senator Robert Morgan, member of the Senate Intelligence Committee (the "Church Committee")[37]

In January 1975, the Senate Select Committee to Study Governmental Operations with Respect to Intelligence came into existence. Chaired by Senator Frank Church, Democrat of Idaho, it became known (gratefully) as the "Church Committee." Its broad mandate was to investigate the government's full range of intelligence activities in an attempt to determine which programs may have been "illegal, improper, or unethical."[38] The Committee was to give special attention to the Rockefeller Commission's uncompleted work on assassinations.

The Committee and The CIA Code of Silence

"The Company was hung out to dry by the White House...Presidents come and go, but the agencies that serve them—be it the FBI, CIA, or IRS, or any other—continue far beyond any one administration. For the government of the United States to try and save face at the expense of its agencies was no more acceptable then than now."
—**Robert Maheu, CIA-Mafia go-between in the anti-Castro plots**[39]

"The Agency was neither intoxicated with power nor warped in its judgments by hubris. It exerted itself, moreover, only at the direction of the President."
—**Former CIA Director Richard Helms, 1994**[40]

Throughout its one-year probe, the Church Committee attempted to find out from the CIA what the chain of command was for the plots against Castro, only to be met with silence. Church's aide, Loch Johnson, expressed disgust at the CIA's tactic of stonewalling the Committee. He wrote, "No cooperation was forthcoming without constant prodding by the Committee."[41] Another staffer remarked, "The only successful CIA assassination plot has been against the Church Committee itself." Given the CIA's directive of plausible denial, these staffers shouldn't have been surprised.

One of the oldest traditions in the world of secret agencies is their willingness to "take the heat." Richard Helms, and numerous others, have publicly expressed pride for fulfilling their role of "keeping these things out of the Oval Office." CIA historian Thomas Powers explained: "They refused to take the rap, but declined to incriminate the President. They were good soldiers—up to a point. Kennedy Administration officials wisely decided not to press them. Head-scratching bafflement was the only answer these officials chose to give when asked how it [the assassination plotting] could have happened."[42]

The Church Report conceded, however, that the Special Group (Augmented) was designed to insulate the President from the unscrupulous aspects of the CIA and Operation Mongoose. It has already been noted that the assassination project protocol specified "nothing on paper." Thus, even if a CIA officer wanted to break ranks, how could he prove what he knew? Thomas Powers has written:

Any CIA officer who said he'd been told to kill Castro by either Kennedy or his advisors would find himself facing a great many formidable enemies indeed, without many friends to come to his aid. It would be his lonely word against that of a host of much better-known men. The CIA officials who know where the orders were given, and when, and in what words, not only don't want to explain their explicit pledge to keep quiet, they do not quite dare. They would be destroyed in the process.[43]

...Can anyone doubt the response of the Kennedy people, and very likely the Committee itself, if some CIA official had risked the complete absence of a single piece of paper to back him up and had said, "Well, who do you think ordered Castro's assassination, the office boy? It was John F. Kennedy and his brother Bobby." If Helms had said that (which in my opinion he could have), he not only would have been the target of some extremely caustic comment, but from that day forward he would have lunched alone.[44]

"Helms," of course, was Richard Helms, who in 1961 succeeded Richard Bissell as the CIA's chief of Clandestine Services, and three years later was named CIA Director by LBJ. Helms was a member of the Eastern/liberal/Democratic wing of the CIA that had so much in common with the Kennedys. Like Jack Kennedy, Richard Helms was a Harvard-educated Navy man. When it came to covert action, however, Richard Helms differed with the Kennedys.

Long-considered an opponent of large-scale covert action, preferring instead covert intelligence gathering, Helms tried to distance himself from operations like the Bay of Pigs, ZR/RIFLE, and Bobby Kennedy's Cuba Project. Still, he participated in these activities when so directed. And no matter how much he disagreed with these activities, he was not about to talk about them out of school. Adhering strictly to his CIA secrecy oath later earned Helms the moniker (and book title), "The Man Who Kept the Secrets." His loyalty to both the CIA and the Oval Office is the stuff of legend, having consistently chosen to take the heat for operations often ordered by others.

Time and time again, Helms refused to tell Congressional investigators about presidentially-ordered covert directives with which he had dutifully complied. Whether it was the Kennedy-inspired Cuba Project, or the Nixon-ordered coup in Chile in 1970 (dubbed, of all things, Project Camelot), Richard Helms would not be drawn out. In fact, CIA officers such as Dulles and Helms have publicly admitted that they would lie to a Congressional oversight committee to protect the president. By 1977, Congress had had enough, and Helms was cited for perjury for his testimony denying CIA involvement in the Chilean coup. At that time, Helms explained to the Justice Department:

I found myself in a position of conflict. I had sworn my oath to protect certain secrets. I didn't want to lie. I didn't want to mislead the Senate. I was simply trying to find my way through the very difficult situation in which I found myself.[45]

Helms' friend from the Mexico City Station, Dave Phillips, wrote that, "Helms was Director during a period when it was axiomatic to respond any way possible to Presidents. He had learned to understand them. And, in the process, he had held the umbrella to catch the crap so CIA's people could get on with their job."[46] Helms would later say, "I just think we all had the feeling that we're hired to keep those things out of the Oval Office." However, he would admit to having the clear impression from the Kennedys that "if he [Castro] had disappeared from the scene, they would not have been unhappy."[47]

Helms and his colleagues, unlike many of their critics, are well-aware of the true nature of the CIA's role. That role was defined by the Agency's founder, President Harry S Truman, who said unambiguously, "I got a couple of admirals together and they formed the Central Intelligence Agency for the benefit and convenience of the President of the United States."[48] Since the CIA's inception in 1948, Truman's dictum had been honored.

The CIA's Sam Halpern puts it this way: "We are the Praetorian Guard. It's our job to protect the president. We work for the President of the United States and then he goes to the American public. We're the fall guys. We take the blame and that's the way it works." Even E. Howard Hunt, who was a CIA officer assisting in the Bay of Pigs planning, recalled the Taylor Commission's investigation of that fiasco, but could just as easily been describing the Church Committee dynamic, when he wrote:

> No one in the Agency, needless to say, was allowed to rebut even the most glaring fabrication...however, [the investigation's] unannounced aim became clear: to whitewash the New Frontier by heaping guilt on the CIA.[49]

This whitewashing clearly benefited Robert Kennedy as well. As one former high-ranking CIA officer told CIA historian Leonard Mosely, "Where Castro and Cuba were concerned, Bobby Kennedy went further than Henry II, and everybody covered up for him."[50]

Finally, in 1997, Richard Helms, exhausted from thirty-plus years of "catching the crap," gave up "The Big Secret," telling a TV producer what he hadn't been ready to tell the Church Committee: "There isn't any doubt as to who was running that effort. It was Bobby Kennedy on behalf of his brother. It wasn't anybody else!"[51]

The CIA, fed up with having the blame pointed at them, finally passed the buck. Timothy Crouse, of the *Village Voice*, wrote at the time of the hearings, "A subtle pattern begins to emerge. One suspects that the Agency may be trying to peddle certain crimes of its own choice, trying to guide the Church Committee toward certain items and away from...God knows what." In 1994, Senator Richard Schweiker, who headed the Kennedy assassination portion of the Committee's inquiry, stated, "It seems to me that we were intentionally misdirected."[52] The CIA, offering the public a patsy at which to direct its anger, essentially gave up the Mafia as a "limited hangout" (In Washington parlance, a "limited hangout" usually refers to making some minor admission of error.)

Although Helms' testimony and his 1967 Inspector General report pointed the finger at the Mafia, Harvey, and FitzGerald (who had died by the time of the Church hearings), Helms himself adamantly denied any hands-on involvement with the plots. His testimony may have been, at best, disingenuous.

On July 16, 1975, the Committee heard from Colonel L. Fletcher Prouty who, during the Kennedy administration, was the liaison officer between the Air Force and the CIA. Prouty was asked if he had any knowledge of U.S. efforts to assassinate Castro. Without hesitation, Prouty described an incident that took place (pre-Kennedy) in early 1960:

> *The only time that the assassination of an individual was ever put in so many words that I knew of was the night or the day that I was told to set up an airplane to take two men into Cuba, and they were going to assassinate Castro.I needed to decide what kind of plane to send...They showed me photographs...of a little curved road in what looked like a sugar cane area. And they told me it was very close to Havana, as close as they dared go...And they said, 'Well, we can get a light plane in there.' Well, the Agency had a special plane that we call in the Air Force L-28—a Helio Courier. It can land in 120 feet...We set up a plane...We closed down air defense so they wouldn't intercept it...We dummied flight plans so that the FAA wouldn't miss an airplane...The object was assassination.[53]*

When asked who attended the meeting, Prouty responded, "There was CIA Operations division, Air Division, which was Dick Helms, and Des FitzGerald, and the whole crowd, the real pros." Asked why he was certain Helms was there, Prouty answered that not only did he recognize him, but the meeting "was held in his office."

Bolstering Prouty's assertion of Helms' complicity in the assassination projects is a CIA memo that surfaced in the 1970's. The result of a Freedom of Information request, the February 19, 1962 memo from Helms to Bill Harvey authorizes Harvey to hire the assassin known as QJ/WIN for the Executive Action capability code-named ZR/RIFLE. According to Helms' directive, QJ/WIN was to be paid $14,700 per annum in salary and expenses.[54]

The CIA's collective testimony presents a classic example of what has come to be called the "Potomac Two-Step." Frank Church remarked, "When Helms said that the CIA never killed any foreign leader, that statement is correct, but not necessarily complete."[55] In fact, the CIA participated in several assassinations, but would always bring in outside subcontractors.

Like so much other embarrassing testimony that pointed away from the Mafia—and towards the White House—Prouty's testimony was not mentioned in the Church Committee Report, perhaps because the Committee knew this was one escapade that couldn't be explained away by claiming "the Mafia did it."

The CIA was not alone in obfuscating ultimate culpability. One by one, officials from Kennedy administration departments paraded before the Church Committee, professing ignorance, memory loss—or both—when it came to answering the $64,000 question: Did the Kennedys order Castro's assassination? McNamara, Bissell, Bundy, Goodwin, and numerous others, like Helms, took great pains to distance themselves and the White House from the plotting. It became clear that these men had dual motivations: to protect not only the memory of their friend John Kennedy, but their own reputations. Given how long they testified, it could be supposed that at least one official would slip up, much as Kennedy's Mongoose coordinator, Edward Lansdale, had before the Rockefeller Committee. This time, however, with no pressure from Church Committee members, the wall of secrecy remained inviolate.

Sitting at home at the time of the Kennedy officials' testimony was Bill Harvey. As the sole official who admitted under oath that he had been involved in the assassination projects, he was furious. Harvey had friends on Capitol Hill who provided him the galleys of the Church Committee's hearing transcripts. Harvey was astounded to see the extent to which the Kennedy administration officials obfuscated the facts. Harvey read how witness after witness misrepresented the events at the critical SGA meetings on Cuba. "Liar! Liar!" Harvey wrote again and again in the margins of the transcripts. Harvey was particularly rough on McNamara and McCone, pointing out that Mongoose and the assassination plots were McNamara's ideas in the first place.[56]

The CIA's retired Western Hemisphere Chief J.C. King, who had first proposed Castro's assassination to Allen Dulles, believed he could put to rest, once and for all, the question of White House authorization. "Dad was given an office at the CIA for his permanent use after he retired in 1964," says King's son Frank King. "In that office he had a safe. During the Church hearings, he said he had a document that showed Bobby Kennedy had authorized the plots. When he went to retrieve it from the safe, it was missing."[57]

In the end, only Bill Harvey admitted a role in the Castro assassination plots. A committee investigator later recalled, "All these big shots from the Kennedy administration came slinking in, worried about their reputations. And then came Harvey—the assassin himself—saying, 'Yeah, I did it, and I'd do it again if ordered.'"[58]

The secrets CIA officials refused to betray had, in fact, long ago been admitted presidential in nature. JFK, one month before his death, said publicly, "I have looked through the record very carefully over the last nine months, and I can find nothing to indicate that the CIA has done anything but support policy. It does not create policy...I can assure you flatly that the CIA has not carried out independent activities, but has operated under close control of the Director of Central Intelligence, operating with the cooperation of the National Security Council and under my instructions."[59]

Robert Kennedy agreed. Prior to his own 1968 assassination, Bobby said that CIA programs were approved at the highest levels of each administration. "If the policy was wrong, it was not the product of the CIA but of each administration," Bobby advised. "We must not forget that we are not dealing with a dream world, but with a very tough adversary."[60]

With that, the Kennedys' old friend Allen Dulles readily agreed, saying, "The facts are that the CIA has never carried out any action of a political nature...without appropriate approval at a high political level in our government outside the CIA."[61]

Completing the circle, a CIA official who was a key figure in the AM/LASH plots told the author on condition of anonymity, "Nothing would have happened if the White House hadn't signed off on it."[62]

Clearly the main accomplishment of the Church Committee's CIA queries was making public large sections of the 1967 CIA Inspector General's Report, initially commissioned by Lyndon Johnson. This marked the first time that the government officially admitted to undertaking assassination plots against foreign leaders, including Fidel Castro. The committee's chief failure, like that of most such investigations, was its inability to determine "where the buck stopped." In fairness, this failure cannot be blamed entirely on retired CIA and Kennedy administration officials. It is an indisputable fact that the Committee itself was a willing participant in the coverup.

The Church Committee Coverup

"The Church Committee has attempted a coverup from the government's end. The Mafia, by silencing Giancana forever, has clamped down the lid from its end."
   —William Safire, New York Times columnist[63]

"If you can't get it right, at least get it written."
   —Church Committee motto hung on the wall of the staff office

Giving a group of politicians the job of assigning blame to other politicians should be understood by all to be an impossibility of the highest degree. There is a built-in structural problem, best-described by the biblical verse, "Let those without sin cast the first stone." One has only to note the impotence of the 1997 Congressional probe into campaign finance irregularities. The paradigm was also demonstrated in the Iran-Contra Hearings, in which it was shown that illegal activity took place that no one initiated or sanctioned. Like the prevailing definition of God, the public is told that these kinds of activities have no beginning or end. They just are.

Other built-in obstacles blocked the scope and effectiveness of probes into CIA operations. Traditionally, few in Congress ever challenged the CIA's activities, or even exhibited interest in monitoring them. According to Frank Church's aide, Loch Johnson, "Until the establishment of the Church Committee, the CIA, with its thousands of employees, large budget, and risky operations spanning the globe, was subjected to roughly 24 hours of legislative 'probing' in both chambers over an entire year."[64] However, one Congressman who *was* interested was Les Aspin. The Wisconsin Democrat once asked CIA Director William Colby what happens when an oversight committee objects to a CIA operation. Colby "was stunned," according to Aspin. "The question had never come up before. The committees preferred not to get involved."[65]

Frank Church recalled senior Senators on so-called "watch-dog" committees saying, in effect, "We don't watch the dog. We don't know what's going on, and, furthermore, we don't want to know." Senator Hubert Humphrey once declared, in the middle of a Senate hearing on a secret CIA operation in Chile, that, "I have to go now. I'm trying to get jobs for 400 people in Minnesota today. That's a great deal more important to me right now than Chile."[66]

Like every Congressional committee that preceded it, the Church Committee's goal became writing the report. The Committee made only a cursory attempt at determining culpability for the plots. It did so by hauling in dozens of senior CIA officers and confronting them with a question that they knew they couldn't answer: Who ordered the plots? In these respects, the Church Committee was no different from any other potentially scandal-loaded investigation—with one exception: it was crystal clear that the Committee went out of its way to protect not just a politician, but a family: the Kennedys.

Consider the Committee's treatment of the Judy Campbell story: on the one hand, the Committee determined that the CIA had hired the Mafia's Johnny Rosselli to kill Castro. But, when the Committee discovered that John Kennedy was having an affair with a woman who was a close friend of the same Johnny Rosselli, it was deemed unimportant. In the report, Kennedy's mistress, Judy Campbell, was described as "a good friend" of undisclosed sex, and relegated to a footnote. In her brief deposition, Campbell was repeatedly asked if she was a courier for the mob. She was, interestingly, never asked if she had performed that same function for Jack Kennedy. She had.

In truth, Republican Senator Curtis Smothers had wanted to ask this obvious question, but was not permitted to do so. Another Republican, and Church Committee Vice-Chairman, John Tower, recalled, "Smothers was overruled. The members of the Church Committee had no stomach for dredging up the martyred President's indiscretions. The line of inquiry was terminated, and all eleven of us voted not to disclose [Judith] Campbell's name or sex."[67]

The Committee also falsely claimed that John Kennedy ended his contact with Campbell after Hoover "informed" Kennedy in March 1962 of Campbell's mob connection; the Committee actually had in its possession phone records proving that the contact continued for the rest of the year. Actually, Hoover had no need to tell Kennedy what he already knew. Hoover was letting Kennedy know what he—Hoover—knew.

Furthermore, if the Church Committee had wanted to get to the bottom of the relationship, it could have called Frank Sinatra to testify, for he had introduced Campbell both to Kennedy and to Mafioso Sam Giancana. Sinatra also knew players such as Johnny Rosselli, Peter Lawford, and Marilyn Monroe. The Committee, however, demurred when it came to the idea of hauling in the "Chairman of the Board."

Everything the Church Committee learned tended to invite further investigation. Instead, the Committee essentially pretended that Jack Kennedy had no idea that Campbell was linked to the Mafia, that Kennedy himself was oblivious to the entire milieu. To believe otherwise would have taken the Kennedy-mob skeleton out of the closet.

During the Church Committee hearings, both Rosselli and Giancana, men who knew the most sensitive secrets of both the CIA and the Kennedys, were violently murdered. Giancana was shot six times in the head at his home on June 19, 1975. Rosselli's body washed ashore in Miami's Dumbfoundling Bay on August 7, 1976. His partially decomposed body was stuffed into a fifty-five-gallon oil drum. He had been smothered, shot, sliced open from chest to navel, and had his legs hacked off—presumably by a chainsaw. No suspects were ever arrested.

Church Committee staffers did determine that Navy Commander John Gordon was essentially correct about anti-Castro plots based in Guantanamo, Cuba. (Gordon had said that these plots were ordered by Bobby Kennedy.)[68] Church Committee staffer Andy Postal was allowed to study the Guantanamo files held by the Office of Naval Intelligence (ONI), and he learned that ONI, in 1964, had investigated Gordon's claims. The ONI report, written by Clyde Roach, affirmed the coded names offered by Gordon—OP 922 HIE, and OP-921D. The report also names people (included on Gordon's "list") who were aware that Alonzo Gonzalez was provided a Springfield rifle, model 1903—a classic "sniper" rifle. Roach summarized the ONI's conclusions:

> *It appears that there was a contemplated assassination plot (OP-922HIE) by individual members of FIO-GITMO [Field Intelligence Office-Guantanamo] to take place in early 1962. The plan failed, apparently due to the unavailability of a silencer and telescopic sight for the Springfield rifle already provided to Alonzo Gonzalez. Knowledge of the plot was closely held, and Gordon was not informed. He apparently did learn of some of the planning during his tenure as OIC-FIO [Officer in Charge, Field Intelligence Office].[69]*

The report also casts doubts on the denials of Gordon's "Gitmo" assistant, Jack Modesset. According to ONI, "Lt. Modesset was interviewed by Naval authorities. He admitted knowledge of the plot and the passing of the Springfield rifle to Gonzalez." Modesset further admitted that he "did help to get a silencer and did test fire the weapon with Gonzalez." The Committee's last words on the subject were crucial:

> *It would appear that there was an assassination plot, or at least some assassination planning, which took place at GITMO [Guantanamo] in May, June and July, 1961. While John Gordon was not involved, apparently he did learn of some of the plans...It appears that [the plot] was not authorized by ONI...There exists the possibility of a back channel authorization...It is conceivable that the Mongoose task force, or perhaps the CIA, was involved.*

However, the Church Committee decided, according to internal memoranda, not to pursue this inquiry because "this case does not warrant such an allocation of resources." It was a very curious decision, in light of the fact that the Church Committee was conceived for precisely the purpose of investigating assassination plots against foreign leaders.

But then again, "Mongoose" meant Robert Kennedy. And it was politically much safer to talk about plots involving Washington's favorite whipping boys—the Mafia. Thus, the treatment of the Gordon information was much like that of the Prouty testimony.

Senate investigator Andy Postal recently stated that, until informed by the author in 1997, he was unaware of another curious linkage:[70] apparently, Jack Modesset's father (Jack, Sr.) and Bobby Kennedy's father (Joe) had been partners in the oil business in Corpus Christi, Texas. Their joint venture was named Mokeen Oil ("Mo" from Modessett, and "Ke" from Kennedy).

The Committee's analysis of the Gordon story was not included in its public report, and only surfaced in 1994, when the Clinton-appointed JFK Review Board forced the release of the Church Committee's internal memoranda. The only mention of the Guantanamo story that made it into the official Church Report was a footnote. But it is pregnant with implications. It tells of an unnamed CIA officer who was informed that:

> The Attorney General wanted to see a man who had contact with a small group of Cubans who had a plan for creating an insurrection, or something like that. The contact recommended by the Attorney General, referred the official to five or six Cubans who claimed to have connections within Cuba...The Attorney General ordered [the contact] to go to Guantanamo Naval Base in Cuba "using whatever assets we could get to make contact with people inside Cuba, and start working and developing this particular group." When the official protested that the CIA had agreed not to work out of Guantanamo, the Attorney General responded, "We will see about that." The official said that he then reported his conversation with the Attorney General to [William] Harvey, who replied: "There was a meeting about that this morning. I forgot to tell you about it. I will take care of it."[71]

This Church Report footnote raises a myriad of questions. The most important is: Was "the contact" Jack Modesset?

"After dad [John Gordon] died, my mother destroyed a box of his most sensitive government documents," Heather Gordon recalls, "but we saved this." Hidden in the Gordon attic all these years, after being carted around from continent to continent, was an object that the late John Gordon told his family it was important to save. Heather Gordon didn't know its importance until the author contacted her in 1994. Without knowing the contents of the ONI report, she retrieved the object, and in a telephone conversation, told the author, "I was told by a local gunsmith that it's a sniper rifle. On the barrel it says 'Springfield Model 1903.'"[72]

The Church Committee was also made aware of Cuban exile leader Antonio Veciana's 1961 plot to kill Castro. However, because Veciana's contacts in Washington were administration officials, not organized crime, this too was deemed irrelevant. In point of fact, neither Gordon nor Veciana is mentioned in the Church Report. Just as it was in the Inspector General's Report, culpability in Washington was traded for a more politically acceptable villain—the Mafia.

Lastly, the Church Committee's shortcomings were partly due to the conflict of interest felt by the Committee members themselves, especially Senator Frank Church. A close observer of the Church hearings pointed out that "all the Committee members had one thing in common: they had all served with Jack Kennedy and most were friends of his."

The friendship of Frank Church and John Kennedy extended back to the late 1950s, when the two worked together crafting civil rights legislation. Forrester Church, the son of the now-deceased Church, called his father a close personal friend of JFK.[73] As an example of their close alliance, he cites the fact that Church delivered the keynote address at the 1960 Democratic National Convention nominating Kennedy for the presidency.[74]

Members of the panel were not oblivious to how Church's agenda tainted the Committee's impartiality. While chairing the Committee, Church was considering his own run at the presidency, and virtually everyone connected with the investigation knew this priority affected Church's objectivity. Senator Schweiker recently said that, "In spite of good leads, Senator Church cut off the investigation of Kennedy's knowledge of the plots. Church was gearing up for a presidential bid in 1976, and he wanted the Kennedy family's blessing."[75]

Staff investigator David Bushong agrees. "Frank Church was understandably sensitive to the Kennedy bloc of votes in the country," Bushong recalled in 1997.[76] CIA officer Jim Flannery, who knew Church, said of the Senator, "He was very much a political animal in those days."[77] Former Church staffer Loch Johnson recalled, "At Church's office, I told him—without mentioning presidential politics—that 'several of the staff think you are spreading yourself too thin.' He stopped writing long enough to look at me. 'They'll just have to live with it,' he said with a quick flair of temper." Committee Counsel Fritz Schwarz said, "Church is trying to carry water on both shoulders." Staff director William Miller agreed, saying "Church isn't doing his homework."[78]

Not surprisingly, in a July 19, 1975 press conference, Frank Church proceeded to point the finger of blame at the CIA, not the White House. The CIA had acted like a "rogue elephant," Church intoned. When that catch-phrase gained quick public acceptance, the Church coverup was complete.

A recent disclosure points out that Church's protection of the Kennedys may have been coordinated with the Kennedys themselves. Staff investigator Andy Postal revealed in 1997 that there was secret contact between Frank Church and the Kennedy family. "Pressure came from many quarters, including Senator Ted Kennedy," remembered Postal. "During the deliberations, Kennedy appeared before the committee and requested that this [Campbell] story not be told. The meeting was not made public."[79] Postal added that when the Kennedys were absolved in the final report, a key investigator and a senior Democratic staff member "almost came to blows over whether the Kennedys were being held to a different standard than others being investigated."

Senator Richard Schweiker headed the Church Committee's investigation into the Kennedy assassination's possible connection to intelligence activities. He has said, "My impression is that the presidents not only knew but ordered these policies by and large...Past presidents have used the CIA as their secret police at home and their secret army abroad."[80]

Perhaps the most forthright Committee member was Senator Barry Goldwater of Arizona. At the time of the hearings, Goldwater remarked that there was friction on the Committee between "those who want to protect the Kennedys and those who want to tell the truth."[81] Years later, he stated it more succinctly, saying, "We spent nine of the ten months trying to get Kennedy's name out of it." When asked by the press who was behind the attempts on Castro's life, Goldwater motioned toward the White House and said, "Everything points right down there."[82]

The Paper Trail

"Allen, as you know, much of the important material of the Kennedy administration does not exist in written form."
—Robert F. Kennedy, in a letter to Allen Dulles, January 7, 1964[83]

Richard Reeves, a political biographer of President Kennedy, is among those who believe the Kennedys planned and knew everything. Reeves' study convinced him that "the Kennedy pressure on the CIA and other agencies was mostly verbal."[84] It was reflected in the Harvey memo, which paradoxically decried putting in writing the term "liquidation of foreign leaders," while Harvey himself wrote it. It also popped out in the October 5, 1961 memo to Robert Woodward discussing the assassination "contingency"—a memo directing that all such details be given "orally."

The Church Committee minimally observed the forms by faulting Bobby Kennedy for not ending the plots when the FBI allegedly "informed" him of them. The Committee cited him for "dereliction of duty"—the equivalent of a posthumous slap on the wrist. Regarding Church's "rogue elephant" decree, the official report refused to go that far—it acknowledged the truth. In a futile attempt to preserve its historical value, it buried in Volume Seven of the Final Report a swipe at the Committee's own chairman, stating, "After having heard the CIA described as a rogue elephant run rampant, it is gratifying that the Committee now finds the CIA is not out of control."[85]

Recently, the author asked Committee staff attorney Jim Johnston directly if the Committee had protected the Kennedys. Johnston responded, "It's pretty obvious, isn't it?"[86]

Why Frank Church avoided assigning the Kennedys some measure of responsibility is perhaps best expressed by Church himself, who said, "I will have no part in pointing a finger of guilt toward any former President."[87]

Despite the insulation provided for "Camelot," the committee couldn't avoid drawing another critical conclusion, buried so deep in its volumes as to go practically unnoticed by the press and the public:

The conspiratorial atmosphere of violence which developed over the course of three years of CIA and exile group operations should have led the CIA investigators to ask whether Lee Harvey Oswald...who was known to have at least touched the fringes of the Cuban community...was influenced by that atmosphere.[88]

On June 8, 1976, exactly one year after his testimony before the Church committee, William King Harvey died of heart failure. He had been rushed to the hospital the previous day, suffering from chest pains. Tests revealed that a lifetime of cigarettes, alcohol, and weight fluctuations had left his heart valves irreparably damaged. His doctors gave him a tough choice: either undergo experimental surgery to replace the valves, or die in a matter of days. Worst of all, his heart was so weak that anesthesia during surgery was out of the question.

Harvey knowingly elected to go ahead with the operation, which ultimately failed. "His doctor said Bill was the bravest man he had ever met—he cried when Bill died the next day," recalls a family member present at the time of Harvey's death. A CIA officer said that Harvey "was asked to do things that nobody should have been asked to do." At his funeral, Harvey's widow, "C.G.," lost control. Bitter that her late husband was clearly the chosen scapegoat in the assassination plots, she railed against "that awful Frank Church."[89]

The House Select Committee on Assassinations

Since practically the moment Chief Justice Warren handed Lyndon Johnson his commission's report, there were calls for a new investigation of President Kennedy's death. Public clamor rose exponentially with each new book critical of the Warren Commission. Unfortunately, most of the published books shared one characteristic: they were written by amateur investigators (and often amateur writers), with limited ability to evaluate eyewitness or scientific testimony. Most of these books were written by well-intentioned doubters, and a few by unscrupulous money-mongers.[90]

After the report of the Church Committee, a variety of questions demanded closure. For the first time, the government admitted to having planned assassinations. Was Kennedy's death an act of retribution that investigators never considered in 1963, or worse, did some clique in our own government use this assassination capability to effect a coup?

Public opinion polls and the Church findings notwithstanding, it was old-fashioned partisan politics that finally put the wheels in motion for a new investigation. In 1976, Coretta King, the widow of the slain civil rights leader Martin Luther King, Jr., paid a visit to the Democratic Speaker of the House, Thomas P. "Tip" O'Neill. Mrs. King told O'Neill, "I have to know what really happened to Martin." What happened next was inevitable. The Congressional Black Caucus put its considerable weight behind the proposed investigation.

The important 1978 Congressional elections were in the back of its mind, and the Democratic majority was concerned with solidifying alliances, not fracturing them. Investigator Scott Malone introduced the Black Caucus' Donovan Gay to Rick Feeney of Congressman Thomas Downing's office. Downing had long maintained a desire to reopen the JFK case. It was determined that the King case would be reopened, and the Kennedy case would be tacked on to the legislation, conveniently assuaging pressure from that camp at the same time.

Consequently, in September 1976, the House, by a margin of 280 to 65, passed HR 1540, establishing the House Select Committee on Assassinations (HSCA). With two bills extending its life span, the Committee operated until January of 1979, and spent a total of $5.4 million for both the Kennedy and King investigations. The first year found the committee mired in political infighting and procedural matters. Its first Chief Counsel was Richard Sprague.

Sprague had earned his reputation as a tough, tenacious, and independent Philadelphia prosecutor—he had compiled a record of 69 homicide convictions in 70 cases brought to trial. His approach was to use hard-line techniques such as lie-detectors, voice-stress analysis, and concealed tape recorders. In an effort to unearth its best-kept secrets, Sprague planed a full assault on the CIA. The Sprague strategy clearly cut against the Congressional grain—most of those in Congress who had approved the Committee's formation did so only as a nod to the Black Caucus. They never intended to wage war against the CIA. Staff investigator Gaeton Fonzi recently stated, "Every member of the HSCA didn't want to even be there."[91]

Before the first year was out, Sprague was forced from his position. He was quoted as saying that during his tenure, the staff spent "point zero one percent" of its time examining the actual evidence. With this setback, serious investigation didn't commence until December 1978, giving the investigators just one year to solve the crimes and write a twenty-seven volume report.

With Sprague's departure came the appointment of a new Chief Counsel, G. Robert Blakey. Blakey, a 41 year-old law professor at Cornell University, had toiled in the early 1960s a junior attorney in the Organized Crime division of Robert Kennedy's Justice Department. Although Blakey is clearly an honorable and well-intentioned man, there is no doubt that his previous experiences would slant his investigative strategy towards the Mafia and away from his friend Bobby Kennedy and his possible, negligent instigation of JFK's assassination.

Blakey's key mistake may have been accepting the impossible position in the first place. He was given one year to investigate and issue an in-depth report on what was arguably the most complicated crime in history—with less money than the D.C. Police Department later allotted to the sting operation against Mayor Marion Barry. In addition, Blakey knew what the Congressional Chairman Louis Stokes knew, and said: "There was absolutely no will in the Congress to further extend the life of the Committee. Congress was not remotely interested in dealing with this issue."[92] That realistically left no time or money for the staff to even consider making a dent in the voluminous and arcane wilderness of top secret CIA/White House projects and files.

At that point, Blakey made a bold, if unwise, decision: he would focus the committee's limited resources on a group which had threatened Kennedy, and which had "means, motive, and opportunity" to kill him—the Mafia (surprise). Blakey knew that there were truckloads of paperwork already available on organized crime. He knew of rumors that Jack Ruby had had contact with criminals—not unlike many other Dallas nightclub owners. He knew as well that Oswald's uncle occasionally worked for someone who knew Carlos Marcello, the mob boss, who, according to one dubious source, had threatened a Kennedy's life (most likely Bobby's). The point was never made that virtually everyone in New Orleans knew someone who knew Marcello.

Blakey's first accomplishment was appointing Mafia experts to key investigative positions. Once again, the deck was stacked, the findings a foregone conclusion. Interviewed by HSCA investigators in New Orleans, Layton Martens quickly perceived the committee's bias. "They kept trying to lead me—to get me to say the mob did it," recalls Martens. "It was unconscionable."

The HSCA's original Deputy Counsel, a hard-nosed homicide attorney from the New York District Attorney's Office named Robert Tanenbaum, resigned in disgust. Tanenbaum told the author, "I didn't want my kids to know that their father participated in a fabrication of history."[93] New Orleans-based HSCA investigator L.J. Delsa recently remarked:

It was very frustrating. Coming from law enforcement, we were used to following our leads. When Blakey came in, that pretty much ended—and we had some strong leads. Had we been allowed to play this thing out, we would have probably found out what really happened. Sprague and Tanenbaum were more traditional, using standard police techniques. Sprague ran the investigation like a normal homicide. Blakey, on the other hand, acted just like a professor, a director, or a teacher. Near the end, it was terrible. We had to fight to be allowed to interview people.[94]

In his book, The Last Investigation, HSCA investigator Gaeton Fonzi expanded on this theme:

At that initial staff meeting, [Blakey], in clear and carefully defined terms reminiscent of a Political Science 101 lecture to a class of frosh, explained the differences between the functions of a legislative body and the goals of a law enforcement agency. Our primary duty, he pointed out, was not to conduct a criminal investigation...Our goals were to gather evidence to be presented at public hearings and, after that, produce a final report.[95]

During the next year, approximately 5,000 interviews were conducted, with 335 witnesses formally deposed. Although the volume of interviews seems impressive, the staff knew the 335 live witnesses were just the tip of the iceberg. By the time the staff had gotten up to speed on the case, it was time to wind the investigation down. Fonzi recalls, "There were only seven months of actual investigation. Then most investigators were fired. Writing the report became the priority...Blakey was giving the Congressmen what they wanted—a report. Not a single investigator on the HSCA staff believes there was a complete investigation. In fact, most were left bitter and frustrated."[96] Staff investigator Leslie Wizelman agreed: "It was the most frustrating experience of my life."[97]

In 1978, the HSCA took the testimony of Sergio Arcacha Smith, but never asked him about his relationship with Robert Kennedy or other Washington officials—nor did Arcacha volunteer any information on the subject.[98]

The CIA, for its part, was true to form: it wasn't going to give up its information willingly. After all, the very nature of its job is to ferret out and keep secrets. Fonzi had a revealing discussion with a former high-ranking CIA officer who wasn't one to mince words. He explained to the investigator that the "clandestine mentality that is drilled into CIA operatives until it is instinctual would permit most of them to commit perjury because, in their view, their secrecy oath supersedes any other." The officer told Fonzi, "You represent the United States Congress. What the hell is that to the CIA?"[99]

Another oft-noted CIA rationale is the Agency's unwritten mandate to protect its relationship with the White House, especially a Kennedy White House which still had allies at Langley. In addition, the CIA, which debriefed Lee Harvey Oswald, may have felt there was nothing to be gained from acknowledging its benign contact with Kennedy's killer. Worse still is the possibility that the CIA learned in advance of Oswald's threat against JFK, but failed to give it significance. Consequently, the Committee's request for the CIA's voluminous files on the Kennedy assassination was stonewalled for months—so many months, in fact, that when the truckload of files finally arrived at the eleventh hour of the Committee's life, there was no time left to read or evaluate them—the written report had already been completed.

The CIA Director at the time of the HSCA, Admiral Stansfield Turner, recently attempted to explain the Agency's performance: "We gave [Chairman] Stokes everything we had. There was no attempt to impede the Committee by stalling on the document delivery. The problem was that the [CIA] guys at the lower level didn't want to do the work."[100]

Whatever the motive, this last-minute document delivery had a chilling effect on serious scholars. After the HSCA went out of business, it sealed its records, as most committees do, for 50 years. This was done because Blakey and Chairman Stokes had anticipated a follow-up investigation by the Department of Justice, and wanted to maintain the chain of evidence. The anticipated investigation never occurred. However, the document-sealing had the effect of making hundreds of thousands of government documents immune to public requests under the Freedom of Information Act.

In spite of all this, Blakey did achieve some noteworthy accomplishments. His decision to throw hard, state-of-the-art science at the assassination was inspired. The best scientific minds available were brought to bear on the physical remnants of the crime, and, with one exception, their work settled a number of nagging questions. Some issues will never be settled in everyone's mind, but for those who take the time to read and evaluate the HSCA's work, the over-whelming majority of professionals agree that these issues have now been finally resolved. Among the issues that were cleared up:

- *The famous backyard photos were found to be authentic, and not an attempt to frame Oswald. Critics had pointed to strange shadows and other artifacts in the photos that seemed to hint at forgery. Even experts from Scotland Yard and the Canadian Department of Defense supported the critics' view. However, when the HSCA photo team showed the experts the lack of unusual artifacts in the original prints and negatives, previously unavailable to them, they retracted their criticism, agreeing that the photos were genuine.*

- *Likewise, early critics saw sinister implications in the number of "mysteri-ous" deaths in the wake of the Kennedy assassination. They had pointed to the fact that The London Sunday Times had hired an actuary who con-cluded that the odds of 18 people—related to the Kennedy case—dying by unnatural causes within three years was one hundred thousand trillion to one. Not only had the sum of unnatural deaths (18) been carelessly com-piled and submitted by an amateur researcher, but The Times was not informed that the list was culled from over 10,000 names cited in the Warren Commission Report. When so informed by the HSCA, The Times retracted its absurd calculation, calling it "a careless journalistic mistake." In fact, only 14 of the deaths were unnatural, and actuarial tables show that 14 such deaths over three years from a pool of 10,000 is well below the norm. Therefore, one could infer that a connection to the Kennedy case would actually tend to increase one's longevity.*

- *During the HSCA's investigation, the recovered bullets and bullet fragments, through sophisticated nuclear technology, were traced to a rifle that proved to be owned by Oswald. This reality was further confirmed in 1993, when the author obtained the Dallas Police's high-contrast photos of the rifle (dusted-for-prints)—photos not reviewed by the FBI in 1963, or by the HSCA. The pictures were analyzed in the 1993 Frontline production, "Who Was Lee Harvey Oswald?" The results were dramatic: previously unseen fin-gerprints were located two inches from the trigger and were positively matched to Lee Oswald.*

- *Kennedy's autopsy was also reviewed by the HSCA, and, although it had been far from ideal, it was nonetheless proven to have accurately determined the cause of death—one shot to the back of the head, with another shot, which entered the upper back, traversing the president's body. Like the back-yard photos, the autopsy photos were also determined untampered-with and authentic.*

- *Lastly, the HSCA also determined that the trajectory of the shots through the victims could be traced back to the southeast sixth floor window of the Texas School Book Depository, an area from which three spent shells were recov-ered, and an area literally blanketed with Oswald's prints. The trajectory study also showed that Governor Connally was in direct line to receive the bullet that exited Kennedy's throat—the governor was not, as had been popularly depicted, sitting out of range of the projectile. (For further proof of this, see Appendix A: "The Shooting of the President.")*

Blakey's one scientific misstep occurred when he attempted to have static-filled audio tapes analyzed. The tapes were recorded by the Dallas Police Department on the afternoon of the assassination, and were the product of raw recordings ("dictabelts") of police communications made while motorcycles traveled the parade route. On one tape made that afternoon are the distinct sounds of police sirens. Assuming that these tapes were made at the time of the assassination, the Committee sought to determine if gunshots could be heard on the recordings. If so, one could possibly determine the source and number of the shots fired at the president.

To the human ear, there were no gunshots audible on the recording. However, two scientists testified that four sub-sonic sound wave patterns could be detected that had a high probability of being gunshots. When the echo patterns of Dealey Plaza were analyzed, three of these impulse patterns appeared to emanate from Oswald's window, and one from the infamous grassy knoll.

Later, the HSCA's acoustic work was reviewed by the National Academy of Sciences. The Academy appointed a panel of twelve distinguished scientists, chaired by Harvard Professor Norman Ramsey, to conduct the review. It reached its conclusion in 1982 that the HSCA's work was "seriously flawed," with no basis for a claim of any shots being recorded on the tape.[101]

The HSCA scientists, narrowly focusing on just a few seconds of the tape, neglected to notice that the sound of police voices came immediately prior to the suspected "impulses." Those voices were later traced to events that took place two minutes after the assassination, and miles away. The HSCA scientists also pinpointed the officer whose open microphone made the recording, supposedly only a few feet from the Presidential limousine. However, after the Committee closed shop, this officer would state unequivocally that he was nowhere near the assassination. In fact, the officer who had the open microphone had been at the Dallas Trade Mart, miles from Dealey Plaza at the time of the shooting.

Because the committee did not spend nearly enough time to determine if there was a conspiracy, the acoustical findings, which were arrived at in the last month of its existence, forced its hand. The Committee therefore concluded that the acoustical analysis proved a conspiracy, and that its best guess was that some "individual members" of organized crime may have been involved. The Committee, however, had no names or hard proof to support that conclusion.

1988: Rosselli/Anderson Redux

In the fall of 1988, columnist Jack Anderson submitted a secret report to President-elect George Bush in which he provided more details about his initial

1967 disclosure of the anti-Castro assassination plots and Robert Kennedy's links to them. Anderson informed the President that his sources included not only Johnny Rosselli, but the CIA's William Harvey, as well as other high-ranking Agency officers. Anderson also admitted that he was provided with copies of "two memos from the CIA's most sensitive files, which summarize the whole operation."

The disclosure of Harvey as a source comes as no surprise, because, according to the CIA's own documents, Harvey was professionally associated with the law firm of Rosselli's attorney, Ed Morgan, the acknowledged original source of the Rosselli-hit team story.[102] Among the items revealed to President Bush were:

- *Allen Dulles had proposed that Fidel Castro be assassinated in conjunction with the Bay of Pigs operation, saying that the invaders would stand a better chance of success if Castro was kept from rallying his forces. This suggestion had traditionally been ascribed to E. Howard Hunt.*

- *William Harvey was convinced that Oswald operated as Castro's agent. He communicated this to his CIA superiors, who had already confirmed this suspicion from "independent sources."*

- *Santos Trafficante was indeed the mole in the assassination plots, reporting back to Fidel Castro. This was confirmed by other participants such as Sam Giancana, Joe Shimon, and Johnny Rosselli. Referring to Trafficante, Giancana allegedly said, "Frankly, he's a rat."[103]*

There is no information regarding what, if anything, Bush did about the Anderson report.

In December of 1991, filmmaker Oliver Stone released his conspiratorial classic, "JFK," which, regretfully, combined the Garrison lunacy with powerful cinematic imagery. The resultant uproar, created by both the audience which believed the Stone/Garrison thesis, *and* by the accused conspirators, produced an interesting alliance, with both groups asserting that a total release of government files would vindicate their position.

Congress proceeded to launch a series of public hearings which resulted in the passage of The President John F. Kennedy Assassination Records Collection Act of 1992. The law mandated the creation of a five-member panel to oversee compliance with the new act, which in turn called for total disclosure by all federal agencies, and private individuals, in possession of relevant material.

In an ironic twist, scrutiny of the over three-million pages released due to the Stone furor virtually demolishes Stone's hero, Jim Garrison. The documents amplify not only the corrupt nature of the Garrison probe, but also the extent to which he missed the real story: the Kennedy administration's links to both Castro assassination plots and the exile community in New Orleans, the latter of which Garrison chose to indict for Kennedy's murder.

But the released papers are also of real historical value. They provide hitherto unavailable insight into the anti-Castro policies of the Kennedy administration, and thus make finally possible an understanding of why no one wanted a complete investigation of the Kennedy assassination's possible links to Cuban intrigue: if the public had known in 1963 of the Kennedy obsession with replacing the Castro regime (when it already knew a pro-Castroite killed their beloved President), the consequences might have been horrific.

The last show of official interest in the Kennedy killing allegedly occurred early in the first term of President Bill Clinton. In 1993, according to President Clinton's one-time Associate Attorney General Webb Hubbell, Clinton requested Hubbell to see if he could learn "Who killed President Kennedy?" Hubbell wrote that his cursory exploration resolved nothing.[104]

CHAPTER TWENTY

THE FINAL CHAPTER

"When the right to kill is so universally accepted, we should not be surprised if our young President was slain."
—I.F. Stone, journalist, November 1963[1]

"John Kennedy had a kind of fixation about Castro—an obsession is a better word. He couldn't abide the fact that this cocky, arrogant young man was in charge in Cuba just a few miles off our shores and willing to defy the great United States."
—Senator George McGovern, 1988[2]

John and Robert Kennedy knew what they were doing. They waged a vicious war against Fidel Castro—a war someone had to lose. The Kennedys were clearly convinced the loser would be Castro. But like the Kennedys, Lee Harvey Oswald also knew what he was doing. As Oswald stated in his New Orleans radio debate, "I think that the United States government, through certain agencies, mainly the State Department and the CIA, has made monumental mistakes in its relations with Cuba." Oswald eventually decided that this problem called for a monumental solution.

The question that must be considered is: Were either the Kennedys or Oswald morally justified? The argument can be made that John Kennedy, in his obsessive, prideful, competitive hatred of Fidel Castro, took millions of people to the brink of nuclear death on a number of occasions. Lee Oswald decided to put an end to what he perceived as the Kennedy brothers' treachery, and he succeeded, though he, too, ought to have known the huge negative consequences of success or failure.

In fact, JFK's actions towards Castro were so provocative that had it not been Oswald, someone else was bound to take a shot at him. Because of the Cuban policies he and his brother carried out, when President Kennedy rode down the street in an open limousine, he might just as well have had a sign on his back proclaiming "Shoot me" to Castro's adherents.

Ed Butler, the New Orleans radio host on whose program Oswald appeared three months before the assassination, opines, "The key factor is that Oswald was someone to be taken seriously at the time. One of the big mistakes that's been made since is to trivialize him." Commentator Alexander Cockburn offered this interpretation and prediction:

Perhaps one day Oswald will be properly recognized as a leftist who came to the conclusion that the only way to relieve the pressure on Cuba and obstruct the attempts on Castro was by killing Kennedy. In his calculations, he was correct...Too bad that this radical exponent of propaganda of the deed should be now presented by assassination buffs as a pawn of the right.[3]

Ed Butler, the New Orleans radio host who debated Oswald, concluded:

To me, there were three very simple reasons for why Oswald did what he did. First, he wanted to make a name for himself, to be a world historical figure. You could see his desire, the need to be famous and heard and attended to. The second thing he was out for was to save Castro. He saved Castro by that act, and as we speak, Castro's still the Generalisimo in Cuba. The third thing Oswald wanted to do, and again he succeeded, was to get America by smashing Kennedy, the top symbol of authority in this country.

After years of sifting through the documents, photographs, and interview transcripts, I reached the conclusion that John Kennedy's assassination was almost inevitable—the consequence of the combined inexperience of the Kennedy brothers, especially Bobby. Before his 1961 appointments as de jure head of the Department of Justice and de facto head of the CIA, Bobby Kennedy had spent only a few months of his 36 years as a very junior attorney in the DOJ, and not a single day in the CIA. A senior officer in the Kennedy State Department recently said, "Bobby was an action man who wanted to take action on things he knew nothing about." While seasoned professionals watched in amazement at their unprofessional maneuvers, the brothers believed their intellect and fierce determination would carry the day. This was the imperative that their father had suffused on their upbringing.

Both brothers held long-entrenched bureaucratic protocols in contempt. Both believed they could short-circuit the wisdom of their more experienced minions with ad hoc committees and hands-on policies—a belief that obliterated the notions of deniability and control.

Inexperience and self-assurance proved a fatal combination when the Kennedys formulated their anti-Castro policy. They represented the "Peter Principle" even before the term was coined. Late in the day, they began to worry that someone would find out about their "secret war" and take action. When the assassination occurred, Bobby immediately grasped the implications, and made sure his brother's character was not assassinated as well.

Robert Kennedy knew that his brother had likely died as a result of their policy initiatives. But his actions and inactions in the realm of his brother's assassination, especially in hiding the truth from the world, greatly contributed to the great public mistrust in government which dates back to the days of the Warren Commission report. Many observers have pointed to the government response to the assassination as the original cause of America's "loss of innocence"—one occurring long before Watergate. Thus, it is unfortunately the case that Lee Oswald and Robert Kennedy unleashed a wave of cynicism from which the country will likely not recover in the foreseeable future.

Lyndon Johnson had to be aware that he was contributing to that mistrust as well. However, his decision was predicated upon his refusal to have an international investigation of the assassination jeopardize millions of lives—American and other. As he saw it, Johnson was faced with a terrible choice: risk a war, or risk public cynicism stemming from a Washington coverup. He wisely chose the latter, but suffered greatly for it.

The CIA, more than willing to go along, also helped trigger the more than three decades of often-justified public mistrust of it.

Clare Booth Luce, the diplomat and Time-Life heiress who gave financial support to the Cuban exiles, reached her own conclusions about the government's reaction to the assassination, citing her high-level government sources as the basis for them. Luce stated that, "Unable to prove that the assassination was backed by the Castroites—but perhaps suspicious of it—the Kennedys and the Johnsons and the whole government decided to say nothing about it since even to raise the suspicion might have plunged us into a war with Cuba."[4]

Who Killed John F. Kennedy?

"Condemn me. It does not matter. History will absolve me!"
   —**Fidel Castro, March 1953, at his sentencing for leading insurrections against the Cuban Army**[5]

"No question in my mind...I think Castro hit Kennedy because of the Bay of Pigs invasion."
   —**Johnny Rosselli, 1966**[6]

History will eventually record without equivocation that Lee Harvey Oswald killed President Kennedy. However, the ensuing coverup of Oswald's motives rendered it forever impossible to precisely determine if Win Scott, Des FitzGerald, Lyndon Johnson, Robert Kennedy, and many others were correct in their suspicions of Castro involvement. Even back in 1964, it would have proved difficult to verify Oswald's "missing days" on the shadowy back streets of Mexico City (and possibly Havana). Thirty-five years later, it is nearly impossible.

The question will probably always remain: Did Castro, or the climate implicit in his regime, play a role in the murder of John Kennedy? Given the American assault on his person and his regime, he certainly had the motive. And when Oswald appeared in Mexico City, Castro's agents were undoubtedly handed the means and opportunity—but did they act on it?

On the one hand, the lofty social goals of Castro's revolution prompted his supporters to give Fidel a Christlike persona. However, this is but one facet of a man who, like John Kennedy, is highly complex and compartmentalized.

For years, the story has been told of how Castro claimed to be shocked and dismayed on hearing of Kennedy's death. That account was clearly a piece of fiction. "Castro is an artist, a great actor," says Manuel Artime's secretary Nilo Messer. "He should get an Oscar. He hated Kennedy so much."[7] Obviously, it was in Cuba's interest for Castro to claim shock and dismay, and it still is in 1998, as Castro, the Pope, President Clinton, and others try to normalize Cuba's trade and other relations with the United States.

Not only had Castro threatened the lives of U.S. leaders two months before the assassination, but his brother Raul expressed strong feelings about the Kennedys' "secret war." Raul was the man responsible for his brother's security detail—a key lieutenant known to direct Cuban terrorism through agents such as Fabian Escalante. In 1975, Senator George McGovern visited the Castro brothers in Havana to obtain details of the Kennedy administration's anti-Castro assassination plots. Raul told him, "Let me tell you, had any one of those attacks succeeded, I would have found some way to retaliate."[8]

All this is not to say that Castro ever uttered the words, "Kill Kennedy." Almost assuredly he did not. Castro's September 1963 threat may easily have been perceived by his agents in Mexico City and elsewhere to be like Becket's plea, "Who will rid me of this man?" As Jean Davison points out, "The irony is that the CIA plots [against Castro] may have evolved in the same manner."[9]

The similarities between both countries' plots were mirrored by the similarities between the men themselves. A recent biographer of Castro, Robert E. Quirk, is quick to draw the parallels between his subject and John Kennedy:

> *In their family and social backgrounds the two men had much in common. Both had wealthy, aggressive, and politically influential fathers. Both inherited the Roman Catholicism of their ancestors, and each was sent away to a private school. Both were the scions of recent immigrants. The pushiness of the Irish-Americans that took [the Kennedys] to the forefront of the church hierarchy and of city and state politics was matched by the vitality of the Galician latecomers in independent Cuba.*[10]

Chicago attorney Constantine "Gus" Kangles takes the parallel one step further. Kangles, in the rare position of having known both the Kennedy brothers and both Castro brothers, opines, "John Kennedy was Fidel, and Bobby was Raul." Jack, he explains, mirrored Fidel's charisma and charm, while Bobby's often arrogant, charmless demeanor could also be found in the hot-tempered Raul.[11]

Colonel Jack Hawkins, the military planner of the ill-fated Bay of Pigs invasion, recently observed, "The Kennedys lived in a dream world. They didn't understand the realities at all. The whole concept of using covert action to overthrow dictators just doesn't hold water. Kennedy was using the resources and the people of the United States as a play toy. And he almost got us blown away. The whole thing was just silly—to spend $100 million to get a few people killed."[12]

Even more disturbing is the fact that Castro's intelligence corps was known to have been trained by the Soviet KGB in Minsk, where many, like Warren Commissioner Richard Russell, worried they may have had contact with Oswald. General Al Haig concluded, "Castro was behind this [assassination], but with KGB help. Like Kennedy, the Pope's assassination had KGB footprints all over it. I mean, these Soviets were bloody-minded people—probably even more bloody-minded than Castro."[13]

Brimming with abundant self-confidence, the Castro brothers became the immovable object, while the Kennedy brothers, no less full of themselves, operated as the irresistible force. Given their backgrounds, it was predictable that neither would back down from their entrenched positions. But the consequences of that were huge. As historian Thomas G. Paterson concluded, "Had there been no exile expedition at the Bay of Pigs, no destructive covert activities, no assassination plots, no military maneuvers and plans, and no economic and diplomatic steps to harass, isolate, and destroy the Castro government in Havana, there would not have been a Cuban missile crisis."[14] There also would have been no assassination of John Kennedy.

E. Howard Hunt—the CIA propagandist who worked so closely with such Kennedy allies as Harry Williams, Manuel Artime, Richard Helms, Allen Dulles, and Sergio Arcacha Smith's Cuban Revolutionary Council—concluded as much in his autobiography. In one passage, he writes of the influence that the Fair Play for Cuba Committee had on Oswald: "But for Castro and the Bay of Pigs disaster, there would have been no such 'committee.' And perhaps no assassin named Lee Harvey Oswald."[15]

The ill feelings towards Cuba fostered during the Kennedy administration remain to this day, although most Americans have no inkling of their origins. At this writing, the Clinton administration still refuses to lift most economic sanctions on Cuba, yet at the same time strikes deals with nations as far removed from the "Jeffersonian ideal" as Indonesia, North Korea, and China. In January 1995, the U.S. moved to normalize relations with Vietnam, a country whose military, only two decades earlier, took almost 60,000 American lives. As these lines are written, President Clinton is in Beijing, China, pandering to a repressive, totalitarian regime that has thought nothing of running tanks over the defenseless bodies of hundreds of college students. As bad as Castro was, especially during the early stages of his revolution and his later consolidation of power, he did not brutally train weapons on unarmed students. A Cuban official, recently addressing the obvious paradox, wondered why "it is only with Cuba that America continues the Cold War."[16]

Perhaps, as Mike McLaney said, "They have long memories up there in Washington." Perhaps the memories include those of Washington insiders still suspecting that Fidel Castro's henchmen played a hand in the murder of our 35th president. The Warren Commission, for example, was aware of Oswald's premeditated threat/offer in the Cuban Embassy in Mexico City. Yet, the public was not told of this until one of the last Commission documents was released in 1995 (CD 1359). A statement by Oswald such as "I'm going to kill that bastard" was ostensibly just what the Commission would have expected to bolster its conclusion of Oswald's guilt. Perhaps the fact that it was made to the Cubans tied the Commission investigators' hands.

In November 1961, Bobby Kennedy, then setting up MONGOOSE, wrote: "My idea is to stir things up on the island...[I] do not know if we will be successful in overthrowing Castro, but we have nothing to lose in my estimate."[17]

Bobby Kennedy soon came to realize how tragically wrong his prediction had been. He would agonize over whether "we did not pay a very great price for being more energetic than wise about a lot of things, especially Cuba." It can be argued that the "very great price" was his brother John's life.

In the months after Dallas, immersed in the world of existentialism and Greek tragedies, Bobby Kennedy underlined a passage in one of his books by the Greek poet Aeschylus. It may have been Bobby's conclusion about the meaning of his brother's death, and with hindsight it should have been a guiding mantra for any investigation of John Kennedy's death. The underlined passage read, "All arrogance will reap a harvest rich in tears. God calls men to a heavy reckoning for overweening pride."[18]

Those in a position to place the assassination in its true perspective were to remain silent because of their friendship and loyalty to the Kennedy family—or because of their calling as professional "secret keepers." Among the numerous examples that illustrate this conflict of interest:

- *Two years after JFK's murder, Robert Kennedy recorded his oral history in which he lauded Allen Dulles.*

- *JFK's friendships with such key figures as Earl Warren, John McCloy, and John McCone were well-known.*

- *RFK's loyalists such as Manuel Artime and Harry Williams were aware of the AM/LASH and re-invasion plans, but never told the Warren Commission of these potential provocations.*

- *Sergio Arcacha and others knew of RFK's links to 544 Camp Street in New Orleans, but waited thirty years to divulge that key information.*

- *FBI and CIA officials loyal to the Kennedys were aware of the coverup in Mexico City, but only spoke of it recently in public.*

Thus, the assassination coverup was never a complex conspiracy, but resulted, for the most part, from the Kennedys having numerous "friends in high places," including the media. Virtually every facet of the Kennedys' social milieu played into the hands of the continued secrecy. From the perspective of the Kennedy family, the narrowed investigation served its purpose: From a fallen charismatic leader with promise, John Kennedy was elevated to an Arthurian myth.

Those who knew him were confounded. As longtime presidential counsel Clark Clifford observed, "While John F. Kennedy was alive, no one imagined that he would, after his death, become a mythical figure in American culture and history."[19] Like many others, Clifford underestimated Bobby's devotion to that end.

The sad, fascinating, and epic history of the assassination and coverup yields at least a handful of major conclusions, a great many questions and gaps, and only a few irreproachable lessons.

To any sort of moral certainty, it is probably impossible to prove precisely why Lee Harvey Oswald assassinated John F. Kennedy. Indeed, his inside-the-head motivations—a narrowly specific single reason why he acted—may never be known for certain.

We can't be sure, for example, to what extent Oswald committed the act because he wanted to be a hero to Fidel. We can't be sure to what extent he knew, independently or with Cubans whispering in his ear, that Castro had been the target of so many assassination plots traceable back to the U.S. and to the Kennedy brothers, and that Cuba wanted revenge. We can't know for sure to what extent Oswald was otherwise encouraged by the Cubans to pull the trigger.

Despite the millions of declassified documents that have been released in recent years, we still cannot know for certain if Oswald truly acted on his own, whether he was hired to do the job by a foreign adversary, or if he merely was encouraged to act by a foreign nation. The single most important piece of evidence—the details of Oswald's Cuban embassy visits—remains conspicuously missing, despite the presence of numerous electronic "bugs" and double agents. And although the CIA's Win Scott wrote that he had Oswald watched closely in Mexico City, what became of the reports of that surveillance? Scott was well-known to keep meticulous and voluminous files.

To further specify Oswald's motivations, we are left to educated guesses. But we can safely say that those who knew most about Oswald's Mexico City visit—people such as Win Scott, U.S. Ambassador Thomas Mann, or Al Haig—were unanimous in believing that Oswald likely became mixed up in some sort of intrigue. Their higher-ups, especially Lyndon Johnson, had likewise seen enough. Rightly or wrongly, Johnson quickly concluded that it was best for the U.S. and the world if Oswald's possible foreign connections were simply left uninvestigated, or cursorily examined. Had an investigation of any integrity been authorized, it would have become apparent, at the very least, that the ardent pro-Castro Oswald had been privy to Kennedy secrets from the exile-hotbed of New Orleans.

Oswald's shooting of John F. Kennedy has been portrayed by some as an accident of history. Certainly to the Soviets, and to the Americans, Oswald seemed an inconsequential figure before the assassination. Neither of these sophisticated countries had much use for him, or took him seriously. The Soviets and the Americans rebuffed him, and repeatedly marginalized him. Cuban diplomats, likewise fearing accusations of involvement, may have steered clear of Oswald as well.

Given what has been reported about his contacts and surroundings, though, Cuban intelligence agents may have challenged Oswald to be the man of action he apparently vowed to be. Logic dictates that, with Castro's regime and very life being threatened by the Kennedys, a quick fix in the form of a bullet would not have been unwelcomed in certain Cuban circles.

It is, of course, easy to oversimplify Oswald. But, based on an examination of the last period of Oswald's life, he *can* be understood. Like everyone who frequented Lafayette Square in New Orleans, Oswald was aware of the administration's most sensitive efforts training a Cuban exile force that would launch a re-invasion from Central America. Oswald, we know, was upset over U.S. policy towards Cuba. We know he wanted to change it—to, in some way, hinder, delay, or cancel the U.S. invasion of Cuba he saw coming soon. We know that he regarded assassination as a way to accomplish that change. And we now know he had already demonstrated his capacity for political violence in trying to kill retired General Edwin Walker, a visible, vocal opponent to civil rights.

Moreover, it is clear from the mounting record *(please read the three appendices for additional clarification)* that, in committing the assassination, Oswald had means (a powerful rifle and considerable shooting skills), a motive (to prove his worth to the Cubans, or to put an end to the invasion plans unfolding in New Orleans), and opportunity (he was in Dallas when the president came to the city).

During the summer of 1998, as this book was going to press, the U.S. Secret Service released an extensive report, "Preventing Assassination," which studied all 83 people who had attacked or tried to attack an American political figure between 1938 and 1998. *Its chief conclusion:* Americans' stereotypical views of assassins are entirely off-base. Assassins, the Secret Service concluded, are not deranged madmen, or lonely losers obsessed with their targets. Nor do their attacks usually follow verbal threats.

Lee Harvey Oswald combined all the traits the Secret Service identified: 1) he considered more than one target (Eisenhower, Walker, Kennedy); 2) he had suffered a trauma (his wife had thoroughly rebuffed him, as had the U.S., the Soviet Union, and possibly Cuba); 3) he clearly suffered from emotional problems (recall his suicide attempt after first arriving in the Soviet Union); 4) he chose a prominent victim (no one was better known in the world than President John F. Kennedy); and 5) he came to see assassination as necessary to stop the U.S.' planned invasion of Cuba.

After reviewing the mountain of new evidence, including the rather startling conclusions of the Secret Service, even skeptics, and especially those who accepted the accuracy of the Warren Commission's findings, must conclude something they never thought truly possible—that Oswald acted at least in part for political reasons, and that, in murdering John F. Kennedy, Lee Harvey Oswald clearly thought he was acting on Cuba's behalf. This single conclusion—that Lee Harvey Oswald was operating on November 22, 1963, for political purposes—in and of itself, alters our view of history.

Similarly, it is quite possible to prove, to a moral certainty, why Oswald's possible foreign connections were not more intensively investigated. The Warren Commission itself wasn't so much a coverup as a deliberately limited investigation. The hours and days immediately after the Kennedy assassination were full of uncertainty and terror. In a world that already seemed so dangerous (the superpowers had come nearly to a nuclear exchange the year before), even the President of the United States was not safe. In America, fear and anger ran extraordinarily high.

For both Lyndon Johnson and Robert Kennedy, for very different reasons, the Warren Commission was a necessary evil, and both opted to make the best of a potentially bad situation. Having the Commission reach the quick, tentative conclusion that a lone nut had committed the act served *both* their purposes. Virtually all of Johnson's experience and instincts made him primarily interested in domestic, not foreign, matters. He never relished the idea of being a wartime president. His passion was saved for domestic matters, from Medicare, to education, to civil rights.

Robert Kennedy had little use for Johnson, but concluded from the start that it was more important to him and his family to cover up the secret war against Cuba than to find out who had killed his brother, and why. For Bobby, it was quite useful to have the country and world conclude that the assassination was the act of a crazy man, not that of someone operating for political reasons.

Knowing all that we know, it might be considered quite strange that Lyndon Johnson and Robert Kennedy agreed on something so important. Johnson, who hated Robert Kennedy, surely had reason to expose the Kennedys' secret war — he could have permanently destroyed Robert Kennedy's political viability in the process. And, with clean hands on the subject of Cuba, he must have been sorely tempted to do so.

But he made the early judgment that the nation needed stability. Cutting off the Warren Commission's investigation made good sense to him. A wider, deeper investigation, he knew, would deprive him of a needed sense of control. If he had required the FBI, the CIA, and the Warren Commission to meticulously investigate the possible anti-U.S. reasons that motivated Oswald to act, the Warren Commission might well have turned up convincing evidence that Oswald acted to stop a coming invasion of Cuba, and continued assassination attempts on Castro, which Oswald had stumbled upon while in New Orleans.

Had he publicly recited just some of the evidence of Oswald as a Castroite, Lyndon Johnson might have been forced to wage a war of retaliation against Cuba. The cycle of violence might have continued, and grown exponentially.

Johnson was smart enough to realize that such a war, while easily justifiable, was best avoided because, he thought, it could plunge the world into a nuclear holocaust. In retrospect, we suspect that the Soviet Union probably would not have used nuclear weapons on the U.S. civil population—that it would have had second thoughts about doing so—and may not have been willing to again use nuclear weapons to defend Cuba. But, in that Cold War climate, the level of mistrust on both sides was outsized. Neither nation trusted the other to refrain from hitting the nuclear button. We can be feel especially grateful that, in such an atmosphere, President Johnson did not take a hawk-like approach towards Cuba. Excoriated for escalating the Vietnam War, Johnson deserves great praise for his restraint immediately after the assassination.

In so acting, Johnson made a momentous decision that worked in the short-term and long-term interests of the U.S. and the world. It also served the interests of the Kennedy family, sparing denunciation by generations of the American people. Kennedy, it turns out, had precipitated the missile crisis with his secret Cuban war, then convinced the world that the U.S. had been the innocent victim of communist aggression in the western hemisphere.

But President Johnson's decision, however essential, badly served the long-term relationship of the U.S. government and its people. In the view of many historians, President Kennedy made an inestimable contribution to the U.S. by encouraging the nation's best and brightest to work, at least part of their careers, in government. How sad it is that the reckless and secret war he and his brother waged against Castro, which had to be covered up in the wake of JFK's death, produced 35 years of active mistrust of the U.S. government.

How fitting, somehow, that Cuba played such a huge, unsung role in Watergate, which added to public mistrust.

And how ironic, too, that Oswald accomplished his chief goals of changing American policy towards Cuba, and rising to heroic proportions in Cuban eyes. A politically-motivated assassin does not usually produce his hoped-for results. Usually, a nation's second-in-command can be counted on to continue the policy of his immediate predecessor. In 1963, there was little reason to doubt that Johnson would have continued the Kennedys' policy towards Cuba. By the same token, there was no reason to doubt that Raul Castro would continue his brother's policies had Fidel been assassinated. Oswald shot against the grain, and succeeded, from a policy standpoint, far beyond realistic expectations.

It is worth noting that the mid 1960s were a far simpler, more innocent, less skeptical age—an age when the media was less aggressive and less antagonistic toward presidents. In this current period of intense media competition, it is unimaginable that such presidential miscalculations and misdeeds as the Kennedy brothers committed on Cuba would go unscrutinized, or that leads from Mexico City, or links from Oswald's New Orleans neighborhood that traced right to Robert Kennedy, would not be pursued.

To Fidel Castro, the assassination offers both benefits and concerns. The Cuban leader could contribute greatly to history if he would finally discuss his agents' true dealings with Oswald, either inside or outside the Cuban Embassy in Mexico City. The case has been firmly established here that the Kennedys recklessly went after Castro personally. Today, 35 years since the secret war and the assassination, the likelihood of U.S. repercussions is infinitesimal, while the lessons to be learned from Castro could be extensive.

Early in his administration, Castro sought the help of the U.S., and was rebuffed. He formed an alliance with the Americans' chief rival (the Soviet Union), thus antagonizing the U.S. In what amounted to a carryover from the previous presidential administration, a fearful U.S. sponsored an unsuccessful invasion of Cuba in 1961. Finally, because turning back communism's advance was the chief tenet of U.S. foreign policy, and because it had been embarassed by the Bay of Pigs fiasco, the Kennedy administration launched an undeclared war against Cuba, and repeatedly sought to assassinate Castro. With Soviet help, Castro protected himself and his nation, several times warning the U.S. to desist, other times trying to quietly strike a peaceful resolution of the dispute. (In foreign affairs, as in domestic law, self-defense greatly mitigates against the crime of murder.)

The brothers Kennedy, for personal and political reasons, refused Castro's overtures and did not sufficiently protect themselves from his threats. When Oswald voluntarily appeared, offering, on his own, to remove President Kennedy from the scene, Cuban agents had to have been delighted. In a best-case scenario—one where Oswald succeeded and Cuba's official involvement was unprovable —the U.S.' secret war against Cuba would be abruptly halted. Far better at the game of deniability than the the Kennedys, Castro had little to lose, and everything to gain, by pushing Oswald's buttons, by telling him of the American attempts on his life and his government, by merely suggesting through underlings that Cuba's leader would appreciate his efforts.

As I see it, my job has been to research the newly enlarged historical record, come to grips with it, and document what I learned and how I learned it. Put as succinctly as possible, I draw five, well-supported and critical conclusions:

- *Oswald did it.*

- *He did it for Cuba.*

- *President Lyndon Johnson and then Attorney General Robert Kennedy, for different reasons, undertook a coverup of his motives, but both acted because of the need to coverup the Kennedys' secret war against Cuba.*

- *Despite tantalizing leads about a possible Cuban conspiracy with Lee Harvey Oswald, the fact that those leads weren't followed when fresh may forever keep us from conclusively ruling a conspiracy in or out. This is one of the great enduring tragedies of the coverup.*

- *In the wake of the coverup, President Johnson aborted an imminent invasion of Cuba.*

In an event as gripping as the Kennedy assassination, there is a compelling desire to determine what great truths can be learned—what lessons there are to take away and apply. The Church Committee thought the lesson was to persuade Congress to pass tough oversight legislation to control the nation's intelligence apparatus. The Committee was naive. The legislation was enacted, and five years later "Iran-Contra" reared its ugly head.

But there are at least two important lessons to be learned from this tragedy. Playing the game of political assassination is an extremely dangerous business. Virtually every foreign leader, even of outwardly terrorist nations, refrains from assassination attempts on other foreign leaders.

Not that there aren't great temptations. The President of the United States, especially a charismatic one, commands such obsequiousness that there will always be a Des FitzGerald or an Oliver North willing to skirt the law to make the chief happy. If and when these national leaders appear, the population would be well-advised to restock the fallout shelters.

Second, if presidents choose to live dangerously, as John F. Kennedy did, it may cost them their lives—even if they think they can somehow insulate themselves from their government's official decisions. The immutable law of agency, it turns out, cannot be ignored. Other nations are likely to impute to a U.S. president the actions of his or her apparent agents. Thus, heads of state who countenance the murder of other foreign leaders can begin a never-ending series of top-level assassinations likely to throw their nations and, potentially the world, into turmoil or conflict.

In recent times, our lack of historical perspective has given rise to imprudent calls for the assassination of Iraqi President Saddam Hussein—most notably by Bill Clinton's youthful former advisor, George Stephanapoulos. Unlike Stephanapoulos, the CIA's Richard Helms is no stranger to historical dilemmas. Helms recently advised, "President Kennedy organized his entire administration to get rid of Castro. Where is Castro? Right where he used to be. It isn't so easy to get rid of these fellas."[20]

As Robert Kennedy came to realize after his brother's assassination, all political foes need not be demonized to Hitlerian proportions, or pursued as such. The moral questions are easy—the ends do not justify the means—and the risks are just too great.

The Biblical words of a noted religious leader may be simple and ancient, but the cautionary advice is doubtlessly eternal: "He who lives by the sword shall die by the sword."[21]

APPENDIX A

OSWALD'S SHOOTING
OF THE PRESIDENT

A ny attempt to prove Oswald's guilt as the lone Dealey Plaza shooter is certain to invite criticism from Oswald's diminishing yet enthusiastic group of defenders. A brief appendix on a subject that could alone fill hundreds of pages will likewise invite scrutiny. I would prefer not to address the subject at all, but the decision represents a "Catch 22": not to address the actual shooting might lead to speculation that I was unaware of details that, some believe, detract from my thesis, while to address it with the space it deserves would drag down the narrative thrust of the Kennedy-Cuba story. The better course, I've decided, is to give a thumbnail sketch of the work I've undertaken that shows Oswald to be the lone shooter.

It should be stated at the outset that in over twenty years of research, I have reviewed virtually all the available research material (both pro and con), and interviewed numerous first-hand witnesses, some speaking for the first time. In addition, advice has been sought from scores of scientists in fields such as ballistics, forensics, and physics. To those who choose to question this summary of my findings, other works and references that deal with the subject in detail are cited. In addition, a partial listing of interviewees follows this essay. The function of this discussion is only to summarize the findings—findings that are powerful not only in their unanimity, but in the eminence of their sources.

Skeptical readers are invited to question my sources and judge for themselves. *(Hint: if readers wish to enter this morass, they should do so only by contacting first-hand sources.)* It should also be noted that from the time of the assassination until the early 1980s, I was among those who doubted Oswald's lone guilt in the shooting. But that was before I was able to interview in detail the scientific experts and to review newly-acquired technology that renders Oswald's culpability a virtual certainty. In addition, the Warren Commission had enough evidence to establish, even to most critics' satisfaction, that Oswald was involved to some degree in the crime. To wit, a sampling of the damning evidence:

- *Oswald's rifle, with three spent cartridges and one unfired bullet, was found in the building behind the assassination's victims. The rifle was clearly Oswald's because: 1) his handwriting was on the order form, 2) a thread from the shirt he was arrested in was found on the rifle, 3) his palm print was found under the rifle barrel, and 4) as it was learned in 1993, his fresh fingerprints were on the metal guard one inch from the trigger.*

Initially, only Oswald's partial palm print was identified under the barrel of the rifle (10 points of identification are usually required for a positive ID). In 1992, I met with Rusty Livingston, a former Dallas policeman assigned to the crime lab at the time of the assassination. Livingston had saved high contrast photo prints of the rifle, taken before it was shipped to FBI headquarters in Washington. The photos contained evidence that had gone unnoticed, and when Frontline had them analyzed, Oswald's guilt seemed even more certain. Vincent Scalice, a renowned fingerprint expert and HSCA consultant, was engaged by Frontline and expressed astonishment at what he saw—three fingers from Oswald's right hand had left their mark just inches from the trigger.

Scalice, in fact, had located a whopping 18 points of identification. After the production aired, he continued his work and increased the total to 24 points. "If I had seen these four photographs in 1978," says Scalice, "I would have been able to make an identification at that point in time. After this reexamination, I definitely conclude these are Oswald's prints. There is no doubt about it."[1] Other experts pointed out that the prints were "fresh" because they would not last long on a smooth, oily metal surface such as the trigger guard housing.

- *The spent shells found in the sixth floor window matched the Mannlicher Carcano bullet and bullet fragments recovered from the victims. The shells were found near a freshly-constructed sniper's nest, and Oswald was the only Depository employee whose prints were found there—in five locations, and very fresh (investigators later left their own prints on the book boxes). Rusty Livingston, who initially scrutinized the boxes for the Dallas PD Crime Lab, had no doubt that the last person to touch the boxes before the shooting was Oswald. "When you have a print on paper, the oils from your skin over time cause the ridges of the print to spread out," says Livingston. "Oswald's prints that I found were fresh prints with good ridge detail. His were the freshest prints on the boxes."[2]*

- *Oswald alone left the premises, went home to grab his pistol, and killed a police officer (both the eyewitness and ballistic evidence point to Oswald's guilt in that crime).*

- *Although Oswald denied his guilt under police interrogation, he lied about so many things that his denial must be seen in that light. In addition, when he was initially apprehended, Oswald's statements were cryptic, bizarre, and wholly out of character for an innocent bystander: "I didn't do anything I'm ashamed of." He made the same statement to at least two observers. When asked directly if he had killed the president, Oswald replied, "You find out your own way," or words to that effect. What sort of person would answer this way? Is it logical that an innocent person would not have been hysterically protesting his innocence of such a heinous crime?*

- *Oswald's capacity for violence was clearly established. In the months before the Kennedy murder, he had attempted to kill General Walker, proposed hijacking a plane to Cuba, and had to be restrained by his wife from killing Richard Nixon, whom he thought was visiting Dallas—all this is in addition to his history of spousal abuse.*

Despite this and other evidence, early confusion about the type of weapon recovered, the wounds received by the victims, and the marksmanship required by one shooter fueled speculation that Oswald had been set up to take the rap for others. (A small minority of critics even believed in Oswald's total innocence. I was never in that category.)

President Kennedy's death at the hands of a man like Oswald was difficult for many to accept. For some, it was impossible. Doubters rightfully pointed out that the Kennedys had many more capable enemies, including Jimmy Hoffa, the Mafia, and impassioned Cuban exiles cut off from the Cuba Project. Many mistakenly believed that Kennedy's brief falling out with the CIA after the Bay of Pigs had not been alleviated, making the Agency a powerful enemy as well. Further, the secrecy surrounding the autopsy of the president (which was later shown to be inadequate for the purposes) led many to conclude that information about Kennedy's wounds was being withheld.

Then there was Oswald. The Warren Commission staff, unaware of the Castro plots, could provide no motive for Oswald's alleged act. This lack of motive made the official conclusion a relatively easy target for critics. And there were still other problems with Oswald. Doubters of the official Warren Commission conclusion seized upon the following facts about the accused killer to sow more seeds of doubt:

- *Oswald had no felonious criminal record.*
- *He was not known to be a marksman.*
- *He had allegedly used a $13 rifle (in the murder of the century) to shoot a moving target two or more times.*
- *At his interrogation, he insisted on his innocence—rare for political assassins.*

His innocence seemed bolstered when paraffin wax molds were taken of Oswald's right cheek and no nitrate gunpowder residue (which cannot be washed away) was observed. This was clearly the most ill-considered criticism, because rifles rarely leave this residue. After the assassination, an FBI sharpshooter, using Oswald's rifle, fired three rapid-fire rounds and immediately took paraffin tests. Both his hands and cheek tested negative.[3] Dallas police interrogators were cagey enough to guess that although they knew of the test's unre-liability, the suspect perhaps didn't. It was a classic "good ol' boy" bluff that often worked to induce a confession. In fact, homicide chief Will Fritz, a leg-endary Texas interrogator, later said that he was convinced that Oswald was about to crack when Ruby intervened.

Armed with these seeming contradictions, a growing army of writers and amateur investigators began combing the official record for the error that, in iron-clad fashion, would prove a conspiracy. Clearly these investigators, with no subpoena power, had no real hope of proving a conspiracy by obtaining a con-fession from the other conspirator(s). The skeptics quickly determined that in order to prove a conspiracy in JFK's death, they would have to rely on the phys-ical record of the shooting itself. In essence, this meant that the critics would have to:

I. Prove by inductive reasoning the existence of two or more shooters—in effect, with hard evidence.

II. Show that Oswald was physically incapable of performing the mur-der alone with his weapon.

III. Show that the wounds suffered by the victims displayed two differ-ent trajectories, or could not be accomplished by one person in the given timing. This deductive reasoning would logically imply at least two shooters.

I will address each of these "proofs" in turn.

I. Was there direct evidence of two or more shooters?

This issue is the easiest to dispatch. Impossibly blurry photographs notwith-standing, there has never been direct, hard proof of a second shooter; no con-sistent witness, no clear photo, no other weapon found, and no confession from anyone with a scintilla of believability. The confessions of such characters as "Tosh the pilot," "Hugh the shooter," "James the shooter," "Chauncey the tramp" and others are so replete with contradictions, absurdities, and profiteer-ing that they deserve no consideration. "James," for instance, has included in his scenario the "fact" that Nazi war criminal Josef Mengele was in the Book Depository at the time of the assassination. "Tosh" claims to have met Lee Oswald in a secret North Carolina spy school at a time when Oswald was known to be in Minsk. More importantly, none of these "confessions" comes accom-panied by any proof of their claims.

II. The Mechanics of Murder: Oswald's ability and the rifle's capability

Oswald's Ability

One of the earliest criticisms of the Warren Commission's "Oswald alone" conclusion was based on the official Marine reports of Oswald's marksmanship. The Marine scale starts with "marksman" (the lowest qualifying score), moves upward to "sharpshooter," and ends at "expert" (the top score). On Oswald's last test with the Marines, he qualified with the score of marksman. This rating is misleading for two reasons:

1. Oswald's scores were hampered by the fact that they were averaged between sitting and standing positions. When in a sitting position, bracing the rifle for steadiness (as was clearly done in the JFK killing), Oswald often scored as a sharpshooter. Dr. John Lattimer, a former World War II wound ballistics specialist for the Army, purchased Oswald's original rifle scorebook from his days with the Marine Corps. The book reveals that in two rapid-fire tests at 200 yards, Oswald scored a 48 and 49 (out of 50). For these tests, Oswald used the .30 caliber M-1 Garand, which is much heavier, and with a stronger recoil, than the light-weight .257 caliber (6.5 mm) Mannlicher-Carcano used to kill Kennedy. In addition, the M-1 was not equipped with a scope, as was the Carcano. And whereas JFK was less than a hundred yards away, the Marine tests were conducted at distances ranging from 200 to 500 yards.

2. A Marine marksman or sharpshooter is anything but a bad shot, as some critics have implied. In 1964, the head of the Marine Marksmanship branch in Quantico, Virginia was Major Eugene D. Anderson. When reviewing Oswald's records for the Warren Commission, Anderson concluded: "As compared to a civilian who had not received this intensive training, he [Oswald] would be considered as a good to excellent shot."[4] The head of training at the Marine Quantico unit, Master Sergeant James A. Zahm, concurred: "I would say that…as compared to the average male of his age throughout the civilian [population], throughout the United States, he is an excellent shot."[5]

Among the numerous marksmen and current Marine trainers I consulted, there is total unanimity on this point. Using expressions such as "shooting fish in a barrel" and "virtually point blank," the experts call the Kennedy shooting a simple feat for a former Marine marksman.

The Rifle's Capability

If Oswald was up to the task, surely his cheap ($13) rifle was incapable of such a performance, other critics assert. Upon close examination, this too proves to be an inaccurate oversimplification.

Originally manufactured in 1891 for the Italian Army, the bolt-action 6.5

mm Mannlicher-Carcano rifle Oswald owned has been widely maligned as too inferior to be used in the assassination. The truth is that this weapon is so powerful—and accurate—at the range of the Kennedy murder that it should be among the last choices for a weapon someone would want pointed at them from that distance.

At the turn-of-the-twentieth-century, for example, the Mannlicher-Carcano was the weapon of choice for those competing in 1,000-yard shooting contests! It was preferred because it was one of the first to incorporate the new idea of "gain twist," popularized by the famous 19th century American gun-barrel maker, Harry Pope. Gain twist means simply that the grooves inside of the rifle barrel were designed to make the bullet spiral as it exited, much like a well-thrown football. Just as in football, the imparted spiral, or twist, increases the stability and accuracy of the bullet. The Mannlicher has a slightly higher twist ratio (1:8") than the current military issue M-16 (1:7").

The rifle has been further ridiculed because of its bolt-action mechanism, which obviously impedes the ability to fire off multiple shots in rapid succession—presumably necessary under the circumstances. This criticism, however, ignores the fact that the knob on the end of the bolt is not there for either aesthetic reasons or comfort. This practical addition allows the well-practiced shooter minimal hand movement when cycling from the trigger to the bolt—essentially rotating the trigger hand in one plane past the knob, with no extraneous movement. This is easier demonstrated than described. Someone skilled in the weapon's use could recycle the weapon in under two seconds, much less than was actually needed in the Kennedy case.

Oswald may very well have been so skilled. I noted earlier in the text that Marina Oswald was disturbed by Lee's repeated dry-firing speed drills on their New Orleans front porch. Witnesses in Dallas recall the speed and accuracy with which he performed at the shooting range in the days just prior to Kennedy's murder.

Oswald's ammunition was similarly deadly. The Mannlicher Carcano bullets are full-metal jacketed, hyper-velocity (2,700 fps—feet per second), and heavy-loaded (160 grains—twice the amount of today's bullets of the same caliber). In addition, they are extremely long projectiles, giving them (especially in combination with the gain twist rifle barrel) increased stability. HSCA ballistics expert Larry Sturdivan testified that the Mannlicher-Carcano bullet is "one of the most stable bullets we have ever done experimentation with."

After the infamous dum-dum bullets (which caused massive fatal injuries) were outlawed at the end of World War I, this Mannlicher rifle/bullet combination became extremely popular because of its amazing penetrating abilities, which are legendary among big game hunters and ballistics experts. Outlawing the combination was in fact welcomed by military planners because even though the bullet, when striking the torso, caused fewer fatalities, it often disabled two or more soldiers—this, combined with the two men who had to carry out the wounded, showed how economical and strategic one well-placed bullet could be. Mannlicher ammunition has often been the ammunition of choice for big game hunters because it penetrates even the thick skulls of elephants.

In experiments conducted by Dr. John Nichols and Dr. John Lattimer, using identical bullets (and rifle) as Oswald's, the bullets cleanly penetrated four feet of ponderosa pine and two feet of elm wood, emerging undamaged. Furthermore, these bullets are considered "over-stabilized," meaning that after the first penetration, they begin spinning like helicopter blades, which causes even more injury to the second person hit. Sound familiar? In the Kennedy killing, the penetrating abilities of this ammunition allowed one bullet to wound two victims, with the second victim, Governor Connally, suffering massive torso damage from the spinning, "over-stabilized" bullet.

In summary, the Mannlicher Carcano, when combined with its accompanying ammunition, is clearly a weapon to be reckoned with.

III. Do the victims' wounds prove a conspiracy?

This aspect of the killing, augmented by the secrecy surrounding JFK's autopsy, has led to the most confusion and argument in the entire assassination debate. The wounds in question, to Kennedy's head and to the torsos of both Kennedy and Governor Connally, inspire the following debates:

1. Toward what source(s) do the entrance wounds point?
2. As a matter of mechanics, did a single shooter, from any position, have the time necessary to inflict the wounds, with their given trajectories? The timing was established by the famous Zapruder film of the murder (now available to the public on videotape). Because neither victim was wounded before disappearing behind a road sign, and the wounding was complete when Kennedy's head was struck, it is a simple matter to conclude, using the film, that all the wounding occurred over a period of 5.4 seconds.

1. Source of the gunfire

There were dozens of eye and earwitnesses to the events in Dealey Plaza. However, there are many considerations to be addressed when judging their testimony *(see Appendix B)*. Suffice it to say that the vast majority of those witnesses agree with the official findings: three shots from behind the victims. The fact is that all of the witnesses' statements can be totally ignored and a solution can still be arrived at using "circumstantial" evidence. In any murder case, the strongest evidence is the hard circumstantial evidence: prints on the murder weapon, and artifacts left behind by the perpetrator(s), buttressed by the suspect's stated motive. As to the source of the gunshots, the "best evidence" is clearly the wounds suffered by the victims.

Readers can access many sources for the details, but the controversy over the source of the shots can most easily be summarized as follows. Although it is conceded by even the most vociferous critics that JFK's spine wound and Governor

Connally's torso wound were inflicted from the rear, the real difficulty in determining direction stems from JFK's head and throat wounds.

Regarding the throat wound, the controversy arose over the fact that the small wound seemed too small for an exit wound originating from the rear of the president. Furthermore, there was no autopsy description of the wound because it was obliterated by an emergency tracheostomy performed in Dallas. This issue was to be firmly resolved when the HSCA examined JFK's X-rays and photos. Here is a sampling of what they learned:

- *Exit wounds leave distinct "abrasion collars" which were detected in the Kennedy photos of his throat (the tracheostomy had left one edge of the exit wound intact).*

- *The X-rays showed wounds to the internal structures of the neck, strongly suggesting that the spine wound, clearly one of entrance, was directly connected to the throat exit wound. The HSCA also pointed out, in an impressive trajectory study, that the downward, right-to-left direction through Kennedy tracked right back towards the window where Oswald's rifle was found.*

- *Kennedy's shirt displayed a bullet hole in the front of the neck band with the fibers splayed out—still more evidence of an exiting bullet.*

In addition, the only doctors who saw the throat wound (at Dallas's Parkland Memorial Hospital) have voiced their agreement that the wound could have easily been a wound of exit.

The head wound controversy revolves essentially around two issues: first, the doctors at Parkland Hospital and the autopsies at Bethesda gave confusing descriptions of the massive damage; second, when the Zapruder film was finally aired nationally in 1975, the public saw that when Kennedy's head was struck, it jerked backwards, strongly suggesting a shot from the front.

As with the throat wound, when the doctors who actually examined JFK's body, and the best scientists in the nation review the evidence, there is no controversy. It has already been noted in the body of the text that the Parkland doctors spent no time in describing or studying JFK's wounds. Emergency room physicians are trained to restore vital functions, not to measure wounds while the patient lays dying. It is not until the patient is stabilized and the wound treated in the operating room that the wound itself is closely scrutinized—and JFK never made it to the operating room. Therefore, with regard to this critical aspect, the emergency room personnel become mere eyewitnesses, accompanied by all the problems inherent with eyewitness testimony (*to be detailed in the next appendix*). But even these doctors, after viewing the autopsy x-rays, overwhelmingly agree with the conclusion that Kennedy was struck in the rear of the head.

As stated, the doctors at Bethesda showed little interest in accurately measuring the entrance and exit points of the wound—they perceived their role as determining the cause of death, not the exact source of the cause of death. In doing so, the autopsies rendered a correct opinion: Kennedy died because part of his head was shot off. To learn about the direction of the shots, a better autopsy was needed but not administered. Once Kennedy was buried, the "best evidence" became the photos and x-rays of his wounds. Thus it fell to later scientific review, utilizing x-rays and photos of the deceased president (stored at the National Archives), to resolve the mystery. And it has been resolved.

Commencing with a 1967 report commissioned by then-Attorney General Ramsey Clark and continuing to the present time, many dozens of qualified experts have viewed the X-ray and photographic materials. Included among these experts are eminent forensic specialists, radiologists, pathologists, general practitioners, physics scholars, photo analysts, etc. Estimates by the National Archives place the total number of experts who have seen the material at over 150. Given their expertise, the fact that 99 percent of them agree on everything is conclusive. Among their findings:

- *All of the photographic and X-ray materials depict John F. Kennedy, and are authentic and unaltered.*

- *The entrance and exit wounds are clearly defined and show that Kennedy was hit from behind, near his cowlick, with a large portion of the bullet exiting above his right temple.*

- *The size of the entrance wound is consistent with Oswald's ammunition.*

Only one person who has viewed the material has stated a belief that these photographs are forgeries. Not coincidentally, this person has no photo analysis schooling, no medical expertise, and in fact no college education. He was allowed to view the material only because he was a member of the HSCA photo panel, a post given him because he was a well-known critic, and not because of his academic expertise. Among many observers, it is accepted fact that his appointment was viewed by the committee as an appeasement of the more vocal critics.

This same critic was largely responsible for the furor over the last key element of the head shot controversy—the Zapruder film, having displayed a bootlegged copy of the film on the conspiracy convention circuit.[6] The bootlegged copies of the Zapruder film clearly show JFK's head snapping backwards after being struck. It furnished proof that the shot came from the front—or so many of us thought. That conclusion, it turns out, suffers from two key errors:

- *On a clear, first-generation copy of the film—available at the time only to Congressional investigators—Kennedy's head can be seen jerking forward before the back snap. In fact, one early critic, Josiah Thompson, perceived this forward motion when he was granted a rare viewing of the film at the National Archives. He mistakenly deduced that this demonstrated a rear shot, followed in one-eighteenth of a second by a frontal shot. We shall see that there is a much more plausible explanation.*

- *Few who saw the Zapruder film ever visited the scene of the crime. Upon visiting Dealey Plaza, it becomes instantly apparent that there is no available sniper's nest in front of Kennedy from which a shot could be fired! (More on this in the trajectory discussion.)*

If the shot originated from the rear, then why the backward snap? Every human instinct and experience tells us that the struck object should continue in the same direction as the projectile. How could Sir Isaac Newton have been wrong when he postulated as much in his second law of motion, describing the conservation of momentum? The answer is that our instincts are occasionally wrong, and Newton was postulating about solid objects, not a projectile piercing a thin shell of bone under pressure, which also involves the conservation of energy. Everything changes when these critical distinctions are taken into account. To be specific, one billiard ball striking another is not analogous to a bullet piercing a living human skull.

On numerous occasions, scientists have attempted to study this phenomenon. Every time the Kennedy assassination has been experimentally simulated, whether by a Nobel Prize-winning physicist (Luis Alvarez), a longtime Army wound ballistics specialist (Dr. John Lattimer), or the best scientific team that Congress could assemble, the results are the same: A bullet that cleanly enters a pressurized human skull produces minimal resistance—thus minimal forward momentum. This momentum is greatly overshadowed by what Alvarez referred to as the "jet effect." When the bullet traverses the brain, it causes a pressure cavity to form behind the bullet. This pressure continues to build until the head literally explodes in all directions. The greatest mass of brain tissue exits in the area of least resistance—near the larger exit wound already created by the bullet. If that wound is in the front, then this escaping material rockets the head backwards. Thus, as Alvarez wrote in his 1976 paper, if one considers all the interacting forces—the bullet, the skull, and the pressurized brain—then both the laws of momentum and energy are taken into account.

Having concluded that the shots could indeed have come from the rear, it must be ascertained where exactly to the rear the shooter was located. Once again, when the best scientific minds are brought to bear on this question (on four occasions thus far), there is no controversy. Using powerful computers applied to the known surveys of the plaza and blueprints of the Presidential limousine, and merged with the position of the President as seen in the Zapruder film and other films and photographs, the wounds have been plotted through JFK's body. *The unanimous conclusion*: The shots originated in the area of the southeast sixth floor window of the Texas School Book Depository, where Lee Harvey Oswald left so many traces of himself.

The first such study was the HSCA's "trajectory study" (1978). This was followed by the studies rendered to video by the PBS science series "Nova" (1988), the tests of the legal profession's preeminent crime reenactment firm, Failure Analysis Associates (1992), and the computer graphics rendering by Microtech

Graphics & Animation (1995). Utilizing the most state-of-the-art equipment yet, Dale Myers' work for Microtech is not only consistent with the previous studies, and is much more dramatic, but resolves virtually all the remaining nagging mysteries of Dealey Plaza.

Like the preceding studies, Myers' work is conclusive that the wounds track back to the sixth floor window where Oswald's prints and ammunition were found—just a few steps from where his rifle was stashed (and, lest we forget, from where Howard Brennan saw Oswald shoot). Myers' work puts still another nail in the coffin of a sensational allegation, long dispensed with by noted ballistic and forensic scientists—the legend, or rather myth, of a shooter from the infamous "Grassy Knoll."

The Myth of the Grassy Knoll Gunman

The oft-repeated belief in a shooter from the knoll (to the right of JFK) originated as a result of the following:

A. Three railroad workers standing on the overpass bridge thought they saw smoke rise from behind the fenced-in knoll area just after the shots—this area fences in a parking lot behind the knoll to the north.
B. Within minutes of the shooting, dozens of people followed a police officer up to the knoll and behind the fence.
C. Three witnesses who rushed the knoll talked of encountering mysterious "government agents" in that area, although government agencies readily admitted having none there.
D. A few earwitnesses (12 percent) believed one shot emanated from behind the knoll/fence area.

When these facets were added to the potentially misleading head snap depicted in the Zapruder film, the myth of the grassy knoll gunman took hold. Later information regarding the knoll would be developed, such as the acoustics tape already dealt with in the text, and impossibly blurred photos of the knoll which are too unconvincing to merit discussion. *(The eyewitnesses' accounts of the grassy knoll story are discussed in Appendix B.)*

Taking these points in order:

A. The Smoke

Since the days of the Civil War, pistol and rifle ammunition has been smokeless when fired. (I was on hand for the filming of the 1991 film, "JFK," where the smoke on the knoll is seen rising. However, when it came time to film the scene, a number of rifles were trotted out, none of which emitted any smoke. Eventually, the special-effects team was brought in. Now the truth can be told: when the film audience sees the "smoke behind the fence" scene, what they are seeing are the effects of a production assistant kneeling behind the fence, armed with a smoke machine.

Other witnesses provide a plausible explanation for what was described: one said he saw smoke from a policeman's motorcycle abandoned near the knoll; another saw smoke that he described as exhaust fumes emanating from the parking lot behind the fence; still another saw steam being vented from a steam pipe running along the fence (on which a police officer later burned his hand).

B. The Crowd on the Knoll

When those who ran up the hill are questioned (I have spoken to six of these witnesses), they have no explanation other than that they were merely following the person in front of them. Some have said that the area just appeared to be a logical place to check out, while others were looking for a place to hide. The vast majority of those charging the hill did so after motorcycle patrolman Bobby Hargis raced up to inspect the area. Therefore, they had reason to suspect something had happened there. However, Hargis told me that he went up there only because he deduced that there were just two places where the shooter could have been: the overpass near the knoll, or the Texas School Book Depository: in fact, he saw or heard nothing suspicious in the knoll area. As Hargis testified, "There wasn't any way in the world I could tell where they [the shots] were coming from." Nonetheless, it was Hargis' curiosity that started a virtual stampede.

C. The Agents on the Knoll

Three of the eyewitnesses—Jean Hill, Malcolm Summers, and policeman Joe Marshall Smith—have told of encountering a government agent in the vicinity of the knoll. In fact, eyewitness Summers told me that his encounter was well in front of the white retaining wall in front of the knoll. Eyewitness Hill's account, which has been exponentially and dramatically enhanced each year, is considered too inconsistent to merit discussion *(the phenomena of Jean Hill and other questionable eyewitnesses is discussed in the following appendix).*

By far the most serious account comes from policeman Smith, who had been directing traffic at the corner of Elm and Houston streets. After the shooting, a woman told Smith she believed the shots were coming from the bushes near the knoll. Smith then rushed to the parking lot behind the picket fence, where he inspected both the bushes and the parked cars. Smith, however, found nothing out of the ordinary. At one point, he stopped a man in a sports shirt who displayed Secret Service credentials. Smith had seen these Treasury Department credentials before and, recognizing them as authentic, left the man and continued his search of the area.

Years later, when all the federal protective agencies (including the Secret Service, which is a branch of the Treasury Department) were queried, they replied that they had placed no agents in the knoll area. This fueled speculation that impostors had shot the president from

behind the grassy knoll. There is, however, another, more plausible explanation for Smith's encounter with someone having Secret Service credentials.

Secret Service agent Mike Howard had been in charge of security for the Fort
Worth leg of the JFK trip. As he told me in 1993, there was coincidentally a
"grassy knoll" on the way to the Ft. Worth Airport. These kinds of topography
were clear security risks, says Howard, who adds, "We placed two deputies there.
This is routine. Sorrells [Forrest Sorrells, the Secret Service Agent in charge of the
Dallas motorcade] did the same thing in Dallas." Howard was told by the now
deceased Sorrells that, like Howard, he had placed security people in all the
obvious areas. Howard elaborated:

> We deputized everybody we could get our hands on—including agents from
> ATF [the Bureau of Alcohol, Tobacco and Firearms], customs, border patrol,
> reserve police, deputy sheriffs, etc. The motorcade route in Dallas was crawl-
> ing with these people, especially in Dealey Plaza and the overpass.[7]

Howard adds that many of these security reinforcements were technically
off-duty, and wouldn't appear on any "official" listing of posted officers. In addition, many of these agents had the standard ATF ID's, which were virtually identical to Secret Service cards, both being issued by the Treasury Department.
Compounding the confusion is the fact that the ATF and Secret Service were
often perceived as interchangeable in 1963. Frank Ellsworth, a Dallas ATF agent
at the time of the assassination, told me, "In 1963, if you would have asked me
if I was a Secret Service agent, I most likely would have answered yes—our roles
overlapped that much."[8] Robert Gemberling, the FBI agent in Dallas who investigated Oswald after his arrest, told me that he remembers being told that two
Customs Agents who worked at the Post Office building across Dealey Plaza
were, in fact, spending their lunch break helping with security in the knoll area.
Gemberling says he was informed by an assassination researcher that the two
agents have in fact been identified.[9]

Finally, the grassy knoll shooter is in and of itself illogical, given: 1) the
available sight lines of a potential grassy knoll shooter, and 2) the absurdity of
an assassin choosing a spot within ten feet of potential witnesses—who never
saw or heard the killer.

D. The Sight Lines

When one first stands behind the picket fence, he/she is struck by a number of
sensations. First, there is no clear shot at the middle lane of Elm street until the
instant of the head shot, allowing for no earlier shots or tracking of the moving
target. It turns out that the intended victim is obscured by road signs and a
white retaining wall about ten feet in front of the fence.

An even more compelling problem was driven home during the filming of
"JFK." I was fortunate to be able to stand near the camera as this scene was reen-

acted. With the street crowd added as it appeared on the day of the shooting, it became clear that, insofar as the first two shots are concerned, a grassy knoll shot was also obstructed by the crowd that lined the sidewalk. The assassin would thus had to shoot through the white wall, the road signs, and bystanders to get to the president. If the assassin shot Kennedy in the head, he had to shoot in the first second the car emerged from behind the retaining wall, again past (or through) the heads of spectators.

Standing behind the picket fence, it is also apparent that if the shot were from the front, then it couldn't have originated behind the fence: the fence is at a 90 degree angle to Kennedy's head—tilted 34 degrees left of center when hit—at the time the president was struck. A virtual broadside hit. Such a shot would not have forced JFK's head forward or backward, but side to side, with the bullet exiting near Kennedy's left ear, hitting Jackie. Of course, none of this happened.

In Dale Myers' meticulous reconstruction of the event, he asked the computer to draw a line from low in the back of Kennedy's head—where some have erroneously stated a wound existed—to the wound in the right temple area. Giving the front-shooter theorists the benefit of the doubt, and negating all the autopsy X-rays and photos, Myers then followed the line forward to determine where such a shooter had to be located. It turns out that if the shooter were in front of Kennedy, in a line with his wounds and front-to-back axis of movement, the assailant could only be in one place: thirty feet in the air above the southernmost point of the railroad overpass. This, of course, also never happened.

Finally, would a shooter place him/herself so perilously close to witnesses? It is well-known that there were three men on the knoll steps, barely twenty feet below the fence, between a potential shooter and JFK. It is also well-known that Abraham Zapruder stood filming the presidential motorcade about the same distance to the east of the fence. But there were spectators even closer to the fence, according to Marilyn Sitzman, Zapruder's secretary, who held his legs steady as he filmed standing atop the white pergola. From at least 1966, when she was first asked, until her death in 1993, Sitzman told a consistent story that renders the idea of a grassy knoll shooter even more implausible.

"I tried to tell that [writer] Mark Lane when he interviewed me in 1966, but he didn't want to hear about it," Sitzman told me in 1992, 10 months before her death.[10] What she was trying to tell Lane, she also told me, as well as writer Josiah Thompson: on November 22, 1963, between the picket fence and the retaining wall, there was a bench on which a young couple sat watching the motorcade. That bench has not been there for many years, and is a fact not known by most grassy knoll theorists. As Sitzman told Thompson:

> There was a colored couple. I figured they were between 18 and 21, a boy and a girl sitting on a bench...between that [concrete slab] and the wooden fence...They were eating their lunch, because they had little lunch sacks, and

they were drinking Coke. The main reason I remember them is that, after the last shot, I recall hearing—I heard a crash of glass, and I looked over there, and the kids had thrown down their Coke bottles, just threw them down and started running towards the back...The pop bottle crashing was much louder than the shots were.[11]

In still photographs taken from the corner of Elm and Houston, some fifty yards away, the young black man appears as a blurry figure behind the wall.[12] Unbeknownst to him, this photo would give him a kind of infamy among conspiracy theorists as the mysterious "black dog man."

Sitzman further told me emphatically that there was no one shooting in the area of the fence. "That's absurd. I was only a few feet away, and I didn't hear or see anything suspicious," said Sitzman. "And that black couple was only a couple feet in front of the fence, and what did they do after the shooting but run behind the fence. Would they run right to the shooter?" And would the shooter post himself a mere five feet behind them?

Sitzman's recollections are bolstered by photos and films taken on that day. Just prior to the shooting, photos and films show a black man standing behind the wall, and a soda bottle placed on the wall. The bottle is missing in photos taken after the shooting. In a film taken by John Martin (and shown on the 1993 Frontline program), the bench, with a large paper sack on it, is clearly visible behind the wall. The black couple has never come forward, nor been identified.

2. The Mechanics of the Shooting

Regarding the mechanics of the shooting, and the question of whether it was possible for one person to accomplish the assassination as it occurred, another major consideration is timing. Using the Zapruder film as a clock, the question becomes: Could the rifle be fired three times in the amount of time allowed, causing all the wounds? Because 88 percent of those present heard three and only three shots, and because three spent shells were found near Oswald's rifle, this hypothesis is necessary to drive home Oswald's guilt.

In using the Zapruder film as a clock, both the Warren Commission and the early critics made a serious misjudgment about timing that made the lone assassin theory just barely possible. In the film, the only obvious wound that can be precisely clocked is the final shot to JFK, the one causing the massive head wound. Five-point-six seconds prior to that, Kennedy disappeared behind a road sign unscathed. When he emerged, he had been shot through the back, with the spinal injury causing his arms to splay upwards in the "Thorburn" position.

The Warren Commission decided that, if it could show the entire attack taking place within those 5.6 seconds, all three major wounds (Kennedy's back, Connally's back, Kennedy's head) could conveniently jibe with the three known shots—consistent with Oswald's culpability. The chief problem with this approach is the later determination that two of the major wounds were caused by just one bullet. Therefore, the shooter had to shoot just twice in 5.6 seconds. One shot obviously missed at a time that is impossible to determine.

Still, for years, experts and amateurs debated whether anyone could score three separate hits in 5.6 seconds. They were trying to prove something that never happened. In their March 27, 1964 reconstruction of the shooting, the Warren Commission's experts, using Oswald's rifle, came close, but not close enough, to validating the mistaken hypothesis. Like Oswald, they achieved their best results in the seated position. Their results were as follows:

- *3 experts achieved 2 hits in 5.6 seconds.*

- *3 experts achieved 2 hits in under 7 seconds.*

- *1 expert made 2 hits in 8.13 seconds.*

It was not until 1967, in a meticulous reconstruction commissioned by CBS News—it used a six-story tower and a moving target—that a number of experts achieved 3 hits in 5.6 seconds, with one scoring even better. (Using a rifle and ammunition virtually identical to Oswald's, expert marksman Howard Donahue was, amazingly, able to score three hits in 4.8 seconds.)

In 1968, Dr. John Lattimer, as well as his 14 and 17-year-old sons, were able to consistently score 3 hits (within 6 inches of the target) in 6.5 seconds. These tests were likewise meticulous reconstructions, using duplicate weaponry, and using three targets placed the appropriate distances between them. More importantly, they had no difficulty accurately shooting the weapon twice in under 5.6 seconds (the Warren Commission's experts had long ago achieved the same result).

By far the most impressive testing was performed in 1994 by independent researcher Todd Vaughn. Vaughn acquired rifle and ammunition of the same year and lot as Oswald's, and proceeded to set up targets at the appropriate distances. In preparation, Vaughn dry-fired the weapon only a few times on the day he received it. Until the test was conducted a month and a half later, Vaughn did not touch the weapon again. Todd Vaughn had never received any formal firearms training, had never been in the military, had never worked a bolt-action weapon, and had never even fired a high-powered rifle before.

On the day of the tests, Vaughn fired fourteen shots to make sure the rifle worked at all, and to familiarize himself with the scope. With his assistant's digital stop watch at the ready, and with only ten minutes of practice with a high-powered, bolt-action rifle, Vaughn fired off four sets of three rapid-fire shots each, with the following results:

- *First attempt: 3 hits in 6.29 seconds (not using scope)*

- *Second attempt: 2 hits in 7.53 seconds (using scope)*

- *Third attempt: 2 hits in 9.11 seconds (not using scope)*

- *Fourth attempt: 3 hits in 8.25 seconds (not using scope)*

Vaughn even attempted four rapid-fire shots, as some have mistakenly theorized Oswald pulled off. On that attempt, he was able to accomplish all four shots, with two hits, in 6.93 seconds.

(When I later learned what Todd Vaughn accomplished, I recalled a meeting I had with a member of the Dallas Police Department. As we peered down from Oswald's sixth floor perch, I informed the officer that I had never fired a rifle. He responded, "I could teach you to hit these shots in a half hour.")

In assessing all the above simulations, the key point is that at least once in every series of attempts, experts were able to achieve two hits in 5.6 seconds. For that timing to be the linchpin, one bullet must account for two sets of wounds—and it did.

When first proposed by the Warren Commission, it was known as "The Single Bullet Theory." With its verification by current, high-powered computer reconstructions, it should be called "The Single Bullet *Fact.*" In order to show that one bullet from Oswald's perch struck both Kennedy and Connally, two key questions must be resolved:

- *Is there a straight line of trajectory through both men's wounds?*

- *Could one Mannlicher Carcano bullet cause so much damage and emerge in the condition of the bullet recovered at the hospital?*

The Trajectory

Initially, critics of the single bullet theory (SBT) used sketches to "prove" that the wounds didn't line up (*see illustrations*). These drawings, however, were absurdly over-simplified, and failed to take into account such not-so-minor details as the measurements of the limousine in which both men were seated, and the precise locations of the four entrance/exit wounds through the victims' torsos. When these considerations were eventually taken into account, there was no question about what had occurred in Dealey Plaza. As Robert Groden, an assassination lecturer, has explained, "The effect of angle or trajectory can be easily manipulated or obscured." [13]

First verified by the HSCA's science experts in 1978, it is now a certainty that the bullet wounds through JFK's back tracked backwards towards "Oswald's perch" and forwards into Governor Connally. Starting in the 1980s, with the advent of computer modeling, the HSCA's work has been verified on the three known occasions this technology has been brought to bear on the controversy. Unlike the critics' sketches, these efforts utilized precise measurements taken from surveyors maps, the limousine's blueprints, and all the information from available films and photos of the shooting.

In truth, the first computer model (for the PBS science series "Nova" in 1988), was crude by today's standards. It was unable to achieve an accurate overhead picture of the victims' position at the time of the shot. However, it concluded that, contrary to the critics' contentions, it was at least possible that they were indeed in line at the time of the shot.

In 1993, a more powerful computer model was rendered for Court TV by Failure Analysis Associates, which specializes in computerized crime reconstructions for the legal profession. For the first time, the computer viewer was able to "fly over" the victims. It was clear that Kennedy and Connally were indeed in line for the shot, which tracked back to Oswald's sixth floor lair in the Texas School Book Depository.

Drawn without scientific basis, sketches such as the one below created the myth of the "magic bullet."

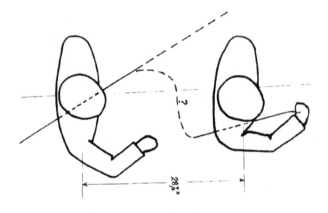

However, when the car blueprints, body sizes, surveyors' maps, and exact measurements are considered, it is clear that Connally's wounds track back through JFK to Lee Harvey Oswald's perch in the Book Depository, as the Myers computer renderings clearly demonstrate.

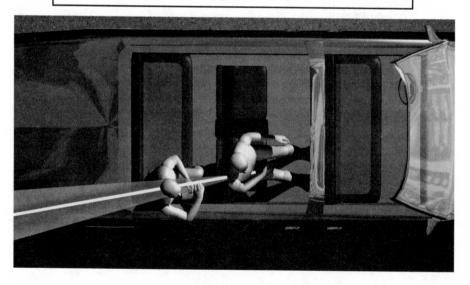

Computer modeling courtesy Dale Myers Animation.

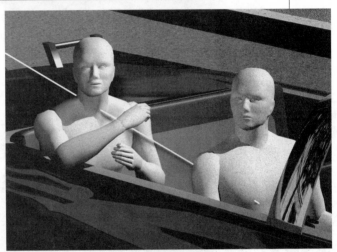

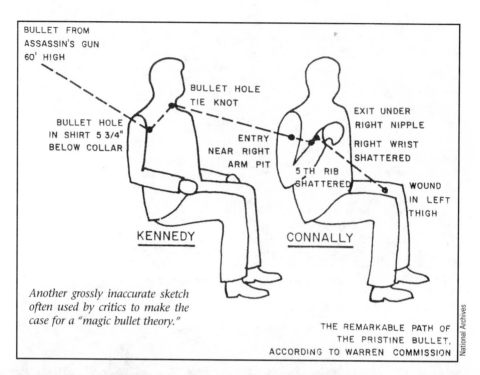

BULLET FROM
ASSASSIN'S GUN
60' HIGH

BULLET HOLE
TIE KNOT

BULLET HOLE
IN SHIRT 5 3/4"
BELOW COLLAR

EXIT UNDER
RIGHT NIPPLE

ENTRY
NEAR RIGHT
ARM PIT

RIGHT WRIST
SHATTERED

5 TH RIB
SHATTERED

WOUND
IN LEFT
THIGH

KENNEDY

CONNALLY

Another grossly inaccurate sketch often used by critics to make the case for a "magic bullet theory."

THE REMARKABLE PATH OF
THE PRISTINE BULLET,
ACCORDING TO WARREN COMMISSION

National Archives

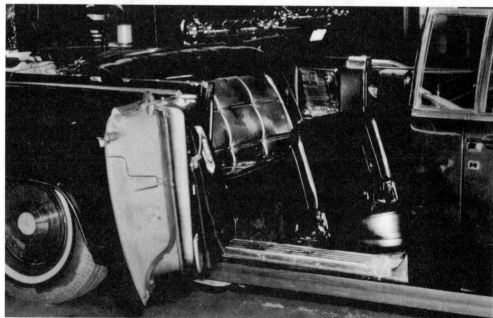

This previously unpublished photo of Kennedy's limousine was taken the night of the assassination and shows the true relationship of Kennedy's back seat and Connally's jump seat.

By far the most sophisticated and impressive computer model was completed in 1995, after two years of work by Dale Myers of Microtech. In addition to verifying the work of his predecessors, Myers was further able to ask the computer to resolve the ultimate conspiratorial question: If all the hard evidence is forged, and if the torso wound trajectories went from front to rear, where would the shooter have to be located? Myers' answer is that the driver of JFK's own limousine would have had to stop the car, lay down in its floor-well, and shoot upwards through Connally.

The still frames in the photo section are from Myers' reconstruction. They show the true trajectory through the victims.

The Condition of the Recovered Bullet

Soon after the victims left the emergency rooms, a spent Mannlicher Carcano bullet was found on Governor Connally's stretcher in Parkland Hospital. In 1964, FBI ballistics experts determined that this bullet, CE 399, and two large fragments recovered from another bullet, were indeed fired from Oswald's Mannlicher Carcano, and could not have been fired by any other weapons. This conclusion was reached in two ways:

1. *Rifling.* The interiors of all rifle barrels are etched lengthwise with grooves that twist to the right or left. These grooves, referred to as rifling, cause the bullet to spiral, or twist, thus increasing accuracy. Every rifle model has its own unique rifling, which makes its imprint on the exiting bullet. The patterns left on the stretcher bullet, and the other fragments large enough to study, clearly indicated that they emanated from a Mannlicher Carcano rifle.

2. *Microscopic etchings.* Because rifle parts are not manufactured using identical molds, but with mechanical filings and carvings, each rifle has thousands of microscopic scars unique to itself. This is true of the bolt, hammer, interior of the barrel, and other metal parts. These scars become incontestably unique given every weapon's peculiar history of cleanings, corrosion, and actual firing; they, in effect, are imprinted on bullets fired from the weapon. When these "fingerprints" from Oswald's rifle were compared to those on the recovered bullet, there was a perfect match. Thus, the bullet came from the rifle clearly linked to Lee Harvey Oswald.

According to the HSCA, it was "highly probable" that the elemental makeup of the stretcher bullet (already shown in 1964 to have come from Oswald's rifle) was responsible for the bullet fragments left in Connally's wrist. (The operative thesis is that one bullet traversed JFK's neck, and entered Connally's back, emerging from his chest, and leaving fragments in his wrist. The body of the bullet struck Connally's thigh, later to fall down his pants leg onto his stretcher. As odd as this sounds to the layman, this type of multiple wounding is not uncommon to wartime MASH units, or to modern urban emergency room physicians.)

The HSCA further determined that all the other recovered fragments originated from one, and only one, other bullet—one of whose fragments had enough rifling scars to prove it also came from Oswald's rifle. (Using a technique known as neutron activation analysis, the HSCA received supporting testimony from Dr. Vincent Guinn, one of the country's top experts in the field of neutron activation. Although at the time, Guinn would only use the words "highly probable," he later published two articles in which he makes it clear that by "highly probable" he meant 99.99% probable.)[14]

Although the bullet was now traced to the miniscule fragments in Connally, in a trajectory previously proven to have had JFK in its path, critics, most with no background in science, were unconvinced. Among other things, they pointed to the condition of the bullet itself, which has quite mistakenly been referred to as "pristine." When photographed at one angle, the bullet indeed appears pristine. However, these photographs are intellectually dishonest. Massad Ayoob, a ballistics expert with *American Handgunner* magazine, has written of this bullet: "Turned over a quarter revolution, it is bent like a banana—consistent with passing through ribs [and] wristbones (at greatly reduced velocity by that time, which would also reduce deformation)."[15]

The fact is that the metal-jacketed Mannlicher Carcano bullet has great "sectional density," making it very hard to deform. This is especially true of a slowed-down bullet, whose speed was diminished from a muzzle velocity of 2,000 feet per second (fps) when it hit Kennedy's back to 900 fps when it hit Connally's wrist. The bullet's nose appears unscathed because it tumbled (as designed) after it hit Kennedy, with its rear portion breaking Connally's rib and radius bone (wrist). Ballistics and wound specialists have testified ad nauseum that a slowed down, metal-jacketed bullet could easily break two bones with its rear portion and end up looking the same as CE 399 did.

In 1964, the FBI had little success in duplicating the bullet's appearance when firing full velocity at cadaver bones. Critics trotted out the test photos, showing grossly deformed bullets that had struck bones at full velocity (and head-on) to demonstrate that they bore no resemblance to the "pristine" stretcher bullet. It was a dishonest analogy. However, it wasn't until three decades later that experimenters finally demonstrated what ballistics experts had long known:

- *In 1992, Failure Analysis Associates reduced the powder charge of a Mannlicher Carcano bullet in order to reduce its velocity. It was then fired through a cadaver wrist, breaking the radius bone. According to Dr. Martin Fackler, who conducted the tests, "The test bullet was non-deformed. It was not flattened in the least and had nowhere near the damage of CE 399."[16]*

- *In 1994, Dr. John Lattimer went to great lengths to duplicate the murder conditions. In addition to using identical weaponry as Oswald, Lattimer slowed down his bullet by firing through pork muscle with the same dimensions as JFK's neck. Twenty-four inches in front of that, Lattimer placed a rack of ribs (clothed like Connally), and a radius bone the size of Connally's. When fired through all three targets, the recovered bullet emerged virtually identical to CE 399.[17] At a later point, Lattimer actually went so far as to acquire two recently-deceased human cadavers with which to experiment. Again, he achieved the same results.*

The Missed Shot

If, in fact, two bullets caused all the wounds, what happened to the third shot heard by so many, and implied by the three spent cartridges found in the Depository? The simple answer is we will never know. However, the best evidence appears to reside once again in the clear print of the Zapruder film. At about frame Z 155, three occupants of the presidential limousine appear to suddenly react to some stimulus. Both JFK and his wife, as well as Connally, stop waving and turn quickly to their right. At the same time, a small girl who had been running on the sidewalk stops suddenly and turns away from the president's car, which she was following, and looks back. She would later say that she stopped when she heard the first shot, and turned to look back at what she thought was the source of the shot, the Book Depository.

If what the film seems to show—and the girl's perceptions—are accurate, the first shot missed, with the next two commencing four to five seconds later. Why Oswald missed, and where the bullet ended up, are anyone's guess (one possibility is suggested in the text). The bullet could have been deflected by a tree branch and buried itself in the turf, yet to be discovered by some lucky archeologist.

The fact that the "single bullet theory" was initially proposed by now-Senator Arlen Spector, considered by some to be exceedingly arrogant, has made it harder for some to accept. It is a classic example of the maxim that sometimes one must accept the message, in spite of one's feelings about the messenger. (No one is more upset than the author over the fact that Anita Hill's basher-in-chief was correct about the single bullet, but in fact, he was.)

Those critics who absolutely refuse to alter their views in light of the new scientific developments suffer from what psychologists have alternately referred to as "groupthink," or the "pathology of knowledge."[18] This phenomenon allows the critic, hyped-up by passion, paranoia, or greed, to fall back on any number of arguments in order to maintain his/her position. The most common methods consist of either finding inconsistencies in FBI "raw data" reports, or taking testimony far out of context.

A good example is the way Constable Seymour Weitzman's testimony has been treated. Anyone who has ever interviewed an FBI agent is aware that preliminary reports are just that—preliminary. They are not meant to be a show of proof for a courtroom. Weitzman, a knowledgeable gun enthusiast, was the official who discovered Oswald's rifle on the sixth floor of the Depository. In his FBI summary interview, he described the rifle as a "Mauser bolt-action" type.

But critics seized on this to show evidence of Oswald's innocence. Of course, when a detailed briefing of Weitzman was undertaken, he made it clear that he was not describing the manufacturer of the rifle, only the generic bolt type. In fact, Weitzman was more correct than he may have known, for the Mannlicher Carcano company had licensed Mauser's bolt assemblies *from* Mauser.

The out-of-context approach is typified by an oft-cited Jack Ruby interview with Earl Warren. Ruby had begged Warren to bring him to Washington so he could feel free to talk about the "conspiracy." Out of context, this is a bombshell. In context, it amounts to nothing. If one reads the entire interview, it quickly becomes apparent that Ruby was referring to a Dallas-based "conspiracy" to frame the Jews in the murder of JFK. Ruby wanted Warren to know that he knew nothing of a Jewish conspiracy to kill Kennedy. Because Warren had no such suspicions, he felt no need to bring the increasingly-delusional Ruby to Washington.

As a last resort, the critic may play the demagogue, utilizing the paranoid's impossible-to-debate argument: government law enforcement officers are corrupt by nature and, therefore, planted or lied about all the evidence. This is an argument that, thank God, is rarely taken seriously when trial time comes. If it were, virtually all criminal suspects would have to be set free. This is especially true of a murder investigation, imperfect by nature, where there is no confession. But there is a preponderance of good evidence in the Kennedy assassination, and it points clearly to Lee Harvey Oswald's guilt.

But don't take my word for it. If the history of this case teaches us anything, it is that the main enemy of the truth of Dealey Plaza has been oversimplification. Because this is a book about people, not science, these considerations were merely summarized. Interested readers are urged to go to the first-hand sources—the scientists and reports cited below—and judge for themselves. Or better still, get to know some law enforcement officials and learn an important lesson: the overwhelming majority are motivated by patriotism and community service and would not allow the minority to perpetrate a murder conspiracy.

(For more details and sources regarding the shooting of the President, see the sources for Appendix A.)

APPENDIX A SOURCES

Interviews

The following is a representative, albeit partial, list of interviews conducted by the author in support of Appendix A.

1) Dealey Plaza witnesses:

Carolyn Arnold, Amos Lee Euins, Buell Frazier, Jean Hill, James Jarman, Bill & Gayle Newman, Arnold Rowland, Bill Shelley, Marilyn Sitzman, Malcolm Summers, Carolyn Walther, Bonnie Ray Williams, Phil Willis.

2) Federal, state, and local officials:

D.A. William Alexander, Off. Marrion Baker, Off. Billy Bass, David Belin, Det. Paul Bentley, G. Robert Blakey, Off. T.F. Bowles, Off. Elmer Boyd, Det. Michael Callahan, Off. Elmo Cunningham, Lt. Carl Day, Agent Vincent Drain, Off. Harold Elkins, Agent Frank Ellsworth, Off. J.W. Foster, Agent Robert Gemberling, Off. B.D. Gossett, Burt Griffin, Off. Bobby Hargis, Agent Wally Heitman, Off. J.B. Hicks, Det. Gerald Hill, Agent Jim Hosty, Agent Mike Howard, Off. Murry Jackson, Agent Sebastian Latona, Det. Jim Leavelle, Off. C. L. "Lummie" Lewis, Det. Rusty Livingstone, Sheriff Al Maddox, Off. Tom McMillan, Agent J. Walton Moore, Off. R.C. Nelson, Off. Billy Preston, Lt. Jack Revill, Ferris Rookstool, Sen. Richard Schweiker, Cong. Louis Stokes, Off. Tom Tilson, Off. Ray Vaughn, D.A. Henry Wade, Off. Marvin Wise.

3) Medical personnel and scientific experts:

Dr. Robert Artwohl, Massad Ayoob, Dr. Michael Baden, Dr. Jack Barnnett, Audrey Bell, G. Robert Blakey, George Bonebrake, Dr. David Dennis, Howard Donohue, Josh Grant, Joseph Hagen, Paul Hoch (assistant to Luis Alvarez), Dr. Pepper Jenkins, Dr. Lou Kartsonis, Cecil Kirk, Dr. John Lattimer, Paul O'Connor, Tom Robinson, Dr. Earl Rose, Dr. Lee Russo, Vincent Scalese, Dr. Robert Shaw, John Stringer, Josiah Thompson, Paul Vallandigham, Prof. Mark Weiss, Dr. Michael West, Ronald Wittmus.

Books, Articles, Films, and Goverment Documents

Luis W. Alvarez, "A Physicist Examines the Kennedy Assassination Film," *American Journal of Physics*, Vol. 44. No. 9, September 1976, p. 819.

Massad Ayoob, "The JFK Assassination: A Shooter's Eye View," in *The American Handgunner*, March/April, 1993, p. 102.

James C. Bowles, *The Kennedy Assassination Tapes: A Rebuttal to the Acoustical Evidence Theory* (Unpublished, Dallas, 1979).

Dennis L. Breo, "JFK's Death: The Plain Truth from the Doctors Who Did the Autopsy," *JAMA*, Volume 267, No. 20, May 27, 1992.

——, "JFK's Death, Part Two: Dallas MDs Recall Their Memories," *JAMA*, Volume 267, No. 20, May 27, 1992.

Francis Corbett, "John Kennedy Assassination Film Analysis, " Itek Corporation, 1975.

Vincent DiMaio, "Gunshot Wounds: Practical Aspects of Firearms, Ballistics and Forensic Techniques."

Howard Donahue reconstruction on CBS News Inquiry, "The Warren Report," Parts 1-4, June 25-28, 1967.

Tom Filsinger, "Groupthink and JFK Assassination Research." in *The Third Decade,* Vol. 8, #6, September, 1992.

Dr. Dennis Ford, "Assassination Research and the Pathology of Knowledge." *The Third Decade,* Volume 8, # 5, July, 1992.

Vincent Guinn, "NAA of Bullet Lead Evidence Specimens in Criminal Cases," in *The Journal of Radioanalytical Chemistry,* Vol. 72, No. 1 & 2, 1982; and "The Elemental Comparison of Bullet Lead Evidence Specimens" in *The Chemistry of Crime,* Samuel M. Gerber ed., Washington, DC, 1983.

HSCA Hearings, Volumes I & III (ballistics and trajectory).

Dr. John Lattimer, *Kennedy and Lincoln: Medical and Ballistic Comparisons of Their Assassinations* (Harcourt, Brace, Jovanovich), 1980.

———, "Experimental Duplication of the Important Physical Evidence...", *Journal of the American College of Surgeons,* May, 1994, Vol. 178.

Jeffrey Lotz computer analysis of Zapruder Film for Failure Analysis Associates, Inc., (Menlo Park, CA) presented by Dr. Martin Fackler, president of the International Wound Ballistics Association, at the annual meeting of the American Bar Association, San Francisco, CA, 1992.

Dale K. Myers, "The Secrets of a Homicide;" computer video reconstruction for Microtech (1995).

National Research Council report—"Reexamination of Acoustic Evidence in the Kennedy Assassination," by the Committee on Ballistic Acoustics, chaired by Prof. Norman Ramsey (1982), published in Science, vol. 218 (1982).

Nova, "Who Shot President Kennedy?'" *PBS,* November 15, 1988.

Alfred G. Olivier & Arthur J. Dziemian, "Wound Ballistics of 6.5mm Mannlicher Carcano Ammunition," U.S. Army Edgewood Arsenal, March, 1965.

Frank Scott, "Report of Autopsy Color Photograph's Authenticity," August 15, 1978, *HSCA* Vol. VII.

Todd Vaughn Report of Shooting Reconstruction, September 18, 1994 (unpublished).

The Warren Report; esp. 79-194, 547-592

Dr. Michael West (with Johann Rush and Dr. John Lattimer), "Nix Film Analysis," Itek Corporation, May 18, 1967, "The Shots Seen Round the World" video, and manuscript, 1992.

APPENDIX B

EYEWITNESSES

"Believing is Seeing."
—Dr. Jim Gray

The details of the shooting in Dealey Plaza have been argued about incessantly since the moment it occurred. The debate has often been personal and vitriolic. The basic points of contention are the same as would be brought to bear in a criminal prosecution. In any crime, the two key types of evidence used to convict a suspect are eyewitness testimony and physical evidence—suspects are often singled out by either linking them to the evidence, or by demonstrating that they possess "means, motive, and opportunity."

In the case of the president's murder, eyewitnesses' contradictory statements fueled the rumors of multiple shooters in Dealey Plaza, with some theories suggesting Oswald's complete innocence. These statements have often led the amateur investigator to make mistakes that a professional, familiar with the inherent peculiarities of eyewitness testimony, would have foreseen.

For many who have written about or researched the assassination, this is the only crime they have ever scrutinized. Those who evaluate evidence as a profession speak in virtual unison about the pitfalls of relying too heavily on eyewitnesses.

Eyewitnesses are most useful when they are numerous, and when the vast majority agree on the important details. In the case of President Kennedy's assassination, they do. The contradictions are produced by a distinct minority of the witnesses.

In 1993, author Gerald Posner conducted a thorough review of all the eyewitness testimony gathered by both the Warren Commission and the later House Select Committee on Assassinations, numbering almost two-hundred witnesses.[1] His work in this area was meticulous and definitive. It was also not well-received by those holding out for shots from other directions (especially the infamous "grassy knoll" located to Kennedy's right front). Here is what Posner discovered:

The number of shots:

- *88% of the witnesses heard three, and only three shots.*

- *Only 5% heard four or more.*

The origin of the shots (which is much more difficult to determine):

- *44% had no idea of the origin.*

- *28% thought the shots originated from the Book Depository.*

- *12% pointed to the grassy knoll area.*

- *Only 2% felt that the shots had more than one point of origin.*

The two percent view—actually four people who thought the two shots originated from two different spots—came to their point of view between the Warren Commission Report of 1964 and the House Select Committee research in 1978. None of them made such an assertion about a second gunman when they gave their original statements. Therefore, it must be considered that their perceptions and memory may have been "enhanced" by fourteen years of allegations by amateur investigators. This is further complicated by the phenomenon known as "memory merge," wherein memories of entirely different events are blurred together. Author Harrison Livingstone has written of "memory merge:"

> *During periods of great stress, in a crisis or emergency when events are unfolding with great rapidity—such as the events of November 22, 1963—the mind plays tricks and does not register each detail. Some events are imprinted in the brain and merge with others, missing connecting links....We think we saw something we did not.[2]*

Of the legal reference material available on the subject of eyewitness testimony, there is virtual unanimity on this issue: eyewitness testimony is fraught with difficulties, all of which must be taken into account before the testimony is accepted. This section merely scratches the surface of the subject. For the eyewitness testimony, the bottom line is: it is most likely accurate when taken immediately after the event, and when corroborated by other testimony. Experts point out the especially troubling accuracy rate of so-called "flashbulb memory." This refers to completely unexpected momentary occurrences—such as the Kennedy assassination.

One seeking to arrive at a better understanding of the phenomenon of "enhanced memory" and "flashbulb memory" might wish to consult (for example):

Loftus, Dr. Elizabeth. *Memory: Surprising New Insights Into How We Remember and How We Forget.* Reading, MA, Addison-Wesley, 1980.

Loftus, Dr. Elizabeth and James McBride. *Eyewitness Testimony: Civil and Criminal.* New York, Kluwer Law Books, 1987.

Loftus, Dr. Elizabeth and Katherine Ketcham. *The Myth of Repressed Memory.* New

York, St. Martin's, 1994.

———— *Witness for the Defense.* New York, St. Martin's, 1991.

Sobel, Nathan. *Eyewitness Identification: Legal and Practical Problems.* New York, Clark Boardman Co., 1972.

Wells, Gary L. and Amy L. Bradfield. "Good, You Identified the Suspect:" Feedback to Eyewitnesses Distorts Their Reports of the Witnessing Experience. *Journal of Applied Psychology,* June, 1998, Vol. 83, No. 3.

Yarmey, A. Daniel. *Psychology of Eyewitness Testimony.* New York, Free Press, 1979.

Attorneys Mark Zaid and Dennis Ford authored a 1993 monograph which summarized the legal and scientific communities' historic skepticism about the accuracy of eyewitness testimony, with specific emphasis on the Kennedy assassination. Entitled "Eyewitness Testimony, Memory, And Assassination Research," it relied heavily on the acknowledged expertise in this field of Elizabeth Loftus and Patrick Doyle.

JACK RUBY

"All I wanted to do was just be a hero, but it looks like I just fouled things up good."
—Jack Ruby to Dallas Detective Jim Leavelle, Nov 24, 1963

"After Oswald's death, we wanted to find out if there was any conspiracy involved, if there was a connection between Ruby and Oswald. We spent many, many, many man-hours running down every lead possible, and all proved futile. We were never at any time able to make any connection between Ruby and Oswald...and had to conclude there was none."
—Jim Leavelle, Dallas Homicide detective

Author's Note: During my research on Jack Ruby, I was fortunate to obtain three key sources of information, one of them never before disclosed. First was a rarely-heard tape of Ruby's "Deathbed Interview" with his rabbi, Hillel Silverman. The emotional interview was conducted just days before Ruby's death from cancer in January 1967.

Second, I was able to obtain over a dozen letters and notes Ruby wrote from his cell. Lastly, in conversations with Jack's brother Earl, I learned of a "Jailhouse Diary" Ruby kept during his three-year incarceration. The existence of this 100-page diary, written at Earl's urging, has never before been disclosed. Through an exclusive arrangement with collector Robert White, a current partial owner of the Jack Ruby estate, I was provided the original diary. Like the known statements of Ruby and his friends, these artifacts offer clear and consistent evidence of Ruby's motive for killing Oswald.

When an assassin is "taken out," as in the case of Lee Harvey Oswald, serious consideration has to be given to the possibility that the assassin's death was an attempt, by any remaining "conspirators," to silence him. This possibility must, of course, be balanced with the knowledge that high-profile killers occasionally inspire an otherwise uninvolved individual to seek revenge.

Abraham Lincoln's assassin was felled by an over-zealous Union soldier who felt it was his "calling" from God. Serial killer Jeffrey Dahmer was slain by a fellow inmate. However, Jack Ruby, like Oswald, led such a colorful life, at the fringes of "normalcy," that conspiratorial possibilities held more than a little potential.

Much has been made of Ruby's underworld acquaintances, leading some to claim proof of mob involvement in both Kennedy's and Oswald's murders. However, Ruby's true history, like Oswald's, has been turned inside out in order to make the mental leaps necessary to conclude that the mob was involved.

So who was Jack Ruby, and what was his motive? Recent interviews, combined with a newly-discovered journal Ruby kept in jail, give clear and consistent answers to these questions. To understand why Ruby was driven to kill Oswald, one must first comprehend Jack Ruby's manic-obsessive nature and his fierce temper. The key recipients of Ruby's obsessive love were Dallas, JFK, the police, and Judaism. These facets of Ruby's personality leave his friends and relatives in total agreement about why he shot Lee Oswald.

Who Was Jack Ruby?

Born in Chicago in 1911, Jacob Rubenstein (later changed to Jack Ruby) was an Orthodox Jew whose childhood eerily paralleled that of Lee Oswald. His father physically abused his mother, which led to their divorce when Jack was ten years old. This left him, like Oswald, at the mercy of his mother. Chicago social workers described Fanny Rubinstein as "disturbed" and "mentally deficient," words that conjure up the professionals' descriptions of Oswald's mother, Marguerite.

The Jewish Social Service Bureau knew Ruby (and family) well because it had been called in to deal with his truancy—again, like Oswald. The Bureau concluded that Fanny was "thoroughly inadequate in the further training of this boy." The courts thus placed Jack and his two brothers and one sister into a foster home. Fanny was eventually committed to a mental institution.[1]

Upon his release from the foster home, Ruby took to the streets, where he became known as a neighborhood tough guy who survived by his wits. An admirer and lifelong friend of champion boxer Barney Ross, Jack Ruby prided himself on his penchant for quickdraw fisticuffs. Ruby's temper was volatile and legendary, earning him the nickname "Sparky." Jack's younger brother, Earl, says of his infamous sibling, "He was always highly temperamental. You couldn't insult him. He got into a lot of fights. He would just stick up for his rights, like whenever anyone made derogatory remarks about the Jews, or when anybody insulted or annoyed our sisters."[2] Invariably, however, Ruby would soon calm down and render a heartfelt apology for his uncontrollable outbursts. Ruby's temper would escalate during his later years in Dallas.

In his younger years, Jack earned money by selling racing tip sheets, and, with his brother Earl, hawking novelty items such as medicinal snake oils, costume jewelry, vitamins, bottle openers, stainless steel razor blades, etc. Such a street-wise, seat-of-the-pants existence inevitably led to contact with the criminal element. For a time as a youngster, Jack "Sparky" Rubenstein even gained the acquaintance of infamous crime boss Al Capone. According to Ruby's life-long friend Barney Ross, Ruby and Ross were two of twelve teenagers to whom the mobster would pay a dollar "to run innocuous errands."[3] Ruby's actions were so innocuous, in fact, that he never incurred any major legal problems. And there is absolutely no evidence that Ruby attempted to parlay this association into an ascension up the ranks of organized crime.

After a brief attempt to succeed on the West Coast in the 1930's, Ruby returned to Chicago to try his hand at union organizing. Bill Roemer, a Chicago FBI agent and leader of the city's anti-crime effort, recently recalled, "We checked that union out. Ruby was nothing in that union. The mob came in and took it over later."

The takeover occurred after Ruby's friend, union secretary Leon Cooke, was murdered in self-defense by union president John Martin (acquitted of pre-med-itated murder at his trial). "It was a legitimate union when Jack was involved," says Jack's brother, Earl. "But the mob was pressuring the union all the time, and then they eventually grabbed control and forced Jack out...The mob came in and took control of the union after Cooke was killed."[4]

In the re-telling, the Cooke murder has become so distorted that Ruby somehow became involved in it—that it became his first "hired" assassination. In reality, Ruby's friendship with Cooke was so strong that when Ruby would later change his name legally to "Ruby," he added the middle name Leon, in honor of his friend.

In 1947, after military service during World War II, Ruby moved to Dallas and legally changed his name to "Jack Leon Ruby." Texas reporter Lonnie Hudkins says Ruby told him he was run out of Chicago after becoming an informant for the FBI. "He had to leave Chicago," claims Hudkins. Ruby was cer-tainly a P.C.I. (Potential Criminal Informant) for the FBI when he lived in Dallas. The FBI retains documentary proof of Bureau contact with him. Also, according to its records, the FBI assigned agent Charles Flynn as Ruby's case officer, who proceeded to contact Ruby on at least nine documented occasions.

Partnering with his sister, Eva, who had previously relocated to Dallas, Ruby now tried his hand at the nightclub business. Managing and owning "show-bars" would be Ruby's vocation until his arrest for the Oswald murder in 1963. With names like the Singapore, the Silver Spur, Bob Wills' Ranch House, the Vegas Club, the Sovereign, and finally, the Carousel, Ruby's clubs never man-aged to provide him the success and notoriety he craved. More often than not, his ventures led to bankruptcy. However, these failures failed to dampen his enthusiasm for a city which gave him numerous chances for a fresh start. As Ruby wrote in his "Jail Diary:"

> I loved Dallas so much, I would boast to people what a wonderful city this is...I used to boast about the skyline, about our master plan. I just know Dallas was going to be the most beautiful city in the world. This is the city that if you

wanted to sell anything at all, you could walk into a millionaire's office and they would listen to you.

Ruby called these times his "bucket of blood" days. Joe Cavagnaro, a later employee of Ruby, recalled, "I saw him hit a guy one night for taking advantage of a girl. He hit the guy clear across the sidewalk."[5] Ruby was known to deck patrons for merely putting their feet up on the tables. He was notorious for his hobby of throwing patrons down the stairs from his second-floor Carousel Club. Officer Joe Cody recalled, "Jack was a fighter, there was no question about that. We'd get a disturbance call down there and we'd just wait at the bottom of the stairs because in just a few minutes, whoever was creating the disturbance was gonna come falling down the stairs. He was pretty violent."[6] Wally Weston, Master-of-Ceremonies at the Carousel Club in the fall of 1963, said Ruby "did his own bouncing in the club. He didn't need anyone else."[7]

Ruby himself would often be injured in the altercations, but that only made him madder. He rendered one victim unconscious after realizing his opponent had inflicted a serious stab wound upon him. Once, when in a fistfight with club guitarist Willis "Dub" Dickerson, Jack threw a punch which came to rest on Dickerson's mouth. Dickerson proceeded to bite Ruby's index finger until it was mangled so badly that it had to be amputated. True to character, Ruby quickly forgot the fight, and remained Dickerson's friend.

Ruby's "Jail Diary" is a virtual paean to his pugilistic prowess. In it are numerous anecdotes of throwing people down the stairs, or dismantling an entire gang with a baseball bat in defending the honor of a woman he didn't even know. There are repeated tales of knocking out someone's teeth with his pistol, or with monogrammed brass knuckles. He would seize upon the slightest excuse to "mix it up" with someone. As he wrote:

Once, when some smart aleck came to the door and tried to give me a hard time, and I tried to be very pleasant to him, and he was becoming all the more belligerant [sic], and I finally had to hit him and knocked some of his teeth out.

One nite a fellow got into a hassle with our comedian Wally Weston, and Wally threw a punch at him, and the fellow said some remark about Wally to go to Russia. Anyway, I picked him up and bodily threw him down the stairs.

One evening some fellow had broken a beer bottle over this man's head and it just made me sick, and I hit this other fellow with my pistol and he went down. They both pleaded with me that they would never come back if I would just let them go.

The fights in the club escalated to such a point that Ruby soon decided to carry a pistol. After that, he almost always was "packing heat." He wrote:

Some drunk tried to throw a heavy wooden chair at me. I decided in time to save my life and I started to hit him and beat him up—close to death. I then realized how important it was for me to always have my pistol on me if I wanted to stay alive.

"Jack carried quite a bit of money around in his pocket, twenty-five hundred, three-thousand dollars," remembers Ruby's friend, Dallas policeman Joe Cody. "He wanted a safe to start with and I explained to him the safe was gonna cost him three or four thousand dollars. He said, 'I can't afford it.' I said, 'Well, why don't you get a gun?' And so we went to Ray Brantly's hardware store, looked all the guns over, and he said, 'I don't know what to get.' I told him I carried a Colt Cobra. He said, 'That'll be fine.' So we bought the Cobra. I never saw it again until on television."[8]

Ruby's tenure in Dallas was highlighted by his affection not only for policeman Joe Cody, but for all his brethren on the Dallas Police force. With free drinks and other "courtesies" provided the men in blue, Ruby's clubs became a favorite cop hangout. "He was a stickler for the law," remembered Bob Larkin, an employee at Ruby's Vegas Club. "He thought of himself as a kind of cop."[9]

Another Ruby friend, reporter Lonnie Hudkins, testified that Ruby had been issued a card by Justice of the Peace Glen Bird, which read, "The Bearer is an honorary Deputy Justice of the Peace."[10] Ruby's friend, Dallas Police Deputy Al Maddox, recalls his friend fondly, saying, "Jack was always very hospitable to us [the Dallas Police]. There was always plenty of liquor, dancing girls, or anything else if Jack Ruby knew that you were a law enforcement officer...He always thought it may help him in case he got fined or got into jail—that we'd be able to help him, and we probably would have."[11]

Ruby's civic interests extended far beyond the boundaries of Dallas. He became fascinated with U.S. presidents after the Japanese attack on Pearl Harbor (in 1941). From that point on, Ruby became a fierce, sometimes violent, defender of the nation's highest office. One of his business ventures included selling busts of Franklin Delano Roosevelt, whose death (in 1945) had caused Ruby to weep. Ruby's younger brother Earl recalled, "He had fights about Roosevelt, even Eisenhower, later on."[12] In the diary, he writes: "It's a terrible feeling one has knowing you had such a great love for your country and your president, and that someone can frame you and completely reverse that."

Ruby was nothing if not a manic personality who saw the world of politics in black and white. It was the white knights of the Oval Office versus "those lousy commies." And those who knew him best have no doubt who was Ruby's main knight—John F. Kennedy.

Jack Ruby's sister, Eva Grant, testified that "one of the things he loved about this President, he didn't care what you were, you were a human being and Jack felt that this was one time in history that Jews are getting the break. He [Kennedy] put great Jewish men in office."[13]

On the night before the assassination, Ruby jumped to the stage of the Carousel Club, demonstrating his newest get-rich idea, the "twist board." Ruby told his audience, "Even President Kennedy tells us to get more exercise." When a heckler yelled out, "That bum!" Ruby screamed. "Don't ever talk that way about the President."[14]

Wally Weston recalls a similar Ruby anecdote reflecting his high opinion of

President Kennedy: one morning, Ruby got the idea that he could promote his club by getting one of his stars to become the first person in Dallas to answer JFK's call to participate in 50-mile walks. Showing up unannounced at Weston's apartment, Ruby directed Weston to get dressed. The last piece of clothing Weston donned were his rigid leather performing shoes. Ruby proceeded to drive Weston 50 miles outside of town, whereupon he informed him of his patriotic walking mission. Ruby then drove back to Dallas. That night, having successfully completed his walk, Weston performed at Ruby's club, sitting down, with his swollen feet in a bucket of ice. He retains photos of that performance to this day.

Weston well-remembers Ruby reading the riot act to comics who made anti-Kennedy or other unpatriotic jokes. In his diary, Ruby wrote: "I tried to correct Wally [Weston] on some things he said about our President." Once, when Ruby, a rabid anti-communist, saw an acquaintance with some right-wing literature, he grabbed the material away, saying, "I'm going to send this stuff to Kennedy. Nobody has the right to talk like this about our government."[15] (The literature, from oil millionaire H.L. Hunt's propaganda mill, was found in Ruby's trunk after he killed Oswald. In a typical truth-reversal, some critics used this to link Ruby with JFK's right-wing haters.)

Dozens of Ruby's friends and relatives testified, as with one voice, that when Kennedy was killed, Jack Ruby was devastated. They described him as sobbing uncontrollably all weekend. Using words like "incoherent," "deeply disturbed," and "emotionally devastated," one might guess that they were describing a member of Kennedy's immediate family (who ironically appeared stoic and controlled). Many said it was the first time they had ever seen him cry. Jack's brother Hyman testified about Ruby's loud weeping at his synagogue the day after the assassination: "They didn't believe a guy like Jack would ever cry. Jack never cried in his life. He is not that kind of guy to cry."[16] Ruby told his sister Eva Grant that "I never felt so bad in my life, even when Ma and Pa died...Someone tore my heart out."

Ruby's attorney Phil Burleson remembers that Ruby admired Kennedy, not only as a leader but as a father of young children. According to Burleson, Ruby felt that "Oswald didn't just kill the President, he killed the father of the First Family."[17]

Joe Cavagnaro, a Ruby employee at the Vegas Club, recalled Ruby in the wake of the assassination: "He felt very remorseful for Mrs. Kennedy and the family. He carried on like you would if it were your own cousin or brother." (Later, in jail, Ruby sobbed on the phone to Tony Zoppi, "Those poor kids, without a father. I grew up without a father." In that same jail, Ruby kept a picture of President Kennedy, which he kissed daily.) In jail, two weeks after killing Oswald, Ruby wrote a friend, saying, "I loved my President and was in such deep mourning about his tragic passing."[18] Further, in his jail diary he wrote:

Saturday morning before I left the house, I watched television and they had a prayer service for the President. And Rabbi Silverman was speaking [about]

how the President was so courageous and fearless and fought every adver-
sary—and to have someone shoot him from behind, this broke what little
pieces were left of my heart.

Kennedy's death clearly put Ruby over the edge. From the moment Oswald was arrested until the day Jack Ruby died three years later, Ruby referred to Lee Oswald as "that lousy Commie." Disconsolate over what Oswald had done to the Kennedy family, Ruby called his old Chicago friend, Lawrence Meyers, and said, "Those poor people, I have got to do something about it."

It would later be learned that Ruby, who spent much of the assassination's tragic weekend at police headquarters, had decided that if the opportunity presented itself, he would heal the nation with his ever-present pistol. After he was arrested, Ruby spoke candidly with another police friend, Detective Jim Leavelle, who remembers, "Jack said he'd thought about it from Friday night on."[19] Ruby made a similar admission to *Look* magazine writer T. George Harris. "In fact, he attempted to get a shot off Saturday night in the hall of Justice, but we [the press] were blocking him," says Harris.[20] Ruby said much the same to Lonnie Hudkins, when he told the Houston reporter before his trial, "I was afraid of hitting one of you guys."[21]

Although Ruby stalked Oswald all weekend, his first opportunity for a clear shot arrived when he least expected it. Just after 11 a.m. on Sunday morning, Ruby drove past the City Police station on his way to the Western Union office, located one block east of the station. Because Oswald's transfer to the County jail had been slated for 10 a.m., Ruby may have abandoned his vendetta, assuming Oswald to now be in the more secure county lockup.

Ruby later told police, "When I passed the station, I looked down the ramp to my right and saw a lot of people down in the basement. So when I finished with Western [Union], I walked west and down the ramp just out of curiosity."[22] ATF agent Frank Ellsworth remembers, "Jack had walked up and down that ramp two or three times a day for years. He practically lived at the police station. He was a police nut."[23] In Ruby's "deathbed tape," he testifies:

The ironic part is this—hadn't I made an illegal turn behind the bus to the
parking lot—had I gone the way I was supposed to go, straight down Main
street, I would never have met this fate. Because the difference in meeting this
fate was 30 seconds one way or the other...So I walked down the ramp. I
noticed a police squad car at the head of the ramp, and an officer leaning over
talking to him with his back to me. All I did was walk down there—down to
the bottom of the ramp, and that's when the incident happened, at the bottom
of the ramp.

At his trial, Ruby testified that Oswald "came out [into the police basement] all of a sudden, with a smirky, defiant, cursing, vicious, communist expression on his face. I can't convey what impression he gave me. I lost my senses."[24]

"You rat, sonofabitch! You shot the President!" Ruby screamed as he got off a shot.[25] Before he could get off another, Ruby was wrestled to the ground and dragged to a holding room. On the way, Ruby yelled, "I hope I killed the sonofabitch! I hope I killed the sonofabitch!"[26] Dallas Police Detective D. R. Archer said to Ruby, "Jack, I think you killed him." To which Ruby responded, "I intended to shoot him three times."[27] In his jail diary, he wrote: "No one felt as indebted to this city as I. It has been so good to me. I guess I owed more to Dallas than anyone. My heart was broken. I was so proud of Dallas."

When Jim Leavelle spoke with Ruby immediately after the shooting, Ruby's bravado had been muted by the reality that had set in. Realizing that he had now prevented authorities from learning if Oswald had accomplices, Ruby told Leavelle, "All I wanted to do was just be a hero, but it looks like I just fouled things up good." (A similar realization was voiced a century earlier, when Lincoln's assassin, John Wilkes Booth, realized he had done more harm than good to the South's cause.)

Later, this statement started Leavelle thinking about an incident with Ruby thirteen years prior. "I was in Jack's Silver Spur Club," remembered Leavelle, "and while talking to him he made the statement that he always wanted to see two police officers in a life and death struggle, about to lose their life, so he could jump in there and save them. So it made him truthful to me when he said, 'All I want to do is be a hero.'"[28]

After his incarceration, Ruby's visitors found him to be the least bit repentant. To Joe Campisi, Ruby bragged, "Well, Jews have got class. Nobody but me could do it...Somebody had to kill him."[29] To Carousel comic Breck Wall: "I was right to kill Oswald." To Tony Zoppi of the *Dallas Morning News*, Ruby said he did it to prove that "Jews have balls."[30]

He reiterated this theme to his Carousel Club M.C., Wally Weston. On Weston's first visit to Ruby in jail, Ruby greeted him with these words, "I've got balls, ain't I baby?" "Yeah, Jack," Weston replied, "and they're going to hang you by them too." Weston, who of course knew Ruby well, was utterly convinced that his boss acted on personal motives alone: his intense desire to be a hero. "He wanted everybody to know that Jewish guys had guts," remembers Weston. "That was what it was all about—'I've got balls and that's it.'"[31]

Dallas Policeman Elmo Cunningham knows what Ruby may have concluded in making his murderous decision: "In those days in Texas, a murderer could have expected two to ten years, with time off for good behavior."[32] Indeed, Carousel Club bartender Andrew Armstrong, after visiting Ruby in jail, said, "Jack talked as if it would be no time before he was back running things."[33] An attorney friend of Ruby, Jim Martin, added, "He never expected to spend a night in jail." In fact, Ruby's lawyer, Tom Howard, was even granted a writ for Ruby's release on bond. When [D.A.] Bill Alexander heard this, he "hit the roof" and immediately had it changed to a "dry writ"—one that demands a hearing before a prisoner can be let out.[34]

Ruby's first lawyer was Tom Howard, who often defended pimps and prostitutes, but had the rare distinction of never having lost a capital case to D.A. Henry Wade.[35] Wade was prosecuting the Ruby case, and had a legendary reputation in Dallas for securing convictions. The convicted men were known as

"the Wade Parade," as one local journalist put it, adding, "Henry sent more people to the electric chair than even Tom Dewey."

If Ruby had calculated he would serve a short term, it was a reasonable
deduction. In Texas, there existed a "murder without malice" charge that could
have been applied to a person as emotionally wrung-out as Ruby. It carried a
maximum five-year sentence. However, Ruby made a fatal miscalculation, firing
Howard and replacing him with the high-profile attorney Melvin Belli. Belli
refused to defend Ruby on the grounds that he had temporarily "lost it."
Instead, he tried to convince the jury that Ruby was clinically insane. Taking
advantage of Belli's flawed strategy, Wade soon won his familiar electric-chair
conviction against Jack Ruby.

"Belli took a good five-year murder-without-malice case and made it into a
death penalty for his client," recalls former Dallas Assistant D.A. Bill Alexander.
"He put on this God-awful defense...Instead of Jack's being a hero, Belli was
bringing out all this stuff about Jack's mother being in the insane asylum and
how Jack himself was sick. [Ruby] just wanted to get on the stand and say, 'I
shot the guy because he killed my President,' but Belli hacked away at his family in public. It was humiliating for Ruby. I actually felt sorry for him. It took
away whatever dignity he had left."[36]

In March 1964, after he was convicted and sentenced to death, Jack Ruby's
already delicate mental state deteriorated rapidly. He now saw conspiracies
everywhere. But they weren't conspiracies against Kennedy. They were directed
at the Jews.

Earl Warren, Chairman of the Warren Commission, visited Ruby in jail
when the Commission was in Dallas gathering evidence. Warren found Ruby to
be in bad mental shape. "The fellow was clearly delusional when I talked to him.
He took me aside and said, 'Hear those voices? Hear those voices?' He thought
there were Jewish children and Jewish women who were being put to death in
the building there."[37] He mentioned as much to his sister Eva Grant, saying, "25
million Jews have been slaughtered on the floor below." His jailers remember
Ruby placing his ears to the jail wall, whispering to them, "Shhh! Do you hear
their screams? They are torturing the Jews again down in the basement."[38]

Ruby begged Warren—and repeated his plea at least eight times, in and out
of Warren's presence—to take him to Washington so he could tell him the truth.

*I may not live tomorrow to give any further testimony...I can't say it here...It
can't be said here...Gentlemen, if you want to hear any further testimony, you
will have to get me to Washington soon...I want to tell the truth and I can't
tell it here...Gentlemen, unless you get me to Washington, you can't get a fair
shake out of me.[39]*

An early proponent of conspiracy theories—his treatment of Ruby's testimony to Chief Justice Warren has been called "a surgical masterpiece"—offered
this as evidence that Ruby killed Oswald in furtherance of a conspiracy. Now,
the theory went, Ruby could not tell the truth about the "conspiracy" because
he too would be killed by an agent of the other "conspirators."

This theory conveniently ignores the context of Ruby's remarks. Ruby did use the word "conspiracy" in his ramblings—but what he was talking about was a conspiracy against the Jews. He imagined Dallasites believing there to be a Jewish conspiracy to kill President Kennedy. He was trying to say that there was no such Jewish conspiracy—the only conspiracy was the one to frame the Jews for Kennedy's death. Ruby feared talking in Dallas because he was obsessed by thoughts of this alleged Jewish persecution. His paranoia drove him to talk and write frequently of pogroms, genocide, and another holocaust. Specifically, he feared that unless he was present in Washington, his fears about Jewish persecution would not be entered into the record.

Ruby clearly thought that, by killing Oswald, he was doing everyone a favor, and would be treated as a hero. In fact, he was not far from wrong. Certainly many in Dallas, if not the rest of the world, despised Oswald. Max Rudberg, a bail bondsman friend of Ruby, remembered, "Everyone was saying, 'The sonofabitch needs killing,' and Jack was anxious to please."[40]

Detective Jim Leavelle echoes this sentiment, recalling, "I had a lot of people tell me, 'Oh, if I could have got to him on Friday, my anger was such that I would have killed him without looking back.' There's a lot of people that felt that way."

Even the wife of Supreme Court Justice William O. Douglas exclaimed when Oswald was shot, "Good! Give it to him again!"[41] As Ruby's sister Eva Grant says, "Millions of red-blooded Americans wanted to kill Oswald. Jack was there. That's all."[42]

Wally Weston, Ruby's frequent jail cell visitor, recalled, "Jack wanted everybody to know that he did it, and he had the guts to do what everybody in Dallas probably wanted to do, including myself."[43]

After his arrest, Ruby's police friends predictably gave him the best possible treatment. He was given two jail cells for his comfort, with meals often sent in from the outside. Regarding his overlarge cell, Ruby friend and Dallas Police Deputy Al Maddox says, "I don't even know that it was ever locked."[44]

Despite this mountain of consistent testimony and evidence, some critics postulate that Jack Ruby was a cold-blooded Mafia assassin. Casting aside Ruby's stated motive, this scenario ignores the larger subject: the modus operandi of crime figures. Many Mafia experts have disputed the logic of letting Oswald live two days before shooting him. Most agree that if it had been a mob conspiracy, Oswald would not have left the Book Depository alive. And if that opportunity had been missed, another one later on Friday would never have been passed up.[45]

Downplayed by the Warren Commission was the fact that Ruby had an acquaintanceship with some shady characters linked to organized crime. However, for this mob hit scenario to play out in actuality, Ruby necessarily would have needed direct, meaningful contact with organized criminals, and they in turn needed to be linked to Oswald—this kind of speculation blithely assumes that organized crime was linked to Oswald, and thus had a need to eliminate him. Those linkages have never been made. The fact is that for every witness who claims that Ruby had direct contact with the Mafia, there are hundreds who know that to be an absurdity.

But the critics parlayed the "he-knew-somebody-who-knew-somebody" catch-all to show Ruby involved in a conspiracy. If that kind of logic carried legal weight, virtually everyone would be involved in conspiracies on a daily basis.

One of the so-called "connected" people close to Ruby was professional gambler Lewis McWillie, who had close ties to numerous underworld figures, especially Santos Trafficante, from his days as a pre-Castro casino operator in Havana. On one occasion, in late 1959, Ruby travelled to Havana to visit McWillie. Ruby later passed polygraph tests, stating that the excursion was merely a pleasure trip. No evidence to the contrary has ever surfaced.

After the assassination, testimony from Ruby's associates indicated that he had sent guns to Havana, via McWillie. Thus began the legend of "Ruby the gunrunner," sending weapons to Cuban haters of JFK. Once again, the truth is far different. In a letter Ruby wrote from jail, he explained:

What happened was that a friend of mine by the name of McWillie called from Havana, Cuba in 1959—that was during peace negotiations with Cuba—and we really hadn't found out what kind of person Castro was. What this Mr. McWillie wanted me to do was to call a Ray Brantly of Ray's Hardware, and Mac wanted him to send four Cobra pistols to him, and all I did was relay the message. Mac wanted these guns because he was managing the gambling casino and wanted some protection for himself, and his wife, and that was all I had to do with it.

Those who actually knew Ruby during his Dallas period know that he was never a mob functionary. Ruby's close friend, officer Joe Cody, who purchased Jack's pistol for him, remembers, "My partner and I would go down to his club every night when we got off and, to my knowledge, I have never seen Jack Ruby associate with any members of organized crime or anything."[46] Another Ruby friend, Detective Jim Leavelle, suggests that "Ruby was a name-dropper. The mob would never hire him—he had such a loud mouth."[47] ATF agent Frank Ellsworth, who knew Ruby well, concludes, "the mob wouldn't have hired Jack Ruby to be a janitor."[48]

Dallas Police Detective Elmo Cunningham summed up his friend, Ruby, this way: "Jack loved Dallas. It was the center of his universe. After two days of watching his idols being pilloried—Dallas, the cops, the Jews, and his President—he just lost it."[49]

Perhaps Ruby himself deserves the last word. In 1966, nearing death from cancer, Ruby spoke to his rabbi from a hospital bed in what amounted to a deathbed-taped confession.[50] In a shaky voice, the dying man said again, as he had from the first, that he had not been part of any conspiracy. "It all happened," he said, "because I was so emotionally upset."

BIBLIOGRAPHY

Books and Journals

Abel, Elie. *The Missile Crisis*. Philadelphia: J.B. Lippincott, 1966.

Adelson, Alan. *The Ruby-Oswald Affair*. Seattle: Romar Books, 1988

Agee, Phillip. *CIA Diary: Inside The Company*. New York: Bantam, 1975.

Ambrose, Stephen E. *Ike's Spies: Eisenhower and the Espionage Establishment*. New York: Doubleday, 1981.

———. *Eisenhower. Vol. 2*. New York: Simon & Schuster, 1984.

Andrew, Christopher. *For the President's Eyes Only: Secret Intelligence and the American Presidency from Washington to Bush*. New York: HarperCollins, 1995.

Artime, Judith. *"The Golden Boy."* Thesis, September, 1996.

Ashman, Charles. *The CIA-Mafia Link*. New York: Manor Books, 1975.

Attwood, William. *The Twilight Struggle*. New York: Harper & Row, 1987.

Ayers, Bradley Earl. *The War That Never Was*. New York: Bobbs-Merrill, 1975.

Badeaux, Hubert J. *The Underworld of Sex*. New Orleans: The Herald Press, 1959.

Baden, Dr. Michael. *Unnatural Death: Confessions of a Medical Examiner*. New York: Random House, 1989.

Bain, Donald. *The Control of Candy Jones*. Chicago: Playboy Press, 1976.

Bakatin, Vadim. *Izbavlenie ot KGB*. Moskva: Novosti, 1992.

Baker, Bobby. *Wheeling and Dealing*. New York: W.W. Norton, 1978.

Bamford, James. *The Puzzle Palace: Inside the National Security Agency*. Boston: Houghton Mifflin, 1982.

Baughman, U.E. *Secret Service Chief*. New York: Harper, 1962.

Beck, Melvin. *Secret Contenders*. New York: Sheridan Square, 1984.

Belin, David. *Final Disclosure*. New York: Scribner's, 1988.

———. November 22: *You Are the Jury*. New York: Quadrangle, 1973.

Bennett, Arnold. Jackie, *Bobby, and Manchester*. New York: Bee-Line, 1967.

Beschloss, Michael R. *Taking Charge: The Johnson White House Tapes 1963-1964*. New York: Simon & Schuster, 1997.

———. *The Crisis Years: Kennedy and Khrushchev, 1960-1963*. New York: HarperCollins, 1991.

———. *Mayday: Eisenhower, Khrushchev, and the U-2 Affair*. New York: Harper & Row, 1986.

Bird, Kai. *The Chairman*. New York: Simon & Schuster, 1992.

Bishop, Jim. *The Day Kennedy Was Shot*. New York: Random House, 1968.

Bissell, Richard M. *Reflections of a Cold Warrior*. New Haven: Yale University Press, 1996.

Blakey, Robert G. and Richard Billings. *The Plot to Kill The President*. New York: Times Books, 1981.

Blight, James, and David Welch. *On the Brink: Americans and Soviets Reexamine the Cuban Missile Crisis*. New York: Hill & Wang, 1989.

———— and Peter Kornbluh, eds. *Politics of Illusion: The Bay of Pigs Invasion Reexamined.* Boulder: Lynne Rienner, 1998.

Blum, William. *CIA: A Forgotten History.* London: Zed Books, 1986.

Blumenthal, Sid, and Harvey Yazijian, eds. *Government by Gunplay.* New York: New American Library, 1976.

Bonsal, Philip. *Cuba, Castro, and the United States.* Pittsburgh: University of Pittsburgh Press, 1971.

Bowart, W.H. *Operation Mind Control.* New York: Dell, 1978.

Bradlee, Ben. *Conversations With Kennedy.* New York: W. W. Norton, 1975.

Brashier, William. *The Don: The Life and Death of Sam Giancana.* New York: Harper & Row, 1977.

Brener, Milton E. *The Garrison Case: A Study in the Abuse of Power.* New York: Potter, 1969.

Brennan, Howard, and J. Edward Cherryholmes. *Eyewitness to History.* Waco, TX: Texian Press, 1987.

Breuer, William B. *Vendetta: Castro and the Kennedy Brothers.* New York: John Wiley. 1997.

Brill, Steven. *The Teamsters.* New York: Simon & Schuster, 1978.

Bringuier, Carlos J. *Operacion Judas.* Miami: Ediciones Universal, 1993.

————. *Red Friday: Nov 22, 1963.* Chicago: Chas. Hallberg, 1969.

Broadwater, Jeff. *Eisenhower and the Anti-Communist Crusade.* Chapel Hill: University of North Carolina Press, 1992.

Brown, Madeleine. *Texas in the Morning.* Dallas: 1991 (reviewed as an unpublished manuscript, and later published).

Brownstein, Ronald. *The Power and The Glitter: The Hollywood-Washington Connection.* New York: Pantheon, 1990.

Brugioni, Dino A. *Eyeball to Eyeball: The Inside Story of the Cuban Missile Crisis.* New York: Random House, 1991.

Burke, Richard E. *The Senator: My Twelve Years With Ted Kennedy.* New York: St. Martin's Press, 1992.

Califano, Joseph A., Jr. *The Triumph and Tragedy of Lyndon Johnson.* New York: Simon & Schuster, 1991.

Carbonell, Néstor T. *And the Russians Stayed: The Sovietization of Cuba.* New York: William Morrow, 1989.

Carillo, Justo. *A Cuba Le Toco Perder.* Unpublished, no date.

Caro, Robert A. *The Years of Lyndon Johnson: The Path to Power.* New York: Knopf, 1982.

————. *The Years of Lyndon Johnson: Means of Ascent.* New York: Knopf, 1990.

Carpenter, Arthur E. *"Social Origins of Anti-Communism: The Information Council of the Americas."* Louisiana History Quarterly 30 (spring, 1989): 117.

Chang, Laurence, and Peter Kornbluth, eds. *The Cuban Missile Crisis: 1962.* New York: The New Press, 1992.

Chomsky, Noam. *Rethinking Camelot.* Boston: South End Press, 1993.

Church, F. Forrester. *Father and Son.* Boston: Faber and Faber, 1985.

Clifford, Clark, with Richard Holbrooke. *Counsel to the President.* New York: Random House, 1991.

Colby, Gerard, and Charlotte Dennett. *Thy Will Be Done: The Conquest of the Amazon.* New York: HarperCollins, 1995.

Collier, Peter and David Horowitz. *The Kennedys, An American Drama.* New York: Warner Books, 1985.

Connally, John. *In History's Shadow.* New York: Hyperion, 1993.

Cook, Blanche Wiesen. *The Declassified Eisenhower: A Divided Legacy.* New York:

Doubleday & Co., 1981.

Cooney, John. *The American Pope: The Life and Times of Francis Cardinal Spellman.* New York: Times Books, 1984.

Corn, David. *Blond Ghost.* New York: Simon & Schuster, 1994.

Corson, William R., Susan B. Trento, and Joseph J. Trento. *Widows.* New York: Crown, 1989.

Cray, Ed. *Chief Justice: A Biography of Earl Warren.* New York: Simon & Schuster, 1997.

Currey, Cecil B. Edward Lansdale: *The Unquiet American.* Boston: Houghton Mifflin, 1988.

Curry, Jesse. *The JFK Assassination File.* Dallas: American Poster, 1969.

Dargo, George. *Jefferson's Louisiana.* Boston: Harvard University Press, 1975.

David, Lester and Irene David. *Bobby Kennedy, The Making of a Folk Hero.* New York: Dodd, Mead & Co., 1986.

Davis, John H. *Mafia Kingfish.* New York: New American Library, 1989.

———. *The Kennedys: Dynasty and Disaster.* New York: S.P.I., 1992.

Davison, Jean. *Oswald's Game.* New York: W.W. Norton, 1983.

Dawkins, Richard. *The Selfish Gene.* Oxford: Oxford University Press, 1976.

Demaris, Ovid. *Captive City: Chicago in Chains.* New York: Lyle Stuart, 1969.

———. *The Last Mafioso: Jimmy "The Weasel" Fratianno.* New York: Times Books, 1981.

Dever, Joseph. *Cushing of Boston: A Candid Portrait.* Boston: Bruce Humphries, 1965.

de Toledano, Ralph. *R.F.K.: The Man Who Would Be President.* New York: G.P. Putnam's Sons, 1967.

Dinges, John. *Our Man in Panama.* New York: Random House, 1990.

Divine, Robert A., ed. *The Cuban Missile Crisis.* New York: Markus Wiener, 1988.

Dorman, Michael. *Payoff: The Role of Organized Crime in American Politics.* New York: Berkley, 1972.

———. *Vesco: The Infernal Money Making Machine.* New York: Berkley Books, no date.

Drosnin, Michael. *Citizen Hughes.* New York: Holt, Rinehart and Winston, 1985.

Dulles, Allen. *The Craft of Intelligence.* New York: Harper & Row, 1965.

Eisenberg, Dennis, Yri Dan, and Eli Landau. *Meyer Lansky, Mogul of the Mob.* New York: Paddington Press, 1979.

Epstein, Edward Jay. *Counterplot: The Assassination Chronicles.* New York: Carroll & Graf, 1992.

———. *Inquest: The Assassination Chronicles.* New York: Carroll & Graf, 1992.

———. *Legend: The Assassination Chronicles.* New York: Carroll & Graf, 1992.

Estes, Pam. *Billie Sol: King ot the Texas Wheeler-Dealers.* Abilene, Tex.: Noble Craft, 1983.

Exner, Judith and Ovid Demaris. *Judith Exner: My Story.* New York: Grove Press, 1978.

Fay, Paul B., Jr. *The Pleasure of His Company.* New York: Harper & Row, 1966.

Fensterwald, Bernard, Jr., and Michael Ewing. *Coincidence or Conspiracy.* New York: Zebra Books, 1977.

Fermoselle, Rafel. *Cuban Leadership After Castro: Biographies of Cuba's Top Commanders.* Miami: Institute of Interamerican Studies, University of Miami, 1987.

Fite, Gilbert C. *Richard B. Russell, Jr.: Senator From Georgia.* Chapel Hill: University of North Carolina Press, 1991.

Fitzgerald, Ray. *"Uncle Joe—Senators' Cuban Connection."* The Sporting News, 21 June 1980.

Flammonde, Paris. *The Kennedy Conspiracy.* New York: Meredith Press, 1969.

Flitner, Jr., David. *The Politics of Presidential Commissions.* Dobbs Ferry, NY: Transnational Pub., 1986.

Fonzi, Gaeton. *The Last Investigation.* New York: Thunder's Mouth Press, 1993.

Ford, Gerald and John Stiles. *Portrait of the Assassin*. New York: Simon & Schuster, 1965.

Franco, Joseph, and Richard Hammer. *Hoffa's Man*. New York: Dell, 1987.

Franklin, Jane. *Cuba and the United States: A Chronological History*. Melbourne: Ocean Press, 1997.

Friedman, Allen, and Ted Schwarz. *Power and Greed: Inside the Teamsters Empire of Corruption*. New York: Watts, 1989.

Furati, Claudia. ZR RIFLE: *The Plot to Kill Kennedy and Castro*. Havana: Ocean Press, 1994.

Fursenko, Aleksandr and Timothy Naftali, *"One hell of a gamble": Khrushchev, Castro, and Kennedy, 1958-1964*, New York: W.W. Norton, 1997.

Gage, Nicholas. *Mafia, USA*. Chicago: Playboy, 1972.

Gannon, Robert I. *The Cardinal Spellman Story*. New York: Doubleday, 1962.

Garrison, Jim. *On the Trail of the Assassins*. New York: Sheridan Square,1988.

———. *A Heritage of Stone*. New York: Berkley, 1970.

Garwood, Darrell. *Under Cover: Thirty-Five Years of CIA Deception*. Stafford, VA: Dan River Press, 1980.

Gentry, Curt, J. *Edgar Hoover: The Man and the Secrets*. New York: Plume, 1992.

Geyer, Georgie Anne. *Guerrilla Prince: The Untold Story of Fidel Castro*. Boston: Little Brown, 1991.

Giancana, Antoinette and Thomas Renner. *Mafia Princess: Growing Up in Sam Giancana's Family*. New York: William Morrow & Co., 1984.

Giancana, Sam and Chuck Giancana. *Double Cross: The Explosive, Inside Story of the Mobster who Controlled America*. New York: Warner Books, 1992.

Goodwin, Doris Kearns. *The FitzGeralds and the Kennedys*. New York: Simon & Schuster, 1987.

———. *Lyndon Johnson and the American Dream*. New York: Harper & Row, 1976.

Goodwin, Richard. *Remembering America: A Voice From the Sixties*. Boston: Little Brown, 1988.

Graham, Allison. *Essence of Decision*. Boston: Little Brown, 1971.

Groden, Robert. *The Killing of a President*. New York: Viking Studio Books, 1994.

Grose, Peter. *Gentleman Spy: The Life of Allen Dulles*. New York: Houghton Mifflin, 1994.

Guthman, Edwin. *We Band of Brothers*. New York: Harper & Row, 1971.

——— and Jeffrey Shulman (ed.). *Robert Kennedy: In His Own Words*. New York: Bantam Books, 1988.

Gulley, Bill and Mary Ellen Reese. *Breaking Cover*. New York: Simon & Schuster, 1980.

Haas, Edward F. DeLesseps S. *Morrison and The Image of Reform*. New Orleans: Louisiana State University Press, 1974.

Haig, Alexander M., Jr. *Inner Circles: How America Changed the World*. New York: Warner Books, 1992.

Halberstam, David. *The Best and the Brightest*. New York: Random House, 1969.

Haldeman, H.R., with Joseph DiMona. *The Ends of Power*. New York: Times Books, 1978.

———. *The Haldeman Diaries: Inside the Nixon White House*. New York: Putnam, 1994.

Hamilton, Nigel. *JFK: Reckless Youth*. New York: Random House, 1992.

Hammer, Ellen J. *A Death in November: America in Vietnam, 1963*. Oxford: Oxford University Press, 1989.

Hartogs, Renatus and Lucy Freeman. *The Two Assassins*. New York: Crowell, 1965.

Hellerman, Michael and Thomas C. Renner. *Wall Street Swindler*. New York: Doubleday, 1977.

Henggeler, Paul R. *In His Steps: Lyndon Johnson and the Kennedy Mystique.* Chicago: Ivan R. Dee, 1991.

Hepburn, James [pseud.]. *Farewell America.* Vaduz, Liechtenstein: Frontiers, 1968.

Hersh, Burton. *The Old Boys: The American Elite and the Origins of the CIA.* New York: Scribner's, 1992.

Hersh, Seymour. *The Dark Side of Camelot.* New York: Little Brown, 1997.

Heymann, C. David. *A Woman Named Jackie.* New York: Signet, 1989.

Hidalgo, Barney. *Hey Spic.* Baltimore: American Literary Press, 1997.

Higgins, Trumball. *The Perfect Failure: Kennedy, Eisenhower, and the CIA at the Bay of Pigs.* New York: W.W. Norton, 1987.

Hinckle, Warren. *If You Have a Lemon, Make Lemonade.* New York: G.P. Putnam's Sons, 1973.

——— and William Turner. *Deadly Secrets: The CIA-Mafia War Against Castro and the Assassination of J.F.K.* (previously published as *The Fish is Red*) New York: Thunder's Mouth Press, 1992.

Hine, Thomas. *Populuxe.* New York: Knopf, 1986.

Horne, Alistair. *Harold MacMillan. Vol. 2, 1957-1986.* New York: Viking, 1989.

Hougan, Jim. *Spooks.* New York: Morrow, 1978.

———. *Secret Agenda.* New York: Ballantine, 1984.

Hubbell, Webb. *Friends in High Places.* New York: Morrow, 1997.

Hurst, Lewis. *The Sweetest Little Club in the World: The U.S. Senate.* Englewood Cliffs, NJ: Prentice-Hall, 1980.

Hunt, E. Howard. *Give Us This Day.* New Rochelle, New York: Arlington House, 1973.

———. *Under Cover. Memoirs of an American Secret Agent.* New York: Berkley, 1974.

Hunt, Linda. *Secret Agenda.* New York: St. Martin's Press, 1991.

Hurt, Henry. *Reasonable Doubt.* New York: Holt, Rinehart & Winston, 1985.

James, Rosemary and Jack Wardlaw. *Plot or Politics: The Garrison Case and its Cast.* New Orleans: Pelican, 1967.

Johnson, Haynes. *The Bay of Pigs.* New York: Dell, 1964.

Johnson, Loch. *A Season of Inquiry.* Lexington, KY: University Press of Kentucky, 1985.

———. *America's Secret Power: The CIA in American Society.* Oxford: Oxford University Press, 1989.

Johnson, Lyndon B. *The Vantage Point: Perspectives of the President, 1963-1969.* New York: Holt, Rinehart & Winston, 1971.

Kantor, Seth. *The Ruby Cover-Up.* New York: Zebra Books, 1978.

Kaplan, John and Jon Waltz. *The Trial of Jack Ruby.* New York: MacMillan, 1965.

Kellerman, Barbara. *The Political Presidency: The Practice of Leadership from Kennedy through Reagan.* Oxford: Oxford University Press, 1984.

Kelley, Clarence M. *Kelley: The Story of a FBI Director.* Kansas: Andrews, McMeel & Parker, 1987.

Kennedy, John F. *Profiles in Courage.* New York: Harper & Row, 1955.

———. *The Strategy of Peace.* New York: Harper & Brothers, 1960.

———. *The Kennedy Wit.* Edited by Bill Adler. New York: Bantam Books, 1964.

———. *More Kennedy Wit.* Edited by Bill Adler. New York: Bantam Books, 1965.

Kennedy, Robert F. *Thirteen Days: A Memoir of the Cuban Crisis.* New York: New American Library, 1969.

———. *In His Own Words: The Unpublished Recollections of the Kennedy Years.* Edited by Edwin O. Guthman and Jeffrey Shulman. New York: Bantam, 1988.

Kern, Montague, Patricia W. Levering, and Ralph B. Levering. *The Kennedy Crises: The Press, the Presidency and Foreign Policy.* Chapel Hill: The University of North

Carolina Press, 1983.

Kerrane, Kevin. *Dollar Sign on the Muscle: The World of Baseball Scouting.* New York: Beaufort Books, 1984.

Kessler, Ronald. *Inside the CIA.* New York: Pocket Books, 1992.

———. *The Sins of the Father.* New York: Warner Books, 1996.

Kirkpatrick, Lyman B., Jr. *The Real CIA.* New York: MacMillan, 1968.

Kirkwood, James. *American Grotesque: An Account of the Clay Shaw-Jim Garrison Kennedy Assassination Trial in New Orleans.* New York: Harper Perennial, 1992.

Koskoff, David. *Joseph P. Kennedy: A Life and Times.* New York: Prentice-Hall, 1974.

Kunz, Diana, ed. *The Diplomacy of the Crucial Decade.* New York: Columbia University, 1994.

Kurtz, Michael. *Crime of the Century.* Knoxville, Tenn.: University of Tennessee Press, 1982.

Lacey, Robert. *Little Man: Meyer Lansky and the Gangster Life.* Boston: Little Brown, 1991.

Lane, Sheldon. *For Bond Lovers Only.* New York: Dell, 1965.

Lasky, Victor. *JFK: The Man and the Myth.* New York: Macmillan, 1963.

———. *It Didn't Start With Watergate.* New York: The Dial Press, 1978.

Latham, Earl, ed. *J. F. Kennedy and Presidential Power.* Lexington, Mass.: Heath, no date.

Lattimer, Dr. *John K. Kennedy and Lincoln: Medical and Ballistic Comparisons of their Assassinations.* New York: Harcourt Brace Jovanovich, 1980.

Lawford, Patricia Seaon. *The Peter Lawford Story.* New York: Carroll & Graf, 1988.

Lazo, Mario. *Dagger in the Heart.* New York: Funk and Wagnalls, 1968.

Leary, William M, ed. *The Central Intelligence Agency: History and Documents.* University of Alabama, 1984.

Lewis, Richard W., and Lawrence Schiller. *The Scavengers and the Critics of the Warren Report.* New York: Dell, 1967.

Lincoln, Evelyn. *Kennedy and Johnson.* New York: Holt, Rinehart, and Winston, 1968.

———. *My Twelve Years with John F. Kennedy.* New York: Bantam Books, 1965.

Lisagor, Nancy and Frank Lipsius. *A Law Unto Itself.* New York: Paragon House, 1989.

Livingstone, Harrison Edward. *High Treason II.* New York: Carroll and Graf, 1992.

Louis, J. C., and Harvey Z. Yazijian. *The Cola Wars.* New York: Everest House, 1980.

Lukas, Anthony. *Nightmare.* New York: Bantam, 1977.

Madsen, Alex. *Gloria and Joe.* New York: Morrow, 1988.

Maheu, Robert and Richard Hack. *Next to Hughes.* New York: HarperCollins, 1992.

Mailer, Norman. *Oswald's Tale: An American Mystery.* New York: Random House, 1995.

Manchester, William. *The Death of a President.* New York: Harper & Row, 1967.

———. *Portrait of a President.* New York: McFadden Books, 1962.

Mangold, Tom. *Cold Warrior: James Jesus Angleton.* New York: Simon & Schuster, 1991.

Marchetti, Victor, and John Marks. *The CIA and The Cult of Intelligence.* New York: Knopf, 1974

Marks, John. *The Search for the "Manchurian Candidate": The CIA and Mind Control.* New York: Times Books, 1979.

Martin, David C. *Wilderness of Mirrors.* New York: Harper & Row, 1980.

Martin, Ralph G. *A Hero For Our Time.* New York: Macmillan, 1982.

———. *Seeds of Destruction: Joe Kennedy and His Sons.* New York: Putnam, 1995.

Mazo, Earl and Stephen Hess. *Nixon: A Political Portrait.* London: Macdonald & Co.,1968.

McCarthy, Edward V. *Working Press.* New York: Vantage, 1997.

McClintock, Michael. *Instruments of Statecraft: US Guerrilla Warfare, Counterinsurgency, and Counterterrorism, 1940-1990.* New York: Pantheon, 1992.

McMillan, Priscilla. *Marina and Lee.* New York: Harper & Row, 1977.

Meagher, Sylvia. *Accessories After the Fact.* New York: Vintage Books, 1976.

Melanson, Philip H. *Spy Saga: Lee Harvey Oswald and U.S. Intelligence.* New York: Praeger, 1990.

Messick, Hank. *John Edgar Hoover.* New York: David McKay, 1972.

———. *Lansky.* New York: Berkley, 1973.

Miller, Merle. *Plain Speaking: An Oral History of Harry S. Truman.* New York: Berkley, 1973.

———. *Lyndon.* New York: Putnam, 1980.

Miller, Nathan. *Stealing From America: A History of Corruption from Jamestown to Reagan.* New York: Paragon House, 1992.

Mitchell, Greg. *Tricky Dick and the Pink Lady: Richard Nixon vs. Helen Gahagan Douglas.* New York: Random House, 1998.

Model, F. Peter and Robert J. Groden. *JFK: The Case for Conspiracy.* New York: Manor Books, 1976.

Moldea, Dan. *Interference: How Organized Crime Influences Professional Football.* New York: Morrow, 1989.

———. *The Hoffa Wars.* New York: Paddington Press, 1978.

Mollenhoff, Clark R. *Despoilers of Democracy.* New York: Doubleday, 1965.

Moore, Jim. *Conspiracy of One.* New York: The Summit Group, 1991.

Morrison, Delesseps S. *Latin American Mission: An Adventure in Hemisphere Diplomacy.* New York: Simon & Schuster, 1965.

Morrow, Robert. *Betrayal.* New York: Warner, 1976.

———. *First Hand Knowledge.* New York: SPI, 1992.

Mosley, Leonard. *Dulles.* New York: Dial, 1977.

Murphy, David E., Sergei Kondrashev, and George Bailey. *Battle Ground Berlin: CIA vs KGB in the Cold War.* New Haven: Yale University Press, 1997.

Myers, Dale K. *With Malice: Lee Harvey Oswald and the Murder of Officer J.D. Tippit.* Milford, MI: Oakcliff Press, 1998.

Navasky, Victor S. *Kennedy Justice.* New York: Atheneum, 1971.

Nechiporenko, Oleg Maximovich. *Passport to Assassination: The Never-Before-Told Story of Lee Harvey Oswald by the KGB Colonel Who Knew Him.* New York: Birch Lane Press, 1993.

Nevins, Allan ed. *President John F. Kennedy: The Burden and the Glory.* New York: Harper & Row, 1964.

Newfield, Jack. *Robert Kennedy: A Memoir.* New York: Dutton, 1969.

Newman, John M. *JFK and Vietnam.* New York: Warner Books, 1992.

———. *Oswald and the CIA.* New York: Carroll and Graff, 1995.

Newhouse, John. *War and Peace in the Nuclear Age.* New York: Vintage Books, 1988.

Nicholas, William. *The Bobby Kennedy Nobody Knows.* Greenwich, CT: Fawcett, 1967.

Nixon, Richard. *Memoirs.* New York: Grossett and Dunlap, 1978.

North, Mark. *Act of Treason: The Role of J. Edgar Hoover in the Assassination of President Kennedy.* New York: Carroll & Graf Publishers, 1991.

O'Donnell, Kenneth P. and David F. Powers. *Johnny, We Hardly Knew Ye.* Boston: Little, Brown, 1972.

Oglesby, Carl. *The Yankee and Cowboy War: Conspiracies from Dallas to Watergate and Beyond.* New York: Berkley Books, 1977.

Olesak, Michael M. and Mary Adams. *Beisbol: Latin Americans and the Grand Old*

Game. Grand Rapids, MI: Master's Press, 1991.

O'Neill, Thomas P. ("Tip"), Jr. *Man of the House*. New York: Random House, 1987.

Oppenheimer, Jerry. *The Other Mrs. Kennedy*. New York: St. Martin's Press, 1994.

Oswald, Robert. *Lee: A Portrait of Lee Harvey Oswald By His Brother*. New York: Coward-McCann, 1967.

O' Toole, G.J.A. *The Encyclopedia of American Intelligence and Espionage*. New York : Facts on File, 1988.

Parenti, Michael. *The Sword and the Dollar: Imperialism, Revolution, and the Arms Race*. New York: St. Martin's Press, 1989.

Parker, Robert, and Richard Rashke. *Capitol Hill in Black and White*. New York: Dodd, Mead, 1986.

Parmet, Herbert S. JFK: *The Presidency of John F. Kennedy*. New York: Penguin, 1983.

Paterson, Thomas J. *Kennedy's Quest for Victory*. Oxford: Oxford University Press, 1989.

———. *Contesting Castro*. Oxford: Oxford University Press, 1994.

Pearson, John. *The Life of Ian Fleming*. New York: McGraw-Hill, 1966.

Persons, Albert C. *Bay of Pigs: A Firsthand Account of the Mission by a U.S. Pilot in Support of the Cuban Invasion Force in 1961*. Jefferson, NC: McFarland & Co., 1990.

Peters, James Edward. *Arlington National Cemetery*. Woodbine House, 1986.

Phelan, James. *Scandals, Scamps, and Scoundrels*. New York: Random House, 1982.

Phillips, David Atlee. *The Night Watch*. New York: Atheneum, 1977.

Potter, John Mason. *Plots Against Presidents*. New York: Astor-Honor, 1968.

Plaster, John. *SOG: The Secret Wars of American Commandos in Vietnam*. New York: Simon & Schuster, 1997.

Posner, Gerald. *Case Closed: Lee Harvey Oswald and the Assassination of JFK*. New York: Random House, 1993.

Powers, Francis Gary. *Operation Overflight*. New York: Holt Rinehart and Winston, 1978.

Powers, Richard. *Secrecy and Power: The Life of J. Edgar Hoover*. New York: Macmillan, 1987.

Powers, Thomas. *The Man Who Kept The Secrets*. New York: Knopf, 1979.

Prados, John. *Presidents' Secret Wars*. New York: Morrow, 1986.

Prouty, L. Fletcher. *The Secret Team: The CIA and Its Allies in Control of the United States and the World*. Englewood Cliffs, NJ: Prentice-Hall, 1973.

Quirk, Robert E. *Fidel Castro*. New York: W.W. Norton, 1993.

Rachlin, Harvey. *The Kennedys: The Chronological History*. New York: Ballantine Books, 1986.

Ranelagh, John. *The Agency: The Rise and Decline of The CIA*. New York: Simon & Schuster, 1986.

Rappleye, Charles and Becker, Ed. *All-American Mafioso: The Johnny Roselli Story*. New York: Doubleday, 1991.

Rather, Dan. *The Camera Never Blinks: Adventures of a TV Journalist*. New York: Morrow, 1977.

Reeves, Richard. *President Kennedy: Profile of Power*. New York: Simon & Schuster. 1993.

Reid, Ed. *The Grim Reapers: The Anatomy of Organized Crime in America, City by City*. Chicago: Regnery, 1969.

Reston, James. *Deadline: A Memoir*. New York: Random House, 1991.

Reston, James, Jr. *The Lone Star: The Life of John Connally*. New York: Harper & Row, 1989.

Riebling, Mark. *The Wedge: The Secret War Between the FBI and the CIA*. New York: Knopf, 1994.

Roberts, Allen, *Robert Francis Kennedy: Biography of a Compulsive Politician*. Brookline: Braden Press, 1984.

Roosevelt, Kermit. *Countercoup: The Struggle for the Control of Iran*. New York: McGraw Hill, 1979.

Rodriguez, Felix I. *Shadow Warrior*. New York: Pocket Books, 1989.

Roemer, William F., Jr. *War of the Godfathers*. New York: Ballantine Books, 1990.

———. *Roemer: Man Against the Mob*. New York: D.I. Fine, 1989.

Rogers, Warren. *When I Think of Bobby: A Personal Memoir of the Kennedy Years*. New York: HarperCollins, 1993.

Rositzke, Harry. *The CIA's Secret Operations: Espionage, Counterespionage and Covert Action*. New York: Reader's Digest Press, 1977.

Rostow, W.W., *The Diffifusion of Power. An Essay in Recent History*. New York: Macmillan, 1972.

Royko, Mike. *Boss: Richard J. Daley of Chicago*. New York: Dutton, 1971.

Rubin, Barry. *Secrets of State: The State Department and the Struggle Over U.S. Foreign Policy*. New York: Oxford University Press, 1985.

Russell, Dick. *The Man Who Knew Too Much*. New York: Carroll and Graf, 1992.

Sahl, Mort. *Heartland*. New York: Harcourt Brace Jovanovich, 1976.

Savage, Gary. *JFK First Day Evidence*. Monroe, LA: The Shoppe Press, 1993.

Schecter, Jerold and Vyacheslav V. Luchkoved, ed. *Khrushchev Remembers: The Glasnost Tapes*. Boston: Little, Brown & Co., 1990.

Scheim, David E. *Contract on America: The Mafia Murder of President John F. Kennedy*. New York: Zebra Books, 1988.

Schlesinger, Arthur M., Jr. *A Thousand Days: John F. Kennedy in the White House*. Boston: Houghton Mifflin, 1965.

———. *Robert Kennedy and His Times*. Boston: Houghton Mifflin, 1978.

Schlesinger, Stephen and Stephen Kinzer. *Bitter Fruit*. New York: Doubleday, 1982.

Schorr, Daniel. *Clearing the Air*. Boston: Houghton Mifflin, 1977.

Schreiber, G.R. *The Bobby Baker Affair*. Chicago: Regnery, 1964.

Scott, P.D. *Deep Politics and the Death of JFK*. Berkeley: University of California Press, 1993.

———. Paul Hoch, Russell Stetler, and Josiah Thompson. *"Beyond Conspiracy: The Hidden Dimensions of the John F. Kennedy Assassination."* Unpublished manuscript, 1980.

Shackley, Theodore. *The Third Option: An American View of Counterinsurgency Operations*. New York: Bantam, 1981.

Shannon, William V. *The Heir Apparent: Robert Kennedy and the Struggle for Power*. New York: Macmillan, 1967.

Shapley, Deborah. *Promise and Power: The Life and Times of Robert McNamara*. Boston: Little, Brown, 1993.

Sheridan, Walter. *The Fall and Rise of Jimmy Hoffa*. New York: Saturday Review Press, 1972.

Shesol, Jeff. *Mutual Contempt: Lyndon Johnson, Robert Kennedy, and the Feud that Defined a Decade*. New York: W.W. Norton, 1997.

Sidey, Hugh. *John F. Kennedy: President*. New York: Crest Books, 1964.

Simpson, Christopher. *The Splendid Blond Beast*. New York: Grove Press, 1993.

Sinatra, Nancy. *Frank Sinatra: An American Legend*. Santa Monica, CA: General Publishing Group, 1995.

Smith, Hedrick. *The Power Game*. New York: Random House, 1989.

Smith, Joseph Burkholder. *Portrait of a Cold Warrior*. New York: G.P. Putnam's Sons, 1976.

Smith, Russell Jack. *The Unknown CIA: My Decades With the Agency*. Washington:

Pergamon-Brassey's, 1989.

Sorensen, Theordore C. *Kennedy*. New York: Harper & Row, 1965.

———. *The Kennedy Legacy: A Peaceful Revolution for the Seventies*. New York: MacMillan, 1969.

Spada, James. *Peter Lawford: The Man Who Kept the Secrets*. New York: Bantam, 1991.

Speriglio, Milo. *The Marilyn Conspiracy*. New York: Pocket Books, 1986.

Stafford, Jean. *A Mother in History*. New York: Bantam, 1965.

Steinberg, Alfred. *Sam Johnson's Boy*. New York: Macmillan, 1968.

Stockwell, John. *In Search of Enemies: A CIA Story*. New York: W.W. Norton, 1978.

Stone, I.F. *In a Time of Torment*. New York: Vintage Books, 1968.

Strober, Gerald S. and Deborah H. Strober. *Let Us Begin Anew: An Oral History of the Kennedy Presidency*. New York: HarperCollins, 1993.

Sullivan, William. *The Bureau*. New York: Pinnacle, 1982.

Summers, Anthony. *Conspiracy*. New York: Paragon House, 1989.

———. *Official and Confidential: The Secret Life of J. Edgar Hoover*. New York: G.P. Putnam's Sons, 1993.

———. *Goddess: The Secret Lives of Marilyn Monroe*. New York: MacMillan, 1985.

Szulc, Tad. *Compulsive Spy: The Strange Career of E. Howard Hunt*. New York: Viking, 1974.

———. *Fidel: A Critical Portrait*. New York: Morrow, 1986.

——— and Karl Meyer. *The Cuban Invasion: The Chronicle of a Disaster*. New York, Ballantine Books, 1962.

Taylor, Maxwell D., and Luis E. Aguilar, *Operation Zapata*, Frederick, MD: Aletheia Books: University Publications of America, 1981.

terHorst, J.F., and Col. Ralph Albertazzie. *The Flying White House: The Story of Air Force One*. New York: Coward, McCann & Geoghegan, 1979.

Thayer, George. *The Farther Shores of Politics*. New York: Simon & Schuster, 1968.

Thomas, Evan and Walter Isaacson. *The Wise Men: Six Friends and the World They Made*. New York: Simon & Schuster, 1986.

———. *The Man To See: Edward Bennett Williams*. New York: Simon & Schuster, 1991.

———. *The Very Best Men*. New York: Simon & Schuster, 1995.

Thomas, Gordon. *Journey into Madness: The True Story of Secret CIA Mind Control and Medical Abuse*. New York: Bantam Books, 1989.

Thompson, Josiah. *Six Seconds in Dallas*. New York: Bernard Geis, 1967.

Thompson, Nelson. *The Dark Side of Camelot*. Chicago: Playboy Press, 1976.

Thompson, Robert Smith. *The Missiles of October: The Declassified Story of John F. Kennedy and the Cuban Missile Crisis*. New York: Simon & Schuster, 1992.

Tower, John G. *Consequences: A Personal and Political Memoir*. Boston: Little, Brown, 1991.

Tucille, Jerome. *Kingdom: The Story of the Hunt Family of Texas*. New York: Paperjacks, 1987.

Tully, Andrew. *CIA: The Inside Story*. New York: Morrow, 1962.

Turner, William W. *Hoover's FBI*. New York: Thunder's Mouth, 1993.

Valenti, Jack. *A Very Human President*. New York: W.W. Norton, 1975.

vanden Heuvel, William and Milton Gwirtzman. *On His Own: RFK 1964-68*. New York: Doubleday, 1970.

Van Gelder, Lawrence. *The Untold Story: Why the Kennedys Lost the Book Battle*. New York: Award, 1967.

Volkman, Ernest, and Blaine Baggett. *Secret Intelligence: The Inside Story of America's Espionage Empire*. New York: Doubleday, 1989.

vonHoffman, Nicholas. *Citizen Cohn: The Life and Times of Roy Cohn*. New York:

Doubleday, 1988.

Wallechinsky, David and Irving Wallace, eds. *The People's Almanac #3*. New York: Morrow, 1981.

Weidenfeld, Lord George. *Remembering My Good Friends: An Autobiography*. New York: HarperCollins, 1994.

Weisberg, Harold. *Oswald in New Orleans*. New York: Canyon Books, 1967.

———. *Whitewash. 4 vols*. Hyattstown, MD: Weisberg, 1974.

Weisberger, Bernard. *Cold War, Cold Peace, The United States and Russia Since 1945*. New York: Houghton Mifflin, 1984.

Whalen, Richard J. *The Founding Father: The Story of Joseph P. Kennedy*. New York: New American Library, 1964.

White, G. Edward. *Earl Warren: A Public Life*. Oxford: Oxford University Press, 1982.

White, Theodore H. *The Making of the President: 1960*. New York: Atheneum, 1962.

Wicker, Tom. *JFK and LBJ: the Influence of Personality Upon Politics*. New York: Morrow, 1968.

———. *Kennedy Without Tears: The Man Beneath the Myth*. New York: Morrow, 1964.

———. *On Press*. New York: Viking, 1978.

Wills, Garry. *The Kennedy Imprisonment: A Meditation on Power*. Boston: Atlantic Monthly Press, 1981.

———. and Ovid Demaris. *Jack Ruby*. NewYork: New American Library, 1967.

Winks, Robin. *Cloak and Gown: Scholars and the Secret War, 1931-1961*. New York: Morrow, 1987.

Winoker, Jon. *True Confessions*. New York: Dutton, 1992.

Winter-Berger, Robert N. *The Washington Payoff*. New York: Dell, 1972.

Wise, David. *MoleHunt*. New York: Random House, 1992.

———. *The Invisible Government*. New York: Random House, 1964.

——— and Thomas B. Ross. *The Espionage Establishment*. New York: Random House, 1967.

Witcover, Jules. Crapshoot: *Rolling the Dice on the Vice Presidency*. New York: Crown, 1992.

Wofford, Harris. *Of Kennedys and Kings: Making Sense of the Sixties*. New York: Farrar, Straus and Giroux, 1980.

Wrone, David, R. *The Assassination of John F. Kennedy: An Annotated Bibliography*. Madison: State Historical Society of Wisconsin, 1973.

Wyden, Peter. *The Bay of Pigs: The Untold Story*. New York: Simon & Schuster, 1979.

Yarmolinsky, Adam. *The Military Establishment: Its Impacts on American Society*. New York: Harper & Row, 1971.

Zeifman, Jerry. *Without Honor: The Impeachment of Richard Nixon and the Crimes of Camelot*. New York: Thunder's Mouth, 1995.

Zeller, Barbie. *Covering the Body: The Kennedy Assassination, the Media, and the Shaping of the Collective Memory*. Chicago: University of Chicago Press, 1992.

Zirbel, Craig I. *The Texas Connection: The Assassination of President John F. Kennedy*. Scottsdale, Ariz.: The Texas Connection Company, 1991.

Government Reports

Senate Interim Report of the Select Committee to Study Government Operations with Respect to Intelligence Activities, Alleged Assassination Plots Involving Foreign Leaders. U.S. Government Printing Office, 1975.

FBI Oversight Hearings. Before the Subcommittee on Civil and Constitutional Rights of the Committee on the Judiciary , House of Representatives, 94th Congress, 1st and 2nd Sessions, Part 3, U.S. Government Printing Office, 1974.

Investigation of the Assassination of President John F. Kennedy: Performance of The
    Intelligence Agencies, final report, Books I—V, Select Committee to Study
    Government Operations with Respect to Intelligence Activities, 94th Congress,
    2nd Session, U.S Senate, U.S. Government Printing Office, 1976.

Investigation of the Assassination of President John F. Kennedy, Final Report, and
    appendix to Hearings Before the Select Committee on Assassinations of the US
    House of Representatives, 95th Congress, Vols. I -XII, U.S. Government Printing
    Office, 1979.

The President's Commission on Obscenity and Pornography. New York: Bantam Books,
    1970.

Public Papers of the Presidents. John F. Kennedy, 1963. Washington: U.S.
    Government Printing Office, 1964.

Report of the President's Commission on the Assassination of President John F.
    Kennedy [Warren Commission Report], and accompanying 26 volumes of hearings
    and exhibits. U.S. Government Printing Office, 1964.

ABBREVIATIONS

CCIR—*Church Committee Interim Report* (Alleged Assassination Plots Involving Foreign Leaders, Interim Report of the Select Committee to Study Government Operations with Respect to Intelligence Activities, U.S. Senate, U.S. Government Printing Office, 1975).

CCR—*Church Committee Report* final report and supporting volumes (especially Book V: Investigation of the Assassination of President John F. Kennedy: Performance of the Intelligence Agencies; Select Committee to Study Government Operations with Respect to Intelligence Activities, 94th Congress, 2nd session, U.S. Senate, U.S. Government Printing Office, 1976).

FL—*Frontline* In 1992-1993, the author, with W. Scott Malone, served as a reporter on the three-hour PBS Frontline special "Who Was Lee Harvey Oswald?" (Broadcast Nov. 16, 1993). In preparing the special, more than 500 interviews were conducted, generating many thousands of pages of transcripts, most of which could not be included on the program that aired. Interviews were conducted as well by the other members of the Frontline team, including: Ben Loeterman, Miri Navasky, Joe Rosenbloom, Michael Sullivan, and Robbyn and Anthony Summers. The author wishes to thank series producer Mike Sullivan for granting permission to use this vast amount of raw data.

FRUS—*Foreign Relations of the United States* Issued by the State Department. Especially 1961-1963, The Kennedy Years.

HSCA—*House Select Committee on Assassinations* (Investigation of the Assassination of President John F. Kennedy, Final Report, and appendix to Hearings Before the Select Committee on Assassinations of the U.S. House of Representatives, 95th Congress, Vols. I-XII, U.S. Government Printing Office, 1979).

WC—*Warren Commission* (Report of the President's Commission on the Assassination of President John F. Kennedy [Warren Commission Report], and accompanying 26 volumes of testimony and exhibits. U.S. Government Printing Office, 1964).

CD—*Commission Document* (Warren Commission.)

CIA and FBI documents—Unless otherwise noted, these can be found in the JFK Collection at the National Archives, College Park, MD.

ENDNOTES

Chapter One (The Story Begins)

1 Beschloss, *The Crisis Years*, 91.
2 Hinckle and Turner, 105.
3 Manolo Reboso, interview by author, 10 February 1994.
4 Oppenheimer, 211.
5 Oleksak and Oleksak, 45; also see Kerrane, *Dollar Sign on the Muscle: The World of Baseball Scouting*, 278; Fitzgerald, "Uncle Joe—Senators' Cuban Connection," The Sporting News, June 21, 1980, 17; and Truby, "Now Pitching for the Giants...Fidel Castro," Sports History II, March 1989, 12.
6 Paterson, *Contesting Castro*, 50-51.
7 Hinckle and Turner, 82.
8 Paterson, *Contesting Castro*, 38.
9 John Lantigua, "Bay of Pigs Secrets," *Miami Herald*, 17 April 1997.
10 Ross Crozier, interview by author, 19 September 1997.
11 Hinckle and Turner, 60.
12 For a thorough discussion of Coca-Cola's losses, see *The Coca-Cola Wars*.
13 See esp. Ray Kerrison, "Face of Evil Meets Face of Goodness," *New York Post*, January 1998.
14 Szulc, *Fidel*, 326.
15 Beschloss, *The Crisis Years*, 97.
16 Paterson, *Contesting Castro*, 120.
17 Weisberger, 204.
18 Quoted in Davison, 217-218.
19 Thomas, *The Very Best Men*, 119.
20 For details of the Eisenhower covert dealings, see: Cook, *The Declassified Eisenhower*; Prados, *Presidents' Secret Wars*; Thomas, *The Very Best Men*; Rubin, *Secrets of State*; Ambrose, *Eisenhower*; Beschloss, *Vol. 2*; Roosevelt, *Countercoup*; Broadwater, *Eisenhower and the Anti-Communist Crusade*; Ambrose, *Ike's Spies*; and Andrew, *For the President's Eyes Only*.
21 Richard Nixon, *Reader's Digest*, November 1964.
22 Quoted in Rappleye and Becker, 176.
23 Rappleye and Becker, 179.
    Although unconfirmed by this author, Nixon is reputed to have appeared on Jack Parr's late-night talk show four days prior to the 1960 election, and, in an effort to advance his candidacy, bragged that he had spearheaded the anti-Castro effort in the White House.
24 Colonel Philip Corso, interview by author, 6 February 1996.
25 Wyden, *The Bay of Pigs*, 29.
26 Andrew Goodpaster, interview by author, 6 February 1996.
27 Nixon to Henry Kissinger, Memorandum, in Stephen Ambrose, *Eisenhower, Vol. II: The President*, 639.
28 Beschloss, *The Crisis Years*, 99.
29 Kennedy, *The Strategy of Peace*, 132-133.
30 Ibid, 101.
31 Darrell Garwood, 158.
32 Mitchell; see also Chris Matthews, *Kennedy and Nixon*.

In point of fact, Kennedy and Nixon were not only friends (they had been since their freshman Senate year of 1950), but shared many more policy views than one might suspect. Nixon's hard-line anti-Communism was so in tune with the Kennedys' that, to Nixon's 1950 Senate campaign, it was recently learned, Joe Kennedy donated $1,000.

33 Weisberger, 209.
34 Richard Goodwin, 125.
35 Ibid, 124-125.
36 Richard Goodwin, interview by author, 20 January 1994.
37 Richard Goodwin, interview by author, 20 January 1994.
38 Richard Goodwin, 125.
39 Seymour Hersh, 175-178.
40 Barney Hidalgo, interview by author, 7 April 1998.
41 Wofford, 205.
42 White House Cuba Special Assistant Richard Goodwin, "Relations with the Revolutionary Council," Memorandum, 9 September 1961.
43 *HSCA*, vol. 10, 57-60.
44 Nino Diaz, interview by author, 4 January 1998.
45 Wyden, 164.
46 Higgins, 89; see also Smathers Oral History, interview #1, JFK Library, 6, 7-8. This suggestion was not intended to be made public and Smathers was incensed when he learned that the library accidentally released it.
47 Turner and Hinckle, 85.
48 James Wilcott, HSCA interview, 26 March 1978; James Wilcott, interview by Hinckle and Turner, February 1979, in Hinkle and Turner.
49 The provocation idea would be floated by Bobby sixteen months later, during his stepped-up campaign against the Cuban leader. In addition, according to anti-Castro operative Gerry Hemming, U.S. Marines were to be murdered during the landing not far from Guantanamo (Gerry Hemming, interview by author, 16 November 1997). Jorge Mas-Canosa (the future Miami millionaire exile leader) and Bernie de Torres led the assassins, according to Hemming. Diaz recently confirmed Mas' presence on the Santa Ana, but says he knew nothing of a murder plot.
    Interestingly, in 1997, four exiles were arrested off the coast of Puerto Rico with sniper rifles. One of the arrestees admitted that the weapons were to be used to murder Fidel Castro. Their boat was registered to a director of the Cuban American National Foundation, lead and founded by Mas-Canosa (*Miami Herald*, 1 November 1997).
50 Jack Hawkins, interview by author, 7 April 1998.
51 Lyman Lemnitzer to Robert McNamara, "Military Evaluation of Cuban Plan," Memorandum, 3 February 1961, *Taylor Report*, Annex 9, 1-3, 10, 26-27, 31-32, 6.
52 Bissell, 167.
53 Bissell, 155-156.
54 Thomas, *The Very Best Men*, 298.
55 Kirkpatrick, 188.
56 Bonsal, 135.
57 Raphael Quintero, interview by author, 6 November 1997.
58 Albert C. "Buck" Persons, interview by author, 18 May 1994.
59 Kirkpatrick, 197.
60 Rafael Nuñez, interview by author, 12 April 1995.
61 *New Orleans Times-Picayune*, 1, 3 April 1961; *HSCA*, vol. 10, 57.
62 *Foreign Broadcast Information Service Report*, 10 April 1961, National Archives.
63 Jack Hawkins, interview by author, 7 April 1998.
64 Grose, 560.
65 Grose, 527.
66 Richard Goodwin, 177.
67 Wofford, 345.
68 Parmet, 159.

69 Bissell, 190.
70 Constantine "Gus" Kangles, interview by author, 12 August 1996.
71 George Smathers, interview by Ralph Martin, in *Seeds of Destruction,* 327.
72 Seymour Hersh, 200-201.
73 Bissell, 185.
74 Jack Hawkins, "Classified Disaster," *National Review,* 31 December 1997.
75 Wofford, 350.
76 Jack Hawkins, interview by author, 7 April 1998.
77 Capt. Eduardo Ferrer, interview by author, 14 May 1994.
78 Jake Esterline, interview by author, 28 March 1998.
79 Jack Hawkins, "Classified Disaster," *National Review,* 31 December 1997.
80 O'Donnell and Powers, 274.
81 Wofford, 363.
82 Nestor Carbonell, 190.
83 Hinckle and Turner, 105.
84 Richard Goodwin, 185.
85 Wofford, 355.
86 Richard Goodwin, 171.
87 Manolo Reboso, interview by author, 28 February 1994.
88 Jan Weininger, interview by author, 14 January 1994.
89 Allen Dulles Papers, Boxes 138, 244, Princeton University.
90 McCone to Bissell, letter, 19 August 1985; see also Bissell, 194.
91 McCone to Bissell, letter, 1986; see also Bissell, 196.
92 Kennedy's fury was also in evidence. According to Hinckle and Turner (104), he
   unleashed a savage indictment "in Navy blue language" of his advisors—the
   CIA, Joint Chiefs of Staff, and members of his own staff—saying, "I was assured
   by every son of a bitch I checked with—all the military experts and the CIA—
   that the plan would be a success."
93 Nixon, 234-235.
94 Wofford, 352.
95 David and David, 157.
96 RFK to JFK, Memorandum, April 19, 1961, *President's Office Files,* Cuba, General,
   JFK Library.
97 RFK, Memorandum, 1 June 1961. Cited in Schlesinger, *Robert Kennedy and His
   Times,* 508.
98 Richard Goodwin, 130.
99 Wofford, 354.
100 Beschloss, *The Crisis Years,* 143-145.
101 Arthur Schlesinger to John F. Kennedy, *Memo for the President,* "Cuba: Political,
   Diplomatic, and Economic Problems," 10 April 1961.
102 Arthur Schlesinger to John F. Kennedy, *Memo for the President,* "Protection of the
   President," 10 April 1961.
103 Allen Dulles Papers, Boxes 138, 244, Princeton University.
104 Mosely, 473.
105 Thomas Powers, 115.
106 Hunt, *Give Us This Day,* 215.
107 Tom Wicker, et al., "CIA, Maker of Policy, or Tool?" *New York Times,* 25 April
   1966.
108 Grose, 530.
109 Schlesinger, *A Thousand Days,* 288-289.
110 Grose, 530.
111 Ibid, 276.
112 Wofford, 347.
113 Wofford, 354.
114 Hinckle and Turner, 107-108.
115 David and David, 158.
116 Taylor and Aguilar, 36-37.
117 Wofford, 347.

118 Richard Goodwin, 187.
119 Quoted in Beschloss, *The Crisis Years,* 147.
120 Wofford, 364.
121 Strober and Strober, 349.
122 Wofford, 373.
123 William Hundley, interview by author, 7 October 1993.
124 Hinckle and Turner, 108.
125 Hamilton, 356, 381.
126 Richard Goodwin, 187.
127 Taylor Branch and George Crile III, "The Kennedy Vendetta," *Harper's Magazine,* August 1975.
128 Christopher Marquis, "Kennedy Rejected Peace Talks," *Miami Herald,* 29 April 1996.
129 Richard Goodwin, "Cigars & Che & JFK," *Cigar Afficianado,* Fall 1996.
130 Beschloss, *The Crisis Years,* 132.
131 Bissell, 201.
132 John Davis, *The Kennedys,* 82.
133 David and David, 111.
134 Nicholas, 15.
135 Shannon, 44.
136 For more sources on the Kennedys' upbringing, see: Nicholas; John Davis, *The Kennedys;* Shannon; Hamilton; Doris Kearns Goodwin, *The Fitzgeralds and The Kennedys;* Ralph deToledano; David and David; Collier and Horowitz; and Richard Goodwin.
137 Schlesinger, *Robert Kennedy and His Times,* 660.
138 Ibid, 643.
139 Cited in Hinckle and Turner, 119.
140 Ibid, 214.
141 Ralph de Toledano, 32.
142 Joseph Kennedy Sr., quoted in Steven Brill, *The Teamsters,* 30.
143 Collier and Horowitz, 308.
144 "Cronkite Remembers," videotape, 1996.
145 David and David, 138.
146 Evelyn Lincoln, interview by author, 10 May 1989.
147 David and David, 224.
148 Wofford, 340.
149 Branch and Crile, "The Kennedy Vendetta," *Harper's Magazine,* August 1975.
150 Ibid.
151 Burton Hersh, 426-427.
152 Parmet, 161.
153 Allen Dulles Oral History, 5 December 1964, JFK Library.
154 Cited in (among other sources) *Signel,* August 1993; and AFCEO (a journal of the Armed Forces Communication Electronics Association).
155 Colonel Alan D. Campen, interview by author, 18 August 1994.
156 Beschloss, *The Crisis Years,* 103.
157 See Koskoff, esp. 239-273.
158 Simpson, 122-123.
    After World War I, Dulles ran the Berlin office of Sullivan & Cromwell, which in turn represented a firm owned by Marcus Wallenberg, who manufactured critical parts of the German Army's communication system. When World War II broke out, S&C helped set up a "dummy" Swedish corporation, to make it appear as if the firm were foreign owned, thus permitting it to stay in business. Dulles, who was then in charge of the Bern, Switzerland headquarters of the Office of the Office of Strategic Services, has been roundly criticized for his profiteering from the war. This is not to imply that Dulles was pro-Hitler. Quite to the contrary, Dulles worked with the SS underground, which was trying to assassinate Hitler. In addition, Dulles' espionage network was critical to the successful bombing of Hitler's V-2 rocket research center. However, with

Germans unilaterally hated in the West, Dulles' friendship with any Germans was viewed as suspicious. To make matters worse, Dulles, after the war, helped negotiate sweetheart deals for his SS friends, who turned themselves in with no punishment (Operation Sunrise). These negotiations were kept secret from America's Soviet allies. This operation then led to Project Paperclip, which repatriated Nazi scientists into the United States to assist in forming the backbone of the U.S. effort against the Soviet Union. Many (including the Russians) have therefore pointed to Dulles as being a critical component to the origins of the Cold War. It was, however, Dulles' original isolationist stance that placed him in the same political universe as Joe Kennedy.
Excellent books on this subject are listed in bibliography: Mosely, Grose; Linda Hunt; Simpson, and Lisagor and Lipsius.

159 Allen Dulles Oral History, Dec 5, 1964, JFK Library,159.
160 RFK, interview by John B. Martin, 1 March 1964, RFK Oral History at the Kennedy Library.
161 RFK, interview by Arthur Schlesinger, Jr., 27 February 1965, RFK Oral History at the Kennedy Library.
162 Beschloss, *The Crisis Years,* 102-103.
163 Thomas C. Reeves, *A Question of Character,* 56.
164 Ironically, because of the transfer, JFK was stationed in the Pacific, aboard the PT-109, leading to the birth of his heroic legend—not exactly what Hoover had in mind.
165 Later, both President Kennedy and Johnson would express an interest in firing Hoover, but were prevented from doing so out of fear that Hoover would leak his "Official and Confidential" files.

   LBJ aide Marty Underwood tells a typical story: "I remember a day not long after the assassination when I spoke with Johnson outside the Oval Office. He told me, 'Today's the day. Hoover's coming in here soon and I'm giving him his walking papers. He's out.' It wasn't long before Hoover arrived with this self-satisfied grin, and a stack of files under his arm. I waited in the hall. After about 15 or 20 minutes, Hoover left, strutting past me with the same smile, and still holding the files. After gathering my courage, I went into the office and encountered a limp Johnson seated behind his desk. He was pale as a ghost. It looked like his mother had just died. He said, 'That son of a bitch knows everything. I could never fire him.'" (Marty Underwood, interview by author, 10 May 1993)

   For more on Hoover's use of blackmail, see Summers, *Official and Confidential;* Richard Powers; and Curt Gentry.
166 Dean Rusk, testimony before the Church Committee, 10 July 1975, 90.
167 E. Howard Hunt, interview on Jack Anderson's TV special, "Who Shot JFK?" in 1988.
168 Peter Grose, 538.
169 JFK to Dulles, letter, JFK Library, WH Name File.
170 Bissell, 203-204.
171 Wise and Ross, 157.
172 Newfield, 79.
173 Ranelagh, 377-378.

Chapter Two (The Cuba Project)

1 Sam Halpern, interview by author, 15 September 1993.
2 Richard Goodwin, 172.
3 Bissell, 160.
4 Quoted in Wofford, 364.
5 Schlesinger, *A Thousand Days,* 428.
6 David Wise and Thomas B. Ross, quoted in de Toledano, 262.
7 Rappleye, 196.

8 Wofford, 386.

9 Cited in Parmet, 215, based on a Bissell interview, 5 March 1982.

10 Quoted in Wyden, 23.

11 Thomas Powers, 174.

12 CIA Inspector General's Report, 23 May 1967 (released in 1993), 33.

13 RFK Memo, 7 November 1961, RFK papers, quoted in Beschloss, *The Crisis Years*, 375.

14 Quoted in Schlesinger, *A Thousand Days,* 341.

15 Field Circular (FC) 100-20, 1986, cited in McClintock, 417.

16 Cited in Michael McClintock, 34-35.

17 Ibid, p. xvii.

18 The details of the SOG units only surfaced in 1997, when SOG Major John Plaster wrote his detailed account, listed in the bibliography. See esp. 19.

19 Ibid, 164-165.

20 Fletcher Knebel, "Washington in Crisis," *Look,* 18 December 1962.

21 Bissell, 202.

22 Currey, p. x.

23 Newman, *JFK and Vietnam,* 3-4.

24 Quoted in Schlesinger, *A Thousand Days,* 985-986.

25 Currey, 224.

26 Ibid, 227.

27 Goodwin to President Kennedy, Memo, 1 November 1961, in *FRUS* vol. X, 664.

28 JFK to Special Group, Memo, 30 November 1961, in *FRUS,* vol. X, 688-689.

29 Guthman, 116.

30 Lansdale to Special Group, Memo, 20 Feb 1962.

31 Marguerita King, interview by author, 16 May 1998; Eloise King, interview by author, 20 June 1998.

32 Sam Halpern, interview by author, 26 January 1998.

33 In that position, Shackley was responsible, in part, for the Agency's efforts to overthrow Salvadore Allende of Chile.

34 Quoted in Taylor Branch and George Crile III, "The Kennedy Vendetta," *Harper's Magazine,* August 1975.

35 Grayston Lynch, interview on BBC production *Time Machine,* "The CIA," broadcast on 13 November 1992.

36 Thomas Powers, 136.

37 Also, in Allen Dulles' Oral History in JFK Library.

38 Pearson, 321-322.

39 Allen Dulles, "The Spy Boss Who Loved Bond," in Lane, Sheldon, *For Bond Lovers Only,* 155-56.

40 Cited in *Riebling,* 165.

41 Thomas, *The Very Best Men,* 288.

42 CCIR, 139.

43 Harvey Notes, 19 January 1962; disclosed by the Church Committee.

44 This was the nickname given RFK by Bill Harvey and others at CIA.

45 Thomas, *The Very Best Men,* 297.

46 Blight and Kornbluh (ed.), 140.

47 Jack Hawkins, interview by author, 7 April 1998.

48 *Harper's Magazine,* August 1975.

49 Wofford, 386.

50 Thomas Parrott, interview by Seymour Hersh, 19 June 1998. Notes of this interview are in the author's possession.

51 Guthman and Shulman (ed.), 378.

52 Frank Sturgis, interview by author, 12 September 1993.

53 Ayers, 76-77, 146-147.

54 Corn, 66.

55 Dino Brugioni, interview by author, 27 January 1998.

56 Brugioni, 68.

Chapter Three (Murder and Missiles)

1 Lumumba was eventually murdered, but not by the U.S.. According to the Church Committee, which investigated Lumumba's death, "[There was] no U.S. involvement in bringing about the death of Lumumba." (CCIR, 52.)

2 Anthony Summers, "JFK and The Mob," *New York Daily News,* 6 October 1991.

3 Allen Dulles, Meet the Press, 31 December 1961; cited in *Szulc and Meyer,* 103.

4 Richard M. Bissell to Lucien S. Vanden Broucke, in his article, "The Confessions of Allen Dulles: New Evidence on the Bay of Pigs," *Diplomatic History,* Fall 1984.

5 Eloise King, interview by author, 20 June 1998.

6 Marguerita King, interview by author, 28 May 1998.

7 *CCIR,* 92.

8 Jake Esterline, interview by author, 28 March 1998.

9 Moldea, *The Hoffa Wars,* 127.

10 Constantine "Gus" Kangles, interview by author, 12 August 1996.

11 Paul Meskil, "How the U.S. Made Unholy Alliance with the Mafia," *New York Daily News,* 23 April 1975.

12 *Time Magazine,* 9 June 1975.

13 Hinckle and Turner, 54

14 At the time of the Watergate break-in, prior to the 1972 Presidential election, Republicans worried that Maheu, a later partner of Democratic Chairman Larry O'Brien, might give the Democrats intelligence regarding what skeletons were in whose closets.

15 Maheu and Hack, 114-115.

16 Ibid, 116.

17 Rappleye and Becker, 190.

18 Jack Anderson, "Report to President George Bush: Who Murdered John F. Kennedy?" 1988.

19 Giancana told Rosselli that he thought the whole assassination idea to be a folly, and only volunteered a few names to Maheu. "I'm not in it," Sam said. "Maheu's conning the hell out of the CIA...How you gonna kill that guy over there? He's an assassin. He knows all the tricks." (Rosselli to Church Committee; also Rappeleye, *All American Mafioso.*) Giancana's FBI case officer in Chicago, Bill Roemer, wrote that, "Giancana's part in the scheme was a ruse," the intention of which was to make the White House believe he held a "marker" on them— they owed him one. (Roemer, *Man Against the Mob,* 149-150). The CIA's Bill Harvey suspected a Giancana scam when he terminated his contacts, calling him "untrustworthy." Giancana's son-in-law Robert McDonnell remembers the don mocking the plots. "Sam thought it was hilarious that the government was paying him to kill Castro, very humorous. He never took it seriously" (Interview of *McDonnell,* June 28, 1997). Even RFK's Justice Department believed Giancana to be pulling a scam. In an August 1963 article, the *Chicago Sun Times,* quoting Department of Justice sources, concluded that Giancana only pretended to go along with the CIA operation. He did this, the article noted, "in the hopes that the Justice Department's drive to put him behind bars might be slowed—or at least affected by his ruse of cooperation with another government agency." (*Chicago Sun Times,* August 8, 1963.) The author has interviewed many of Giancana's contemporaries, family and friends, all whom laugh at the con they believe Sam pulled on the Kennedy administration.

20 Rodriguez, *Shadow Warrior,* 65-66.

21 Flora May Stephens, interview by author, 22 December 1994.

22 John Henry Stephens, Church Committee interview by Bob Kelley, 30 May 1975.

23 Blight and Kornbluh (ed.), 86-87.

24 Cables, in Mason Cargill, Church Committee Memo, 21 May 1975, from DPD files, CIA.

5 Loch Johnson, *A Season of Inquiry,* 50-51.

26 *CCIR* (Elder not named in report), 142.

27 ONI Officer, interview by author, 10 August 1994.

28 "I've got three degrees, and John was the most knowledgeable historian I ever met—absolutely brilliant." So says Mack Daniels, Gordon's predecessor at the South Carolina college they both had directed (Mack Daniels, interview by author, 3 March 1994). His successor, Dr. Stewart Strothers, agreed: " He was a genius—a brilliant man" (Dr. Stewart Strothers, interview by author, 2 March 1994).

29 *CCIR*, 93.

30 Jack Anderson, column, "Break-in at naval hero's office should be investigated," 1995 [month unknown].

31 *CCIR*, 92.

32 Jack Modesset, interview by author, 10 April 1994.

33 Mack Daniels, interview by author, 5 March 1994.

34 Heather Gordon, interview by author, 21 February 1994.

35 Balbuena was interviewed by Miami Police Intelligence detective Charles Sapp in 1963. Sapp reported: "Early in 1959, Balbuena was the contact between U.S. Naval Intelligence and the Oriente (anti-Castro Cuban) underground." In the 1970's, respected researcher Paul Hoch supplied Senator Richard Schweiker with details about when the United States similarly utilized Cuban nationals in a Castro murder plot. CIA-sponsored Antonio Veciana and Reynol Gonzalez coordinated this failed attempt. Veciana escaped to Florida, while Gonzalez and others were arrested. Amador Odio was imprisoned in Cuba for harboring Gonzalez. Amador's daughter, Sylvia Odio, would later say that Oswald showed up on her doorstep in September 1963 with two Cuban members of JURE, a group supported by Robert Kennedy. The veracity of the Odio account has never been established, but, if true, it raises the disturbing possibility that a Castro-worshipping Lee Harvey Oswald learned of the Kennedys' Cuban plotting directly from those involved. For, as will be seen, immediately after the alleged "Odio incident," Oswald went to the Cuban Embassy in Mexico City and began formulating his attack on Kennedy.

36 Documents in the author's possession were given to Senator George McGovern by Fidel Castro in 1972. They detail the extent to which Castro double agents had penetrated the Arleigh Burke/ ONI/Guantanamo plots.

37 Anti-Castro activist and sometime CIA contact Gerry Hemming told the author that he had a memory of a Marine Captain and a Lieutenant who "blew away" a Castro double agent who had picked up on the Guantanamo schemes and was going to blow the lid on Robert Kennedy.

38 F. Lee Bailey, interview by author, 20 March 1993 and 11 April 1993.

39 A 1976 Congressional investigation had access to information that verified many of Gordon's allegations. That information would also cast doubt on the denials of Jack Modesset. However, in an effort to protect JFK's image, the investigators would not disclose the evidence.

40 Evan Thomas, *The Very Best Men*, 310.

41 *CCIR*, 184-185.

42 Reeves, 713-714.

43 Jan Weininger, interview by author, 24 January 1994.

44 Jan Weininger, interview by author, 24 January 1994.

45 *CIA Inspector General's Report*, 37.

46 Sidney Gottlieb, interview by Seymour Hersh, 1994, in Seymour Hersh, 191.

47 CIA file, in David C. Martin, 122.

48 Years later, this would change. "At lunch, he'd have five martinis before he took his first bite. But he was great to work for—very loyal," remembers his assistant Sam Halpern (Sam Halpern, interview by author, 15 September 1993).

49 David Murphy, interview by author, 8 December 1997.
   In 1997, Murphy collaborated on a book with his KGB Berlin counterpart Sergei Kondrashev in which both agree that the Berlin Tunnel was a coup for the West. See Murphy, Kondrashev, and Bailey, esp. 236 and 423-428; Darrell

Garwood, *Under Cover,* 270-271.

50 Thomas Powers, 137.

51 William Harvey, testimony, 25 June 1975, Church Committee, 15.

52 Mankel was recruited by someone whose name has long been withheld—CIA contract agent David Dzitzichvili, also known as WI/ROGUE. ROGUE was described by the CIA as a man who "learns quickly and carries out any assignment without regard for danger...in a word, he can rationalize all actions" (*CCIR, 46*).

53 *CCIR,* 43.

54 *CIA dispatch,* 24 April 1964.

55 Congressional investigators would later locate documents in the CIA's files which verified that ZR/RIFLE activity against Castro had operated out of the Miami area (Mason Cargill to David Belin, Memorandum, 1 May 1975).

56 Richard Helms, testimony, *CCIR,* in Rappleye, 198.

57 Davis, *The Kennedys,* 394.

58 Jake Esterline, interview by author, 29 November, 1993.

59 Congressional testimony, in *Ranelagh,* 385.

60 *CIA 1967 Inspector General's Report,* 78.

61 *CIA 1967 Inspector General's Report,* 78-132.

62 *CCIR,* 141.

63 Christopher Marquis, "Behind the Scenes after the Bay of Pigs," *The Miami Herald,* 29 April 1996.

64 George Lardner, Jr., "Aide Tells JFK's View on Killings," *New York Post,* 21 July 1975, in Ralph G. Martin, *Seeds of Destruction,* 338.

65 Theodore Szulc, "Cuba on Our Mind," *Esquire,* November 1975.

66 Senator George Smathers, in Anthony Summers and Robbyn Summers, "The Ghost of November," *Vanity Fair,* December 1994, 100.

67 Grayston Lynch, interview by author, 1 January 1994.

68 *CCIR,* 143-144.

69 For more on Joe Kennedy's contacts with the underworld, see forthcoming volume two of this book, *Live By the Sword: Supplements and Key Documents,* soon to be available from Bancroft Press. Also see Seymour Hersh.

70 Sam Halpern, interview by author, 15 September 1993.

71 Although the aforementioned officer is now deceased, Halpern nonetheless would not initially volunteer the man's name, in deference to his family. In 1997, after a micro-examination of RFK's phone messages, veteran journalist Seymour Hersh told Halpern he knew the name of the agent. At that point, Halpern supplied the name. Also see Max Holland, "The Key to the Warren Report," *American Heritage,* November 1995.

72 Halpern noticed that Ford often wore monogrammed shirts, and thus came up with a name that matched Ford's real initials, lest he be caught in a lie by his mob contacts.

73 *HSCA Hearings,* vol. 10, 183.

74 Norman Rothman, HSCA interview, 6 April 1978; see also FBI Memos: SAC Charlotte to Director, 24 June 1961; Evans to Belmont, 26 June 1961.

75 Angelo Kennedy, interview by author, 4 January 1998.

76 It will later be seen that when the CIA, in 1967, wrote its own internal history of the assassination plots, the Rothman and Ford escapades were nowhere to be found. This continued a coverup that omitted any assassination plots that could be linked to the Kennedys. John and Robert Kennedy may have utilized both the military and intelligence apparati to have Castro murdered. Many, however, scoff at the thought of presidential liaisons to the Mafia. To assess such a possibility, one may wish to examine the long history of evidence that links the Kennedy family to organized crime. See volume two of this book, *Live By the Sword: Supplements and Key Documents: The Kennedys and the Mob.* Judy Campbell, lover to both JFK and Sam Giancana, also claims knowledge of a Kennedy/mob plot against Castro. Campbell has stated that between 1961 and 1962 she delivered secret anti-Castro intelligence from Kennedy to Giancana.

Recently, this controversial claim was corroborated by her longtime friend, Johnny Grant, who told both Seymour Hersh and ABC's Peter Jennings that a distraught Judy confided this to him at the time it was happening *(See The Dark Side of Camelot /or/ ABC's Dangerous World, The Kennedy Years)*. This would have clearly been a delicate dichotomy, because by early 1961, Robert Kennedy had launched an all-out war against the Chicago don, in spite of any pre-election deals Papa Joe may have made.

77 Michael McLaney, interview by author, 15 May 1994.
McLaney, who played golf with the president, noted that JFK's swing suffered from his back ailments. Did he ever hustle JFK? "Never. You don't do that kind of thing with the President. I think we bet $5 once," he says.

78 Steve Reynolds, interview by author, 19 May 1994.
Steve Reynolds disclosed few details about his boss and lifelong friend Mike McLaney at our initial interview, saying, "There was contact made. That's all I can say. I can't open up that can of worms. Not as long as Mike is alive." As fate would have it, Mclaney died four months later, on September 9, 1994.

79 Mike McLaney, HSCA testimony, 7 April 1978.

80 Larry Murphey, interview by author, 10 July 1994.

81 Both mob groups were familiar with the Kennedys. See volume two of this book, *Live By the Sword: Supplements and Key Documents: The Kennedys and the Mob*. Also see Moldea, *Interference*, 94-95.

82 Gerry Hemming, interview by author, 3 June 1994.

83 Jack Anderson, "Washington Merry-Go-Round," *San Francisco Chronicle*, 4 May 1963, in Hinckle and Turner, 181.

84 Gerry Hemming, interview by author, 21 February 1994.

85 Steve Reynolds, interview by author, 21 December 1994.

86 Hinckle and Turner, 244.

87 Michael McLaney, HSCA testimony, 7 April 1978.

88 Steve Reynolds, interview by author, 23 April 1997.

89 McLaney filed, and lost, a $4.2 million lawsuit against his former partner, but it helped trigger an NFL investigation in which McLaney, supported by affadavits, charged that Rosenbloom had fixed Colts' games. McLaney and Reynolds told the author of sitting in the owner's box at the 1958 Colts-Giants championship game—the so-called "Greatest Game Ever Played"—with Rosenbloom. With the game tied, sudden-death overtime was invoked under which the championship went to the first team to score. The Colts came within easy range of kicking what would have been a winning field goal, but in a controversial move, coach Weeb Eubank ordered his team to go for a much more difficult touchdown, which they made. Reynolds says, "Everything depended on the point spread and the side bets." Since the Colts were favored by 3 and 1/2 points, a three-point victory would have been meaningless. According to both McLaney and Reynolds, when the decision had to be made, Eubank looked back to Rosenbloom's box seats. "He saw four monkeys nodding in unison," laughs Reynolds. "I spent the next week flying around the country picking up bagfuls of cash from lockers. Even Joe Kennedy had a piece of the action. The Colts were given huge bonuses by Rosenbloom. Everybody was happy." To the insiders, it became known as "the greatest fix ever made."

Many observers believed that the charges of corruption against Rosenbloom were rock-solid and that the Kennedy Justice Department turned a blind eye to them because of the family friendship with Rosenbloom. "During the 1960 campaign, Rosenbloom sent the Colt team to West Virginia to help get out the vote for JFK," remembers Steve Reynolds. Rosenbloom and Joe Kennedy were so close that on JFK's election night, Rosenbloom was one of only three people invited to spend the day with the Kennedy family at Hyannis Port. This incident is mentioned by Kennedy biographer Doris Kearns Goodwin (Goodwin, 804). McLaney's aide, Steve Reynolds, verifies it. Robert F. Kennedy once received a game ball signed by all the Colts, which he kept on his desk in the Attorney General's office. Steve Reynolds says that Rosenbloom had direct access to the "red phone" in the Oval Office. Investigative journalist Dan Moldea writes:

> *Rosenbloom was a great, great friend of Joe Kennedy," says Rosenbloom's longtime friend and business partner Tex McCrary. "And he was a great friend of Jack Kennedy. Carroll worshipped Jack Kennedy. And he used to love quoting old Joe. He used to love telling a joke Joe Kennedy used to tell him: 'Never trust an Irishman with a bottle of booze or a Jew with a pack of matches (Moldea, Interference, 110)."*

90 *CCIR*, 126.
91 Pappich, Church Committee interview by Andy Postal, 25 August 1975.
92 Richard Reeves, *President Kennedy*, 288.
93 Thomas Powers, 155.
94 For a thorough discussion of this episode, see *CCIR*, 124-134. Later, in 1967, when it was thought New Orleans District Attorney Jim Garrison was learning of the Kennedy administration's plots, Bobby had his secretary retrieve the document from the FBI files, in case he needed it.
95 *CCIR*, 124-134, also quoted in Rappleye and Becker, 217.
   It is not known if Hoover, Harvey, or Edwards were aware of RFK's duplicitous dealings with the McLaney element, Charlie "Fiscalini," or Norman Rothman.
96 Director to Attorney General, FBI Memorandum, 29 October 1962.
97 Thomas Powers, 143.
98 Bruce Cheever, Church Committee interview [undated].
99 Chamberlain, CIA, to Knoche, Memorandum, 30 April 1975 in Ford Library holdings, JFK Collection, National Archives.
100 Thomas Parrott, "Memo for the Record," 5 October 1961.
101 Lonnie Hudkins, interview by author, 20 August 1993.
   Incredibly, Hudkins can corroborate his early inside knowledge of these plots. He retains copies of a December 12, 1963 Secret Service report in which he told them of the plots. The plots would not become publicly known until the Rockefeller and Church Committee investigations of the 1970's. Regarding Cheddi Jagan, newly-released documents give credence to the Hudkins story. The documents describe a series of covert operations approved by JFK against Jagan's Marxist-populist regime. These included start-up of a clandestine radio network, and inciting crippling labor strikes, followed by mysterious fires. Much of this activity was believed to be coordinated by a CIA-backed organization called the Institute for Free Labor Development, headed by William Doherty, Jr. Although Jagan was driven from office for over twenty years, he eventually returned and was elected Prime Minister in 1992. Ironically, the Clinton administration appointed the same William Doherty, Jr. as its new ambassador to Guyana.
102 Howard Burris, interview by author, 25 June 1998.
103 *New Times Magazine*, 11 July 1975, 14-15.
104 *CCIR*, 141.
105 Evan Thomas, *The Very Best Men*, 297.
106 Thomas Powers, 141.
107 Brugioni, 69.
108 *CCIR*, 146 and 152.
109 Richard Goodwin, *Remembering America*, 189; also David Aaron to Bill Miller, Church Committee Memo of Conversation with Dick Goodwin, 27 May 1975.
110 Taylor Branch and George Crile III, "The Kennedy Vendetta," *Harper's Magazine*, August 1975.
111 Grayston Lynch, interview by author, 20 January 1994.
112 Lynch later said he ran 113 raids and went on five. He told Jan Weininger recently that when he was preparing to hit the beach on one raid, General Maxwell Taylor demanded to know if he, Lynch, had permission from Bobby.
113 McCone to Director, CIA Memo, 14 April 1967.
114 *CCR*, 102.

115 Ibid, 106.
116 Ibid, 102.
117 Brennan to Sullivan, FBI Memo, 5 April 1968; re: interview of Harvey.
118 *CCIR*, 311.
119 CIA official who attended the seminar, interview by author, 13 September 1994.
120 McCone to Belin, Memorandum, 1 May 1975.
121 See JCS documents in the JFK Assassination Collection at the National Archives, College Park, MD, esp. JFK to Lansdale, "Justification for U.S. Military Intervention in Cuba," Memorandum, 13 March 1962.
122 Reminiscences of Admiral Robert Lee Dennison, U.S. Navy (Ret.), U.S. Naval Inst., Annapolis, MD (1975). See also Brugioni, 368, fn. *.
123 "Memo For Lansdale from Brigadier General W. H. Craig, 17 Jan 1962," JCS Papers in Kennedy Collection.
124 The "brink" analogy has been widely misinterpreted to mean that the Soviets might have launched their Cuban-based missiles at the U.S.. This was never a possibility. In fact, the requisite nuclear-tipped warheads that would have given the missiles potency were never even found to be on the island. Also there was no mobilization, or war-making preparedness, in the USSR detected by U.S. intelligence. A few weeks after the crisis, JFK assured German Chancellor Konrad Adenauer that the missiles were in fact removed. However, Kennedy admitted, "We don't even know if they [the missiles] were ever there at all" (Russell Jack Smith, 160). CIA analyst Dino Brugioni says that in the following weeks, CIA came to believe that the warheads were in fact on the island. This conclusion was reached when the CIA obtained photos of special vans, which were custom-built to carry nuclear material (see Brugioni, *Eyeball to Eyeball*).
   Even if the warheads weren't in Cuba, a major confrontation could have occurred in one of two ways: if the Soviets engaged the U.S. in a gunfight at the blockade line, or, if the U.S., in invading the island, sought to take the missiles out by force. In that instance, the Soviets might have employed their tactical nuclear weapons (with a 30-mile range) on the battlefield. *Those weapons were known to be operational.*
125 Fursenko and Naftali, 152-154.
126 Ibid, 150.
127 Ibid, 182.
128 Beschloss, *The Crisis Years,* 390.
129 Serge Mikoyan Oral History, 13 Oct 1987, JFK Library.
130 McNamara remarks, Tripartite Conference on the October Crisis of 1962, Havana, 9 January 1992.
131 Report by the Department of Defense and the Joint Chiefs of Staff on the Caribbean Survey Group, "Justification for U.S. Intervention in Cuba," 9 March 1962.
132 CIA Memo for File, 21 August 1962.
133 It is not known if this was also proposed by Robert Kennedy (See The Santa Ana).
134 See esp. Richard Reeves, *President Kennedy,* 367.
135 The Dennison Report was obtained by WGBH-TV and is available at the National Security Archives in Washington, D.C.
136 Arthur Schlesinger, *Robert Kennedy and His Times,* 493
137 Currey, 239-240.
138 Martin, "The CIA's Loaded Gun," *Washington Post,* 10 September 1976, C1.
139 Sam Halpern, interview by Seymour Hersh, 21 February 1997.
140 Sam Halpern, interview by author, 15 September 1993.
141 Thomas Powers, 142.
142 Ibid.
143 Sam Halpern, interview by author, 15 September 1993.
   There is yet another twist to the tale of Harvey and his dismissal after the missile crisis—one that makes Harvey out to be the unrecognized hero of the affair. It must be acknowledged that the allegation is sensational, and stems from only

one source, "John Evans," but due to "Evans'" intimate association with Harvey, it bears mentioning. By the summer of 1962, the CIA had begun to take seriously the warnings of its spies in Cuba. Stepping up the Cuban overflights of the U-2 spyplane, the CIA observed thousands of Soviet military technicians, increased cargo tonnage, and surface to air (SAM) missiles arriving in Cuba. By October 15, the President was advised that U-2 photos now appeared to show missiles with a range of over 2,000 miles (IRBM's) on the island. With the "Missile Crisis" now in full swing, Kennedy and his advisors debated both interpretation of the photos and the U.S. strategy of response. However, Bill Harvey, according to John Evans, had known for months that the Cubans were building a nuclear capability, and he possessed even more frightening information that would force Kennedy into action.

"Bill had been trying to get the missile information to Jack for months, but Bobby cut off his access to the President, and showed disdain for the accuracy of the reports," says Evans. "Bill mounted an operation inside Cuba that would prove to Bobby what had been happening." Top secret Cuban documents were spirited off the island in an operation that cost the lives of nine of Bill's agents. "Bill never forgave Bobby for their deaths, but at least now he had the proof." The proof was a document from the Kremlin that gave Castro full authority to launch the missiles, even suggesting a date, October 29, for the launch."

Harvey received the document on October 19, while Kennedy was maintaining appearances on the campaign trail in Chicago. Evans remembers, "Bill had tears in his eyes as he paced the floor saying, 'How am I going to get this to Jack?'" Harvey flew to Chicago, proceeding directly to Kennedy's Hotel, the Sheraton Blackstone. He implored Secret Service Agent Paul Cotter to let him in, saying, "I've got to see the President!" Shortly, Harvey was in Kennedy's suite, handing the documents to a stunned president. (Confidential aide to Harvey, interview by author, 12 March 1995.) Later that night, Presidential aide Kenny O'Donnell advised Kennedy press spokesman Pierre Salinger, "The President may have to develop a cold tomorrow" (Abel, 75).

Entering the Presidential suite at 8 am the next morning, Salinger found Kennedy with a scarf around his neck. Kennedy handed Salinger a note written on hotel stationery: "Slight upper respiratory infection. 1 degree temperature. Weather raw and rainy. Recommend return to Washington." Salinger wasn't buying any of it. Pressed by Salinger, Kennedy admitted that the story was a fiction. He then told his press secretary about the missiles in Cuba (Brugioni, 304). Flying directly back to Washington, Kennedy moved decisively to initiate a blockade of Cuba. Over the next two days, the military was placed on maximum alert, foreign allies alerted, and an address to the nation delivered on the following Monday night. Khrushchev eventually backed down on October 28, diffusing the crisis. "When the crisis ended, we were 18 hours from Armageddon," says Evans.

144 General Charles E. Johnson III, Church Committee interview, 28 July 1975.
145 Jake Esterline, interview by author, 29 November 1993.
146 Demaris, *The Last Mafioso,* 238.
147 "John Evans" [pseud.], interview by author, 12 March 1995.
148 David C. Martin, 147.
149 *Grose,* 326.
150 CIA officer, interview by author, 2 January 1995.
151 Sam Halpern, interview by author, 15 October 1993; Jim Flannery, interview by author, 23 December 1993; Frankie FitzGerald and Nora Camman, interview by author, 26 January 1994.

Cuba Desk executive assistant Sam Halpern had heard that FitzGerald and the President were related. So had Mexico City Station officer Jim Flannery, saying, "Like Sam, I heard that Des was related to the Kennedys." A distant family relationship is certainly a possibility. Although FitzGerald's daughter and niece claim there was no direct relationship, they agree that the bond may have something to do with the fact that Des' grandfather was from JFK's hometown of Brookline Massachussets, and both of Des' parents' last names were FitzGerald, as was JFK's grandfather's.

152 Evan Thomas, *The Very Best Men,* 297.

153 Edwin O. Guthman and Jeffrey Shulman, *Robert Kennedy: In His Own Words,* (New York: Bantam Books, 1988), 379.

154 Evan Thomas, *The Very Best Men,* 291.

155 Thomas Powers, 143.

156 Sam Halpern, interview by author, 23 December 1993.

157 Evan Thomas, *The Very Best Men,* 295.

158 George McGovern, press release, 30 July 1975.

159 "ZR/RIFLE (Executive Action)," documentary, *Cuba Vision Network,* 27 November 1993.

160 Thomas G. Patterson, Kennedy's *Quest for Victory* (Oxford: Oxford University Press, 1989), 129.

161 Wofford, 342.

Chapter Four (The Child is the Father to the Man)

1 Quoted on *FL,* 16 November 1993.

2 Epstein, *Legend,* 87.

3 Interview of James Bothelho, 7 December 1992 *(FL).*

4 Interview of Ed Butler, 6 May 1993 *(FL).*

5 In October 1963—a month before the assassination—Oswald would move to a rooming house in Dallas. The daughter of the owner would remember him as a nice, quiet man who played ball with her young children. Interview of Fay Puckett, 5 May 1993 *(FL).*

6 Interview of Priscilla McMillan, 19 August 1993 *(FL).*

7 Interview of Ruth Paine, 2 July 1993 *(FL).*

8 On the 30th anniversary of the assassination, even so respected a commentator as Nicholas von Hoffman described Oswald as a "psychotic jerk." (*New York Observer,* 20 December 1993)

9 Psychiatrist's report quoted in Hartogs and Freeman, *The Two Assassins,* 319.

10 Later, when her own mental state deteriorated after having her children, some would cite the possible effects of being raised without a mother (psychologists say this can be more devastating than being raised without a father).

11 Report of Evelyn Strickman [Siegel], Youth House, April 30, 1953 *(FL).*

12 Ford and Stiles, 71.

Immediately after the assassination, Marguerite would behave in ways that astonished those who saw her. She hadn't seen much of Lee for months, yet, when she arrived at Dallas Police Headquarters, where he was being held after the shooting, she behaved in a pushy, proprietary manner, as if the entire assassination drama were a way for her to at last receive the attention she deserved. Throughout that weekend, she displayed a kind of self-absorption that might have been mistaken for a parody in less serious circumstances. While the rest of the world was gripped by the drama and sorrow of what had happened to the President, she cared only for Lee—and not really Lee, but how she appeared because of her son. This continued after he was shot by Jack Ruby. In the protective custody of the Secret Service, she demanded beers for herself and a state funeral for her son; above all, she demanded attention for herself. (Mike Howard, interview by author, 7 December 1993.)

13 Mike Howard (one of the Secret Service agents who sequestered the Oswald family in the days following the assassination), interview by author, 7 December 1993.

14 John Pic, testimony, *WC* vol. XI, 74.

15 Report of Evelyn Strickman [Siegel], Youth House, 30 April 1953.

16 From the *Book Week* quote used on the dust jacket of *A Woman in History.*

17 From the *Saturday Review* quote used on the dust jacket of A Woman in History.

18 Allen Campbell, interview by author, 8 February 1994.

Campbell, who was older than Lee at the time, remembered being so depressed one day that he sobbed on a nearby riverbank. Approaching Campbell, Oswald comforted him, saying, "Allen, there's someone out there who loves us. One day we'll find them."

19 Interview of Alan Campbell, 5 May 1993 *(FL)*.

There is some evidence that Lee might also have suffered brain damage. When he was five years old and his brother Robert was 12, Marguerite made one of the many moves of their childhood, this time from a house in Fort Worth. As the moving van backed out of the driveway, Robert cut behind it on his bicycle. Lee followed on his tricycle, and the driver slammed on his brakes when a worker shouted a warning. The sudden stop caused a chest of drawers to slide from the back of the van and onto young Lee. He was unconscious for eight days. A doctor warned Marguerite that "if the boy comes to at all, he's going to have a problem." From then on, Lee would suffer occasional black outs. He began doing things of which he'd have no memory, such as walking out in the middle of a class and wandering school hallways. When a teacher asked where he was going, he'd ask in return what the questioner was talking about. (Former Secret Service agent Mike Howard—who helped sequester the Oswald family immediately after the assassination—interview by author, 7 December 1993.)

Based on the above account, Dr. Lee Russo, a distinguished neurosurgeon, does not preclude the possibility of temporal lobe damage, which could cause petit-mal seizures. Dr. Russo has speculated that even if the damage did not lead to anti-social behavior, seizures might have made classmates think Oswald weird, which could have made him withdraw. (Dr. Lee Russo, interview by author, 10 December 1993.)

20 Oswald's sea bag was stored in the Paines' garage. The finding of a Minox camera and undeveloped film in what was thought to be the sea bag became, for several decades, a principal source of conjecture that Oswald might have been employed by Soviet or American intelligence. Very few Americans had that kind of camera in 1963; it was largely restricted to intelligence agents and camera buffs. The mystery continued when the FBI seemingly deleted the camera from its inventory of items in the garage, compiled after the assassination. The Dallas police insisted that it had been on its list, but the FBI made no mention of the camera. The mystery deepened when copies of the developed film were obtained under the Freedom of Information Act, and the photographs included what appeared to be reconnaissance of foreign border areas and coastlines, mixed with tourist pictures of European cities Oswald was never known to have visited. But, it turned out that the FBI was right not to list the camera, for it belonged not to Oswald but to Michael Paine, who cleared up the mystery, at the author's instigation, in a 1993 interview for *Frontline*. Paine not only identified the camera as his, but also specified that he had taken each of the photos.

21 Interview of Ruth Paine, 2 July 1993 *(FL)*.
22 Oswald, 53. *WC* vol. XI, 38-39—cited in Posner, 10.
23 CD 1245, FBI report of interview with Mrs. Clyde Livingston, 4 June 1964. *WC* vol. XXV, 119—cited in Posner, 8.
24 Interview of Pat O'Connor, 14 June 1993 *(FL)*.
25 Interview of John Clark Carro, 21 May 1993 *(FL)*.
26 Interview of Evelyn Strickman Siegel, 21 May 1993 *(FL)*.
27 John Carro, testimony, *WC* vol. VIII, 207-208.
28 From Oswald's social and psychiatric reports, by Dr. Renatus Hartogs and Evelyn Strickman, as quoted in Hartogs, Renatus, and Lucy Freeman, *The Two Assassins,* New York: Crowell, 1965, 319-320.
29 Robert Oswald, testimony, *WC* vol. I, 60 (quoted in Posner, 14).
30 Hiram Conway, testimony, *WC* vol. VIII, 86.
31 Transcript of *WC* executive session, 23 June 1964.
32 Interview of Robert Oswald, 13 June 1993 *(FL)*.
33 Interview of Robert Oswald, 13 June 1993 *(FL)*.
34 Osborne, Mack, affidavit, *WC* vol. XIII, 322.

35 McMillan, 76; and see (CD 352) CE 1385 *WC* vol. XXII, 703, Aline Mosby's notes of an interview in Moscow in November 1959.
36 Interview of Owen Dejanovich, 29 April 1993 *(FL)*.
37 McMillan, 76.
38 Interview of Willy Wulf, 4 June 1993 *(FL)*.
39 Ibid.
40 Edward Voebel, testimony, *WC*, vol. III, 9.
41 Ibid, 13.
42 His Russian associates would later doubt Oswald's sincerity to the Marxist cause. A number of them told PBS's Frontline in 1993 that they were suspicious of Oswald because he never attended any Marxist meetings during his entire 2 1/2 year stay in the Soviet Union.
43 CE 2240, 2.
44 Posner, 19.
45 Interview of Dan Powers, 10 June 1993 *(FL)*.
46 Interview of Owen Dejanovich, 29 April 1993 *(FL)*.
47 Epstein, *Legend*, 88.
48 Ibid.
49 Posner, op cit., 29.
50 Gerry Hemming, interview by author, 5 June 1992.
  The Consul's name was Manuel Valasquez. His house was in Monterey Park, a suburb of Los Angeles with poor bus service and too far—some nine miles—from the city for anything approaching ordinary walking. In January of the same 1959, the Monterey Park Police were called to break up a reported quarrel at Valasquez' house. Paul Bartlett, a photographer for the local *Post Advocate*, took ten photographs of some 35 Cubans present, nine of whom were taken to the station. After Kennedy's assassination, Hank Osborne, the editor of the *Los Angeles Times*, heard that Oswald was among those photographed. He assigned a reporter named Boris Yaro to the story. The Monterey Park police told Yaro that a CIA agent had just visited the station and removed several of the photographs, which were never returned. Oswald did not appear in the photographs that remained. (Boris Yaro, interview by author, 19 October 1991.)
51 Epstein, *Legend*, 89.
52 Ibid.
53 Nelson Delgado, testimony before Warren Commission; extracted in Epstein, *Legend*, 89 Years later, when the Rockefeller Commission would investigate the Warren Commission's performance, Ray Rocca, the CIA liaison to the Warren Commission, wrote that the Delgado story was credible and should not have been overlooked by the official investigators into the President's death. Rocca wrote that Delgado's testimony suggests "more of a possible operational significance than is reflected by the language of the Warren Report, and its implications do not appear to have been run down or developed by investigation." As noted, the author attempted to learn more of this incident in 1991—hence the Hemming story.
54 Interview of Robert Oswald, 13 June 1993 *(FL)*.
55 Oswald wrote to his mother shortly before boarding the ship that would take him to Europe: "Just remember above all else that my values are different from Robert's or yours...Just remember this is what I must do. I did not tell you about my plans because you could hardly be expected to understand." (Lee Oswald to his mother, letter, CE 200, *WC* vol. XVI, 580.) The letter was postmarked 19 September 1959. Oswald's ship, a freighter named Marion Lykes, left New Orleans for Le Havre the following day.
56 Lee to Robert Oswald, letter, 8 November 1959 (CE 294), 57. Interview of Rimma Shirakova, 4 April 1993 *(FL)*.
58 For years, a remark attributed to Oswald's wife fueled speculation that Oswald arrived in Russia already proficient in the language, leading to the conjecture that he may have been trained by the military as a spy. Marina Oswald's statement that when she met him, she thought he was from "the Baltic States" was

the basis of this theory. Her remark actually was based on the fact that the Baltic citizens spoke poor Russian. In 1992, Marina would tell Gerald Posner, "Baltics don't speak Russian very well." Oswald himself remarked to a Moscow reporter: "I can get along in restaurants, but my Russian is very bad." (CE 1385) Vyacheslev Nikonnov, the KGB officer who reviewed the KGB file on Oswald after the fall of communism, said in 1993, "I don't think her impression of Oswald being from a Baltic State really reflects his good knowledge of Russian because most people from the Baltic States do not speak good Russian. In fact, they are foreigners." (I.V. 8 April 1993, [FL].)

Rimma Shirakova says that Oswald knew only a few words of Russian, like "how are you?" (I.V. 21 January 1993 [FL].) She elaborates, "As for the Russian, I helped him a bit. But I can't say that he was very good at languages " (Interview, 4 April 1993 [FL].) His first Russian girlfriend, Ella Germann, says his Russian was poor, and she agreed to help him with it. Dr. Lydia Mikhailina, who treated Oswald after his suicide attempt, says, "Oswald spoke not a word of Russian." (Interview January 1993 [FL]). Margarita Gracheva, who disbursed tourist tickets at the Hotel Berlin, where Oswald initially stayed, remembers him well, and says he spoke no Russian (Interview, 18 January 1993 [FL].)

Numerous other hotel employees confirm that Oswald definitely could not speak the language. In fact, many expressed pity for him because of the fact that, with no one to talk to, he stayed in his room alone for weeks on end. Stanisalv Shshkevich, then a teacher [foreigners were assigned], and later chairman of the Parliament of Belarus, says, "I personally taught the Russian language to the man who is considered the murderer of Kennedy. I can't say that he was very good at languages. So though he spent many hours, the result wasn't very good." (UPI story from Moscow, 23 January 1994.) Even near the end of his life, after spending over two and a half years with his Russian-speaking wife, Oswald's linguistic skills were weak. Oleg Nechiporenko, the KGB agent who saw him in the Soviet embassy in Mexico City in September 1963, says he spoke poor Russian even then. Their discussions were conducted in a "cocktail" of Russian, English, and Spanish (Interview, 27 January 1993 [FL]).

59 CE 1385, WC vol. XXII, 702, 706.
60 Interview of Rimma Shirakova, 4 April 1993 (FL).
61 Interview of Dr. Lydia Mikhailina, January 1993 (FL).
62 Nechiporenko, 54.
63 Interview of Vladimir Semichastny, 6 April 1993 (FL).
64 Dino Brugioni, interview by author, 27 January 1998.
65 Interview of son of Vasili Petrov (who asks that his name be withheld), 10 January 1993 (FL).
66 Nechiporenko, 62.
67 Izvestya, "KGB Case File No. 31451 on Lee Harvey Oswald," 11 August 1992, 3.
68 Interview of Vladimir Semichastny, 6 April 1993 (FL).
69 Nechiporenko, 61.
70 Interview of Vladimir Semichastny, 6 April 1993 (FL).
71 Interview of Pavel Golovachev, 8 April 1993 (FL).
72 Interview of Allen Campbell, 2 February 1993 (FL).
73 Interview of Richard Snyder, 19 August 1993 (FL).
Because he had CIA experience, Snyder's estimation of Oswald's appeal to the KGB rings true. Snyder continues, "All intelligence agencies, certainly ours and the KGB, used foreign nationals for their work. But I don't think they'd have touched him with a ten-foot pole. He was a flaky kid. I saw absolutely no reason to believe that Oswald was anything but what he appeared, this kid standing before me who really didn't know beans about what he thought he was going to do." Snyder subjected Oswald's knowledge of Marxism to a kind of quick oral test, and found it almost non-existent in terms of the basic theories on which the credo was based. "I never really considered him a Marxist in the sense that I believed what he said when he came in. He had all the earmarks of a sopho-more Marxist, someone who'd just discovered a religion...I had no reason to

believe he even knew what Marxism was in any serious sense." The consular/CIA official also dismissed the possibility that Oswald was a fake defector. Says Snyder, "I can't possibly imagine where the fake would arise and for what purpose. Whom was he faking it *for*?"

74 Many still insist, without any hard evidence, that Oswald was a fake defector, working for a U.S. intelligence service. A high-ranking CIA official told the author in 1993 that a program using fake defectors was considered, but never implemented. He said, "Although the Soviets had fake defectors, we in the U.S. didn't have the capability. Practically speaking, who in their right mind would defect from the U.S. in 1959 and spend the rest of their lives in Russia? On the other hand, the Soviets, I'm sure, had no shortage of volunteers." (Confidential interview by author, 15 October 1993)

Also interviewed in 1993 was Senator Richard Schweiker, who headed the Church Subcommittee looking into the JFK murder in 1975. Asked about fake defectors, he paused, looked at his aide, took a breath, and said, "Oh, I guess I can say this now. Hell, it's been thirty years, the Cold War is over. (PAUSE) I was told by knowledgeable CIA brass that there was a fake defector program. However, I was assured in a most convincing manner that Oswald was not a part of it. I agreed not to mention the program in my report." (Interview of Senator Richard Schweiker , 7 July 1993 *[FL]*.)

75 See Yuri Nosenko, interview by Gerald Posner, in Posner, 58.

76 Interview of Ernst Titovets, 6 April 1993 *(FL)*.

77 Interview of Vacheslav Nikonov, 12 April 1993 *(FL)*.

78 Quoted in "Literati Probing Oswald's Days in Minsk," *The Chicago Tribune,* 29 January 1993, 1.

79 Quoted in "Literati Probing Oswald's Days in Minsk," *The Chicago Tribune,* 29 January 1993, 1.

80 Bakatin, 163-166.

81 Interview of Vacheslav Nikonov, January 1993 *(FL)*.

82 Ivan Ivanovich Lunyov, interview by author, 14 January 1993.

83 Interview of Vacheslav Nikonov, 12 April 1993 *(FL)*.

84 Some writers such as former CIA agent Frank Camper (*The MK/ULTRA Secret*) suggest that Oswald was sent to the Soviet Union as a guinea pig—with no specific mission, but to test the viability of the concept of mind control. Camper further suggests that the Soviets knew this about Oswald, and the only reason they allowed him to stay in the Soviet Union was to study him. This remains at least logically possible. Most now agree that Oswald wasn't an espionage agent. (This theory at least explains Oswald's detached, dysfunctional attitude, his later nightmares, and his interest in LSD.)

American attempts at mind control were largely prompted by American fury and dismay over the "Communist brain-washing" that forced American prisoners in Korea to attack their homeland and government using Communist terms.

Project Artichoke, as it was named in 1952, had started earlier, with CIA attempts to duplicate suspected Soviet use of drugs and hypnosis—as demonstrated as long before as the Moscow purge trials—to alter states of mind: to strip subjects of their own desires and identities and to give them new ones. One of the possible objects of such a transformation was to see if a person could be induced to commit an assassination against his/her will. The agency had an intense interest in this possibility, and "authorized a virtually unlimited use of unaccountable funds for the project." (Gordon Thomas, 96) The first practical steps to test the possibility of breaking and re-making human minds took place during the summer of 1950. Rapid alternating injections of powerful depressants and stimulants were used, then massive electroshock and a variety of drugs (including LSD and heroin) and hypnotic techniques, including inducing amnesia so that the subject would not remember the "treatment." Quite a few doctors and scientists from various disciplines were recruited. Although it would be unfair to say that none of them had moral concerns or scruples, all fit Allen Dulles' insistence that the ethics of every member of the staff "must be such

that he would be completely cooperative in any phase of our program, regardless of how revolutionary it may be." The objects of the most dangerous experiments were captured spies, defectors, suspected double agents, etc.
(Simultaneously, the Navy was carrying out tests on unwitting American college students. The chief doctor knew this was "unethical," but felt he had to do it "for the good of the country.")
In April 1953, Artichoke (see Gordon Thomas) became MK/ULTRA, to which behavioral research was transferred in 1954 (Marks, 186). The link to Oswald, for some, is the fact that he was stationed at the Atsugi U-2 base ,which is believed to be one of the two foreign CIA stations where MK/ULTRA experiments were conducted.

When the Americans took over Atsugi after World War II, they were amazed to find an "entire city" underground. The Japanese had used it for storing records, including all the documentation of Colonel Ishi, the father of Japan's chemical and biological warfare. Some believe that the CIA wanted to capture and occupy the city for that reason. One of Ishi's experiments was infecting fleas with botulism. Few realized that Japan's only way of reaching the U.S. with its botulism weapons were a few hundred balloons—which were filled with the infected fleas. Luckily, Isihi wasn't able to keep the fleas alive during their voyage.

Under the Kennedy administration, the most extreme experiments were terminated, but more remained than changed. When John McCone became the new CIA director, Richard Helms persuaded him that the Agency was close to cracking the secret of mind control, and McCone was impressed enough to urge RFK to allow MK/ULTRA to continue. "The Agency may have acquired new heads, but the body politic remained as intact as it had been under Dulles." (Gordon Thomas, 232)

Behavioral research of this type was supposedly terminated in 1963 (Marks, 212)—but actually went on much longer under a different name. The records were destroyed in 1973.

Many CIA officers have told the author that the technique was never perfected, let alone deployed. They have further stated that the research was inspired by fears that the Soviets had already perfected the technique. In typical Cold War paranoia, the Soviets pointed to equivalent fears about the U.S. as the basis for their experiments.

One New York psychologist has said: "It cannot be done consistently, but it can be done." (Marks, 187)

(See also: Brackman, Arnold C., *The Other Nuremberg*, New York: Morrow, 1987; and Williams, Peter and David Wallace, *Unit 731*, New York: Free Press, 1989. For stories of extraordinarily cruel use of these experiments and techniques, see the bibliography under Bain and Bowart.)

85 Interview of Ella Germann, 5 April 1993 *(FL)*.
86 Oswald's Historic Diary (CE24), entry for 2 January 1961; cited in Posner, 60.
87 Interview of Ella Germann, 5 April 1993 *(FL)*.
88 Ibid, 103.
89 Interview of Yuri Merezhinski, 14 April 1993 *(FL)*.
90 Ibid, 55.
91 Interview of Oleg Pavlovich Tarusin, 21 January 1993 *(FL)*.
92 Interview of Vanda Ivanova Kuznetsova, 21 January 1993 *(FL)*.
93 Interview of Galya Vasylievna Printseva, 21 January 1993 *(FL)*.
Many interviewees in 1993 were not so kind to Marina. A number of acquaintances claimed that she was "an easy lay" and that Oswald was her ticket out of the country. Many firmly believe that she was run out of Leningrad with a band of prostitutes. She was said to cheat on Oswald constantly, from the very beginning of their marriage. Marina admitted one such tryst to her biographer, Priscilla McMillan (McMillan, 129). After the assassination, with all Marina's communication monitored, Marina earned the name "hot pants," as the FBI agents in charge would later tell the HSCA. There are numerous stories of

Marina's many liaisons with government employees during the 1964 investigation. One reporter told the author that Buell Frazier, Marina's young neighbor who gave Lee the ride to work on the fateful day, admitted to having an affair with Marina during her separation from Lee.

94 Interview of Oleg D. Kalugin, 13 January 1993 (*FL*).

95 McMillan, 39.

On the surface, it may seem trivial to examine the background of Marina in a study of the death of President Kennedy. However, it will be one thesis of this work that the lack of communication between Lee and Marina would play a large role in Oswald's desperation at the end of his life. This is not meant to imply that Marina was responsible for the events of 22 November 1963. Only a rare woman could have penetrated Oswald's wall of emotional isolation. It is important to realize, however, that Marina Prusakova was in no way suited to the task.

96 Ibid, 54.

97 Interview of Vacheslav Nokonov, 12 April 1993 (*FL*).

98 Interview of Vacheslav Nokonov, 12 April 1993 (*FL*).

99 Quoted in Mailer, 285.

100 Nechiporenko, 63.

101 Ibid, 63.

102 Broadcast on "Who Was Lee Harvey Oswald?" *Frontline* (PBS), 16 November 1993.

103 Interview of Vladimmir Semichastny, 6 April 1993 (*FL*).

104 McMillan, 546.

Chapter Five (Back in the USA)

1 Interview of Jim Hosty, 25 April 1993 (*FL*).

2 Interview of Edward Butler, 6 April 1993 (*FL*).

3 Appendix A offers a summary of recent, conclusive evidence establishing that Oswald shot alone. Appendix B shows seemingly contradictory testimony to be mistaken conjecture.

4 McMillan, 340-341; also, interview of Priscilla McMillan (*FL*).

5 Posner, 321.

6 McMillan, 340.

7 *The Militant,* 11 March 1963, 7.

8 *The New York Times,* 17 October 1961.

9 *The Militant,* 7 October 1963; Michael Paine, testimony, *WC*, 414.

10 Meticulous examination after the assassination would show that Oswald almost certainly took some of the photographs to a local drug store for development. It is possible he developed one of them himself at the Jaggars-Chiles-Stovall Company, a commercial photography firm where he had been working as a trainee since the previous October, four months after returning from the Soviet Union.

Using many techniques, including microscopic examination of the emulsion, which is impossible to fake, the House Select Committee on Assassinations (HSCA) decisively showed that the photos were not forged. Critics have also questioned the inscription on the back of one of the photos given to an Oswald friend, George DeMohrenschildt. After examining examples of his handwriting taken from all parts of his life, a panel of experts concluded with no qualifications that he had indeed written, "to my friend George, from Lee Oswald." The puzzle was, who added "Hunter of fascists, ha-ha—ha!!!" in Russian—but in a hand unaccustomed to writing it—on the back with Oswald's inscription? Experts established that that handwriting wasn't Oswald's. Neither was it the handwriting of Marina or DeMohrenschildt. Who, then, was the mysterious fourth person who had access to this incriminating photograph? Was it someone whose function was to set up Lee? If so, wasn't that powerful evidence of a conspiracy? Over the decades, many researchers have suspected that this might be true. DeMohrenschildt's wife Jeanne seems to provide the answer. In 1993, Ferris Rookstool, who inherited the DeMohrenschildts' possessions (including the original photo), pointed out to the author that the handwriting is identical to Jeanne's, and that among her favorite expressions was a protracted "Ha ha ha!"

11 Interview of Michael Paine, 19 August 1993 *(FL)*.

Paine later took Oswald to a meeting of the American Civil Liberties Union "because I wanted him to see the activity of a group that was doing some of the things he wanted and doing them in a nonviolent way." But Oswald said that that activity "wasn't political enough. And he also said he didn't want to be defending the right of people on the far right—fascists—to free speech." Still later, when Paine was to learn that Oswald had in fact joined the ACLU, he assumed it was because Oswald thought that if he was a member, "they might more readily come to his defense if he ever needed them."

12 Interview of Dovid Ofstein, 16 June 1993 *(FL)*.

13 Oswald conceivably also sent a print to the Secret Service office in the White House, where an agent named John Norris would adamantly remember seeing it pasted on a wall before the assassination, then noticed it gone on November 22nd. That has not been confirmed by fellow agents, although Norris feels they too should be able to remember the photograph. It is almost unthinkable that Oswald was planning to kill the President in March or April (or even through the summer of 1963). Memories play odd tricks on people involved in celebrated cases. But if Oswald did, in fact, send a print to the White House, it would be further evidence not of his criminal intent at this time, but of his inordinate hunger for recognition and appreciation.

14 Interview of Michael Paine, 19 August 1993 *(FL)*.

15 Interview of Sylvia Weinstein, 12 June 1993 *(FL)*.

Four months later, Weinstein would again hear about Oswald, after his arrest for handing out leaflets of the Fair Play for Cuba Committee in New Orleans. The "big worry" at *The Militant's* office then was, "Who is this guy? Why is he causing all these problems?" After the assassination, Farrell Dobbs directed that the photograph, together with "every scrap of paper" mentioning Oswald, including his subscription plate, be swept from the files and given to William Kunstler, the well-known civil-rights attorney who represented the publication.

16 Interview of Volkmar Schmidt, 17 June 1993 *(FL)*.

17 Oswald would use the alias Alik Hidell on several forged documents as well. According to Marina, Oswald most likely would have pronounced the alias Heedel, the Russian pronunciation, which perhaps not coincidentally rhymed with Oswald's hero Fidel.

18 Interview of Volkmar Schmidt, 17 June 1993 *(FL)*.

About "logical suicide," Schmidt said that a man who knows his powers but who hasn't been given a good set of values to use them may eventually kill himself. Schmidt asserts, "Whatever happened, he would have found a victim because he was so obsessed with doing something. His assassinations were literally a means of substitute suicide: killing somebody else instead of killing himself."

19 Max Clark, testimony, *WC* vol. VIII, 350.

20 CE 100, *WC* vol. XVI, 437.

21 Interview of Priscilla McMillan, 19 August 1993 *(FL)*.

22 Interview of Volkmar Schmidt, 17 June 1993 *(FL)*.

23 Myrna Blyth and Jane Farrell, "Marina Oswald: Twenty-Five Years Later," *Ladies Home Journal*, November 1988, 237.

24 The book by Kennedy was his *Profiles in Courage*. The book about him was William Manchester's *Portrait of a President*. From an early age, Oswald's reading set him apart from his schoolmates and others around him. A friend of his mother called him "a bookworm" at the age of seven (Marilyn Murret, testimony, *WC* vol. VIII, 51). While fellow Marines played cards or "shot the shit"

538 NOTES TO CHAPTER FIVE

or perhaps gawked at issues of a relatively new magazine called *Playboy* on a troopship delivering them to Japan in August and September, 1957, Oswald read Walt Whitman's *Leaves of Grass,* hardly typical Marine Corps reading. Oswald liked history, especially military history, but his interests also included biography and science fiction. As for his feelings about John Kennedy before 1963, the evidence is inconclusive. A Russian friend would remember that Oswald "liked" the President (Ernst Titovets, interview by author, 15 April 1993). Marina would tell the same thing to a Dallas friend named Ruth Paine (Ruth Paine, interview by author, 2 July 1993), but provide more details to Priscilla McMillan, author of *Marina and Lee*, a book about their relationship and history. According to McMillan, Marina specifically praised Kennedy for his stance on civil rights—although, he added, Kennedy's father had bought him everything and paved the way for him to become President. She also told McMillan that he expressly criticized the president for the Bay of Pigs invasion. When the Kennedys' infant son Patrick Bouvier would die on November 7th, 1963, both Marina and Lee Oswald, whose second daughter had been born two weeks earlier, took the tragedy personally, suffering with the President and First Lady.

Whatever Oswald's feelings were for John Kennedy personally and as a fellow father, his political convictions and own personal ambition almost certainly superseded them. Oswald consistently argued that capitalism had to be destroyed. When the time came—a time when Oswald had almost certainly learned of new Kennedy threats to Cuba well after the Bay of Pigs—he no doubt concluded that the most any individual could do to destroy it was strike at the person on top, and the more effective leader he was, the harder the blow to capitalism.

25 According to Priscilla McMillan, author of *Marina and Lee,* Lee told Marina that he would be President or Prime Minister in 20 years. She made fun of him for that claim, answering that right now, she needed a new pair of pants. Lee said that "the child they were about to have would be President or Prime Minister, and he didn't seem to distinguish or realize that there's no Prime Minister in the United States" (Interview of Marina, 19 August 1993 *[FL]*). A Dallas friend of Oswald's named George DeMohrenschildt once asked him—teasingly, he thought, in response to Oswald's Marxist pronouncements—whether he'd like to be a commissar in the United States. DeMohrenschildt saw that the idea delighted Oswald. "To me, it was a ridiculous question to ask. But he took me seriously" (George DeMohrenschildt, testimony, *WC* vol. IX, 241).

26 Blakey and Billings, 147.
According to a young man who did messenger work with a 15-year-old Oswald in 1955, Oswald said then that he would like to kill President Eisenhower—who "exploit[ed] the working people"—if he had the opportunity (FBI report about an affidavit of Palmer McBride, 26 November 1963).

27 By that time, DeMohrenschildt's mental state had deteriorated too badly to trust his memory about anything significant. But his clear-headed wife, Jeanne, disputed the description of Oswald by the Warren Commission and the mass media as "a complete loner, a total failure, both as a man and a father" (Jim Marrs, *Crossfire: The Plot that Killed Kennedy,* (New York: Carroll & Graf Publishers, 1989, 285).

28 Hinckle and Turner, 406.

29 It seemed incredible not only to proponents of conspiracy theories. FBI agent Jim Hosty, who looked after Oswald in Dallas for a time, would join the "anti-conspiracy-believers" who also doubted that a debriefing of Oswald hadn't been conducted.

30 Not all Intourist guides fulfilled that role, but a great many did, one way or another.

31 Anthony Summers, *Conspiracy.*

32 Sober scholars of Cold War practices long speculated that the CIA could not and

did not pass up its opportunity with Oswald. Many assassination researchers surmised that DeMohrenshildt was, at most, Oswald's CIA handler, his contact and watcher in the middle, or his debriefer at the least. Edward Jay Epstein, for example, stated that DeMohrenschildt was Oswald's debriefer, and strongly implied that a friend of DeMohrenschildt functioned as his case officer in the matter. That friend was J. Walton Moore, the CIA's Domestic Contact officer in Dallas. Moore would not comment about this for 30 years, but recently denied any such thing to the author, saying he "never even heard of Lee Oswald until one night at dinner, when George mentioned he was helping a Russian woman named Marina, who was having marital problems [with Oswald]. I encouraged George to help her as a Good Samaritan. That's the extent of it" (J. Walton Moore, interview by author, 25 April 1993).

33 Casasin, HSCA Staff interview, 17 August 1978, and Walter P. Haltigan, HSCA Staff interview, 13 June 1978, in HSCA Staff Notes section of the JFK Collection, National Archives. The HSCA verified that Haltigan's assistant, Robert G. Lamprell, in fact delivered the memo to CIA headquarters.

34 Interview of Donald Denesleya, 10 May 1993 *(FL)*.

35 HSCA Outside Contact Report, 17 October 1978, HSCA Staff Notes Section of JFK Collection, National Archives.

36 Interview of Michael Paine, 19 August 1993 *(FL)*.

37 Interview of Volkmar Schmidt, 17 June 1993 *(FL)*.

38 Interview of Volkmar Schmidt, 17 June 1993 *(FL)*.

39 "James Hepburn" [pseud.], 139.

40 Max Holland, "Cuba, Kennedy, and the Cold War," *The Nation,* 29 November 1993.

41 Jim Hosty, interview by author, 22 June 1993.
"This is a possibility," Hosty would speculate, "just as I think Castro put the idea into Oswald's mind to shoot President Kennedy for attempting to overthrow him (Castro)."

42 Marina Oswald, testimony, *WC* vol. I, 17.
Lee's revelation that he had shot at Walker came the morning after the event, when he learned from the radio—to his disgust—that he had missed. At that point, Marina thought him "sick...not a stable-minded person."

43 General Walker's own investigators, privately hired to find out who tried to kill him, tracked down a man named Bill Duff, who told them he had fired the shot. However, there is very little controversy about the conclusion that the shooter was actually Oswald. Marina would testify convincingly about his activities and statements both before and after the shooting, which leave little doubt that her husband was responsible. The bullet retrieved from General Walker's dining room was too damaged to match ballistically to Oswald's Mannlicher-Carcano 6.5 exclusively, but it was determined to be the same type of ammunition, made by the same manufacturer, as the bullets that killed President Kennedy (Posner, 116).

44 Elmo Cunningham, interview by author, 8 December 1993.

45 Larry Schmidt allegedly told Brad Angers that he and his brother Bob Schmidt gave Oswald the idea to shoot Walker when the three were driving around drunk. Later, according to Schmidt, Bob and Oswald did just that. This lends support to the eyewitness testimony of neighbor Kirk Coleman, who saw two men fleeing Walker's house immediately after the shooting (Interview of Brad Angers, 19 March 1993 (FL); interview of Walter Kirk "Case" Coleman, 15 June 1993 *(FL)*).
Hosty suspects the shooting might have been an inside job. (Some of Walker's own people were angry with him because of his recent arrest in Oxford, Mississippi, for inciting a riot there—Hosty was in charge of that investigation, so he was familiar with the personnel. Bob Schmidt was his driver.) Hosty also suggests the shooting was arranged by Walker himself as a publicity stunt—in fact, the Dallas Police considered these as possibilities and were working on them.

Mary Brengel, New Orleans detective Guy Banister's temporary secretary, lived for a time in Dallas. She says Walker was gay and often had young boys from Europe at his house. Walker would twice be arrested and fined for making lewd sexual advances to undercover policemen in the men's rooms in two Dallas public parks (*Dallas Times Herald*, 17 March 1977). Although they were American citizens, Bob and Larrie Schmidt were raised in Europe.

46 Hinckle and Turner, 249.
47 Kent Courtney, interview by author, 7 February 1994.
    Walker had described the incident in detail to Courtney, his fellow conservative from Louisiana.
48 Elmo Cunningham, interview by author, 8 December 1993.
49 When Schmidt had to go abroad soon afterward, he left money with friends for a large party for the Oswalds. After the assassination, Marina stayed for a time with one of the couples she would meet at that party.
50 Michael Paine, testimony, *WC* vol. II, 403, also in Posner, 112.
51 Marina Oswald, testimony, *WC* vol. I, 17, also in Posner, 116.
52 McMillan, 279-281.
53 Marina Oswald, testimony, *WC* vol. I, 17, also in Posner, 116.
54 Interview of Priscilla McMillan, 19 August 1993 *(FL)*.
55 Interview of Case Coleman, 15 June 1993 *(FL)*.
56 Interview of Owen Dejanovich, 29 April 1993 *(FL)*.
57 Interview of Dovid Ofstein, 16 June 1993 *(FL)*.
58 McMillan, 239.
59 McMillan, 262-263.
60 Ibid, 281.
61 Dallas Chief of Police Jesse Curry, Memorandum, 15 May 1964, CE 1409; also in *Dallas Times Herald*, 9 Dec 1963, 18.

Chapter Six (Washington, New Orleans, and Cuba)

1 Interview of Stephen Tyler, 12 February 1993 *(FL)*.
2 Sergio Arcacha Smith, interview by author, 30 June 1994.
3 Layton Martens, interview by author, 26 July 1994.
4 Davis, *Mafia Kingfish*, 22.
5 For more on Louisiana and the Napoleonic Code, see *Jefferson's Louisiana*, by George Dargo (Boston: Harvard University Press, 1975).
6 While "codified law" makes Louisiana unique in the U.S., it puts it very much in step with the rest of the world.
7 "New Orleans in the Early 1960s," *Win Magazine*, February 1969, 5.
8 Arthur Carpenter, "Social Origins of Anticommunism," *Louisiana History*, 119.
9 Layton Martens, interview by author, 12 May 1993.
10 "New Orleans in the Early 1960s," *Win Magazine*, February 1969, 5.
11 William Dalzell, interview by author, 5 February, 1994.
12 Sergio Arcacha Smith, interview by author, 30 June, 1994.
13 Julian Buznedo, interview by author, 13 July, 1994.
14 CIA Internal Memo, "CIA Involvement with Cubans and Cuban Groups," 8 May 1967.
15 "New Orleans in the Early 1960s," *Win Magazine*, February 1969, 9.
16 Sergio Arcacha Smith, interview by author, 30 June, 1994.
17 Warren C. DeBrueys, HSCA testimony, 13 May 1978, 7.
18 Morrison, 33.
19 Locals claim that Morrison was never actually a reform candidate, and that, in fact, he was only able to defeat the powerful R.D.O. (Regular Democratic Organization) machine with the help of local Mafia don Carlos Marcello.
20 Morrison had served in the state legislature with Ross Banister, who recommended his brother Guy to the mayor as a possible facilitator for the "reforms."
21 Allen Campbell, interview by author, 8 February 1994.

Campbell would later work for Banister in New Orleans.

22 Joe Newbrough, interview by author, 8 February 1994.

For more on the Morrison controversy, see Haas (in Bibliography). Banister intended to record his methods in what would become a textbook for use throughout the country. But the work did not end well. When Banister's investigations started to hit close to home, Morrison attempted to divert Banister by assigning him to root out the Communists of New Orleans. Knowing that this was Banister's passion, the Mayor hoped he would back away from the graft investigations. It didn't work. By this time, Banister had the audacity to align himself with a chief gadfly of the administration, Aaron Kohn of the Metropolitan Commission. Together, Banister and Kohn relentlessly pursued corruption, pitting themselves against prominent administrators, regardless of who had appointed them. The inevitable soon followed. (Interview of Joe Newbrough, 6 April 1993 *[FL]*).

23 The actual circumstances behind Banister's eviction from the police department were clouded by an episode that took place during Mardi Gras in 1957. Banister reportedly pulled a gun on a waiter. Some insisted that he had been provoked or even set up by enemies. Banister employees, such as Joe Newbrough, were convinced that the entire episode was a setup. Letters among Morrison's papers reflect a mayor under pressure to dismiss Banister. At one point, however, Morrison interceded with the Police Commissioner to lift Banister's suspension.

24 Interview with Joe Newbrough, 6 April 1993 *(FL)*.

25 "Louisiana Intelligence Digest," vol. 1, number 1, 1961.

26 Delphine Roberts, interview by author, 8 February 1994.

Testimony by Mary Brengel, Banister's one-time secretary, illustrates the uncountable number of circumstances that can be considered suspicious by people with that inclination. Brengel could not remember Roberts bringing a radio to the office at any time before the fateful day, November 22, 1963. She does remember that someone telephoned Roberts in mid-morning "and she turned on the radio real quickly...and we listened until the President was dead." No one can stop people from interpreting such slim evidence as indication that Roberts had advance knowledge of the event in Dealey Plaza. In any case, she seems to confirm both Roberts' elation at the news and Banister's quite different reaction. "Then [after hearing the news on the radio], she jumped up from her desk, twirled around the office, and said, 'Oh, he's dead, he's dead, he's dead!' And that was strange to me because although I was not a follower of President Kennedy, I respected his office, and I think most conservatives did. We wouldn't get out and want him assassinated" (Mary Brengel, interview by author, 6 June 1993).

27 *New Orleans Times-Picayune*, 18 April 1961, 9.

28 *HSCA*, vol X, 127.

29 Sergio Arcacha Smith, interview by author, 14 May 1994.

30 *HSCA*, vol. X, 57.

31 Ibid; see also CIA Internal Memo, "CIA Involvement with Cubans and Cuban Groups," 8 May 1967.

32 Lou Ivon, Memorandum, based on an interview with Richard Rolfe, 13 January 1968.

33 CIA document 1363-501, 26 October 1967.

CIA documents also state that one of Arcacha's regular FBI contacts was Banister—which supports the evidence of Banister's files that he never stopped working for J. Edgar Hoover.

34 Dick Billings' Internal Memo, *Life Magazine*, April 1967.

The memo concluded that Arcacha was "doing all sorts of things to help start a revolution to help free his native land, and was considered by United States agencies as an ally of the U.S."

35 There are a host of conceivable ways for the introduction to have occurred: first, through any one of a number of exile leaders who were mutual acquaintances of both RFK and Arcacha, such as Artime and Ray. Secondly, the papers of

Mayor Morrison, also Bobby's good friend, reflect a friendship with the mayor and Arcacha. Arcacha once gave Morrison a certificate of appreciation from the local CRC chapter for his help with the exiles. Finally, the local FBI agents Warren DeBrueys and Ernest Wall acted as liaisons between the Cubans and Washington, and could have facilitated the introductions.

36 *New York Times,* "Anti-Castro Units Trained..." 7 April 1961.

37 Ronnie Caire, New Orleans District Attorney's office, interview by author, January 23, 1967.

38 *New Orleans Times-Picayune,* 11 April 1961, sec. 3, 4.

39 Sergio Arcacha Smith, interview by author, 24 April 1997.

40 Sergio Arcacha Smith, interview by author, 14 May 1994.

41 Martin Underwood, interview by author, 9 September 1997.

42 Corn, 76.

43 Kirkpatrick, 189.

44 *New Orleans Times-Picayune,* 5 January 1961, 2.

45 *New Orleans Times-Picayune,* 11 April 1961, sec. 3, 4.

46 *New Orleans Times-Picayune,* 8 April 1961, 9.

47 Sergio Arcacha Smith, interview by author, 14 May 1994.

48 *HSCA,* vol. X, 107.
   Ferrie was not in the minority in expressing his outrage. As we have seen, even JFK's advisors criticized him severely after the 1961 event. JFK was even harsh on himself.

49 Nick Caridas, owner of a concession at Lakefront Airport where Ferrie regularly ate. Interview by author, 7 February 1994.

50 Interview of Layton Martens, 12 May 1993 *(FL).*

51 Al Beauboeuf, interview by author, 26 January 1994.

52 Morris Brownlee, interview by author, 29 November 1993.

53 Morris Brownlee, interview by author, 29 November 1993.

54 Layton Martens, interview by W. Scott Malone, 25 February 1993 *(FL).*

55 Gerry Hemming, interview by author, 15 February 1994.
   The story that blew the operation was written by Bill Stuckey of the *New Orleans States Item* on July 21, 1962.

56 Sergio Arcacha Smith, interview by author, 14 May 1994.

57 Sergio Arcacha Smith, interview by author, 14 May 1994.

58 Layton Martens, interview by author, 5 July 1994.

59 Sergio Arcacha Smith to Eddie Rickenbacker, letter, 18 July 1961, cited in Fensterwald and Ewing, 496.

60 To this day, everywhere one goes in New Orleans one hears tales of David Ferrie's inspirational prowess.

61 Morris Brownlee, interview by author, 7 July 1994.

62 Interview of Layton Martens, 12 May 1993 *(FL).*
   Another possibility for RFK contact with Ferrie involves Ferrie's piloting abilities. Testimony was given to D.A. Jim Garrison that Ferrie had flown a high official of Freeport Sulphur Company, located near New Orleans, to Cuba along with local businessman Clay Shaw (whom Garrison later indicted for conspiring with Ferrie to kill Kennedy). The New York sales manager for Freeport Sulphur, former Senator Paul Douglas, was a close friend of Bobby Kennedy (James Cogswell, interview, *HSCA* Outside Contact Report, 6 July 1978).

63 Herbert Wagner, deposition to the New Orleans District Attorney Office, 6 December 1967.

64 David Ferrie to Eastern Airlines, letter, 30 October 1961, FAA copy on file in *HSCA* JFK Collection, box 284, file 014904.

65 Morris Brownlee, interview by author, 5 February 1994.

66 Interview of Layton Martens, 7 July 1993 *(FL).*

67 Martens believes that Ferrie and Arcacha took the materials, believing that Martens was too young to hold on to them, and because he would have no use for them after he returned to school.

68 HSCA Memo of interview with Ross Crozier, submitted by Gaeton Fonzi to

Robert Blakey, 16 January 1978.

69 Fonzi, 360.

Gerry Hemming, an anti-Castro activist, has said that the Cuban underground furnished him with the missile information at least six months prior to the crisis (Gerry Hemming, interview by author, 3 November 1993). Hemming's group, Interpen, passed this information along to Republican Senator Kenneth Keating, who then went on the Senate floor on August 31, 1962 to reveal what he knew. (See Keating's article in *Look Magazine,* "My Advance View of the Cuban Crisis," November 3, 1964.) CIA executive Sam Halpern says, "We were aware that Keating had sources on the missiles, but we were never able to determine who they were." (Sam Halpern, interview by author, 15 October 1993).

70 Fursenko and Naftali, 193.

71 Morris Brownlee, interview by author, 29 November 1993.

72 *New Orleans Times-Picayune,* 29 December 1961.

73 Joe Newbrough, interview by author, 8 February 1994.

George Faraldo, a Cuban exile with extensive knowledge of aerial photography and espionage techniques, may have been the original source of the Ferrie/Arcacha photos. He told HSCA investigator Gaeton Fonzi that he had "taken shots of the Russian missiles in Cuba long before Kennedy announced that they existed." Faraldo said, "I was told I was working for the U.S. Information Agency," but all along he believed he was working for the CIA (Fonzi, 65).

74 Louis Rabel Nuñez, interview by author, 6 February 1994.

75 Phillips, 124-125.

Allegedly, the British also had advance knowledge of the missiles. According to British Royal Air Force (RAF) squadron leader Anthony M. Eaton, British overflights in October 1960 took reconnaissance photos that "clearly indicated IRBM emplacements being set up in several locations." Eaton says the information was passed on to the U. S. State Department (Affidavit of Eaton to Robert Morrow, 3 June 1976).

CIA contract agent Robert Morrow has long insisted that the underground apparatus of Cuban "president-in-exile" Mario Garcia Kohly also had learned of the missiles in 1961 and had reported it to President Kennedy. The exiles were infuriated when Kennedy did nothing (See Morrow, *Betrayal* and Morrow, *First Hand Knowledge*).

76 Ed Dolan, interview by author, 17 October 1997.

77 Rafael Nuñez, interview by author, 12 April 1995.

78 Layton Martens, interview by author, 3 February 1994.

The members of Arcacha's CRC were not the only New Orleans exiles receiving the missile reports. Carlos Bringuier, leader of the Cuban Student Directorate in New Orleans, recently stated, "The leaders of the Student Directorate had a list of all the sites where Castro had deployed the missiles long before the crisis" (Carlos Bringuier, interview by author, 28 February 1994). Kent Courtney, Banister associate and publisher, corroborates him, saying, "Carlos Bringuier told me about the missiles very early on." (Kent Courtney, interview by author, 7 February 1994). Layton Martens believes this early knowledge of the missiles helps explain the Kennedy obsession with killing Castro. "It was known in our office that the Kennedys wanted Castro dead," says Martens. "We were told that the CIA was 'under the presidential hammer' to get the job done."

79 Of this similar trouble spot, Kennedy aide Arthur Schlesinger, Jr. wrote that Kennedy "had never really given it [Vietnam] his full attention." Kennedy had once remarked that one of his favorite books was David Cecil's *Melbourne,* a biography of the British Parliamentarian, Lord Melbourne. One of Melbourne's most famous precepts was "When in doubt, do nothing."

80 Cited in 2 August 1976 press conference by Congressman Thomas Downing, first chairman of the HSCA.

81 In 1967, Martens would undergo a polygraph (lie detector) examination for the New Orleans D.A.'s office. Among other things, he would disclose his and

Arcacha's relationship with Bobby Kennedy. The test results indicated no evidence of deception. The test was administered by Richard O'Donnell for the New Orleans District Attorney, Jim Garrison.

82 Memorandum for Chief [deleted], 19 October 1967.

83 Special Agent in Charge to J. Edgar Hoover, FBI Memorandum, New Orleans office, 20 April 1967.

84 Guy Johnson, interview by Bernard Fensterwald, 24 August 1967, Assassination Archives and Research Center, Washington, D.C.

85 Jack Martin and David Lewis, affidavit to New Orleans District Attorney Jim Garrison, 20 February 1968, 33.

More on the Regis Kennedy/ Guy Banister relationship:

The inference that Regis Kennedy sanctioned the arms transfer jibes with testimony regarding an incident six months later. In early 1962, Regis Kennedy visited Frank DeLabarre, nephew of Gus DeLabarre, who owned the property being used as one of the exile training camps. Kennedy offered DeLaBarre a chance to do some gun-running. DeLaBarre asked, "What the hell are you talking about?" Kennedy replied, "Well my old boss, Banister, he's back doing something" (Frank DeLaBarre affidavit to New Orleans District Attorney Jim Garrison; also Frank DeLaBarre, interview by author, 5 February 1994). Banister's secretary in 1963, Mary Brengel, said that Banister formed a group of ex-FBI men, with Regis Kennedy given the task of guarding the Mississippi Test Site (Mary Brengel, interview by [FNU] Navarre, 1 June 1967).

Banister assistant Jack Martin wrote, "We often met Regis Kennedy during this period in Banister's office. Sometimes we'd run into him several times a day." He claimed that daily reports on Cuban activities were written by Regis Kennedy, and forwarded to FBI Assistant Director Mohr. Regis Kennedy himself admitted going to Banister's office and seeing Jack Martin there (Jack Martin and David Lewis, affidavit to New Orleans District Attorney Jim Garrison, 20 February 1968, 35; also Regis Kennedy, Memo to Special Agent in Charge, New Orleans, 18 May 1967).

Betty Parrot, a friend of Bill Dalzell (a founder with Banister and Jack Martin of the Friends of Democratic Cuba), also said that Regis Kennedy was working with Dalzell and Friends of Democratic Cuba. Parrot said they were involved in shipments of men and supplies to Cuba. "He came by the house many times to discuss it" (Betty Parrot, interview by New Orleans DA staff investigator Andrew Sciambra, 1 April 1967 and 18 September 1967).

Former CIA agent Dalzell had numerous contacts with New Orleans CIA agent Lloyd Ray (Dalzell called him Logan), a fact which was confirmed by CIA personnel. Dalzell reportedly admitted to the *New Orleans States-Item* that he was "CIA" and that his advisors were Logan and Regis Kennedy. Dalzell recounted how he first met Kennedy: "The day after the Bay of Pigs, Regis Kennedy came to my door. I thought he wanted to bust me for my work with Cubans. I explained the situation to him and he said, 'There is no Mr. Ray of the CIA.' So I walked him across the street to the Masonic Building, where the CIA was headquartered, and introduced him to Mr. Ray." Mr. Ray removed Dalzell from any trouble (William Dalzell, interview by author, 5 February 1994). (Lloyd Ray may also have been involved in an Oswald debriefing.)

These interrelationships go a long way to explaining why any investigation of 544 Camp street after the assassination was relegated to a quick phone call to Banister. On June 1st, 1964, as the Warren Commission raced to meet its deadline, Banister ran into Jack Martin. He asked Martin, "You haven't been circulating anything about me you shouldn't, have you?" Martin responded, "Your old buddy Regis Kennedy has pretty well taken care of things" (Martin and Lewis, affidavit to New Orleans District Attorney Jim Garrison, 11). Regis was still an FBI agent—one of the men who did the investigating for the Warren Commission, through Hoover.

86 Jack Martin and David Lewis, affidavit to New Orleans District Attorney Jim Garrison, 20 February 1968, 35.

87 Frank Hernandez, Sergio Arcacha's attorney, interview by author, 18 February 1994.
88 Interview of Gordon Novel, 2 June 1993 *(FL)*.
89 Ronnie Caire, *NODA* interview, 23 January 1967.
90 Carlos Quiroga, deposition to HSCA, 19 June 1978.
Quiroga said he was introduced to Arcacha by the FBI's Warren DeBrueys, who recommended that Quiroga work with them.
91 Carlos Quiroga, statement to NODA, [undated].
92 Luis Rabel Nunes, interview by author, 6 February 1994.
Much as Luis Rabel was linked to RFK's "Cuba Project" through the CRC, his brother Ricardo became the key component of another secret, Kennedy-inspired Cuban operation in 1963, known as AM/TRUNK. The dramatic details were given the author by family members, and supplemented by recent CIA disclosures.
93 Luis Rabel Nunes, testimony to HSCA, 11 May 1978.
94 Delphine Roberts, interview by author, 8 February 1994.
95 Mary Brengel, interview by author, 6 June 1993 *(FL)*.
96 *New Orleans States-Item*, 25 April 1967; in Flammonde, 119.
97 FBI bio of Ferrie supplied to FAA, 30 October 1961.
98 There are also indications that an earlier raid was undertaken before the Bay of Pigs, as some Schlumberger weapons were seen in the hold of the Santa Ana, piloted by Nino Diaz from New Orleans to Cuba (Turner and Hinckle, 85).

Chapter Seven (The Kennedys and the Communists)

1 Graham, 193.
2 Haynes Johnson, 213.
3 Lazo, 378.
4 The details of the individual raids are found in *HSCA*, vol. X, 12-14. Robert Morrow, who helped the exiles counterfeit Cuban currency, described a raid on his operation in his book *Betrayal*.
5 Article cited in Weisberg, *Oswald in New Orleans*, 147.
6 Kennedy to McNamara, Memo, *FRUS*, 1961-1963, vol. XI, 379.
7 Kennedy to McNamara, Memo, *FRUS*, 1961-1963, vol. XI, 381.
8 "Cuban Missile Crisis and its Aftermath," State Dept. Release, 1997.
(Summarized in Associated Press, "Papers: Kennedy Broke Pledge," 6 April 1997.)
9 Hinckle and Turner, 176.
10 *CCR*, 171; also *FRUS*, 1961-1963, vol. XI, 781-782.
11 Kennedy's knowledge of history made him skeptical of unqualified statements, and cautious about predictions. But writing a year later, Arthur Schlesinger, Jr., Kennedy's aide and biographer, had time to consider the results of the "Peace Speech." Schlesinger entitled his chapter on the missile crisis "The Great Turning."
12 Until recently, opposing tests had been regarded as "madness, if not treason," as summarized by one of American's soberest political commentators, Tom Wicker.
13 What everyone then knew was substantially less than the whole truth. The dismantling of the Soviet missiles was as much a horse trade as a clear-cut victory for Kennedy, who secretly promised to remove American Jupiter missiles from Turkey, installation of which had been one of the chief threats to the neighboring Soviet Union that prompted Khrushchev to take his extremely risky gamble on Cuba. As agreed, almost a year later, the Jupiters were withdrawn—so quietly that no public link would be made with the Soviet "blink" and retreat from Cuba. Kennedy insisted that the bargain not be revealed, and Khrushchev complied.
14 Remarkably, the Soviet press interrupted its distorting and censoring to publish the full text of the speech, which many citizens tore from newspapers to preserve. Many also heard a Russian translation on the Voice of America, whose

broadcasts were not jammed except for the paragraph about the "baseless and incredible" Soviet claims that the United States intended to achieve world domination by war. The Soviets stopped jamming most Western broadcasts soon thereafter. During the following years, they would resume and stop again, in accordance with fluctuating Cold War temperatures.

15 Parmet, 352.
16 Ayers, 76-77.
17 Memo for the Special Group, 19 June 1963, 1; cited in *CCIR*, 173, fn. 2.
18 Al Haig, interview by author, 26 February 1998.
19 Excerpted from "Memo For General Lansdale: Ideas in Support of Project, from: DOD Caribbean Survey Group," 2 February 1962, *Califano Papers*, compiled 1 May 1963.
20 Haig, 109-110.
21 Al Haig, interview on ABC's *Nightline*, 29 December 1997.
22 Al Haig, interview by author, 26 February 1998.
23 CIA to Church Committee, Memo, "Approved CIA Covert Operations into Cuba," 11 July 1975; cited in *CCIR*, 173.
24 CIA, "Memo for SAS," 17 July 1963.
25 Manolo Reboso, Roberto San Román, John Nolan, interviews by author, 1993-94.
26 Haynes Johnson, 161-162.
27 Harry Williams, interview by Hinckle and Turner, quoted in Hinckle and Turner *(The Fish is Red)*, 168.
28 Hinckle and Turner, 168
29 Guthman and Shulman, 377.
30 Harry Williams, interview by author, 22 December 1993.
31 Harry Williams, interview by Hinckle and Turner, quoted in Hinckle and Turner *(The Fish is Red)*, 170.
32 Harry Williams, interview by author, 22 December 1993.
33 Harry Williams, interview by author, 22 December 1993.
34 Hunt wrote his own account of his involvement with the Cubans entitled *Give Us This Day*, listed in the bibliography.
35 Szulc, *Compulsive Spy*, 96.
36 Frank Sturgis, interview by Andrew St. George, *True Magazine*, August 1974.
37 Dinges, 61.
38 *Associated Press* dispatch, 10 May 1963.
39 Morrow, *First Hand Knowledge*, 187.
40 Ibid.
41 Lamar Waldron, interview by author, 1 May 1998.
42 Anthony Summers and Robbyn Summers, "The Ghost of November," *Vanity Fair*, December 1994, 100-101.

Chapter Eight (Yet Another Invasion Plan)

1 Hinckle and Turner, 36.
2 L. Fletcher Prouty, interview by Aureliano Sanchez Arango, Jr., 7 May 1998; also Prouty, 50.
3 Bernard "Macho" Barker, interview by Judith Artime, in Artime, 16.
4 Carillo, 182-184, cited in Artime.
5 Angelo Kennedy, interview by author, 8 January 1998.
6 Roberts, 99.
7 Christopher Marquis, "Behind the Scenes after the Bay of Pigs," *Miami Herald*, 29 April 1996. The article drew on newly-released State Departnment documents.
   The dungeons were built in 1774. The 1,179 prisoners had one toilet, for which the wait was two days. They slept on concrete floors in dimly lit cells. The men told of how they were rarely fed, and even then their food was a horrific concoction that tasted like dirt mixed with water. Sometimes their meals consisted of a stew made from small animals—the heads of rats or cats often

surfaced in the pots. There was no medicine for the hepatitis and gastroenteritis which raged in the overcrowded cells.

8 "We Are Frantic," *Newsweek,* 13 August 1962.
9 Haynes Johnson, 328.
10 Angelo Kennedy, interview by author, 24 April 1997.
11 *Orlando Sentinel Star,* 12 June 1977.
12 Pam Turnure started seeing Kennedy in the late fifties when Jack was a (married) Senator. The conjugal visits to the 21 year-old Turnure's Georgetown apartment so infuriated her landlady, Florence Kater, that she began surveilling the lovers. In her personal effort to thwart Kennedy's rising political star, Kater photographed and recorded the goings-on. JFK then had Turnure (whom the president had hired as an "assistant") move in with another of his mistresses, Mary Meyer. After winning the election, Jack got Turnure hired as Jackie's appointments secretary, the effect of which was said to be a daily embarrassment to the First Lady.
13 Bernard "Macho" Barker, interview by Judith Artime, in Artime, 39.
14 Manuel Hernandez would go on to become a history professor at Georgetown University.
15 H.L. Hunt, *Memo For the Record,* 5 April 1963.
16 Haig, 111.
17 Hinckle and Turner, 170.
18 *Miami News,* "Profile of Artime," 27 July 1977.
19 Nilo Messer, interview by Judith Artime, in Artime, 46-47.
20 Manuel Hernandez, interview by author, 5 January 1998.
21 *HSCA*, vol. X, 68.
22 Haig, 112.
23 Manuel Artime, interview, in HSCA Memo, Gonzales to Blakey, 3 November 1977.
24 Letter from CIS to Robert Kennedy, 26 January 1963, National Archives JFK Collection.
25 Hinckle and Turner, 165.
26 Files of CIA/DDO "Ray," vol. XVI, Memo for Director of Central Intelligence, 9 July 1964, from Des FitzGerald, Subj: "Chronology of Concept of Autonomous Operations and Summary of Financial Support to Manuel Artime," in HSCA Staff notes, Gaeton Fonzi, JFK Collection.
27 *Orlando Sentinel Star,* 12 June 1977.
28 Profile of Artime, *Miami News,* 27 July 1977.
29 *Orlando Sentinel Star,* 12 June 1977.
30 Raphael Quintero, interview by author, 6 November 1997.
31 Blight and Kornbluh, 122.
   Quintero knows what he is talking about in making this comparison: he would become a major player in North's and Casey's "Iran-Contra" resupply scheme of the 1980's.
32 Ted Shackley, interview by author, 12 December 1997.
33 Colonel James Patchell to Joseph Califano, Trip Report, 30 June 1963; in Joseph Califano Papers, JFK Collection, National Archives.
34 Corn, 98.
35 Sam Halpern, interview by author, 9 March 1998.
36 Blight and Kornbluh, 121.
37 CIA Memo for SAS, 17 July 1963.
38 Des FitzGerald to DCI, "Chronology and Concept of Autonomous Operations and Summary of Financial Support to Manuel Artime," Memorandum, 1964.
39 CIA, "Blind Memo," 21 Aug 1963.
40 Rodriguez, 116-118.
41 *Orlando Sentinel Star,* 12 June 1977.
42 Corn, 98.
43 Tom Clines, interview by David Corn, 98.
44 Corn, 82.

45 Ibid, 100.
46 Sam Halpern, interview by author, 1 July 1995.
47 FitzGerald to Bundy, Memorandum, August 9, 1963, in *FRUS*, 1961-1963, vol. XI, 853-855.
48 Hinckle and Turner, 165.
A CIA document verifies Artime's access to the President, stating that his organization "was supported by both the CIA and the White House," and that "Manuel Artime...[and] the CRC had direct access to President Kennedy and top Executive Branch aides" (CIA Internal Memo, "CIA Involvement with Cubans and Cuban Groups," 8 May 1967).
49 *New Orleans States Item,* 29 November 1956, 1.
50 Rolando Cubela Secades, *HSCA* interview, 28 August 1978.
The description of the officer points to the possibility that it was David Atlee Phillips, Cuba Counterintelligence Specialist at the Mexico City Station.
51 *CCIR*, 86.
52 Secretary of the Army Cyrus Vance to Assistant Secretary of Defense, "Future U.S. Policy Toward Cuba," Memorandum, 3 September 1963; in Joseph Califano Papers, JFK Collection, National Archives.
53 *CC Final Report,* bk. V, 100; also Beschloss, The Crisis Years, 639-640.
54 Raphael Quintero, interview by author, 6 November 1997.
55 Sam Halpern, interview by author, 15 October 1993.
56 *FRUS,* 1961-1963, vol. XI, 114.
57 *CC Final Report,* bk. V, 14, fn. 17.
58 *CC Final Report,* bk. V, 19.
59 Joint Chiefs of Staff Draft Memo for the President, 4 December 1962, JCS Papers, JFK Collection, National Archives.
60 The relevant documents are located in the JFK Collection at the National Archives in College Park, MD. See the personal papers of Joseph Califano, the Army, and the JCS Papers. Released in November 1997, the papers comprise over 1,500 pages.
61 Taylor Memo of Meeting with JFK, 28 February 1963, *FRUS,* 1961-1963, vol. XI, 711-712.
62 Memo from Kennedy to McNamara, 29 April 1963, *FRUS,* 1961-1963, vol. XI, 791.
63 Memo from McNamara to Kennedy, 7 May 1963, in *FRUS,* 1961-1963, vol. XI, 802-803.
64 JCS Memo for the Chairman, "Draft State-Defense Contingency Plan for Cuba (S), Sept. 26, 1963," JCS Papers, JFK Collection, National Archives.
65 Dean Rusk, interviewed by Anthony Summers and Robbyn Summers, "The Ghosts of November," *Vanity Fair,* December 1994, 105.
66 *CCIR*, 86.
MH/APRON is referred to in the CIA's 1967 Inspector General's Report on Castro Assassination Plots, 79 (it is censored in most available versions of this report).
67 CIA Interim Working Draft, "AMTRUNK Operation," 14 February 1977.
68 Andrew, 303.
69 Seymour Hersh, 282-283.
70 Hurwitch, who later became Ambassador to the Dominican Republic, specialized in Cuban affairs, and had been instrumental in RFK's Brigade prisoner release negotiations.
71 CIA Interim Working Draft, "AMTRUNK Operation," 14 February 1977.
72 Robert Stevenson, interview by author, 22 February 1996.
73 In a dramatic postscript with parallels to Romeo and Juliet, Ricardo and Sylvia never abandoned their attempts to reunite. On September 7, 1963, having given up on the CIA and desperate to take her family to Miami, Sylvia tracked Castro to his beach house at Santa Maria Beach. Encountering the dictator swimming, Sylvia made her plea, "Commandante, please let me leave." To that, Castro responded, "You will never leave Cuba. Your husband was a traitor to the revolution." In 1965, after much planning, Ricardo borrowed a "cigarette" style

motorboat, and traveled 90 miles across the ocean alone to a prearranged, secluded coastal point to pick up his wife. However, Castro's omniscient intelligence apparatus, not Sylvia, met him upon arrival. After three years of aiding in the CIA AM/TRUNK operation, Ricardo Rabel was sentenced to thirty years imprisonment, and thrown into the infamous Cuban dungeons. After one year, he was transferred to the regular prison, where he died four years later. Sylvia and her family eventually made it to the U.S. during the 1980 Mariel boatlift.

74 Other key participants were Jorge Volsky (USIA), Alfonso Rodriguez (CIA), and Colonel Albert C. Davies, on loan to the CIA from the Army.

75 AM/TRUNK officer, interview by author, 8 February 1995. Background on AM/TRUNK operation from author interviews with Luis Rabel, Sylvia Rabel, and other family members, February 6, 1994. CIA documents from AM/TRUNK file, released to the National Archives in 1994.

76 Ted Shackley, interview by author, 12 December 1997.

77 Alexander Haig, interview by author, 26 February 1998.

78 Hinckle and Turner, 230.

79 CIA documents released in 1993 confirmed the existence of a training camp located at the Naval Ammunition Depot in Belle Chasse, Louisiana. See David A. Phillips, Memo for the Chief of Counterintelligence, 26 October 1967.

80 Bill Stuckey, "Cuban Force Trained Here For Invasion," *New Orleans States Item*, 16 April 1962.

81 *New Orleans States Item*, 1 August 1963, 1.

82 Flammonde, 119.

83 Harold Weisberg, *Oswald in New Orleans*, 374.

84 Wannell to Sullivan, FBI Memo, 29 July 1963.

85 William McLaney, interview by author, 10 April 1994.

86 Gerry Hemming, interview by Lamar Waldron, 10 April 1996.

87 SAS to DCI, CIA Telex, 10 September 1963.

88 John Crimmins, Memo of conversation, 17 August 1963.

89 It is a virtual certainty that Sierra's Chicago-based "Junta" was part of the "autonomous operations" package approved by JFK in June.

90 Arthur Schlesinger, *Robert Kennedy and His Times*, 587.

91 SAC New Orleans to Director, FBI Airtel, 7 March 1967, #62-109060-4758.

92 SAC New Orleans to Director, FBI Airtel, 7 March 1967, #62-109060-4758.

93 CIA Internal Memo, "CIA Involvement with Cubans and Cuban Groups," 8 May 1967.

94 "Anti-Castro Units Trained..." *New York Times*, April 7, 1961.

95 *HSCA*, vol. X, 71.

96 Milo Messer, interview by Judith Artime, 49.

97 Al Burt, "Cuban Exiles, The Mirage of Havana," *The Nation*, 25 January 1965, 76-79.

98 Luis Arrizurieta, interview by Judith Artime, 46.

99 "Juan" [pseud.], interview by author, 14 May 1994.

100 Frank DeLaBarre, interview by author, 5 February 1994.

101 Angel Vega, testimony to New Orleans District Attorney Jim Garrison, 5 February 1967.

102 Frank DeLaBarre, HSCA interview, undated.

103 Frank DeLaBarre, interview by author, February 5, 1994.

104 Julian Buznedo, interview by author, 13 July 1994.

105 Interview of Joe Newbrough, 6 May 1993 (*FL*).

106 Morris Brownlee, interview by author, 17 July 1994.

107 Various *Miami News* sources, cited in Weisberg, *Oswald in New Orleans*, 158-159.

108 UPI, *The Charge*, by Adolfo Merino, 3 Sept 1964.

109 Weisberg, *Oswald in New Orleans*, 154-155.

110 Hinckle and Turner, 226.

111 FBI Report of 25 February 1963, File #55-29, "Threat Against the President of the United States." Also, Report of Miami FBI Agent Peter J. Nero to Secret Service, 7 February 1963, File #105-6932.

Chapter Nine (Kennedy and Oswald: Colliding Obsessions)

1 McMillan, 417.
2 McMillan, 397.
3 Marina Oswald to Ruth Paine, letter, 25 May 1963, CE 408.
4 Jesse Garner, testimony before the Warren Commission, 267.
5 McMillan, 412.
6 Ibid, 413.
7 Lynne Loisel to Jim Garrison, Memo about interview of Henry Gogreve, 7 March 1967.
8 L.J. Delsa (HSCA investigator who located the witnesses), interview by author, 10 May 1993.
9 McMillan, 452.
10 Charles LeBlanc, testimony, *WC* vol. X, 214.
11 McMillan, 452.
12 *HSCA,* vol. II, 252.
13 Jay Epstein, *Frontline* interview, 1993.
14 *HSCA Report,* 176.
15 Kennedy, *Profiles In Courage,* 11.
16 Ibid, 16.
17 One of the empty offices in the building was the former headquarters of Sergio Arcacha Smith. If Oswald had followed up and rented an office, the chances are good that he would have held Arcacha's space—adding still another ironic twist to the Kennedy/Oswald story.
18 Morris Brownlee, interview by author, 17 July 1994.
19 "Juan," confidential interview by author, 14 May 1994.
20 V.T. Lee, "Cuban Counter-Revolutionaries In the United States." Pamphlet found among Oswald's possessions on 22 November 1963.
21 McMillan, 410.
22 Interview of Joe Newbrough, 5 May 1993 (FL).
23 As we have seen, Oswald was a compulsive liar, prone to exaggerate his own importance. According to the building's landlord, James Arthus, someone, possibly Oswald, approached him that summer to rent an office, but never followed up. At the time, Oswald worked one block away at the Reily Coffee Company. He had been denied his request to set up a New Orleans office for a local Fair Play For Cuba Committee, but he pretended to have leadership approval anyway, and therefore needed a physical office and address. Passing by the Camp street lobby, Oswald would have noticed the bank of mailboxes in the lobby. Joe Newbrough describes the scene, saying, "In the front, you would see a wall on your right side with multiple mailboxes—more mailboxes than were necessary for the number of occupants in the building." Oswald's use of the address therefore served multiple purposes. (Interview of Joe Newbrough, May 5, 1993 *[FL].)*
24 Ross Banister, HSCA interview by L.J. Delsa, 11 August 1978. (Information from interviewer's notes.)
25 Marina Oswald, testimony, *WC,* vol. V, 401.
26 Warren C. DeBrueys, testimony before the HSCA, 13 May 1978, 26.
27 Ernesto Rodriguez, interview by Earl Golz of the *Dallas Morning News,* 7 March 1979.
28 Philip Geraci, testimony, *WC,* vol. X, 77.
29 Ibid, 77.
30 Carlos Bringuier, pamphlet: "Oswald: A Castro Agent In the United States."
31 Carlos Bringuier, interview by author, 10 July 1994.
32 CE 93, *WC,* vol. XVI, 341.
33 Interview of Carlos Bringuier, 5 May 1993 (FL).
34 *WC,* V.T. Lee Exhibit 6; vol. XX, 261, cited in Posner, 158.
35 "Juan," confidential interview by author, 14 May 1994.
Juan told the author that "after the assassination, the FBI interviewed me for three days, and all they wanted to know was, 'Was Castro behind it?'"

36 Carlos Bringuier, testimony, *WC*, vol. X, 39.
   Much of what we know of Quiroga's conversation stems from the fact that he reported it to Carlos Bringuier.
37 CD 75, 705.
38 Warren C. DeBrueys, testimony before the HSCA, 13 May 1978.
39 *HSCA*, vol. X, 62.
40 Lynne Loisel to Jim Garrison, Memo about interview of Henry Gogreve, 7 March 1967.
41 McMillan, 351.
42 INCA's specialty was taping interviews with refugees from communist countries and distributing them to radio stations in Central America.
43 Interview of Carlos Bringuier, 5 May 1993 *(FL)*.
44 Interview of Ed Butler, 6 May 1993 *(FL)*.
45 Interview of Ed Butler, 6 May 1993 *(FL)*.
46 Interview of Carlos Bringuier, 5 May 1993 *(FL)*.
47 Carlos Bringuier, interviewed by Posner, cited in Posner, 162.
48 Interview of Ed Butler, 6 May 1993 *(FL)*.
49 McMillan, 441.
50 Interview of Carlos Bringuier, 5 May 1993 *(FL)*.
51 *WC* Exhibit #1145, vol. 22, 168-169.
52 Johnson Exhibit *(WC)*, #4A, vol. XX, 265 (cited in McMillan, 443).
53 McMillan, 443-447.
54 Ibid, 444.
55 Ibid, 449-450.
56 CD 1203, 21. Also see Evaristo Rodriguez, testimony before the *WC*, 4 April 1964.
57 Interview of Carlos Bringuier, 10 July 1994.
58 Warren C. DeBrueys, New Orleans Field Office Report, 17 July 1964.
59 Oswald had applied for a new passport on 24 June, and received it on 25 June. He stated his desire to travel to England, France, Germany, Holland, USSR, Finland, Italy, and Poland. Oswald received Passport # D 092526. According to Passport Office records, Pena also went to the Passport Office on 24 June 1963. (CE 950, 278, 285-286; Hoover to Lee Rankin [*WC* attorney], letter regarding Pena passport, 1 July 1964.)
60 Weisberg, *Oswald in New Orleans*, 317.
61 *WC*, vol. XI, 325-339.
   This is seemingly corroborated by a recent discovery. While working on PBS's 1993 Frontline program "Who Was Lee Harvey Oswald?" researcher Miri Navasky was given exclusive access to the working notes of Marina's biographer, Priscilla McMillan *(Marina and Lee)*. Navasky found that according to one handwritten note of an interview with Marina, she apparently told McMillan that "Lee was very often in the company of Cubans in New Orleans."
   By far the most sensational allegation is that of Oswald's friend Adrian Alba. Alba told Frontline investigator Scott Malone that RFK's network in New Orleans had considered recruiting Oswald for the Castro assassination plot. "Oswald was one of ten dossiers given to RFK to assassinate Castro." Alba's sources for this information were John Rice of the Secret Service (who parked his car in Alba's garage), and a writer from a local paper named "Fitz." His sources also told him that after the assassination, RFK was seen in the Justice Department wailing, "I've killed my own brother!" (Adrian Alba, interview W. Scott Malone, 27 February 1993.) Alba repeated this story to the author in 1994, and to author Gerald Posner.
62 Pavel Golovachev, interview by Peter Wronski, printed in *The Third Decade*, May 1992.

Chapter Ten (Mexico City: The Parallax View)

1 This is a photographic term that refers to the difference between the image seen in the viewfinder of a non-reflex camera, and what actually appears in the picture-taking lens—a fancy way of saying "things aren't what they seem." The term was used as the title of a fictional 1974 film about an assassination.

2 Fonzi, 266.

3 Phillips, 114.

4 Coincidentally, the same West Indian Creoles who settled in Louisiana helped Mexico gain its independence from Spain in the nineteenth century. Mexico City shares still another similarity with "the Big Easy." It is infamous for its history of political corruption.

5 Russell, 229.

6 Nechiporenko, 72.

7 *New York Times,* 27 February 1994.

8 Another problem in the trade, so to speak, is the treachery a triple agent poses by picking and choosing from both troughs.

9 It is not common knowledge, but in a few rare instances the FBI was allowed a permanent overseas presence. Mexico City was one of those rarities.

10 Ibid, 98.

11 Beck, 85.

12 Phillips, 113-114.

13 Agee, 537-538.

14 Raphael Quintero, interview by author, 6 November 1997.

15 Krulak, Memo, "To Service, Joint Staff..." 5 March 1963; in Joseph Califano Papers.

16 Nechiporenko, 70.

17 The week he would spend here cost him an estimated $85, including transportation, hotel, and food. ("Analysis of Lee Harvey Oswald's Finances from June 13, 1962 through November 22, 1963," *WC* Appendix XIV, 741.)

18 Affidavit of John Bryan and Merlyn McFarland, *WC* vol. XXV, 749-750 (cited in Posner, 172) Summers, *Conspiracy,* 343.

19 Warren Report, 735 (cited in Posner, 190).

20 Interview of Sylvia Duran, 8 May 1993 *(FL).*

21 Interview of Mrs. Eusebio Azcue, 8 May 1993 *(FL).*

22 Nechiporenko, 68-69.

23 Ibid, 70.

24 Ibid, 69.

25 Interview of Sylvia Duran, 8 May 1993 *(FL).*

26 Nechiporenko, 77.

27 Valery Kostikov, interview by author, 3 May 1993.

28 Nechiporenko, 78-79.

29 Interview of Pavel Yatskov, 3 May 1993 *(FL).*

30 Nechiporenko, 81.

31 Ibid, 80.

32 Police Officer Charles Thomas, Memo, 10 December 1965.

33 "Mexico City Report," *HSCA,* 206-257.

34 "Mexico City Report," *HSCA,* 206.

35 June Cobb Sharp, interview by John Newman, 4 March and 17 March 1995; cited in Newman, *Oswald and the CIA,* 380.

36 "Willard Curtis," Memo for files, 25 November 1964. ("Curtis" was the codename of Station Chief Win Scott.)

37 "Mexico City Report," *HSCA,* 213.

38 Ibid, 195.

The source was undoubtedly Luis Alberu, a cultural attaché in the Embassy. According to recently-released CIA documents, Alberu was doubling as an agent for the CIA. This document took the form of a request for approval of Alberu's counterintelligence work. In the document dated 27 July 1962, both Alberu's

"201" number (328609), and his Office of Security (OS) number (OS-279-089) are divulged.

39 Ibid, 195-196.

40 Ibid, 197 (interview of David Phillips, 3 August 1978).

41 Lonnie Hudkins, interview by author, 20 August 1993.

42 Harold Weisberg to Jim Garrison, Memo, 17 March 1968.

43 "Mexico City Report," *HSCA*, 254.

44 CIA Memo for "Willard C. Curtis" (Win Scott), 13 June 1967.

45 Newman, *Oswald and the CIA*, 388.

46 Ibid, 388.

47 "Mexico City Report," *HSCA*, 201.

48 Gaeton Fonzi to G. Robert Blakey, Memo (telephone interview of Alvaro Proenza), 14 April 1978.

49 Elizabeth Mora, testimony, in "FBI LEGAT Mexico City to Director," 24 January 1964.

50 MIAMI SAC to Director, FBI Teletype, 4 January 1964.
It may have also reached the CIA's Cuba specialist in Mexico City, David Phillips, as Verson was also one of Phillips' agents. ("Afterword: The Search for Maurice Bishop," *Lobster #10,* January 1986.)

A possible link between Oswald and the Cuban officials is viewable through the story of Oscar Contreras. It should be noted that Contreras has been inconsistent about the time frame of the occurrence. However, it is not inconceivable that, in the context of what we now know about the Mexico City episode, other parts of his story deserved more attention in 1963 than they were given.

Oscar Contreras, a member of a pro-Castro student group, recalls encountering Oswald during his "missing days." At the time, Contreras was a law student at the National Autonomous University of Mexico City. One day in the cafeteria, a young man walked up to Contreras' table and introduced himself as Lee Harvey Oswald, at one point spelling out his entire name. Oswald made quite a stir over his desire to obtain a Cuban visa, and wondered if Contreras and his friends could help. Coincidentally, Contreras did have contacts in the Cuban Consulate, and, although they were suspicious of Oswald's real motivation, agreed to help. (Contreras, *HSCA* Report, 124-25, fn. 17, cited in Summers, 351)

A later FBI interview with Contreras established that he "belonged to a clandestine pro-Castro revolutionary group...[which] visited Cuba and met Castro and [his brother] Raul." (FBI Memo for Director, 30 June 1967). The document continued, "The group allowed Oswald to accompany them the rest of the day, that night (at a group safehouse), and part of the next day." When pressed for details of what the group discussed with Oswald, Contreras refused to answer. He was a no-show for a scheduled follow-up interview. The FBI was clearly disturbed by Contreras' refusal to discuss the details, and by his failure to appear.

51 Interview of Dr. Eduardo Borrell Navarros, May 10, 1993 *(FL)*. Navarros added, "For anyone who knows anything about Castro and his personal history, I think they can believe anything. He has absolutely altered the hemisphere. He was capable of sending soldiers to Angola. He is a governor with, you could almost say, psychopathic characteristics, someone who wants to become a leader of all Latin America, who took soldiers to Grenada where forty-five Cubans were killed. How can anyone doubt, in fact, Castro's participation, whether direct or indirect, in Kennedy's assassination?"

52 Cited in Epstein, *Legend,* 237.

53 *The Miami Herald,* 23 October 1975.

54 WAVE to Director, cable, 30 November 1963.

55 FBI report of agent William Stevens, File # 105-655, 24 October 1962.

56 *Dallas Morning News,* 24 September 1975, from a *Los Angeles Times* story by Charles Ashman.

57 Jim Hosty, interview by author, 13 March 1994. See also "Hoover Said to Have Been Told Oswald Disclosed Plans to Cubans," *New York Times,* 12 November

1976. On "Solo" mission, see "Lee Harvey Oswald in Mexico: New Leads," *Lobster #6*, November 1984.
58 *The Wall Street Journal*, 18 October 1993, A18.
59 SAC New York to Director, FBI AirTel, 12 June 1964 (released on 30 March 1995).
60 Schorr, 177. (The Clark story was ghost-written by Nina Gadd.)
61 Blakey, 145.
62 "Comer Clark Allegation," HSCA Summary.
63 *HSCA Final Report* (Bantam Edition), 142.
64 *New Times Magazine*, 11 July 1975, 13-14.
65 *Miami Herald*, 22 March 1976 and 13 November 1976; *Chicago Sun-Times*, 19 November 1976.
66 WC Exhibit No. 103, vol. XVI, 443-444.
67 Raymond Rocca, Church Committee interview by Dan Dwyer and Ed Greissing, 15 March 1976. Also, CIA Review of Oswald File, 23 May 1975.
68 CIA Blind Memo, 7 May 1964.
69 Transcript, CIA JFK Segregated File, at the National Archives.
70 CIA Review of Oswald File, 23 May 1975, 19.
71 Blakey, 154.
72 CIA Blind Memo, 7 May 1964.
73 Blakey, 148, 155.
74 Autilio Ramirez Ortiz, HSCA interview, 25 August 1977 (Doc # 005134).
75 Summers, *Conspiracy*, 451.
76 Herminio Portell-Villa, FBI interview, 21 May 1964. (HSCA Box 465, folder 1.)
77 Secret Service Field Report of Ernest Aragon: interview of Cuban exile and attorney, Dr. Fernando Penebaz, 29 November 1963. Included in the Secret Service interview of Penebaz is the following footnote: "Reference is made to the file involving a Cuban plot to assassinate the President under file SC-2-32-682, dated December 14, 1962, wherein Machado is prominently mentioned. 'The source [of that report] cautions that Quinton Pino Machado should be considered a dangerous person.'" See also *HSCA Final Report*, 147.
78 *HSCA Final Report*, 147-148.
79 *The Boston Record American*, 31 March 1963.
80 Edward McCarthy, *Working Press*, 9-19.
81 *HSCA Final Report* (Bantam Edition), 316-324.
82 *HSCA Final Report*, 320, fn. 2.
83 "Mexico City Report," HSCA, 178.
84 *CCIR*, 173.
85 Jose Aleman, Church Committee interview by Andy Purdy, 10 March 1977; Aleman HSCA testimony, 27 September 1978.

Chapter Eleven (Two Tracks to Oblivion)

1 Reeves, 655-657; also Beschloss, *The Crisis Years*, 641-642.
2 Colby and Dennett, 404-407.
The Kennedy camp also feared the potential candidacy of the devout Mormon Governor of Michigan George Romney. "We have to watch Romney," advised Robert Kennedy. "People buy that God and country stuff."
"Romney could be tough," the President responded. "You have to be a little suspicious of somebody as good as Romney. No vices whatsoever, no smoking and no drinking. Imagine someone we know going off for twenty-four or forty-eight hours to fast and meditate, awaiting a message from the Lord whether to run or not...Give me Barry. I won't even have to leave the Oval Office" (Reeves, 655-657).
3 Over the years, debate has raged as to whether Kennedy had set his mind on pulling out of Vietnam in his second term. There is much evidence to support that interpretation. However, there seems to be even more evidence that

Kennedy was flexible to a fault on this issue—seemingly inclined to change his mind from week to week. As CIA agent Grayston Lynch says, "Kennedy was one of those guys who, you know—whoever talks to him last has his way. He just blew with the wind. They spent so much time trying not to embarrass themselves that they brought on the very embarrassment they sought to avoid." (Grayston Lynch, interview by author, 20 January 1994). Marine Major General Victor Krulak, appointed by Kennedy as the Special Assistant for Counterinsurgency and Special Activities, was one of Kennedy's closest military advisors on Vietnam policy. Krulak told the author in 1994, "If there was a plan to pull out of Vietnam, I never saw it. The truth of the matter is we had no more of an idea of what to do than you or anyone else. It was total confusion" (General Victor Krulak, interview by author, 22 April 1994).

4 Captain Eduardo Ferrer, who commanded the exile air force in the Bay of Pigs invasion, said in 1994, "Today, ninety percent of the Cubans are Republicans because of Kennedy" (Eduardo Ferrer, interview by author, 14 May 1994).

5 Kern, Levering, and Levering, 100.

6 Kern, Levering, and Levering, 100.

7 Ibid, 107.

8 Beschloss, *The Crisis Years,* 667.

9 Paterson, *Kennedy's Quest For Victory,* 154.

10 Attwood, 258.

11 *CCR,* bk. V, 21.

12 *CCIR,* 174.

13 *CCR,* bk. V, 21.

14 Flammonde, 255-261.

15 Ibid, 259.

16 Hinckle and Turner, 222.

17 FBI testimony, cited in Adolfo Merino, "The Charge," *UPI,* 3 September 1964.

18 *New York Times* and *Washington Post,* 19 November 1962; *New York Times,* 20 November 1962; *Baltimore Sun,* 21 November 1962; Breuer, 1-5.

19 Mexico Station to Director, CIA Classified Message, #7065, 96-572, 25 November 1963.

In a 1995 interview with Anthony Summers, Duran denied the Oswald affair, but openly admitted the Lechuga relationship, adding that Lechuga had petitioned Castro for permission to marry Duran. Castro denied the request (Newman, *Oswald and the CIA,* 281-282).

20 Newman, *Oswald and the CIA,* 255-261.

21 Anthony Summers and Robbyn Summers, "The Ghosts of November," *Vanity Fair,* December 1994, 101.

22 Beschloss, *The Crisis Years,* 667.

23 ONI officer, interview by author, 10 August 1994.

24 CIA to Church Committee, "Approved CIA Covert Operations into Cuba," Memorandum, 11 July 1975, in *CCIR,* 173.

25 Robert Kennedy Oral History, Kennedy Library; conducted by John Martin, 1 March 1964.

26 Ayers, 147-149; also Turner and Hinckle, 218-219.

27 Jim Flannery, interview by author, 23 December 1993.

28 "Case Officer" [Nestor Sanchez], testimony to Church Committee, 29 July 1975, 42.

29 "Case Officer" [Nestor Sanchez], testimony to Church Committee, 29 July 1975, 12.

30 *CCR,* bk. V, 14.

31 CIA Inspector General's Report, 87.

32 RFK Phone Logs, National Archives.

Neither Helms nor FitzGerald was ever confronted with the RFK phone logs proving an October 11 conversation with FitzGerald. (It was then that the Cubela pot was boiling.) The logs were only released in 1994. FitzGerald died in 1967.

33 Des FitzGerald, "Contact Plan for Meeting with AM/LASH," October 1963.
34 Rolando Cubela Secades, HSCA interview, 28 August 1978, 8.
35 Rolando Cubela Secades, HSCA interview, 28 August 1978, 10.
36 Rolando Cubela Secades, testimony in *CCR*, bk. V, 19.
37 Sam Halpern, interview by Seymour Hersh, 21 February 1997.
38 Joseph Langosch, HSCA testimony, 30 August 1978.
39 *CCIR*, 175.
40 The name of Cubela's case officer has been a closely held government secret. According to newly-released CIA documents, confirmed by confidential sources, he was CIA agent Nestor Sanchez. Cubela knew him only by his pseudonym, "Nicolas Sanson."
41 Richard Schweiker, interview by author, 23 June 1994.
42 Richard Helms, interview by author, 30 July 1994.
43 CIA official, interview by author, 2 January 1995.
44 CIA official, interview by author, 8 February 1995.
45 Alexander Haig, interview by author, 26 February 1998.
46 Johnny Rosselli, Church Committee testimony, 22 September 1975, 4.
47 *U.S. News and World Report*, 29 April 1963.
48 Arthur Schlesinger, Jr. to JFK, Memorandum, Subject: Miro Cardona Statement, 13 April 1963.
49 Johnny Rosselli, Church Committee testimony, 11 September 1975, 5-7.
50 Demaris, *The Last Mafioso*, 238.
51 Rappleye, 209.
52 Hougan, *Spooks*, 270.
   After many years of working for the family, he went on to become chief investigator for the Senate Watergate Committee (many observers point out that Bellino looked out for Kennedy interests in that investigation when it became known that key Watergate figures such as Howard Hunt, Richard Helms, Richard Nixon and others had inside knowledge of the Kennedys' secret war against Cuba). Maheu's relationship with the Kennedys is clearly a sensitive subject for Maheu. In 1971, Will Wilson, assistant Attorney General in the Criminal Division, was attempting to gather ammunition for an upcoming prosecution of Sam Giancana. Although Wilson received helpful cooperation from former FBI man Maheu, the mood changed abruptly when the name Kennedy was brought up. "Maheu flatly refused to talk about the Kennedys," recalls Wilson. (Will Wilson, interview by author, 6 February 1995).
53 Grayston Lynch, interview by author, 20 January 1994.
54 CIA Memo for the Record, 24 April 1975, Rockefeller Commission Records, #1781000210225.
55 Corn, 85.
56 Hal Hendrix, "Backstage With Bobby," *Miami News*, 14 July 1963.
57 Furati, 150 (See sample infiltration reports released by Escalante).
58 Ted Shackley, interview by author, 12 December 1997.
59 "Names and Individuals Involved in Assassination Attempts Provided to Senator George McGovern By Prime Minister Fidel Castro," May 1975, documents provided to author; also McGovern press conference transcript, 30 July 1975.
60 Israel Behar, interview, in *Time Machine: The CIA*, BBC/U.S. production, broadcast in U.S. on 13 November 1992.
61 Thomas and Isaacson, *The Very Best Men*, 300.
62 Juan Falaifel, interviewed on "ZR/RIFLE," 19 November 1993.
63 Miami Field Office to HQ, FBI Memo, 10 October 1963; also Miami SAC to Director, FBI AIRTEL, 5 July 1962.
64 Joseph Langosch, affidavit to HSCA, Exhibit F-512.
65 *CCR*, bk. V, 17, fn. 32.
66 Ibid, 17.
67 Thomas, *The Very Best Men*, 300
68 Sam Halpern, interview by author, 15 September 1993.
69 *Newsweek*, 22 November 1993, 71.

70 Noted in Church Committee review of AM/LASH file at CIA; Johnston to Senator Hart, Memorandum, 27 January 1976.
71 In some instances, Castro was said to be waiting at the airport for the arrival of the "assassins."
72 Jose Aleman, HSCA testimony, vol. V, 314-315.
73 *AARC Quarterly*, Winter 1995-96, 4.
74 Santos Trafficante, Jr., HSCA testimony, vol. V, 368.
75 Riebling, 169-170.
76 Jack Anderson's TV special, "Who Shot JFK?" 1988.
77 Demaris, *The Last Mafioso*, 235.
78 *CIA Inspector General's Report*, 103-104.
79 *HSCA*, vol. X, 184.
80 Ibid.
81 William Harvey, Rockefeller Commission testimony, 1 May 1975, 5.
82 See *CCR*, bk. V: 14, fn. 17; 17; 19; 31.
83 Juan Falaifel, interviewed on "ZR/RIFLE," 19 November 1993.
84 CIA Interim Working Draft, "AM/TRUNK Operation," 14 February 1977.
85 Corn, 104.
86 "CBS Reports: Who Killed JFK?" 19 November 1993.
87 Rafael Nuñez, interview by author, 12 April 1995.
88 Schecter and Luchkoved.
89 Geyer, 299.
90 *AP and New Orleans Times-Picayune*, 9 September 1963, also Daniel Schorr, *Clearing the Air*, 165.
91 *New York Times*, 8 October 1963.
92 Richard Goodwin, Church Committee testimony, 18 July 1975, 4; 11.
93 Alexander Haig, interview by author, 26 February 1998.
94 DOD, Memo for the Record, 13 September 1963, Minutes of Cuban Coordinating Committee; in *CCR*, bk. V, 15.
95 Coordinator of Cuban Affairs to the Interdepartmental Coordinating Committee of Cuban Affairs, Memorandum, 27 September 1963, Subject: Contingency Paper Assignments re Possible Retaliatory Actions by Castro Government; in *CCR*, bk. V, 16.
96 Tad Szulc, "Before Dallas, RFK Formed Covert Unit to Probe Possible Cuban Death Plots," *The Boston Globe*, 28 May 1976.
97 Tad Szulc, interview by author, 6 August 1994.
Szulc was not the only *New York Times* staffer privy to the secrets of the Kennedys. Distinguished *Times* executive editor, Washington bureau chief, and longtime syndicated columnist James (Scotty) Reston knew both Bobby and Jack well. There was no doubt in Reston's mind who was behind the Castro assassination plots. In his autobiography, *Deadline*, Reston stated flatly, "Bobby monkeyed around with amateur plots to assassinate Castro" (James Reston, 377).
98 Manolo Reboso, interview by author, 28 February 1994.
99 Carlos Bringuier, interview by author, 28 February 1994.
100 Des FitzGerald to DCI, "Chronology and Concept of Autonomous Operations and Summary of Financial Support to Manuel Artime," CIA Memo, 1964.
101 JCS/J5 Report, "Courses of Action Related to Cuba," 4 October 1963, JCS Papers, JFK Papers, National Archives.
102 Thomas and Isaacson, *The Very Best Men*, 302-304.
103 Special Group Memo for the Record, 12 November 1963, in FRUS, 1961-1963, vol. XI, 885-888.

Chapter Twelve (The Eye of the Hurricane)

1 LBJ to Katzenbach, phone call, 10:45 a.m. 5 December 1966, LBJ tape K66.01, LBJ Library.
2 Merle Miller, *Lyndon*, 309.

The civil war among the Texas Democratic factions had been caused by a familiar mixture of ideological, political, and personal contention. Rooted in a fundamental split between populist/labor and conservative/commercial interests, it was bloody every way but literally. The feud had vented itself into open expression as long ago as during President Roosevelt's bid for a third term, which the conservatives opposed. Since then, there had been periods of truce and attempts at reconciliation, but smoldering hatreds—sometimes stronger within the party than against outsiders, as in many families—often erupted into vitriolic words and acts of vengeance against supposedly "fellow" Democrats. Now the chieftains were Senator Yarborough, a smooth-talking liberal, and Governor John Connally, a smooth-talking "moderate" who was much liked by the conservatives. He was Republican, many observed, in everything but name only. Soon in name too, when Connally switched to the GOP. Connally was known to some as "Lyndon's Boy." The first big boost to his career came, as Johnson's had, when he was hired to help in a Washington office—in this case, Johnson's. More than twenty years before this trip, Connally had been Johnson's administrative assistant. The protege also roughly followed his mentor's path in conquering wretched Texas poverty by the power of his ambition and cunning. More recently, he had worked wonders to humiliate and politically emasculate Yarborough, no mean in-fighter himself.

3 John Connally, "Why Kennedy Went To Texas," *Life Magazine,* 24 November 1967, 86B.

4 Heymann, 406.

5 O'Donnell and Powers, 10.

6 LBJ to Robert Kintner, phone call, 20 December 1966, LBJ tape K66.01, side B, LBJ Library.

7 John Connally, "Why Kennedy Went To Texas," *Life Magazine,* 24 November 1967, 86B.

8 Manchester, *The Death of a President,* 36.

9 Ibid.

10 Heymann, 408.

11 The details of this planning were thoroughly investigated by the HSCA, which interviewed numerous Kennedy aides, advancemen, Secret Service, Dallas Police, etc; see *HSCA* vol. XI, 507-531.

12 *WC,* 737.

13 McMillan, 472.

14 Interview of Leon Lee, 10 May 1993 *(FL).*

15 McMillan, 479.

16 Interview of Fay Puckett, 12 May 1993 *(FL).*

17 McMillan, 476.

18 Ibid, 475-478.
Lee Oswald would be dead in a month, continuing a pattern established by his father—dying young, leaving a widow with young children.

19 Kelley, 297.
Ironically, the death of President Kennedy brought about an end to the Third Agency Rule, thus allowing more contact between the agencies, the very kind of contact that would have spared Kennedy on November 22, 1963.

20 Interview of Jim Hosty, 22 June 1993 *(FL).*
Hosty cites Title 18 U.S. Code, Section 781 as the rule which forbade his picking up Oswald ahead of time. Hosty also says, "All the Secret Service wanted were direct threats against the President. Oswald, to my knowledge at the time, never made such a threat. Oswald didn't fit their criteria for referral…Look at what happened to Sara Jane Moore. She in fact made an implied threat against President Ford and they still didn't arrest her" (Jim Hosty, interview by author, 6 December 1993 (Note: Sara Jane Moore later shot at Ford).

21 McMillan, 495.

22 Senate Intelligence Committee, *Performance of Intelligence Agencies,* "Appendix B: Hearings on FBI Oversight before House Subcommittee on Civil and

Constitutional Rights," ser. 2, pt..3, 21 October and 11-12 December 1975.

23 Ibid, 21 October 1975.

24 Robert Gemberling, interview by author, 30 July 1993.

25 Wallechinsky and Wallace, 287-288.

26 Church Committee, "Cuban Threats" file.

27 Hugh Aynesworth, "Oswald Practicing Told," *Dallas Morning News,* 9 December 1963.

28 Interview of Dema (Mrs. Howard) Price, 28 July 1993 *(FL).*

29 LBJ to Robert Kintner, phone call, 20 December 1966, LBJ tape K66.01, side B, LBJ Library.

30 O'Donnell, and Powers, 10; also Hugh Aynesworth, "Oswald Practicing Told," *Dallas Morning News,* 9 December 1963.

31 Homer Wood, interviewed by Anthony Summers, in Summers, *Conspiracy,* 380.

32 Homer Wood, interview by W. Scott Malone, 1 May 1993 *(FL).*

33 Ken Longley, interview by W. Scott Malone, 2 May 1993 *(FL).*

34 Solidifying Wood's fear was his belief (unsubstantiated by the author) that his attacker had been Alan Tippit, the son of the policeman slain by Oswald during his getaway attempt. The author assured Wood that only a handful of the thousands of "mysterious" incidents were really mysterious after all, and that, though Alan Tippit may have had a reputation for this kind of behavior, other alleged victims had no connection with the events of November 22.

35 "Further Oswald Tie To Range Revealed." *Dallas Morning News,* 11 December 1963.

36 *WC,* exhibits 2931 and 2932.

37 Interview of Leon Lee, 10 May 1993 *(FL).*
In 1964, FBI agents would interview Mrs. Edna Walker, who owned the Oriental Barber Shop, located at the corner of Zangs Boulevard and Beckley Street, barely 50 feet from Oswald's apartment. Walker reported observing Oswald on several occasions standing in the company of a female, possibly at the bus stop. Curiously, Walker claimed that their appearance indicated that they were "Cuban refugees" (FBI Report of Agents Vernon Mitchem and John Thomas Kesler, 23 January 1964).

38 Lucille Slack, FBI interview by Alfred Neeley, 10 September 1964.

39 Buell Wesley Frazier, interview by author, 16 February 1987.

40 In 1991, the author set up a meeting between Frazier and Oliver Stone, who wanted Frazier's input for Stone's movie *JFK,* which was in pre-production. Unlike the hundreds of people who came out of the woodwork to get a piece of Stone's "action," Frazier had only one concern—that no meetings conflicted with his little league practice. When Stone's people wanted another meeting on the spur of the moment, Frazier declined, citing his team commitment. Stone's minions were uncomprehending. Didn't Frazier understand the importance of this high-budget movie? Was he alone immune to the seductive power of Hollywood? For his part, Frazier was confused that the filmmakers didn't grasp the importance of *his* commitment. The production assistants called him again and again, offering ever-escalating amounts of money to show up for a meeting. With everyone else fighting for a meeting with Stone, Frazier was a refreshing change. The whole episode disgusted Frazier, who again retreated from interviews.

41 Interview of Hubert Anderson Morrow, 11 June 1993 *(FL).*

42 Interview of Viola Sapp, 15 July 1993 *(FL).*

43 Interview of G. Claude Hallmark, 17 July 1993 *(FL).*

44 Cristobal Espinosa Landivar, FBI interview, 2 December 1963.

45 W. D. Tyra, interview, *WC,* CD 206, 484.

46 Interview of Jack Cody, 20 June 1993 *(FL).*

47 The most obvious problem with the Yates story is the fact that Oswald's timecards show that he was at work at the time Yates claims to have given him the ride (although Oswald could have conceivably gotten to Beckley Street during the lunch hour, Yates' worksheet for that day shows him on the road until after

the lunch hour). On the other hand, during an FBI interview. Dempsey Jones clearly recalled that on Wednesday, November 20, Yates came in and told him of his strange rider who discussed shooting the President from a building. (FBI interview of Ralph Yates, 26 November 1963; also FBI interview of Dempsey Jones, 28 November 1963).

48 Interview of Hugh Slough, 6 June 1993 *(FL)*; also interview of Jerry Duncan, 2 July 1993 *(FL)*.
49 "Oswald's Room Yields Map of Bullets' Path," *Dallas Morning News*, 25 November 1963.
50 Interview of Elmo Cunningham, 8 December 1993 *(FL)*.
51 McMillan, 521.
52 McMillan, 523.
53 The Warren Commission decided to not include psychiatric conclusions in its report on Oswald. In executive session, however, three eminent psychiatrists told the commissioners that Marina unknowingly held it in her power to alter the course of history. One of the doctors, Dr. Dale Cameron, testified, "I think what Marina had a chance to do unconsciously that night was to veto his plan without ever knowing of its existence, but she didn't. She really stamped it down hard...At any rate, she was capable of fitting into his pathology."(*WC* executive session transcript, 9 July 1964, in Posner, 221-222, fn. *).

The Warren Commission hired several psychiatrists to explore the Oswalds' relationship, and much has been said about Marina's inadvertent blame for the Kennedy assassination. One doctor of psychiatry, Dr. David Rothstein, concluded: "[Marina] is what psychiatrists would often call a castrating woman... who is building up her own importance, her own feeling of importance by depreciating him." Applying Freudian logic, Dr. Dale Cameron concluded, "Oswald was unconsciously assassinating both his mother and his wife" when he shot the President.
54 For example, see Dawkins *(The Selfish Gene)*.
55 Crimmons to Joseph Califano, "The Future of Cuba," State Department Memorandum, 7 November 1963, Joseph Califano Papers, JFK Papers, National Archives.
56 Beschloss, *The Crisis Years*, 667.
57 Hinckle and Turner, 166-167.
58 Hinckle and Turner, 167.
59 Beschloss, *The Crisis Years*, 666-667.
60 "Robert G. O'Connor, Memo for the Record," U.S. Army file, National Archives.
61 Ted Shackley, interview by author, 12 December 1997.
62 From the CIA's AM/TRUNK file, summarized in "AM/TRUNK Chronology dispatch."
63 *CCR*, bk. V, 19.

Chapter Thirteen (Die by the Sword)

1 John Davis, interview by Peter Korn, as related to the author, 10 April 1994.
2 Guthman, 244.
3 Knowing his advice would not sit well with Kennedy, who put a high premium on courage, Stevenson withdrew it. This saddened him deeply after the assassination, when he spoke of "how right my first instinct was."
4 Manchester, *The Death of a President*, 34.
5 Harry Williams, interview by author, 22 December 1993.
6 *CCR*, bk. V, 20.
7 James Johnston (congressional investigator), interview by Seymour Hersh, in Seymour Hersh *(The Dark Side of Camelot*, 440, fn.).
8 It is a well-established fact that the CIA regularly plants stories in newspapers to relay intelligence messages (Grose, 365).
9 Tom Wicker, *Kennedy Without Tears*, 39.

10 Manchester, *The Death of a President,* 35.

11 *New York Times,* 13 May 1976.

12 Marty Underwood, interview by author, 10 May 1993.

13 O'Donnell and Powers, 22.

14 Ibid, 25.

15 Ibid, 404.

16 So far, there had been little progress toward mending the feud between Johnson and Ralph Yarborough, despite attempts by Kennedy staffer Bill Moyers and others. Calculated insults and bruised feelings continued to be the order of the day following the president's arrival in San Antonio. Stung by more evidence of foul play, Yarborough, although he promised a few concessions, still refused to ride with Johnson. Bitter wrangling followed over who would sit where in the Dallas motorcade the following morning. Kennedy tried to pressure Yarborough and placate Connally in an attempt to avoid an airing of grievances that would have dredged up old wounds. The common good demanded that the split be mended now; good politics required reason. But this meeting with Johnson was no reasoned exchange between the top national leaders or even an "active discussion" about the party's future. First, there was the business of Yarborough. Johnson proposed, "Let's kick the sonovabitch out." The next day, Kennedy was overheard by Mike Howard, of the Secret Service, telling Yarborough, "If you don't ride with Johnson, you'll walk." Yarborough relented (Mike Howard, interview by author, 7 December 1993; also in Merle Miller, Lyndon, 311).

17 Marty Underwood, interview by author, 10 May 1993 (who witnessed the exchange).

18 Marty Underwood, interview by author, 10 May 1993.

19 Henggeler, 56.

20 Horace Busby, interview by author, 7 October 1993.

21 Howard Burris, interview by author, 4 April 1994.

22 Merle Miller, *Lyndon,* 308.

23 Lincoln, *Kennedy and Johnson,* 205.

24 Walt Perry, interview by author, 6 June 1992.

25 Baker, 117.

26 Ibid.

27 Davis, *Mafia Kingfish,* 301.

28 Documents released to author in 1998; esp. Director to Attorney General, July 17, 1962, Evans to Belmont, July 17, 1963.

29 Van Kirk, interview by Seymour Hersh, 12 December 1993.

30 Henggeler, 60.

31 Howard Burris, interview by John Newman, 21 November 1992.

32 Merle Miller, *Lyndon,* 309.

33 Ibid.

34 Harry Provence, interview by author, 8 October 1993.

35 Horace Busby, interview by author, 7 October 1993.

Madeleine Brown has long spoken of her illicit affair with Johnson during those years (she even says that she bore an illegitimate son by Johnson). Brown alleges that on the morning of the assassination, Johnson contacted her and fumed, "Those Goddamned Kennedys. After today, they'll never embarrass me again. That's no threat, that's a promise." Even assuming the veracity of the statement, it remains a mystery as to exactly what Johnson meant by it. Many, including Brown, assert that Johnson knew what fate awaited Kennedy in downtown Dallas. In the 1940's and 1950's, Johnson's reputation was tainted by enemies' frequent accusations of violent retaliation against them, but there is no evidence that Johnson had anything but high regard for John Kennedy (that was not the case with Bobby). Furthermore, Johnson's behavior after the assassination is telling: witnesses speak of a frightened puppy, alternately crying, shaking, and hiding under tables thinking he was next—not exactly the demeanor of a fellow conspirator. The true meaning of such a statement, if made, is much simpler and innocent: by leaving the Vice-Presidency, Johnson would no longer be in a position to be humiliated by the Kennedys (Madeleine Brown, interview by author, 7 April 1992).

36 Howard Burris, interview by author, 25 June 1998.

Burris held the documents with him in San Antonio on November 22nd, in preparation for meeting Johnson at the ranch in Austin that night. When he received word of the President's death, he was ordered by Johnson to head for Washington immediately. The military aide to the now President hopped a two-seater jet fighter with his sensitive cargo. Halfway there, the pilot slipped into unconsciousness, forcing Burris, a World War II Air Force pilot, to seize the unfamiliar controls and land the plane. He never learned what became of the pilot who, on landing, was transported away by ambulance.

37 CIA Dispatch summarizing AMTRUNK Operation, 25 April 1977, JFK Papers, National Archives.

38 Director to GPFLOOR, CIA Telex, 5 December 1963.

39 Marty Underwood, interview by author, 10 May 1993.

40 Kennedy had also missed a reference to himself in the previous morning's edition of the same paper—more precisely, to the address he would deliver at lunch in the city's Trade Mart. "If the speech is about boating," a sports columnist had written, "you will be among the warmest of admirers. If it is about Cuber, civil rights, taxes or Viet Nam, there will sure as shootin' be some who heave to and let go with a broadside of grapeshot in the presidential rigging."

41 Manchester, *The Death of a President,* 126.

42 H. L. Hunt had most recently been involved in a letter-writing campaign to try to persuade prominent southern Democrats to block Kennedy's renomination in order to "save the nation" (H. L. Hunt to Senator Harry Byrd, letter, 11 July 1963, Byrd Papers, University of Virginia). His son Bunker was believed to have been interested in training shooters to assassinate liberal politicians—some have said that he even attempted to launder money to have Kennedy assassinated. After Kennedy was assassinated, strong evidence suggests that Oswald's widow, Marina, was taken to H. L. Hunt's downtown office to have a private meeting with him (the author has interviewed a number of Texans who witnessed the Marina/Hunt rendezvous). Rumor has it that Hunt proffered financial assistance to Mrs. Oswald. Marina herself admitted to author Dick Russell in 1992 that "I was taken to somebody's office, but I have no idea what I went there for....Yes, it is very possible that I went to see the oil millionaire, but I can't remember the face" (Russell, 602). All this would further confuse future attempts to discern who may have been behind Oswald's act. In fact, the Hunts were among many powerful groups who hated Kennedy, some of whom casually discussed killing the President, and many of whom donated money to Marina after the assassination. The groups included the Mafia, Cuban exiles who felt betrayed, rabid anti-communists, pro-Castro Cubans, etc. The problem, as HSCA Counsel G. Robert Blakey has pointed out, is in tying one of these groups to the man who fired the shots, Lee Oswald. The consistent mountain of evidence linking Oswald to pro-Castro groups dwarfs the tenuous links some have drawn between Oswald and the other groups.

43 Joe Dealey, son of the publisher, was also appalled. When he saw the startling page after returning to Dallas from a trip late the previous day, he told his father it was "like inviting someone to dinner and then throwing tapioca in his face." Publisher E. M. "Ted" Dealey rejected the reproach, arguing that the ad merely represented "what we've been saying editorially."

Anti-Kennedy sentiment was less pronounced in the *Dallas Times-Herald,* the city's other major newspaper, which refused to print the ad. But the headline of a column published two days earlier made the same point about the local feeling. "Why Do So Many Hate the Kennedys?" it asked. The text stressed that the hatred was not only for the President, a man whose "money still stinks," "but extended to his wife, father, brothers, daughter Caroline and to some extent, even the little tyke, John Jr."

44 Manchester, *The Death of a President,* 121.

45 Buell Frazier, interview by author, 16 February 1987.

46 Jack Dougherty, testimony, *WC*, vol. VI, 377.

47 Memo For the Secretary of the Army/Attn: Jos. Califano, "Training of Cuban Refugees in Nicaragua," 11 December 1963.

48 Hinckle and Turner, 251.

49 When Baker himself testified after the assassination, Johnson confided his own concern to House Speaker John McCormack. McCormack's public relations manager Robert Winter-Berger describes the scene:

> *I heard the private door open [to McCormack's office]. I immediately recognized the rather tall, broad-shouldered man in the dark suit. I had never seen such anguish on a man's face before. It was Lyndon Baines Johnson, the President of the United States. A Secret Service man hovered behind him, but he remained in the hall as the door swung shut. Stunned, I froze in my chair...Johnson disregarded me, but I can never forget the sight of him, crossing the room in great strides. In a loud, hysterical voice, he said: "John, that son of a bitch is going to ruin me. If that cocksucker talks, I'm gonna go to jail." By the time he had finished these words, he had reached the chair at McCormack's desk, sat down, and buried his face in his hands...I could see he was crying...[Johnson said], "He should have known better. Now we're all up shit creek. We're all gonna rot in jail. They'll get him in front of an open committee and all the crap will come out and it'll be my neck. Jesus Christ, John, my whole life is at stake!" (Winter-Berger, 65-68).*

If it wasn't already clear, later in the conversation Johnson revealed that "he" was Bobby Baker. Johnson was frantic, even proposing a payoff. "Get to him. Find out how much more he wants, for Chrissake," Johnson implored. "I've got to be kept out of this. You've got to get to Bobby, John. Tell him I expect him to take the rap for this on his own. Tell him I'll make it worth his while. Remind him that I always have."

50 Van Kirk, interview by Seymour Hersh, 12 December 1993.

51 Merle Miller, *Lyndon*, 297.

52 Rolando Cubela, HSCA interview, 28 August 1978.

53 *CCIR*, 89.

54 *CCIR*, 88, fn. 2.

55 Heymann, 256.

56 Jackie Kennedy, interview by Theodore White, 29 November 1963, in "The Camelot Documents," 26 May 1995, Kennedy Library.

57 It has been alleged that the turn violated Secret Service rules. The author inspected the Secret Service guidebook in use in 1963, "Principles of Protection of the President and Other Dignitaries," and found this not to be the case. Rules 8 through 18 deal with motorcades, and are intentionally flexible, allowing the agents on the scene to define the amount of risk to take. There are very few specific rules, and none that prohibit any specific turning radius.

58 *WC*, CE 295.

59 Carlos Bringuier, interview by author, 28 February 1994.

60 Ranelagh, 390.

61 Cortlandt Cunningham, WC testimony, vol. IV, 224.

62 Interview of Harold Norman, June 13, 1993 *(FL)*.

63 Amos Lee Euins, interview by Gerald Posner, in Posner, 247.

64 Posner, 248, from Brennan and Cherryholmes; also Howard Brennan, WC testimony, vol. III, 143.

65 Hartogs and Freeman, 11.

66 Interview of Leonid Tsagoika, 14 April 1993 *(FL)*.

67 Amos Euins, WC Testimony, vol. II, 204.

68 James Worrel, WC Testimony, vol. II, 193; also Posner, 247.

69 Ibid., 200.

70 Mike Howard, interview by author, 7 December 1993.

71 Malcolm Couch, WC testimony, vol. VI, 158; also Bob Jackson, vol. VI, 173.

72 Interview of Harold Norman, 13 June 1993 *(FL)*.
73 Posner, 242.
74 Brennan and Cherryholmes; also Posner, 248.
75 The time is established because Oswald was given a bus transfer with the time stamped on it.
76 Dr. Robert Artwohl, interview by author, 9 September 1994.
77 William Manchester, *The Death of a President,* 187.
78 Posner, 291.
79 *Journal of the American Medical Association,* 27 May 1992, 2805.
80 For a good discussion of this controversy, see Posner, 304-316.
81 Manchester, *Death of a President,* 294; also Bishop, 187.
82 Guthman, 244.
83 Arthur M. Schlesinger, Jr., *Robert Kennedy and His Times,* 656 (Howard University is a predominantly African-American university in Washington, D.C.).
84 RFK Oral history, in Arthur M. Schlesinger, Jr., *Robert Kennedy and His Times,* 655.
85 Oppenheimer, 263.
86 Summers, *Official and Confidential,* 315.
87 Anthony Summers and Robbyn Summers, "The Ghost of November," *Vanity Fair,* December 1994, 109; also *Washington Post,* 20 November 1983.
88 Evan Thomas, "The Real Coverup," *Newsweek,* 22 November 1993.
89 Ibid.
90 *CCIR,* 89.
91 Rolando Cubela, HSCA interview, 28 August 1978.
92 CIA officer, interview by author, 8 December 1997.
93 Brigadier General Godfrey McHugh, HSCA interview, 11 May 1978.
94 Marty Underwood, interview by author, 10 May 1993.
Underwood kept one copy of the speech and invitation as souvenirs, and graciously provided the author with a photocopy. Underwood also maintains many other mementos of his years with the White House, most notably a famous Kennedy rocking chair used at the president's Camp David retreat.

Chapter Fourteen (The Suburban Net Closes)

1 Elcan Elliott, interview by author, 9 September 1994.
2 Belin, November 22, 425-428.
The question has never been answered as to what else Oswald may have attempted to do with the bus transfer.
3 Belin, *Final Disclosure,* 213.
4 Ibid, 215.
5 Jim Hosty, interview by author, 19 January 1994.
6 British author Matt Smith, in his book *Vendetta,* also talks of the Cuban Air Force and Redbird. In 1992, Smith received a phone call from "Hank Gordon" (pseudo.) of Arizona. Gordon said he hadn't spoken to anyone in thirty years, in fear for his life. He stated that in 1963 he had worked for Roburn, Inc., an aircraft company that flew DC-3's from Redbird. On November 18, he was asked to inspect the planes for a new owner, a Cuban who said he had served in the Cuban Air Force. Gordon continued his inspection until the afternoon of November 21st, when a pilot friend of the new Cuban owner told him, "They're going to kill your President. They're going to kill Robert too if he becomes President. They want Robert real bad."
7 Interview of Wayne January, 19 January 1994.
Two days earlier, on November 18, a man named Billy Kemp was at work at a defense plant in Dallas, when a fellow employee offered him and a partner $25,000 for a "no-questions-asked" flight to take two passengers from Dallas to Mexico City on November 22. Highly suspicious, Kemp refused. "It was going to be a one-way trip," recalls Kemp. "Leave the plane there, come back on a

commercial flight." (Billy Kemp, interview by writer John Moulder, 1974.)

8 Louis Gaudin, interview by author, 20 January 1994; see also FBI Dallas Field Office File #62-109060, 4755, 10 March 1967.

9 Merritt Gobel, interview by author, 19 January 1994.

10 CIA Headquarters to Mexico Station, cable, 1 December 1963; cited in CCFR, Book V, 60-61, and fn. 68.

A CIA memo on Casas' biography bears the document number ""979-927AX." The number "927" also appears on CIA surveillance photos of a man identified originally as Oswald entering the Cuban and Soviet Embassies. The man is clearly not Oswald. Research seems to indicate that the mystery man bears no connection to the assassination of the president. The CIA identified the man as either a Mexican national named Gutierrez, or a KGB officer named Yuri Ivanovich Moskalev ("Mexico City Report," *HSCA*, 139, 179). The late Bernard Fensterwald, D.C. based attorney and assassination researcher, believed him to be Edmund Meunier, a mercenary based in Lieges, Belgium. Anti-Castro activist Gerry Hemming has offered the names of Cuban exile Tauler Saggue, or Johnny Mitchell Devereaux, as candidates.

11 CIA Dispatch (routing classified), 31 January 1964.

12 Deputy Director of Plans to FBI Director Hoover, CIA Memo, 23 December 1964.

13 Interview of Jim Hosty, 22 June 1993 *(FL)*.

14 Transcript in CIA JFK Segregated File at the National Archives.

15 Slawson to Record, WC Memo, "Trip to Mexico City," 24 April 1964, 24.

16 GPFLOOR to Mexico Station, CIA Telex, 6 December 1963. For more on Oswald and FPCC, see this book's chapter"The Child is the Father to the Man."

17 Nilo Messer, interview by author, 20 May 1998.

18 James Johnston, testimony before the House Committee on Government Operations, 17 November 1993.

19 Mexico to HQ, CIA Classified Message Cable, 19 March 1964.

20 *HSCA Final Report*, 141.

21 From combined sources: Earl Golz, "Cuban Rebels Told Ex-Envoy...", *Dallas Morning News*, 10 May 1979; Summers, *Conspiracy*, 420-422; and Fonzi, 53-59.

22 Tippit was married, with two sons, the youngest having recently been born. Feeling the financial pinch, Tippit had been moonlighting at the Oak Cliff restaurant, Austin's Barbecue. By many accounts, he entered into an affair with a young waitress there named Johnnie Maxie Witherspoon, who had been separated from her husband. Witherspoon reconciled with her husband two months prior to the assassination. However, when they finally divorced in 1968, her husband alleged that a child born to them in June 1964 was fathered by Tippit (some who have seen the child claim a strong resemblance to Tippit). It has been posited that it Tippit was attempting to call Witherspoon (some have even proposed that the jealous husband had killed Tippit, although the evidence is overwhelming that Oswald committed the crime).

23 Interview of Jack Tatum, 18-20 June 1993 *(FL)*.

24 Oswald, 85.

25 Curry, 65.

26 Interview of Gerald Hill, 21 June 1993 *(FL)*.

27 Henry Hurt, 157.

28 Interview of Gerald Hill, 21 June 1993 *(FL)*.

29 Interview of Paul Bentley, 30 July 1993 *(FL)*.

30 Interview of Lonnie Hudkins, 21 June 1993 *(FL)*

Chapter Fifteen (The Aftermath)

1 Steinberg, Alfred. *Sam Johnson's Boy*, 608.

2 Wicker, *JFK and LBJ*, 229.

3 Clifford, 336.

4 David and David, 227.

5 Ibid, 147.

6 Navasky, 65.

When Miller arrived in Dallas, the FBI virtually ignored him.

7 James Johnston, interview by author, 27 December 1993.

A Counsel to the Church Committee, Johnston attempted, in vain, to locate these tapes at the Kennedy Library in Boston.

8 *The Boston Globe,* 31 March 1993.

9 Burke, 44-45, 61, 128; also Burke, interview by author with Seymour Hersh, 29 January 1997.

10 Beschloss, *The Crisis Years,* 673.

11 Manchester, *The Death of a President,* 349-350.

12 Ibid, 390.

Years after, some would allege a conspiracy that reached as far as the autopsy suite, where the conspirators allegedly altered the Presidential wounds, or intentionally lied about bullets retrieved from the body. The theory continued that the autopsy doctors burned their notes in order to conceal their crime. This theory ignores the obvious: Jackie chose the autopsy site, and as shall be seen, she and Robert Kennedy were the only ones attempting to exert any influence on the proceedings.

13 *JAMA,* 27 May 1992, 2796.

14 Manchester, *The Death of a President,* 419

15 *JAMA,* 27 May 1992, 2799.

16 Ibid, 430.

17 Livingstone, 179-190.

18 Memo of contact (Robert Karnei, interview by Kelly and Purdy), HSCA, 29 August 1977.

19 Manchester, *The Death of a President,* 427.

20 Brigadier General Godfrey McHugh, HSCA testimony, 11 May 1978.

21 HSCA Outside Contact Report with John Stover, 11 May 1978.

22 Memo of contact (Jay Boswell, interview by Andy Purdy), HSCA, 17 August 1977.

23 Francis X. O'Neill, Jr., HSCA interview by Andy Purdy, 10 January 1978.

24 *JAMA,* 7 October 1992, 1737.

25 *JAMA,* 7 October 1992, 1737

26 Ibid, 1752.

27 *JAMA,* 27 May 1992, 2803.

28 Herbst Clinical Notes, 1950-1963, Medical File, MS 83-38, Kennedy Library; also Hamilton, 808-809; and Reeves, 668, fn. 42.

29 Pierre Finck, testimony, *State of Louisiana v. Clay Shaw,* 24-25 February 1969.

30 Travell, Memo for the file, 6 December 1963, WHCSF Box 104, JFK Library.

31 Posner, 300, fn. *.

32 *JAMA,* 27 May 1992, 2799.

33 *JAMA,* 7 October 1992, 1748.

34 In 1975, Janos testified to a Senate investigator, and said that he was told the story by the wife of a high-ranking Johnson aide. Janos would not divulge the woman's name directly, but hinted strongly that it was the wife of LBJ Chief of Staff Bob Hardesty. Janos also interviewed Johnson in retirement. When contacted by the same Senate investigator, Hardesty claimed no knowledge of the file. (Leo Janos, Church Committee interview by Rhett Dawson, 14 October 1975; SSCI Box 337, folder 2.) Also: Leo Janos, interview by Seymour Hersh, 17 April 1994.

35 Merle Miller, *Lyndon,* 324.

36 Layton Martens, interview by author, 10 September 1994.

37 Al Beaubeouf, interview by author, 13 September 1994.

Garrison also made much of the fact that Ferrie later said that they intended to go "duck hunting" on the trip, but took no rifles with them. Beaubeouf says, "While we were on the road, I suggested we go deer hunting, not duck hunting, in Alexandria, Louisiana. I had plenty of relatives in the area from whom we could borrow rifles if we needed them. We ended up not hunting after all." (Al Beaubeouf, interview by author, 13 September 1994.)

38 Results in author's possession; Mutual Protective Association, Inc., 10 May 1967.
39 Layton Martens, interview by author, 3 February 1994.

Stories abound in New Orleans regarding Garrison's alleged bisexuality. There was indeed an incident on the roof of the Men's Athletic Club where Garrison was accused of indecency with another male. The incident was not resolved. Garrison's later persecution of homosexual businessman Clay Shaw is perceived by some as a vendetta for a long-standing sexual feud. The story goes that Shaw and Garrison attended college together and both had vied for the affections of the same older man. Shaw allegedly prevailed and Garrison subsequently held it against Shaw.

Nick Caridas owns the concessions at Lakefront Airport where Banister aide and pilot Dave Ferrie often ate. Caridas also went to law school and knew Garrison well. His comments are fairly typical of those heard in New Orleans. "We used to hear rumors that Jim's wife took a boyfriend because Jim was more interested in his male friends," says Caridas. (Nick Caridas, interview by author, 7 February 1994.)

At to why Garrison associated David Ferrie with the Kennedy assassination, many of Banister's employees agree this was pure revenge for Ferrie's role in helping Banister assemble "the bomb" on Garrison.

40 Layton Martens, interview by author, 10 September 1994.
41 Morris Brownlee, interview by author, 10 September 1994.
42 Ibid.
43 Cited in Mailer, 291.
44 Interview of Jim Leavelle, 19 June 1993 *(FL)*.
45 Posner, 344, fn. *.
46 Interview of Jim Leavelle, 19 June 1993 *(FL)*.
47 Interview of Frank Ellsworth, 29 April 1993 *(FL)*.
48 Elmo Cunningham, interview by author, 8 December 1993.
49 Interview of Jim Hosty, 22 June 1993 *(FL)*.
50 A Warren Commission memo notes that Dallas Deputy Sheriff Raymond "Buddy" Walthers reported finding a set of metal file cabinets at Ruth Paine's Irving house (where Oswald stored his things) that appeared to contain the "names and activities of Cuban sympathizers." Walthers turned the cabinets over to the Secret Service. They have not surfaced since. (Arthur Marmor to Norman Redlich, Memo, 22 July 1964).
51 Ibid.
52 Bill Alexander, interview by Gerald Posner, 6 March 1992, cited in Posner, 348, fn. *.
53 *WC* Exhibits 1414, 3119.
54 Guy Banister, interview by Ernest Wall, FBI Report of interview, 25 November 1963.
55 David and David, 223.
56 Manchester, *The Death of a President,* 435.
57 Ibid, 443.
58 Oppenheimer, 264.
59 Schlesinger, *Robert Kennedy and His Times,* 659.
60 Interview of Paul Bentley, 30 July 1993 *(FL)*.

This detail was corroborated for the author by the FBI's Robert Gemberling and Homicide detective Jim Leavelle. There are a few cops who hint that Oswald's civil rights were in fact abused while in custody. Two Dallas policemen, requesting anonymity, told the author that this happened, but would only hint at the details: the abuse was mental, not physical. When pressed, one of the policemen said, "I'll take that to my grave." For an indication of how touchy a subject this was for the Dallas police, note the different photos taken of Oswald on the day he was shot. At the time of his shooting, pictures of his face show only a minor scrape over his right eye. But in autopsy pictures taken only a few hours later, he has a severe black eye. Dallas police officials have admitted that they put makeup on his face so that he would appear unmarked when the press viewed his transfer (Oswald autopsy photos in CIA "201" file on Oswald, box 24, National Archives).

After Oswald's death, the FBI ordered an investigation of the Dallas police to determine if any abuses had occurred. The investigation was headed by agent Vincent Drain. When asked if he was aware of these allegations, Drain responded, "I just wouldn't want to comment on that." (Vincent Drain, interview by author, 18 October 1993.)

61 Interview of Jim Leavelle, 19 June 1993 *(FL)*.
62 Kaplan and Waltz, 143-150.
63 Quoted in Posner, 397.
64 Interview of Jim Leavelle, 19 June 1993 *(FL)*.
65 Malcolm Kilduff, interview by author, 18 September 1996.
66 McMillan, 547-548.
67 Ibid, 557.
68 Mike Howard, interview by author, 7 December 1993.
69 Mike Cochran, "No Answers...", *Houston Post,* 15 November 1993.
70 Ibid.
71 Scott Malone, interview by author, 10 October 1993.
72 *CCR,* Book V, 26.
73 Evan Thomas, "The Real JFK Coverup," *Newsweek Magazine,* 22 November 1993.
74 *CCR,* Book V, 78.
75 *CCR,* Book V, 27.
76 Dino Brugioni, interview by author, 27 January 1998.
77 Hal Hendrix, "U.S. Seeks Link To Cuba in Kennedy Slaying," *Scripps-Howard,* 24 November 1963.
78 This CIA-Cuba chronology is summarized in *CCR,* Book V, 103-104.
79 Haig, 116.
80 After his retirement, Ryan learned that he himself had been on Castro's "hit list." After the Cold War ended, when Ryan happened to meet his Cuban intelligence counterpart, he told his former adversary: "I hope you know now it wasn't me pushing to get Castro killed. So why the hell did you put me on that hit list?" The Castro agent replied, "Oh, we took you off that list in 1979." (Former CIA Station Chief, interview by author, 10 January 1998.)
81 JMWAVE to CIA Director, Memo, 4 February 1964; CIA Segregated file, JFK Collection.
82 Confidential interview by author, 18 March 1998.
83 David Slawson For the Record, Memo, "Trip to Mexico City," *WC,* 22 April 1964.
84 For a complete chronology of this activity, see *CCR,* Book V, especially Appendix C.
85 James Johnston, interview in Riebling, 202.
86 "Willard C. Curtis" (Win Scott) to HQ, CIA cable, 27 November 1963.
87 Interview of Thomas Mann, 12 May 1993 *(FL)*.
88 Russell, 453.
89 *The Miami News* (from the *Chicago Sun Times*), 24 June 1976.
90 Cited in "Retired FBI Agent...", *Wall Street Journal,* 18 October 1993, A18.
91 Interview of Jim Hosty, 22 June 1993 *(FL)*.
   DeGuire passed away in the early 1990's.
92 "Schweiker Report," *CCFR,* Book V, 25.
93 Richard Helms to Warren Commission Senior Attorney J. Lee Rankin, Memo, "Translation of Interrogation Reports of Sylvia Duran," 21 February 1964; in CIA Segregated File in the National Archives JFK Collection.
94 "Mexico City Report," *HSCA,* 213.
95 *HSCA Hearings*, vol. III, 304.
96 Ibid , 228.

97 Mexico City to McGeorge Bundy, White House, CIA Teletype, 27 November 1963.
98 LEGAT MEXICO CITY to DIRECTOR, FBI cable, 26 November 1963.
99 CIA Cable from Mexico City, 28 November 1963.
100 LEGAT MEXICO CITY TO DIRECTOR, FBI Memo, 6 March 1964. Also, CD's 564, 566.3, 663.4, and 896.3.
101 The Church Committee later pointed out that the CIA "reported other information from a sensitive and reliable source which tended to confirm Alvarado's story that Oswald may have been paid by the Cubans to assassinate President Kennedy. This report has never been satisfactorily explained, although it was made available to the Warren Commission." (*CCR*, Book V, 28)
102 Mexico Station to McGeorge Bundy, CIA Teletype, 27 November 1963.
103 Alvaro Proenza, interview by Gaeton Fonzi, HSCA Memo, 14 April 1978.
104 [Source deleted] to Director, CIA Teletype, 7 December 1963.
105 "Debriefing of AMMUG-1, May 5, 1964," CIA Counterintelligence Memo.
106 The CIA, ever loyal to Kennedy, performed one last function on his behalf. Because there were no large printing facilities available on such short notice, the CIA utilized its extensive printing facilities at its Langley headquarters to print the mass cards and programs for JFK's memorial service (Manchester, *Death of A President*, 549).
107 Manchester, *Death of a President*, 568.
108 McMillan, 557.
109 Interview of Jerry Herald, 14 June 1993 *(FL)*.
Years later, after coming under the influence of the local assassination "buffs," and a British journalist with a bizarre body-switching scenario, Marina would question whether Lee was buried that day, having possibly been replaced by a decoy. However, as first documented by William Manchester (in *The Death of A President*, 568), Oswald's casket was opened before being put in the ground. Manchester wrote: "The lid was raised. Forty reporters peered over the officers' shoulders. Marina, who had been following TV and was learning about images, kissed her husband and put her ring on his finger." Robert Oswald also spoke of this detail in the *Dallas Morning News* (11 September 1981). Jerry Herald was one of those doing the peering, and he adds another detail: "After the casket was placed on the rack at the burial site, the Secret Service or FBI opened the casket and asked Marina to identify the body. She did. They closed it, had their little church service. There was a priest or a minister of some type there. Said the little prayer, and dropped him into the ground—very few people there, only the three family members and the two children." A security man assigned to the Oswalds, Miles Lankford, added that Lee's mother and brother also identified the body. In spite of this, Marina would gain permission in 1981 to have the body exhumed for the purposes of identification. Just as Marina, Robert and Marguerite had done in 1963, the team of forensics experts again identified the body as Lee Oswald's. (*New York Post*, 5 October 1981)
110 Mike Howard, interview by author, 7 December 1993.
111 RFK to J. Edgar Hoover, Memo of approval, 24 February 1964.
Soon, according to FBI agent Thomas Trettis, who monitored the eavesdropping, Marina's activities would resurrect her Russian reputation for "loose" behavior. Trettis and other agents gave Marina the nickname "hot pants." (Thomas Trettis, Church Committee interview, 17 January 1976.) During their stay in protective custody, Agent Mike Howard introduced Marina to the manager of the Inn, Jim Martin. Within days, Marina had moved into Martin's home. She also traveled with him to Washington in February 1964, when she testified before the Warren Commission. Marina's reputation was further sullied by this liaison, and by her admission of having sex with Martin during the Washington stay. (Vada [Mrs. Robert] Oswald, FBI Statement, 24 February 1964; see also HSCA, Box 15, Section 86 at National Archives.)

Chapter Sixteeen (The Investigations)

1 Interview of Laurence Keenan, 1993 *(FL)*.
2 FBI Internal Memo, in *Associated Press*, 8 December 1977.
3 John Scelso, HSCA testimony, [undated].
  As likely candidates for true Scelso identity, pundits have proposed John Whitten, William Broe, or Walter Kaufmann.
4 *CCR*, bk. V, 58-59 (emphasis added).
5 Boris Tarassoff, HSCA testimony, 12 April 1978.
6 *HSCA Mexico City Report,* 125.
7 CIA Internal Memo 256, 12 March 1964, 4.
8 David Helms, interview by John M. Newman, 23 August 1994, in Newman, *Oswald and the CIA,* 418.
9 The Memo is entitled "Progress Report on Defection and Recruitment Activity in Latin America." The document not only states, "Since around January 1960 Station Mexico has been involved in 11 defections and recruitments of Cuban officials, mostly from the Cuban Embassy," but actually names them. (CIA Document, rec. #104-10102, file 80T01357A).
10 *HSCA Mexico City Report,* 49.
11 David Philips to Deputy Director of Operations, recommedation, 21 June 1973.
12 Mexico City Station to Headquarters, classified message, 20 July 1963.
13 T. Jeremy Gunn, investigator for the Assassination Records Review Board, interview by author, 5 May 1995.
14 CIA document, "Information Developed by CIA on the Activity of Lee Harvey Oswald in Mexico City," 31 January 1964.
15 Shackley Outside Contact Report with HSCA Counsel Blakey and Fonzi, [undated], in Fonzi, 360.
16 Raymond Rocca, Church Committee interview by Dan Dwyer and Ed Greissing, 15 March 1976.
17 James Angleton, HSCA interview by Surell Brady, 15 June 1978.
18 Nicholas Katzenbach to Bill Moyers, Memorandum, 25 November 1963.
19 *The Washington Post,* 14 November 1993, 1.
20 Ibid.
21 Alan Belmont to Sullivan, Memorandum, 26 November 1963.
22 Nicholas Katzenbach, "CBS Reports: Who Killed JFK," 19 November 1993.
23 Summers, *Official and Confidential,* 317.
24 *CCR*, bk. V, 36.
25 Ibid, 37.
26 Sullivan, 51.
27 *CCR*, 37.
28 Laurence Keenan, interview by author, 11 April 1995.
29 *CCR*, bk. V, 42-43.
30 Laurence Keenan, interview by author, 11 April 1995.
31 For a thorough discussion of this rivalry, and its terrible consequences through the years, see Mark Reibling's *The Wedge.*
32 Interview of Laurence Keenan, 1993 (FL).
33 Interview of Laurence Keenan, 1993 (FL).
34 Laurence Keenan, interview by author, 11 April 1995.
35 "The President's Commission on Obscenity and Pornography," Minority Report, 583.
36 George Lardner, "The Assassination Files," *Washington Post,* 14 November 1993.
37 This conclusion was uttered in the wake of the missile crisis; cited in numerous books, e.g. Sorensen, *Kennedy,* 321, and Pollard, *Truman to Johnson,* 100-105.
38 LBJ with Joseph Alsop, conversation, 25 November 1963, in LBJ Tapes, National Archives.
39 LBJ to Abe Fortas, 16 December 1966, Oval Office tape, K66.01, Side B, LBJ Library.
  RFK's affection for Dulles is underscored by an event that took place in June

1964. Days earlier, three student civil rights volunteers had disappeared in Meridian, Mississippi, and were feared murdered (a fear later realized). The country galvanized against Southern extremists, and more violence was feared. At this point, Lyndon Johnson called Dulles and asked him to go to Mississippi to try to diffuse the situation. Before hanging up the phone, Johnson said, "Now hold the line a minute." Johnson handed the phone to Bobby Kennedy, who may have suggested the use of Dulles. Kennedy then told Dulles to meet him at his [Kennedy's] office. The next morning, before leaving for Mississippi, Dulles had a private briefing in the Attorney General's office (Grose, 556-557).

40 George Lardner, "The Assassination Files," *Washington Post*, 14 November 1993.
41 Cray, 427 and 429.
42 Fensterwald and Ewing, 72.
43 Jeffrey Warren, interview by author, 3 October 1994.
44 G. Edward White, 203.
45 Cray, 413.
46 Ibid, 414.
47 "Eulogies to the Late President," 24 November 1963, Senate Document #46, 89th Congress, 1st Session.
48 Ibid, 194 and 197.
49 Among these back channels, according to Jeffrey Warren, would have been the attorney famed for defending individuals associated with organized crime. "Edward Bennett Williams was my grandfather's best friend in the whole world. You can be sure that he was asked if Oswald had any ties to organized crime" (Jeffrey Warren, interview by author, 3 October 1994).
50 Connally, 186.
51 LBJ with Richard Russell, conversation, 29 November 1963, LBJ Tapes, National Archives.
52 General Wheeler, Memo For the Record, "Meeting With the President on Cuba," 19 December 1993.
53 Lyndon Johnson, 48.
54 Burt Griffin, interview by Gerald Posner, 23 January 1992, in Posner, 409.
55 Weidenfeld, 350.
56 Bird, 18.
57 Ibid, 543-544.
58 Anthony Summers and Robbyn Summers, "The Ghost of November," *Vanity Fair*, December 1994, 90.
59 Burt Griffin to Mrs. Martin Parker, letter, 30 July 1976.
60 David Belin to Rockefeller Commission, Memorandum, 20 May 1975; also *CCR*, bk. V, 73.
61 J. Lee Rankin, HSCA testimony, undated.
62 Loch Johnson, *A Season of Inquiry*, 6-7.
63 WC Executive Session, 27 January 1964, in Weisberg, *Whitewash IV*, 60-63.
64 Ibid.
65 Allen Dulles Oral History, 5 December 1964, JFK Library.
66 Thomas Powers, 305.
67 Fonzi, 210.
68 David Belin, interview, *Face the Nation*, CBS, 23 November 1975.
69 Demaris, *The Last Mafioso*, 239.
70 *CCIR*, 13-70.
71 *CCIR*, 55.
72 Robert Johnson, interview by author, 9 February 1996.
73 Garwood, 57-58.
74 *CCR*, 94-95.
75 Church Committee testimony of Sheffield Edwards, April 9, 1975, 5.
76 Peter Grose, 539
77 *CCIR*, 264
78 Donald Chamberlain to Knoche, Memorandum, 15 April 1975.
79 Ibid, 544.

80 Ibid, 553-554.
81 Mosley, 477-478.
82 J. Edgar Hoover to Gale and Tolson, note, 10 December 1963; summarized in *CCR*, bk. V, 50-57.
83 J. Edgar Hoover to Belmont, note, 24 September 1964; J. Edgar Hoover to Tolson, note, 1 October 1964.
84 Sullivan, 50.
85 *CCR*, bk. V, 49, fn. 15.
86 Interview of Senator Richard Schweiker, 26 June 1993 (FL).
87 *WC* transcript, 16 December 1963, 52; in Bird, 549.
88 Wesley Liebeler, interview by Edward Jay Epstein, in Epstein, 105.
89 *HSCA*, vol. XI, 259.
90 *U.S. News and World Report,* 17 August 1992, 30.
91 Ibid, 30.
92 Slawson, "Trip to Mexico City," Memorandum, 22 April 1964.
93 Belin, *Final Disclosure,* 217-218.
94 Ibid, 218.
95 O'Neill, 178.
96 Cray, 425.
97 Wofford, 415-416.
98 *U.S. News and World Report,* 17 August 1992, 40.
99 Ibid.
100 Max Holland, "The Key to the Warren Report," *American Heritage Magazine,* November 1995.
101 Burt Griffin, interview by Gerald Posner, 23 January 1992, in Posner, 411-412.
102 Fensterwald and Ewing, *Coincidence or Conspiracy,* 96.
103 *The Washington Post,* 19 January 1970.
104 Russell, 500.
105 Gilbert Fite, 423.
106 Colonel Philip Corso, interview by author, 6 February 1996; also Colonel Philip Corso, interview by Anthony Summers, July 1993 (FL). Transcript in author's possession.
107 Weisberg, *Whitewash IV,* esp. 208-209.
108 Cartha DeLoach to Mohr, FBI Memo, 12 December 1963.
109 Transcript of show (name unknown) in author's files.
110 President Gerald R. Ford to Phil Buchen, Memorandum, 7 March 1975, Ford Library Box, JFK Collection, National Archives.
111 Wayne Thevenot, interview by author, 20 May 1996.
112 Judge Burt Griffin, interview by author, 5 April 1993.
113 Lee Rankin, interview by Mike Ewing, HSCA Outside Contact Report, 31 May 1978.
114 Jeffrey Warren, interview by author, 3 October 1994.
115 Cray, 423.
116 Fensterwald and Ewing, 80.
117 Anthony Summers and Robbyn Summers, "The Ghost of November," *Vanity Fair,* December 1994, 101.
118 Leo Janos, *Atlantic Monthly,* July 1973.
119 Jack Martin and Lewis, affidavit to New Orleans District Attorney Jim Garrison, 20 February 1968, 48.
120 Lyndon B. Johnson to Mike Mansfield, phone conversation, 28 September 1964, LBJ Library; also Beschloss, *Taking Charge,* 561.
121 Kelley, 298.
122 Livingstone, 438.
123 General Alexander Haig, interview by author, 26 February 1998.
124 Beschloss, *The Crisis Years,* 682.
125 Leo Janos, LBJ speechwriter, Church Committee interview by Rhett Dawson, 14 October 1975; also in the report is a follow-up interview with Bob Hardesty, SSCI box 337, folder 2.

126 *Fort Worth Star Telegram,* 15 December 1993.
127 Leo Janos, LBJ speechwriter, Church Committee interview by Rhett Dawson, 14 October 1975.
128 Model and Groden, 94-95.
129 *New York Times,* 25 June 1976.
     Smith recalls the "confidential" conversation, only releasing the statement during the Church Committee hearings, well after Johnson's death in 1972. The recollections were based on "thorough notes." Smith recalled, "I was rocked all right. I begged for details. He [Johnson] refused, saying, 'It will all come out one day.'"
130 Schorr, 178.
131 Weidenfeld, 350.
132 Russell, 454.
133 *CCR,* bk. V, 6-7.
134 Ibid, 60.
135 *HSCA,* vol. XI, 260.
136 Ibid, 256-257.
137 Ibid, 260-261.
138 Ibid, 261.
139 CIA Review of Oswald File, 5 May 1975, 5-6.
140 David and David, 230.
141 *Panorama,* BBC, March 1978.
142 Judge Burt Griffin, HSCA testimony.

Chapter Seventeen (Bobby Alone)

1 Wofford, 426.
2 David and David, 3.
3 Guthman, 244.
4 Wofford, 384.
5 Harry Williams, interview by author, 22 December 1993.
6 John Davis, interview by author, 20 November 1993.
7 Sergio Arcacha Smith, interview by author, 24 April 1997.
8 William Vanden Heuvel, interview by author, 7 August 1993.
9 David and David, 217.
10 William Vanden Heuvel, interview by author, 7 August 1993.
11 Oppenheimer, 265.
12 G. Robert Blakey, interview by author, 22 July 1992.
13 David and David, 219.
14 Ibid, 217.
15 Ibid, 220.
16 Ibid, 221.
17 David and David, 215.
18 Ibid.
19 Ibid, 217.
20 Leo Janos, Church Committee interview by Rhett Dawson, Memo for the Record, 14 October 1975.
21 Arthur Schlesinger, Jr. "JFK: Truth and Fiction," *Wall Street Journal,* 10 January 1992.
22 Nilo Messer, interview by author, 20 May 1998.
     Messer was Artime's secretary.
23 Schlesinger, *Robert Kennedy and His Times,* 664.
24 Newfield, 29.
25 David and David, 221.
26 Quoted in David and David, 216, fn. 6.
27 Richard Goodwin, 463.
28 Quoted in Belin, *Final Disclosure,* 217.

29 Ibid.
30 HSCA box 18, section 88, National Archives.
31 Seymour Hersh, 450-451.
32 Julius Draznin, interview by Seymour Hersh, 17 April 1994.
33 Interview of Al Maddox, 12 June 1993 (*FL*).
34 Vincent Drain, interview by author, 18 October 1993.
35 After this trip, according to sources close to the Kennedy circle, Bobby contacted "my best friend in the Justice Department," Daniel Patrick Moynihan.
Moynihan was charged with resolving two questions: 1) Was the Secret Service bought off on the day of the assassination? and 2) Was Bobby's nemesis Jimmy Hoffa involved? After a short period of involvement on his investigative task, Moynihan reported negatively on both counts. Moynihan was confronted with this allegation by a writer from *Ramparts* magazine in 1968. According to authors Bill Turner and Warren Hinckle: "Moynihan jumped as if a live grenade was rolling toward him. In CIA fashion, he declared he would neither confirm nor deny his secret mission for Bobby Kennedy. After leaving the room to use the phone, the suddenly unamiable Irishman returned and announced that he had nothing more to say." (Hinckle and Turner, 260)
In March 1964, Secret Service Agent Mike Howard witnessed an incident that may relate to Bobby's interest in a Hoffa connection. At the time, Howard had been assigned to Jackie Kennedy, with whom he would become quite close. (Howard recalled her having terrifying nightmares. He would often spend the night just outside her bedroom, sometimes rushing in to comfort her when she would wake up screaming, then sit on the edge of her bed until she fell back asleep.) One morning in April 1964, Howard remembered going down to the kitchen in Jackie's house in suburban Virginia, and being startled to see Robert Kennedy there. RFK asked Howard to drive him to a section of Dulles Airport where private planes were parked, and Howard drove onto the tarmac, where Jimmy Hoffa was disembarking from a plane that had just landed.
Approaching each other without shaking hands, Kennedy and Hoffa spoke in conversational tones for some ten minutes. Not wanting to eavesdrop, Howard heard none of the conversation until its end, when he heard Hoffa ask, "Is that all right with you?" "Yes," replied Kennedy. On March 4th, 1964, the Justice Department had just obtained a conviction of Hoffa for complicity in jury tampering, and would push for a second conviction in April, when Hoffa and seven others would go on trial in Chicago for defrauding the Central States Pension Fund of over $20 million. That might have been the subject of the conversation at the airport—but that spring, Robert Kennedy remained too shattered by his brother's assassination to undertake any serious work as Attorney General. There was, of course, another possibility—the assassination. Did Kennedy want to look into Hoffa's eyes while asking him if he had anything to do with his brother's killing—as he had done with, among others, John McCone of the CIA? (Mike Howard, interview by author, 7 December 1993)
Although Moynihan declined to divulge any information, other sources, albeit second-hand ones, have disclosed that Bobby Kennedy's next foray into the mystery of his brother's death came after the release of the Warren Commission Report. At that time, Kennedy said, "I just can't believe that guy [Oswald] acted alone. I'm going to contact someone independent of this government to get to the bottom of this." Bobby then contacted a lifelong friend of the Kennedy family, then working in Britain's intelligence agency, known as MI6. The friendship dated back to the days when Papa Joe Kennedy was the U.S. Ambassador to England. Undertaking this highly secretive mission, the MI6 agent contacted two French intelligence operatives who proceeded to conduct, over a three year period, a quiet investigation that involved hundreds of interviews in the United States. One agent was the head of the French Secret Service, Andre Ducret. The second was known only as "Philippe"—believed to be Philippe Vosjoly, who was a former French Intelligence Chief in the United States. Over the years, Ducret and Philippe hired men to infiltrate the Texas

oil industry, the CIA, and Cuban mercenary groups in Florida. Their report, replete with innuendo about Lyndon Johnson and right-wing Texas oil barons, was delivered to Bobby Kennedy only months before his own assassination in June of 1968.

There is no information concerning Bobby's reaction to the document. After Bobby's death, the MI6 agent contacted the last surviving brother, Senator Ted Kennedy, inquiring as to what to do with the material. Teddy said the family wasn't interested. The agent proceeded to hire a French writer by the name of Hervé LaMarre to fashion the material into a book. Published in Europe and authored under the pseudonym of "James Hepburn," the book was entitled *Farewell, America*. It contains highly exaggerated prose combined with a large dose of poetic license. Because the anecdotes about LBJ and others could be considered downright libelous, the book was never published in America. Over the years, however, through private dealers, the book obtained an "underground" distributorship in the United States. One of the dealers approached Dave Powers, Kennedy intimate and curator of the John F. Kennedy Museum, for his opinion of the book. Echoing Moynihan, Powers responded, "I can't confirm or deny the European connection, but Bobby definitely didn't believe the Warren Report." (Al Navis, interview by author, 19 November 1993. In the 1980's, Navis conducted inquiries about RFK's investigation with members of the Kennedy family inner-circle.)

For more background on the "European Connection," see the notes of former FBI agent William Turner on file at the Assassination Archive and Research Center in Washington, D.C. Turner and his partner Warren Hinckle traveled extensively, interviewing a number of those enlisted in the Bobby Kennedy investigation.

36 This same doctor went on to become part of the cottage industry that has ghoulishly surrounded the Kennedy assassination. In what seemed to many to be demagogue-like fashion, he has appeared on countless panel discussions and television programs trumpeting the theme that the government lied to the public about the manner of Kennedy's death, but never offering any proof of his contention. To the contrary, he originally emerged from his viewing of the autopsy photographs admitting that there was no evidence of a shot from the front. He eventually left his place of employment in 1983 under a cloud of accusations that he had misappropriated hundreds of thousands of dollars in public funds. By 1993, the doctor had repaid $200,000 to his local government.

37 Initial chronology compiled in *HSCA* vol. VII, 23-34.

38 *JAMA*, 27 May 1992, vol. 267, no. 20, 2803.

39 Ibid, 2803.

40 CE 391.

41 National Archives, Memo of Transfer, 26 April 1965.

42 Angela Novello, interview by author, 26 April 1994.

43 Thomas, *The Man to See*, 162.

44 After Bobby Kennedy's assassination in 1968, Evelyn Lincoln began to wonder what had happened to the president's brain. She called Ted Kennedy, who assured her that everything was under control.

45 George Burkley, HSCA interview, 1 September 1977.

46 The author made attempts to contact both Giordiano and Dalton for interviews. Efforts included a brief telephone call to Joseph Giordano, 10 May 1994, when he declined an interview request, and a letter to Dalton in 1992, which was not answered.

47 Thomas J. Kelly, Asst. SS Director, Memo for file, 13 February 1969.

48 *HSCA*, vol. VII, 29.

49 G. Robert Blakey, Outside Contact Report, 22 March 1976.

50 Both the HSCA and the author spoke to numerous people present at the gravesite for the reinterment, none of whom saw anything but the coffin rebur-

ial. After the Committee ended its work, Blakey told the author that he was informed that a National Archives employee knew the brain was in the ground. The employee denied this to the author. A friend of the Archive employee believes that the employee knows about the brain, but prefers to have the Kennedy family verify it.

51 Robert Tanenbaum, interview by author, 5 April 1992.

52 Frank Mankiewicz, interview by author, 19 January 1994.
Jack Metzler, Jr., current Arlington Superintendent (and son of the Superintendent in 1967), researched all gravesite records for the author and reported that no other groundbreaking occurred besides the original burial and the reinterment. He said, however, that security is very lax at night, and it would be easy to sneak in, bury material, carefully replace the sod, and never be detected.

53 Manchester, *The Death of a President*, 378

54 Hinckle and Turner *(The Fish is Red)*, 238.

55 Thomas Powers, 143.

56 CIA Headquarters to JM/WAVE, cable, 23 November 1963, cited in Corn, 106.

57 Loch Johnson (Church Committee staff), memo on his inspection of classified Cuba documents, 21 July 1975, LBJ Library.

58 Nilo Messer, interview by author, 20 May 1998.

59 Blight and Kornbluh, 122.

60 Guthman and Shulman, 379.

61 Rene Cancio, interview by Judith Artime, 61.

62 Al Haig, interview on ABC's *Nightline*, 12 December 1997.

Chapter Eighteen (Assault on Camelot)

1 Through an informant, FBI agent Jack Barron learned that Rosselli had lied in testifying to the Kefauver Committee about his birth in Chicago. According to Barron's information, Rosselli was actually born Filippo Sacco in Esteria, Italy in 1911. After emigrating to Boston six years later, young Filippo fell into a world of crime, eventually burning down his family home in an arson for insurance scam. He then fled to Chicago, changed his name to Johnny Rosselli, and began working for Al Capone (Demaris, 232).

2 Demaris, 233.

3 *CCIR*, 85, fn. 4.

4 Luncheon Meeting with William K. Harvey, Howard Osborn, CIA Memo For the Record, 4 October 1967.

5 Edward Morgan, Church Committee testimony, 19 March 1976.

6 *CCR*, bk. V, 80.

7 Henggler, 40-41.

8 Henggler, 37.

9 Parker and Rashke, 92.

10 Henggler, 40-41.

11 Arthur Schlesinger, *Robert Kennedy and His Times*, 715.

12 Thomas and Isaacson, *The Man to See*, 182.

13 Henggler, 81.

14 Arthur Schlesinger, *Robert Kennedy and His Times*, 711.

15 Ibid, 715-716.

16 Ibid, 716.

17 Henggler, 198.

18 Ibid, 206.

19 For more details, see Van Gelder and Bennett (in the Bibliography).

20 Shesol, 366.

21 This confrontation recalls what Johnson aides have long claimed to have been Johnson's biggest, self-admitted mistake—retaining the original JFK advisors, whom he came to believe ill-served him.

22 Among other interviewees, Johnson's Military Aide and lifelong friend, Colonel Howard Burris, recalled this LBJ view for the author. Also, LBJ Special Assistant, Martin Underwood, who shared many an after-hour drink with Johnson in the residence area of the White House, said Johnson was firm on this fact.
23 Henggler, 209.
24 LBJ with Governor John Connally, phone conversation, 2 March 1967; LBJ library tape 67.02.
25 Leo Janos, *Atlantic Monthly*, July 1973.
26 Kirkwood, 180.
27 William Hundley, interview by author, 7 October 1993.
28 We know Garrison knew the story, because John Connally told LBJ that he learned the story from sources in Garrison's office (LBJ with Governor John Connally, taped conversation, JFK Collection, National Archives). Also, the CIA pointed out that Rosselli himself was in touch with Garrison when the two of them were in Las Vegas at the same time as Ed Morgan in March 1967 (CIA Inspector General Report, 120). Rosselli himself admitted that he spoke with Garrison in Las Vegas, referring to the D.A. as a "phoney" and a "publicity seeker" (Sheffield Edwards, CIA Memo For The Record, 11 December 1968).
29 Garrison, *On the Trail of the Assassins*, 13.
30 Kirkwood, 79.
31 Ferrie was dogged for years with allegations of improper activity with young boys. However, he was never convicted of any such offense. In addition, interviews with many of his so-called victims bring rapid denials that Ferrie ever made a pass at any of them. As for his appearance, Ferrie suffered from Alopecia Totalis, a condition which often involves total loss of body hair. This occurred late in life, and there are numerous conjectures as to how or why it occurred. Ferrie didn't help matters by insisting on wearing an ugly toupee while sporting painted-on eyebrows. In any event, it must be remembered that none of this has any bearing on who killed JFK.
32 SAC New Orleans to Director, FBI AIRTEL, 20 December 1966.
33 Ramsey Clark to LBJ, phone conversation, 22 February 1967, LBJ Library; see also Beschloss, *The Crisis Years*, 564.
34 Layton Martens, interview by author, 10 September 1994.
35 Interview of Nicky Chetta, Jr., 10 January 1993 *(FL)*.
36 *CCR*, bk. V, 106.
37 Richard Helms, Church Committee testimony, 29 June 1975.
38 DeLoach to Tolson, FBI Memorandum, 20 March 1967.
39 Richard Helms, Church Committee testimony, 28 June 1975.
40 Thomas Powers, 157-158.
41 The details of the operation are revealed in several documents of the Military District of Washington, including a Daily Staff Journal of Duty Officer's Log, a list entitled "Military Personnel for the Military District of Washington That Will Be Present During the Re-interment of President John F. Kennedy," and several memoranda and receipts. They were released by the Gerald Ford Library to the National Archives on August 25th, 1993.
42 According to one Lieutenant Colonel, a *Washington Post* reporter who appeared at 1:30 in the morning "was immediately escorted from the Cemetery" (Lieutenant Colonel James Mason, Memorandum for the Record, March 15, 1967).
43 Colonel J. B. Conmy, interview by author, 3 December 1993.
44 Frank Mankiewicz, interview by author, 19 January 1994.
Mankiewicz said that he never got to give Kennedy his final opinion on Garrison, because Kennedy himself was assassinated halfway through the New Orleans investigation.
    In a more bizarre take on RFK's involvement with the Garrison proceedings, Gordon Novel, a self-professed CIA "contract operative," once told John Lear (of "LearJet"), "Bobby Kennedy personally asked me to help him. Allen Dulles handed me a bagful of cash and then went off to Mexico on my advice to avoid

a Garrison subpoena." Novel explained that his job was to feed Garrison bogus information that would steer him away from the Castro-retaliation story. (Gordon Novel to John Lear, phone conversation transcript, undated).

45 Hougan, *Spooks,* 125-132.
In 1994, the Church Committee released its transcribed testimony from, and interviews of, witnesses regarding the Kennedy assassination. By far the most censored transcript is that of Walter Sheridan, with entire pages blackened out. In 1995, the presidentially-appointed JFK Review Board sought to obtain more details from Sheridan regarding his investigation of the Garrison case. Sources on the board told the author that Sheridan was "uncooperative," refusing to turn over his notes. Sheridan passed away soon after, his obituary suggesting a donation to the Robert Kennedy Memorial Fund in lieu of flowers. As of this writing, the board remains very interested in the workings of the "Five Eyes."

46 Sheridan, 426-427.
47 Phelan, 168-169.
48 Arthur Schlesinger, *Robert Kennedy and His Times,* 665.
49 Kirkwood, 540-541.
50 Flammonde, 317.
51 Frank Hernandez, interview by author, 29 June 1994.
52 *Dallas Times-Herald,* 4 April 1967.
53 Martens' letter offering help to Arcacha was still in Arcacha's possession at the time of the 1978 HSCA investigation. Arcacha handed it over to the investigators. A copy of it was located in the recently-released HSCA working files.
54 J.S. Martin to Louis Ivon, Subject: Investigation of Layton Martens, Memorandum from DA's office, 4 April 1968.
55 FBI Memo, File 62-10960, 30 March 1967.
56 Sergio Arcacha Smith, interview by author, 12 October 1994.
57 After much prodding, Arcacha, who considers his relationship with Bobby both private and personal, produced the tie-clip from his its hiding place and showed it to the author.
58 Sergio Arcacha Smith, interview by author, 24 April 1997.
59 The test was administered by John M. Spoonmore of Scientific Security Service, on March 8, 1967, and is in the author's possession.
60 Two years after the assassination, Layton Martens, like so many other New Orleaneans, would meet the ubiquitous Clay Shaw. When it was later revealed that Martens' college address appeared in Clay Shaw's address book, more fuel was added to the theory that Shaw must have known Ferrie. "I first met Shaw during the 1965 Mardi Gras," remembers Martens. "We were on Bourbon Street, when a mutual friend spotted Shaw in full regalia—a monk's outfit—and introduced us." Later, Shaw and Martens met again at the New Orleans Chess Club, where Shaw, as a member, was helping with the historic preservation of the club's headquarters. "Shaw was a 'B' player," says Martens. "We played often after that, a number of times in his home." Martens is adamant that he never saw Shaw with Ferrie, and indeed Martens himself didn't meet Shaw until 1965 (Layton Martens, interview by author, 6 April 1995).
61 Layton Martens, interview by author, 6 February 1994.
62 Brener, 164-171.
63 Layton Martens, interview by author, 1 September 1995.
64 Brener, 138.
Perry Russo may have accidentally stumbled onto a kernel of truth with this one. According to Martens, it was known to those in Arcacha's office, including Ferrie, that the administration was trying to kill Castro. "Ferrie talked about it. We all talked about it," recalls Martens. In addition, Banister's assistant, Joe Newbrough, told Frontline in 1993 that he had seen Banister and Ferrie discussing the possibility of Castro being assassinated.
65 Sal Panzeca, interview by author, 24 February 1994.
66 Kirkwood, 25.
67 Brener, 226.

68 Michael Dorman, interview by author, 19 November 1993.

69 Dorman, *Payoff,* 174-175.

70 That evidence included correspondence between Johnson and Halfen that Halfen's lawyer removed from his safe to show Dorman. (When contacted by the author in 1993, Halfen's widow expressed no interest in opening up her safe.) Other Big Fix papers were in the safekeeping of a Louisiana racketeer known as Bill "Nitro," who wasn't one for fantasizing: his sobriquet developed from his signature car bombs used against his enemies. He spoke of "all Lyndon did for us."

In addition to written exhibits, Halfen would claim to have photographs and films of himself with Lyndon and Lady Bird Johnson on hunting trips. He also claimed that Johnson's protege John Connally was among "his" prominent politicians, telling an investigator for the Senate's Permanent Subcommittee on Investigations, popularly known as the rackets committee, that some of his transactions with Connally—who was elected Governor of Texas in 1962—took place in a Bahamas bank.

Halfen supported his assertions about bribe recipients with enough detailed evidence and names of corroborating witnesses to convince the most skilled, skeptical interrogators. His disclosures were bi-partisan (Dorman, *Vesco,* 62).

Although no official explanation was made of the Senate subcommittee's failure to pursue Halfen's allegations, observers believe that members and aides feared the consequences of investigating the powerful, prestigious likes of Connally and Bush. While Halfen's motive was to reduce his sentence, a close Connally associate was reported to have threatened Halfen with a life in prison for fingering the former Governor.

71 Apparently, Halfen (who was given a copy of Dorman's manuscript) had showed a copy of the manuscript to his civil lawyer, Moise Simon, who showed it to his friend and Johnson aide, Jim Novy. Both were members of Austin's tight-knit Jewish community. Interestingly, Moise Simon was also on Marcello's staff briefly in 1972, when the Mafioso was re-tried for assaulting an FBI agent (Michael Dorman, interview by author, 10 August and 16 August 1992).

72 Rostow to McNamara, Memorandum, 24 April 1961, *FRUS* vol. X, 327-330.

73 The document was discovered by researcher G.R. Dodge in the handwriting file at the LBJ Library in Austin, TX. Dodge provided the author with a copy.

Chapter Nineteen (The Myth Unravels)

1 Michael Scott, interview in Russell, 462.

2 "Mexico City Report," CIA, 98-99.

3 Robert Krandle, HSCA interview, 27 March 1978.

4 *HSCA Final Report,* 323.

5 The officers were: Phillip Agee, Daniel Stanley Watson, Joseph Piccolo, Joseph B. Smith, and Daniel Niescuir.

6 Unnamed by Summers, the official was most assuredly Allen P. White.

7 Anthony Summers, interview by author, 26 January 1995.

8 In 1994, the Summers also interviewed Homer Bono, who told them that he met Oswald at Sanborn's Restaurant outside Mexico City in 1963. Oswald left in the company of a Quaker from Philadelphia named Steve Kennan [sic?]. Oswald was a passenger on Kennan's motorbike as the two drove off to the Cuban Embassy to try to secure a visa for Oswald. Kennan has never been found or interviewed.

9 "Mexico City Report," *HSCA,* 22, 91, and 114, respectively.

10 Russell, 461.

11 Win Scott, *Foul Foe,* 187.

12 Ibid, 190.

13 Ibid, 192.

14 Nixon's knowledge of anti-Castro activities was firsthand. As Vice President, he was the primary mover in a secret Cuban project known as "Operation 40." He also held intense conversations in the summer of 1960 about "delicate" Cuban matters with the very people who were later found to be the chief go-betweens in the first (pre-Kennedy) phase of the Castro assassination plots. For more details, see Beschloss, *The Crisis Years,* 135-137.

15 Earlier in 1971, Nixon told aide John Ehrlichman to order the CIA to turn over "the full file" on the Cuban project, "or else." Ehrlichman's notes make it clear that the President "must have the file." He had been "deeply involved." This may have been a partial motivation for the Watergate break-in, as the man whose office was broken into, Democratic National Committee Chairman Larry O'Brien, had been working recently with the very people Richard Nixon had been consulting in the first phase of the Castro assassination projects. (See fn. 14 and previous text references to Nixon.)

16 Just the day before, an incident occurred that may have inspired the Nixon gambit. On 19 June 1972, Hunt's White House safe was drilled open by FBI agents investigating the Watergate affair. L. Patrick Gray, Acting Director of the FBI, proceeded to burn the politically sensitive documents in Hunt's possession. One of the documents concerned the Kennedy assassination.

Reportedly, both Hunt and Cuban exile activist/Watergate burglar Frank Sturgis, at various times, had privately voiced suspicion over whether elements of the Castro government could have been involved in the Kennedy assassination. Based on a Frank Sturgis tip, Hunt, along with other Watergaters (Sturgis, Barker and Martinez) wrote a report in June 1971 of an interview they conducted of a Cuban woman in Miami with Fidel Castro when he heard of Kennedy's death. One copy of the report went to CIA Director Richard Helms and one copy was kept in Hunt's safe. This may have been among the documents burned on 19 June. The question remained: Who ordered Hunt to investigate the Kennedy assassination?

Also taken from Hunt's safe at that time was a document based on another "plumber's" probe that has gotten little attention. The Nixon White House had maintained an interest in damaging the possible presidential bid of Ted Kennedy. Hunt felt it would be possible to link the Kennedy family to the assassination of South Vietnamese President Diem three weeks before John Kennedy's own murder. Hunt reported to Nixon aide Chuck Colson that secret State Department cables made it obvious that JFK had complicity in Diem's death—but no single cable proved it. Hunt used a razor blade and a photocopying machine to produce a bogus single cable, which he gave to *Life Magazine* (see Lukas, 83-85). This document on the Diem murder was contained in Hunt's safe, and it too was taken.

Ted Kennedy was not the only Democratic contender whom Nixon intended to link to an assassination (albeit via his brother). In the December 14, 1993 issue of the *New Yorker Magazine,* investigator Seymour Hersh detailed an interview with Nixon aide Chuck Colson. Colson admitted to Hersh that Nixon proposed planting George McGovern's campaign literature in the apartment of Arthur Bremer, the convicted assailant of another presidential hopeful, Alabama governor George Wallace. Hersh wrote that Nixon was "energized and excited by what seems to be the ultimate political dirty trick" against the Democrats' presidential nominee, George McGovern.

(Sources: Mike Ewing to HSCA, "Hunt" memo, released in August 1993. Also, E. Howard Hunt, interview in *Providence Journal,* November 1975; and Seymour Hersh, *The New Yorker,* 14 December 1993.)

17 Haldeman with DiMona, 52-70.

18 Brent Scowcroft, Memo of conversation, 4 January 1975; Ford Library file of the JFK Collection, National Archives.

19 Schorr, 143-144.

20 Tom Wicker, *The New York Times,* 7 January 1975.

21 Belin, *Final Disclosure,* 93.

22 Colby and Dennett, 736, quoting from Rockefeller's oral history.
23 Belin, *Final Disclosure*, 117.
24 Ibid, 121.
25 Ibid, 124.
26 Robert McNamara, testimony before Church Committee, 11 July 1975, cited in *CCIR*, 158.
27 Ibid, 118-119.
28 FitzGerald died at the age of 56 while playing tennis at his Virginia home. Bobby Kennedy attended his funeral. FitzGerald was posthumously awarded the National Security Medal by President Johnson. (Thomas, *The Very Best Men*, 333.)
29 Beschloss, *The Crisis Years*, 138-139.
30 Richard Helms, testimony before the Church Committee, 96.
31 David Martin, *The Morning News* (of Wilmington, Delaware), 31 May 1975.
32 *CCIR*, 167-169.
33 Quoted in Belin, *Final Disclosure*, 119.
34 Belin, *Final Disclosure*, 118.
35 Richard Goodwin, interview by author, 20 January 1994.
36 David and David, 228.
37 *Human Events*, 24 July 1976, 13-15.
38 *CCIR*, 1.
39 Maheu, 112, 130.
40 Richard Helms, "Reflections on a 'Gentleman Spy,'" *World Intelligence Review*, vol. 13, no. 3, 1994.
41 Johnson, *A Season of Inquiry*, 270.
42 Thomas Powers, quoted in Beschloss, *The Crisis Years*, 138, fn.
43 Thomas Powers, 156.
44 Ibid, 7.
45 Quoted in Thomas Powers, 304.
46 Phillips, 290.
47 Johnson, *A Season of Inquiry*, 60.
48 Cited in Merle Miller, *Plain Speaking*, 420 n.
49 Hunt, *Give Us This Day*, 213-214.
50 Mosely, 473.
51 "The CIA: America's Secret Warriors," *The Discovery Channel*, 1997.
52 Senator Richard Schweiker, interview by author, 23 June 1994.
53 L. Fletcher Prouty, Church Committee testimony, 16 July 1975. This testimony was not released until 1994. The JFK Records Act forced Congress and other agencies to release all their JFK records.
54 Richard Helms to William K. Harvey, Memo (Subject: "Authorization of ZRRIFLE Agent Activities"), 19 February 1962. Author's files.
55 Schorr, 149
56 These documents are retained by a Harvey family member, and represent the only physical record of Harvey's work. It had been rumored that Harvey brought sensitive operational documents home, which were destroyed upon his death by his widow. This was not the case. The author was assured by someone in a position to know that "Bill *never* brought paperwork home!"
57 Frank King, interview by author, 30 April 1998.
58 Martin, 220.
59 Dulles, 177.
60 Wise and Ross, 157.
61 Ibid, 174-175.
62 CIA officer, confidential interview by author, 8 February 1995.
63 William Safire, "The President's Friend," *New York Times*, 15 December 1975.
64 Loch Johnson, *A Season of Inquiry*, 7.
65 Ibid, 6.
66 Ibid, 8.
67 Tower, 135.
68 Bolstering this Bobby Kennedy link (as if more bolstering were needed), the

committee obtained testimony from a CIA employee who stated that "a very high level source in the CIA had once told him that Bobby Kennedy had, in fact, been active in pursuing the idea of an assassination attempt against Castro, and that Bobby Kennedy had not been in the position of simply receiving such a proposal from the Agency." (Confidential CIA source, interview by David Aaron, cited in Aaron to William Miller, Memo, 1 April 1975.)

69 Andy Postal to Church Committee, Memo for the Record, 15 January 1976.
70 Andy Postal, interview by author, 1 August 1997.
71 *CCIR*, 150, fn. 2.
72 Heather Gordon, interview by author, 9 September 1994.
73 Church, 57.
74 Ibid, 57.
75 Interview of Senator Richard Schweiker, 26 July 1993 (FL).
76 David Bushong, interview by author, 1 August 1997.
77 Jim Flannery, interview by author, 23 December 1993.
78 Johnson, *A Season of Inquiry*, 176.
79 Andy Postal, interview by author, 1 August 1997.
80 Richard Schweiker, quoted in Johnson, *A Season of Inquiry*, 57.
81 Johnson, *A Season of Inquiry*, 70.
82 Ibid, 187.
83 Letter on file in Dulles Collection at the Mudd Library, Princeton, NJ.
84 Reeves, 265-266.
85 *CCR*, vol. VII, 182.
86 Jim Johnston, interview by author, 27 December 1993.
87 Quoted in Max Holland, "After Thirty Years: Making Sense of the Assassination," *Reviews in American History #22*, June 1994, 205.
88 Church Report, vol. III, 59.
89 Harvey family member, interview by author; also David Martin, 222.
90 The author counts himself among those teenagers impressed by the arguments raised by a number of these books. However, after over thirty years of following the twists and turns in the evidence, and having the opportunity to conduct thousands of interviews, including many with members of the scientific community, the author has come to the realization that approximately 90% of the books and witnesses are, in fact, worthless.
91 Gaeton Fonzi, interview by author, 4 April 1993.
92 Congressman Louis Stokes, interview by author, 6 April 1992.
93 Robert Tanenbaum, interview by author, 3 April 1993.
94 Interview of L.J. Delsa, 10 January 1993 (FL).
95 Fonzi, 210-211.
96 Gaeton Fonzi, interview by author, 4 April 1993.
97 Leslie Wizelman, interview by author, 4 April 1993.
98 Sergio Arcacha Smith, HSCA testimony, 7 July 1978; National Archives, College Park, MD.
99 Fonzi, 302.
100 Admiral Stansfield Turner, interview by author, 10 October 1991.
101 For an excellent summary of this subject, see Posner, 237-243; see also the appendix to Savage, by Sheriff Jim Bowles.
102 Howard Osborne, CIA Memo for the Record, 19 December 1967.
103 Jack Anderson, Report to President George Bush: Who Murdered John F. Kennedy? (1988)
104 Hubbell, 282.

Chapter Twenty (The Final Chapter)

1 "We All had a Finger on that Trigger," *I.F. Stone's Weekly*, December 1963.
2 George McGovern, interviewed on Jack Anderson's TV special, "Who Shot JFK?" in 1988.

3 Alexander Cockburn, "Propaganda of the Deed," *The New Statesman,* 19 November 1993.

4 Earl Golz, *Dallas Morning News,* 10 May 1979.

5 Quoted in numerous sources, including the *New York Times,* 17 October 1953. Castro biographer Robert Quirk has pointed out "the remarkable resemblance" to Adolf Hitler's famous declaration at one of his early trials: "The eternal court of History will smile and tear up the indictment of the prosecutor and the verdict of the judges. She will acquit us!"

6 Demaris, *The Last Mafioso,* 235.

7 Nilo Messer, interview by author, 20 May 1998.

8 George McGovern, interviewed on Jack Anderson's TV special, *"Who Shot JFK?"* in 1988.

9 Davison, 184.

10 Quirk, 356.

11 Constantine "Gus" Kangles, interview by author, 12 August 1996.

12 Jack Hawkins, interview by author, 7 April 1998.

13 Al Haig, interview by author, 26 February 1998.

14 Paterson, 260.

15 Hunt, *Give Us This Day,* 14-15.

16 *Washington Post,* National Weekly Edition, 5-11 July 1993.

17 RFK Memo, 7 November 1961; cited in Andrew, 275; and Beschloss, *The Crisis Years,* 375.

18 Quoted in Max Holland, "After Thirty Years: Making Sense of the Assassination," *Reviews in American History #22,* June 1994, 202.

19 Clifford, 303.

20 *The NewsHour with Jim Lehrer,* 18 February 1998.

21 Matthew 26:52.

Appendix A (Oswald's Shooting of the President)

1 Vincent Scalice, interview by author, 25 November 1993.

2 Quoted in Savage, 173.
An ongoing mystery has surrounded one identifiable fingerprint that was nonetheless never identified. For years, speculation about the identity of this print (a possible co-conspirator) has been rife. The main candidate, according to some researchers, was a violent Cuban exile named Manuel Rodriguez. Rodriguez was known to have been acquainted with a Dallas gun dealer named John Thomas Masen, who sold Mannlicher Carcano ammunition. Masen told the author in 1992 that he never sold this type of ammunition to the Cubans. Ironically, John Masen was a dead ringer for Lee Harvey Oswald, and some felt that he may have been the Oswald-looking character rumored to have gotten into a fistfight with Jack Ruby in his night club. Masen told the author that he had been in Ruby's club only once (with his wife), and he never met or fought with Jack Ruby. (John Thomas Masen, interview by author, 28 April 1993.)
An FBI source told the author that, in the years after the assassination, the Bureau solved the mystery of an unidentified fingerprint on several of the ixth floor boxes—it belonged to Dallas Police homicide chief, Captain Will Fritz, who in 1964 couldn't be bothered having his own fingerprints made for comparison purposes (the other law enforcement officials permitted the comparison prints). Just prior to his death in 1984, Fritz relented and let the FBI do the comparison print, resolving the mystery. (Dallas FBI official, interview by author, 10 May 1993.)

3 Warren Report, 561-562.

4 *WC* Report, 192.

5 Ibid.

6 Twenty years later, this same unschooled critic was the only person the O.J. Simpson defense team could unearth to opine that the photos showing

Simpson wearing the murderer's shoes were also faked. The same critic has at times claimed that the Zapruder film is forged as well.
7 Mike Howard, interview by author, 7 December 1993.
8 Frank Ellsworth, interview by author, 16 February 1994.
9 Robert Gemberling, interview by author, 30 July 1993.
10 Marilyn Sitzman, interview by author, 25 October 1992.
11 Marilyn Sitzman, interview by Josiah Thompson, 29 November 1966, 3-5, transcript on file at the Assassination Archives and Research Center, Washington, D.C.
12 See photo by Phil Willis.
13 Groden, 125.
14 The Guinn articles are: "NAA of Bullet Lead Evidence Specimens in Criminal Cases," *The Journal of Radioanalytical Chemistry*, vol. 72, no. 1-2, 1982; and Samuel M. Gerber ed., "The Elemental Comparison of Bullet Lead Evidence Specimens." The Chemistry of Crime, Washington, D.C., 1983.
15 Massad Ayoob, "The JFK Assassination: A Shooter's Eye View," *The American Handgunner,* March/April, 1993, 102.
16 Dr. Martin Fackler, testimony, American Bar Association mock trial of Lee Harvey Oswald, 10 August 1992.
17 Dr. John Lattimer, "Experimental Duplication of the Important Physical Evidence," *Journal of the American College of Surgeons,* May 1994, vol. 178.
18 Dr. Dennis Ford, "Assassination Research and the Pathology of Knowledge," *The Third Decade,* vol. VIII, no. 5, July 1992; also, Tom Filsinger, "Groupthink and JFK Assassination Research," *The Third Decade*, vol. VIII, no. 6, September 1992.

Appendix B (Eyewitnesses)

1 Posner, 236.
Posner, a distinguished New York attorney, was quite familiar with the pitfalls in eyewitness testimony. He cited as an example the story of the Titanic. When the 900 foot-long liner sank in 1912, the seven hundred survivors were split over whether the ship went down in one or two pieces.
2 Livingstone, 126.

Appendix C (Jack Ruby)

1 For details and specific citations, see Posner, 350-365.
2 Barry Boesch, "Jack Ruby: Obsessions and Contradictions," *Dallas Morning News,* JFK Memorial edition, 1983.
3 CE 1288.
4 Earl Ruby and Bill Roemer, interviews by Gerald Posner (1992), cited in Posner, 352.
5 Barry Boesch, "Jack Ruby: Obsessions and Contradictions," *Dallas Morning News,* JFK Memorial edition, 1983.
6 Joe Cody, interview by author, 12 June 1993.
7 Wally Weston, interview by author, 12 June 1993.
8 Ibid.
9 Wills and Demaris, 6.
10 CD 87.
11 Al Maddox, interview by author, 12 June 1993.
12 Barry Boesch, "Jack Ruby: Obsessions and Contradictions," *Dallas Morning News,* JFK Memorial edition, 1983.
13 Eva Grant, testimony, *WC,* vol. XIV, 469, 484.
14 Wills and Demaris, "You all know me! I'm Jack Ruby!" *Esquire,* May 1967.
15 Wills and Demaris, 218.
16 An excellent compilation of Ruby's acquaintances' testimony can be found in Posner, 374-379.

17 Barry Boesch, "Jack Ruby: Obsessions and Contradictions," *Dallas Morning News,* JFK Memorial edition, 1983.

18 Jack Ruby to "Bill," letter from jail, 4 December 1963. Copy of letter in author's possession.

19 Jim Leavelle, interview by author, 19 June 1993.

20 T. George Harris, interview by author, 8 March 1993.

21 Lonnie Hudkins, interview by author, 19 June 1993.

22 Ruby to Dallas police, statement, CE 1253.

23 Frank Ellsworth, interview by author, February 16, 1994.

24 Cited in Kaplan and Waltz, 66.

25 Kaplan and Waltz, 143.

26 Ibid, 150.

27 Kaplan and Waltz, 143.

28 Jim Leavelle, interview by author, 19 June 1993.

29 Joe Campisi, HSCA testimony.

30 Wills and Demaris, 72-72.

31 Wally Weston, interview by author, 6 June 1993.

32 Elmo Cunningham, interview by author, 8 December 1993.

33 Wills and Demaris, 72.

34 Ibid, 73.

35 One day soon after the crime, Howard sat in Ruby's Carousel Club trying to think of a convincing defense. "In those days," reporter Lonnie Hudkins would recall, "defense attorneys trusted reporters enough to tell them their plans." Hudkins listened while Howard "threw out possible defenses, and tried to figure out how they sounded. He's the one who came up with the possible defense that Ruby just could not stand the thought of the First Lady having to come to Dallas and testify—that's why he shot Oswald. George Harris, a senior editor of *Look* magazine, was with me. We just sat there in amazement."

36 Bill Alexander, interview by Gerald Posner, 1992, in Posner, 400.

37 Miller, *Lyndon,* 348.

38 Wills and Demaris, 255.

39 Warren Report, 5 Hearings, 181 ff.

40 Wills and Demaris, "You all know me! I'm Jack Ruby!" *Esquire,* May 1967.

41 Wills and Demaris, 262.

42 Barry Boesch, "Jack Ruby: Obsessions and Contradictions," *Dallas Morning News,* JFK Memorial edition, 1983.

43 Wally Weston, interview by author, 12 June 1993.

44 Al Maddox, interview by author, 12 June 1993.

45 There is also a question of whether the "Dallas city fathers" desired Oswald's death as a way of atoning for Kennedy's murder. It is known that Ruby attempted to make contact all weekend with Gordon McLendon, one of his icons. McLendon was the Walter Cronkite of Dallas at station WLIF, and a powerful city figure. One informed source claims that Ruby did see McLendon, who gave him the idea to kill Oswald—but if this is true, it was probably simply by saying something like, "That son of a bitch ought to be killed." Ruby employees at the Carousel Club told Ruby the same thing. (Lonnie Hudkins, interview by author, 20 August 1993.)

46 Joe Cody, interview by author, 12 June 1993.

47 Jim Leavelle, interview by author, 20 October 1994.

48 Frank Ellsworth, interview by author, 16 February 1994.

49 Elmo Cunningham, interview by author, 8 December 1993.

50 A tape of the conversation was recorded by Ruby's rabbi, a copy of which is in the author's possession.

INDEX

This index does not cover all of the "Endnotes."
Readers with a special interest are strongly encouraged to read them.

Gaudin, Louis D., 309
Gay, Donovan, 441
Gemberling, Robert, 260, 473
Genovese, Vito, 414
Germann, Ella, 106, 107
Geyer, Georgie Anne, 248
Giancana, Sam
  Castro assassination plans and, 45, 52, 241, 523 n 19
  emissary of, meets with McLaney and JFK, 70
  Kennedy family and, 242
  murder of, 436
  RFK's coverup of, 72–73
  Sinatra and, 435
  wiretapping and, 71
Gil, G. Wray, 329
Gilpatrick, Roswell, 231–32
Giordano, Joseph, 389
Gleichauf, Justin, 143
Gobel, Merritt, 309
Goldwater, Barry, 231, 254, 439
Golovachev, Pavel, 103, 105, 111, 121, 205–6
Gonzalez, Alonzo, 59, 436
Goodpaster, Andrew, 9
Goodpasture, Ann, 353
Goodwin, Doris Kearns, 397
Goodwin, Richard
  on Castro assassination plan, 75
  on Castro's power in Cuba, 26
  Cuba Project and, 43
  Guevara and, 27, 63
  on JFK's anti-Castro campaign, 13, 22
  on JFK's reaction to Bay of Pigs, 27
  on Kennedy family dynamic, 28
  on Lansdale's admissions, 428
  RFK avoiding JFK assassination questions and, 385
  writing JFK's anti-Castro campaign speeches, 11–12
Gordon, Caroline, 58
Gordon, Heather, 58, 59, 437
Gordon, John, III, 436, 437
  post-Bay of Pigs plots and, 57–60
Gottlieb, Sidney, assassination poisons and, 61
government, U.S.
  CIA role in, 431
  continued Cold War with Cuba and, 453–54
  Cuban Revolutionary Council and, 141
  Oswald's inconsequence to, 455–56
  public distrust of, JFK assassination and, 451, 458
  Ruby's patriotism and, 495–96
GPFOCUS. *See* Kennedy, Robert F.
GPIDEAL
  11/22/63, Cuban journalist reports killing of, 285

See also Kennedy, John F.
Granello, Sal, 51
Grant, Eva, 493, 495, 496, 499
grassy knoll gunman, 471–75
  agents on knoll and, 472–73
  crowd on knoll and, 472
  sight lines problem, 473–75
  smoke problem, 471–72
Graves, L. C., 335
Great Lakes Carbon, 4, 31
Greer, Bill, 298
Gregory, Peter, 116
Griffin, Burt, 362, 363, 371, 374
Griffith, Clark, 4
Groden, Robert, 477
Gromyko, Andrei, 176–77
Grose, Peter, 34, 82, 366
Guantanamo, 58–60, 162, 436
Guatemala, PBSUCCESS and, 8
Guatemalan Lumber Company, 186
Guevara, Che, 27, 51, 63
Guin Diaz, Ramon Tomas, 247
Guinn, Vincent, 482
gunfire source, 467–75
  witnesses and, 298–300, 467
  wounds and, 468
Gurvich, William, 407–8
Guthman, Edwin, 302, 381, 390
Gutierrez, Pedro, 222, 345
Guy Banister and Associates, 139, 140, 142–43, 152–53
  See also Banister, Guy

Hackett, Dave, 382
Haig, Alexander, Jr., 171
  on Castro's threats, 249–50, 455
  on Cuba Project demise, 391
  Cuban Coordinating Committee and, 162
  on JFK assassination, 453
  JFK funeral plans and, 341
  on LBJ and Warren Commission report, 376–77
  on RFK and CCC, 163–64
  on RFK support of Cubela, 241
  on unprovoked U.S.-supported invasion of Cuba, 182–83
Halberstam, David, 158
Haldeman, H. R. (Bob), 150, 422–23
Halfen, Jack, 283–84, 413, 414–16, 579 n 70
Hallmark, Claude, 267
Halperin, Maurice, 7
Halpern, Sam, 176
  on CIA role in U.S. government, 431
  on Cuba Project, 37
  on Cubela antagonizing/not assassinating Castro, 240
  on funding Cuba re-invasion, 173
  on Harvey/Kennedy run-ins, 80, 81
  on JM/WAVE reaction to Artime's

on Soviet military in Caribbean, 178–79
timetable for Castro overthrow, 157
Jones, Dempsey, 268
Jordan, Everett, 284
Jorge, Luis, 54
Juan (MDC para-military training camps manager), 186
on Castro infiltrator, 187, 188
suspicions of Oswald, 200–201
on talkative nature of Cubans, 195

Kahn, Herman, 388
Kalugin, Oleg, 108
Kangles, Constantine "Gus," 18, 66, 452
Karamessines, Thomas, 344
Karnei, Robert, 325
Karpel, Craig, 237
Katzenbach, Nicholas, 253
on LBJ and *Death of a President*, 399
LBJ independent investigation of Oswald-Castro connection and, 377
Mexico City development reports to, 343
on RFK and Warren Commission, 371
running Justice after assassination, 382
Keating, Charles, 359
Keating, Kenneth, 233, 235, 398
Keenan, Laurence, 220, 351, 357, 358
Kelley, Clarence, 258
Kennedy, Angelo, 170, 171
Kennedy, Caroline, 17
Kennedy, Edward M. "Ted," 322–23, 389, 406, 426
Kennedy, Ethel Skakel, 28, 274
Kennedy, Eunice, 28
Kennedy, Jacqueline
crowd turnout, Texas trip and, 280–81
decision to do Dallas trip, 278
Hill and, 298
home movie on JFK's assassination and, 277
on JFK and death, 276, 278
JFK autopsy and, 323
at JFK re-internment, 406
motorcade 11/22/63, 291–94
on open car, 291
puts wedding ring in JFK coffin, 301
refuses to leave Dallas without JFK body, 304
RFK edits her Warren Commission transcript, 371
security objections, Texas trip, 255
Warren and, 361
Kennedy, John F., 1–84
after Cuban missile crisis, Castro plans, 156
authorizing OPLAN 380-63, 178

autonomous projects and, 161–63, 173–74
Campbell and, 72
on Castro, 271
character of, 29–30
on CIA, 33–34
on CIA policy support, 433
compared to Fidel, 452–54
counterinsurgency and, 39–41
courage, need to show, 25–26
CRC and, 17
Cuba invasion aftermath and, 20–21, 27–28
Cuba invasion planning, 1962, and, 77
on Cuba invasion planning media leaks, 16
Cuba ties/sympathy toward, 10–11
Cuban situation meeting 11/19/63, 271–72
on *Dallas Morning News* anti-JFK ad, 287–88
death and, 276–78
delaying action on LBJ kick-back rumors, 281–82
Dulles (Allen) connection and, 31–32
Dulles (Allen) resignation and, 23–24
early inside information on Cuba invasion, 12
on early reports of Soviet missiles in Cuba, 149, 150
facing 1964 elections, 231–33
family ties to Cuba, 4
FBI McLaney camp raid and, 184
as "Fifth Avenue cowboy," 31
FitzGerald and, 82–83
gonorrhea and, 326–27
home movie on his assassination, 277
inattention to Cuba, 13
inexperience/self-assurance of, 450
invasion/assassination strategy, 237–38
James Bond books and, 45–46
Lansdale's Vietnam report and, 42–43
LBJ's attacks on, 1960 Democratic race, 395–96
McLaney and, 67–71
meets Artime, 169
meets with Gromyko, 176–77
Morrison and, 139
motorcade 11/22/63, 291–94
Nixon and, 22
Oswald's anger toward, 118, 119, 120
peace speech, USSR and, 157–61
peace strategy, Cuban, 234–37
possibility Cuba Project might backfire and, 249
Profiles in Courage, 194–95
re-internment, 389, 404–6

ACKNOWLEDGEMENTS

"You need a mess of help to stand alone."
—Brian Wilson

Special Thanks

My sincere thanks go first to all those who trusted me with their memories. Every attempt was made to keep your interview words accurate, and in context. This book owes its existence to veteran producer Harry Moses, who convinced me that my work should have a wider audience. Harry, I hope you were right. If not, I'm blaming everything on you. Thanks to Mary Ferrell, for her years of gracious support. To Joseph Howell and Craig and Debby Witzke: thanks for believing in and supporting my work. Cinda Elser, not only the best skip tracer in the biz, but a guaranteed giggle—your contributions are visible (to me at least) on every page. My old high school chum Doug Kearns made an initial effort at line editing an early unwieldy behemoth of a manuscript.

Sy Hersh was always gracious in allowing access to his voluminous files and contacts. He was also considerate in not taking advantage of my second serve. Peter Matson at Sterling Lord—thanks for the Herculean effort. Michael Sullivan, W. Scott Malone, Miri "The Glue" Navasky, and David Fanning at Frontline all provided a great and collegial work experience. The late Bud Fensterwald, who encouraged my early work (and that of numerous other truth seekers), was a constant source of help in those important years.

It was Linda Jackson-Patterson who suggested I approach Bancroft Press at a book fair we were attending. So she shares the blame with Harry Moses, I suppose. To my publisher Bruce Bortz—thanks for taking the chance, while allowing me to retain my own voice throughout. Also at Bancroft, thanks to Evonne Smitt for a painstaking line edit. Jonathan Sachsman labored hard to manage both structural and computer gremlins. Robert Aulicino contributed a terrific jacket design. Susan Mangan not only functioned as last-minute trouble shooter, but in partnership with Steven Parke of What ?Design, added the artistic touch to the final design and photo spread. Deborah Patton, with very little notice, provided a thorough and meticulous index. Sarah Azizi managed the Bancroft office with great humor and professionalism, while also playing the role of prototypical reader with little background on or interest in the subject. (Her enthusiasm for the book was, therefore, especially appreciated.) Fred White and Melinda Russell both made significant contributions in the book's early stages.

I'd be greatly remiss if I didn't single out Dr. Abe Bortz for his vital contributions to the book. A professional historian trained at Harvard under Arthur Schlesinger, Sr., Dr. Bortz devoted a significant part of his career to writing, studying, and teaching American history. For this book, he painstakingly read each draft, always asked the right questions, continually made astute suggestions, and constantly praised my efforts. This book was purposely written to be of use to adults of three distinct generations: the young (who have little knowledge of the Kennedy assassination), the middle-aged (the people who, like me and my publisher, grew up on a staple of Kennedy assassination information, and didn't quite know what to believe), and Dr. Bortz's generation (who are inclined to support the Warren Commission's findings). It was edited by three generations of editors. When my youngest editors said they understood the story, when my publisher said it proved a paradigm shift from what his (and my) generation understood, and when Dr. Bortz, in reading the manuscript's various versions, said he was "almost persuaded," then "persuaded," then "absolutely persuaded," I sensed that this gigantic effort had succeeded.

Jim Lesar of the Assassination Archives and Research Center has shared his insights (and files) with me for three decades. Steve Tilley of the National Archives JFK Collection went above and beyond the call of duty to keep the documents flowing. Sam Halpern graciously made himself available for late-night calls and fact checking. Ross Crozier was a great help in providing background and photos on Castro's early years.

To Mom—thanks for your love and support, especially in the form of spaghetti dinners. Ditto—Aunt Marie Young. To my landlords, Steve and Janet Nugent—thanks for your patience. Thanks, too, to Scout and Mrs. Teasdale; they showed unflinching love and loyalty in the face of my constant absences. Lastly, Geraldine Monsant, who now dwells with her own kind—angels: Thanks for the passion and love you showed for everyone and their work. I wanted you, more than anyone, to see the final product.

The Supporting Cast

At the risk of omitting someone, I would like to cite a partial list of key contributors to my work over the years. This book represents nothing less than the sum total of your support and encouragement. In alphabetical order, much thanks to: Mark Allen, Steve Allen and the Meadowlane staff, Sergio Arcacha Smith and Marisol, the Assassinations Record Review Board (especially David Marwell, John Tunheim, Tom Samoluk, and Ann Buttimer, Jeremy Gunn, and Eileen Sullivan), Dr. Robert Artwohl, F. Lee Bailey, Richard Bakst, Kathleen Boyle, Jane Brody, Ed Butler, Josh Butler, Doug Carlson, Dr. Jeffrey Caufield, John Cirovolo, Matt Coogan, Bill Cran and Invisions, John Davis, L. J. Delsa, Ron Devillier, Gary Dodge, Capt. J. E. (Ned) Dolan, Brian Donegan, Mike Dorman, Dennis Lee Effle, Wayne Everard, George Feifer, Bernie Fensterwald, Bill Gable and Dani

Minnick, Steve Glauber, Jim Gray, Dr. Larry Haapanen.

Also Alexander Haig, Linda Hanson and Claudia Anderson at the LBJ Library, Kristina Hare, Bob Harris, Ed Haslam, Sandy Heberer, Jenn Hengen, Paul Hoch, Jim Hougan, Kathleen Hutera, Harold Hyde, Mal Hyman, Peter Jennings, Doug Kearns, Phillip Knightley, Andy Kolis, Jennifer Lawson, Taimi and Jim Leavelle, Rusty Livingstone, Ben Loeterman, Layton Martens, Daniel Martinez, Jim Marrs, Erin McCarthur, Bob Mergehenn, Eve Morra, John Morton, Dale Myers, Jennifer Nelson, Sue and John Newman, Mark Obenhaus and the Lancer staff (especially Sally Rosenthal, Trina Quagliaroli, Linda Patterson, Richard Robbins, Ed Gray, Eric Davies, Kristina Kaplan), Lyndon Olson, Otto Otepka, Linda and Tom Patterson, Nicki and Dave Perry, Fletcher Prouty, Trisha and Gerald Posner, Tom Queeney, Dan Rather, Kristina Rebelo, Peter Robbins, Peggy Adler Robohm, Dan Rodericks, Joe Rosenbloom.

And Jane Rusconi, Dick Russell, Mort Sahl, Gary Savage, Senator Richard Schweiker, J. Gary Shaw, Jerry Shields, Jerry Shinley, Marion Slack at Framingham State College, Dan Smith, Cindy Smolovik, Dutch Snedeker, Oliver Stone, Stoneleigh Hotel and Stacey O'Neil, Robbyn and Anthony Summers, Stan Szerszen, Ed Tatro, William Turner, Marty Underwood, Todd Vaughn, Hal Verb, Lamar Waldron, Kevin Walsh, Larry Warren, Rick Waybright, Kate L. M. Webb, Harold Weisberg, Robert White, Jason Wiener, Brian Wilson, Gordon Winslow, Elizabeth "Lizzo" Woodbury, Dr. Bob Yaffee, Janet Yang, Mark Zaid, Azita Zendel, and last but not least, Julie "i mani" Ziegler.

It must be said that the support of all the people above does not imply their agreement with any of this book's conclusions. Nor, above all, does it absolve me of any errors that appear on these pages.

ABOUT THE AUTHOR

An acclaimed investigative reporter and longtime student of the Kennedy presidency, author Gus Russo was one of the lead reporters on Frontline's landmark 1993 documentary, "Who Was Lee Harvey Oswald?" Most recently, he served as chief investigative reporter for ABC's "Dangerous World: The Kennedy Years," hosted by Peter Jennings. He has assisted authors Gerald Posner, Seymour Hersh, and Anthony Summers with their books on Kennedy-related subjects, and has served as consultant to numerous network television specials, books, and magazine articles. For more than 20 years (and with no preconceived conclusions), Russo has sought to compile a credible account of President Kennedy's assassination and the foreign policy errors that set the stage for it. Using first-time, on-the-record interviews, newly discovered photographs, and recently declassified U.S. government documents, he has crafted the definitive chronicle of a critical episode in American history.

Gus Russo lives in Baltimore, MD, where he earned a B.A. in political science from the University of Maryland. As a professional musician, he has composed commercial music and film scores.